Experimental Design and Data Analysis for Biologists

An essential textbook for any student or researcher in biology needing to design experiments, sampling programs or analyze the resulting data. The text begins with a revision of estimation and hypothesis testing methods, covering both classical and Bayesian philosophies, before advancing to the analysis of linear and generalized linear models. Topics covered include linear and logistic regression, simple and complex ANOVA models (for factorial, nested, block, split-plot and repeated measures and covariance designs), and log-linear models. Multivariate techniques, including classification and ordination, are then introduced. Special emphasis is placed on checking assumptions, exploratory data analysis and presentation of results. The main analyses are illustrated with many examples from published papers and there is an extensive reference list to both the statistical and biological literature. The book is supported by a website that provides all data sets, questions for each chapter and links to software.

GERRY QUINN is in the School of Biological Sciences at Monash University, with research interests in marine and freshwater ecology, especially river floodplains and their associated wetlands.

MICHAEL KEOUGH is in the Department of Zoology at the University of Melbourne, with research interests in marine ecology, environmental science and conservation biology.

Both authors have extensive experience teaching experimental design and analysis courses and have provided advice on the design and analysis of sampling and experimental programs in ecology and environmental monitoring to a wide range of environmental consultants, university and government scientists.

Experimental Design and Data Analysis for Biologists

Gerry P. Quinn
Monash University

Michael J. Keough
University of Melbourne

CAMBRIDGE
UNIVERSITY PRESS

CAMBRIDGE UNIVERSITY PRESS
Cambridge, New York, Melbourne, Madrid, Cape Town, Singapore, São Paulo, Delhi

Cambridge University Press
The Edinburgh Building, Cambridge CB2 8RU, UK

Published in the United States of America by Cambridge University Press, New York

www.cambridge.org
Information on this title: www.cambridge.org/9780521009768

First published in 2002
Reprinted with corrections 2003
Seventh printing 2008

Printed in the United Kingdom at the University Press, Cambridge

A catalogue record for this book is available from the British Library

Library of Congress Cataloguing in Publication data

Quinn, G.P. (Gerald Peter), 1956–
    Experimental design and data analysis for biologists / G.P. Quinn, Michael J. Keough.
        p.   cm.
    Includes bibliographical references (p.).
    ISBN 0 521 81128 7 (hb) – ISBN 0 521 00976 6 (pb)
    1. Biometry. I. Keough, Michael J. II. Title.

    QH323.5 .Q85 2002
    570′.1′5195–dc21   2001037845

ISBN 978-0-521-00976-8 paperback

Contents

Preface

Statistical analysis is at the core of most modern biology, and many biological hypotheses, even deceptively simple ones, are matched by complex statistical models. Prior to the development of modern desktop computers, determining whether the data fit these complex models was the province of professional statisticians. Many biologists instead opted for simpler models whose structure had been simplified quite arbitrarily. Now, with immensely powerful statistical software available to most of us, these complex models can be fitted, creating a new set of demands and problems for biologists.

We need to:

- know the pitfalls and assumptions of particular statistical models,
- be able to identify the type of model appropriate for the sampling design and kind of data that we plan to collect,
- be able to interpret the output of analyses using these models, and
- be able to design experiments and sampling programs optimally, i.e. with the best possible use of our limited time and resources.

The analysis may be done by professional statisticians, rather than statistically trained biologists, especially in large research groups or multidisciplinary teams. In these situations, we need to be able to speak a common language:

- frame our questions in such a way as to get a sensible answer,
- be aware of biological considerations that may cause statistical problems; we can not expect a statistician to be aware of the biological idiosyncrasies of our particular study, but if he or she lacks that information, we may get misleading or incorrect advice, and
- understand the advice or analyses that we receive, and be able to translate that back into biology.

This book aims to place biologists in a better position to do these things. It arose from our involvement in designing and analyzing our own data, but also providing advice to students and colleagues, and teaching classes in design and analysis. As part of these activities, we became aware, first of our limitations, prompting us to read more widely in the primary statistical literature, and second, and more importantly, of the complexity of the statistical models underlying much biological research. In particular, we continually encountered experimental designs that were not described comprehensively in many of our favorite texts. This book describes many of the common designs used in biological research, and we present the statistical models underlying those designs, with enough information to highlight their benefits and pitfalls.

Our emphasis here is on dealing with biological data – how to design sampling programs that represent the best use of our resources, how to avoid mistakes that make analyzing our data difficult, and how to analyze the data when they are collected. We emphasize the problems associated with real world biological situations.

In this book

Our approach is to encourage readers to understand the models underlying the most common experimental designs. We describe the models that are appropriate for various kinds of biological data – continuous and categorical response variables, continuous and categorical predictor or independent variables. Our emphasis is on general linear models, and we begin with the simplest situations – single, continuous variables – describing those models in detail. We use these models as building blocks to understanding a wide range of other kinds of data – all of the common statistical analyses, rather than being distinctly different kinds of analyses, are variations on a common theme of statistical modeling – constructing a model for the data and then determining whether observed data fit this particular model. Our aim is to show how a broad understanding of the models allows us to deal with a wide range of more complex situations.

We have illustrated this approach of fitting models primarily with parametric statistics. Most biological data are still analyzed with linear models that assume underlying normal distributions. However, we introduce readers to a range of more general approaches, and stress that, once you understand the general modeling approach for normally distributed data, you can use that information to begin modeling data with nonlinear relationships, variables that follow other statistical distributions, etc.

Learning by example

One of our strongest beliefs is that we understand statistical principles much better when we see how they are applied to situations in our own discipline. Examples let us make the link between statistical models and formal statistical terms (blocks, plots, etc.) or papers written in other disciplines, and the biological situations that we are dealing with. For example, how is our analysis and interpretation of an experiment repeated several times helped by reading a literature about blocks of agricultural land? How does literature developed for psychological research let us deal with measuring changes in physiological responses of plants?

Throughout this book, we illustrate all of the statistical techniques with examples from the current biological literature. We describe why (we think) the authors chose to do an experiment in a particular way, and how to analyze the data, including assessing assumptions and interpreting statistical output. These examples appear as boxes through each chapter, and we are delighted that authors of most of these studies have made their raw data available to us. We provide those raw data files on a website http://www.zoology.unimelb.edu.au/qkstats allowing readers to run these analyses using their particular software package.

The other value of published examples is that we can see how particular analyses can be described and reported. When fitting complex statistical models, it is easy to allow the biology to be submerged by a mass of statistical output. We hope that the examples, together with our own thoughts on this subject, presented in the final chapter, will help prevent this happening.

This book is a bridge

It is not possible to produce a book that introduces a reader to biological statistics and takes them far enough to understand complex models, at least while having a book that is small enough to transport. We therefore assume that readers are familiar with basic statistical concepts, such as would result from a one or two semester introductory course, or have read one of the excellent basic texts (e.g. Sokal & Rohlf 1995). We take the reader from these texts into more complex areas, explaining the principles, assumptions, and pitfalls, and encourage a reader to read the excellent detailed treatments (e.g. for analysis of variance, Winer *et al.* 1991 or Underwood 1997).

Biological data are often messy, and many readers will find that their research questions require more complex models than we describe here. Ways of dealing with messy data or solutions to complex problems are often provided in the primary statistical literature. We try to point the way to key pieces of that statistical literature, providing the reader with the basic tools to be able to deal with that literature, or to be able to seek professional (statistical) help when things become too complex.

We must always remember that, for biologists, *statistics is a tool* that we use to illuminate and clarify biological problems. Our aim is to be able to use these tools efficiently, without losing sight of the biology that is the motivation for most of us entering this field.

Some acknowledgments

Our biggest debt is to the range of colleagues who have read, commented upon, and corrected various versions of these chapters. Many of these colleagues have their own research groups, who they enlisted in this exercise. These altruistic and diligent souls include (alphabetically) Jacqui

Brooks, Andrew Constable, Barb Downes, Peter Fairweather, Ivor Growns, Murray Logan, Ralph Mac Nally, Richard Marchant, Pete Raimondi, Wayne Robinson, Suvaluck Satumanatpan and Sabine Schreiber. Perhaps the most innocent victims were the graduate students who have been part of our research groups over the period we produced this book. We greatly appreciate their willingness to trade the chance of some illumination for reading and highlighting our obfuscations.

We also wish to thank the various researchers whose data we used as examples throughout. Most of them willingly gave of their raw data, trusting that we would neither criticize nor find flaws in their published work (we didn't!), or were public-spirited enough to have published their raw data.

Chapter 1

Introduction

Biologists and environmental scientists today must contend with the demands of keeping up with their primary field of specialization, and at the same time ensuring that their set of professional tools is current. Those tools may include topics as diverse as molecular genetics, sediment chemistry, and small-scale hydrodynamics, but one tool that is common and central to most of us is an understanding of experimental design and data analysis, and the decisions that we make as a result of our data analysis determine our future research directions or environmental management. With the advent of powerful desktop computers, we can now do complex analyses that in previous years were available only to those with an initiation into the wonders of early mainframe statistical programs, or computer programming languages, or those with the time for laborious hand calculations. In past years, those statistical tools determined the range of sampling programs and analyses that we were willing to attempt. Now that we can do much more complex analyses, we can examine data in more sophisticated ways. This power comes at a cost because we now collect data with complex underlying statistical models, and, therefore, we need to be familiar with the potential and limitations of a much greater range of statistical approaches.

With any field of science, there are particular approaches that are more common than others. Texts written for one field will not necessarily cover the most common needs of another field, and we felt that the needs of most common biologists and environmental scientists of our acquaintance were not covered by any one particular text.

A fundamental step in becoming familiar with data collection and analysis is to understand the philosophical viewpoint and basic tools that underlie what we do. We begin by describing our approach to scientific method. Because our aim is to cover some complex techniques, we do not describe introductory statistical methods in much detail. That task is a separate one, and has been done very well by a wide range of authors. We therefore provide only an overview or refresher of some basic philosophical and statistical concepts. We strongly urge you to read the first few chapters of a good introductory statistics or biostatistics book (you can't do much better than Sokal & Rohlf 1995) before working through this chapter.

1.1 | Scientific method

An appreciation of the philosophical bases for the way we do our scientific research is an important prelude to the rest of this book (see Chalmers 1999, Gower 1997, O'Hear 1989). There are many valuable discussions of scientific philosophy from a biological context and we particularly recommend Ford (2000), James & McCulloch (1985), Loehle (1987) and Underwood (1990, 1991). Maxwell & Delaney (1990) provide an overview from a behavioral sciences viewpoint and the first two chapters of Hilborn & Mangel (1997) emphasize alternatives to the Popperian approach in situations where experimental tests of hypotheses are simply not possible.

Early attempts to develop a philosophy of scientific logic, mainly due to Francis Bacon and John Stuart Mill, were based around the principle of induction, whereby sufficient numbers of confirmatory observations and no contradictory observations allow us to conclude that a theory or law is true (Gower 1997). The logical problems with inductive reasoning are discussed in every text on the philosophy of science, in particular that no amount of confirmatory observations can ever prove a theory. An alternative approach, and also the most commonly used scientific method in modern biological sciences literature, employs deductive reasoning, the process of deriving explanations or predictions from laws or theories. Karl Popper (1968, 1969) formalized this as the hypothetico-deductive approach, based around the principle of falsificationism, the doctrine whereby theories (or hypotheses derived from them) are *disproved* because proof is logically impossible. An hypothesis is falsifiable if there exists a logically possible observation that is inconsistent with it. Note that in many scientific investigations, a description of pattern and inductive reasoning, to develop models and hypotheses (Mentis 1988), is followed by a deductive process in which we critically test our hypotheses.

Underwood (1990, 1991) outlined the steps involved in a falsificationist test. We will illustrate these steps with an example from the ecological literature, a study of bioluminescence in dinoflagellates by Abrahams & Townsend (1993).

1.1.1 Pattern description

The process starts with observation(s) of a pattern or departure from a pattern in nature. Underwood (1990) also called these puzzles or problems. The quantitative and robust description of patterns is, therefore, a crucial part of the scientific process and is sometimes termed an observational study (Manly 1992). While we strongly advocate experimental methods in biology, experimental tests of hypotheses derived from poorly collected and interpreted observational data will be of little use.

In our example, Abrahams & Townsend (1993) observed that dinoflagellates bioluminesce when the water they are in is disturbed. The next step is to explain these observations.

1.1.2 Models

The explanation of an observed pattern is referred to as a model or theory (Ford 2000), which is a series of statements (or formulae) that explains why the observations have occurred. Model development is also what Peters (1991) referred to as the synthetic or private phase of the scientific method, where the perceived problem interacts with insight, existing theory, belief and previous observations to produce a set of competing models. This phase is clearly inductive and involves developing theories from observations (Chalmers 1999), the exploratory process of hypothesis formulation.

James & McCulloch (1985), while emphasizing the importance of formulating models in science, distinguished different types of models. Verbal models are non-mathematical explanations of how nature works. Most biologists have some idea of how a process or system under investigation operates and this idea drives the investigation. It is often useful to formalize that idea as a conceptual verbal model, as this might identify important components of a system that need to be included in the model. Verbal models can be quantified in mathematical terms as either empiric models or theoretic models. These models usually relate a response or dependent variable to one or more predictor or independent variables. We can envisage from our biological understanding of a process that the response variable might depend on, or be affected by, the predictor variables.

Empiric models are mathematical descriptions of relationships resulting from processes rather than the processes themselves, e.g. equations describing the relationship between metabolism (response) and body mass (predictor) or species number (response) and island area (first predictor) and island age (second predictor). Empiric models are usually statistical models (Hilborn & Mangel 1997) and are used to describe a relationship between response and predictor variables. Much of this book is based on fitting statistical models to observed data.

Theoretic models, in contrast, are used to study processes, e.g. spatial variation in abundance of intertidal snails is caused by variations in settlement of larvae, or each outbreak of

Mediterranean fruit fly in California is caused by a new colonization event (Hilborn & Mangel 1997). In many cases, we will have a theoretic, or scientific, model that we can re-express as a statistical model. For example, island biogeography theory suggests that the number of species on an island is related to its area. We might express this scientific model as a linear statistical relationship between species number and island area and evaluate it based on data from a range of islands of different sizes. Both empirical and theoretic models can be used for prediction, although the generality of predictions will usually be greater for theoretic models.

The scientific model proposed to explain bioluminescence in dinoflagellates was the "burglar alarm model", whereby dinoflagellates bioluminesce to attract predators of copepods, which eat the dinoflagellates. The remaining steps in the process are designed to test or evaluate a particular model.

1.1.3 Hypotheses and tests

We can make a prediction or predictions deduced from our model or theory; these predictions are called research (or logical) hypotheses. If a particular model is correct, we would predict specific observations under a new set of circumstances. This is what Peters (1991) termed the analytic, public or Popperian phase of the scientific method, where we use critical or formal tests to evaluate models by falsifying hypotheses. Ford (2000) distinguished three meanings of the term "hypothesis". We will use it in Ford's (2000) sense of a statement that is tested by investigation, experimentally if possible, in contrast to a model or theory and also in contrast to a postulate, a new or unexplored idea.

One of the difficulties with this stage in the process is deciding which models (and subsequent hypotheses) should be given research priority. There will often be many competing models and, with limited budgets and time, the choice of which models to evaluate is an important one. Popper originally suggested that scientists should test those hypotheses that are most easily falsified by appropriate tests. Tests of theories or models using hypotheses with high empirical content and which make improbable predictions are what

Popper called severe tests, although that term has been redefined by Mayo (1996) as a test that is likely to reveal a specific error if it exists (e.g. decision errors in statistical hypothesis testing – see Chapter 3). Underwood (1990, 1991) argued that it is usually difficult to decide which hypotheses are most easily refuted and proposed that competing models are best separated when their hypotheses are the most distinctive, i.e. they predict very different results under similar conditions. There are other ways of deciding which hypothesis to test, more related to the sociology of science. Some hypotheses may be relatively trivial, or you may have a good idea what the results can be. Testing that hypothesis may be most likely to produce a statistically significant (see Chapter 3), and, unfortunately therefore, a publishable result. Alternatively, a hypothesis may be novel or require a complex mechanism that you think unlikely. That result might be more exciting to the general scientific community, and you might decide that, although the hypothesis is harder to test, you're willing to gamble on the fame, money, or personal satisfaction that would result from such a result.

Philosophers have long recognized that proof of a theory or its derived hypothesis is logically impossible, because all observations related to the hypothesis must be made. Chalmers (1999; see also Underwood 1991) provided the clever example of the long history of observations in Europe that swans were white. Only by observing all swans everywhere could we "prove" that all swans are white. The fact that a single observation contrary to the hypothesis could disprove it was clearly illustrated by the discovery of black swans in Australia.

The need for disproof dictates the next step in the process of a falsificationist test. We specify a null hypothesis that includes all possibilities except the prediction in the hypothesis. It is much simpler logically to disprove a null hypothesis. The null hypothesis in the dinoflagellate example was that bioluminesence by dinoflagellates would have no effect on, or would decrease, the mortality rate of copepods grazing on dinoflagellates. Note that this null hypothesis includes all possibilities except the one specified in the hypothesis.

So, the final phase in the process is the experimental test of the hypothesis. If the null hypothesis is rejected, the logical (or research) hypothesis, and therefore the model, is supported. The model should then be refined and improved, perhaps making it predict outcomes for different spatial or temporal scales, other species or other new situations. If the null hypothesis is not rejected, then it should be retained and the hypothesis, and the model from which it is derived, are incorrect. We then start the process again, although the statistical decision not to reject a null hypothesis is more problematic (Chapter 3).

The hypothesis in the study by Abrahams & Townsend (1993) was that bioluminesence would increase the mortality rate of copepods grazing on dinoflagellates. Abrahams & Townsend (1993) tested their hypothesis by comparing the mortality rate of copepods in jars containing biolumi-nescing dinoflagellates, copepods and one fish (copepod predator) with control jars containing non-bioluminescing dinoflagellates, copepods and one fish. The result was that the mortality rate of copepods was greater when feeding on bioluminescing dinoflagellates than when feeding on non-bioluminescing dinoflagellates. Therefore the null hypothesis was rejected and the logical hypothesis and burglar alarm model was supported.

1.1.4 Alternatives to falsification

While the Popperian philosophy of falsificationist tests has been very influential on the scientific method, especially in biology, at least two other viewpoints need to be considered. First, Thomas Kuhn (1970) argued that much of science is carried out within an accepted paradigm or framework in which scientists refine the theories but do not really challenge the paradigm. Falsified hypotheses do not usually result in rejection of the over-arching paradigm but simply its enhancement. This "normal science" is punctuated by occasional scientific revolutions that have as much to do with psychology and sociology as empirical information that is counter to the prevailing paradigm (O'Hear 1989). These scientific revolutions result in (and from) changes in methods, objectives and personnel (Ford 2000). Kuhn's arguments have been described as relativ-

istic because there are often no objective criteria by which existing paradigms and theories are toppled and replaced by alternatives.

Second, Imre Lakatos (1978) was not convinced that Popper's ideas of falsification and severe tests really reflected the practical application of science and that individual decisions about falsifying hypotheses were risky and arbitrary (Mayo 1996). Lakatos suggested we should develop scientific research programs that consist of two components: a "hard core" of theories that are rarely challenged and a protective belt of auxiliary theories that are often tested and replaced if alternatives are better at predicting outcomes (Mayo 1996). One of the contrasts between the ideas of Popper and Lakatos that is important from the statistical perspective is the latter's ability to deal with multiple competing hypotheses more elegantly than Popper's severe tests of individual hypotheses (Hilborn & Mangel 1997).

An important issue for the Popperian philosophy is corroboration. The falsificationist test makes it clear what to do when an hypothesis is rejected after a severe test but it is less clear what the next step should be when an hypothesis passes a severe test. Popper argued that a theory, and its derived hypothesis, that has passed repeated severe testing has been corroborated. However, because of his difficulties with inductive thinking, he viewed corroboration as simply a measure of the past performance of a model, rather an indication of how well it might predict in other circumstances (Mayo 1996, O'Hear 1989). This is frustrating because we clearly want to be able to use models that have passed testing to make predictions under new circumstances (Peters 1991). While detailed discussion of the problem of corroboration is beyond the scope of this book (see Mayo 1996), the issue suggests two further areas of debate. First, there appears to be a role for both induction and deduction in the scientific method, as both have obvious strengths and weaknesses and most biological research cannot help but use both in practice. Second, formal corroboration of hypotheses may require each to be allocated some measure of the probability that each is true or false, i.e. some measure of evidence in favor or against each hypothesis. This goes to the heart of one of the most long-standing and vigorous debates in statistics, that between frequentists and Bayesians (Section 1.4 and Chapter 3).

Ford (2000) provides a provocative and thorough evaluation of the Kuhnian, Lakatosian and Popperian approaches to the scientific method, with examples from the ecological sciences.

1.1.5 Role of statistical analysis

The application of statistics is important throughout the process just described. First, the description and detection of patterns must be done in a rigorous manner. We want to be able to detect gradients in space and time and develop models that explain these patterns. We also want to be confident in our estimates of the parameters in these statistical models. Second, the design and analysis of experimental tests of hypotheses are crucial. It is important to remember at this stage that the research hypothesis (and its complement, the null hypothesis) derived from a model is not the same as the statistical hypothesis (James & McCulloch 1985); indeed, Underwood (1990) has pointed out the logical problems that arise when the research hypothesis is identical to the statistical hypothesis. Statistical hypotheses are framed in terms of population parameters and represent tests of the predictions of the research hypotheses (James & McCulloch 1985). We will discuss the process of testing statistical hypotheses in Chapter 3. Finally, we need to present our results, from both the descriptive sampling and from tests of hypotheses, in an informative and concise manner. This will include graphical methods, which can also be important for exploring data and checking assumptions of statistical procedures.

Because science is done by real people, there are aspects of human psychology that can influence the way science proceeds. Ford (2000) and Loehle (1987) have summarized many of these in an ecological context, including confirmation bias (the tendency for scientists to confirm their own theories or ignore contradictory evidence) and theory tenacity (a strong commitment to basic assumptions because of some emotional or personal investment in the underlying ideas). These psychological aspects can produce biases in a given discipline that have important implications for our subsequent discussions on research

design and data analysis. For example, there is a tendency in biology (and most sciences) to only publish positive (or statistically significant) results, raising issues about statistical hypothesis testing and meta-analysis (Chapter 3) and power of tests (Chapter 7). In addition, successful tests of hypotheses rely on well-designed experiments and we will consider issues such as confounding and replication in Chapter 7.

1.2 | Experiments and other tests

Platt (1964) emphasized the importance of experiments that critically distinguish between alternative models and their derived hypotheses when he described the process of strong inference:

- devise alternative hypotheses,
- devise a crucial experiment (or several experiments) each of which will exclude one or more of the hypotheses,
- carry out the experiment(s) carefully to obtain a "clean" result, and
- recycle the procedure with new hypotheses to refine the possibilities (i.e. hypotheses) that remain.

Crucial to Platt's (1964) approach was the idea of multiple competing hypotheses and tests to distinguish between these. What nature should these tests take?

In the dinoflagellate example above, the crucial test of the hypothesis involved a manipulative experiment based on sound principles of experimental design (Chapter 7). Such manipulations provide the strongest inference about our hypotheses and models because we can assess the effects of causal factors on our response variable separately from other factors. James & McCulloch (1985) emphasized that testing biological models, and their subsequent hypotheses, does not occur by simply seeing if their predictions are met in an observational context, although such results offer support for an hypothesis. Along with James & McCulloch (1985), Scheiner (1993), Underwood (1990), Werner (1998), and many others, we argue strongly that manipulative experiments are the best way to properly distinguish between biological models.

There are at least two costs to this strong inference from manipulative experiments. First, experiments nearly always involve some artificial manipulation of nature. The most extreme form of this is when experiments testing some natural process are conducted in the laboratory. Even field experiments will often use artificial structures or mechanisms to implement the manipulation. For example, mesocosms (moderate sized enclosures) are often used to investigate processes happening in large water bodies, although there is evidence from work on lakes that issues related to the small-scale of mesocosms may restrict generalization to whole lakes (Carpenter 1996; see also Resetarits & Fauth 1998). Second, the larger the spatial and temporal scales of the process being investigated, the more difficult it is to meet the guidelines for good experimental design. For example, manipulations of entire ecosystems are crucial for our understanding of the role of natural and anthropogenic disturbances to these systems, especially since natural resource agencies have to manage such systems at this large spatial scale (Carpenter *et al.* 1995). Replication and randomization (two characteristics regarded as important for sensible interpretation of experiments – see Chapter 7) are usually not possible at large scales and novel approaches have been developed to interpret such experiments (Carpenter 1990). The problems of scale and the generality of conclusions from smaller-scale manipulative experiments are challenging issues for experimental biologists (Dunham & Beaupre 1998).

The testing approach on which the methods in this book are based relies on making predictions from our hypothesis and seeing if those predictions apply when observed in a new setting, i.e. with data that were not used to derive the model originally. Ideally, this new setting is experimental at scales relevant for the hypothesis, but this is not always possible. Clearly, there must be additional ways of testing between competing models and their derived hypotheses. Otherwise, disciplines in which experimental manipulation is difficult for practical or ethical reasons, such as meteorology, evolutionary biology, fisheries ecology, etc., could make no scientific progress. The alternative is to predict from our models/hypotheses in new settings that are not experimentally derived. Hilborn & Mangel (1997), while arguing for experimental studies in ecology where possible, emphasize the approach of "confronting" competing models (or hypotheses) with observational data by assessing how well the data meet the predictions of the model.

Often, the new setting in which we test the predictions of our model may provide us with a contrast of some factor, similar to what we may have set up had we been able to do a manipulative experiment. For example, we may never be able to (nor want to!) test the hypothesis that wildfire in old-growth forests affects populations of forest birds with a manipulative experiment at a realistic spatial scale. However, comparisons of bird populations in forests that have burnt naturally with those that haven't provide a test of the hypothesis. Unfortunately, a test based on such a natural "experiment" (*sensu* Underwood 1990) is weaker inference than a real manipulative experiment because we can never separate the effects of fire from other pre-existing differences between the forests that might also affect bird populations. Assessments of effects of human activities ("environmental impact assessment") are often comparisons of this kind because we can rarely set up a human impact in a truly experimental manner (Downes *et al.* 2001). Well-designed observational (sampling) programs can provide a refutationist test of a null hypothesis (Underwood 1991) by evaluating whether predictions hold, although they cannot demonstrate causality.

While our bias in favor of manipulative experiments is obvious, we hope that we do not appear too dogmatic. Experiments potentially provide the strongest inference about competing hypotheses, but their generality may also be constrained by their artificial nature and limitations of spatial and temporal scale. Testing hypotheses against new observational data provides weaker distinctions between competing hypotheses and the inferential strength of such methods can be improved by combining them with other forms of evidence (anecdotal, mathematical modeling, correlations etc. – see Downes *et al.* 2001, Hilborn & Mangel 1997, McArdle 1996). In practice, most biological investigations will include both observational and experimental approaches. Rigorous and sensible statistical analyses will be relevant at all stages of the investigation.

1.3 | Data, observations and variables

In biology, data usually consist of a collection of observations or objects. These observations are usually sampling units (e.g. quadrats) or experimental units (e.g. individual organisms, aquaria, etc.) and a set of these observations should represent a sample from a clearly defined population (all possible observations in which we are interested). The "actual property measured by the individual observations" (Sokal & Rohlf 1995, p. 9), e.g. length, number of individuals, pH, etc., is called a variable. A random variable (which we will denote as Y, with y being any value of Y) is simply a variable whose values are not known for certain before a sample is taken, i.e. the observed values of a random variable are the results of a random experiment (the sampling process). The set of all possible outcomes of the experiment, e.g. all the possible values of a random variable, is called the sample space. Most variables we deal with in biology are random variables, although predictor variables in models might be fixed in advance and therefore not random. There are two broad categories of random variables: (i) discrete random variables can only take certain, usually integer, values, e.g. the number of cells in a tissue section or number of plants in a forest plot, and (ii) continuous random variables, which take any value, e.g. measurements like length, weight, salinity, blood pressure etc. Kleinbaum *et al.* (1997) distinguish these in terms of "gappiness" – discrete variables have gaps between observations and continuous variables have no gaps between observations.

The distinction between discrete and continuous variables is not always a clear dichotomy; the number of organisms in a sample of mud from a local estuary can take a very large range of values but, of course, must be an integer so is actually a discrete variable. Nonetheless, the distinction between discrete and continuous variables is important, especially when trying to measure uncertainty and probability.

1.4 | Probability

The single most important characteristic of biological data is their uncertainty. For example, if we take two samples, each consisting of the same number of observations, from a population and estimate the mean for some variable, the two means will almost certainly be different, despite the samples coming from the same population. Hilborn & Mangel (1997) proposed two general causes why the two means might be different, i.e. two causes of uncertainty in the expected value of the population. Process uncertainty results from the true population mean being different when the second sample was taken compared with the first. Such temporal changes in biotic variables, even over very short time scales, are common in ecological systems. Observation uncertainty results from sampling error; the mean value in a sample is simply an imperfect estimate of the mean value in the population (all the possible observations) and, because of natural variability between observations, different samples will nearly always produce different means. Observation uncertainty can also result from measurement error, where the measuring device we are using is imperfect. For many biological variables, natural variability is so great that we rarely worry about measurement error, although this might not be the case when the variable is measured using some complex piece of equipment prone to large malfunctions.

In most statistical analyses, we view uncertainty in terms of probabilities and understanding probability is crucial to understanding modern applied statistics. We will only briefly introduce probability here, particularly as it is very important for how we interpret statistical tests of hypotheses. Very readable introductions can be found in Antelman (1997), Barnett (1999), Harrison & Tamaschke (1984) and Hays (1994); from a biological viewpoint in Sokal & Rohlf (1995) and Hilborn & Mangel (1997); and from a philosophical perspective in Mayo (1996).

We usually talk about probabilities in terms of events; the probability of event A occurring is written $P(A)$. Probabilities can be between zero and one; if $P(A)$ equals zero, then the event is impossible; if $P(A)$ equals one, then the event is certain. As a simple example, and one that is used in nearly every introductory statistics book, imagine the toss of a coin. Most of us would state that the probability of heads is 0.5, but what do we really mean by that statement? The classical interpretation of probability is that it is the relative frequency of an event that we would expect in the long run, or in a long sequence of identical trials. In the coin tossing example, the probability of heads being 0.5 is interpreted as the expected proportion of heads in a long sequence of tosses. Problems with this long-run frequency interpretation of probability include defining what is meant by identical trials and the many situations in which uncertainty has no sensible long-run frequency interpretation, e.g. probability of a horse winning a particular race, probability of it raining tomorrow (Antelman 1997). The long-run frequency interpretation is actually the classical statistical interpretation of probabilities (termed the frequentist approach) and is the interpretation we must place on confidence intervals (Chapter 2) and P values from statistical tests (Chapter 3).

The alternative way of interpreting probabilities is much more subjective and is based on a "degree of belief" about whether an event will occur. It is basically an attempt at quantification of an opinion and includes two slightly different approaches – logical probability developed by Carnap and Jeffreys and subjective probability pioneered by Savage, the latter being a measure of probability specific to the person deriving it. The opinion on which the measure of probability is based may be derived from previous observations, theoretical considerations, knowledge of the particular event under consideration, etc. This approach to probability has been criticized because of its subjective nature but it has been widely applied in the development of prior probabilities in the Bayesian approach to statistical analysis (see below and Chapters 2 and 3).

We will introduce some of the basic rules of probability using a simple biological example with a dichotomous outcome – eutrophication in lakes (e.g. Carpenter et al. 1998). Let $P(A)$ be the probability that a lake will go eutrophic. Then $P(\sim A)$ equals one minus $P(A)$, i.e. the probability of not A is one minus the probability of A. In our

example, the probability that the lake will not go eutrophic is one minus the probability that it will go eutrophic.

Now consider the $P(B)$, the probability that there will be an increase in nutrient input into the lake. The joint probability of A and B is:

$$P(A \cup B) = P(A) + P(B) - P(A \cap B) \tag{1.1}$$

i.e. the probability that A or B occur $[P(A \cup B)]$ is the probability of A plus the probability of B minus the probability of A and B both occurring $[P(A \cap B)]$. In our example, the probability that the lake will go eutrophic or that there will be an increase in nutrient input equals the probability that the lake will go eutrophic plus the probability that the lake will receive increased nutrients minus the probability that the lake will go eutrophic and receive increased nutrients.

These simple rules lead on to conditional probabilities, which are very important in practice. The conditional probability of A, given B, is:

$$P(A \mid B) = P(A \cap B)/P(B) \tag{1.2}$$

i.e. the probability that A occurs, given that B occurs, equals the probability of A and B both occurring divided by the probability of B occurring. In our example, the probability that the lake will go eutrophic given that it receives increased nutrient input equals the probability that it goes eutrophic and receives increased nutrients divided by the probability that it receives increased nutrients.

We can combine these rules to develop another way of expressing conditional probability – Bayes Theorem (named after the eighteenth-century English mathematician, Thomas Bayes):

$$P(A \mid B) = \frac{P(B \mid A)P(A)}{P(B \mid A)P(A) + P(B \mid \sim A)P(\sim A)} \tag{1.3}$$

This formula allows us to assess the probability of an event A in the light of new information, B. Let's define some terms and then show how this somewhat daunting formula can be useful in practice. $P(A)$ is termed the prior probability of A – it is the probability of A prior to any new information (about B). In our example, it is our probability of a lake going eutrophic, calculated before knowing anything about nutrient inputs, possibly determined from previous studies on eutrophication in lakes. $P(B|A)$ is the likelihood of B being observed, given that A did occur [a similar interpretation exists for $P(B|\sim A)$]. The likelihood of a model or hypothesis or event is simply the probability of observing some data assuming the model or hypothesis is true or assuming the event occurs. In our example, $P(B|A)$ is the likelihood of seeing a raised level of nutrients, given that the lake has gone eutrophic (A). Finally, $P(A|B)$ is the posterior probability of A, the probability of A after making the observations about B, the probability of a lake going eutrophic after incorporating the information about nutrient input. This is what we are after with a Bayesian analysis, the modification of prior information to posterior information based on a likelihood (Ellison 1996).

Bayes Theorem tells us how probabilities might change based on previous evidence. It also relates two forms of conditional probabilities – the probability of A given B to the probability of B given A. Berry (1996) described this as relating inverse probabilities. Note that, although our simple example used an event (A) that had only two possible outcomes, Bayes formula can also be used for events that have multiple possible outcomes.

In practice, Bayes Theorem is used for estimating parameters of populations and testing hypotheses about those parameters. Equation 1.3 can be simplified considerably (Berry & Stangl 1996, Ellison 1996):

$$P(\theta|\text{data}) = \frac{P(\text{data}|\theta)P(\theta)}{P(\text{data})} \qquad (1.4)$$

where θ is a parameter to be estimated or an hypothesis to be evaluated, $P(\theta)$ is the "unconditional" prior probability of θ being a particular value, $P(\text{data}|\theta)$ is the likelihood of observing the data if θ is that value, $P(\text{data})$ is the "unconditional" probability of observing the data and is used to ensure the area under the probability distribution of θ equals one (termed "normalization"), and $P(\theta|\text{data})$ is the posterior probability of θ conditional on the data being observed. This formula can be re-expressed in English as:

posterior probability $\propto$ likelihood $\times$
prior probability $\qquad (1.5)$

While we don't advocate a Bayesian philosophy in this book, it is important for biologists to be aware of the approach and to consider it as an alternative way of dealing with conditional probabilities. We will consider the Bayesian approach to estimation in Chapter 2 and to hypothesis testing in Chapter 3.

1.5 | Probability distributions

A random variable will have an associated probability distribution where different values of the variable are on the horizontal axis and the relative probabilities of the possible values of the variable (the sample space) are on the vertical axis. For discrete variables, the probability distribution will comprise a measurable probability for each outcome, e.g. 0.5 for heads and 0.5 for tails in a coin toss, 0.167 for each one of the six sides of a fair die. The sum of these individual probabilities for independent events equals one. Continuous variables are not restricted to integers or any specific values so there are an infinite number of possible outcomes. The probability distribution of a continuous variable (Figure 1.1) is often termed a probability density function (pdf) where the vertical axis is the probability density of the variable [$f(y)$], a rate measuring the probability per unit of the variable at any particular value of the variable (Antelman 1997). We usually talk about the probability associated with a range of values, represented by the area under the probability distribution curve between the two extremes of the range. This area is determined from the integral of the probability density from the lower to the upper value, with the distribution usually normalized so that the total probability under the curve equals one. Note that the probability of any particular value of a continuous random variable is zero because the area under the curve for a single value is zero (Kleinbaum et al. 1997) – this is important when we consider the interpretation of probability distributions in statistical hypothesis testing (Chapter 3).

In many of the statistical analyses described in this book, we are dealing with two or more variables and our statistical models will often have more than one parameter. Then we need to switch from single probability distributions to joint

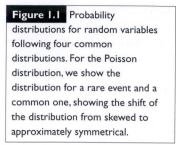

Figure 1.1 Probability distributions for random variables following four common distributions. For the Poisson distribution, we show the distribution for a rare event and a common one, showing the shift of the distribution from skewed to approximately symmetrical.

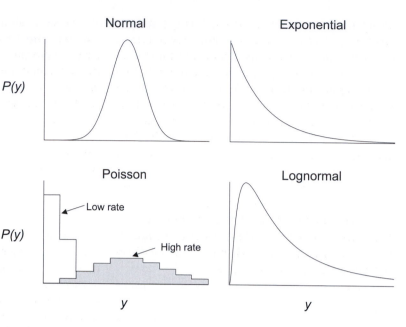

probability distributions where probabilities are measured, not as areas under a single curve, but volumes $P(y)$ under a more complex distribution. A common joint pdf is the bivariate normal distribution, to be introduced in Chapter 5.

Probability distributions nearly always refer to the distribution of variables in one or more populations. The expected value of a random variable $[E(Y)]$ is simply the mean (μ) of its probability distribution. The expected value is an important concept in applied statistics – most modeling procedures are trying to model the expected value of a random response variable. The mean is a measure of the center of a distribution – other measures include the median (the middle value) and the mode (the most common value). It is also important to be able to measure the spread of a distribution and the most common measures are based on deviations from the center, e.g. the variance is measured as the sum of squared deviations from the mean. We will discuss means and variances, and other measures of the center and spread of distributions, in more detail in Chapter 2.

1.5.1 Distributions for variables

Most statistical procedures rely on knowing the probability distribution of the variable (or the error terms from a statistical model) we are analyzing. There are many probability distributions that we can define mathematically (Evans *et al.* 2000) and some of these adequately describe the distributions of variables in biology. Let's consider continuous variables first.

The normal (also termed Gaussian) distribution is a symmetrical probability distribution

with a characteristic bell-shape (Figure 1.1). It is defined as:

$$f(y) = \frac{1}{\sqrt{2\pi\sigma^2}} e^{-(y-\mu)^2/2\sigma^2} \tag{1.6}$$

where $f(y)$ is the probability density of any value y of Y. Note that the normal distribution can be defined simply by the mean (μ) and the variance (σ^2), which are independent of each other. All other terms in the equation are constants. A normal distribution is often abbreviated to $N(Y:\mu,\sigma)$. Since there are infinitely many possible combinations of mean and variance, there is an infinite number of possible normal distributions. The standard normal distribution (z distribution) is a normal distribution with a mean of zero and a variance of one. The normal distribution is the most important probability distribution for data analysis; most commonly used statistical procedures in biology (e.g. linear regression, analysis of variance) assume that the variables being analyzed (or the deviations from a fitted model) follow a normal distribution.

The normal distribution is a symmetrical probability distribution, but continuous variables can have non-symmetrical distributions. Biological variables commonly have a positively skewed distribution, i.e. one with a long right tail (Figure 1.1). One skewed distribution is the lognormal distribution, which means that the logarithm of the variable is normally distributed (suggesting a simple transformation to normality – see Chapter 4). Measurement variables in biology that cannot be less than zero (e.g. length, weight, etc.) often follow lognormal distributions. In skewed distributions like the lognormal, there is a positive relationship between the mean and the variance.

There are some other probability distributions for continuous variables that are occasionally used in specific circumstances. The exponential distribution (Figure 1.1) is another skewed distribution that often applies when the variable is the time to the first occurrence of an event (Fox 1993, Harrison & Tamaschke 1984), such as in failure time analysis. This is a single parameter (λ) distribution with the following probability density function:

$$f(y) = \lambda e^{-\lambda y} \tag{1.7}$$

where $1/\lambda$ is the mean time to first occurrence. Fox (1993) provided some ecological examples.

The exponential and normal distributions are members of the larger family of exponential distributions that can be used as error distributions for a variety of linear models (Chapter 13). Other members of this family include gamma distribution for continuous variables and the binomial and Poisson (see below) for discrete variables.

Two other probability distributions for continuous variables are also encountered (albeit rarely) in biology. The two-parameter Weibull distribution varies between positively skewed and symmetrical depending on parameter values, although versions with three or more parameters are described (Evans et al. 2000). This distribution is mainly used for modeling failure rates and times. The beta distribution has two parameters and its shape can range from U to J to symmetrical. The beta distribution is commonly used as a prior probability distribution for dichotomous variables in Bayesian analyses (Evans et al. 2000).

There are also probability distributions for discrete variables. If we toss a coin, there are two possible outcomes – heads or tails. Processes with only two possible outcomes are common in biology, e.g. animals in an experiment can either live or die, a particular species of tree can be either present or absent from samples from a forest. A process that can only have one of two outcomes is sometimes called a Bernoulli trial and we often call the two possible outcomes success and failure. We will only consider a stationary Bernoulli trial, which is one where the probability of success is the same for each trial, i.e. the trials are independent.

The probability distribution of the number of successes in n independent Bernoulli trials is called the binomial distribution, a very important probability distribution in biology:

$$P(y = r) = \frac{n!}{r!(n-r)!} \pi^r (1 - \pi)^{n-r} \tag{1.8}$$

where $P(y = r)$ is the probability of a particular value (y) of the random variable (Y) being r successes out of n trials, n is the number of trials and π is the probability of a success. Note that n, the number of trials is fixed, and therefore the value of a binomial random variable cannot exceed n. The binomial distribution can be used to calculate probabilities for different numbers of successes out of n trials, given a known probability of success on any individual trial. It is also important as an error distribution for modeling variables with binary outcomes using logistic regression (Chapter 13). A generalization of the binomial distribution to when there are more than two possible outcomes is the multinomial distribution, which is the joint probability distribution of multiple outcomes from n fixed trials.

Another very important probability distribution for discrete variables is the Poisson distribution, which usually describes variables representing the number of (usually rare) occurrences of a particular event in an interval of time or space, i.e. counts. For example, the number of organisms in a plot, the number of cells in a microscope field of view, the number of seeds taken by a bird per minute. The probability distribution of a Poisson variable is:

$$P(y = r) = \frac{e^{-\mu} \mu^r}{r!} \tag{1.9}$$

where $P(y = r)$ is the probability that the number of occurrences of an event (y) equals an integer value ($r = 0, 1, 2...$), μ is the mean (and variance) of the number of occurrences. A Poisson variable can take any integer value between zero and infinity because the number of trials, in contrast to the binomial and the multinomial, is not fixed. One of the characteristics of a Poisson distribution is that the mean (μ) equals the variance (σ^2). For small values of μ, the Poisson distribution is positively skewed but once μ is greater than about five, the distribution is symmetrical (Figure 1.1).

The Poisson distribution has a wide range of applications in biology. It actually describes the occurrence of random events in space (or time) and has been used to examine whether organisms have random distributions in nature (Ludwig & Reynolds 1988). It also has wide application in many applied statistical procedures, e.g. counts in cells in contingency tables are often assumed to be Poisson random variables and therefore a Poisson probability distribution is used for the error terms in log-linear modeling of contingency tables (Chapter 14).

A simple example might help in understanding the difference between the binomial and the Poisson distributions. If we know the average number of seedlings of mountain ash trees (*Eucalyptus regnans*) per plot in some habitat, we can use the Poisson distribution to model the probability of different numbers of seedlings per plot, assuming independent sampling. The binomial distribution would be used if we wished to model the number of plots with seedlings out of a fixed number of plots, knowing the probability of a plot having a seedling.

Another useful probability distribution for counts is the negative binomial (White & Bennetts 1996). It is defined by two parameters, the mean and a dispersion parameter, which measures the degree of "clumping" in the distribution. White & Bennetts (1996) pointed out that the negative binomial has two potential advantages over the Poisson for representing skewed distributions of counts of organisms: (i) the mean does not have to equal the variance, and (ii) independence of trials (samples) is not required (see also Chapter 13).

These probability distributions are very important in data analysis. We can test whether a particular variable follows one of these distributions by calculating the expected frequencies and comparing them to observed frequencies with a goodness-of-fit test (Chapter 14). More importantly, we can model the expected value of a response variable [$E(Y)$] against a range of predictor (independent)

variables if we know the probability distribution of our response variable.

1.5.2 Distributions for statistics

The remaining theoretical distributions to examine are those used for determining probabilities of sample statistics, or modifications thereof. These distributions are used extensively for estimation and hypothesis testing. Four particularly important ones are as follows.

1. The z or normal distribution represents the probability distribution of a random variable that is the ratio of the difference between a sample statistic and its population value to the standard deviation of the population statistic (Figure 1.2).

2. Student's t distribution (Figure 1.2) represents the probability distribution of a random variable that is the ratio of the difference between a sample statistic and its population value to the standard deviation of the distribution of the sample statistic. The t distribution is a symmetrical distribution very similar to a normal distribution, bounded by infinity in both directions. Its shape becomes more similar with increasing sample size (Figure 1.2). We can convert a single sample statistic to a t value and use the t distribution to determine the probability of obtaining that t value (or one smaller or larger) for a specified value of the population parameter (Chapters 2 and 3).

3. χ^2 (chi-square) distribution (Figure 1.2) represents the probability distribution of a variable that is the square of values from a standard normal distribution (Section 1.5). Values from a χ^2 distribution are bounded by zero and infinity. Variances have a χ^2 distribution so this distribution is used for interval estimation of population variances (Chapter 2). We can also use the χ^2 distribution to determine the probability of obtaining a sample difference (or one smaller or larger) between observed values and those predicted by a model (Chapters 13 and 14).

4. F distribution (Figure 1.2) represents the probability distribution of a variable that is the ratio of two independent χ^2 variables, each

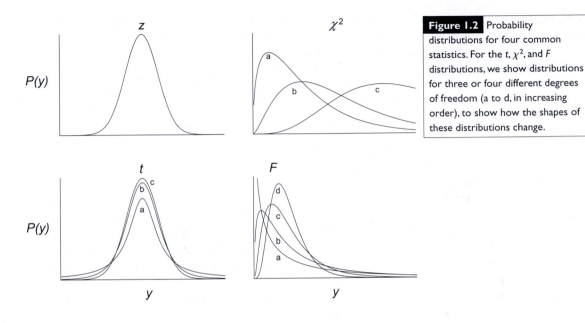

Figure 1.2 Probability distributions for four common statistics. For the t, χ^2, and F distributions, we show distributions for three or four different degrees of freedom (a to d, in increasing order), to show how the shapes of these distributions change.

divided by its df (degrees of freedom) (Hays 1994). Because variances are distributed as χ^2, the F distribution is used for testing hypotheses about ratios of variances. Values from the F distribution are bounded by zero and infinity. We can use the F distribution to determine the probability of obtaining a sample variance ratio (or one larger) for a specified value of the true ratio between variances (Chapters 5 onwards).

All four distributions have mathematical derivations that are too complex to be of much interest to biologists (see Evans *et al.* 2000). However, these distributions are tabled in many textbooks and programmed into most statistical software, so probabilities of obtaining values from each, within a specific range, can be determined. These distributions are used to represent the probability distributions of the sample statistics (z, t, χ^2 or F) that we would expect from repeated random sampling from a population or populations. Different versions of each distribution are used depending on the degrees of freedom associated with the sample or samples (see Box 2.1 and Figure 1.2).

Chapter 2

Estimation

2.1 | Samples and populations

Biologists usually wish to make inferences (draw conclusions) about a population, which is defined as the collection of all the *possible* observations of interest. Note that this is a statistical population, not a biological population (see below). The collection of observations we take from the population is called a sample and the number of observations in the sample is called the sample size (usually given the symbol n). Measured characteristics of the sample are called statistics (e.g. sample mean) and characteristics of the population are called parameters (e.g. population mean).

The basic method of collecting the observations in a sample is called simple random sampling. This is where any observation has the same probability of being collected, e.g. giving every rat in a holding pen a number and choosing a sample of rats to use in an experiment with a random number table. We rarely sample truly randomly in biology, often relying on haphazard sampling for practical reasons. The aim is always to sample in a manner that doesn't create a bias in favour of any observation being selected. Other types of sampling that take into account heterogeneity in the population (e.g. stratified sampling) are described in Chapter 7. Nearly all applied statistical procedures that are concerned with using samples to make inferences (i.e. draw conclusions) about populations assume some form of random sampling. If the sampling is not random, then we are never sure quite what population is represented by our sample. When random sampling from clearly defined populations is not possible, then interpretation of standard methods of estimation becomes more difficult.

Populations must be defined at the start of any study and this definition should include the spatial and temporal limits to the population and hence the spatial and temporal limits to our inference. Our formal statistical inference is restricted to these limits. For example, if we sample from a population of animals at a certain location in December 1996, then our inference is restricted to that location in December 1996. We cannot infer what the population might be like at any other time or in any other place, although we can speculate or make predictions.

One of the reasons why classical statistics has such an important role in the biological sciences, particularly agriculture, botany, ecology, zoology, etc., is that we can often define a population about which we wish to make inferences and from which we can sample randomly (or at least haphazardly). Sometimes the statistical population is also a biological population (a group of individuals of the same species). The reality of random sampling makes biology a little different from other disciplines that use statistical analyses for inference. For example, it is often difficult for psychologists or epidemiologists to sample randomly because they have to deal with whatever subjects or patients are available (or volunteer!).

The main reason for sampling randomly from a clearly defined population is to use sample statistics (e.g. sample mean or variance) to estimate population parameters of interest (e.g. population mean or variance). The population parameters cannot be measured directly because the populations are usually too large, i.e. they contain too many observations for practical measurement. It is important to remember that population parameters are usually considered to be fixed, but unknown, values so they are not random variables and do not have probability distributions. Note that this contrasts with the Bayesian approach where population parameters are viewed as random variables (Section 2.6). Sample statistics are random variables, because their values depend on the outcome of the sampling experiment, and therefore they do have probability distributions, called sampling distributions.

What are we after when we estimate population parameters? A good estimator of a population parameter should have the following characteristics (Harrison & Tamaschke 1984, Hays 1994).

- It should be unbiased, meaning that the expected value of the sample statistic (the mean of its probability distribution) should equal the parameter. Repeated samples should produce estimates which do not consistently under- or over-estimate the population parameter.
- It should be consistent so as the sample size increases then the estimator will get closer to the population parameter. Once the sample includes the whole population, the sample statistic will obviously equal the population parameter, by definition.
- It should be efficient, meaning it has the lowest variance among all competing estimators. For example, the sample mean is a more efficient estimator of the population mean of a variable with a normal probability distribution than the sample median, despite the two statistics being numerically equivalent.

There are two broad types of estimation:

1. point estimates provide a single value which estimates a population parameter, and

2. interval estimates provide a range of values that might include the parameter with a known probability, e.g. confidence intervals.

Later in this chapter we discuss different methods of estimating parameters, but, for now, let's consider some common population parameters and their point estimates.

2.2 | Common parameters and statistics

Consider a population of observations of the variable Y measured on all N sampling units in the population. We take a random sample of n observations $(y_1, y_2, y_3, \ldots y_i, \ldots y_n)$ from the population. We usually would like information about two aspects of the population, some measure of location or central tendency (i.e. where is the middle of the population?) and some measure of the spread (i.e. how different are the observations in the population?). Common estimates of parameters of location and spread are given in Table 2.1 and illustrated in Box 2.2.

2.2.1 Center (location) of distribution

Estimators for the center of a distribution can be classified into three general classes, or broad types (Huber 1981, Jackson 1986). First are L-estimators, based on the sample data being ordered from smallest to largest (order statistics) and then forming a linear combination of weighted order statistics. The sample mean ($\bar{y}$), which is an unbiased estimator of the population mean (μ), is an L-estimator where each observation is weighted by $1/n$ (Table 2.1). Other common L-estimators include the following.

- The median is the middle measurement of a set of data. Arrange the data in order of magnitude (i.e. ranks) and weight all observations except the middle one by zero. The median is an unbiased estimator of the population mean for normal distributions, is a better estimator of the center of skewed distributions and is more resistant to outliers (extreme values very different to the rest of the sample; see Chapter 4).
- The trimmed mean is the mean calculated after omitting a proportion (commonly 5%) of the highest (and lowest) observations, usually to deal with outliers.
- The Winsorized mean is determined as for trimmed means except the omitted observations are replaced by the nearest remaining value.

Second are M-estimators, where the weightings given to the different observations change

Table 2.1 Common population parameters and sample statistics

Parameter	Statistic	Formula
Mean (μ)	$\bar{y}$	$\dfrac{\sum_{i=1}^{n} y_i}{n}$
Median	Sample median	$y_{(n+1)/2}$ if n odd $(y_{n/2} + y_{(n/2)+1})/2$ if n even
Variance (σ^2)	s^2	$\sum_{i=1}^{n} \dfrac{(y_i - \bar{y})^2}{n-1}$ ← SS sum of squares
Standard deviation (σ)	s	$\sqrt{\sum_{i=1}^{n} \dfrac{(y_i - \bar{y})^2}{n-1}}$
Median absolute deviation (MAD)	Sample MAD	$\text{median}[|y_i - \text{median}|]$
Coefficient of variation (CV)	Sample CV	$\dfrac{s}{\bar{y}} \times 100$
Standard error of $\bar{y}$ ($\sigma_{\bar{y}}$)	$s_{\bar{y}}$	$\dfrac{s}{\sqrt{n}}$
95% confidence interval for μ		$\bar{y} - t_{0.05(n-1)}\dfrac{s}{\sqrt{n}} \leq \mu \leq \bar{y} + t_{0.05(n-1)}\dfrac{s}{\sqrt{n}}$

gradually from the middle of the sample and incorporate a measure of variability in the estimation procedure. They include the Huber M-estimator and the Hampel M-estimator, which use different functions to weight the observations. They are tedious to calculate, requiring iterative procedures, but maybe useful when outliers are present because they downweight extreme values. They are not commonly used but do have a role in robust regression and ANOVA techniques for analyzing linear models (regression in Chapter 5 and ANOVA in Chapter 8).

Finally, R-estimators are based on the ranks of the observations rather than the observations themselves and form the basis for many rank-based "non-parametric" tests (Chapter 3). The only common R-estimator is the Hodges–Lehmann estimator, which is the median of the averages of all possible pairs of observations.

For data with outliers, the median and trimmed or Winsorized means are the simplest to calculate although these and M- and R-estimators are now commonly available in statistical software.

2.2.2 Spread or variability

Various measures of the spread in a sample are provided in Table 2.1. The range, which is the difference between the largest and smallest observation, is the simplest measure of spread, but there is no clear link between the sample range and the population range and, in general, the range will rise as sample size increases. The sample variance, which estimates the population variance, is an important measure of variability in many statistical analyses. The numerator of the formula is called the sum of squares (SS, the sum of squared deviations of each observation from the sample mean) and the variance is the average of these squared deviations. Note that we might expect to divide by n to calculate an average, but then s^2 consistently underestimates σ^2 (i.e. it is biased), so we divide by $n-1$ to make s^2 an unbiased estimator of σ^2. The one difficulty with s^2 is that its units are the square of the original observations, e.g. if the observations are lengths in mm, then the variance is in mm², an area not a length.

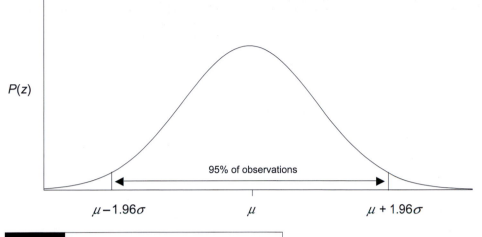

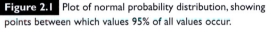

$P(z)$

95% of observations

$\mu - 1.96\sigma$ μ $\mu + 1.96\sigma$

Figure 2.1 Plot of normal probability distribution, showing points between which values 95% of all values occur.

The sample standard deviation, which estimates σ, the population standard deviation, is the square root of the variance. In contrast to the variance, the standard deviation is in the same units as the original observations.

The coefficient of variation (CV) is used to compare standard deviations between populations with different means and it provides a measure of variation that is independent of the measurement units. The sample coefficient of variation CV describes the standard deviation as a percentage of the mean; it estimates the population CV.

Some measures of spread that are more robust to unusual observations include the following.

• The median absolute deviation (MAD) is less sensitive to outliers than the above measures and is the sensible measure of spread to present in association with medians.
• The interquartile range is the difference between the first quartile (the observation which has 0.25 or 25% of the observations below it) and the third quartile (the observation which has 0.25 of the observations above it). It is used in the construction of boxplots (Chapter 4).

For some of these statistics (especially the variance and standard deviation), there are equivalent formulae that can be found in any statistics textbook that are easier to use with a hand calculator. We assume that, in practice, biologists will use statistical software to calculate these statistics and, since the alternative formulae do not assist in the understanding of the concepts, we do not provide them.

2.3 | Standard errors and confidence intervals for the mean

2.3.1 Normal distributions and the Central Limit Theorem

Having an estimate of a parameter is only the first step in estimation. We also need to know how precise our estimate is. Our estimator may be the most precise of all the possible estimators, but if its value still varies widely under repeated sampling, it will not be very useful for inference. If repeated sampling produces an estimator that is very consistent, then it is precise and we can be confident that it is close to the parameter (assuming that it is unbiased). The traditional logic for determining precision of estimators is well covered in almost every introductory statistics and biostatistics book (we strongly recommend Sokal & Rohlf 1995), so we will describe it only briefly, using normally distributed variables as an example.

Assume that our sample has come from a normally distributed population (Figure 2.1). For any normal distribution, we can easily determine what proportions of observations in the

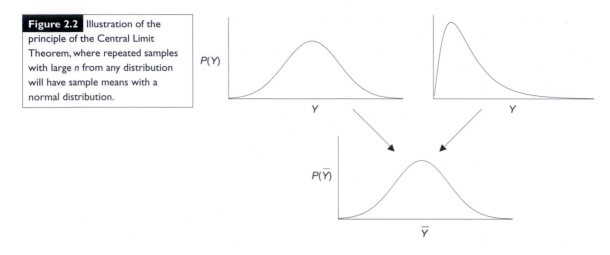

Figure 2.2 Illustration of the principle of the Central Limit Theorem, where repeated samples with large *n* from any distribution will have sample means with a normal distribution.

population occur within certain distances from the mean:

- 50% of population falls between $\mu \pm 0.674\sigma$
- 95% of population falls between $\mu \pm 1.960\sigma$
- 99% of population falls between $\mu \pm 2.576\sigma$.

Therefore, if we know μ and σ, we can work out these proportions for any normal distribution. These proportions have been calculated and tabulated in most textbooks, but only for the standard normal distribution, which has a mean of zero and a standard deviation (or variance) of one. To use these tables, we must be able to transform our sample observations to their equivalent values in the standard normal distribution. To do this, we calculate deviations from the mean in standard deviation units:

$$z = \frac{y_i - \mu}{\sigma} \qquad (2.1)$$

These deviations are called normal deviates or standard scores. This *z* transformation in effect converts any normal distribution to the standard normal distribution.

Usually we only deal with a single sample (with *n* observations) from a population. If we took many samples from a population and calculated all their sample means, we could plot the frequency (probability) distribution of the sample means (remember that the sample mean is a random variable). This probability distribution is called the sampling distribution of the mean and has three important characteristics.

- The probability distribution of means of samples from a normal distribution is also normally distributed.

- As the sample size increases, the probability distribution of means of samples from any distribution will approach a normal distribution. This result is the basis of the Central Limit Theorem (Figure 2.2).
- The expected value or mean of the probability distribution of sample means equals the mean of the population (μ) from which the samples were taken.

2.3.2 Standard error of the sample mean

If we consider the sample means to have a normal probability distribution, we can calculate the variance and standard deviation of the sample means, just like we could calculate the variance of the observations in a single sample. The expected value of the standard deviation of the sample means is:

$$\sigma_{\bar{y}} = \frac{\sigma}{\sqrt{n}} \qquad (2.2)$$

where σ is the standard deviation of the original population from which the repeated samples were taken and *n* is the size of samples.

We are rarely in the position of having many samples from the same population, so we estimate the standard deviation of the sample means from our single sample. The standard deviation of the sample means is called the standard error of the mean:

$$s_{\bar{y}} = \frac{s}{\sqrt{n}} \qquad (2.3)$$

where *s* is the sample estimate of the standard deviation of the original population and *n* is the sample size.

The standard error of the mean is telling us about the variation in our sample mean. It is termed "error" because it is telling us about the error in using $\bar{y}$ to estimate μ (Snedecor & Cochran 1989). If the standard error is large, repeated samples would likely produce very different means, and the mean of any single sample might not be close to the true population mean. We would not have much confidence that any specific sample mean is a good estimate of the population mean. If the standard error is small, repeated samples would likely produce similar means, and the mean of any single sample is more likely to be close to the true population mean. Therefore, we would be quite confident that any specific sample mean is a good estimate of the population mean.

2.3.3 Confidence intervals for population mean

In Equation 2.1, we converted any value from a normal distribution into its equivalent value from a standard normal distribution, the z score. Equivalently, we can convert any sample mean into its equivalent value from a standard normal distribution of means using:

$$z = \frac{\bar{y} - \mu}{\sigma_{\bar{y}}} \qquad (2.4)$$

where the denominator is simply the standard deviation of the mean, $\sigma/\sqrt{n}$, or standard error. Because this z score has a normal distribution, we can determine how confident we are in the sample mean, i.e. how close it is to the true population mean (the mean of the distribution of sample means). We simply determine values in our distribution of sample means between which a given percentage (often 95% by convention) of means occurs, i.e. between which values of $(\bar{y} - \mu)/\sigma_{\bar{y}}$ do 95% of values lie? As we showed above, 95% of a normal distribution falls between $\mu \pm 1.960\sigma$, so 95% of sample means fall between $\mu \pm 1.96\sigma_{\bar{y}}$ (1.96 times the standard deviation of the distribution of sample means, the standard error).

Now we can combine this information to make a confidence interval for μ:

$$P\{\bar{y} - 1.96\sigma_{\bar{y}} \leq \mu \leq \bar{y} + 1.96\sigma_{\bar{y}}\} = 0.95 \qquad (2.5)$$

This confidence interval is an interval estimate for the population mean, although the probability statement is actually about the interval, not about the population parameter, which is fixed. We will discuss the interpretation of confidence intervals in the next section. The only problem is that we very rarely know σ in practice, so we never actually know $\sigma_{\bar{y}}$; we can only estimate the standard error from s (sample standard deviation). Our standard normal distribution of sample means is now the distribution of $(\bar{y} - \mu)/s_{\bar{y}}$. This is a random variable called t and it has a probability distribution that is not quite normal. It follows a t distribution (Chapter 1), which is flatter and more spread than a normal distribution. Therefore, we must use the t distribution to calculate confidence intervals for the population mean in the common situation of not knowing the population standard deviation.

The t distribution (Figure 1.2) is a symmetrical probability distribution centered around zero and, like a normal distribution, it can be defined mathematically. Proportions (probabilities) for a standard t distribution (with a mean of zero and standard deviation of one) are tabled in most statistics books. In contrast to a normal distribution, however, t has a slightly different distribution depending on the sample size (well, for mathematical reasons, we define the different t distributions by $n - 1$, called the degrees of freedom (df) (see Box 2.1), rather than n). This is because s provides an imprecise estimate of σ if the sample size is small, increasing in precision as the sample size increases. When n is large (say >30), the t distribution is very similar to a normal distribution (because our estimate of the standard error based on s will be very close to the real standard error). Remember, the z distribution is simply the probability distribution of $(y - \mu)/\sigma$ or $(\bar{y} - \mu)/\sigma_{\bar{y}}$ if we are dealing with sample means. The t distribution is simply the probability distribution of $(\bar{y} - \mu)/s_{\bar{y}}$ and there is a different t distribution for each df $(n - 1)$.

The confidence interval (95% or 0.95) for the population mean then is:

$$P\{\bar{y} - t_{0.05(n-1)}s_{\bar{y}} \leq \mu \leq \bar{y} + t_{0.05(n-1)}s_{\bar{y}}\} = 0.95 \qquad (2.6)$$

where $t_{0.05(n-1)}$ is the value from the t distribution with $n - 1$ df between which 95% of all t values lie and $s_{\bar{y}}$ is the standard error of the mean. Note that the size of the interval will depend on the sample size and the standard deviation of the sample, both of which are used to calculate the standard

Box 2.1 Explanation of degrees of freedom

Degrees of freedom (df) is one of those terms that biologists use all the time in statistical analyses but few probably really understand. We will attempt to make it a little clearer. The degrees of freedom is simply the number of observations in our sample that are "free to vary" when we are estimating the variance (Harrison & Tamaschke 1984). Since we have already determined the mean, then only $n-1$ observations are free to vary because knowing the mean and $n-1$ observations, the last observation is fixed. A simple example – say we have a sample of observations, with values 3, 4 and 5. We know the sample mean (4) and we wish to estimate the variance. Knowing the mean and one of the observations doesn't tell us what the other two must be. But if we know the mean and two of the observations (e.g. 3 and 4), the final observation is fixed (it must be 5). So, knowing the mean, only two observations ($n-1$) are free to vary. As a general rule, the df is the number of observations minus the number of parameters included in the formula for the variance (Harrison & Tamaschke 1984).

error, and also on the level of confidence we require (Box 2.3).

We can use Equation 2.6 to determine confidence intervals for different levels of confidence, e.g. for 99% confidence intervals, simply use the t value between which 99% of all t values lie. The 99% confidence interval will be wider than the 95% confidence interval (Box 2.3).

2.3.4 Interpretation of confidence intervals for population mean

It is very important to remember that we usually do not consider μ a random variable but a fixed, albeit unknown, parameter and therefore the confidence interval is not a probability statement about the population mean. We are not saying there is a 95% probability that μ falls within this specific interval that we have determined from our sample data; μ is fixed, so this confidence interval we have calculated for a single sample either contains μ or it doesn't. The probability associated with confidence intervals is interpreted as a long-run frequency, as discussed in Chapter 1. Different random samples from the same population will give different confidence intervals and if we took 100 samples of this size (n), and calculated the 95% confidence interval from each sample, 95 of the intervals would contain μ and five wouldn't. Antelman (1997, p. 375) summarizes a confidence interval succinctly as ". . . one interval generated by a procedure that will give correct intervals 95% of the time".

2.3.5 Standard errors for other statistics

The standard error is simply the standard deviation of the probability distribution of a specific statistic, such as the mean. We can, however, calculate standard errors for other statistics besides the mean. Sokal & Rohlf (1995) have listed the formulae for standard errors for many different statistics but noted that they might only apply for large sample sizes or when the population from which the sample came was normal. We can use the methods just described to reliably determine standard errors for statistics (and confidence intervals for the associated parameters) from a range of analyses that assume normality, e.g. regression coefficients. These statistics, when divided by their standard error, follow a t distribution and, as such, confidence intervals can be determined for these statistics (confidence interval $= t \times$ standard error).

When we are not sure about the distribution of a sample statistic, or know that its distribution is non-normal, then it is probably better to use resampling methods to generate standard errors (Section 2.5). One important exception is the sample variance, which has a known distribution that is not normal, i.e. the Central Limit Theorem does not apply to variances. To calculate confidence intervals for the population variance, we need to use the chi-square (χ^2) distribution, which is the distribution of the following random variable:

$$\chi^2 = \frac{(y - \mu)^2}{\sigma^2}$$

(2.7)

Box 2.2 | Worked example of estimation: chemistry of forested watersheds

Lovett *et al.* (2000) studied the chemistry of forested watersheds in the Catskill Mountains in New York State. They chose 39 sites (observations) on first and second order streams and measured the concentrations of ten chemical variables (NO_3^-, total organic N, total N, NH_4^-, dissolved organic C, SO_4^{2-}, Cl^-, Ca^{2+}, Mg^{2+}, H^+), averaged over three years, and four watershed variables (maximum elevation, sample elevation, length of stream, watershed area). We will assume that the 39 sites represent a random sample of possible sites in the central Catskills and will focus on point estimation for location and spread of the populations for two variables, SO_4^{2-} and Cl^-, and interval estimation for the population mean of these two variables. We also created a modified version of SO_4^{2-} where we replaced the largest value (72.1 µmol l^{-1} at site BWS6) by an extreme value of 200 µmol l^{-1} to illustrate the robustness of various statistics to outliers.

Boxplots (Chapter 4) for both variables are presented in Figure 4.3. Note that SO_4^{2-} has a symmetrical distribution whereas Cl^- is positively skewed with outliers (values very different from rest of sample). Summary statistics for SO_4^{2-} (original and modified) and Cl^- are presented below.

Estimate	SO_4^{2-}	Modified SO_4^{2-}	Cl^-
Mean	61.92	65.20	22.84
Median	62.10	62.10	20.50
5% trimmed mean	61.90	61.90	20.68
Huber's M-estimate	61.67	61.67	20.21
Hampel's M-estimate	61.85	61.62	19.92
Standard deviation	5.24	22.70	12.38
Interquartile range	8.30	8.30	7.80
Median absolute deviation	4.30	4.30	3.90
Standard error of mean	0.84	3.64	1.98
95% confidence interval for mean	60.22–63.62	57.84–72.56	18.83–26.86

Given the symmetrical distribution of SO_4^{2-}, the mean and median are similar as expected. In contrast, the mean and the median are different by more than two units for Cl^-, as we would expect for a skewed distribution. The median is a more reliable estimator of the center of the skewed distribution for Cl^-, and the various robust estimates of location (median, 5% trimmed mean, Huber's and Hampel's M-estimates) all give similar values. The standard deviation for Cl^- is also affected by the outliers, and the confidence intervals are relatively wide.

The modified version of SO_4^{2-} also shows the sensitivity of the mean and the standard deviation to outliers. Of the robust estimators for location, only Hampel's M-estimate changes marginally, whereas the mean changes by more than three units. Similarly, the standard deviation (and therefore the standard error and 95%

confidence interval) is much greater for the modified variable, whereas the inter-quartile range and the median absolute deviation are unaffected by the outlier.

We also calculated bootstrap estimates for the mean and the median of SO_4^{2-} concentrations, based on 1000 bootstrap samples ($n = 39$) with replacement from the original sample of 39 sites. The bootstrap estimate was the mean of the 1000 bootstrap sample statistics, the bootstrap standard error was the standard deviation of the 1000 bootstrap sample statistics and the 95% confidence interval was determined from 25th and 975th values of the bootstrap statistics arranged in ascending order. The two estimates of the mean were almost identical, and although the standard error was smaller for the usual method, the percentile 95% confidence interval for the bootstrap method was narrower. The two estimates for the median were identical, but the bootstrap method allows us to estimate a standard error and a confidence interval.

	Usual	Bootstrap
Mean	61.92	61.91
Standard error	0.84	0.88
95% confidence interval	60.22–63.62	60.36–63.59
Median	61.72	61.72
Standard error	NA	1.34
95% confidence interval	NA	58.60–63.40

The frequency distributions of the bootstrap means and medians are presented in Figure 2.4. The distribution of bootstrap means is symmetrical whereas the bootstrap distribution of medians is skewed. This is commonly the case and the confidence interval for the median is not symmetrical around the bootstrap estimate. We also calculated the bias corrected bootstrap confidence intervals. Forty nine percent of bootstrap means were below the bootstrap estimate of 61.91, so the bias-corrected confidence interval is basically the same as the standard bootstrap. Forty four percent of bootstrap medians were below the bootstrap estimate of 61.72, so $z_0 = -0.151$ and $(2z_0 + 1.96) = 1.658$ and $(2z_0 - 1.96) = -2.262$. The percentiles, from the normal cumulative distribution, are 95.2% (upper) and 1.2% (lower). However, because so many of the bootstrap medians were the same value, these bias-corrected percentiles did not change the confidence intervals.

This is simply the square of the standard z score discussed above (see also Chapter 1). Because we square the numerator, χ^2 is always positive, ranging from zero to ∞. The χ^2 distribution is a sampling distribution so, like the random variable t, there are different probability distributions for χ^2 for different sample sizes; this is reflected in the degrees of freedom ($n - 1$). For small df, the probability distribution is skewed to the right (Figure 1.2) but it approaches normality as df increases.

Now back to the sample variance. It turns out that the probability distribution of the sample variance is a chi-square distribution. Strictly speaking,

$$\frac{(n-1)s^2}{\sigma^2} \qquad (2.8)$$

is distributed as χ^2 with $n - 1$ df (Hays 1994). We can rearrange Equation 2.8, using the chi-square distribution, to determine a confidence interval for the variance:

$$P\left\{\frac{s^2(n-1)}{\chi^2_{n-1}} \leq \sigma^2 \leq \frac{s^2(n-1)}{\chi^2_{n-1}}\right\} = 0.95 \qquad (2.9)$$

where the lower bound uses the χ^2 value below which 2.5% of all χ^2 values fall and the upper bound uses the χ^2 value above which 2.5% of all χ^2 values fall. Remember the long-run frequency interpretation of this confidence interval – repeated sampling would result in confidence intervals of which 95% would include the true population variance. Confidence intervals on

| **Box 2.3** | Effect of different sample variances, sample sizes and degrees of confidence on confidence interval for the population mean |

We will again use the data from Lovett et al. (2000) on the chemistry of forested watersheds in the Catskill Mountains in New York State and focus on interval estimation for the mean concentration of SO_4^{2-} in all the possible sites that could have been sampled.

Original sample

Sample ($n = 39$) with a mean concentration of SO_4^{2-} of 61.92 and s of 5.24. The t value for 95% confidence intervals with 38 df is 2.02. The 95% confidence interval for population mean SO_4^{2-} is $60.22 - 63.62$, i.e. 3.40.

Different sample variance

Sample ($n = 39$) with a mean concentration of SO_4^{2-} of 61.92 and s of 10.48 (twice original). The t value for 95% confidence intervals with 38 df is 2.02. The 95% confidence interval for population mean SO_4^{2-} is $58.53 - 65.31$, i.e. 6.78 (cf. 3.40).

So more variability in population (and sample) results in a wider confidence interval.

Different sample size

Sample ($n = 20$; half original) with a mean concentration of SO_4^{2-} of 61.92 and s of 5.24. The t value for 95% confidence intervals with 19 df is 2.09. The 95% confidence interval for population mean SO_4^{2-} is $59.47 - 64.37$, i.e. 4.90 (cf. 3.40).

So a smaller sample size results in wider interval because our estimates of s and $s_{\bar{y}}$ are less precise.

Different level of confidence (99%)

Sample ($n = 39$) with a mean concentration of SO_4^{2-} of 61.92 and s of 5.24. The t value for 99% confidence intervals with 38 df is 2.71. The 95% confidence interval for population mean SO_4^{2-} is $59.65 - 64.20$, i.e. 4.55 (cf. 3.40).

So requiring a greater level of confidence results in a wider interval for a given n and s.

---

variances are very important for the interpretation of variance components in linear models (Chapter 8).

2.4 | Methods for estimating parameters

2.4.1 Maximum likelihood (ML)

A general method for calculating statistics that estimate specific parameters is called Maximum Likelihood (ML). The estimates of population parameters (e.g. the population mean) provided earlier in this chapter are ML estimates, except for the variance where we correct the estimate to reduce bias. The logic of ML estimation is deceptively simple. Given a sample of observations from a population, we find estimates of one (or more) parameter(s) that maximise the likelihood of observing those data. To determine maximum likelihood estimators, we need to appreciate the likelihood function, which provides the likelihood of the observed data (and therefore our sample statistic) for all possible values of the parameter we are trying to estimate. For example, imagine we have a sample of observations with a sample mean of $\bar{y}$. The likelihood function, assuming a normal distribution and for a given standard

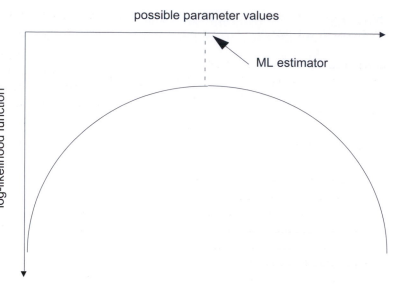

Figure 2.3 Generalized log-likelihood function for estimating a parameter.

deviation, is the likelihood of observing the data for all possible values of μ, the population mean. In general, for a parameter θ, the likelihood function is:

$$L(y; \theta) = \prod_{i=1}^{n} f(y_i; \theta) \qquad (2.10)$$

where $f(y_i; \theta)$ is the joint probability distribution of y_i and θ, i.e. the probability distribution of Y for possible values of θ. In many common situations, $f(y_i; \theta)$ is a normal probability distribution. The ML estimator of θ is the one that maximizes this likelihood function. Working with products (Π) in Equation 2.10 is actually difficult in terms of computation so it is more common to maximize the log-likelihood function:

$$L(\theta) = \ln \left[\prod_{i=1}^{n} f(y_i; \theta) \right] = \sum_{i=1}^{n} \ln[f(y_i; \theta)] \qquad (2.11)$$

For example, the ML estimator of μ (knowing σ^2) for a given sample is the value of μ which maximises the likelihood of observing the data in the sample. If we are trying to estimate μ from a normal distribution, then the $f(y_i; \mu)$ would be the equation for the normal distribution, which depends only on μ and σ^2. Eliason (1993) provides a simple worked example.

The ML estimator can be determined graphically by simply trying different values of μ and seeing which one maximizes the log-likelihood function (Figure 2.3). This is very tedious, however, and it is easier (and more accurate) to use some simple calculus to determine the value of μ that maximizes the likelihood function. ML estimators sometimes have exact arithmetical solutions, such as when estimating means or parameters for linear models (Chapters 8–12). In contrast, when analyzing some non-normal distributions, ML estimators need to be calculated using complex iterative algorithms (Chapters 13 and 14).

It is important to realize that a likelihood is not the same as a probability and the likelihood function is not a probability distribution (Barnett 1999, Hilborn & Mangel 1997). In a probability distribution for a random variable, the parameter is considered fixed and the data are the unknown variable(s). In a likelihood function, the data are considered fixed and it is the parameter that varies across all possible values. However, the likelihood of the data given a particular parameter value is related to the probability of obtaining the data assuming this particular parameter value (Hilborn & Mangel 1997).

2.4.2 Ordinary least squares (OLS)

Another general approach to estimating parameters is by ordinary least squares (OLS). The least squares estimator for a given parameter is the one that minimizes the sum of the squared differences between each value in a sample and the parameter, i.e. minimizes the following function:

$$\sum_{i=1}^{n} [y_i - f(\theta)]^2 \qquad (2.12)$$

The OLS estimator of μ for a given sample is the value of μ which minimises the sum of squared differences between each value in the sample and the estimate of μ (i.e. $\Sigma(y_i - \bar{y})^2$). OLS estimators are usually more straightforward to calculate than ML estimators, always having exact arithmetical solutions. The major application of OLS estimation is when we are estimating parameters of linear models (Chapter 5 onwards), where Equation 2.12 represents the sum of squared differences between observed values and those predicted by the model.

2.4.3 ML vs OLS estimation

Maximum likelihood and ordinary least squares are not the only methods for estimating population parameters (see Barnett 1999) but they are the most commonly used for the analyses we will discuss in this book. Point and interval estimation using ML relies on distributional assumptions, i.e. we need to specify a probability distribution for our variable or for the error terms from our statistical model (see Chapter 5 onwards). When these assumptions are met, ML estimators are generally unbiased, for reasonable sample sizes, and they have minimum variance (i.e., they are precise estimators) compared to other estimators. In contrast, OLS point estimates require no distributional assumptions, and OLS estimators are also generally unbiased and have minimum variance. However, for interval estimation and hypothesis testing, OLS estimators have quite restrictive distributional assumptions related to normality and patterns of variance.

For most common population parameters (e.g. μ), the ML and OLS estimators are the same when the assumptions of OLS are met. The exception is σ^2 (the population variance) for which the ML estimator (which uses n in the denominator) is slightly biased, although the bias is trivial if the sample size is reasonably large (Neter *et al.* 1996). In balanced linear models (linear regression and ANOVA) for which the assumptions hold (see Chapter 5 onwards), ML and OLS estimators of regression slopes and/or factor effects are identical. However, OLS is inappropriate for some common models where the response variable(s) or the residuals are not distributed normally, e.g. binary and more general categorical data. Therefore, generalized linear modeling (GLMs such as logistic regression and log-linear models; Chapter 13) and nonlinear modeling (Chapter 6) are based around ML estimation.

2.5 | Resampling methods for estimation

The methods described above for calculating standard errors for a statistic and confidence intervals for a parameter rely on knowing two properties of the statistic (Dixon 1993).

- The sampling distribution of the statistic, usually assumed to be normal, i.e. the Central Limit Theorem holds.
- The exact formula for the standard error (i.e. the standard deviation of the statistic).

These conditions hold for a statistic like the sample mean but do not obviously extend to other statistics like the median (Efron & Gong 1983). In biology, we would occasionally like to estimate the population values of many measurements for which the sampling distributions and variances are unknown. These include ecological indices such as the intrinsic rate of increase (r) and dissimilarity coefficients (Dixon 1993) and statistics from unusual types of analyses, such as the intercept of a smoothing function (see Chapter 5; Efron & Tibshirani 1991). To measure the precision (i.e. standard errors and confidence intervals) of these types of statistics we must rely on alternative, computer-intensive resampling methods. The two approaches described below are based on the same principle: in the absence of other information, the best guess for the distribution of the population is the observations we have in our sample. The methods estimate the standard error of a statistic and confidence intervals for a parameter by resampling from the original sample.

Good introductions to these methods include Crowley (1992), Dixon (1993), Manly (1997) and Robertson (1991), and Efron & Tibshirani (1991) suggest useful general applications. These resampling methods can also be used for hypothesis testing (Chapter 3).

2.5.1 Bootstrap

The bootstrap estimator was developed by Efron (1982). The sampling distribution of the statistic is determined empirically by randomly resampling (using a random number generator to choose the observations; see Robertson 1991), with replacement, from the original sample, usually with the same original sample size. Because sampling is with replacement, the same observation can obviously be resampled so the bootstrap samples will be different from each other. The desired statistic can be determined from each bootstrapped sample and the sampling distribution of each

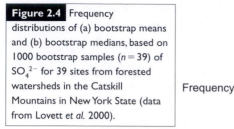

Figure 2.4 Frequency distributions of (a) bootstrap means and (b) bootstrap medians, based on 1000 bootstrap samples ($n = 39$) of SO_4^{2-} for 39 sites from forested watersheds in the Catskill Mountains in New York State (data from Lovett *et al.* 2000).

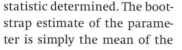

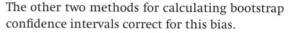

statistic determined. The bootstrap estimate of the parameter is simply the mean of the statistics from the bootstrapped samples. The standard deviation of the bootstrap estimate (i.e. the standard error of the statistic) is simply the standard deviation of the statistics from the bootstrapped samples (see Figure 2.4).

Techniques like the bootstrap can be used to measure the bias in an estimator, the difference between the actual population parameter and the expected value (mean) of the estimator. The bootstrap estimate of bias is simply the difference between the mean of the bootstrap statistics and the statistic calculated from the original sample (which is an estimator of the expected value of the statistic); see Robertson (1991).

Confidence intervals for the unknown population parameter can also be calculated based on the bootstrap samples. There are at least three methods (Dixon 1993, Efron & Gong 1983, Robertson 1991). First is the percentile method, where confidence intervals are calculated directly from the frequency distribution of bootstrap statistics. For example, we would arrange the 1000 bootstrap statistics in ascending order. Based on 1000 bootstrap samples, the lower limit of the 95% confidence interval would be the 25th value and the upper limit of the 95% confidence interval would be the 975th value; 950 values (95% of the bootstrap estimates) would fall between these values. Adjustments can easily be made for other confidence intervals, e.g. 5th and 995th value for a 99% confidence interval.

Unfortunately, the distribution of bootstrap statistics is often skewed, especially for statistics other than the mean. The confidence intervals calculated using the percentile method will not be symmetrical around the bootstrap estimate of the parameter, so the confidence intervals are biased.

The other two methods for calculating bootstrap confidence intervals correct for this bias.

The bias-corrected method first works out the percentage of bootstrap samples with statistics lower than the bootstrap estimate. This is transformed to its equivalent value from the inverse cumulative normal distribution (z_0) and this value used to modify the percentiles used for the lower and upper limits of the confidence interval:

$$95\% \text{ percentiles} = \Phi(2z_0 \pm 1.96) \tag{2.13}$$

where Φ is the normal cumulative distribution function. So we determine the percentiles for the values $(2z_0 + 1.96)$ and $(2z_0 - 1.96)$ from the normal cumulative distribution function and use these as the percentiles for our confidence interval. A worked example is provided in Box 2.2.

The third method, the accelerated bootstrap, further corrects for bias based on a measure of the influence each bootstrap statistic has on the final estimate. Dixon (1993) provides a readable explanation.

2.5.2 Jackknife

The jackknife is an historically earlier alternative to the bootstrap for calculating standard errors that is less computer intensive. The statistic is calculated from the full sample of n observations (call it θ^*), then from the sample with first data point removed (θ_{-1}^*), then from the sample with second data point removed (θ_{-2}^*) etc. Pseudovalues for each observation in the original sample are calculated as:

$$\tilde{\theta}_i = n\theta^* - (n-1)\theta_{-i}^* \tag{2.14}$$

where θ_{-i}^* is the statistic calculated from the sample with observation i omitted. Each pseudo-value is simply a combination of two estimates of the statistic, one based on the whole sample and one based on the removal of a particular observation.

The jackknife estimate of the parameter is simply the mean of the pseudovalues ($\bar{\theta}$). The standard deviation of the jackknife estimate (the standard error of the estimate) is:

$$\sqrt{\frac{n-1}{n} \sum (\theta^*_{-i} - \bar{\theta})^2} \qquad (2.15)$$

Note that we have to assume that the pseudovalues are independent of each other for these calculations (Crowley 1992, Roberston 1991), whereas in reality they are not. The jackknife is not usually used for confidence intervals because so few samples are available if the original sample size was small (Dixon 1993). However, Crowley (1992) and Robertson (1991) suggested that if normality of the pseudovalues could be assumed, then confidence intervals could be calculated as usual (using the t distribution because of the small number of estimates).

2.6 | Bayesian inference – estimation

The classical approach to point and interval estimation might be considered to have two limitations. First, only the observed sample data contribute to our estimate of the population parameter. Any previous information we have on the likely value of the parameter cannot easily be considered when determining our estimate, although our knowledge of the population from which we are sampling will influence the design of our sampling program (Chapter 7). Second, the interval estimate we have obtained has a frequentist interpretation – a certain percentage of confidence intervals from repeated sampling will contain the fixed population parameter. The Bayesian approach to estimating parameters removes these limitations by formally incorporating our prior knowledge, as degrees-of-belief (Chapter 1), about the value of the parameter and by producing a probability statement about the parameter, e.g. there is a 95% probability that μ lies within a certain interval.

2.6.1 Bayesian estimation

To estimate parameters in a Bayesian framework, we need to make two major adjustments to the way we think about parameters and probabilities. First, we now consider the parameter to be a random variable that can take a range of possible values, each with different probabilities or degrees-of-belief of being true (Barnett 1999). This contrasts with the classical approach where the parameter was considered a fixed, but unknown, quantity. Dennis (1996), however, described the parameter being sought as an unknown variable rather than a random variable and the prior and posterior distributions represent the probabilities that this unknown parameter might take different values. Second, we must abandon our frequentist view of probability. Our interest is now only in the sample data we have, not in some long run hypothetical set of identical experiments (or samples). In Bayesian methods, probabilities can incorporate subjective degrees-of-belief (Chapter 1), although such opinions can still be quantified using probability distributions.

The basic logic of Bayesian inference for estimating a parameter is:

$$P(\theta \mid \text{data}) = \frac{P(\text{data} \mid \theta)P(\theta)}{P(\text{data})} \qquad (2.16)$$

where

θ is the population parameter to be estimated and is regarded as a random variable,

$P(\theta)$ is the "unconditional" prior probability of θ, expressed as a probability distribution summarizing our prior views about the probability of θ taking different values,

$P(\text{data} \mid \theta)$ is the likelihood of observing the sample data for different values of θ, expressed as a likelihood function (Section 2.4.1),

$P(\text{data})$ is the expected value (mean) of the likelihood function; this standardization means that the area under the posterior probability distribution equals one, and

$P(\theta \mid \text{data})$ is the posterior probability of θ conditional on the data being observed, expressed a probability distribution summarizing the probability of θ taking different values by combining the prior probability distribution and the likelihood function.

Equation 2.16 can be re-expressed more simply as:

posterior probability $\propto$ likelihood $\times$
prior probability   (2.17)

because the denominator in Equation 2.15, P(data), is a normalizing constant, the mean of the likelihood function (Ellison 1996).

2.6.2 Prior knowledge and probability

Prior probability distributions measure the relative "strength of belief" in possible values of the parameter (Dennis 1996) and can be of two forms (Barnett 1999).

1. Prior ignorance or only vague prior knowledge, where we have little or no previous information to suggest what value the parameter might take. While some Bayesians might argue that scientists will always have some prior information, and that we will never be in a position of complete ignorance, prior ignorance is a conservative approach and helps overcome the criticism of Bayesian statistics that subjectively determined prior opinion can have too much influence on the inferential process. We can represent prior ignorance with a non-informative prior distribution, sometimes called a diffuse distribution because such a wide range of values of θ is considered possible. The most typical diffuse prior is a rectangular (uniform or flat) probability distribution, which says that each value of the parameter is equally likely.

One problem with uniform prior distributions is that they are improper, i.e. the probability distribution does not integrate to one and therefore the probability of any range of values might not be less than one. In practice, this is not a serious problem because improper priors can be combined with likelihoods to produce proper posterior distributions. When we use a non-informative prior, the posterior distribution of the parameter is directly proportional to the likelihood function anyway. The uniform prior distribution can be considered a reference prior, a class of priors designed to represent weak prior knowledge and let the data, and therefore the likelihood, dominate the posterior distribution.

2. Substantial prior knowledge or belief represented by an informative prior probability distribution such as a normal or beta distribution. The construction of these informative prior distributions is one of the most controversial aspects of Bayesian inference, especially if they are constructed from subjective opinion. Crome et al. (1996) illustrated one approach based on surveying a small group of people for the opinions about the effects of logging. Dennis (1996) and Mayo (1996) have respectively highlighted potential practical and philosophical issues associated with using subjective prior information.

2.6.3 Likelihood function

The likelihood function P(data$|\theta$), standardized by the expected value (mean) of likelihood function [P(data)], is how the sample data enter Bayesian calculations. Note that the likelihood function is not strictly a probability distribution (Section 2.4.1), although we refer to it as the probability of observing the data for different values of the parameter. If we assume that our variable is normally distributed and the parameter of interest is the mean, the standardized likelihood function is a normal distribution with a mean equal to the mean of the sample data and a variance equal to the squared standard error of the mean of the sample data (Box & Tiao 1973, Ellison 1996).

2.6.4 Posterior probability

All conclusions from Bayesian inference are based on the posterior probability distribution of the parameter. This posterior distribution represents our prior probability distribution modified by the likelihood function. The sample data only enter Bayesian inference through the likelihood function. Bayesian inference is usually based on the shape of the posterior distribution, particularly the range of values over which most of the probability mass occurs. The best estimate of the parameter is determined from the mean of the posterior distribution, or sometimes the median or mode if we have a non-symmetrical posterior.

If we consider estimating a parameter (θ) with a normal prior distribution, then the mean of the normal posterior distribution of θ is (Box & Tiao 1973, Ellison 1996):

$$\bar{\theta} = \frac{1}{w_0 + w_1}(w_0\bar{\theta}_0 + w_1\bar{y}) \tag{2.18}$$

where $\bar{\theta}_0$ is the mean of the prior distribution, $\bar{y}$ is the mean of the likelihood function (i.e. sample mean from data), w_0 is the reciprocal of the estimate of the prior variance σ_0^2 ($1/s_0^2$), w_1 is the reciprocal of the sample variance times the sample size (n/s^2) and n is the sample size. In other words, the posterior mean is a weighted average of the prior mean and the sample mean (Berry 1996). This posterior mean $\bar{\theta}$ is our estimate of θ, the parameter of interest.

The variance of the posterior distribution equals:

$$\bar{\sigma}^2 = \frac{1}{w_0 + w_1} \tag{2.19}$$

Note that with a non-informative, flat, prior the posterior distribution is determined entirely by the sample data and the likelihood function. The mean of the posterior then is $\bar{y}$ (the mean of the sample data) and the variance is s^2/n (the variance of the sample data divided by the sample size).

The Bayesian analogues of frequentist confidence intervals are termed Bayesian credible or probability intervals. They are also called highest density or probability regions because any value in the region or interval has a higher probability of occurring than any value outside. If we have a normal posterior distribution for a parameter, Bayesian credible intervals for this parameter are:

$$P\{\bar{\theta} - 2\sqrt{D} \le \theta \le \bar{\theta} + 2\sqrt{D}\} = 0.95 \tag{2.20}$$

where $D = \bar{\sigma}^2$, the variance of the posterior distribution (Ellison 1996). Alternatively, the usual methods based on the t distribution can be used (Winkler 1993). Note that because the parameter is considered a random variable in Bayesian inference, the interval in Equation 2.20 is telling us directly that there is a 95% probability that the value of the parameter falls within this range, based on the sample data. With a non-informative (flat) prior distribution, the Bayesian confidence interval will be the same as the classical, frequentist, confidence interval and Edwards (1996) argued that the difference in interpretation is somewhat semantic. He recommended simply

reporting the interval and letting the reader interpret it as required. If we have a more informative prior distribution (i.e. we knew that some values of θ were more likely than others), then the Bayesian credible interval would be shorter than the classical confidence interval.

2.6.5 Examples

We provide a very simple example of Bayesian estimation in Box 2.4, based on the data from Lovett *et al.* (2000) on the chemistry of forested watersheds. Another biological example of Bayesian estimation is the work of Carpenter (1990). He compared eight different models for flux of pesticides through a pond ecosystem. Each model was given an equal prior probability (0.125), data were collected from an experiment using radioactively labeled pesticide and likelihoods were determined for each model from the residuals after each model was fitted using OLS (see Chapter 2). He found that only one of the models had a posterior probability greater than 0.1 (actually it was 0.97, suggesting it was a very likely outcome).

2.6.6 Other comments

We would like to finish with some comments. First, normal distributions are commonly used for both prior and posterior distributions and likelihood functions for the same reasons as for classical estimation, especially when dealing with means. Other distributions can be used. For example, Crome *et al.* (1996) used a mixture of lognormal distributions for an informative prior (see also Winkler 1993) and the beta distribution is commonly used as a prior for binomially distributed parameters.

Second, the data generally are much more influential over the posterior distribution than the prior, except when sample sizes, and/or the variance of the prior, are very small. Carpenter (1990) discussed Bayesian analysis in the context of large-scale perturbation experiments in ecology and he also argued that prior probabilities had far less impact than the observed data on the outcome of the analysis and implied that the choice of prior probabilities was not crucial. However, Edwards (1996) noted that if the prior standard deviation is very small, then differences in the prior mean could have marked effects on

Box 2.4 | Worked example of Bayesian estimation: chemistry of forested watersheds

To illustrate the Bayesian approach to estimation, we will revisit the earlier example of estimating the mean concentration of SO_4^{2-} in first and second order stream sites in the Catskill Mountains in New York State based on a sample of 39 sites (Lovett et al. 2000). Now we will consider the mean concentration of SO_4^{2-} a random variable, or at least an unknown variable (Dennis 1996), and also make use of prior information about this mean, i.e. we will estimate our mean from a Bayesian perspective. For comparison, we will also investigate the effect of more substantial prior knowledge, in the form of a less variable prior probability distribution. We will follow the procedure for Bayesian estimation from Box & Tiao (1973; see also Berry 1996 and Ellison 1996).

1. Using whatever information is available (including subjective assessment; see Crome et al. 1996), specify a prior probability distribution for Y. Note that initial estimates of the parameters of this distribution will need to be specified; a normal prior requires an initial estimate of the mean and variance. Imagine we had sampled the central Catskill Mountains at a previous time so we had some previous data that we could use to set up a prior distribution. We assumed the prior distribution of the concentration of SO_4^{2-} was normal and we used the mean and the variance of the previous sample as the parameters of the prior distribution. The prior distribution could also be a non-informative (flat) one if no such previous information was available.

2. Collect a sample to provide an estimate of the parameter and its variance. In our example, we had a sample of concentration of SO_4^{2-} from 39 streams and determined the sample mean and variance.

3. Determine the standardized likelihood function, which in this example is a normal distribution with a mean equal to the mean of the sample data and a variance equal to the squared standard error of the mean of the sample data.

4. Determine the posterior probability distribution for the mean concentration of SO_4^{2-}, which will be a normal distribution because we used a normal prior and likelihood function. The mean of this posterior distribution (Equation 2.18) is our estimate of population mean concentration of SO_4^{2-} and we can determine credible intervals for this mean (Equation 2.20).

High variance prior distribution

Prior mean = 50.00, prior variance = 44.00.
Sample mean = 61.92, sample variance = 27.47, n = 39.
Using Equations 2.18, 2.19 and 2.20, substituting sample estimates where appropriate:
$w_0 = 0.023$
$w_1 = 1.419$
Posterior mean = 61.73, posterior variance = 0.69, 95% Bayesian probability interval = 60.06 to 62.57.
Note that the posterior distribution has almost the same estimated mean as the sample, so the posterior is determined almost entirely by the sample data.

Low variance prior distribution

If we make our prior estimate of the mean much more precise:
Prior mean = 50.00, prior variance = 10.00.
Sample mean = 61.92, sample variance = 27.47, $n = 39$.
$w_0 = 0.100$
$w_1 = 1.419$
Posterior mean = 61.14, posterior variance = 0.66, 95% Bayesian probability interval = 59.51 to 62.76.

Now the prior distribution has a greater influence on the posterior than previously, with the posterior mean more than half one unit lower. In fact, the more different the prior mean is from the sample mean, and the more precise our estimate of the prior mean is, i.e. the lower the prior variance, the more the prior will influence the posterior relative to the data.

Note that if we assume a flat prior, the posterior mean is just the mean of the data (61.92).

the posterior mean, irrespective of the data. He described this as "editorial", where the results of the analysis are mainly opinion.

Third, if a non-informative prior (like a rectangular distribution) is used, and we assume the data are from a normally distributed population, then the posterior distribution will be a normal (or t) distribution just like in classical estimation, i.e. using a flat prior will result in the same estimates as classical statistics. For example, if we wish to use Bayesian methods to estimate μ, and we use a rectangular prior distribution, then the posterior distribution will turn out to be a normal distribution (if σ is known) or a t distribution (if σ is unknown and estimated from s, which means we need a prior distribution for s as well).

Finally, we have provided only a very brief introduction to Bayesian methods for estimation and illustrated the principle with a simple example. For more complex models with two or more parameters, calculating the posterior distribution is difficult. Recent advances in this area use various sampling algorithms (e.g. Hastings–Metropolis Gibbs sampler) as part of Markov chain Monte Carlo methods. These techniques are beyond the scope of this book – Barnett (1999) and Gelman *et al.* (1995) provide an introduction although the details are not for the mathematically challenged. The important point is that once we get beyond simple estimation problems, Bayesian methods can involve considerable statistical complexity.

Other pros and cons related to Bayesian inference, particularly in comparison with classical frequentist inference, will be considered in Chapter 3 in the context of testing hypotheses.

Chapter 3

Hypothesis testing

3.1 | Statistical hypothesis testing

In Chapter 2, we discussed one component of statistical inference, estimating population parameters. We also introduced the philosophical and statistical differences between frequentist and Bayesian approaches to parameter estimation. The other main component of inference, and one that has dominated the application of statistics in the biological sciences, is testing hypotheses about those parameters. Much of the philosophical justification for the continued use of statistical tests of hypotheses seems to be based on Popper's proposals for falsificationist tests of hypotheses (Chapter 1). Although Jerzy Neyman, Egon Pearson and Sir Ronald Fisher had developed their approaches to statistical testing by the 1930s, it is interesting to note that Popper did not formally consider statistical tests as a mechanism for falsifying hypotheses (Mayo 1996). Hilborn & Mangel (1997, pp. 15–16) stated that "Popper supplied the philosophy and Fisher, Pearson, and colleagues supplied the statistics" but the link between Popperian falsificationism and statistical tests of hypotheses is still controversial, e.g. the contrasting views of Mayo (1996) and Oakes (1986). We will present a critique of statistical hypothesis tests, and significance tests in particular, in Section 3.6.

The remainder of this section will provide an overview of statistical tests of hypotheses.

3.1.1 Classical statistical hypothesis testing

Classical statistical hypothesis testing rests on two basic concepts. First, we must state a statistical null hypothesis (H_0), which is usually (though not necessarily) an hypothesis of no difference or no relationship between population parameters (e.g. no difference between two population means). In many cases, we use the term effect to describe a difference between groups or experimental treatments (or a non-zero regression slope, etc.), so the H_0 is usually an hypothesis of no effect. The philosophical basis for the statistical null hypothesis, at least in part, relates back to Popperian falsificationism, whereby science makes progress by severely testing and falsifying hypotheses. The implication is that rejection of the statistical H_0 is equivalent to falsifying it and therefore provides support ("corroboration") for the research hypothesis as the only alternative (Underwood 1997). We do not test the research hypothesis in this way because it is rarely more exact than postulating an effect, sometimes in a particular direction. Fisher (1935) pointed out that the null hypothesis is exact, e.g. a difference of zero, and is the result we would expect from randomizing observations to different experimental groups when there is no effect of the experimental treatment (Mulaik et al. 1997). The philosophical justification for testing the null hypothesis is still a controversial issue. For example, Oakes (1986) argued that support for the research hypothesis as a result of the null being rejected is not true corroboration and statistical tests, as currently practiced, have only superficial philosophical respectability.

Second, we must choose a test statistic to test the H_0. A test statistic is a random variable and, as such, can be described by a probability distribution. For example, a commonly used test statistic for testing hypotheses about population means is t, where:

$$t = \frac{(\bar{y} - \mu)}{s_{\bar{y}}} \qquad (3.1)$$

We introduced the t statistic and its probability distribution in Chapters 1 and used it in Chapter 2 for determining confidence intervals for population means. Test statistics like t have a number of probability distributions (see Figure 1.2), called sampling distributions, one for each possible degrees of freedom $(n-1)$. These sampling distributions represent the probability distributions of t based on repeated random sampling from populations when the H_0 is true and are sometimes called central distributions. Probabilities associated with particular ranges of values of test statistics are tabled in most statistics textbooks. Note that test statistics are continuous random variables, so we cannot define the probability of a single t value, for example. We can only talk about the probability that t is greater (or less than) a certain value or that t falls in the range between two values.

Before we look at the practical application of statistical tests, some consideration of history is warranted. The early development of statistical hypothesis testing was led primarily by Sir Ronald Fisher, whose influence on statistics was enormous. Fisher (1954, 1956) gave us null hypothesis or significance testing in statistics with the following methodology (Huberty 1993).

1. Construct a null hypothesis (H_0).

2. Choose a test statistic that measures deviation from the H_0 and that has a known sampling distribution (e.g. t statistic).

3. Collect the data by one or more random samples from the population(s) and compare the value of the test statistic from your sample(s) to its sampling distribution.

4. Determine P value, the associated probability of obtaining our sample value of the statistic, or one more extreme, if H_0 is true

5. Reject H_0 if P is small; retain H_0 otherwise.

Fisher proposed that we should report the actual P value (e.g. $P = 0.042$), which is a property of the data and could be viewed as a "strength of evidence" measure against H_0 (Huberty 1994).

Fisher also introduced the idea of a conventional probability (of obtaining our sample data or data more extreme if H_0 is true) for rejecting H_0; this is called a significance level. He suggested a probability of one in twenty (0.05 or 5%) as a convenient level and the publication of tables of sampling distributions for various statistics reinforced this by only including tail probabilities beyond these conventional levels (e.g. 0.05, 0.01, 0.001). Later, however, Fisher (1956) recommended that fixed significance levels (e.g. 0.05) were too restrictive and argued that a researcher's significance level would depend on circumstances. Fisher also introduced the idea of fiducial inference, although this approach is rarely used in the biological sciences – Mayo (1996) and Oakes (1986) provide details.

Jerzy Neyman and Egon Pearson (Neyman & Pearson 1928, 1933) offered a related but slightly different approach, which has sometimes been called statistical hypothesis testing. Their approach differed from Fisher's in a number of important ways (Oakes 1986, Royall 1997).

1. They argued that we should set a level of significance (e.g. 0.05) in advance of the data collection and stick with it – this is sometimes called fixed level testing. The significance level is interpreted as the proportion of times the H_0 would be wrongly rejected using this decision rule if the experiment were repeated many times and the H_0 was actually true. Under the Neyman–Pearson scheme, the P value provides no additional information beyond indicating whether we should reject the H_0 at our specified significance level (Oakes 1986). They emphasized making a dichotomous decision about the H_0 (reject or nor reject) and the possible errors associated with that decision (see below) whereas Fisher was more concerned with measuring evidence against the H_0. Whether P values provide a suitable measure of evidence is a matter of debate (e.g. Royall 1997) that we will consider further in Section 3.6.

2. Another major difference between the Fisher and the Neyman–Pearson approaches was that Neyman and Pearson explicitly incorporated an alternative hypothesis (H_A) into their scheme. The H_A is the alternative hypothesis that must be true if the H_0 is false, e.g. if the H_0 is that two population means are equal, then the H_A is that they are different by some amount. In contrast, Fisher strongly opposed the idea of H_A in significance testing (Cohen 1990).

3. Neyman and Pearson developed the concepts of Type I error (long-run probability of falsely rejecting H_0, which we denote α) and Type II error (long-run probability of falsely not rejecting H_0, which we denote β) and their *a priori* significance level (e.g. $\alpha = 0.05$) was the long-run probability of a Type I error (Gigerenzer 1993). This led naturally to the concept of power (the probability of correctly rejecting a false H_0). Fisher strongly disagreed with Neyman and Pearson about the relevance of the two types of error and even criticized Neyman and Pearson for having no familiarity with practical application of hypothesis testing in the natural sciences (Oakes 1986)!

Statisticians have recently revisited the controversy between the Fisher and Neyman–Pearson approaches to hypothesis testing (Inman 1994, Lehmann 1993, Mulaik *et al.* 1997, Royall 1997), pointing out their similarities as well as their disagreements and the confusion in terminology. Biologists, like psychologists (Gigerenzer 1993), most commonly follow a hybrid approach, combining aspects of both Fisherian inference and Neyman–Pearson decision-making to statistical hypothesis testing.

1. Specify H_0, H_A and appropriate test statistic
2. Specify *a priori* significance level (e.g. 0.05), which is the long-run frequency of Type I errors (α) we are willing to accept.
3. Collect the data by one or more random samples from the population(s) and calculate the test statistic from our sample data.
4. Compare that value of the statistic to its sampling distribution, assuming H_0 true.
5. If the probability of obtaining this value or one greater is less than the specified significance level (e.g. 0.05), then conclude that the H_0 is false and reject it ("significant" result),
6. If the probability of obtaining this value is greater than or equal to the specified significance level (e.g. 0.05), then conclude there is no evidence that the H_0 is false and retain it ("non-significant" result).

The Fisherian aspect of this hybrid approach is that some biologists use $P < 0.05$ (significant), $P < 0.01$ (very significant) and $P < 0.001$ (highly significant) or present the actual P values to indicate strength of evidence against the H_0. Although the latter has been strongly criticized by some in the psychological literature (Shaver 1993), there is some logical justification for providing P values (Oakes 1986). For one thing, it allows readers to use their own *a priori* significance levels to decide whether or not to reject the H_0.

To reiterate, interpretations from classical statistical tests are based on a long-run frequency interpretation of probabilities, i.e. the probability in a long run of identical "trials" or "experiments". This implies that we have one or more clearly defined population(s) from which we are sampling and for which inferences are to be made. If there is no definable population from which random samples are collected, the inferential statistics discussed here are more difficult to interpret since they are based on long-run frequencies of occurrence from repeated sampling. Randomization tests (Section 3.3.2), which do not require random sampling from a population, may be more applicable.

3.1.2 Associated probability and Type I error

Fisher and Neyman & Pearson both acknowledged that probabilities from classical statistical hypothesis testing must be interpreted in the long-run frequency sense, although the latter were more dogmatic about it. The sampling distribution of the test statistic (e.g. t) gives us the long-run probabilities of different ranges of t values occurring if we sample repeatedly from a population(s) in which the H_0 is true. The P value, termed the associated probability by Oakes (1986), then is simply the long-run probability of obtaining our sample test statistic *or one more extreme*, if H_0 is true. Therefore, the P value can be expressed as $P(\text{data}|H_0)$, the probability of observing our sample data, or data more extreme, under repeated identical experiments if the H_0 is true. This is not the same as the probability of H_0 being true, given the observed data – $P(H_0|\text{data})$. As Oakes (1986) has pointed out, there is rarely a sensible long-run frequency interpretation for the probability that a particular hypothesis is true. If we wish to know the probability of H_0 being true, we need to tackle hypothesis testing from a Bayesian perspective (Berger & Berry 1988; see Section 3.7).

The P value is also sometimes misinterpreted as the probability of the result of a specific analysis being due to chance, e.g. a P value of <0.05 means that there is a less than 5% probability that the result is due to chance. This is not strictly correct (Shaver 1993); it is the probability of a result occurring by chance in the long run if H_0 is true, not the probability of any particular result being due to chance.

Traditionally, biologists are correctly taught that a non-significant result (not rejecting H_0) does not indicate that H_0 is true, as Fisher himself stressed. In contrast, the Neyman–Pearson logic is that H_0 and H_A are the only alternatives and the non-rejection of H_0 implies the acceptance of H_0 (Gigerenzer 1993), a position apparently adopted by some textbooks, e.g. Sokal & Rohlf (1995) refer to the acceptance of H_0. The Neyman–Pearson approach is really about alternative courses of actions based on the decision to accept or reject. Accepting the H_0 does not imply its truth, just that one would take the action that results from such a decision.

Our view is that a statistically non-significant result basically means we should suspend judgement and we have no evidence to reject the H_0. The exception would be if we show that the power of our test to detect a desired alternative hypothesis was high, then we can conclude the true effect is probably less than this specific effect size (Chapter 7). Underwood (1990, 1999) has argued that retention of the H_0 implies that the research hypothesis and model on which it is based are falsified (see Chapter 1). In this context, a statistically non-significant result should initiate a process of revising or even replacing the model and devising new tests of the new model(s). The philosophical basis for interpreting so-called 'negative' results continues to be debated in the scientific literature (e.g. see opinion articles by Allchin 1999, Hull 1999 and Ruse 1999 in *Marine Ecology Progress Series*).

The Type I error rate is the long-run probability of rejecting the H_0 at our chosen significance level, e.g. 0.05, if the H_0 is actually true in all the repeated experiments or trials. A Type I error is one of the two possible errors when we make a decision about whether the H_0 is likely to be true or not under the Neyman–Pearson protocol. We will consider these errors further in Section 3.2.

3.1.3 Hypothesis tests for a single population

We will illustrate testing an H_0 with the simplest type of test, the single-parameter t test. We demonstrated the importance of the t distribution for determining confidence intervals in Chapter 2. It can also be used for testing hypotheses about single population parameters or about the difference between two population parameters if certain assumptions about the variable hold. Here we will look at the first type of hypothesis, e.g. does the population mean equal zero? The value of the parameter specified in the H_0 doesn't have to be zero, particularly when the parameter is a mean, e.g. testing an H_0 that the mean size of an organism is zero makes little biological sense. Sometimes testing an H_0 that the mean equals zero is relevant, e.g. the mean change from before to after a treatment equals zero, and testing whether other parameters equal zero (e.g. regression coefficients, variance components, etc.) is very important. We will consider these parameters in later chapters.

The general form of the t statistic is:

$$t_s = \frac{St - \theta}{S_{St}} \tag{3.2}$$

where St is the value of the statistic from our sample, θ is the population value against which the sample statistic is to be tested (as specified in the H_0) and S_{St} is the estimated standard error of the sample statistic. We will go through an example of a statistical test using a one-sample t test.

1. Specify the H_0 (e.g. $\mu = 0$) and H_A (e.g. $\mu \neq 0$).
2. Take a random sample from a clearly defined population.
3. Calculate $t = (\bar{y} - 0)/s_{\bar{y}}$ from the sample, where $s_{\bar{y}}$ is the estimated standard error of the sample mean. Note that if H_0 is true, we would expect t to be close to zero, i.e. when we sample from a population with a mean of zero, most

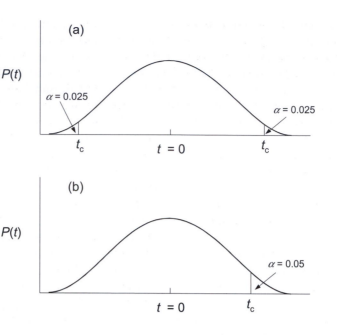

Figure 3.1 Probability distributions of t for (a) two-tailed and (b) one-tailed tests, showing critical t values (t_c).

samples will have means close to zero. Sample means further from zero are less likely to occur if H_0 is true. The probability of getting a sample mean a long way from zero, and therefore a large t, either positive or negative, is less if the H_0 is true. Large t values are possible if H_0 is true – they are just unlikely.

4. Compare t with the sampling distribution of t at $\alpha = 0.05$ (or 0.01 or whatever significance level you choose *a priori*) with $n - 1$ df. Look at the t distribution in Figure 3.1. Values of t greater than $+t_c$ or less than $-t_c$ have a less than 0.05 chance of occurring from this t distribution, which is the probability distribution of t when H_0 is true. This value (t_c) is sometimes called the critical value. If the probability (P value) of obtaining our sample t value or one larger is less than 0.05 (our α), then we reject the H_0. Because we can reject H_0 in either direction, if μ is greater than zero or if μ is less than zero, then large values of the test statistic at either end of the sampling distribution will result in rejection of H_0 (Figure 3.1). This is termed a two-tailed test (see Section 3.1.4). To do a test with $\alpha = 0.05$, then we reject H_0 if our t value falls in the regions where $P = 0.025$ at each end of the sampling distribution ($0.025 + 0.025 = 0.05$). If the probability (P value) of obtaining our t value or one larger is ≥ 0.05, then we do not reject the H_0.

As mentioned earlier, the sampling distribution of the t statistic when the H_0 is true is also called the central t distribution. The probabilities for the t distribution for different degrees of freedom are tabled in most textbooks (usually for $P = 0.05$, 0.01 and sometimes 0.001). In addition, t distributions are programmed into statistical software. When using statistical tables, our value of t is simply compared to the critical t_c value at $\alpha = 0.05$. Larger t values always have a smaller P value (probability of this or a larger value occurring if H_0 is true) so if the statistic is larger than the critical value at 0.05, then H_0 is rejected. Statistical software usually gives actual P values for statistical tests, making the use of tables unnecessary.

We could theoretically use the sampling distribution of the sample mean (which would be a normal distribution) to test our H_0. However, there are an infinite number of possible combinations of mean and variance, so in practice such sampling distributions are not calculated. Instead, we convert the sample mean to a t value (subtracting μ specified in H_0 and dividing by the standard error of the mean), whose central distribution is well defined.

Finally, it is important to note the relationship between the hypothesis test illustrated here and confidence intervals described in Chapter 2. The H_0 that μ equals zero is tested using a t distribution; a confidence interval for μ is also constructed using the same t distribution (based on $n - 1$ df). Not surprisingly then, a test of this H_0 with a 0.05 significance level is the equivalent of seeing whether the 95% (0.95) confidence interval for μ overlaps zero; if it does, we have no evidence to reject H_0.

3.1.4 One- and two-tailed tests

In most cases in biology, the H_0 is one of no effect (e.g. no difference between two means) and the H_A (the alternative hypothesis) can be in either direction; the H_0 is rejected if one mean is bigger than the other mean or vice versa. This is termed a two-tailed test because large values of the test statistic at either end of the sampling distribution will result in rejection of H_0 (Figure 3.1). The H_0 that a parameter equals a specific value is sometimes called a simple hypothesis or a point hypothesis (Barnett 1999). To do a test with $\alpha = 0.05$, then we use critical values of the test statistic at $\alpha = 0.025$ at each end of the sampling distribution. Sometimes, our H_0 is more specific than just no difference. We might only be interested in whether one mean is bigger than the other mean but not the other way. For example, we might expect increased density of organisms to induce competition and reduce their growth rate, and we can think of no mechanism whereby the organisms at the higher density would increase their growth. Here our H_0 is that the population mean growth rate for increased density is greater than or equal to the population mean growth rate for lower density. Our H_A is, therefore, that the population mean growth rate for increased density is less than the population mean growth rate for lower density. This is a one-tailed test, the H_0 being directional or composite (Barnett 1999), because only large values of the test statistic at one end of the sampling distribution will result in rejection of the H_0 (Figure 3.1). To do a test with $\alpha = 0.05$, then we use critical values of the test statistic at $\alpha = 0.05$ at one end of the sampling distribution.

We should test one-tailed hypotheses with care because we are obliged to ignore large differences in the other direction, no matter how tempting it may be to deal with them. For example, if we expect increased phosphorous (P) to increase plant growth compared to controls (C) with no added phosphorous, we might perform a one-tailed t test ($H_0: \mu_P \leq \mu_C$; $H_A: \mu_P > \mu_C$). However, we cannot draw any formal conclusions if growth rate is much less when phosphorous is added, only that it is a non-significant result and we have no evidence to reject the H_0. Is this unrealistic, expecting a biologist to ignore what might be an important effect just because it was in the oppo-

site direction to that expected? This might seem like an argument against one-tailed tests, avoiding the problem by never ruling out interest in effects in both directions and always using two-tailed tests. Royall (1997) suggested that researchers who choose one-tailed tests should be trusted to use them correctly, although he used the problems associated with the one-tail versus two-tail choice as one of his arguments against statistical hypothesis testing and P values more generally. An example of one-tailed tests comes from Todd & Keough (1994), who were interested in whether microbial films that develop on marine hard substrata act as cues inducing invertebrate larvae to settle. Because they expected these films to be a positive cue, they were willing to focus on changes in settlement in one direction only. They then ignored differences in the opposite direction from their *a priori* one-tailed hypothesis.

Most statistical tables either provide critical values for both one- and two-tailed tests but some just have either one- or two-tailed critical values depending on the statistic, so make sure you look up the correct P value if you must use tables. Statistical software usually produces two-tailed P values so you should compare the P value to $\alpha = 0.10$ for a one-tailed test at 0.05.

3.1.5 Hypotheses for two populations

These are tests of null hypotheses about the equivalent parameter in two populations. These tests can be one- or two-tailed although testing a point null hypothesis with a two-tailed test is more common in practice, i.e. the parameter is the same in the two populations. If we have a random sample from each of two independent populations, i.e. the populations represent different collections of observations (i.e. sampling or experimental units), then to test the H_0 that $\mu_1 = \mu_2$ (comparing two independent population means):

$$t = \frac{\bar{y}_1 - \bar{y}_2}{s_{\bar{y}_1 - \bar{y}_2}} \tag{3.3}$$

where

$$s_{\bar{y}_1 - \bar{y}_2} = \sqrt{\frac{(n_1 - 1)s_1^2 + (n_2 - 1)s_2^2}{n_1 + n_2 - 2}\left(\frac{1}{n_1} + \frac{1}{n_2}\right)} \tag{3.4}$$

Equation 3.4 is the standard error of the difference between the two means. This is just like the one-parameter t test except the single sample statistic is replaced by the difference between two sample statistics, the population parameter specified in the H_0 is replaced by the difference between the parameters of the two populations specified in the H_0 and the standard error of the statistic is replaced by the standard error of the difference between two statistics:

$$t = \frac{(\bar{y}_1 - \bar{y}_2) - (\mu_1 - \mu_2)}{s_{\bar{y}_1 - \bar{y}_2}} \qquad (3.5)$$

We follow the steps in Section 3.1.1 and compare t to the t distribution with $n_1 + n_2 - 2$ df in the usual manner. This H_0 can also be tested with an ANOVA F-ratio test (Chapter 8).

We will illustrate tests of hypotheses about two populations with two examples. Ward & Quinn (1988) studied aspects of the ecology of the intertidal predatory gastropod *Lepsiella vinosa* on a rocky shore in southeastern Australia (Box 3.1). *L. vinosa* occurred in two distinct zones on this shore: a high-shore zone dominated by small grazing gastropods *Littorina* spp. and a mid-shore zone dominated by beds of the mussels *Xenostrobus pulex* and *Brachidontes rostratus*. Both gastropods and mussels are eaten by *L. vinosa*. Other data indicated that rates of energy consumption by *L. vinosa* were much greater in the mussel zone. Ward & Quinn (1988) were interested in whether there were any differences in fecundity of *L. vinosa*, especially the number of eggs per capsule, between the zones. From June to September 1982, they collected any egg capsules they could find in each zone and recorded the number of eggs per capsule. There were 37 capsules recorded from the littorinid zone and 42 from the mussel zone. The H_0 was that there is no difference between the zones in the mean number of eggs per capsule. This is an independent comparison because the egg capsules were independent between the zones.

Furness & Bryant (1996) studied energy budgets of breeding northern fulmars (*Fulmarus glacialis*) in Shetland (Box 3.2). As part of their study, they recorded various characteristics of individually labeled male and female fulmars. We will focus on differences between sexes in metabolic rate. There were eight males and six females labeled. The H_0 was that there is no difference

between the sexes in the mean metabolic rate of fulmars. This is an independent comparison because individual fulmars can only be either male or female.

If we have a random sample from a population and we have recorded two (paired) variables from each observation, then we have what are commonly called paired samples, e.g. observations at two times. To test whether the population mean difference between the two sets of observations equals zero, we basically use a test for a single population (Section 3.1.3) to test the H_0 that $\mu_d = 0$:

$$t = \frac{\bar{d}}{s_{\bar{d}}} \qquad (3.6)$$

where $\bar{d}$ is the mean of the pairwise differences and $s_{\bar{d}}$ is the standard error of the pairwise differences. We compare t with a t distribution with $n - 1$ df in the usual manner. This H_0 can also be tested with a two factor unreplicated ANOVA F-ratio test (Chapter 10).

For example, Elgar *et al.* (1996) studied the effect of lighting on the web structure of an orb-spinning spider (Box 3.3). They set up wooden frames with two different light regimes (controlled by black or white mosquito netting), light and dim. A total of 17 orb spiders were allowed to spin their webs in both a light frame and a dim frame, with six days' "rest" between trials for each spider, and the vertical and horizontal diameter of each web was measured. Whether each spider was allocated to a light or dim frame first was randomized. The null hypotheses were that the two variables (vertical diameter and horizontal diameter of the orb web) were the same in dim and light conditions. Elgar *et al.* (1996) correctly treated this as a paired comparison because the same spider spun her web in a light frame and a dark frame.

We can also test whether the variances of two populations are the same. Recall from Chapter 2 that variances are distributed as chi-squares and the ratio of two chi-square distributions is an F distribution, another probability distribution that is well defined. To test the H_0 that $\sigma_1^2 = \sigma_2^2$ (comparing two population variances), we calculate an F-ratio statistic:

$$F = \frac{s_1^2}{s_2^2} \qquad (3.7)$$

Box 3.1 | Fecundity of predatory gastropods

Ward & Quinn (1988) collected 37 egg capsules of the intertidal predatory gastropod *Lepsiella vinosa* from the littorinid zone on a rocky intertidal shore and 42 capsules from the mussel zone. Other data indicated that rates of energy consumption by *L. vinosa* were much greater in the mussel zone so there was interest in differences in fecundity between the zones. The H_0 was that there is no difference between the zones in the mean number of eggs per capsule. This is an independent comparison because individual egg capsules can only be in either of the two zones.

Zone	n	Mean	Median	Rank sum	Standard deviation	SE of mean	95% CI for mean
Littorinid	37	8.70	9	1007	2.03	0.33	8.03–9.38
Mussel	42	11.36	11	2153	2.33	0.36	10.64–12.08

Note that standard deviations (and therefore the variances) are similar and box-plots (Figure 4.4) do not suggest any asymmetry so a parametric *t* test is appropriate.

Pooled variance test:

$$t = -5.39, df = 77, P < 0.001.$$

We would reject the H_0 and conclude there was a statistically significant difference in mean number of eggs per capsule between zones.

Effect size (difference between means) $= -2.65$ (95% CI: -1.674 to -3.635)

Separate variance test:

$$t = -5.44, df = 77, P < 0.001.$$

Note that the *t* values were almost identical and the degrees of freedom were the same, not surprising since the variances were almost identical.

Although there was little justification for a non-parametric test, we also tested the H_0 that there was no difference in a more general measure of location using the Mann–Whitney–Wilcoxon test.

$$U = 304.00, \chi^2 \text{ approximation} = 21.99 \text{ with 1 df}, P < 0.001.$$

Again we would reject the H_0. In this example, the parametric pooled and separate variance *t* tests and non-parametric test all give *P* values < 0.001.

A randomization test was done to test the H_0 that there is no difference between the mean number of eggs per capsule so that any possible allocation of observations to the two groups is equally likely.

Mean difference $= -2.65$, $P < 0.001$ (significant) for difference as or more extreme than observed based on 10 000 randomizations.

where s_1^2 is the larger sample variance and s_2^2 is the smaller sample variance. We compare this *F*-ratio with an *F* distribution with $n_1 - 1$ df for numerator (sample one) and $n_2 - 1$ df for denominator (sample two). We will consider *F*-ratio tests on variances in more detail in Chapters 5 onwards.

3.1.6 Parametric tests and their assumptions

The *t* tests we have just described for testing null hypotheses about population means are classified as parametric tests, where we can specify a probability distribution for the populations of the

Box 3.2 | Metabolic rate of male and female fulmars

Furness & Bryant (1996) studied energy budgets of breeding northern fulmars (*Fulmarus glacialis*) in Shetland. As part of their study, they recorded various characteristics of individually labeled male and female fulmars. We will focus on differences between sexes in metabolic rate. There were eight males and six females labeled. The H_0 was that there is no difference between the sexes in the mean metabolic rates of fulmars. This is an independent comparison because individual fulmars can only be either male or female.

Sex	n	Mean	Median	Standard deviation	SE of mean	95% CI for mean
Male	8	1563.78	1570.55	894.37	316.21	816.06 − 2311.49
Female	6	1285.52	1226.15	420.96	171.86	843.74 − 1727.29

Note that variances are very different although the boxplots (Figure 4.5) do not suggest strong asymmetry. The small and unequal sample sizes, in conjunction with the unequal variances, indicate that a *t* test based on separate variances is more appropriate.

Separate variance test:

$t = 0.77$, df $= 10.5$, $P = 0.457$.

We would not reject the H_0 and conclude there was no statistically significant difference in mean metabolic rate of fulmars between sexes.

The effect size (difference between means) = 278.26 (95% CI: −518.804 to 1075.321).

Note that the confidence interval on the mean difference includes zero, as expected given the non-significant result from the test.

The very different variances would make us reluctant to use a rank-based non-parametric test. Even a randomization test might be susceptible to unequal variance, although the results from such a test support the previous conclusion.

Mean difference = 278.26, $P = 0.252$ (not significant) for difference as or more extreme than observed based on 10 000 randomizations.

variable from which our samples came. All statistical tests have some assumptions (yes, even so-called "non-parametric tests" – see Section 3.3.3) and if these assumptions are not met, then the test may not be reliable. Basically, violation of these assumptions means that the test statistic (e.g. *t*) may no longer be distributed as a *t* distribution, which then means that our *P* values may not be reliable. Although parametric tests have these assumptions in theory, in practice these tests may be robust to moderate violations of these assumptions, i.e. the test and the *P* values may still be reliable even if the assumptions are not met. We will describe the assumptions of *t* tests here and

introduce ways of checking these assumptions, although these methods are presented in more detail in Chapter 4. The assumptions themselves are also considered in more detail as assumptions for linear models in Chapters 5 onwards.

The first assumption is that the samples are from normally distributed populations. There is reasonable evidence from simulation studies (Glass *et al.* 1972, Posten 1984) that significance tests based on the *t* test are usually robust to violations of this assumption unless the distributions are very non-symmetrical, e.g. skewed or multimodal. Checks for symmetry of distributions can include dotplots (if *n* is large enough), boxplots and

Box 3.3 | Orb spider webs and light intensity

Elgar *et al.* (1996) exposed 17 orb spiders each to dim and light conditions and recorded two aspects of web structure under each condition. The H_0s are that the two variables (vertical diameter and horizontal diameter of the orb web) were the same in dim and light conditions. Because the same spider spun her web in both light conditions, then this was a paired comparison. Boxplots of paired differences for both variables suggested symmetrical distributions with no outliers, so a parametric paired *t* test is appropriate.

Horizontal diameter (cm):

Mean difference = 46.18, SE difference = 21.49.
$t = 2.15$, df = 16, $P = 0.047$ (significant).

So we would reject the H_0 and conclude that, for the population of female orb spiders, there is a difference in the mean horizontal diameter of spider webs between light and dim conditions.

Wilcoxon signed rank $z = -1.84$, $P = 0.066$ (not significant), do not reject H_0. Note the less powerful non-parametric test produced a different result.

Vertical diameter (cm):

Mean difference = 20.59, SE difference = 21.32.
$t = 0.97$, df = 16, $P = 0.349$ (not significant), do not reject H_0.

So we would not reject the H_0 and conclude that, for the population of female orb spiders, there is no difference in the mean vertical diameter of spider webs between light and dim conditions.

Wilcoxon signed rank $z = -0.78$, $P = 0.434$ (not significant). In this case, the non-parametric test produced the same conclusion as the *t* test.

---

pplots (see Chapter 4). Transformations of the variable to a different scale of measurement (Chapter 4) can often improve its normality. We do not recommend formal significance tests for normality (e.g. Shapiro–Wilk test, Lilliefors test; see Sprent 1993) because, depending on the sample size, these tests may reject the H_0 of normality in situations when the subsequent *t* test may be reliable.

The second assumption is that samples are from populations with equal variances. This is a more critical assumption although, again, the usual *t* test is very robust to moderately unequal variances if sample sizes are equal (Glass *et al.* 1972, Posten 1984). While much of the simulation work relates to analysis of variance (ANOVA) problems (see Day & Quinn 1989, Wilcox *et al.* 1986, Chapter 8), the results also hold for *t* tests, which are equivalent to an ANOVA *F*-ratio test on two groups. For example, if *n* equals six and the ratio

of the two standard deviations is four or less, simulations show that the observed Type I error rate for the *t* test is close to the specified rate (Coombs *et al.* 1996). If sample sizes are very unequal, especially if the smaller sample has the larger variance, then Type I error rates may be much higher than postulated significance level. If the larger sample has the larger variance, then the rate of Type II errors will be high (Judd *et al.* 1995, Coombs *et al.* 1996). Coombs *et al.* (1996) illustrated this with simulation data from Wilcox *et al.* (1986) that showed that for sample sizes of 11 and 21, a four to one ratio of standard deviations (largest standard deviation associated with small sample size) resulted in a Type I error rate of nearly 0.16 for a nominal α of 0.05. Note that unequal variances are often due to skewed distributions, so fixing the non-normality problem will often make variances more similar. Checks for this assumption include

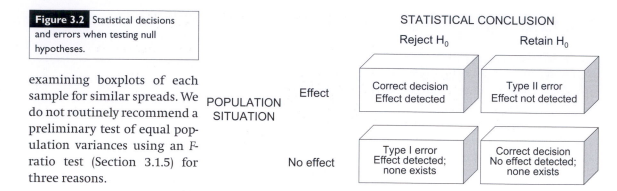

Figure 3.2 Statistical decisions and errors when testing null hypotheses.

examining boxplots of each sample for similar spreads. We do not routinely recommend a preliminary test of equal population variances using an F-ratio test (Section 3.1.5) for three reasons.

- The F-ratio test might be more sensitive to non-normality than the t test it is "protecting".
- Depending on sample size, an F-ratio test may not detect variance differences that could invalidate the following t test, or it might find unequal variances (and hence recommend the following analysis not be done), which would not adversely affect the subsequent t test (Markowski & Markowski 1990). This dependence of the results of a statistical hypothesis test on sample size is well known and will be discussed further in Section 3.6.
- Statistical hypothesis testing should be used carefully, preferably in situations where power and effect sizes have been considered; this is rarely the case for exploratory checks of assumptions.

The third assumption is that the observations are sampled randomly from clearly defined populations. This is an assumption that must be considered at the design stage. If samples cannot be sampled randomly from populations, then a more general hypothesis about differences between samples can be tested with a randomization test (see Section 3.3.2).

These t tests are much more sensitive to assumptions about normality and equal variances if sample sizes are unequal, so for this reason alone, it's always a good idea to design studies with equal sample sizes. On an historical note, testing differences between means when the variances also differ has been a research area of long-standing interest in statistics and is usually called the Behrens–Fisher problem. Solutions to this problem will be discussed in Section 3.3.1.

An additional issue with many statistical tests, including parametric tests, is the presence of outliers (Chapter 4). Outliers are extreme values in a sample very different from the rest of the observations and can have strong effects on the results of most statistical tests, in terms of both Type I and Type II errors. Note that both parametric t tests and non-parametric tests based on ranks (Section 3.3) are affected by outliers (Zimmerman 1994), although rank-based tests are less sensitive (Zimmerman & Zumbo 1993). Detection and treatment of outliers is considered in Chapter 4.

3.2 | Decision errors

3.2.1 Type I and II errors
When we use the Neyman–Pearson protocol to test an H_0, there are four possible outcomes based on whether the H_0 was actually true (no effect) or not (real effect) for the population (Figure 3.2). A rejection of a H_0 is usually termed a significant result (statistically significant, not necessarily biologically significant – see Box 3.4) and implies that some alternative hypothesis (H_A) is true. Clearly, two of the outcomes result in the right statistical decision being made; we correctly reject a false H_0 or we correctly retain a true H_0. What about the two errors?

- A Type I error is when we mistakenly reject a correct H_0 (e.g. when we conclude from our sample and a t test that the population parameter is not equal to zero when in fact the population parameter does equal zero) and is denoted α. A Type I error can only occur when H_0 is true.
- A Type II error is when we mistakenly accept an incorrect H_0 (e.g. when we conclude from

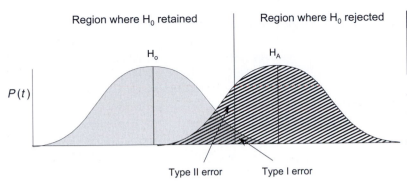

Region where H_0 retained   Region where H_0 rejected

H_0 H_A

$P(t)$

Type II error   Type I error

our sample and a t test that the population parameter equals zero when in fact the population parameter is different from zero). Type II error rates are denoted by β and can only occur when the H_0 is false.

Both errors are the result of chance. Our random sample(s) may provide misleading information about the population(s), especially if the sample sizes are small. For example, two populations may have the same mean value but our sample from one population may, by chance, contain all large values and our sample from the other population may, by chance, contain all small values, resulting in a statistically significant difference between means. Such a Type I error is possible even if H_0 $(\mu_1 = \mu_2)$ is true, it's just unlikely. Keep in mind the frequency interpretation of P values also applies to the interpretation of error rates. The Type I and Type II error probabilities do not necessarily apply to our specific statistical test but represent the long-run probability of errors if we repeatedly sampled from the same population(s) and did the test many times.

Examine Figure 3.3, which shows the probability sampling distribution of t when the H_0 is true (left curve) and the probability sampling distribution of t when a particular H_A is true (right curve). Of course, we never know what this latter distribution looks like in practice because if H_0 is false, we don't know what the real H_A is. For a particular df, there will be a different distribution for each possible H_A but only one sampling distribution for H_0. The critical value of t for $\alpha = 0.05$ is indicated. If H_0 is actually true, any t value greater than this critical value will lead to a rejection of H_0 and a Type I error. If H_0 is actually false and H_A is true, any

value equal to or smaller than this critical value will lead to non-rejection of H_0 and a Type II error. Note that if H_0 is, for example, no difference between means, then H_A is a difference between means. The bigger the difference, the further the t distribution for H_A will be to the right of the t distribution for H_0 and the less likely will be a Type II error.

Traditionally, scientists have been most concerned with Type I errors. This is probably because statistically significant results imply falsification of a null hypothesis and therefore progress in science and maybe because we wrongly equate statistical significance with biological significance (see Box 3.4). Therefore, we protect ourselves (and our discipline) from false significant results by using a conservative significance level (e.g. 0.05); this means that we are controlling our Type I error rate to 0.05 or 5%. If the probability of obtaining our sample when the H_0 is true is less than 0.05, then we reject that H_0; otherwise we don't reject it. Why don't we use an even lower significance level to protect ourselves from Type I errors even more? Mainly because for most statistical tests, for a given sample size and level of variation, lowering the Type I error rate (the significance level) results in more Type II errors (imagine moving the vertical line to the right in Figure 3.3) if it turns out that the H_A is true.

For some activities, especially environmental monitoring and impact assessment and experiments involving human health issues, Type II errors may be of much greater importance than Type I. Consider a monitoring program, and the consequences of the two kinds of errors. A Type I error results in an erroneous claim of a significant environmental change. In an ideal world, the result would be a requirement by the relevant regulatory authority for some mitigation or cessation of the activity causing that change. The

Box 3.4 | Biological versus statistical significance

It is important to distinguish between biological and statistical significance. As mentioned in Section 3.6.1, if we take larger and larger samples, we can detect even very small differences. Whenever we get a (statistically) significant result, we must still decide whether the effects that we observe are biologically meaningful. For example, we might measure 100 snails in each of two populations, and we would almost certainly find that the two populations were different in size. However, if the mean size differed by $\approx 1\%$, we may struggle to explain the biological meaning of such a small difference.

What is biologically significant? The answer has nothing to do with statistics, but with our biological judgment, and the answer will vary with the questions being answered. Small effects of experimental treatments may be biologically significant when we are dealing with rates of gene flow, selection, or some physiological measurements, because small differences can have important repercussions in population genetics or organism health. For example, small changes in the concentration of a toxin in body tissues may be enough to cause mortality. In contrast, small effects may be less important for ecological processes at larger spatial scales, especially under field conditions.

It is important for biologists to think carefully about how large an effect has to be before it is biologically meaningful. In particular, setting biologically important effect sizes is crucial for ensuring that out statistical test has adequate power.

"costs" would be purely financial – the cost of (unnecessary) mitigation. A Type II error, on the other hand, is a failure to detect a change that has occurred. The verdict of "no significant impact" results in continuation of harmful activities. There is no added financial cost, but some time in the future the environmental change will become large enough to become apparent. The consequence of this error is that significant environmental degradation may have occurred or become more widespread than if it had been detected early, and mitigation or rehabilitation may be necessary, perhaps at significant cost. A strong argument can therefore be made that for many "applied" purposes, Type II errors are more important than Type I errors. A similar argument applies to other research areas. Underwood (1990, 1997), in describing the logical structure of hypothesis testing, indicates very clearly how Type II errors can misdirect research programs completely.

The inverse of Type II error is power, the probability of rejecting a false H_0. We will consider power in more detail as part of experimental design in Chapter 7.

3.2.2 Asymmetry and scalable decision criteria

One of the problems of fixing our significance level α, even if we then use power analysis to determine sample sizes to minimize the probability of Type II errors, is that there is an implicit asymmetry in the importance of H_0 relative to H_A (Barnett 1999, Oakes 1986). In many practical situations, fixing α to 0.05 will make it difficult to reduce the probability of Type II errors to a comparable level, unless sample sizes or effect sizes are very large. The only solution to this problem, while still maintaining the structure of statistical tests and errors associated with decisions, is to abandon fixed level testing and use decision criteria that provide a more sensible balance between Type I and Type II errors.

Mapstone (1995) has proposed one way of incorporating flexible decision criteria in statistical hypothesis testing in ecology and environmental science. He suggested that we should set the ratio of acceptable Type I and Type II errors *a priori*, based on the relative costs of making each kind of error, and the critical effect size is the most crucial element. Keough & Mapstone (1995) have incorporated this idea into a framework for designing environmental monitoring programs, and included a worked example. Downes *et al.* (2001) have also advocated scalable decision criteria for assessing environmental impact in freshwater ecosystems. The logic of considering costs of making errors in statistical decision making is much closer to the Bayesian approach to making decisions, although Bayesians eschew the long-run frequency view of probability (Section 3.7).

3.3 | Other testing methods

The statistical tests most commonly used by biologists, and the tests based on the *t* distribution we have just described, are known as parametric tests. These tests make distributional assumptions about the data, which for *t* tests are that the distributions of the populations from which the samples came are normal. Most textbooks state that parametric tests are robust to this assumption, i.e. the sampling distribution of the *t* statistic still follows the appropriate mathematical distribution even if the variable has a non-normal distribution. This means that the conclusions from the test of H_0 are still reliable even if the underlying distribution is not perfectly normal. This robustness is limited, however, and the assumption of normality (along with other assumptions inherent in all statistical tests – see Section 3.1.6) should always be checked before doing a parametric analysis.

3.3.1 Robust parametric tests
A number of tests have been developed for the H_0 that $\mu_1 = \mu_2$ which do not assume equal variances. For example, there are approximate versions of the *t* test (called variously the Welch test, Welch–Aspin test, the Satterthwaite-adjusted *t* test, Behrens–Fisher test, separate variances *t* test), which are available in most statistical software. The most common version of this test recalculates the df for the *t* test as (Hays 1994):

$$\frac{(s_1/\sqrt{n_1} + s_2/\sqrt{n_2})^2}{(s_1/\sqrt{n_1})^2/(n_1 + 1) + (s_2/\sqrt{n_2})^2/(n_2 + 1)} - 2 \quad (3.8)$$

This results in lower df (which may not be an integer) and therefore a more conservative test.

Such a test is more reliable than the traditional *t* test when variances are very unequal and/or sample sizes are unequal.

Coombs *et al.* (1996) reviewed all the available tests for comparing two population means when variances may be unequal. They indicated that the Welch test is suitable when the samples come from normally distributed populations but recommended the Wilcox *H* test, based on M-estimators and bootstrapped estimates of variance (Chapter 2), for skewed distributions. Unfortunately, this test is not available in most software.

Some common types of null hypotheses can also be tested with non-parametric tests. Non-parametric tests do not assume that the underlying distribution of the population(s) from which the samples came is normal. Before looking at "classical" non-parametric tests based on ranks, let's consider another type of statistical test called a randomization test.

3.3.2 Randomization (permutation) tests
These tests resample or reshuffle the original data many times to generate the sampling distribution of a test statistic directly. Fisher (1935) first proposed that this method might be suitable for testing hypotheses but, without computers, could only analyze very small data sets. To illustrate randomization tests, we will revisit the example described in Section 3.1.5 where Ward & Quinn (1988) wished to test the H_0 that there is no difference between the mussel and littorinid zones in the mean number of eggs per capsule of *L.vinosa*. The steps in the randomization test are as follows (Manly 1997).

1. Calculate the difference between the mean numbers of eggs per capsule of the two groups (D_0).

2. Randomly reassign the 79 observations so that 37 are in the littorinid zone group and 42 are in the mussel zone group and calculate the difference between the means of the two groups (D_1).

3. Repeat this step a large number of times, each time calculating the D_i. How many randomizations? Manly (1997) suggested 1000 times for a 0.05 test and 5000 times for a

0.01 test. With modern computer power, these numbers of randomizations only take a few seconds.

4. Calculate the proportion of all the D_is that are greater than or equal to D_0 (the difference between the means in our samples). This is the "*P* value" and it can be compared to an *a priori* significance level (e.g. 0.05) to decide whether to reject the H_0 or not (Neyman–Pearson tradition), or used as a measure of "strength of evidence" against the H_0 (Fisher tradition – see Manly 1997).

The underlying principle behind randomization tests is that if the null hypothesis is true, then any random arrangement of observations to groups is equally possible (Crowley 1992). Randomization tests can be applied to situations where we are comparing groups or testing whether a set of observations occurs in a random order (e.g. time series). They are particularly useful when analyzing data for which the distribution is unknown (Potvin & Roff 1993), when random sampling from populations is not possible (e.g. we are using data that occurred opportunistically, such as museum specimens – see Manly 1997) or perhaps when other assumptions such as independence of observations are questionable, as when testing for temporal trends (Manly 1997). There are some potential interpretation problems with randomization tests that users should be aware of. First, they involve resampling the data to generate a probability distribution of the test statistic. This means that their results are more difficult to relate to any larger population but the positive side is that they are particularly useful for analyzing experiments where random sampling is not possible but randomization of observations to groups is used (Ludbrook & Dudley 1998). Crowley (1992, p. 432) argued that the difficulty of making inferences to some population is a problem "of greater theoretical than applied relevance" (see also Edgington 1995), particularly as randomization tests give similar *P* values to standard parametric tests when assumptions hold (Manly 1997). Manly (1997) also did not see this as a serious problem and pointed out that one of the big advantages of randomization tests is in situations when a population is not

relevant or the whole population is effectively measured. Second, the H_0 being tested then is not one about population parameters, but simply that there is no difference between the means of the two groups, i.e. is the difference between group means "greater then we would expect by chance". Finally, the *P* value is interpreted differently from the usual "classical" tests. In randomization tests, the *P* value is the proportion of possible data rearrangements (e.g. between two groups) that are equal to, or more extreme than, the one we observed in our sample(s). Interestingly, because the *P* value is determined by a (re)sampling process, confidence intervals for the *P* value can be determined (Crowley 1992).

Randomization tests for differences between group means are not free of assumptions. For example, randomization tests of the H_0 of no difference between means are likely to be sensitive to differences in variances (Boik 1987, Stewart-Oaten *et al.* 1992). Indeed, randomization tests of location (e.g. mean) differences should be considered to have an assumption of similar distributions in the different samples, and transformations used where appropriate (Crowley 1992). So these tests should not be automatically applied to overcome problems of variance heterogeneity.

Manly (1997) is an excellent introduction to randomization tests from a biological perspective and Crowley (1992) critically summarized many applications of randomization tests in biology. Other good references for randomization tests are Edgington (1995) and Noreen (1989).

3.3.3 Rank-based non-parametric tests

Statisticians have appreciated the logic behind randomization tests for quite a long time, but the computations involved were prohibitive without computers. One early solution to this problem was to rank the observations first and then randomize the ranks to develop probability distributions of a rank-based test statistic. Ranking the observations has two advantages in this situation. First, determining the probability distribution of a rank-based test statistic (e.g. sum of the ranks in each sample) by randomization is relatively easy, because for a given sample size with no ties, the distribution is identical for any set of data. The critical values for such distributions are tabled in many statistics books. In contrast, determining the probability distribution for a test statistic (e.g. difference between means) based on randomizing the original observations was not possible before computers except for small sample sizes. Second, using the ranks of the observations removes the assumption of normality of the underlying distribution(s) in each group, although other assumptions may still apply.

Although there is a wide range of rank-based non-parametric tests (Hollander & Wolfe 1999, Siegel & Castellan 1988, Sprent 1993), we will only consider two here. First, consider a test about differences between two populations. The Mann–Whitney–Wilcoxon test is actually two independently developed tests (Mann–Whitney and Wilcoxon) that produce identical results. The H_0 being tested is that the two samples come from populations with identical distributions against the H_A that the samples come from populations which differ only in location (mean or median). The procedure is as follows.

1. Rank all the observations, ignoring the groups. Tied observations get the average of their ranks.

2. Calculate the sum of the ranks for both samples. If the H_0 is true, we would expect a similar mixture of ranks in both samples (Sprent 1993).

3. Compare the smaller rank sum to the probability distribution of rank sums, based on repeated randomization of observations to groups, and test in the usual manner.

4. For larger sample sizes, the probability distribution of rank sums approximates a normal distribution and the z statistic can be used. Note that different software can produce quite different results depending on whether the large-sample approximation or exact randomization methods are used, and also how ties are handled (Bergmann *et al.* 2000).

Second, we may have a test about differences based on paired observations. For paired samples, we can use the Wilcoxon signed-rank test to test the H_0 that the two sets of observations come from the same population against the H_A that the populations differ in location (mean or median). This test is actually a test of a single population param-eter, analyzing the paired differences, and the procedure is as follows.

1. Calculate the difference between the observations for each pair, noting the sign of each difference. If H_0 is true, we would expect roughly equal numbers of + and − signs.

2. Calculate the sum of the positive ranks and the sum of the negative ranks.

3. Compare the smaller of these rank sums to the probability distribution of rank sums, based on randomization, and test in the usual manner.

4. For larger sample sizes, the probability distribution of rank sums follows a normal distribution and the z statistic can be used, although the concern of Bergmann *et al.* (2000) about differences between the large sample approximation and exact methods for the Mann–Whitney–Wilcoxon test may also apply to the Wilcoxon signed-rank test.

Another non-parametric approach using ranks is the class of rank transformation tests. This is a more general approach that theoretically can be applied to any analysis for which there is a parametric test. The data are transformed to ranks and then these ranks are analyzed using the appropriate parametric analysis. Note that this technique is conceptually no different to transforming data to logs to meet the assumptions of a parametric test (Chapter 4) and is therefore not a true non-parametric test (Potvin & Roff 1993). The rank transform approach will generally give the same answer as the appropriate rank-based test, e.g. rank transform t test is the same as the Mann–Whitney–Wilcoxon test (Zimmerman & Zumbo 1993), although if there are a large number of ties the results will vary a little. Tests based on the rank transform method have also been used for various linear model analyses (Chapters 5, 8 and 9).

Although these non-parametric tests of location differences do not assume a particular shape (e.g. normal) of the underlying distributions, they do assume that the distributions of the populations are similar, so the assumption of equal variances still applies (Crowley 1992, Manly 1997, Sprent 1993, Stewart-Oaten *et al.* 1992, Zimmerman & Zumbo 1993). The common strategy in biological research to use rank-based non-parametric tests to overcome variance heterogeneity is inappropriate. Variance heterogeneity in the two-sample hypothesis test should be dealt with by using a robust test, such as the Welch t test (Section 3.3.1) or by transforming the data to remove the relationship between the mean and variance (Chapter 4).

These non-parametric tests generally have lower power than the analogous parametric tests when parametric assumptions are met, although the difference in power is surprisingly small (e.g. <5% difference for Mann–Whitney–Wilcoxon test versus t test) given the former's use of ranks rather than the original data (Hollander & Wolfe 1999). With non-normal distributions, the non-parametric tests do cope better but because normality by itself is the least critical of all parametric assumptions, its hard to recommend the rank-based tests except in situations where (i) the distributions are very weird, and transformations do not help, or (ii) outliers are present (see Chapter 4). It is sometimes recommended that if the data are not measured on a continuous scale (i.e. the data are already in the form of ranks), then tests like the Mann–Whitney–Wilcoxon are applicable. We disagree because such a test is equivalent to applying a parametric test (e.g. t test) to the ranks, a much simpler and more consistent approach. It is also worth noting that the rank-based randomization tests don't really have any advantage over randomization tests based on the original data, except in terms of computation (which is irrelevant with modern computer power) – see Ludbrook & Dudley (1998). Both have assumptions of equal distributions in the two groups, and therefore equal variances, and neither is very sensitive to non-normality.

Rank-based tests have been argued to be more powerful than parametric tests for very skewed (heavy tailed) distributions. However, this is primarily because rank-based tests deal with outliers more effectively (Zimmerman & Zumbo 1993). Indeed, outliers cause major problems for parametric tests and their identification should be a priority for exploratory data analysis (Chapter 4). The alternative to rank-based tests is to remove or modify the outlying values by trimming or winsorizing (Chapter 2) and using a parametric test. Note that non-parametric tests are not immune to outliers; they are just not affected as much as parametric tests (Zimmerman & Zumbo 1993).

3.4 | Multiple testing

3.4.1 The problem

One of the most difficult issues related to statistical hypothesis testing is the potential accumulation of decision errors under circumstances of multiple testing. As the number of tests increases, so does the probability of making at least one Type I error among the collection of tests. The probability of making one or more Type I errors in a set (or family) of tests is called the family-wise Type I error rate, although Day & Quinn (1989) and others have termed it experiment-wise Type I error rate because it is often used in the context of multiple comparisons of means when analyzing experimental data. The problem of increasing family-wise Type I error rate potentially occurs in any situation where there are multiple significance tests that are considered simultaneously. These include pairwise comparisons of treatment groups in an experiment (Chapter 8), testing pairwise correlations between multiple variables recorded from the same experimental or sampling units (Rice 1989) or multiple univariate analyses (e.g. t tests) of these variables.

If the tests are orthogonal (i.e. independent of each other), the family-wise Type I error can be calculated:

$$1 - (1 - \alpha)^c \qquad (3.9)$$

where α is the significance level (e.g. 0.05) for each test and c is the number of tests. For example, imagine having a random sample from a number of populations and we wish to test the H_0s that each independent pair of population means is equal. We keep these comparisons independent by not using the same population in more than one test. As the number of populations we wish to compare increases, so does the number of pairwise comparisons required and the probability of at least one Type I error among the family of tests (Table 3.1). If the tests are non-orthogonal, then the family-wise Type I error rate will be lower (Ramsey 1993), but cannot be calculated as it will

No. of tests	Family-wise probability of at least one Type I error
3	0.14
10	0.40
45	0.90

Table 3.1 Accumulation of probability of at least one Type 1 error among a "family" of tests

depend on the degree of non-independence among the tests.

The different approaches for dealing with the increased probability of a Type I error in multiple testing situations are based on how the Type I error rate for each test (the comparison-wise Type I error rate) is reduced to keep the family-wise Type I error rate at some reasonable level. Each test will then have a more stringent significance level but as a consequence, much reduced power if the H_0 is false. However, the traditional priority of recommendations for dealing with multiple testing has been strict control of family-wise Type I error rates rather than power considerations. Before describing the approaches for reducing the Type I error rate for each test to control the family-wise Type I error rate, we need to consider two other issues. The first is how we define the family of tests across which we wish to control the Type I error rate and the second is to what level should we control this error rate.

What comprises a family of tests (Shaffer 1995, Hancock & Klockars 1996) for determining error rates is a difficult decision. An extreme view, and not one to which we subscribe, might be to define a family as all the tests a researcher might do in a lifetime (see Maxwell & Delaney 1990 and Miller 1981 for discussion), and try to limit the Type I error rate over this family. Controlling error rates over such a family of tests has interesting and humorous implications for biologists' career structures (Morrison 1991). More generally, a family is defined as some collection of simultaneous tests, where a number of hypotheses are tested simultaneously using a single data set from a single experiment or sampling program.

We agree with Hochberg & Tamhane (1987) that unrelated hypotheses (in terms of intended use or content) should be analyzed separately, even if they are not independent of each other. We recommend that each researcher, in a specific analytical situation, must make an *a priori* decision about what a family of tests is; this decision should be based, at least in part, on the relative importance of Type I versus Type II errors.

The other issue is what level to set for family-wise error rate. It is common practice for biologists to set the family-wise Type I error rate to the same level as they use for individual comparisons (e.g. 0.05). This is not easy to justify, especially as it reduces the comparison-wise Type I error rate to very low levels, increasing the probability of Type II errors if any of the H_0s are false. So this is a very conservative strategy and we should consider alternatives. One may be to use a procedure that controls the family-wise error rate but to set a significance level above 0.05. There is nothing sacred about 0.05 (see Section 3.6) and we are talking here about the probability of any Type I error in a collection of tests. Setting this significance level *a priori* to 0.10 or higher is not unreasonable. Another approach is the interesting proposal by Benjamini & Hochberg (1995). They also argued that control of family-wise Type I error rate may be too severe in some circumstances and recommended controlling the false discovery rate (FDR). This is the expected proportion of Type I errors among the rejected hypotheses.

3.4.2 Adjusting significance levels and/or P values

Whatever philosophy we decide to use, there will be situations when some control of family-wise Type I error rate will be required. The procedures we will describe here are those which are independent of the test statistic used and are based on adjusting the significance levels for each test downwards to control the family-wise Type I error rate. Note that instead of adjusting significance levels, we could also adjust the P values and use the usual significance levels; the two approaches are equivalent.

Bonferroni procedure

This is a general procedure for adjusting significance levels to control Type I error rates in multiple testing situations. Each comparison is tested at

α/c where α is the nominated significance level (e.g. 0.05) and c is the number of comparisons in the family. It provides great control over Type I error but is very conservative when there are lots of comparisons, i.e. each comparison or test will have little power. The big advantage is that it can be applied to any situation where we have a family of tests, so it has broad applicability.

Dunn–Sidak procedure

This is a modification of the Bonferroni procedure that slightly improves power for each comparison, which is tested at $1 - (1 - \alpha)^{1/c}$.

Sequential Bonferroni (Holm 1979)

This is a major improvement on the Bonferroni procedure where the c test statistics (F, t, etc.) or P values are ranked from largest to smallest and the smallest P value is tested at α/c, the next at $\alpha/(c-1)$, the next at $\alpha/(c-2)$, etc. Testing stops when a non-significant result occurs. This procedure provides more power for individual tests and is recommended for any situation in which the Bonferroni adjustment is applicable.

Hochberg (1988) described a similar procedure that works in reverse. The largest P value is tested at α, rejecting all other tests if this one is significant. If not significant, the next largest is tested against $\alpha/2$, and so on. Shaffer (1995) stated that Hochberg's procedure is slightly more powerful than Holm's.

Resampling-based adjusted P values

Westfall & Young (1993a,b) have developed an interesting approach to P value adjustment for multiple testing based around resampling. They defined the adjusted P value as:

$$P_{adj} = P(\min P_{rand} \le P | H_0) \tag{3.10}$$

where P_{rand} is the random P value for any test. Basically, their procedure measures how extreme any particular P value is out of a list of P values from multiple tests, assuming all H_0s are true. Westfall & Young (1993b) argue that their procedure generalizes to Holm's and other methods as special cases and also accounts for correlations among the P values.

3.5 | Combining results from statistical tests

We sometimes need to evaluate multiple studies in which statistical analyses have been used to test similar hypotheses about some biological process, such as the effect of a particular experimental treatment. Our interest is in summarizing the size of the treatment effect across studies and also testing an H_0 about whether there is any overall effect of the treatment.

3.5.1 Combining P values

Fisher (1954) proposed a method for combining the P values from a number of independent tests of the same hypothesis, even though different statistical procedures, and therefore different H_0s, may have been used (see also Hasselblad 1994, Manly 2001, Sokal & Rohlf 1995). For c independent tests, each producing a P value for the test of a commensurate H_0, the P values can be combined by:

$$-2 \sum_{i=1}^{c} \ln(P) \tag{3.11}$$

which is distributed as a χ^2 with $2c$ degrees of freedom. The overall H_0 is that all the H_0s in the collection of tests are true (Sokal & Rohlf 1995). If we reject the overall H_0, we conclude that there is an overall effect of whatever treatment or contrast was commensurate between the analyses. Alternative methods, including ones that weight the outcomes from the different tests differently, are described in Becker (1994) and Manly (2001).

3.5.2 Meta-analysis

The limitation of Fisher's method is that P values are only one piece of information that we use for drawing conclusions from a statistical test. They simply indicate whether we would reject the H_0 at the chosen level of significance. The biological interpretation of that result would depend on the size of the difference or effect, and the sample sizes, so a better approach would incorporate effect sizes, the variances of the effect sizes and sample sizes when combining results from different tests. Such a more sophisticated approach is called meta-analysis. Meta-analysis is used primarily when reviewing the literature on a particular topic, e.g. competition between organisms (Gurevitch *et al.* 1992), and some overall summary of the conclusions from different studies is required.

Basically, meta-analysis calculates, for each analysis being incorporated, a measure of effect size (Rosenthal 1994, see also Chapters 7 and 8) that incorporates the variance of the effect. These effect sizes from the *c* different tests are averaged using the sum of the inverse of the variance of each effect size ("inverse variance weighted average": Hasselblad 1994, p. 695). This average effect size can be used as a summary measure of the overall effect of the process being investigated.

Most meta-analyses are based on fixed effects models (see also Chapter 8) where we are assuming that the set of analyses we are combining share some true effect size for the process under investigation (Gurevitch & Hedges 1993). Under this model, the test of H_0 that the true effect size is zero can be tested by constructing confidence intervals (based on the standard normal distribution) for the true average effect size (Gurevitch & Hedges 1993) and seeing if that confidence interval includes zero at the chosen level (e.g. 95%). We can also calculate a measure of homogeneity (Q) for testing whether all *c* effect sizes are equal. Q is the sum of weighted (by the inverse of the variance of each effect size) squared differences between each effect size and the inverse variance weighted average of the effect sizes. It sounds messy but the computations are quite simple (Gurevitch & Hedges 1993, Hasselblad 1994). Q is distributed as a χ^2 with $c-1$ degrees of freedom. In some cases, the analyses being combined fall into different *a priori* groups (e.g. studies on competition in marine, freshwater and terrestrial environments) and within-group and between-group measures of homogeneity can be calculated (analogous to partitioning the variance in an ANOVA – Chapter 8).

Meta-analysis can be used in any situation where an effect size, and its variance, can be calculated so it is not restricted to continuous variables. Nor is it restricted to fixed effects models, with both random and mixed models possible (Gurevitch & Hedges 1993; see also Chapters 8 and 9). Meta-analyses do depend on the quality of the literature being surveyed. For some studies, not enough information is provided to measure an effect size or its variance. There is also the issue of quality control, ensuring that the design of the studies we have used in a meta-analysis are acceptable, and whether we can combine studies based on experimental manipulations versus those based on weaker survey designs. Nonetheless, meta-analysis is increasing in use in the biological literature and some appreciation of its strengths and weaknesses is important for biologists. One important weakness worth noting is the "file-drawer problem". The database of published papers is highly censored, with non-significant results under-represented, so a meta-analysis of published work should include careful thought about what "population" these published studies represent.

Two detailed texts are Hedges & Olkin (1985) and the volume edited by Cooper & Hedges (1994), although excellent reviews from a biological perspective include Gurevitch & Hedges (1993) and Hasselblad (1994).

3.6 | Critique of statistical hypothesis testing

Significance testing, especially null hypothesis significance testing, has been consistently criticized by many statisticians (e.g. Nester 1996, Salsburg 1985) and, in particular, in the recent psychological and educational literature (e.g. Carver 1978, 1993, Cohen 1990, 1994, Shaver 1993, Harlow *et al.* 1997 and chapters therein). Biologists have also questioned the validity of statistical hypothesis testing (e.g. Johnson 1999, Jones & Matloff 1986, Matloff 1991, Stewart-Oaten 1996). A thorough review of this literature is beyond the scope of our book but a brief discussion of these criticisms is warranted.

3.6.1 Dependence on sample size and stopping rules

There is no question that results for classical statistical tests depend on sample size (Chow 1988, Mentis 1988, Thompson 1993), i.e. everything else being the same, larger sample sizes are more likely to produce a statistically significant result and with very large sample sizes, trivial effects

Box 3.5 | Likelihood inference and the likelihood principle

Oakes (1986) described four major schools of statistical inference, three of which we describe in this chapter – Fisherian and Neyman–Pearson hypothesis testing, aspects of both being used by many biologists, and the Bayesian methods based on subjective probabilities. The fourth school is likelihood inference, based on the likelihood function that we outlined in Chapter 2 (see also Royall 1997). There are two important issues involved. First, the evidence that the observed data provide about the hypothesis is represented by the likelihood function, the likelihood of observing our sample data given the hypothesis. Second, the likelihood principle states that two sets of data that produce proportional likelihood functions are equal in terms of evidence about the hypothesis. One of the arguments often used against statistical significance tests is that they violate the likelihood principle.

Likelihood inference is really about relative measures of evidence of support between competing hypotheses so the focus is on the likelihood ratio:

$$\frac{L(\text{data}|H_1)}{L(\text{data}|H_2)}$$

although, as discussed in Chapter 2, we often convert likelihoods to log-likelihoods and the result is a ratio of log-likelihoods. The likelihood ratio can be viewed as a measure of the relative strength of evidence provided by the data in H_1 compared with H_2.

Likelihoods are relevant to both classical and Bayesian inference. Likelihood ratios can often be tested in a classical framework because, under many conditions, the ratio follows a χ^2 distribution. The observed data contribute to a Bayesian analysis solely through the likelihood function and, with a non-informative, uniform prior, the Bayesian posterior probability distribution has an identical shape to the likelihood function.

can produce a significant result. However, while this is true by definition and can cause problems in complex analyses (e.g. factorial ANOVAs) where there are numerous tests based on different df, designing experiments based on *a priori* power considerations is crucial here. Rather than arbitrarily choosing sample sizes, our sample size should be based on that necessary to detect a desired effect if it occurs in the population(s) (Cohen 1988, 1992, Fairweather 1991, Peterman 1990a,b). There is nothing new in this recommendation and we will consider power analysis further in Chapter 7.

The sample size problem relates to the stopping rule, how you decide when to stop an experiment or sampling program. In classical hypothesis testing, how the data were collected influences how we interpret the result of the test, whereas the likelihood principle (Box 3.5) requires

the stopping rule to be irrelevant (Oakes 1986). Mayo (1996) and Royall (1997) provide interesting, and contrasting, opinions on the relevance of stopping rules to inference.

3.6.2 Sample space – relevance of data not observed

A well-documented aspect of P values as measures of evidence is that they comprise not only the long-run probability of the observed data if H_0 is true but also of data more extreme, i.e. data not observed. The set of possible outcomes of an experiment or sampling exercise, such as the possible values of a random variable like a test statistic, is termed the sample space. The dependence of statistical tests on the sample space violates the likelihood principle (Box 3.5) because the same evidence, measured as likelihoods, can produce different conclusions (Royall 1997). The counter argument, detailed by Mayo (1996), is that likelihoods do not permit measures of probabilities of error from statistical tests. Measuring these errors in a frequentist sense is crucial to statistical hypothesis testing.

3.6.3 *P* values as measure of evidence

Cohen (1994) and others have argued that what we really want to know from a statistical test is the probability of H_0 being true, given our sample data, i.e. $P(H_0|data)$. In contrast, Mayo (1996) proposed that a frequentist wants to know what is "the probability with which certain outcomes would occur given that a specified experiment is performed" (p. 10). What the classical significance test tells us is the long-run probability of obtaining our sample data, given that H_0 is true, i.e. $P(data|H_0)$. As Cohen (1994) and others have emphasized, these two probabilities are not interchangeable and Bayesian analyses (Section 3.7), which provide a measure of the $P(H_0|data)$, can produce results very different from the usual significance test, especially when testing two-tailed "point" hypotheses (Berger & Sellke 1987). Indeed, Berger & Sellke (1987) presented evidence that the *P* value can greatly overstate the evidence against the H_0 (see also Anderson 1998 for an ecological example). We will discuss this further in the next section. In reply to Berger & Sellke (1987), Morris (1987) argued that differences between *P* values and Bayesian posteriors will mainly occur when the power of the test is weak at small sample sizes; otherwise *P* values work well as evidence against the H_0. Reconciling Bayesian measures and *P* values as evidence against the H_0 is still an issue of debate among statisticians.

3.6.4 Null hypothesis always false

Cohen (1990) and others have also argued that testing an H_0 is trivial because the H_0 is always false: two population means will never be *exactly* the same, a population parameter will never be *exactly* zero. In contrast, Frick (1995) has pointed out an H_0 can be logically true and illustrated this with an ESP experiment. The H_0 was that a person in one room could not influence the thoughts of a person in another room. Nonetheless, the argument is that testing H_0s is pointless because most common H_0s in biology, and other sciences, are

always false. Like Chow (1988, 1991) and Mulaik *et al.* (1997), we argue that the H_0 is simply the complement of the research hypothesis about which we are trying to make a decision. The H_0 represents the default (or null) framework that "nothing is happening" or that "there is no effect" (3.1.1). A rejection of the H_0 is not important because we thought the H_0 might actually be true. It is important because it indicates that we have detected an effect worth reporting and investigating further. We also emphasise that H_0s do not have to be of the "no effect" form. There may be good reasons to test H_0s that a parameter equals a non-zero value. For example, in an environmental monitoring situation, we might compare control and impact locations to each other, and look for changes through time in this control–impact difference. We might find that two locations are quite different from each other as a result of natural processes, but hypothesize that a human activity will change that relationship.

3.6.5 Arbitrary significance levels

One long-standing criticism has been the arbitrary use of $\alpha = 0.05$ as the criterion for rejecting or not rejecting H_0. Fisher originally suggested 0.05 but later argued against using a single significance level for every statistical decision-making process. The Neyman–Pearson approach also does not rely on a single significance level (α), just a value chosen *a priori*. There is no reason why all tests have to be done with a significance level fixed at 0.05. For example, Day & Quinn (1989) have argued that there is nothing sacred about 0.05 in the context of multiple comparisons. Mapstone (1995) has also provided a decision-making framework by which the probabilities of Type I and Type II errors are set based on our assessment of the cost of making the two types of error (Section 3.2.2). The point is that problems with the arbitrary use of 0.05 as a significance level are not themselves a reason to dismiss statistical hypothesis testing. Irrespective of which philosophy we use for making statistical decisions, some criterion must be used.

3.6.6 Alternatives to statistical hypothesis testing

In the discussions on significance testing, particularly in the psychological literature, three general alternatives have been proposed. First, Cohen (1990, 1994) and Oakes (1986) and others have argued that interval estimation and determination of effect sizes (with confidence intervals) is a better alternative to testing null hypotheses. While we encourage the use and presentation of effect sizes, we do not see them as an alternative to significance testing; rather, they are complementary. Interpreting significance tests should always be done in conjunction with a measure of effect size (e.g. difference between means) and some form of confidence interval. However, effect sizes by themselves do not provide a sensible philosophical basis for making decisions about scientific hypotheses.

Second, Royall (1997) summarized the view that likelihoods provide all the evidence we need when evaluating alternative hypotheses based on the observed data. Finally, the Bayesian approach of combining prior probability with the likelihood function to produce a posterior probability distribution for a parameter or hypothesis will be considered in the next section.

In summary, biologists should be aware of the limitations and flaws in statistical testing of null hypotheses but should also consider the philosophical rationale for any alternative scheme. Does it provide us with an objective and consistent methodology for making decisions about hypotheses? We agree with Dennis (1996), Levin (1998), Mulaik *et al.* (1997) and others that misuse of statistical hypothesis testing does not imply that the process is flawed. When used cautiously, linked to appropriate hypotheses, and combined with other forms of interpretation (including effect sizes and confidence intervals), it can provide a sensible and intelligent means of evaluating biological hypotheses. We emphasize that statistical significance does not necessarily imply biological importance (Box 3.4); only by planning studies and experiments so they have a reasonable power to detect an effect of biological importance can we relate statistical and biological significance.

3.7 | Bayesian hypothesis testing

One approach that may provide a realistic alternative to classical statistical hypothesis testing in some circumstances is Bayesian methodology. As we discussed in Chapter 2, the Bayesian approach views population parameters (e.g. means, regression coefficients) as random, or at least unknown, variables. Bayesians construct posterior probability distributions for a parameter and use these probability distributions to calculate confidence intervals. They also use prior information to modify the probability distributions of the parameters and this prior information may include subjective assessment of prior probabilities that a parameter may take specific values.

The Bayesian approach rarely incorporates hypothesis testing in the sense that we have been discussing in this chapter and Bayesian do not usually evaluate alternative hypotheses or models with a reject/accept decision framework. They simply attach greater or lesser favor to the alternatives based on the shape of the posterior distributions. Nonetheless, there are some formal ways of assessing competing hypotheses using Bayesian methods.

We might, for example, have two or more rival hypotheses (H_1, H_2, …H_i); in the classical hypothesis testing framework, these would be H_0 and H_A, although a null hypothesis of no effect would seldom interest Bayesians. We can then use a similar version of Bayes theorem as described for estimation in Chapter 2:

$$P(H_1 | \text{data}) = \frac{P(\text{data} | H_1)P(H_1)}{P(\text{data})} \qquad (3.11)$$

where $P(H_1 | \text{data})$ is the posterior probability of H_1, $P(H_1)$ is the prior probability of H_1 and $P(\text{data} | H_1)/P(\text{data})$ is the standardized likelihood function for H_1, the likelihood of the data given the hypothesis. For example, we could test an H_0 using the Bayesian approach by:

posterior probability of H_0 = likelihood of data given $H_0 \cdot$ prior probability of H_0 $\qquad (3.12)$

The posterior probability is obtained by integrating (if the parameter in the H_0 is continuous) or summing (if discrete) under the posterior probability distribution for the range of values of the parameter specified in the H_0. For continuous parameters, the procedure is straightforward for directional (composite) hypotheses, e.g. H_0: θ less than some specified value, but difficult for a point (simple) hypothesis, e.g. H_0: θ equals some specified value, because we cannot determine the probability of a single value in a probability distribution of a continuous variable.

We can present the relative evidence for H_0 and H_A as a posterior odds ratio:

$$\frac{P(H_0 \mid \text{data})}{P(H_A \mid \text{data})} \tag{3.13}$$

i.e. the ratio of the posterior probabilities, given the data, of the competing hypotheses (Reckhow 1990). This posterior odds ratio is also the product of the prior odds ratio with a term called the Bayes factor (Barnett 1999, Ellison 1996, Kass & Raftery 1995, Reckhow 1990). If the two hypotheses were considered equally likely beforehand, then the Bayes factor equals the posterior odds ratio. If the prior odds were different, then the Bayes factor will differ from the posterior odds ratio, although it seems that the Bayes factor is primarily used in the situation of equal priors (Kass & Raftery 1995). Both the Bayes factor and the posterior odds ratio measure the weight of evidence against H_A in favor of H_0, although the calculations can be reversed to measure the evidence against H_0.

When both hypotheses are simple (i.e. θ equals a specified value), the Bayes factor is just the likelihood ratio (Box 3.5):

$$B = \frac{L(\text{data} \mid H_0)}{L(\text{data} \mid H_A)} \tag{3.14}$$

where the numerator and denominator are the maxima of the likelihood functions for the values of the parameter specified in the hypotheses. When one or both hypotheses are more complex, the Bayes factor is still a likelihood ratio but the numerator and denominator of Equation 3.14 are determined by integrating under the likelihood functions for the range of parameter values specific in each hypothesis (Kass & Raftery 1995). We are now treating the likelihood functions more like probability distributions. For complex hypotheses with multiple parameters, this integration may not be straightforward and the Monte Carlo posterior sampling methods mentioned in Chapter 2 might be required.

To choose between hypotheses, we can either set up a decision framework with an *a priori* critical value for the odds ratio (Winkler 1993) or,

more commonly, use the magnitude of the Bayes factor as evidence in favor of a hypothesis. A simpler alternative to the Bayes factor is the Schwarz criterion (or Bayes Information Criterion, BIC), which approximates the log of the Bayes factor and is easy to calculate. Ellison (1996) has provided a table relating different sizes of Bayes factors (both as $\log_{10} B$ and $2 \log_e B$) to conclusions against the hypothesis in the denominator of Equation 3.14. Odds and likelihood ratios will be considered in more detail in Chapters 13 and 14.

Computational formulae for various types of analyses, including ANOVA and regression linear models, can be found in Box & Tiao (1973), while Berry & Stangl (1996) have summarized other types of analyses. Hilborn & Mangel (1997) focused on assessing the fit of models to data using Bayesian methods. In a fisheries example, they compared the fit of two models of the dynamics of hake off the coast of Namibia where one model was given a higher prior probability of being correct than the second model. As another example, Stow et al. (1995) used Bayesian analysis to estimate the degree of resource dependence (ϕ) in lake mesocosms with different ratios of grazing *Daphnia*. Using a non-informative prior, a high value of ϕ, indicating much interference among the predators, had the highest posterior probability. Stow et al. (1995) pointed out that, in contrast, classical statistical analysis would only have shown that ϕ was significantly different to some hypothesized value. A third example is Crome et al. (1996), who compared Bayesian (with a range of prior distributions) and classical linear model analyses of a BACI (Before-After-Control-Impact) design assessing the effects of logging on birds and mammals in a north Queensland rainforest. Although the two approaches produced similar conclusions for some variables, the posterior distributions for some variables clearly favored some effect sizes over others, providing more information than could be obtained from the classical test of a null hypothesis.

When classical P values [$P(\text{data} \mid H_0)$] are compared to Bayes factors or Bayesian posterior probabilities [$P(H_0 \mid \text{data})$], the differences can be marked, even when H_0 and H_A are assigned equal prior probabilities (i.e. considered equally likely).

Berger & Sellke (1987) and Reckhow (1990) argued that the differences are due to the P value being "conditioned" on the sample space, including an area of a probability distribution that includes hypothetical samples more extreme than the one observed (Section 3.6.2). In contrast, the Bayesian posterior probability is conditioned only on the observed data through the likelihood. The differences between P values and Bayesian posterior probabilities seem more severe for two-tailed testing problems (Casella & Berger 1987), where the P value generally overstates the evidence against H_0, i.e. it rejects H_0 when the posterior probability suggests that the evidence against H_0 is relatively weak. Nonetheless, P values will mostly have a monotonic relationship with posterior probabilities of H_0, i.e. smaller P values imply smaller posterior probabilities, and for one-tailed tests (e.g. ANOVA F-ratio tests), there may be equivalence between the P values and posterior probabilities for reasonable sorts of prior distributions (Casella & Berger 1987). So it may be that the relative sizes of P values can be used as a measure of relative strength of evidence against H_0, in the sense that they are related to Bayesian posterior probabilities (but see Schervish 1996; also Royall 1997 for alternative view).

One of the main difficulties classical frequentist statisticians have with Bayesian analyses is the nature of the prior information (i.e. the prior probabilities). We discussed this in Chapter 2 and those issues, particularly incorporating subjective probability assessments, apply just as crucially for Bayesian hypothesis testing.

So, when should we adopt the Bayesian approach? We have not adopted the Bayesian philosophy for the statistical analyses described in this book for a number of reasons, both theoretical and practical. First, determining prior probabilities is not straightforward in those areas of biology, such as ecology, where much of the research is still exploratory and what happened at other times and places does not necessarily apply in a new setting. We agree with Edwards (1996) that initial analyses of data should be "journalistic", i.e. should not be influenced by our opinions of what the outcome might be (prior probabilities) and that there is an argument that using prior (personal) beliefs in analyses should not be

classified as science. While Carpenter (1990) and others have argued that the prior probabilities have relatively little influence on the outcome compared to the data, this is not always the case (Edwards 1996). For the types of analyses we will discuss in this book, any prior information has probably already been incorporated in the design components of the experiment. Morris (1987) has argued that P values are interpretable in well-designed experiments (and observational studies) where the power to detect a reasonable H_A (effect) has been explicitly considered in the design process. Such a well-designed experiment explicitly considering and minimizing Type I and Type II errors is what Mayo (1996) would describe as a severe test of an hypothesis. Second, treating a population parameter as a random variable does not always seem sensible. In ecology, we are often estimating parameters of real populations (e.g. the density of animals in an area) and the mean of that population is a fixed, although unknown, value. Third, Bayesian analyses seem better suited to estimation rather than hypothesis testing (see also Dennis 1996). Some well-known Bayesian texts (e.g. Box & Tiao 1973, Gelman et al. 1995) do not even discuss hypothesis testing in their Bayesian framework. In contrast, the philosophical position we take in this book is clear. Advances in biology will be greatest when unambiguously stated hypotheses are tested with well-designed sampling or preferably experimental methods. Finally, the practical application of Bayesian analyses is not straightforward for complex analyses and there is little software currently available (but see Berry 1996, Berry & Stangl 1996 and references in Ellison 1996). We suspect that if biologists have enough trouble understanding classical statistical analyses, Bayesian analyses, with their reliance on defining probability distributions and likelihood functions explicitly, are more likely to be misused.

There are some circumstances where the Bayesian approach will be more relevant. In environmental management, managers often wish to know the probability of a policy having a certain outcome or the probabilities of different policies being successful. Whether policies are significantly different from one another (or different from some hypothesized value) is not necessarily helpful and Bayesian calculation of posterior probabilities of competing models might be appropriate. Hilborn & Mangel (1997) also emphasize Bayesian methods for distinguishing between competing models. This in itself has difficulties. Dennis (1996) correctly pointed out the danger of various interest groups having input into the development of prior probabilities, although we have argued earlier (Section 3.2.2) that such negotiation in terms of error rates in the classical decision-making framework should be encouraged. One-off, unreplicated, experiments might also be more suited to Bayesian analyses (Carpenter 1990) because the long-run frequency interpretation doesn't have much meaning and the probability of a single event is of interest.

Bayesian approaches are being increasingly used for analyzing biological data and it is important for biologists to be familiar with the methods. However, rather than simply being an alternative analysis for a given situation, the Bayesian approach represents a different philosophy for interpreting probabilities and we, like Dennis (1996), emphasize that this must be borne in mind before it is adopted for routine use by biologists.

Chapter 4

Graphical exploration of data

Graphical displays are very important in the analysis of data. There are four main functions of graphical displays in data analysis (Snee & Pfeifer 1983).

- Exploration, which involves checking data for unusual values, making sure the data meet the assumptions of the chosen analysis and occasionally deciding what analysis (or model) to use.
- Analysis, which includes checking assumptions but primarily ensuring that the chosen model is a realistic fit to the data.
- Presentation and communication of results, particularly summarizing numerical information (Chapter 19).
- Graphical aids, which are graphical displays for specific statistical purposes, e.g. power curves for determining sample sizes.

We describe graphical displays for the first two functions here, and the third in our final chapter, although some graphs are useful for more than one function, e.g. scatterplots of Y against X are important exploratory tools and often the best way of communicating such data to readers.

4.1 Exploratory data analysis

Before any formal statistical analysis is carried out, it is essential to do preliminary checks of your data for the following reasons:

- to reassure yourself that you do actually have some meaningful data,

- to detect any errors in data entry,
- to detect patterns in the data that may not be revealed by the statistical analysis that you will use,
- to ensure the assumptions of the analysis are met,
- to interpret departures from the assumptions, and
- to detect unusual values, termed outliers (Section 4.5).

Exploratory data analysis (EDA) was originally developed by John Tukey (1977) and extended by Hoaglin *et al.* (1983). The aim is basically to describe and find patterns in your data. A good introduction for biologists is given by Ellison (1993).

4.1.1 Exploring samples

It is usually very important to become familiar with your data before doing any formal analysis. What sort of numbers are they? How variable are they? What sort of distribution do they have? For small data sets, simply examining the raw data in rows and columns is possible. For large samples, especially with multiple variables, graphical techniques are much more appropriate.

The most important thing we want to know about our sample data, and therefore about the population from which our data came, is the shape of the distribution. Many of the statistical procedures we describe in this book assume, to some extent, that the variables being analyzed have normal distributions. The best way of examining the distribution of values of a variable

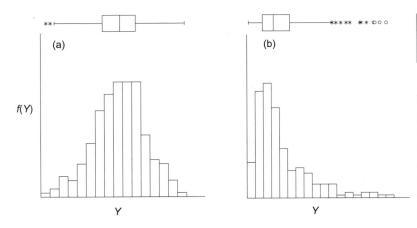

$f(Y)$

(a)

(b)

Y

Y

Figure 4.1 Histograms and boxplots for (a) normal and (b) positively skewed data ($n = 200$).

is with a density plot, where the frequencies ("densities") of different values, or categories, are represented. Many of the graphs described below are density plots and show the shape of a sample distribution.

Histogram

One simple way of examining the distribution of a variable in a sample is to plot a histogram, a graphical representation of a frequency (or density) distribution. A histogram is a type of bar graph (see Chapter 19) grouping the observations into *a priori* defined classes on the horizontal axis and their frequency on the vertical axis (Figure 4.1). If the variable is continuous, the size (width) of the classes will depend on the number of observations: more observations mean that more classes can be used. The values of a discrete variable usually determine the classes. Histograms are very useful for examining the shape of a distribution of observations (Figure 4.1). For example, is the distribution symmetrical or skewed? Is it unimodal or multimodal? The vertical axis of a histogram can also be relative frequency (proportions), cumulative frequency or cumulative relative frequency. Unfortunately, histograms are not always particularly useful in biology, especially experimental work, because we are often dealing with small sample sizes (<20).

A useful addition to a histogram is to superimpose a more formal probability density function. For example, we could include a normal probability distribution function, based on our sample mean and variance. An alternative approach is to not stipulate a specific distribution for the sample

but to use the observed data to generate a probability density curve. This is non-parametric estimation because we are not assuming a specific underlying population distribution for our variable. Our estimation procedure may produce probability density curves that are symmetrical, asymmetrical or multimodal, depending on the density pattern in the observed data. The standard reference to non-parametric density estimation is Silverman (1986) and the most common method is kernel estimation. For each observation, we construct a window of a certain width, like the categories in a histogram. We then fit a symmetric probability density function (called the kernel) to the observations in each window; commonly, the normal distribution is used. The estimated density for any value of our variable is simply the sum of the estimates from the density functions in each window. The calculations are tedious, even when the kernel is a normal distribution, but kernel density estimators are now common options in statistical software.

The window width is sometimes termed the smoothing parameter because it influences the shape of final estimated density function. For standard kernel density estimation, the smoothing parameter is constant for all observations; other approaches allow the smoothing parameter to vary depending on the local density of data (Silverman 1986). If the smoothing parameter is low (narrow windows), then the density function can have numerous modes, many artificial if the sample size is small. If the smoothing parameter is high (wide windows), then the density function will be much smoother but important detail, such as real modes, might be missed. Clearly, kernel estimation requires a large sample size so that there can be enough observations to reliably fit a probability density function (e.g. normal) in each window and also enough windows to represent

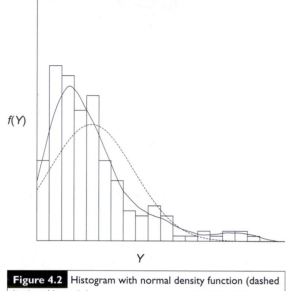

Figure 4.2 Histogram with normal density function (dashed line) and kernel density curve or smooth (solid line) for a positively skewed distribution ($n = 200$). Smoothing parameter for kernel curve equals one.

estimation for bivariate distributions (see Chapter 5) and for determining density functions for use in procedures such as discriminant function analysis (Silverman 1986).

Dotplot

A dotplot is a plot where each observation is represented by a single dot or symbol, with the value of the variable along the horizontal axis (Wilkinson 1999a). Dotplots can be used for univariate and bivariate data (Sasieni & Royston 1996); in the latter case, they are like scatterplots. Univariate dotplots can be very effective ways of representing single samples because skewness and unusually large or small values are easy to detect (Figure 4.3).

Boxplot

A good alternative for displaying the sample observations of a single variable, when we have a sample size of about eight or more, is to use a boxplot (Figure 4.4 and Figure 4.5), also called a box-and-whiskers plot. The boxplot uses the median to identify location and 25% quartiles for the hinges (ends of the box). The difference between the values of the two hinges is called the spread. Unusually large or small values (outliers) are highlighted, although the actual formulae for identifying outliers vary between different textbooks and statistical software (commonly, an outlier is any value greater than 1.5 times the spread outside the closest hinge). The lines (or whiskers) extend to the extreme values within 1.5 times the spread beyond the hinges. Boxplots efficiently indicate several aspects of the sample.

the detail present in the data. The choice of the probability density function fitted in each window is also determined by the user. Symmetrical distributions such as normal are most common, although others are possible (Silverman 1986).

For the positively skewed distribution plotted in Figure 4.2, it is clear that a normal distribution function based on the sample mean and variance is not a good fit to the data. In contrast, the non-parametric kernel smoothing curve is a much more realistic representation of the distribution of the data. The kernel density estimator is particularly useful as an exploratory tool for describing the shape of a distribution if we have a sample of reasonable size and may indicate what more formal parametric distribution should be used in modeling (see Chapter 13). Other uses include density

- The middle of the sample is identified by the median, which is resistant (robust) to unusual values (Chapter 2).

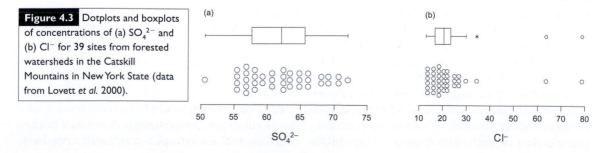

Figure 4.3 Dotplots and boxplots of concentrations of (a) SO_4^{2-} and (b) Cl^- for 39 sites from forested watersheds in the Catskill Mountains in New York State (data from Lovett et al. 2000).

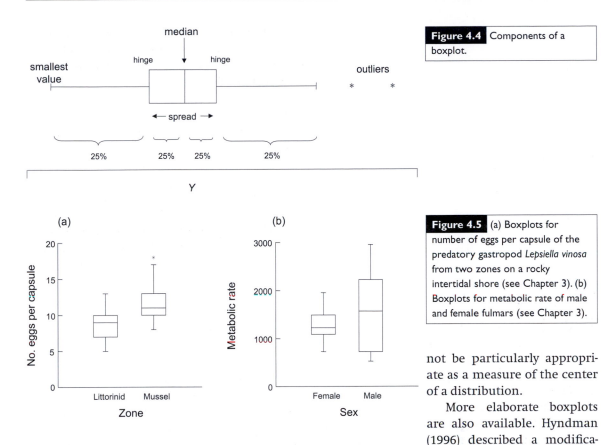

Figure 4.4 Components of a boxplot.

Figure 4.5 (a) Boxplots for number of eggs per capsule of the predatory gastropod *Lepsiella vinosa* from two zones on a rocky intertidal shore (see Chapter 3). (b) Boxplots for metabolic rate of male and female fulmars (see Chapter 3).

- The variability of the sample is indicated by the distance between the whiskers (with or without the outliers).
- The shape of the sample, especially whether it is symmetrical or skewed (Figure 4.1, Figure 4.3).
- The presence of outliers, extreme values very different from the rest of the sample (Figure 4.3).

Because boxplots are based on medians and quartiles, they are very resistant to extreme values, which don't affect the basic shape of the plot very much (Chapter 2). The boxplots and dotplots for the concentrations of SO_4^{2-} and Cl^- from 39 stream sites in the Catskill Mountains are presented in Figure 4.3 (Lovett *et al.* 2000, Chapter 2). The skewness and outliers present in the sample of Cl^- are clear, in contrast to the symmetrically distributed SO_4^{2-}. Boxplots can also be used to graphically represent summaries of data in research publications (Chapter 19) instead of the more traditional means ($\pm$ standard deviations or similar). This is particularly the case when non-parametric analyses are used, as the mean might

not be particularly appropriate as a measure of the center of a distribution.

More elaborate boxplots are also available. Hyndman (1996) described a modification of the boxplot that graphs high-density regions and shows bimodality very well. Rousseeuw *et al.* (1999) described the bagplot, a bivariate version of the boxplot. Both papers provided computer code for these plots.

Scatterplot

When we have two variables, each measured on the same units, we are often interested in the relationship between the variables. A very important graphical technique is the scatterplot, where the vertical axis represents one variable, the horizontal axis represents the other variable and the points on the plot are the individual observations (Chapter 5). Scatterplots are very informative, especially when bordered by boxplots for each variable (Figure 5.3). Nonlinearity and outliers can be identified, as well as departures from fitted linear models.

Scatterplot matrix (SPLOM)

An extension of the scatterplot to three or more variables is the scatterplot matrix (SPLOM). Each

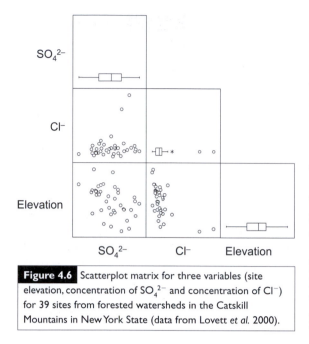

Figure 4.6 Scatterplot matrix for three variables (site elevation, concentration of SO_4^{2-} and concentration of Cl^-) for 39 sites from forested watersheds in the Catskill Mountains in New York State (data from Lovett *et al.* 2000).

context of exploratory data analysis. Sometimes, these assumptions are not critical because the result of your analysis (estimation or hypothesis tests) will be the same even if the assumptions are violated. Such tests are termed robust. Other assumptions are critical because the statistical test may give unreliable results when assumptions are violated.

4.2.1 Assumptions of parametric linear models

The assumptions of linear models apply to the response (or dependent) variable and also to the error terms from the fitted model.

Normality

Linear models are based on OLS estimation and the reliability of interval estimates and tests of parameters depends on the response variable being sampled from a population (or populations) with a normal (Gaussian) distribution. Most analyses are robust to this assumption, particularly if sample sizes are equal. Despite this robustness, the symmetry (roughly equal spreads on each side of the mean or median) of each sample should be checked with a graphical procedure like boxplots. Another way of assessing normality is to use probability plots (pplots). These plots examine a cumulative frequency distribution of your data, and compare the shape of that distribution to that expected of a normal distribution having the same mean and variance. If your data are normal, the pplot will be a straight line; various kinds of skewness, multimodality, etc., will show as a kinked line. A pplot is shown in Figure 4.7 for a normal and a lognormal distribution. We don't suggest that you do any formal analyses of these plots, but just look for major kinks. The method is really only useful for large sample sizes, say 25 or more; with fewer data points, you'll always get a fairly irregular line.

The most common asymmetry in biological data is positive skewness, i.e. populations with a long right tail (Figure 4.1). Positive skewness in biological data is often because the variables have a lognormal (measurement variables) or a Poisson (count) distribution. In our experience, skewed distributions are more common than symmetrical distributions. This makes sense when you

panel in the matrix represents a scatterplot between two of the variables and the panels along the diagonal can indicate which variable forms the horizontal and vertical axes or show other univariate displays such as boxplots or frequency distributions (Figure 4.6). Recently, Murdoch & Chow (1996) illustrated a method for displaying large correlation matrices (Chapter 15), where different shaped and angled ellipses represent the magnitude of the correlation.

Multivariate plots

There are other, more complex, methods for graphing multivariate data, including icon plots, such as Chernoff's faces and the like (see Chapter 15; also Cleveland 1994, Tufte 1983).

4.2 | Analysis with graphs

Most of the analyses that we describe in this book are based on linear models (regression and analysis of variance models). These analyses have important assumptions, besides that of random sampling, that must be assessed before linear models (or even *t* tests) can be applied. We discuss these assumptions in detail in the relevant chapters, but briefly introduce them here in the

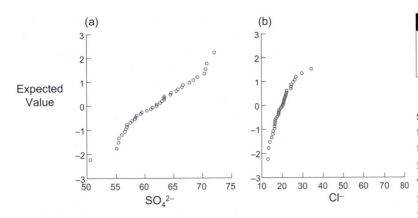

realize that most variables cannot have values less than zero (lengths, weights, counts, etc.) but have no mathematical upper limit (although there may be a biological limit). Their distributions are usually truncated at zero, resulting in skewness in the other direction. Transformations of skewed variables to a different scale (e.g. log or power transformations) will often improve their normality (Section 4.3).

The other distribution that will cause major problems is multimodal, where there are two or more distinct peaks. There is not much that you can do about this distribution; both parametric and non-parametric tests become unreliable. The best option is to treat each peak of the distribution as representing a different "population", and to split your analyses into separate populations. In ecological studies, you might get such a problem with different cohorts in a population of plants or animals, and be forced to ask questions about the mean size of the first, second, etc., cohorts. In physiological or genetic studies, you might get such a result from using animals or plants of different genotypes. For example, allozymes with "fast" and "slow" alleles might produce two different classes of physiological response, and you could analyze the response of fast and slow tissues as an additional factor in your experiment.

One final distribution that often causes problems in biological data is when we have many zeroes, and a few non-zero points. In his case, the distribution is so skewed that no transformation will normalize the distribution; whatever we do to these zeros, they will remain a peak in our distribution. Non-parametric approaches will fare little better, as these values will all be assigned the same (tied) rank. In this situation, our only suggestion is that your data reflect two different processes, such as whether or not a particular replicate has a response or not, and the level of response when it occurs. We could make two different comparisons – does the likelihood of a response differ between groups (Chapters 13 and 14), regarding each replicate as zero or not-zero, and a comparison of the response between groups, using only those replicates in which a response occurred.

Homogeneity of variances

Tests of hypotheses in linear models assume that the variance in the response variable is the same at each level, or combination of levels, of the predictor variables. This is a more important assumption than normality although the analyses are more robust if sample sizes are equal. If the response variable has a normal distribution, then unequal variances will probably be due to a few unusual values, especially if sample sizes are small. If the response variable has a lognormal or Poisson distribution, then we would expect a relationship between the mean (expected or predicted values from the linear model) and unequal variances are related to the underlying distribution. Transformations that improve normality will also usually improve homogeneity of variances.

There are formal tests for variance homogeneity, such as an F-ratio test before a t test. Our reluctance to recommend such tests has already been discussed in Chapter 3 and also applies to the use of Cochran's, Bartlett's or Levene's tests before an ANOVA model (Chapter 8). Less formal, but more useful, checks include side-by-side boxplots for multiple groups, which allow a check of homogeneity of spread of samples (Figure 4.3, Figure 4.5). Note that plots of residuals from the model against predicted values are also valuable exploratory checks (see Chapters 5 and 8).

Linearity

Parametric correlation and linear regression analyses are based on straight-line relationships between variables. The simplest way of checking whether your data are likely to meet this assumption is to examine a scatterplot of the two variables, or a SPLOM for more than two variables. Figure 5.17(a) illustrates how a scatterplot was able to show a nonlinear relationship between number of species of invertebrates and area of mussel clumps on a rocky shore. Smoothing functions through the data can also reveal nonlinear relationships. We will discuss diagnostics for detecting nonlinearity further in Chapter 5.

Independence

This assumption basically implies that all the observations should be independent of each other, both within and between groups. The most common situation where this assumption is not met is when data are recorded in a time sequence. For experimental designs, there are modifications of standard analyses of variance when the same experimental unit is observed under different treatments or times (Chapters 10 and 11). We will discuss independence in more detail for each type of analysis in later chapters.

4.3 | Transforming data

We indicated in the previous section that transformation of data to a different scale of measurement can be a solution to distributional assumptions, as well as related problems with variance homogeneity and linearity. In this section, we will elaborate on the nature and application of data transformations.

The justification for transforming data to different scales before data analysis is based, at least in part, on the appreciation that the scales of measurement we use are often arbitrary. For example, many measurements we take are based on a decimal system. This is probably related to the number of digits we have on our hands; characters from the Simpsons would probably measure everything in units of base eight! Sokal & Rohlf (1995) point out that linear (arithmetic) scale of measurement we commonly use can be viewed in the same way. For example, we might measure the length of an object in centimeters but we could just as easily measure the length in log units, such as log centimeters. In fact, we could do so directly just by altering the scale on our measuring device, like using a slide ruler instead of a normal linear ruler.

Surprisingly, transformations are quite common for measurements we encounter in everyday life. Sometimes, these transformations simply change the zero value, i.e. adding a constant. Slightly more complex transformations may change the zero value but also rescale the measurements by a constant value, e.g. the change in temperature units from Fahrenheit to Celsius. Such transformations are linear, in that the relationship between the original variable and the transformed variable is a perfect straight line. Statistical tests of null hypotheses will be identical, in most cases, for the untransformed and the transformed data.

More commonly in data analysis, particularly in biology, are transformations that change the data in a nonlinear fashion. The most common transformation is the log transformation, where the transformed data are simply the logs (to any base) of the original data. The log transformation, while nonlinear, is monotonic, i.e. the order of data values after transformation is the same as before. A log-transformed scale is often the default scale for commonly used measurements. For example, pH is simply the log of the concentration of H^+ ions, and most cameras measure aperture as f-stops, with each increase in f representing a halving of the amount of light reaching the film, i.e. a $\log_2$ scale.

There are at least five aims of data transformations for statistical analyses, especially for linear models:

- to make the data and the model error terms closer to a normal distribution (i.e. to make the distribution of the data symmetrical),
- to reduce any relationship between the mean and the variance (i.e. to improve homogeneity of variances), often as a result of improving normality,

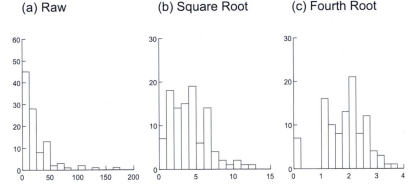

(a) Raw   **(b) Square Root**   **(c) Fourth Root**

Figure 4.8 Distribution of counts of limpets in quadrats at Point Nepean: (a) untransformed (raw), (b) square root transformed, and (c) fourth root transformed. (M Keough & G. Quinn, unpublished data.)

your data, the null hypothesis becomes "mean log-growth does not vary with density", or you might say that in the first case, growth is defined as mg of weight gained, whereas after log-transforming, growth is the log-mg weight gained.

- to reduce the influence of outliers, especially when they are at one end of a distribution,
- to improve linearity in regression analyses, and
- to make effects that are multiplicative on the raw scale additive on a transformed scale, i.e. to reduce the size of interaction effects (Chapters 6 and 9).

The most common use of transformations in biology is to help the data meet the distributional and variance assumptions required for linear models. Emerson (1991), Sokal & Rohlf (1995) and Tabachnick & Fidell (1996) provide excellent descriptions and justification of transformations. These authors are reassuring to those who are uncomfortable about the idea of transforming their data, feeling that they are "fiddling" the data to increase the chance of getting a significant result. A decision to transform, however, is always made before the analysis is done.

Remember that after any transformation, you must re-check your data to ensure the transformation improved the distribution of the data (or at least didn't make it any worse!). Sometimes, log or square root transformations can skew data just as severely in the opposite direction and produce new outliers!

A transformation is really changing your response variable and therefore your formal null hypothesis. You might hypothesize that growth of plants varies with density, and formalize that as the H_0 that the mean growth of plants at high density equals the mean growth at low density. If you are forced to log-transform

4.3.1 Transformations and distributional assumptions

The most common type of transformation useful for biological data (especially counts or measurements) is the power transformation (Emerson 1991, Neter *et al.* 1996), which transforms Y to Y^p, where p is greater than zero. For data with right skew, the square root ($\sqrt{}$) transformation, where $p = 0.5$, is applicable, particularly for data that are counts (Poisson distributed) and the variance is related to the mean. Cube roots ($p = 0.33$), fourth roots ($p = 0.25$), etc., will be increasingly effective for data that are increasingly skewed; fourth root transformations are commonly used for abundance data in ecology when there are lots of zeros and a few large values (Figure 4.8). For very skewed data, a reciprocal transformation can help, although interpretation is a little difficult because then order of values is reversed.

Transforming data to logarithms (the base is irrelevant although base 10 logs are more familiar to readers) will also make positively skewed distributions more symmetrical (Keene 1995; Figure 4.9), especially when the mean is related to the standard deviation. Such a distribution is termed lognormal because it can be made normal by log transforming the values. Use $\log (Y + c)$ where c is an appropriate constant if there are zeros in the data set because you can't take the log of zero. Some people use the smallest possible value for their variable as a constant, others use an arbitrarily small number, such as 0.001 or, most

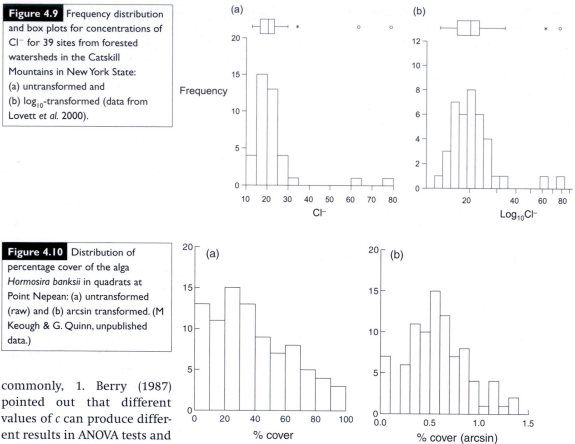

Figure 4.9 Frequency distribution and box plots for concentrations of Cl⁻ for 39 sites from forested watersheds in the Catskill Mountains in New York State: (a) untransformed and (b) $\log_{10}$-transformed (data from Lovett et al. 2000).

Figure 4.10 Distribution of percentage cover of the alga *Hormosira banksii* in quadrats at Point Nepean: (a) untransformed (raw) and (b) arcsin transformed. (M Keough & G. Quinn, unpublished data.)

commonly, 1. Berry (1987) pointed out that different values of c can produce different results in ANOVA tests and recommended using a value of c that makes the distribution of the residuals as symmetrical as possible (based on skewness and kurtosis of the residuals).

If skewness is actually negative, i.e. the distribution has a long left tail, Tabachnick & Fidell (1996) suggested reflecting the variable before transforming. Reflection simply involves creating a constant by adding one to the largest value in the sample and then subtracting each observation from this constant.

These transformations can be considered part of the Box–Cox family of transformations:

$$\frac{Y^\lambda - 1}{\lambda} \text{ when } \lambda \neq 0 \tag{4.1}$$

$$\log(Y) \text{ when } \lambda = 0 \tag{4.2}$$

When $\lambda = 1$, we have no change to the distribution, when $\lambda = 0.5$ we have the square root transformation, and when $\lambda = -1$ we have the reciprocal transformation, etc. (Keene 1995, Sokal & Rohlf 1995). The Box–Cox family of transformations can also be used to find the best transformation, in terms of normality and homogeneity of variance, by an iterative process that selects a value of λ that maximizes a log-likelihood function (Sokal & Rohlf 1995).

When data are percentages or proportions, they are bounded at 0% and 100%. Power transformations don't work very well for these data because they change each end of the distribution differently (Emerson 1991). One common approach is to use the angular transformation, specifically the arcsin transformation. With the data expressed as proportions, then transform Y to $\sin^{-1}(\sqrt{Y})$, and the result is shown in Figure 4.10. It is most effective if Y is close to zero or one, and has little effect on mid-range proportions.

Finally, we should mention the rank transformation, which converts the observations to ranks, as described in Chapter 3 for non-parametric tests. The rank transformation is different from the other transformations discussed here because it is bounded by one and n, where n is the sample size. This is an extreme transformation, as it results in equal differences (one unit, except for ties) between every pair of observations in this ranked set, regardless of their absolute difference. It therefore results in the greatest loss of information of all the monotonic transformations.

For common linear models (regressions and ANOVAs), transformations will often improve normality and homogeneity of variances and reduce the influence of outliers. If unequal variances and outliers are a result of non-normality (e.g. skewed distributions), as is often the case with biological data, then transformation (to log or square root for skewed data) will improve all three at once.

4.3.2 Transformations and linearity

Transformations can also be used to improve linearity of relationships between two variables and thus make linear regression models more appropriate. For example, allometric relationships with body size have a better linear fit after one or both variables are log-transformed. Note that nonlinear relationships might be better investigated with a nonlinear model, especially one that has a strong theoretical justification.

4.3.3 Transformations and additivity

Transformations also affect the way we measure effects in linear models. For example, let's say we were measuring the effect of an experimental treatment compared to a control at two different times. If the means of our control groups are different at each time, how we measure the effect of the treatment is important. Some very artificial data are provided in Table 4.1 to illustrate the point. At Time 1, the treatment changes the mean value of our response variable from 10 to 5 units, a decrease of 5 units. At Time 2 the change is from 50 to 25 units, a change of 25 units. On the raw scale of measurement, the effects of the treatments are very different, but in percentage terms, the effects are actually identical with both showing a 50% reduction. Biologically, which is the most meaningful measure of effect, a change in raw scale or a change in percentage scale? In many cases, the percentage change might be more biologically relevant and we would want our analysis to conclude

Table 4.1 Means for treatment and control groups for an experiment conducted at two times. Artificial data and arbitrary units used.

	Untransformed		Log-transformed	
	Time 1	Time 2	Time 1	Time 2
Control	10	50	1.000	1.699
Treatment	5	25	0.699	1.398

that the treatment effects are the same at the two times. Transforming the data to a log scale achieves this (Table 4.1).

Interpretation of interaction terms in more complex linear models (Chapter 9) can also be affected by the scale on which data are measured. Transforming data to reduce interactions may be useful if you are only interested in main effects or you are using a model that assumes no interaction (e.g. some randomized blocks models; Chapter 10). Log-transformed data may better reflect the underlying nature and interpretation of an interaction term.

4.4 | Standardizations

Another change we can make to the values of our variable is to standardize them in relation to each other. If we are including two or more variables in an analysis, such as a regression analysis or a more complex multivariate analysis, then converting all the variables to a similar scale is often important before they are included in the analysis. A number of different standardizations are possible. Centering a variable simply changes the variable so it has a mean of zero:

$$y_i = y_i - \bar{y} \qquad (4.3)$$

This is sometimes called translation (Legendre & Legendre 1998).

Variables can also be altered so they range from zero (minimum) to one (maximum). Legendre & Legendre (1998) describe two ways of achieving this:

$$y_i = \frac{y_i}{y_{max}} \text{ and } y_i = \frac{y_i - y_{min}}{y_{max} - y_{min}} \qquad (4.4)$$

The latter is called ranging and both methods are particularly useful as standardizations of abundance data before multivariate analyses that examine dissimilarities between sampling units in terms of species composition (Chapter 15).

Changing a variable so it has a mean of zero and a standard deviation (and variance) of one is often termed standardization:

$$y_i = \frac{y_i - \bar{y}}{s} \tag{4.5}$$

The standardized values are also called z scores and represent the values of the variable from a normal distribution with a mean of zero and a standard deviation of one (Chapter 2).

4.5 | Outliers

Outliers (or unusual values) are values of a variable that lie outside the usual range of that variable. They can seriously affect the results of analyses. There are two aspects in dealing with outliers (i) identifying them, and (ii) dealing with them. There are formal tests for detecting outliers, which assume that the observations are normally distributed. Dixon's Q test examines the difference between the outlier and the next closest observation relative to the overall range of the data (Miller 1993, Sokal & Rohlf 1995), although such tests have difficulties when there are multiple outliers. For some linear models (e.g. linear regression), Cook's D statistic indicates the influence of each observation on the result of the analysis (Chapter 5). Outliers are often easier to detect with EDA methods. For example, boxplots will highlight unusually large or small values, plots of residuals from linear models reveal observations a long way from the fitted model, as will scatterplots with an appropriate smoothing function.

Once you identify outliers, you should first check to make sure they are not a mistake, such as an error typing in your data or in writing values down. They often show up as impossible values, e.g. a 3 m ant, a blood pressure that would result in an animal exploding, etc. If you can classify an outlier as a mistake, it should be deleted.

The second kind of outlier can occur if something unusual happened to that particular observation. Perhaps the tissue preparation took longer than usual or an experimental enclosure was placed in an unusual physical location. In this case, you may have had *a priori* cause to be suspicious of that value. It is important to keep detailed notes of your experiments, to identify potential outliers. If you were suspicious of this observation *a priori*, you may be able to delete such an outlier.

In other cases, you may simply have an anomalous value. Although evolutionary biologists might make their reputations from rare variants, they are an unfortunate fact of life for the rest of us. If you have no reason to suspect an outlier as being a mistake, there are two options. First, you can re-run the analysis without the outlier(s) to see how much they influence the outcome of the analysis. If the conclusions are altered, then you are in trouble and should try and determine why those values are so different. Perhaps you are unwittingly counting two very similar species, or have a batch of laboratory animals that came from very different sources. Sometimes thinking about why particular observations are outliers can stimulate new research questions. Second, use statistical techniques that are robust to outliers, e.g. for simple analyses, rank-based tests can provide some protection (Chapter 3). Don't forget that outliers may be a result of a very skewed underlying distribution and transformations will often make the distribution more symmetrical and bring outliers more in line with the rest of the sample.

It is crucial that outliers only be deleted when you have *a priori* reasons to do so – dropping observations just because they are messy or reduce the chance of getting a significant result is unethical, to say the least. The other unacceptable behaviour is to run the analysis and then go back and look for outliers to remove if the analysis is not significant.

4.6 | Censored and missing data

4.6.1 Missing data

A common occurrence in biology is that, despite careful field or laboratory work, we might end up with samples that are missing observations that were originally planned to be collected. It is very important to distinguish between missing values and zero values. The former are observations where we did not record a value for a variable (e.g. there was no response from an experimental unit) or where we did record a value that went subsequently missing (e.g. the observation was lost). The latter are recorded observations where the value of the variable was zero, such as the absence of an organism when we are recording counts. Zero values are real data and do not represent a problem in data analysis except that distributional assumptions might be harder to meet and some transformations do not deal with zeros (e.g. logs). Missing observations can cause great difficulties although these problems are much more severe for multivariate data sets and we will describe methods for handling missing observations in those circumstances in Chapter 15. Note that these methods will be relevant for linear models with multiple continuous predictor variables (multiple regression models; Chapter 6).

For univariate analyses described in Chapter 3 and in subsequent chapters on linear models with categorical predictor variables (ANOVA models), the main difficulty with missing observations is that they might result in unequal sample sizes between the two or more groups that we wish to compare. These are termed unbalanced data. We emphasized in Chapter 3 that the results of t tests comparing two population means are much more sensitive to assumptions about normality and variance homogeneity when sample sizes are unequal. There are three general approaches to handling such missing values. First is to do nothing because linear model analyses can easily handle unequal sample sizes. You need to choose which sum-of-squares to use in factorial models (Chapter 9) and also to check the assumptions of the analyses carefully (Sections 4.2.1, Chapters 5, 8, etc.). There are also difficulties with estimation of variance components (Chapter 8). Second is to delete observations from all samples so that the sample size is equal across groups. It is difficult to recommend this conservative approach; it wastes data and sample sizes in biology are often small, so that power is a real consideration. Third, we can substitute (impute) replacement values for the missing observations. These replacement values might be simply the mean of the remaining values, although these methods result in underestimation

of the variances and standard errors of the estimates of parameters based on these imputed values, i.e. our estimates will be artificially more precise. More complex imputation methods are available for multivariate data sets (Chapter 15).

Our preferred option is to do nothing and analyze the data with unequal sample sizes. However, equal sample sizes make data analysis and interpretation much easier, so every effort must be made during the design and execution stages to achieve this balance.

4.6.2 Censored (truncated) data

A problem related to missing data is that of censored or truncated data, where some of the observations in our data set have values but others are simply recorded as less than or greater than a particular value, or between two values. Clearly we have some information about a censored value independently of the other values whereas we have no information about a missing value. Censored data in biology occur most often in two types of situation.

When we are measuring the concentration of some substance in the environment (e.g. air or water quality monitoring), our field and laboratory analytical equipment will have limits to its sensitivity. Sometimes we might only be able to record the level of a substance as being below a detection limit (BDL), the smallest concentration we are able to record. For example, in their study of chemical characteristics of 39 streams in the Catskill Mountains in New York State (see worked example in Chapter 2, Section 4.1.1), Lovett *et al.* (2000) recorded the concentration of ammonium (NH_4^+). Over the course of the three years, 38% of the values of ammonium concentration were below their detection limit of 1.1 μmol l^{-1}. Data that are below some detection limit are termed left censored. Right censoring is also possible, e.g. counts of organisms in a sampling unit might be integers up to 100 but larger numbers are simply recorded as >100. Left censoring of air and water quality data has been the focus in the literature (Akritas *et al.* 1994). When the detection limit is fixed in advance, such as when we know the limits of our equipment, and the number of observations occurring below this limit is random, then we have Type I censoring.

The second situation in which censored data are common is time-to-event, survival or failure-time analysis (Fox 1993, Lindsey & Ryan 1998). In these studies, sampling or experimental units are observed at regular intervals and we usually only know that an event occurred (e.g. response of patients in a clinical trial, flowering of plants or germination of seeds, etc.) after the last recording. These data are nearly always right censored but since the observation is actually somewhere in a time interval, the phrase interval-censored is often used. Sometimes our variable of interest might be the time between two events occurring, e.g. the first introduction of an exotic species to a system and the first loss of a native species. Both events will often be interval-censored, i.e. we only know when each occurred within an interval, and such data are termed doubly censored. Doubly censored data are more common in medicine and clinical trials than in general biological research. Unfortunately, the area of survival analysis is beyond the scope of this book (but see Andersen & Keiding 1996, Fox 1993).

The methods for dealing with censored data are related to those for dealing with missing data. We will only provide a brief mention here and recommend Akritas et al. (1994) for a good introduction to the literature for left-censored environmental data.

Estimation of mean and variance

Three methods have been proposed for dealing with censored, especially left-censored, data when the aim is to estimate parameters of a single population.

The first is simple substitution, where the detection limit, half the detection limit (as used by Lovett et al. 2000 for their ammonium data) or zero are substituted for the censored data. A less common alternative is to assume a distribution (e.g. normal or uniform) for the values below the detection limit and substitute random data from the distribution. Parameters are estimated from the complete data set, although these estimates will be biased and the extent of the bias depends on the actual values of the censored observations, which, of course, we do not know. As with missing data, simple substitution is not recommended.

Parametric methods assume a normal distribution and use maximum likelihood methods to estimate parameters, based primarily on the non-censored data but incorporating the size of the censored and non-censored components of the sample (Newman et al. 1989). The ML estimates can also be used to infill the censored data (Akritas et al. 1994). These ML estimates are biased but usually more precise than other methods; restricted ML (REML; see Chapter 8) methods are also available that reduce the bias. There are more robust parametric methods, often based on order statistics (Chapter 2) where the censored values are infilled from predicted values from a regression through a normal or lognormal probability plot fitted to the ordered data. These methods are termed normal or lognormal probability regressions (Akritas et al. 1994) or regressions on expected order statistics (Newman et al. 1989). We have to assume that the censored values are extensions of the same distribution as the uncensored values. The simulations of Newman et al. (1989) indicated that ML estimates are best when distributional assumptions are met, otherwise the probability regression method should be used.

Comparing two or more populations

There is some consensus in the literature that non-parametric, rank-based, tests are most appropriate for hypothesis testing with censored data. Millard & Deveral (1988) compared twelve rank tests for comparing two populations based on sample data with single censoring and multiple censoring (the detection limit varies between groups). For tests like the Mann–Whitney–Wilcoxon (Chapter 3), values below the detection limit are given the same tied rank. Millard & Deverel (1988) recommended score tests (linear rank tests) for comparing two populations, whereas Akritas et al. (1994) preferred a form of the robust Theil–Sen regression (Sprent 1993; see also Chapter 5) in which the predictor variable defines the two groups. For more than two groups, multiple pairwise tests, with a suitable correction for multiple testing (Chapter 3), are probably the simplest approach.

Akritas et al. (1994) also describe regression methods for censored data. For survival data, proportional hazards models can be used. For left-censored data, various non-parametric regression analyses (Chapter 5) are possible, with a form of the Theil–Sen method being the simplest.

4.7 | General issues and hints for analysis

4.7.1 General issues

- Graphical analysis of the data should be the first step in every analysis. Besides allowing you to assess the assumptions of your planned analysis, it allows you to get familiar with your data.

- Many current statistical packages emphasize exploratory data analysis, and make it easy to produce boxplots, residual plots, etc.
- Initial graphical analysis is also very valuable for identifying outliers, which can have a great influence on your analyses.
- Transformations are routinely used to improve the fit of biological data to the assumptions of the planned statistical analyses, especially linear models.
- Data transformations should be monotonic, so that the order of the observations for a variable does not change.

Chapter 5

Correlation and regression

Biologists commonly record more than one variable from each sampling or experimental unit. For example, a physiologist may record blood pressure and body weight from experimental animals, or an ecologist may record the abundance of a particular species of shrub and soil pH from a series of plots during vegetation sampling. Such data are termed bivariate when we have two random variables recorded from each unit or multivariate when we have more than two random variables recorded from each unit. There are a number of relevant questions that might prompt us to collect such data, based on the nature of the biological and statistical relationship between the variables. The next two chapters consider statistical procedures for describing the relationship(s) between two or more continuous variables, and using that relationship for prediction. Techniques for detecting patterns and structure in complex multivariate data sets, and simplifying such data sets for further analyses, will be covered in Chapters 15–18.

5.1 | Correlation analysis

Consider a situation where we are interested in the statistical relationship between two random variables, designated Y_1 and Y_2, in a population. Both variables are continuous and each sampling or experimental unit (i) in the population has a value for each variable, designated y_{i1} and y_{i2}.

Land crabs on Christmas Island
Christmas Island in the northeast Indian Ocean is famous for its endemic red land crabs, *Gecarcoidea natalis*, which undergo a spectacular mass migra-

tion back to the ocean each year to release their eggs. The crabs inhabit the rain forest on the island where they consume tree seedlings. In a study on the ecology of the crabs, Green (1997) tested whether there was a relationship between the total biomass of red land crabs and the density of their burrows within 25 m^2 quadrats (sampling units) at five forested sites on the island. The full analyses of these data are provided in Box 5.1.

5.1.1 Parametric correlation model
The most common statistical procedure for measuring the 'strength' of the relationship between two continuous variables is based on distributional assumptions, i.e. it is a parametric procedure. Rather than assuming specific distributions for the individual variables, however, we need to think of our data as a population of y_{i1} and y_{i2} pairs. We now have a joint distribution of two variables (a bivariate distribution) and, analogous to the parametric tests we described in Chapter 3, the bivariate normal distribution (Figure 5.1) underlies the most commonly used measure of the strength of a bivariate relationship. The bivariate normal distribution is defined by the mean and standard deviation of each variable and a parameter called the correlation coefficient, which measures the strength of the relationship between the two variables. A bivariate normal distribution implies that the individual variables are also normally distributed and also implies that any relationship between the two variables, i.e. any lack of independence between the variables, is a linear one (straight-line; see Box 5.2; Hays 1994). Nonlinear relationships between two variables indicate that the bivariate normal distribution does not apply and we must use other

Box 5.1 | Worked example: crab and burrow density on Christmas Island

Green (1997) studied the ecology of red land crabs on Christmas Island and examined the relationship between the total biomass of red land crabs and the density of their burrows within 25 m² quadrats (sampling units) at five forested sites on the island. We will look at two of these sites: there were ten quadrats at Lower Site (LS) and eight quadrats at Drumsite (DS). Scatterplots and boxplots are presented in Figure 5.3. There was slight negative skewness for biomass and burrow density for LS, and an outlier for burrow density for DS, but no evidence of nonlinearity. Pearson's correlation coefficient was considered appropriate for these data although more robust correlations were calculated for comparison.

Site	Correlation type	Statistic	P value
DS ($n = 8$)	Pearson	0.392	0.337
	Spearman	0.168	0.691
	Kendall	0.036	0.901
LS ($n = 10$)	Pearson	0.882	0.001
	Spearman	0.851	0.002
	Kendall	0.719	0.004

The H_0 of no linear relationship between total crab biomass and number of burrows at DS could not be rejected. The same conclusion applies for monotonic relationships measured by Spearman and Kendall's coefficients. So there was no evidence for any linear or more general monotonic relationship between burrow density and total crab biomass at site DS.

The H_0 of no linear relationship between total crab biomass and number of burrows at LS was rejected. The same conclusion applies for monotonic relationships measured by Spearman and Kendall's coefficients. There was strong evidence of a linear and more general monotonic relationship between burrow density and total crab biomass at site LS.

procedures that do not assume this distribution for quantifying the strength of such relationships (Section 5.1.2).

Covariance and correlation

One measure of the strength of a linear relationship between two continuous random variables is to determine how much the two variables covary, i.e. vary together. If one variable increases (or decreases) as the other increases (or decreases), then the two variables covary; if one variable does not change as the other variable increases (or decreases), then the variables do not covary. We can measure how much two variables covary in a

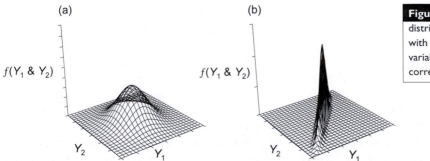

(a)   (b)

$f(Y_1 \& Y_2)$ $f(Y_1 \& Y_2)$

Y_2 Y_1 Y_2 Y_1

Figure 5.1 Bivariate normal distribution for (a) two variables with little correlation and (b) two variables with strong positive correlation.

Table 5.1 Parameters used for parametric correlation analysis and their estimates, with standard error for correlation coefficient. Note that y_{i1} and y_{i2} are the values of the two variables for observation i, $\bar{y}_1$ and $\bar{y}_2$ are the sample means for the two variables and n is the number of observations

Parameter	Estimate	Standard error
Covariance: $\sigma_{Y_1 Y_2}$	$s_{Y_1 Y_2} = \dfrac{\sum\limits_{i=1}^{n}(y_{i1} - \bar{y}_1)(y_{i2} - \bar{y}_2)}{n - 1}$	n/a
Correlation: $\rho_{Y_1 Y_2}$	$r_{Y_1 Y_2} = \dfrac{\sum\limits_{i=1}^{n}[(y_{i1} - \bar{y}_1)(y_{i2} - \bar{y}_2)]}{\sqrt{\sum\limits_{i=1}^{n}(y_{i1} - \bar{y}_1)^2 \sum\limits_{i=1}^{n}(y_{i2} - \bar{y}_2)^2}}$	$s_r = \sqrt{\dfrac{(1 - r^2)}{(n - 2)}}$

Figure 5.2 Scatterplots illustrating (a) a positive linear relationship ($r = 0.72$), (b) a negative linear relationship ($r = -0.72$), (c) and (d) no relationship ($r = 0.10$ and -0.17, respectively), and (e) a nonlinear relationship ($r = 0.08$).

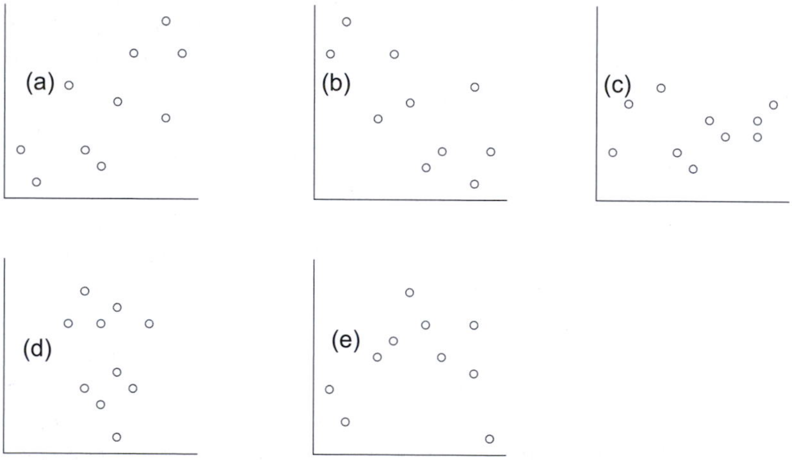

sample of observations by the covariance (Table 5.1). The numerator is the sum of cross-products (SSCP), the bivariate analogue of the sum of squares (SS). The covariance ranges from $-\infty$ to $+\infty$. Note that a special case of the covariance is the sample variance (see Chapter 2), the covariance of a variable with itself.

One limitation of the covariance as a measure of the strength of a linear relationship is that its absolute magnitude depends on the units of the two variables. For example, the covariance between crab biomass and number of burrows in the study of Green (1996) would be larger by a factor of 10^3 if we measured biomass in grams rather than kilograms. We can standardize the covariance by dividing by the standard deviations of the two variables so that our measure of the strength of the linear relationship lies between -1 and $+1$. This is called the Pearson (product–moment) correlation (Table 5.1) and it measures the "strength" of the linear (straight-line) relationship between Y_1 and Y_2. If our sample data comprise a random sample from a population of (y_{i1}, y_{i2}) pairs then the sample correlation coefficient r is the maximum likelihood (ML) estimator of the population correlation coefficient ρ; r actually slightly under-estimates ρ, although the bias is small (Sokal & Rohlf 1995). Along with the means and standard deviations of the two variables, the population correlation coefficient (ρ) is the parameter that defines a bivariate normal distribution. The sample correlation coefficient is also the sample covariance of two variables that are both standardized to zero mean and unit variance (Rodgers & Nicewander 1988; see Chapter 4 for details on standardized variables). Note that r can be positive or negative (Figure 5.2) with $+1$ or -1 indicating that the observations fall along a straight line and zero indicating no correlation. The correlation coefficient measures linear

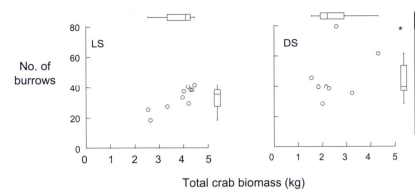

No. of burrows

Total crab biomass (kg)

Figure 5.3 Scatterplots showing the relationship between number of burrows of red land crabs and total crab biomass in 25 m² quadrats at two sites (LS, DS) on Christmas Island (Green 1997). Each plot includes bordered boxplots for each variable separately.

relationships; two variables may have a strong nonlinear relationship but not have a large correlation coefficient (Figure 5.2(e)).

Since the sample correlation coefficient is a statistic, it has a sampling distribution (probability distribution of the sample correlation coefficient based on repeated samples of size n from a population). When ρ equals zero, the distribution of r is close to normal and the sample standard error of r can be calculated (Table 5.1). When ρ does not equal zero, the distribution of r is skewed and complex (Neter et $al.$ 1996) and, therefore, the standard error cannot be easily determined (although resampling methods such as the bootstrap could be used; see Chapter 2). Approximate confidence intervals for ρ can be calculated using one of the versions of Fisher's z transformation (see Sokal & Rohlf 1995) that convert the distribution of r to an approximately normal distribution.

Hypothesis tests for ρ

The null hypothesis most commonly tested with Pearson's correlation coefficient is that ρ equals zero, i.e. the population correlation coefficient equals zero and there is no linear relationship between the two variables in the population. Because the sampling distribution of r is normal when ρ equals zero, we can easily test this H_0 with a t statistic:

$$t = \frac{r}{s_r} \tag{5.1}$$

We compare t with the sampling distribution of t (the probability distribution of t when H_0 is true) with $n - 2$ df. This is simply a t test that a single population parameter equals zero (where t equals the sample statistic divided by the standard error

of the statistic) as described for the population mean in Chapter 3. The value of r can also be compared to the sampling distribution for r under the H_0 (see tables in Rohlf & Sokal 1969, Zar 1996). The results of testing the H_0 using the sampling distribution of t or r will be the same; statistical software usually does not provide a t statistic for testing correlation coefficients.

Tests of null hypotheses that ρ equals some value other than zero or that two population correlation coefficients are equal cannot use the above approach because of the complex sampling distribution of r when ρ does not equal zero. Tests based on Fisher's z transformation are available (Sokal & Rohlf 1995).

Assumptions

Besides the usual assumptions of random sampling and independence of observations, the Pearson correlation coefficient assumes that the joint probability distribution of Y_1 and Y_2 is bivariate normal. If either or both variables have non-normal distributions, then their joint distribution cannot be bivariate normal and any relationship between the two variables might not be linear. Nonlinear relationships can even arise if both variables have normal distributions. Remembering that the Pearson correlation coefficient measures the strength of the linear relationship between two variables, checking for a nonlinear relationship with a simple scatterplot and for asymmetrical distributions of the variables with boxplots is important. Modern statistical software produces these plots very easily (see Figure 5.3).

If the assumption of bivariate normality is suspect, based on either of the two variables having non-normal distributions and/or apparent nonlinearity in the relationship between the two

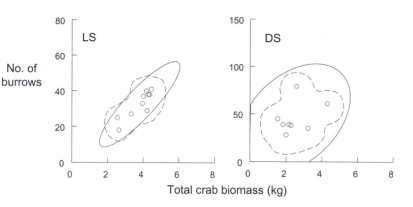

Figure 5.4 Comparison of 95% confidence ellipses (——) and kernel density estimators (------) for the relationship between total crab biomass and number of burrows at sites LS and DS on Christmas Island (Green 1997).

variables, we have two options. First, we can transform one or both variables if they are skewed and their nature suggests an alternative scale of measurement might linearize their relationship (see Chapter 4 and Section 5.3.11). Second, we can use more robust measures of correlation that do not assume bivariate normality and linear relationships (Section 5.1.2).

5.1.2 Robust correlation

We may have a situation where the joint distribution of our two variables is not bivariate normal, as evidenced by non-normality in either variable, and transformations do not help or are inappropriate (e.g. the log of a variable does not make much theoretical sense). We may also be interested in testing hypotheses about monotonic relationships or more general associations between two variables, i.e. one variable increases (or decreases) as the other increases (or decreases) but not necessarily in a linear (straight-line) manner. One general approach for testing monotonic relationships between variables that does not assume bivariate normality is to examine the association of the ranks of the variables; statistical tests based on rank transformations were described in Chapter 3.

Spearman's rank correlation coefficient (r_s) is simply the Pearson correlation coefficient after the two variables have been separately transformed to ranks but the (y_{i1}, y_{i2}) pairing is retained after ranking. An equivalent computation that uses the ranked data directly is also available (e.g. Hollander & Wolfe 1999, Sokal & Rohlf 1995, Sprent 1993). The null hypothesis being tested is that there is no monotonic relationship between Y_1 and Y_2 in the population. An alternative measure is Kendall's rank correlation coefficient, sometimes termed Kendall's tau (τ). The value of

Spearman's r_s will be slightly greater than τ for a given data set (Box 5.1), and both are more conservative measures than Pearson's correlation when distribution assumptions hold. Note that these non-parametric correlation analyses do not detect all nonlinear associations between variables, just monotonic relationships.

5.1.3 Parametric and non-parametric confidence regions

When representing a bivariate relationship with a scatterplot, it is often useful to include confidence regions (Figure 5.4, left). The 95% confidence region, for example, is the region within which we would expect the observation represented by the population mean of the two variables to occur 95% of the time under repeated sampling from this population. Assuming our two variables follow a bivariate normal distribution, the confidence band will always be an ellipse centered on the sample means of Y_1 and Y_2 and the orientation of the ellipse is determined by the covariance (or the Pearson correlation coefficient). The two major axes (length and width) of these ellipses are determined from the variances (or standard deviations) of Y_1 and Y_2. These axes are used for some forms of regression analysis (Section 5.3.14) and also for some statistical procedures that deal with multivariate data sets, such as principal components analysis (Chapters 15 and 16). Note that if the linear relationship between Y_1 and Y_2 is weak, then the bounds of the ellipse may exceed the actual and theoretical range of our data, e.g. include impossible values such as negatives (Figure 5.4, right).

Sometimes we are not interested in the

Box 5.2 | What does "linear" mean?

The term linear model has been used in two distinct ways. First, it means a model of a straight-line relationship between two variables. This is the interpretation most biologists are familiar with. A second, more correct, definition is that a linear model is simply one in which any value of the variable of interest (y_i) is described by a linear combination of a series of parameters (regression slopes, intercept), and "no parameter appears as an exponent or is multiplied or divided by another parameter" (Neter *et al.* 1996, p. 10). Now the term "linear" refers to the combination of parameters, not the shape of the relationship. Under this definition, linear models with a single predictor variable can represent not only straight-line relationships such as Equation 5.3, but also curvilinear relationships, such as the models with polynomial terms described in Chapter 6.

population mean of Y_1 and Y_2 but simply want a confidence region for the observations themselves. In Chapter 4, we introduced kernel density estimators for univariate data (Silverman 1986). The estimated density for a value of Y is the sum of the estimates from a series of symmetrical distributions (e.g. normal, although others are often used) fitted to groups of local observations. In the bivariate case, we determine contours that surround regions of high bivariate density where these contours are formed from summing a series of symmetrical bivariate distributions fitted to groups of local paired observations. Note that the kernel estimators are not constrained to a specific ellipsoid shape and will often better represent the pattern of density of observations in our sample (Figure 5.4, right).

5.2 | Linear models

Most of the analyses in the following chapters are concerned with fitting statistical models. These are used in situations where we can clearly specify a response variable, also termed the dependent variable and designated Y, and one or more predictor variables, also termed the independent variables or covariates and designated X_1, X_2, etc. A value for each response and predictor variable is recorded from sampling or experimental units in a population. We expect that the predictor variables may provide some biological explanation for the pattern we see in the response variable. The

statistical models we will use take the following general form:

$$\text{response variable} = \text{model} + \text{error} \qquad (5.2)$$

The model component incorporates the predictor variables and parameters relating the predictors to the response. In most cases, the predictor variables, and their parameters, are included as a linear combination (Box 5.2), although nonlinear terms are also possible. The predictor variables can be continuous or categorical or a combination of both. The error component represents the part of the response variable not explained by the model, i.e. uncertainty in our response variable. We have to assume some form of probability distribution for the error component, and hence for the response variable, in our model.

Our primary aim is to fit our model to our observed data, i.e. confront our model with the data (Hilborn & Mangel 1997). This fitting is basically an estimation procedure and can be done with ordinary least squares or maximum likelihood (Chapter 2). We will emphasize OLS for most of our models, although we will be assuming normality of the error terms for interval estimation and hypothesis testing. Such models are called general linear models, the term "general" referring to the fact that both continuous and categorical predictors are allowed. If other distributions are applicable, especially when there is a relationship between the mean and the variance of response variable, then ML must be used for estimation. These models are called generalized linear models, generalized meaning that other distributions besides normal and relationships between the mean and the variance can be accommodated.

We nearly always have more than one statistical model to consider. For example, we might have the simplest model under a null hypothesis versus a more complex model under some alternative hypothesis. When we have many possible predictor variables, we may be comparing a large number of possible models. In all cases, however, the set of models will be nested whereby we have a full model with all predictors of interest included and the other models are all subsets of this full model. Testing hypotheses about predictors and their parameters involves comparing the fit of models with and without specific terms in this nested hierarchy. Non-nested models can also be envisaged but they cannot be easily compared using the estimation and testing framework we will describe, although some measures of fit are possible (Hilborn & Mangel 1997; Chapter 6).

Finally, it is important to remember that there will not usually be any best or correct model in an absolute sense. We will only have sample data with which to assess the fit of the model and estimate parameters. We may also not have chosen all the relevant predictors nor considered combinations of predictors, such as interactions, that might affect the response variable. All the procedure for analyzing linear models can do is help us decide which of the models we have available is the best fit to our observed sample data and enable us to test hypotheses about the parameters of the model.

5.3 | Linear regression analysis

In this chapter, we consider statistical models that assume a linear relationship between a continuous response variable and a single, usually continuous, predictor variable. Such models are termed simple linear regression models (Box 5.2) and their analysis has three major purposes:

1. to describe the linear relationship between Y and X,

2. to determine how much of the variation (uncertainty) in Y can be explained by the linear

relationship with X and how much of this variation remains unexplained, and

3. to predict new values of Y from new values of X.

Our experience is that biologists, especially ecologists, mainly use linear regression analysis to describe the relationship between Y and X and to explain the variability in Y. They less commonly use it for prediction (see discussion in Ford 2000, Peters 1991).

5.3.1 Simple (bivariate) linear regression

Simple linear regression analysis is one of the most widely applied statistical techniques in biology and we will use two recent examples from the literature to illustrate the issues associated with the analysis.

Coarse woody debris in lakes

The impact of humans on freshwater environments is an issue of great concern to both scientists and resource managers. Coarse woody debris (CWD) is detached woody material that provides habitat for freshwater organisms and affects hydrological processes and transport of organic materials within freshwater systems. Land use by humans has altered the input of CWD into freshwater lakes in North America, and Christensen et al. (1996) studied the relationships between CWD and shoreline vegetation and lake development in a sample of 16 lakes. They defined CWD as debris greater than 5 cm in diameter and recorded, for a number of plots on each lake, the density (no. km^{-1}) and basal area (m^2 km^{-1}) of CWD in the nearshore water, and the density (no. km^{-1}) and basal area (m^2 km^{-1}) of riparian trees along the shore. They also recorded density of cabins along the shoreline. Weighted averages of these values were determined for each lake, the weighting based on the relative proportion of lake shore with forest and with cabins. We will use their data to model the relationships between CWD basal area and two predictor variables separately, riparian tree density and cabin density. These analyses are presented in Box 5.3.

Species–area relationships

Ecologists have long been interested in how abundance and diversity of organisms relate to the area of habitat in which those organisms are found.

Box 5.3	Worked example of linear regression analysis: coarse woody debris in lakes

Christensen *et al.* (1996) studied the relationships between coarse woody debris (CWD) and shoreline vegetation and lake development in a sample of 16 lakes in North America. The main variables of interest are the density of cabins (no. km^{-1}), density of riparian trees (trees km^{-1}), the basal area of riparian trees (m^2 km^{-1}), density of coarse woody debris (no. km^{-1}), basal area of coarse woody debris (m^2 km^{-1}).

CWD basal area against riparian tree density

A scatterplot of CWD basal area against riparian tree density, with a Loess smoother fitted, showed no evidence of a nonlinear relationship (Figure 5.13(a)). The boxplots of each variable were slightly skewed but the residuals from fitting the linear regression model were evenly spread and there were no obvious outliers (Figure 5.13(b)). One lake (Tenderfoot) had a higher Cook's D_i than the others that was due mainly to a slightly higher leverage value because this lake had the greatest riparian density (X-variable). Omitting this lake from the analysis did not alter the conclusions so it was retained and the variables were not transformed.

The results of the OLS fit of a linear regression model to CWD basal area against riparian tree density were as follows.

	Coefficient	Standard error	Standardized coefficient	t	P
Intercept	−77.099	30.608	0	−2.519	0.025
Slope	0.116	0.023	0.797	4.929	<0.001

Correlation coefficient $(r) = 0.797$, $r^2 = 0.634$

Source	df	MS	F	P
Regression	1	3.205×10^4	24.303	<0.001
Residual	14	1318.969		

The t test and the ANOVA F test cause us to reject the H_0 that β_1 equals zero. Note that $F (24.307) = t^2 (4.929)$, allowing for rounding errors. We would also reject the H_0 that β_0 equals zero, although this test is of little biological interest. The r^2 value (0.634) indicates that we can explain about 63% of the total variation in CWD basal area by the linear regression with riparian tree density.

We can predict CWD basal area for a new lake with 1500 trees km^{-1} in the riparian zone. Plugging 1500 into our fitted regression model:

CWD basal area $= -77.099 + 0.116 \times 1500$

the predicted basal area of CWD is 96.901 m^2 km^{-1}. The standard error of this predicted value (from Equation 5.10) is 37.900, resulting in a 95% confidence interval for true mean CWD basal area of lakes with a riparian density of 1500 trees km^{-1} of ±81.296.

CWD basal area against cabin density

A scatterplot of CWD basal area against cabin density, with a Loess smoother fitted, showed some evidence of a nonlinear relationship (Figure 5.14(a)). The boxplot of cabin density was highly skewed, with a number of zero values. The residuals from fitting the linear regression model to untransformed data suggested increasing spread of residuals with an unusual value (Arrowhead Lake) with a low (negative) predicted value and a much higher Cook's D_i than the others (Figure 5.14(b)). Following Christensen *et al.* (1996), we transformed cabin density to $\log_{10}$ and refitted the linear model. The scatterplot of CWD basal area against $\log_{10}$ cabin density suggested a much better linear relationship (Figure 5.15(a)). The boxplot of $\log_{10}$ cabin density was less skewed but the residuals from fitting the linear regression model still showed increasing spread with increasing predicted values. Lake Arrowhead was no longer influential but Lake Bergner was an outlier with a moderate Cook's D_i. Finally, we fitted a linear model when both variables were $\log_{10}$ transformed. The scatterplot of $\log_{10}$ CWD basal area against $\log_{10}$ cabin density suggested a slightly less linear relationship (Figure 5.16(a)) and the boxplot of $\log_{10}$ CWD basal area was now negatively skewed. The residuals from fitting the linear regression model were much improved with constant spread and no observations were particularly influential.

Overall, transforming both variables seems to result in a linear model that fits best to these data, although we will present the analysis with just cabin density transformed as per Christensen *et al.* (1996). The results of the OLS fit of a linear regression model to CWD basal area against $\log_{10}$ cabin density were as follows.

	Coefficient	Standard error	Standardized coefficient	t	P
Intercept	121.969	13.969	0	8.732	<0.001
Slope	−93.301	18.296	−0.806	−5.099	<0.001
Correlation coefficient (r) = −0.806, r^2 = 0.650					

Source	df	MS	F		P
Regression	1	3.284×10^4	26.004		<0.001
Residual	14	1262.870			

The t test and the ANOVA F test cause us to reject the H_0 that β_1 equals zero. We would also reject the H_0 that β_0 equals zero, although this test is of little biological interest, especially as the slope of the relationship is negative.

For example, it has been shown that as the area of islands increases, so does the number of species of a variety of taxa (Begon *et al.* 1996). On rocky intertidal shores, beds of mussels are common and many species of invertebrates use these mussel beds as habitat. These beds are usually patchy and isolated clumps of mussels mimic islands of habitat on these shores. Peake & Quinn (1993) investigated the relationship between the number of species of macroinvertebrates, and the total abundance of macroinvertebrates, and area of clumps of mussels on a rocky shore in southern Australia. They collected a sample of 25 clumps of mussels in June 1989 and all organisms found within each clump were identified and counted.

We will use their data to model the relationship between two separate response variables, the total number of species and the total number of individuals, and one predictor variable, clump area in dm². These analyses are presented in Box 5.4.

5.3.2 Linear model for regression

Consider a set of $i = 1$ to n observations where each observation was selected because of its specific X-value, i.e. the X-values were fixed by the investigator, whereas the Y-value for each observation is sampled from a population of possible Y-values. The simple linear regression model is:

$$y_i = \beta_0 + \beta_1 x_i + \varepsilon_i \tag{5.3}$$

Box 5.4 | Worked example of linear regression analysis: species richness of macroinvertebrates in mussel clumps

Peake & Quinn (1993) investigated the relationship between the number of species of macroinvertebrates, and the total abundance of macroinvertebrates, and area of clumps of mussels on a rocky shore in southern Australia. The variables of interest are clump area (dm^2), number of species, and number of individuals.

Number of species against clump area

A scatterplot of number of species against clump area, and the plot of residuals against predicted number of species from a linear regression analysis, both suggested a nonlinear relationship (Figure 5.17(a,b)). Although only clump area was positively skewed, Peake & Quinn (1993) transformed both variables because of the nature of the species–area relationships for other seasons in their study plus the convention in species–area studies to transform both variables.

The scatterplot of log number of species against log clump area (Figure 5.18) linearized the relationship effectively except for one of the small clumps. The residual plot also showed no evidence of nonlinearity but that same clump had a larger residual and was relatively influential (Cook's $D_i = 1.02$). Reexamination of the raw data did not indicate any problems with this observation and omitting it did not alter the conclusions from the analysis (b_1 changed from 0.386 to 0.339, r^2 from 0.819 to 0.850, all tests still $P < 0.001$) so it was not excluded from the analysis. In fact, just transforming clump area produced the best linearizing of the relationship with no unusually large residuals or Cook's D_i statistics but, for the reasons outlined above, both variables were transformed.

The results of the OLS fit of a linear regression model to log number of species and log clump area were as follows.

	Coefficient	Standard error	Standardized coefficient	t	P
Intercept	1.270	0.024	0	52.237	<0.001
Slope	0.386	0.038	0.905	10.215	<0.001
Correlation coefficient (r) = 0.905, r^2 = 0.819					
Source	df	MS	F		P
Regression	1	1.027	104.353		<0.001
Residual	23	0.010			

The t test and the ANOVA F test cause us to reject the H_0 that β_1 equals zero. We would also reject the H_0 that β_0 equals zero, indicating that the relationship between species number and clump area must be nonlinear for small clump sizes since the model must theoretically go through the origin. The r^2 value (0.819) indicates that we can explain about 82% of the total variation in log number of species by the linear regression with log clump area.

Number of individuals against clump area

A scatterplot of number of individuals against clump area, with a Loess smoother fitted, suggested an approximately linear relationship (Figure 5.19(a)). The plot of residuals against predicted number of individuals from a linear regression model fitted to number of individuals against clump area (Figure 5.19(b)) showed a clear pattern of increasing spread of residuals against increasing predicted number of individuals (or, equivalently, clump area); the pattern in the residuals was wedge-shaped. The boxplots in Figure 5.19(a) indicated that both variables were positively skewed so we transformed both variables to logs to correct for variance heterogeneity.

The scatterplot of log number of individuals against log clump area (Figure 5.20(a)) showed an apparent reasonable fit of a linear regression model, with symmetrical boxplots for both variables. The residual plot showed a more even spread of residuals with little wedge-shaped pattern (Figure 5.20(b)).

The results of the OLS fit of a linear regression model to log number of individuals and log clump area were as follows.

	Coefficient	Standard error	Standardized coefficient	t	P
Intercept	2.764	0.045	0	60.766	<0.001
Slope	0.835	0.071	0.927	11.816	<0.001
Correlation coefficient (r) = 0.927, r^2 = 0.859					
Source	df	MS	F		P
Regression	1	4.809	139.615		<0.001
Residual	23	0.034			

The t test and the ANOVA F test cause us to reject the H_0 that β_1 equals zero. We would also reject the H_0 that β_0 equals zero, although this test is of little biological interest. The r^2 value (0.859) indicates that we can explain about 86% of the total variation in log number of individuals by the linear regression with log clump area.

The details of the linear regression model, including estimation of its parameters, are provided in Box 5.5.

For the CWD data from Christensen *et al.* (1996), we would fit:

(CWD basal area)$_i$ =
$\beta_0 + \beta_1$(riparian tree density)$_i + \varepsilon_i$ \qquad (5.4)

where $n = 16$ lakes.

For the species–area data from Peake & Quinn (1993), we would fit:

(number of species)$_i$ =
$\beta_0 + \beta_1$(mussel clump area)$_i + \varepsilon_i$ \qquad (5.5)

where $n = 25$ mussel clumps.

In models 5.3 and 5.4:

y_i is the value of Y for the ith observation when the predictor variable $X = x_i$. For example, this is the basal area of CWD for the ith lake when the riparian tree density is x_i;

β_0 is the population intercept, the mean value of the probability distribution of Y when $x_i = 0$, e.g. mean basal area of CWD for lakes with no riparian trees;

β_1 is the population slope and measures the change in Y per unit change in X, e.g. the change in basal area of CWD for a unit (one tree km^{-1}) change in riparian tree density; and

ε_i is random or unexplained error associated with the ith observation, e.g. the error terms for a linear model relating basal area of CWD to riparian tree density in lakes are the differences between each observed value for CWD basal area and the true mean CWD basal area at each possible riparian tree density.

In this model, the response variable Y is a random variable whereas the predictor variable X represents fixed values chosen by the researcher. This means that repeated sampling from the population of possible sampling units would use the same values of X; this restriction on X has important ramifications for the use of

Box 5.5 | The linear regression model and its parameters

Consider a set of $i = 1$ to n observations with fixed X-values and random Y-values. The simple linear regression model is:

$$y_i = \beta_0 + \beta_1 x_i + \varepsilon_i \qquad (5.3)$$

In model 5.3 we have the following.

y_i is the value of Y for the ith observation when the predictor variable $X = x_i$.

β_0 is the population intercept, the mean value of the probability distribution of Y when x_i equals zero.

β_1 is the population slope and measures the change in Y per unit change in X.

ε_i is random or unexplained error associated with the ith observation. Each ε_i measures, for each x_i, the difference between each observed y_i and the mean of y_i; the latter is the value of y_i predicted by the population regression model, which we never know. We must make certain assumptions about these error terms for the regression model to be valid and to allow interval estimation of parameters and hypothesis tests. We assume that these error terms are normally distributed at each x_i, their mean at each x_i is zero [$E(\varepsilon_i)$ equals zero] and their variance is the same at each x_i and is designated σ_ε^2. This assumption is the same as the homogeneity of variances of y_i described in Section 5.3.8. We also assume that these ε_i terms are independent of, and therefore uncorrelated with, each other. Since the ε_i terms are the only random ones in our regression model, then these assumptions (normality, homogeneity of variances and independence) also apply to the response variable y_i at each x_i. We will examine these assumptions and their implications in more detail in Section 5.3.8.

Figure 5.5 illustrates the population linear regression model and shows some important features:

1. For any particular value of X (x_i), there is a population of Y-values with a probability distribution. For most regression applications, we assume that the population of Y-values at each x_i has a normal distribution. While not necessary to obtain point estimates of the parameters in the model, this normality assumption is necessary for determining confidence intervals on these parameters and for hypothesis tests.

2. These populations of Y-values at each x_i are assumed to have the same variance (σ^2); this is termed the homogeneity of variance assumption.

3. The true population regression line joins the means of these populations of Y-values.

4. The overall mean value of Y, also termed the expected value of Y [$E(Y)$], equals $\beta_0 + \beta_1 X$. This implies that we can re-express the linear regression model in terms of means of the response variable Y at each x_i:

$$y_i = \mu_i + \varepsilon_i$$

where μ_i is the population mean of Y-values at each x_i. This type of linear model is particularly useful when the predictor variable is categorical and the effects of the predictor on the response variable are usually expressed in terms of mean values.

As we described in Chapter 2, we can use either of two methods for estimating parameters, (ordinary) least squares (OLS) and maximum likelihood (ML). If we assume normality of the ε_i, it turns out that the OLS and ML estimates of β_0 and β_1 are identical, although, as is usual for variance estimation, the ML estimate of the variance (σ_ε^2) is slightly biased whereas the OLS estimate of σ_ε^2 is not. In this book, we will focus on OLS estimates of these parameters; details of the calculations for ML estimation of regression parameters can be found in Neter et al. (1996).

The OLS estimates of β_0 and β_1 are the values that produce a sample regression line ($\hat{y}_i = b_0 + b_1 x_i$) that minimize $\Sigma(y_i - \hat{y}_i)^2$. These are the sum of the squared deviations (SS) between each observed y_i and the value of y_i predicted by the sample regression line for each x_i. This is the sum of squared vertical distances between each observation and the fitted regression line (Figure 5.6). Note that for any $x_i, \hat{y}_i$ is our best estimate of the mean of y_i in the usual case of only a single y_i at each x_i. In practice, the values of b_0 and b_1 that minimize $\Sigma(y_i - \hat{y}_i)^2$ are found by using a little calculus to derive two new equations, termed normal equations, that are solved simultaneously for b_0 and b_1 (see Neter et al. 1996, Rawlings et al. 1998 for details).

Because we have different populations of Y for each x_i, the estimate of the common variance of ε_i and y_i (σ_ε^2) must be based on deviations of each observed Y-value from the estimated value of the mean Y-value at each x_i. As stated above, our best estimate of the mean of y_i is $\hat{y}_i$. This difference between each observed Y-value and each predicted $\hat{y}_i$ is called a residual:

$$e_i = y_i - \hat{y}_i$$

These residuals are very important in the analysis of linear models. They provide the basis of the OLS estimate of σ_ε^2 and they are valuable diagnostic tools for checking assumptions and fit of our model. The OLS estimate of σ_ε^2 is the sample variance of these residuals and is termed the Residual (or Error) Mean Square (Table 5.2). Remember from Chapter 2 that a variance is also termed a mean square. The numerator of the $MS_{Residual}$ is the sum-of-squares (SS) of the residuals and the quantity that OLS estimation minimizes when determining estimates of the regression model parameters. The degrees of freedom (the denominator) are $n - 2$ because we must estimate both β_0 and β_1 to estimate σ_ε^2. The $SS_{Residual}$ and $MS_{Residual}$ measure the variation in Y around the fitted regression line. Two other attributes of residuals are important: their sum equals zero ($\Sigma_{i=1}^{n} e_i = 0$) and, therefore, their mean must also equal zero ($\bar{e} = 0$). Note that the residuals ($e_i = y_i - \hat{y}_i$) are related to the model error terms ($\varepsilon_i = y_i - \mu_i$) because our best estimate of the mean of Y at each x_i is the predicted value from the fitted regression model.

regression analysis in biology because usually both Y and X are random variables with a joint probability distribution. For example, the predictor variable in the study by Peake & Quinn (1993) was the area of randomly chosen clumps of mussels, clearly a random variable. Some aspects of classical regression analysis, like prediction and tests of hypotheses, might not be affected by X being a random variable whereas the estimates of regression coefficients can be inaccurate. We

will discuss this issue in some detail in Section 5.3.14.

From the characteristics of the regression model summarized in Box 5.5, we assume that (a) there is a population of lakes with a normal distribution of CWD basal areas, (b) the variances of CWD basal area (σ_i^2) are the same for all of these populations and (c) the CWD basal areas in different lakes are independent of each other. These assumptions also apply to the error terms of the

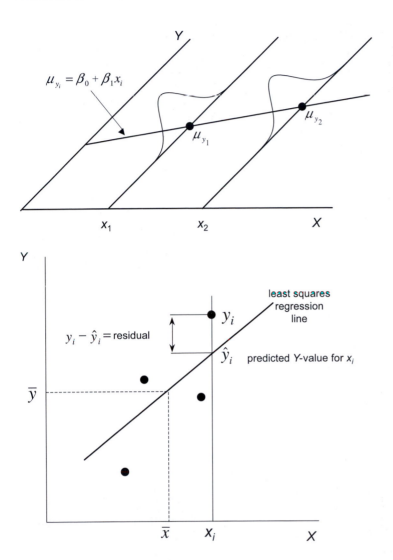

$\mu_{y_i} = \beta_0 + \beta_1 x_i$

μ_{y_1}

μ_{y_2}

X_1 X_2 X

least squares regression line

y_i

$y_i - \hat{y}_i =$ residual

$\hat{y}_i$ predicted Y-value for x_i

$\bar{y}$

$\bar{x}$ x_i X

In model 5.6:

$\hat{y}_i$ is the value of y_i predicted by the fitted regression line for each x_i, e.g. the predicted basal area of CWD for lake i.

b_0 is the sample estimate of β_0, the Y-intercept, e.g. the predicted basal area of CWD for a lake with no riparian trees; and

b_1 is the sample estimate of β_1, the regression slope, e.g. the estimated change in basal area of CWD for a unit (one tree km^{-1}) change in riparian tree density.

The OLS estimates of β_0 and β_1 are the values that minimize the sum of squared deviations (SS) between each observed value of CWD basal area and the CWD basal area predicted by the fitted regression model against density of riparian trees. The estimates of the linear regression model are summarized in Table 5.2.

model, so the common variance of the error terms is σ_ε^2. We will examine these assumptions and their implications in more detail in Section 5.3.8.

5.3.3 Estimating model parameters

The main aim of regression analysis is to estimate the parameters (β_0 and β_1) of the linear regression model based on our sample of n observations with fixed X-values and random Y-values. Actually, there are three parameters we need to estimate: β_0, β_1 and σ_ε^2 (the common variance of ε_i and therefore of y_i). Once we have estimates of these parameters (Box 5.5), we can determine the sample regression line:

$$\hat{y}_i = b_0 + b_1 x_i \qquad (5.6)$$

Regression slope

The parameter of most interest is the slope of the regression line β_1 because this measures the strength of the relationship between Y and X. The estimated slope (b_1) of the linear regression

Table 5.2 Parameters of the linear regression model and their OLS estimates with standard errors

Parameter	OLS estimate	Standard error
β_1	$b_1 = \dfrac{\sum_{i=1}^{n}[(x_i - \bar{x})(y_i - \bar{y})]}{\sum_{i=1}^{n}(x_i - \bar{x})^2}$	$s_{b_1} = \sqrt{\dfrac{MS_{Residual}}{\sum_{i=1}^{n}(x_i - \bar{x})^2}}$
β_0	$b_0 = \bar{y} - b_1\bar{x}$	$s_{b_0} = \sqrt{MS_{Residual}\left[\dfrac{1}{n} + \dfrac{\bar{x}^2}{\sum_{i=1}^{n}(x_i - \bar{x})^2}\right]}$
ε_i	$e_i = y_i - \hat{y}_i$	$\sqrt{MS_{Residual}}$ (approx.)

model derived from the solution of the normal equations is the covariance between Y and X divided by the sum of squares (SS) of X (Table 5.2). The sample regression slope can be positive or negative (or zero) with no constraints on upper and lower limits.

The estimate of the β_1 is based on X being fixed so in the common case where X is random, we need a different approach to estimating the regression slope (Section 5.3.14). Nonetheless, there is also a close mathematical relationship between linear regression and bivariate correlation that we will discuss in Section 5.4. For now, note that we can also calculate b_1 from the sample correlation coefficient between Y and X as:

$$b_1 = r\frac{s_Y}{s_X} \tag{5.7}$$

where s_X and s_Y are the sample standard deviations of X and Y and r is the sample correlation coefficient between X and Y.

Standardized regression slope

Note that the value of the regression slope depends on the units in which X and Y are measured. For example, if CWD basal area was measured per 10 km rather than per kilometer, then the slope would be greater by a factor of ten. This makes it difficult to compare estimated regression slopes between different data sets. We can calcu-late a standardized regression slope b_1^*, termed a beta coefficient:

$$b_1^* = b_1\frac{s_X}{s_Y} \tag{5.8}$$

This is simply the sample regression slope multiplied by the ratio of the standard deviation of X and the standard deviation of Y. It is also the sample correlation coefficient. The same result can be achieved by first standardizing X and Y (each to a mean of zero and a standard deviation of one) and then calculating the usual sample regression slope. The value of b_1^* provides an estimate of the slope of the regression model that is independent of the units of X and Y and is useful for comparing regression slopes between data sets. For example, the estimated slopes for regression models of CWD basal area and CWD density against riparian tree density were 0.116 and 0.652 respectively, suggesting a much steeper relationship for basal area. The standardized slopes were 0.797 and 0.874, indicating that when the units of measurement were taken into account, the strength of the relationship of riparian tree density on CWD basal area and CWD density were similar. Note that the linear regression model for standardized variables does not include an intercept because its OLS (or ML) estimate would always be zero. Standardized regression slopes are produced by most statistical software.

Intercept

The OLS regression line must pass through $\bar{y}$ and $\bar{x}$. Therefore, the estimate (b_0) of the intercept of our regression model is derived from a simple rearrangement of the sample regression equation, substituting b_1, $\bar{y}$ and $\bar{x}$. The intercept might not be of much practical interest in regression analysis because the range of our observations rarely includes X equals zero and we should not usually extrapolate beyond the range of our sample observations. A related issue that we will discuss below is whether the linear regression line should be forced through the origin (Y equals zero and X equals zero) if we know theoretically that Y must be zero if X equals zero.

Confidence intervals

Now we have a point estimate for both σ_ε^2 and β_1, we can look at the sampling distribution and standard error of b_1 and confidence intervals for β_1. It turns out that the Central Limit Theorem applies to b_1 so its sampling distribution is normal with an expected value (mean) of β_1. The standard error of b_1, the standard deviation of its sampling distribution, is the square root of the residual mean square divided by the SS_X (Table 5.2). Confidence intervals for β_1 are calculated in the usual manner when we know the standard error of a statistic and use the t distribution. The 95% confidence interval for β_1 is:

$$b_1 \pm t_{0.05, n-2} s_{b_1} \tag{5.9}$$

Note that we use $n - 2$ degrees of freedom (df) for the t statistic. The interpretation of confidence intervals for regression slopes is as described for means in Chapter 2. To illustrate using 95% confidence interval, under repeated sampling, we would expect 95% of these intervals to contain the fixed, but unknown, true slope of our linear regression model. The standard error (Table 5.2) and confidence intervals for β_0 can also be determined (Neter et al. 1996, Sokal & Rohlf 1995) and are standard output from statistical software.

We can also determine a confidence band (e.g. 95%) for the regression line (Neter et al. 1996, Sokal & Rohlf 1995). The 95% confidence band is a biconcave band that will contain the true population regression line 95% of the time. To illustrate with the data relating number of individuals of macroinvertebrates to mussel clump area from Peake & Quinn (1993), Figure 5.20(a) shows the confidence bands that would include the true population regression line 95% of the time under repeated sampling of mussel clumps. Note that the bands are wider further away from $\bar{x}$, indicating we are less confident about our estimate of the true regression line at the extremes of the range of observations.

Predicted values and residuals

Prediction from the OLS regression equation is straightforward by substituting an X-value into the regression equation and calculating the predicted Y-value. Be wary of extrapolating when making such predictions, i.e. do not predict from X-values outside the range of your data. The predicted Y-values have a sampling distribution that is normal and we provide the equation for the standard error of a new predicted Y-value because these standard errors are not always produced by statistical software:

$$s_{\hat{y}} = \sqrt{MS_{Residual}\left[1 + \frac{1}{n} + \frac{(x_p - \bar{x})^2}{\sum_{i=1}^{n}(x_i - \bar{x})^2}\right]} \tag{5.10}$$

where x_p is the new value of X from which we are predicting and the other terms have already been used in previous calculations. This predicted Y-value is an estimate of the true mean of Y for the new X-value from which we are predicting. Confidence intervals (also called prediction intervals) for this mean of Y can be calculated in the usual manner using this standard error and the t distribution with $n - 2$ df.

This difference between each observed y_i and each predicted $\hat{y}_i$ is called a residual (e_i):

$$e_i = y_i - \hat{y}_i \tag{5.11}$$

For example, the residuals from the model relating CWD basal area to riparian tree density are the differences between each observed value of CWD basal area and the value predicted by the fitted regression model. We will use the residuals for checking the fit of the model to our data in Section 5.3.9.

Table 5.3 | Analysis of variance (ANOVA) table for simple linear regression of Y on X

Source of variation	SS	df	MS	Expected mean square
Regression	$\sum_{i=1}^{n}(\hat{y}_i - \bar{y})^2$	1	$\dfrac{\sum_{i=1}^{n}(\hat{y}_i - \bar{y})^2}{1}$	$\sigma_\varepsilon^2 + \beta_1^2 \sum_{i=1}^{n}(x_i - \bar{x})^2$
Residual	$\sum_{i=1}^{n}(y_i - \hat{y}_i)^2$	$n-2$	$\dfrac{\sum_{i=1}^{n}(y_i - \hat{y}_i)^2}{n-2}$	σ_ε^2
Total	$\sum_{i=1}^{n}(y_i - \bar{y})^2$	$n-1$		

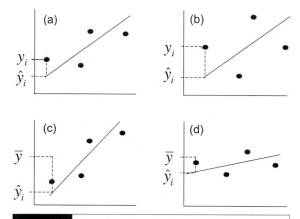

Figure 5.7 Illustration of explained and residual variation in regression analysis. Residual variation: (a) and (b) have identical regression lines but the differences between observed and predicted observations in (b) are greater than in (a) so the $MS_{Residual}$ in (b) is greater than in (a). Explained variation: (c) and (d) have identical $MS_{Residual}$ (the differences between the observed and predicted values are the same) but the total variation in Y is greater in (c) than in (d) and the differences between the predicted values and the mean of Y are greater in (c) than in (d) so $MS_{Regression}$ would be greater in (c) than in (d).

5.3.4 Analysis of variance

A fundamental component of the analysis of linear models is partitioning the total variability in the response variable Y into the part due to the relationship with X (or X_1, X_2, etc. – see Chapter 6) and the part not explained by the relationship. This partitioning of variation is usually presented in the form of an analysis of variance (ANOVA) table (Table 5.3). The total variation in Y is expressed as a sum of squared deviations of each

observation from the sample mean. This SS_{Total} has $n-1$ df and can be partitioned into two additive components. First is the variation in Y explained by the linear regression with X, which is measured as the difference between $\hat{y}_i$ and $\bar{y}$ (Figure 5.7). This is a measure of how well the estimated regression model predicts $\bar{y}$. The number of degrees of freedom associated with a linear model is usually the number of parameters minus one. For a simple linear regression model, there are two parameters (β_0 and β_1) so $df_{Regression} = 1$.

Second is the variation in Y not explained by the regression with X, which is measured as the difference between each observed Y-value and the value of Y predicted by the model ($\hat{y}_i$) (Figure 5.7). This is a measure of how far the Y-values are from the fitted regression line and is termed the residual (or error) variation (see Section 5.3.3). The $df_{Residual} = n-2$, because we have already estimated two parameters (β_0 and β_1) to determine the $\hat{y}_i$.

The SS and df are additive (Table 5.3):

$$SS_{Regression} + SS_{Residual} = SS_{Total}$$
$$df_{Regression} + df_{Residual} = df_{Total}$$

Although the SS is a measure of variation, it is dependent on the number of observations that contribute to it, e.g. SS_{Total} will always get bigger as more observations with different values are included. In contrast to the SS, the variance (mean square, MS) is a measure of variability that does not depend on sample size because it is an average of the squared deviations and also has a known probability distribution (Chapter 2). So the next step in the analysis of variance is to convert the SS into MS by dividing them by their df:

The MS are not additive:

$$MS_{Regression} + MS_{Residual} \neq MS_{Total}$$

and the "MS_{Total}" does not play a role in analyses of variance.

These MS are sample variances and, as such, they estimate parameters. But unlike the situation where we have a single sample, and therefore a single variance (Chapter 2), we now have two variances. Statisticians have determined the expected values of these mean squares, i.e. the average of all possible values of these mean squares or what population values these mean squares actually estimate (Table 5.3).

The $MS_{Residual}$ estimates σ_ε^2, the common variance of the error terms (ε_i), and therefore of the Y-values at each x_i. The implicit assumption here, that we mentioned in Section 5.3.2 and will detail in Section 5.3.8, is that the variance of ε_i (and therefore of y_i) is the same for all x_i (homogeneity of variance), and therefore can be summarized by a single variance (σ_ε^2). If this assumption is not met, then $MS_{Residual}$ does not estimate a common variance σ_ε^2 and interval estimation and hypothesis tests associated with linear regression will be unreliable. The $MS_{Regression}$ also estimates σ_ε^2 plus an additional source of variation determined by the strength of the absolute relationship between Y and X (i.e. β_1^2 multiplied by the SS_X).

Sometimes the total variation in Y is expressed as an "uncorrected" total sum-of-squares ($SS_{Total\ uncorrected}$; see Neter *et al.* 1996, Rawlings *et al.* 1998). This is simply $\sum_{i=1}^{n} y_i^2$ and can be "corrected" by subtracting $n\bar{y}^2$ (termed "correcting for the mean") to convert $SS_{Total\ uncorrected}$ into the SS_{Total} we have used. The uncorrected total SS is occasionally used when regression models are forced through the origin (Section 5.3.12) and in nonlinear regression (Chapter 6).

5.3.5 Null hypotheses in regression

The null hypothesis commonly tested in linear regression analysis is that β_1 equals zero, i.e. the slope of the population regression model equals zero and there is no linear relationship between Y and X. For example, the population slope of the regression model relating CWD basal area to

riparian tree density is zero or there is no linear relationship between number of species and mussel clump area in the population of all possible mussel clumps. There are two equivalent ways of testing this H_0.

The first uses the ANOVA we have described in Section 5.3.4. If H_0 is true and β_1 equals zero, then it is apparent from Table 5.3 that $MS_{Regression}$ and $MS_{Residual}$ both estimate σ_ε^2 because the term $\beta_1^2 \sum_{i=1}^{n}(x_i - \bar{x})^2$ becomes zero. Therefore, the ratio of $MS_{Regression}$ to $MS_{Residual}$ should be less than or equal to one. If H_0 is not true and β_1 does not equal zero, then the expected value of $MS_{Regression}$ is larger than that of $MS_{Residual}$ and their ratio should be greater than one.

If certain assumptions hold (Section 5.3.8), the ratio of two sample variances (the F-ratio) follows a well-defined probability distribution called the F distribution (Chapter 2). A central F distribution is a probability distribution of the F-ratio[1] when the two sample variances come from populations with the same expected values. There are different central F distributions depending on the df of the two sample variances. Therefore, we can use the appropriate probability distribution of F (defined by numerator and denominator df) to determine whether the probability of obtaining our sample F-ratio or one more extreme (the usual hypothesis testing logic; see Chapter 3), is less than some specified significance level (e.g. 0.05) and therefore whether we reject H_0. This F test basically compares the fit to the data of a model that includes a slope term to the fit of a model that does not.

We can also test the H_0 that β_1 equals zero using a single parameter t test, as described in Chapter 3. We calculate a t statistic from our data:

$$t = \frac{b_1 - \theta}{s_{b_1}} \qquad (5.12)$$

In Equation 5.12, θ is the value of β_1 specified in the H_0. We compare the observed t statistic to a t distribution with $(n-2)$ df with the usual logic of

---

[1] *F-ratio versus F.* Hypothesis tests that involve comparisons of variance (ANOVA, ANCOVA, etc.) use an F-ratio, which is the ratio of two variances. This ratio follows an F distribution. Strictly speaking, any test statistic that we calculated as part of an ANOVA or ANCOVA is an F-ratio, but in much of the biological literature, there is reference to the less cumbersome F. We will often use this abbreviation.

a t test. Note that the F test of the H_0 that β_1 equals zero is mathematically identical to the t test; in fact, the F-ratio equals t^2 for a given sample. So, in practice, it does not matter which we use and both are standard output from statistical software. We offer some suggestions about presenting results from linear regression analyses in Chapter 19.

While the test of the H_0 that β_1 equals zero is most common, a test whether β_1 equals some other value may also be relevant, especially when variables have been log transformed. Examples include increases in metabolic rate with body size, an allometric relationship with a predicted slope of 0.75, and the self-thinning rule, that argues that the relationship between log plant size and log plant density would have a slope of $-3/2$ (Begon et al. 1996).

We can also test the H_0 that β_0 equals zero, i.e. the intercept of the population regression model is zero. Just as with the test that β_1 equals zero, the H_0 that β_0 equals zero can be tested with a t test, where the t statistic is the sample intercept divided by the standard error of the sample intercept. Alternatively, we can calculate an F test by comparing the fit of a model with an intercept term to the fit of a model without an intercept term (Section 5.3.6). The conclusions will be identical as the F equals t^2 and the t test version is standard output from statistical software. This H_0 is not usually of much biological interest unless we are considering excluding an intercept from our final model and forcing the regression line through the origin (Section 5.3.12).

Finally, we can test the H_0 that two regression lines come from populations with the same slope using a t test, similar to a test of equality of means (Chapter 3). A more general approach to comparing regression slopes is as part of analysis of covariance (ANCOVA, Chapter 12).

5.3.6 Comparing regression models

Methods for measuring the fit of a linear model to sample data fall into two broad categories based on the way the parameters of the models are estimated (see also Chapter 2).

1. Using OLS, the fit of a model is determined by the amount of variation in Y explained by the model or conversely, the lack of fit of a model is determined by the unexplained (residual) variation. This approach leads to the analysis of variance described above and F tests of null hypotheses about regression model parameters.

2. Using maximum likelihood (ML), the fit of a model is determined by the size of likelihood or log-likelihood. This approach leads to likelihood ratio tests of null hypotheses about regression model parameters and is most commonly used when fitting generalized linear models (GLMs) with non-normal error terms (Chapter 13).

The logic of comparing the fit of different models is the same whichever approach is used to measure fit. We will illustrate this logic based on the OLS estimation we have been using throughout this chapter. We can measure the fit of different models to the data and then compare their fits to test hypotheses about the model parameters. For example, smaller unexplained (residual) variation when a full model that includes β_1 is fitted compared with when a reduced model is fitted that omits β_1 is evidence against the H_0 that β_1 equals zero. Including a slope term in the model results in a better fit to the observed data than omitting a slope term. If there is no difference in the explanatory power of these two models, then there is no evidence against the H_0 that β_1 equals zero.

Let's explore this process more formally by comparing the unexplained, or residual, SS (the variation due to the difference between the observed and predicted Y-values) for full and reduced models (Box 5.6). To test the H_0 that β_1 equals zero, we fit the full model with both an intercept and a slope term (Equation 5.3):

$$y_i = \beta_0 + \beta_1 x_i + \varepsilon_i$$

We have already identified the unexplained SS from the full model as $\sum_{i=1}^{n}(y_i - \hat{y}_i)^2$. This is the $SS_{Residual}$ from our standard regression ANOVA in Table 5.3.

We then fit a reduced model that omits the slope term, i.e. the model expected if the H_0 that β_1 equals zero is true:

$$y_i = \beta_0 + \varepsilon_i \tag{5.13}$$

This is a model with zero slope (i.e. a flat line). The predicted Y-value for each x_i from this model is the intercept, which equals $\bar{y}$. Therefore, the unexplained SS from this reduced model is the sum of squared differences between the observed Y-

Box 5.6 | Model comparisons in simple linear regression

We can use the model relating CWD basal area to riparian tree density to illustrate comparing the fit of full and reduced models to test null hypotheses about population parameters.

Test $H_0: \beta_1$ equals zero:

Full model:

$(\text{CWD basal area})_i = \beta_0 + \beta_1 (\text{riparian tree density})_i + \varepsilon_i$

$SS_{\text{Residual}} = 18\ 465.56$ (14 df).

Reduced model:

$(\text{CWD basal area})_i = \beta_0 + \varepsilon_i$

$SS_{\text{Residual}} = 50\ 520.00$ (15 df).

Reduced SS_{Residual} − Full $SS_{\text{Residual}} = 32\ 054.44$ (1 df). This is identical to $MS_{\text{Regression}}$ from the ANOVA from fitting the original full model (Box 5.3).

Test $H_0: \beta_0$ equals zero:

Full model:

$(\text{CWD basal area})_i = \beta_0 + \beta_1 (\text{riparian tree density})_i + \varepsilon_i$

$SS_{\text{Residual}} = 18\ 465.56$ (14 df).

Reduced model:

$(\text{CWD basal area})_i = \beta_1 (\text{riparian tree density})_i + \varepsilon_i$

$SS_{\text{Residual}} = 26\ 834.35$ (15 df).

Reduced SS_{Residual} − Full $SS_{\text{Residual}} = 8368.79$ (1 df).

values and $\bar{y}$ (i.e. $\sum_{i=1}^{n}(y_i - \bar{y})^2$), which is the SS_{Total} from our standard regression ANOVA.

The difference between the unexplained variation of the full model (SS_{Residual}) and the unexplained variation from the reduced model (SS_{Total}) is simply the $SS_{\text{Regression}}$. It measures how much more variation in Y is explained by the full model than by the reduced model. It is, therefore, the relative magnitude of the $SS_{\text{Regression}}$ (which equals $MS_{\text{Regression}}$ with one df) that we use to evaluate the H_0 that β_1 equals zero (Box 5.6). So describing the $SS_{\text{Regression}}$ or $MS_{\text{Regression}}$ as the variation explained by the regression model is really describing the $SS_{\text{Regression}}$ or $MS_{\text{Regression}}$ as how much more variation in Y the full model explains over the reduced model.

The same logic can be used to test H_0 that β_0 equals zero by comparing the fit of the full model and the fit of a reduced model that omits the intercept:

$$y_i = \beta_1 x_i + \varepsilon_i \tag{5.14}$$

This is the model expected if the H_0 that β_0 equals zero is true and therefore, when x_i equals zero then y_i equals zero (Box 5.6).

For most regression models, we don't have to worry about comparing full and reduced models because our statistical software will do it automatically and provide us with the familiar ANOVA table and F tests and/or t tests. While comparisons of full and reduced models are trivial for linear models with a single predictor variable, the model comparison approach has broad applicability for testing null hypotheses about particular parameters in more complex linear (Chapter 6) and generalized linear models (Chapter 13).

5.3.7 Variance explained

A descriptive measure of association between Y and X is r^2 (also termed R^2 or the coefficient of determination), which measures the proportion of the total variation in Y that is explained by its linear relationship with X. When we fit the full model, it is usually calculated as (Kvalseth 1985, Neter *et al.* 1996):

$$r^2 = \frac{SS_{Regression}}{SS_{Total}} = 1 - \frac{SS_{Residual}}{SS_{Total}} \qquad (5.15)$$

Anderson-Sprecher (1994) argued that r^2 is better explained in terms of the comparison between the full model and a reduced (no slope parameter) model:

$$r^2 = 1 - \frac{SS_{Residual(Full)}}{SS_{Residual(Reduced)}} \qquad (5.16)$$

Equations 5.15 and 5.16 are identical for models with an intercept (see below for no intercept models) but the latter version emphasizes that r^2 is a measure of how much the fit is improved by the full model compared with the reduced model. We can also relate explained variance back to the bivariate correlation model because r^2 is the square of the correlation coefficient r. Values of r^2 range between zero (no relationship between Y and X) and one (all points fall on fitted regression line). Therefore, r^2 is not an absolute measure of how well a linear model fits the data, only a measure of how much a model with a slope parameter fits better than one without (Anderson-Sprecher 1994).

Great care should be taken in using r^2 values for comparing the fit of different models. It is inappropriate for comparing models with different numbers of parameters (Chapter 6) and can be problematical for comparing models based on different transformations of Y (Scott & Wild 1991). If we must compare the fit of a linear model based on Y with the equivalent model based on, say log(Y), using r^2, we should calculate r^2 as above after re-expressing the two models so that Y is on the same original scale in both models (see also Anderson-Sprecher 1994).

5.3.8 Assumptions of regression analysis

The assumptions of the linear regression model strictly concern the error terms (ε_i) in the model, as described in Section 5.3.2. Since these error terms are the only random ones in the model, then the assumptions also apply to observations of the response variable y_i. Note that these assumptions are not required for the OLS estima-

Table 5.4 | Types of residual for linear regression models, where h_i is the leverage for observation i

Residual	$e_i = y_i - \hat{y}_i$
Standardized residual	$\dfrac{e_i}{\sqrt{MS_{Residual}}}$
Studentized residual	$\dfrac{e_i}{\sqrt{MS_{Residual}(1 - h_i)}}$
Studentized deleted residual	$e_i \sqrt{\dfrac{n-1}{SS_{Residual}(1 - h_i) - e_i^2}}$

tion of model parameters but are necessary for reliable confidence intervals and hypothesis tests based on t distributions or F distributions.

The residuals from the fitted model (Table 5.4) are important for checking whether the assumptions of linear regression analysis are met. Residuals indicate how far each observation is from the fitted OLS regression line, in Y-variable space (i.e. vertically). Observations with larger residuals are further from the fitted line that those with smaller residuals. Patterns of residuals represent patterns in the error terms from the linear model and can be used to check assumptions and also the influence each observation has on the fitted model.

Normality

This assumption is that the populations of Y-values and the error terms (ε_i) are normally distributed for each level of the predictor variable x_i. Confidence intervals and hypothesis tests based on OLS estimates of regression parameters are robust to this assumption unless the lack of normality results in violations of other assumptions. In particular, skewed distributions of y_i can cause problems with homogeneity of variance and linearity, as discussed below.

Without replicate Y-values for each x_i, this assumption is difficult to verify. However, reasonable checks can be based on the residuals from the fitted model (Bowerman & O'Connell 1990). The methods we described in Chapter 4 for checking normality, including formal tests or graphical methods such as boxplots and probability plots, can be applied to these residuals. If the assumption is not met, then there are at least two options. First, a transformation of Y (Chapter 4 and Section 5.3.11) may be appropriate if the distribution is positively skewed. Second, we can fit a linear model using techniques that allow other distributions of error terms other than normal. These generalized linear models (GLMs) will be described in Chapter 13. Note that non-normality of Y is very commonly associated with heterogeneity of variance and/or nonlinearity.

Homogeneity of variance

This assumption is that the populations of Y-values, and the error terms (ε_i), have the same variance for each x_i:

$$\sigma_1^2 = \sigma_2^2 = \ldots = \sigma_i^2 = \ldots = \sigma_\varepsilon^2 \text{ for } i = 1 \text{ to } n \quad (5.17)$$

The homogeneity of variance assumption is important, its violation having a bigger effect on the reliability of interval estimates of, and tests of hypotheses about, regression parameters (and parameters of other linear models) than non-normality. Heterogeneous variances are often a result of our observations coming from populations with skewed distributions of Y-values at each x_i and can also be due to a small number of extreme observations or outliers (Section 5.3.9).

Although without replicate Y-values for each x_i, the homogeneity of variance assumption cannot be strictly tested, the general pattern of the residuals for the different x_i can be very informative. The most useful check is a plot of residuals against x_i or $\hat{y}_i$ (Section 5.3.10). There are a couple of options for dealing with heterogeneous variances. If the unequal variances are due to skewed distributions of Y-values at each x_i, then appropriate transformations will always help (Chapter 4 and Section 5.3.11) and generalized linear models (GLMs) are always an option (Chapter 13). Alternatively, weighted least squares (Section 5.3.13) can be applied if there is a consistent pattern of unequal variance, e.g. increasing variance in Y with increasing X.

Independence

There is also the assumption that the Y-values and the ε_i are independent of each other, i.e. the Y-value for any x_i does not influence the Y-values for any other x_i. The most common situation in which this assumption might not be met is when the observations represent repeated measurements on sampling or experimental units. Such data are often termed longitudinal, and arise from longitudinal studies (Diggle et al. 1994, Ware & Liang 1996). A related situation is when we have a longer time series from one or a few units and we wish to fit a model where the predictor variable is related to a temporal sequence, i.e. a time series study (Diggle 1990). Error terms and Y-values that are non-independent through time are described as autocorrelated. A common occurrence in biology is positive first-order autocorrelation, where there is a positive relationship between error terms from adjacent observations through time, i.e. a positive error term at one time follows from a positive error term at the previous time and the same for negative error terms. The degree of autocorrelation is measured by the autocorrelation parameter, which is the correlation coefficient between successive error terms. More formal descriptions of autocorrelation structures can be found in many textbooks on linear regression models (e.g Bowerman & O'Connell 1990, Neter et al. 1996). Positive autocorrelation can result in underestimation of the true residual variance and seriously inflated Type I error rates for hypothesis tests on regression parameters. Note that autocorrelation can also be spatial rather than temporal, where observations closer together in space are more similar than those further apart (Diggle 1996).

If our Y-values come from populations in which the error terms are autocorrelated between adjacent x_i, then we would expect the residuals from the fitted regression line also to be correlated. An estimate of the autocorrelation parameter is the correlation coefficient between adjacent residuals, although some statistical software calculates this as the correlation coefficient between adjacent Y-values. Autocorrelation can therefore be detected in plots of residuals against x_i by an obvious positive, negative or cyclical trend in the residuals. Some statistical software also provides the Durbin–Watson test of the H_0 that the autocorrelation parameter equals zero. Because we might expect positive autocorrelation, this test is often one-tailed against the alternative hypothesis that the autocorrelation parameter is greater than zero. Note that the Durbin–Watson test is specifically designed for first-order autocorrelations and may not detect other patterns of non-independence (Neter et al. 1996).

There are a number of approaches to modeling a repeated series of observations on sampling or experimental units. These approaches can be used with both continuous (this chapter and Chapter 6) and categorical (Chapters 8–12) predictor variables and some are applicable even when the response variable is not continuous. Commonly, repeated measurements on individual units occur in studies that also incorporate a treatment structure across units, i.e. sampling or experimental units are allocated to a number of treatments (representing one or more categorical predictor variables or factors) and each unit is also recorded repeatedly through time or is subject to different treatments through time. Such "repeated measures" data are usually modeled with analysis of variance type models (partly nested models incorporating a random term representing units; see Chapter 11). Alternative approaches, including unified mixed linear models (Laird & Ware 1982, see also Diggle *et al.* 1994, Ware & Liang 1996) and generalized estimating equations (GEEs; see Liang & Zeger 1986, Ware & Liang 1996), based on the generalized linear model, will be described briefly in Chapter 13.

When the data represent a time series, usually on one or a small number of sampling units, one approach is to adjust the usual OLS regression analysis depending on the level of autocorrelation. Bence (1995) discussed options for this adjustment, pointing out that the usual estimates of the autocorrelation parameter are biased and recommending bias-correction estimates. Usually, however, data forming a long time series require more sophisticated modeling procedures, such as formal time-series analyses. These can be linear, as described by Neter *et al.* (1996) but more commonly nonlinear as discussed in Chatfield (1989) and Diggle (1990), the latter with a biological emphasis.

Fixed X

Linear regression analysis assumes that the x_i are known constants, i.e. they are fixed values controlled or set by the investigator with no variance associated with them. A linear model in which the predictor variables are fixed is known as Model I or a fixed effects model. This will often be the case in designed experiments where the levels of X are treatments chosen specifically. In these circum-

stances, we would commonly have replicate Y-values for each x_i and X may well be a qualitative variable, so analyses that compare mean values of treatment groups might be more appropriate (Chapters 8–12). The fixed X assumption is probably not met for most regression analyses in biology because X and Y are usually both random variables recorded from a bivariate distribution. For example, Peake & Quinn (1993) did not choose mussel clumps of fixed areas but took a haphazard sample of clumps from the shore; any repeat of this study would use clumps with different areas. We will discuss the case of X being random (Model II or random effects model) in Section 5.3.14 but it turns out that prediction and hypothesis tests from the Model I regression are still applicable even when X is not fixed.

5.3.9 Regression diagnostics

So far we have emphasized the underlying assumptions for estimation and hypothesis testing with the linear regression model and provided some guidelines on how to check whether these assumptions are met for a given bivariate data set. A proper interpretation of a linear regression analysis should also include checks of how well the model fits the observed data. We will focus on two aspects in this section. First, is a straight-line model appropriate or should we investigate curvilinear models? Second, are there any unusual observations that might be outliers and could have undue influence on the parameter estimates and the fitted regression model? Influence can come from at least two sources – think of a regression line as a see-saw, balanced on the mean of X. An observation can influence, or tip, the regression line more easily if it is further from the mean (i.e. at the ends of the range of X-values) or if it is far from the fitted regression line (i.e. has a large residual, analogous to a heavy person on the see-saw). We emphasized in Chapter 4 that it is really important to identify if the conclusions from any statistical analysis are influenced greatly by one or a few extreme observations. A variety of "diagnostic measures" can be calculated as part of the analysis that identify extreme or influential points and detect nonlinearity. These diagnostics also provide additional ways of checking the underlying assumptions of normality, homogeneity of variance and independence. We will illustrate some of the more common regression diagnostics that are standard outputs from most statistical software but others are available. Belsley *et al.* (1980) and Cook & Weisberg (1982) are the standard references, and other good discussions and illustrations include Bollen & Jackman (1990), Chatterjee & Price (1991) and Neter *et al.* (1996).

Leverage

Leverage is a measure of how extreme an observation is for the X-variable, so an observation with high leverage is an outlier in the X-space (Figure 5.8). Leverage basically measures how much each x_i influences $\hat{y}_i$ (Neter *et al.* 1996). X-values further from $\bar{x}$ influence the predicted Y-values more than those close to $\bar{x}$. Leverage is often given the symbol h_i because the values for each observation come from a matrix termed the hat matrix (**H**) that relates the y_i to the $\hat{y}_i$ (see Box 6.1). The hat matrix is determined solely from the X-variable(s) so Y doesn't enter into the calculation of leverage at all.

Leverage values normally range between $1/n$ and 1 and a useful criterion is that any observation with a leverage value greater than $2(p/n)$ (where p is the number of parameters in the model including the intercept; $p = 2$ for simple linear regression) should be checked (Hoaglin & Welsch 1978). Statistical software may use other criteria for warning about observations with high leverage. The main use of leverage values is when they are incorporated in Cook's D_i statistic, a measure of influence described below.

Residuals

We indicated in Section 5.3.8 that patterns in residuals are an important way of checking regression assumptions and we will expand on this in Section 5.3.10. One problem with sample residuals is that their variance may not be constant for different x_i, in contrast to the model error terms that we assume do have constant variance. If we could modify the residuals so they had constant variance, we could more validly compare residuals to one another and check if any seemed unusually large, suggesting an outlying observation from the fitted model. There are a number of modifications that try to make residuals more useful for detecting outliers (Table 5.4).

Standardized residuals use the $\sqrt{MS_{Residual}}$ as an approximate standard error for the residuals. These are also called semistudentized residuals by Neter *et al.* (1996). Unfortunately, this standard error doesn't solve the problem of the variances of the residuals not being constant so a more sophisticated modification is needed. Studentized residuals incorporate leverage (h_i) as defined earlier. These studentized residuals do have constant variance so different studentized residuals can be validly compared. Large (studentized) residuals for a particular observation indicate that it is an outlier from the fitted model compared to the other observations. Studentized residuals also follow a t distribution with $(n-1)$ df if the regression assumptions hold. We can determine the probability of getting a specific studentized residual, or one more extreme, by comparing the studentized residual to a t distribution. Note that we would usually test all residuals in this way, which will result in very high family-wise Type I error rates (the multiple testing problem; see Chapter 3) so some type of P value adjustment might be required, e.g. sequential Bonferroni.

The deleted residual for observation i, also called the PRESS residual, is defined as the difference between the observed Y-values and those predicted by the regression model fitted to all the observations except i. These deleted residuals are usually calculated for studentized residuals. These studentized deleted residuals can detect outliers that might be missed by usual residuals (Neter *et al.* 1996). They can also be compared to a t distribution as we described above for the usual studentized residual.

Influence

A measure of the influence each observation has on the fitted regression line and the estimates of the regression parameters is Cook's distance statistic, denoted D_i. It takes into account both the size of leverage and the residual for each observation and basically measures the influence of each observation on the estimate of the regression slope (Figure 5.8). A large D_i indicates that removal of that observation would change the estimates of the regression parameters considerably. Cook's D_i can be used in two ways. First, informally by scanning the D_is of all observations and noting if any values are much larger than the rest. Second, by comparing D_i to an $F_{1,n}$ distribution; an approximate guideline is that

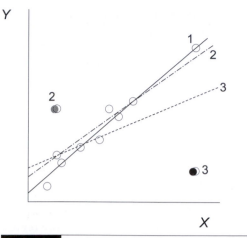

Figure 5.8 Residuals, leverage, and influence. The solid regression line is fitted through the observations with open symbols. Observation 1 is an outlier for both Y and X (large leverage) but not from the fitted model and is not influential. Observation 2 is not an outlier for either Y or X but is an outlier from the fitted model (large residual). Regression line 2 includes this observation and its slope is only slightly less than the original regression line so observation 2 is not particularly influential (small Cook's D_i). Observation 3 is not an outlier for Y but it does have large leverage and it is an outlier from the fitted model (large residual). Regression line 3 includes this observation and its slope is markedly different from the original regression line so observation 3 is very influential (large Cook's D_i, combining leverage and residual).

an observation with a D_i greater than one is particularly influential (Bollen & Jackman 1990). An alternative measure of influence that also incorporates both the size of leverage and the residual for each observation is DFITS$_i$, which measures the influence of each observation (i) on its predicted value ($\hat{y}_i$).

We illustrate leverage and influence in Figure 5.8. Note that observations one and three have large leverage and observations two and three have large residuals. However, only observation three is very influential, because omitting observations one or two would not change the fitted regression line much.

Transformations of Y that overcome problems of non-normality or heterogeneity of variance might also reduce the influence of outliers from the fitted model. If not, then the strategies for dealing with outliers discussed in Chapter 4 should be considered.

5.3.10 Diagnostic graphics
We cannot over-emphasize the importance of preliminary inspection of your data. The diagnostics and checks of assumptions we have just described are best used in graphical explorations of your data before you do any formal analyses. We will describe the two most useful graphs for linear regression analysis, the scatterplot and the residual plot.

Scatterplots
A scatterplot of Y against X, just as we used in simple correlation analysis, should always be the first step in any regression analysis. Scatterplots can indicate unequal variances, nonlinearity and outlying observations, as well as being used in conjunction with smoothing functions (Section 5.5) to explore the relationship between Y and X without being constrained by a specific linear model. For example, the scatterplot of number of species of invertebrates against area of mussel clump from Peake & Quinn (1993) clearly indicates nonlinearity (Figure 5.17(a)), while the plot of number of individuals against area of mussel clump indicates increasing variance in number of individuals with increasing clump area (Figure 5.19(a)). While we could write numerous paragraphs on the value of scatterplots as a preliminary check of the data before a linear regression analysis, the wonderful and oft-used example data from Anscombe (1973) emphasize how easily linear regression models can be fitted to inappropriate data and why preliminary scatterplots are so important (Figure 5.9).

Residual plots
The most informative way of examining residuals (raw or studentized) is to plot them against x_i or, equivalently in terms of the observed pattern, $\hat{y}_i$ (Figure 5.10). These plots can tell us whether the assumptions of the model are met and whether there are unusual observations that do not match the model very well.

If the distribution of Y-values for each x_i is positively skewed (e.g. lognormal, Poisson), we would expect larger $\hat{y}_i$ (an estimate of the population mean of y_i) to be associated with larger residuals. A wedge-shaped pattern of residuals, with a larger spread of residuals for larger x_i or $\hat{y}_i$ as shown for the model relating number of individuals of macroinvertebrates to mussel clump area

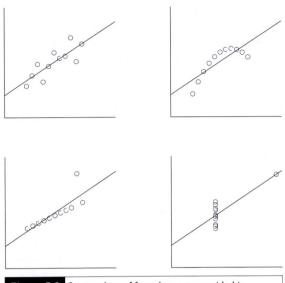

Figure 5.9 Scatterplots of four data sets provided in Anscombe (1973). Note that despite the marked differences in the nature of the relationships between Y and X, the OLS regression line, the r^2 and the test of the H_0 that β_1 equals zero are identical in all four cases: $y_i = 3.0 + 0.5x_i$, $n = 11$, $r^2 = 0.68$, H_0: $\beta_1 = 0$, $t = 4.24$, $P = 0.002$.

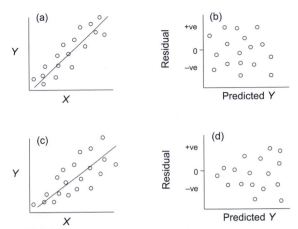

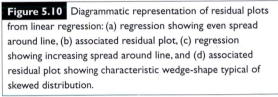

Figure 5.10 Diagrammatic representation of residual plots from linear regression: (a) regression showing even spread around line, (b) associated residual plot, (c) regression showing increasing spread around line, and (d) associated residual plot showing characteristic wedge-shape typical of skewed distribution.

in our worked example (Box 5.4 and Figure 5.19(b)), indicates increasing variance in ε_i and y_i with increasing x_i associated with non-normality in Y-values and a violation of the assumption of homogeneity of variance. Transformation of Y (Section 5.3.11) will usually help. The ideal pattern in the residual plot is a scatter of points with no obvious pattern of increasing or decreasing variance in the residuals. Nonlinearity can be detected by a curved pattern in the residuals (Figure 5.17b) and outliers also stand out as having large residuals. These outliers might be different from the outliers identified in simple boxplots of Y, with no regard for X (Chapter 4). The latter are Y-values very different from the rest of the sample, whereas the former are observations with Y-values very different from that predicted by the fitted model.

Searle (1988) pointed out a commonly observed pattern in residual plots where points fall along parallel lines each with a slope of minus one (Figure 5.11). This results from a number of observations having similar values for one of the variables (e.g. a number of zeros). These parallel lines are not a problem, they just look a little unusual. If the response variable is binary (dichotomous),

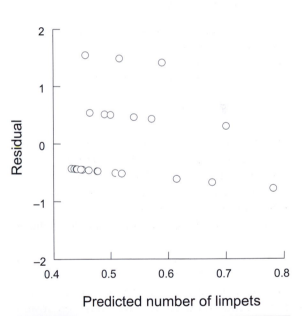

Figure 5.11 Example of parallel lines in a residual plot. Data from Peake & Quinn (1993), where the abundance of the limpets (*Cellana tramoserica*) was the response variable, area of mussel clump was the predictor variable and there were $n = 25$ clumps.

then the points in the residual plot will fall along two such parallel lines although OLS regression is probably an inappropriate technique for these data and a generalized linear model with a binomial error term (e.g. logistic regression) should be used (Chapter 13). The example in Figure 5.11 is from Peake & Quinn (1993), where the response variable (number of limpets per mussel clump) only takes three values: zero, one or two.

5.3.11 Transformations

When continuous variables have particular skewed distributions, such as lognormal or Poisson, transformations of those variables to a different scale will often render their distributions closer to normal (Chapter 4). When fitting linear regression models, the assumptions underlying OLS interval estimation and hypothesis testing of model parameters refer to the error terms from the model and, therefore, the response variable (Y). Transformations of Y can often be effective if the distribution of Y is nonnormal and the variance of y_i differs for each x_i, especially when variance clearly increases as x_i increases. For example, variance heterogeneity for the linear model relating number of individuals of macroinvertebrates to mussel clump area was greatly reduced after transformation of Y (and also X – see below and compare Figure 5.19 and Figure 5.20). Our comments in Chapter 4 about the choice of transformations and the interpretation of analyses based on transformed data are then relevant to the response variable.

The assumption that the x_i are fixed values chosen by the investigator suggests that transformations of the predictor variable would not be warranted. However, regression analyses in biology are nearly always based on both Y and X being random variables, with our conclusions conditional on the x_i observed in our sample or we use a Model II analysis (Section 5.3.14). Additionally, our discussion of regression diagnostics shows us that unusual X-values determine leverage and can cause an observation to have undue influence on the estimated regression coefficient. Transformations of X should also be considered to improve the fit of the model and transforming both Y and X is sometimes more effective than just transforming Y.

The other use of transformations in linear regression analysis is to linearize a nonlinear relationship between Y and X (Chapter 4). When we have a clear nonlinear relationship, we can use nonlinear regression models or we can approximate the nonlinearity by including polynomial terms in a linear model (Chapter 6). An alternative approach that works for some nonlinear relationships is to transform one or both variables to make a simple linear model an appropriate fit to the data. Nonlinear relationships that can be made linear by simple transformations of the variables are sometimes termed "intrinsically linear" (Rawlings et al. 1998); for example, the relationship between the number of species and area of an island can be modeled with a nonlinear power function or a simple linear model after log transformation of both variables (Figure 5.17 and Figure 5.18). If there is no evidence of variance heterogeneity, then it is best just to transform X to try and linearize the relationship (Neter et al. 1996). Transforming Y in this case might actually upset error terms that are already normally distributed with similar variances. The relationship between number of species and area of mussel clump from Peake & Quinn (1993) illustrates this point, as a log transformation of just clump area (X) results in a linear model that best fits the data although both variables were transformed in the analysis (Box 5.4). However, nonlinearity is often associated with non-normality of the response variable and transformations of Y and/or Y and X might be required.

Remember that the interpretation of our regression model based on transformed variables, and any predictions from it, must be in terms of transformed Y and/or X, e.g. predicting log number of species from log clump area, although predictions can be back-transformed to the original scale of measurement if required.

5.3.12 Regression through the origin

There are numerous situations when we know that Y must equal zero when X equals zero. For example, the number of species of macroinvertebrates per clump of mussels on a rocky shore must be zero if that clump has no area (Peake & Quinn 1993), the weight of an organism must be zero when the length of that organism is zero etc. It might be tempting in these circumstances to force our regression line through the origin (Y equals zero, X equals zero) by fitting a linear model without an intercept term:

$$y_i = \beta_1 x_i + \varepsilon_i \qquad (5.14)$$

There are several difficulties when trying to interpret the results of fitting such a no-intercept model. First, our minimum observed x_i rarely extends to zero, and forcing our regression line through the origin not only involves extrapolating the regression line outside our data range but also assuming the relationship is linear outside this range (Cade & Terrell 1997, Neter et al. 1996). If we know biologically that Y must be zero when X is zero, yet our fitted regression line has an intercept different to zero, it suggests that the relationship between Y and X is nonlinear, at least for small values of X. We recommend that it is better to have a model that fits the observed data well than one that goes through the origin but provides a worse fit to the observed data.

Second, although residuals from the no-intercept model are $(y_i - \hat{y}_i)$ as usual, they no longer sum to zero, and the usual partition of SS_{Total} into $SS_{Regression}$ and $SS_{Residual}$ doesn't work. In fact, the $SS_{Residual}$ can be greater than SS_{Total} (Neter et al. 1996). For this reason, most statistical software presents the partitioning of the variance in terms of $SS_{Total\ uncorrected}$ (Section 5.3.4) that will always be larger than $SS_{Residual}$. However, the value of r^2 for a no-intercept model determined from $SS_{Total\ uncorrected}$ will not be comparable to r^2 from the full model calculated using SS_{Total} (Cade & Terrell 1997, Kvalseth 1985). The residuals are still comparable and the $MS_{Residual}$ is probably better for comparing the fit of models with and without an intercept (Chatterjee & Price 1991).

If a model with an intercept is fitted first and the test of the H_0 that β_0 equals zero is not rejected, there may be some justification for fitting a no-intercept model. For example, Caley & Schluter (1997) examined the relationship between local species richness (response variable) and regional species richness (predictor variable) for a number of taxa and geographic regions at two spatial scales of sampling (1% of region and 10% of region). They argued that local species richness must be zero when regional richness was zero and that no-intercept models were appropriate.

Re-analysis of their data showed that when a model with an intercept was fitted to each combination of region and spatial scale, the test of the H_0 that β_0 equals zero was not rejected and the $MS_{Residual}$ was always less for a no-intercept model than a model with an intercept. This indicates that the no-intercept model was probably a better fit to the observed data. So no-intercept models were justified in this case, although we note that the estimates of β_1 were similar whether or not an intercept was included in the models.

Generally, however, we recommend against fitting a model without an intercept. The interpretation is more difficult and we must assume linearity of the relationship between Y and X beyond the range of our observed data.

5.3.13 Weighted least squares

The usual OLS approach for linear regression assumes that the variances of ε_i (and therefore the y_i) are equal, i.e. the homogeneity of variance assumption discussed in Section 5.3.8. If the variance of y_i varies for each x_i, we can weight each observation by the reciprocal of an estimate of its variance (σ_i^2):

$$w_i = \frac{1}{s_i^2} \qquad (5.18)$$

We then fit our linear regression model using generalized least squares which minimizes $\sum_{i=1}^{n} w_i (y_i - \hat{y}_i)^2$. This is the principle of weighted least squares (Chaterjee & Price 1991, Myers 1990, Neter et al. 1996). The difficulty is calculating the w_i because we can't calculate s_i^2 unless we have replicate Y-values at each x_i. One approach is to group nearby observations and calculate s_i^2 (Rawlings et al. 1998), although there are no clear guidelines for how many observations to include in each group. A second approach uses the absolute value of each residual ($|e_i|$) from the OLS regression as an estimate of σ_i. Neter et al. (1996) suggested that the predicted values from an OLS regression of $|e_i|$ against x_i could be used to calculate the weights for each observation, where w_i is the inverse of the square of this predicted value. These weights can be used in statistical software with a weighted least squares option or, equivalently, OLS regression used once y_i and x_i in each pair has been multiplied (i.e. weighted) by w_i.

Box 5.7 | Model II regression.

For the data from Christensen *et al.* (1996), both the response variable (CWD basal area) and the predictor variable (riparian tree density) are random. These variables are measured in different units, so reduced major axis (RMA; also called standard major axis) and ranged MA regression are appropriate. We used the program "Model II regression" from Pierre Legendre at the University of Montreal.

Statistic	RMA	Ranged MA	OLS
b_1	0.145	0.164	0.116
95% CI	0.103 to 0.204	0.109 to 0.275	0.065 to 0.166
b_0	−113.904	−137.108	−77.099
95% CI	−187.152 to −61.767	−275.514 to −70.160	−142.747 to −11.451

The correlation coefficient was nearly 0.8, so we would not expect much difference in the estimates of the regression slope. The estimated regression slope from the RMA model and the ranged MA model were both larger than the OLS estimate, and, not surprisingly, the estimates of the intercept also differed. Note that the width of the confidence interval for β_1 was the same for RMA and OLS, but wider for ranged MA. A randomization test of the H_0 that β_1 equals zero for ranged MA resulted in a P value of 0.001. The test for the OLS regression is the same as the test for the correlation coefficient and provides a test for the RMA slope, with a P value less than 0.001.

Weighted least squares seems to have been rarely applied in the biological literature, most biologists including us preferring to transform one or both variables to meet the assumption of homogeneity of variance or else use generalized linear models (Chapter 13).

5.3.14 *X* random (Model II regression)

The linear regression model we have been using in this chapter is sometimes called Model I regression because *X* is a fixed variable, i.e. the x_i are fixed values set by the investigator and a new sample of observations from the population would use the same x_i. As we have previously discussed, most applications of linear regression in biology are unlikely to involve fixed *X*-values. Although we can usually conceptually distinguish a response variable (*Y*) from a predictor variable (*X*), the (x_i, y_i) pairs are commonly a sample from a bivariate distribution of two random variables, *X* and *Y*. For example, number of species per clump and area of mussel clump were clearly both random variables in the study by Peake & Quinn (1993) because clumps were chosen haphazardly from the shore and both variables recorded from each clump. Fitting a linear regression model for *Y* on *X* to data where both variables are random, and assumed to be jointly distributed with a bivariate normal distribution has been termed Model II regression (Legendre & Legendre 1998, Sokal & Rohlf 1995). It is a topic of some controversy and there are several ways of looking at the problem.

If the main aim of our regression analysis is prediction, then we can use the usual OLS regression model when *Y* and *X* are random as long as the probability distributions of y_i at each x_i are normal and independent. We must constrain our inferences about *Y* to be conditional given particular values of *X* (Neter *et al.* 1996).

If the main aim of our regression analysis is not prediction but to describe the true nature of the relationship between *Y* and *X* (i.e. estimate β_1), then OLS regression might not be appropriate. There is error variability associated with both *Y* (σ_ε^2) and *X* (σ_δ^2) and the OLS estimate of β_1 is biased towards zero (Box 5.7). The extent of the bias depends on the ratio of these error variances

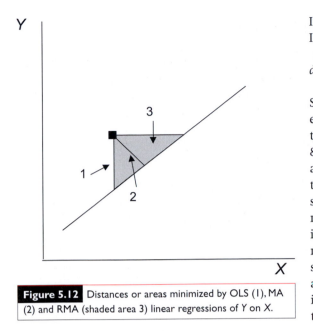

Figure 5.12 Distances or areas minimized by OLS (1), MA (2) and RMA (shaded area 3) linear regressions of Y on X.

(Legendre & Legendre 1998, Prairie *et al.* 1995, Snedecor & Cochran 1989):

$$\lambda = \frac{\sigma_\varepsilon^2}{\sigma_\delta^2} \tag{5.19}$$

If X is fixed then σ_δ^2 equals zero and the usual OLS estimate of β_1 is unbiased; the greater the error variability in X relative to Y, the greater the downward bias in the OLS estimate of β_1. Remember that the usual OLS regression line is fitted by minimizing the sum of squared vertical distances from each observation to the fitted line (Figure 5.12). Here, σ_δ^2 equals zero (fixed X) and λ equals ∞. The choice of method for estimating a linear regression model when both Y and X are random variables depends on our best guess of the value of λ, which will come from our knowledge of the two variables, the scales on which they are measured and their sample variances.

Major axis (MA) regression is estimated by minimizing the sum of squared perpendicular distances from each observation to the fitted line (Figure 5.12). For MA regression, σ_ε^2 is assumed to equal σ_δ^2 so λ equals one. The calculation of the estimate of the slope of the regression model is a little tedious, although it can be calculated using the estimate of the slope of the Model I regression and the correlation coefficients:

$$b_{1(MA)} = \frac{d \pm \sqrt{d^2 + 4}}{2} \tag{5.20}$$

If r is +ve, use the +ve square root and vice versa. In Equation 5.20:

$$d = \frac{b_{1(OLS)}^2 - r^2}{r^2 b_{1(OLS)}} \tag{5.21}$$

Standard errors and confidence intervals are best estimated by bootstrapping and a randomization test used for testing the H_0 of zero slope. Legendre & Legendre (1988) argued that MA regression was appropriate when both variables are measured on the same scales with the same units, or are dimensionless. They described a modification of MA regression, termed ranged MA regression. The variables are standardized by their ranges, the MA regression calculated, and then the regression slope is back-transformed to the original scale. The advantage of ranged MA regression is that the variables don't need to be in comparable units and a test of the H_0 of zero slope is possible (see below).

Reduced major axis (RMA) regression, also called the standard major axis (SMA) regression by Legendre & Legendre (1998), is fitted by minimizing the sum of areas of the triangles formed by vertical and horizontal lines from each observation to the fitted line (Figure 5.12). For RMA regression, it is assumed that σ_ε^2 and σ_δ^2 are proportional to σ_Y^2 and σ_X^2 respectively so λ equals σ_Y^2/σ_X^2. The RMA estimate of β_1 is simply the ratio of standard deviation of Y to the standard deviation of X:

$$b_1 = \frac{s_Y}{s_X} \tag{5.22}$$

This is also the average of the OLS estimate of the slope of Y on X and the reciprocal of the OLS estimate of the slope of X on Y. The standard error for the RMA estimate can be determined by bootstrapping but it turns out that the standard error of β_1 is, conveniently, the same as the standard error of the OLS estimate. Confidence intervals for β_1 can then be determined in the usual manner (Section 5.3.3). The H_0 that β_1 equals some specified value (except zero) can also be tested with a T-statistic (McArdle 1988, modified from Clarke 1980):

$$T = \frac{|\log b_1 - \log \beta_1^*|}{\sqrt{(1 - r^2)(n - 2)}} \tag{5.23}$$

where b_1 is the RMA estimate of β_1, β_1^* is the value of β_1 specified in the H_0 and the denominator is

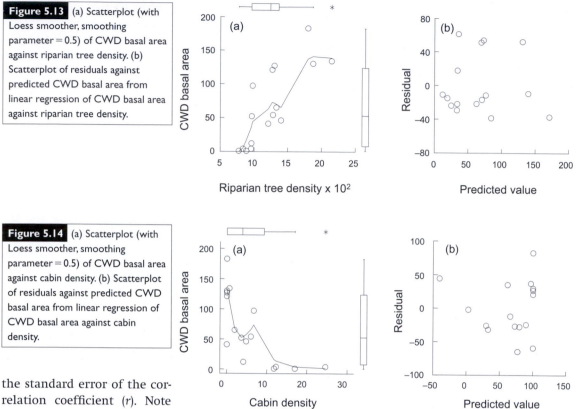

Figure 5.13 (a) Scatterplot (with Loess smoother, smoothing parameter = 0.5) of CWD basal area against riparian tree density. (b) Scatterplot of residuals against predicted CWD basal area from linear regression of CWD basal area against riparian tree density.

Figure 5.14 (a) Scatterplot (with Loess smoother, smoothing parameter = 0.5) of CWD basal area against cabin density. (b) Scatterplot of residuals against predicted CWD basal area from linear regression of CWD basal area against cabin density.

the standard error of the correlation coefficient (r). Note again the close relationship between RMA regression and the correlation coefficient. Testing β_1 against a specific non-zero value is applicable in many aspects of biology, such as the scaling of biological processes with body size of organisms (LaBarbera 1989). The H_0 that β_1 equals zero cannot be tested because log zero is undefined; the RMA regression slope is related to λ and cannot be strictly zero unless σ_Y^2 is also zero, an unlikely occurrence in practice (Legendre & Legendre 1998, McArdle 1988, Sokal & Rohlf 1995). The inability to formally test the H_0 that β_1 equals zero is actually a trivial problem because the H_0 that the population correlation coefficient (ρ) equals zero is essentially the same.

Prairie *et al.* (1995) proposed the slope-range method, which estimates β_1 when X is random from the relationship between the OLS estimate and $(1/s_X^2)$ for subsets of the data covering different ranges of X. This is a modification of methods based on instrumental variables (a third variable which may separate the data into groups). The main limitation of the method is that it needs a reasonably large sample size – at least ten potential groups in the data set with $n > 20$ in each group.

The intercepts are straightforward to calculate for any of these estimates of the slope because each regression line passes through the point ($\bar{y}$, $\bar{x}$) – see Section 5.3.3. The MA and RMA regression lines can be related to principal components analysis (see Chapter 17); the former is the first principal component of the covariance matrix between Y and X and the latter is the first principal component of the correlation matrix between Y and X. The RMA regression line is also the long axis of the bivariate confidence ellipse (Figure 5.4), indicating a close relationship between the correlation coefficient and the RMA regression line that we will elaborate on below.

Note that fitting a regression model of Y on X will produce a different OLS regression line than a regression model of X on Y for the same data because the first is minimizing deviations from the fitted line in Y and the latter is minimizing deviations from the fitted line in X. Interestingly,

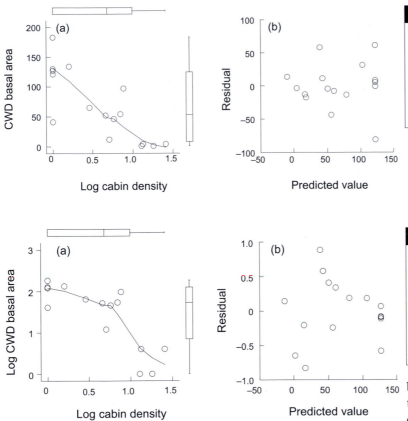

Figure 5.15 (a) Scatterplot (with Loess smoother, smoothing parameter = 0.5) of CWD basal area against $\log_{10}$ cabin density. (b) Scatterplot of residuals against predicted CWD basal area from linear regression of CWD basal area against $\log_{10}$ cabin density.

Figure 5.16 (a) Scatterplot (with Loess smoother, smoothing parameter = 0.5) of $\log_{10}$ CWD basal area against $\log_{10}$ cabin density. (b) Scatterplot of residuals against predicted $\log_{10}$ CWD basal area from linear regression of $\log_{10}$ CWD basal area against $\log_{10}$ cabin density.

as pointed out by Jackson (1991), the RMA line seems to most observers a more intuitive and better "line-of-best-fit" than the OLS line since it lies half way between the OLS line for Y on X and the OLS line for X on Y.

Simulations by McArdle (1988) comparing OLS, MA and RMA regression analyses when X is random showed two important results. First, the RMA estimate of β_1 is less biased than the MA estimate and is preferred, although he did not consider the ranged MA method. Second, if the error variability in X is more than about a third of the error variability in Y, then RMA is the preferred method; otherwise OLS is acceptable. As the correlation coefficient between Y and X approaches one (positive or negative), the difference between the OLS and RMA estimates of β_1, and therefore the difference between the fitted regression lines, gets smaller. Legendre & Legendre (1998) preferred the ranged MA over RMA, partly because the former permits a direct test of the H_0 that β_1 equals zero. We don't regard this as a crucial issue

because the test of the H_0 that the correlation coefficient equals zero is the same test. A more sophisticated decision tree for choosing between methods for Model II regression is provided by Legendre & Legendre (1998), in addition to a detailed but very readable discussion of the issues.

Examples of the application of Model II regression analyses are most common in studies of scaling of aspects of biology with body size of organisms. Herrera (1992) calculated the OLS, MA and RMA estimates of the slope of the linear regression of log fruit width on log fruit length for over 90 species of plants from the Iberian Peninsula. He showed that, averaging across the species, the RMA estimate of the regression slope was greater than MA, which in turn was greater than OLS. He argued that MA regression was appropriate because the error variabilities for log width and log length were similar. Trussell (1997) used RMA regression for describing relationships between morphological characteristics (e.g. shell height, shell length, foot size, etc.) of an intertidal snail. However, he used OLS regressions to compare between shores as part of an analysis of

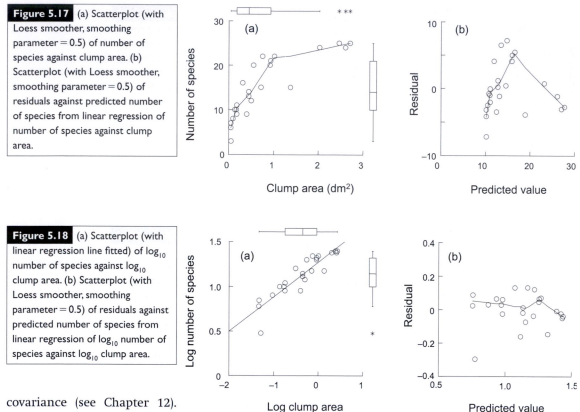

Figure 5.17 (a) Scatterplot (with Loess smoother, smoothing parameter = 0.5) of number of species against clump area. (b) Scatterplot (with Loess smoother, smoothing parameter = 0.5) of residuals against predicted number of species from linear regression of number of species against clump area.

Figure 5.18 (a) Scatterplot (with linear regression line fitted) of $\log_{10}$ number of species against $\log_{10}$ clump area. (b) Scatterplot (with Loess smoother, smoothing parameter = 0.5) of residuals against predicted number of species from linear regression of $\log_{10}$ number of species against $\log_{10}$ clump area.

covariance (see Chapter 12). Both Herrera (1992) and Trussell (1997) tested whether their regression slopes were significantly different from unity, the value predicted if the relationships were simply allometric.

It is surprising that there are not more uses of Model II regression, or acknowledgment of the potential biases of using OLS estimates when both Y and X are random, in biological research literature, particularly given the extensive discussion in the influential biostatistics text by Sokal & Rohlf (1995). This may be partly because many excellent linear models textbooks are based on examples in industry or business and marketing where the assumption of fixed X is commonly met, so the issue X being random is not discussed in detail. Also, biologists seem primarily interested in the test of the H_0 that β_1 equals zero. Since the test is identical for OLS regression of Y on X and X on Y, and both are identical to the test that the correlation coefficient (ρ) equals zero, then it essentially does not matter whether OLS or RMA regression is used for this purpose. Biologists less commonly compare their estimates of β_1 with

other values, so underestimating the true slope may not be costly.

5.3.15 Robust regression

One of the limitations of OLS is that the estimates of model parameters, and therefore subsequent hypothesis tests, can be sensitive to distributional assumptions and affected by outlying observations, i.e. ones with large residuals. Even generalized linear model analyses (GLMs; see Chapter 13) that allow other distributions for error terms besides normal, and are based on ML estimation, are sensitive to extreme observations. Robust regression techniques are procedures for fitting linear regression models that are less sensitive to deviations of the underlying distribution of error terms from that specified, and also less sensitive to extreme observations (Birkes & Dodge 1993).

Least absolute deviations (LAD)
LAD, sometimes termed least absolute residuals (LAR; see Berk 1990), is where the estimates of β_0

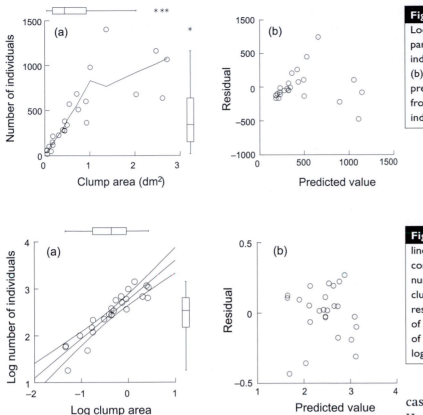

Figure 5.19 (a) Scatterplot (with Loess smoother, smoothing parameter = 0.5) of number of individuals against clump area. (b) Scatterplot of residuals against predicted number of individuals from linear regression of number of individuals against clump area.

Figure 5.20 (a) Scatterplot (with linear regression line and 95% confidence band fitted) of $\log_{10}$ number of individuals against $\log_{10}$ clump area. (b) Scatterplot of residuals against predicted number of individuals from linear regression of $\log_{10}$ number of individuals against $\log_{10}$ clump area.

and β_1 are those that minimize the sum of absolute values of the residuals:

$$\sum_{i=1}^{n} |e_i| = \sum_{i=1}^{n} |(y_i - \hat{y}_i)| \tag{5.24}$$

rather than the sum of squared residuals ($\sum_{i=1}^{n} e_i^2$) as in OLS. By not squaring the residuals, extreme observations have less influence on the fitted model. The difficulty is that the computations of the LAD estimates for β_0 and β_1 are more complex than OLS estimates, although algorithms are available (Birkes & Dodge 1993) and robust regression techniques are now common in statistical software (often as part of nonlinear modeling routines).

M-estimators

These were introduced in Chapter 2 for estimating the mean of a population. In a regression context, M-estimators involve minimizing the sum of some function of e_i, with OLS (minimizing $\sum_{i=1}^{n} e_i^2$) and LAD (minimizing $\sum_{i=1}^{n} |e_i|$) simply being special cases (Birkes & Dodge 1993). Huber M-estimators, described in Chapter 2, weight the observations differently depending how far they are from the center of the distribution. In robust regression analyses, Huber M-estimators weight the residuals (e_i) differently depending on how far they are from zero (Berk 1990) and use these new residuals to calculate adjusted Y-values. The estimates for β_0 and β_1 are those that minimize both $\sum_{i=1}^{n} e_i^2$ (i.e. OLS) when the residuals are near zero and $\sum |e_i|$ (i.e. LAD) when the residuals are far from zero. We need to choose the size of the residual at which the method switches from OLS to LAD; this decision is somewhat subjective, although recommendations are available (Huber 1981, Wilcox 1997). You should ensure that the default value used by your statistical software for robust regression seems reasonable. Wilcox (1997) described more sophisticated robust regression procedures, including an M-estimator based on iteratively reweighting the residuals. One problem with M-estimators is that the sampling distributions of the estimated coefficients are unlikely to be normal, unless sample sizes are large, and the usual calculations for standard errors, confidence intervals and hypothesis testing may not be valid (Berk 1990). Resampling methods such as bootstrap (Chapter 2) are probably the most reliable approach (Wilcox 1997).

Rank-based ("non-parametric") regression
This approach does not assume any specific distribution of the error terms but still fits the usual linear regression model. This approach might be particularly useful if either of the two variables is not normally distributed and nonlinearity is evident but transformations are either ineffective or misrepresent the underlying biological process. The simplest non-parametric regression analysis is based on the $[n(n-1)]/2$ OLS slopes of the regression lines for each pair of X values (the slope for y_1x_1 and y_2x_2, the slope for y_2x_2 and y_3x_3, the slope for y_1x_1 and y_3x_3, etc.). The non-parametric estimator of β_1 (b_1) is the median of these slopes and the non-parametric estimator of β_0 (b_0) is the median of all the $y_i - b_1x_i$ differences (Birkes & Dodge 1993, Sokal & Rohlf 1995, Sprent 1993). A t test for β_1 based on the ranks of the Y-values is described in Birkes & Dodge (1993); an alternative is to simply use Kendall's rank correlation coefficient (Sokal & Rohlf 1995).

Randomization test
A randomization test of the H_0 that β_1 equals zero can also be constructed by comparing the observed value of b_1 to the distribution of b_1 found by pairing the y_i and x_i values at random a large number of times and calculating b_1 each time (Manly 1997). The P value then is the % of values of b_1 from this distribution equal to or larger than the observed value of b_1.

5.4 | Relationship between regression and correlation

The discussion on linear regression models when both Y and X are random variables in Section 5.3.14 indicated the close mathematical and conceptual similarities between linear regression and correlation analysis. We will formalize those similarities here, summarizing points we have made throughout this chapter. The population slope of the linear regression of Y on X (β_{YX}) is related to the correlation between Y and X (ρ_{YX}) by the ratio of the standard deviations of Y and X:

$$\beta_{YX} = \rho_{YX}\frac{\sigma_Y}{\sigma_X} \tag{5.25}$$

Therefore, the OLS estimate of β_1 from the linear regression model for Y on X is:

$$b_{YX} = r_{YX}\frac{s_Y}{s_X} \tag{5.26}$$

The equivalent relationship also holds for the population slope of the linear regression of X on Y with the ratio of standard deviations reversed. Therefore the sample correlation coefficient between Y and X can be calculated from the standardized slope of the OLS regression of Y on X (Rodgers & Nicewander 1988).

These relationships between regression slopes and correlation coefficients result in some interesting equivalencies in hypothesis tests. The test of the H_0 that β_{YX} equals zero is also identical to the test of the H_0 that β_{XY} equals zero, although the estimated values of the regression slopes will clearly be different. These tests that β_{YX} or β_{XY} equal zero are also identical to the test of the H_0 that ρ_{YX} equals zero, i.e. the test of the OLS regression slope of Y on X is identical to the test of the OLS regression slope of X on Y and both are identical to the test of the Pearson correlation coefficient between Y and X, although neither estimated value of the slope will be the same as the estimated value of the correlation coefficient. The sample correlation coefficient is simply the geometric mean of these two regression slopes (Rodgers & Nicewander 1988):

$$r = \pm \sqrt{b_{YX}b_{XY}} \tag{5.27}$$

Simple correlation analysis is appropriate when we have bivariate data and we simply wish to measure the strength of the linear relationship (the correlation coefficient) between the two variables and test an H_0 about that correlation coefficient. Regression analysis is called for when we can biologically distinguish a response (Y) and a predictor variable (X) and we wish to describe the form of the model relating Y to X and use our estimates of the parameters of the model to predict Y from X.

5.5 | Smoothing

The standard OLS regression analysis, and the robust regression techniques, we have described in this chapter specify a particular model that we fit to our data. Sometimes we know that a linear model is an inappropriate description of the relationship between Y and X because a scatterplot shows obvious nonlinearity or because we know theoretically that some other model should apply. Other times we simply have no preconceived model, linear or nonlinear, to fit to the data and we simply want to investigate the nature of the relationship between Y and X. In both situations, we require a method for fitting a curve to the relationship between Y and X that is not restricted to a specific model structure (such as linear). Smoothers are a broad class of techniques that describe the relationship between Y and X, etc., with few constraints on the form the relationship might take (Goodall 1990, Hastie & Tibshirani 1990). The aim of the usual linear model analysis is to separate the data into two components:

$$\text{model} + \text{residual (error)} \qquad (5.28)$$

Smoothing also separates data into two components:

$$\text{smooth} + \text{rough} \qquad (5.29)$$

where the rough component should have as little information or structure as possible (Goodall 1990). The logic of smoothing is relatively simple.

- Each observation is replaced by the mean or the median of surrounding observations or the predicted value from a regression model through these local observations.
- The surrounding observations are those within a window (sometimes termed a band or a neighbourhood) that covers a range of observations along the X-axis and the X-value on which the window is centered is termed the target. The size of the window, i.e. the number of observations it includes, is determined by a smoothing parameter for most smoothers (Hastie & Tibshirani 1990).
- Successive windows overlap so that the resulting line is smooth.

- The mean or median in one window are not affected by observations in other windows so smoothers are robust to extreme observations.
- Windows at the extremes of the X-axis often extend beyond the smallest or largest X-value and must be handled differently (see Section 5.5.5).

Smoothing functions are sometimes termed non-parametric regressions; here, non-parametric refers to the absence of a specified form of the relationship between Y and X rather than the distribution of the error terms from the fit of a model. Smoothing functions don't set any specific conditions for Y or X. For example, the observations may come from a joint distribution of Y and X (both Y and X random) or X may be considered fixed (Hastie & Tibshirani 1990). There are numerous varieties of smoothers and our descriptions are based on Goodall (1990) and Hastie & Tibshirani (1990).

5.5.1 Running means

A running (moving) means (averages) smoother is determined from the means of all the observations in a window. Each window is centered on the target X-value and the remaining X-values included in the window can be determined in two ways: (i) including a fixed number of observations both sides of the target X-value, or (ii) including a fixed number of nearest observations to the target x_i irrespective of which side of the target they occur (Hastie & Tibshirani 1990, Neter et al. 1996). The latter tend to perform better (Hastie & Tibshirani 1990), especially for locally weighted smoothers (see Cleveland's Loess below). Note that any observation might be included in a number of neighbouring windows. Using running medians instead of means makes the smoothing more resistant to extreme observations, i.e. more robust (Figure 5.21(a,b)). Running means or medians have been used commonly for analyzing data from simple time series (Diggle 1990), although the resulting line is rarely smooth (Hastie & Tibshirani 1990).

5.5.2 LO(W)ESS

A simple modification of running means or medians is to calculate the OLS regression line

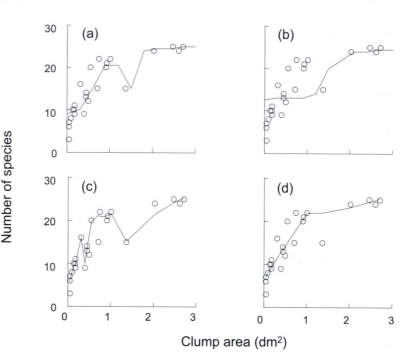

Figure 5.21 Smoothing functions through species–area data from Peake & Quinn (1993). (a) Running median smoother with smoothing parameter of 0.25, (b) running median smoother with smoothing parameter of 0.75, (c) Loess smoother with smoothing parameter of 0.25, and (d) Loess smoother with smoothing parameter of 0.75. Plotted in SYSTAT.

within a window and replace the observed y_i with that predicted by the local regression line for the target X-value. A modification of this approach is locally weighted regression scatterplot smoothing (Loess or Lowess; Cleveland 1979, 1994; see Figure 5.21). Here, the observations in a window are weighted differently depending on how far they are from the target X-value using a tri-cube weight function (see Hastie & Tibshirani 1990 and Trexler & Travis 1993 for details). In essence, observations further from the target X-value are downweighted compared with values close to the target X-value (Goodall 1990). Further refinement can be achieved by repeating the smoothing process a number of times during which observations with large residuals (difference between observed y_i and those predicted by the smooth) are downweighted. The final Loess smooth is often an excellent representation of the relationship between Y and X, although the choice of smoothing parameter (window size) can be important for interpretation (see Section 5.5.5). A related smoother is distance weighted least squares (DWLS) that also weights observations differently within each window. DWLS is slightly less sensitive to extreme observations than Loess for a given smoothing parameter.

5.5.3 Splines

Splines approach the smoothing problem by fitting polynomial regressions (see Chapter 6), usually cubic polynomials, in each window. The final smoother is termed a piecewise polynomial.

The windows are separated at user-defined break-points termed knots and the polynomials within each window are forced to be continuous between windows, i.e. two adjacent polynomials join smoothly at a knot (Hastie & Tibshirani 1990). The computations are complex and a rationale for the choice of the number of knots, that will influence the shape of the smooth, is not obvious. Our experience is that regression splines are less useful than Loess smoothers as an exploratory tool for bivariate relationships.

5.5.4 Kernels

We have already discussed kernel functions as non-parametric estimators of univariate (Chapter 2) and bivariate (Section 5.1.3) probability density functions. Hastie & Tibshirabni (1990) also described a kernel smoother for Y versus X relationships. Within a window, observations are weighted based on a known function (e.g. normal distribution), termed the kernel, so that the weights decrease the further the observation is from the target X-value (just like in Loess smoothing). The estimated smoother results from the means of the Y-values within each window. Again, a smoothing parameter sets the size of the window and this, along with the kernel (the function that sets the weights of the observations within each window), are defined by the user. Kernels are not often used as smoothers for estimating the relationship between Y and X but are useful as more general univariate or bivariate density estimators.

5.5.5 Other issues

All the above smoothers describe the relationship between Y and X, and a predicted Y-value ($\hat{y}_i$) can be determined for each x_i. Therefore, residuals ($y_i - \hat{y}_i$) can also be calculated for each observation, and are produced from some statistical software. These residuals can be used in a diagnostic fashion to assess the fit of the smooth to the data, similar to the methods described in Section 5.3.10 for OLS linear regression. In particular, large residuals might indicate influential observations, although most smoothing techniques are considered robust to outliers because the components of the smoother are fitted to local observations within windows. Also, standard errors for $\hat{y}_i$ can be determined using bootstrap techniques (Efron & Tibshirani 1991; Chapter 2) and hypotheses about $\hat{y}_i$ tested with randomization procedures (Chapter 3).

There are several important issues related to the practical application of all the smoothers described here. First, whichever smoothing method is used, an important decision for the user is the value for the smoothing parameter, i.e. how many observations to include in each window. Hastie & Tibshirani (1990) have discussed this in some detail. Increasing the number of observations in each window (larger smoothing parameter) produces a flatter and "smoother" smooth that has less variability (Figure 5.21(a,c)) but is less likely to represent the real relationship between Y and X well (the smooth is probably biased). In contrast, fewer observations in each window (smaller smoothing parameter) produces a "jerkier", more variable, smooth (Figure 5.21(b,d)) but which may better match the pattern in the data (less biased). Hastie & Tibshirani (1990) have described complex, data-based methods for choosing the smoothing parameter (window-size) and producing a smooth that best minimizes both variance and bias. These methods might be useful if low variance is important because the smooth is being used as part of a modeling process, e.g.

generalized additive modeling (GAM; see Chapter 13). Lower variance will result in predictions from such models being more precise. Trexler & Travis (1993) recommended the approach of Cleveland (1994) for Loess smoothing whereby the smoothing parameter (window-size) is as large as possible without resulting in any relationship between the residuals and X. In our experience, such a relationship is not common irrespective of the value of the smoothing parameter so this recommendation does not always work. Since smoothers are most commonly used as an exploratory tool rather than for model-fitting, we recommend trying different values of smoothing functions as part of the phase of exploring patterns in data before formal analyses.

A second issue is what we do when the endpoints (the smallest and largest X-values) are the targets, because their windows will usually exceed the range of the data. Goodall (1990) suggested a step-down rule so that the window size decreases as the largest and smallest X-values are approached, although he emphasized that definitive recommendations are not possible.

In summary, smoothing functions have a number of applications. First, they are very useful for graphically describing a relationship between two variables when we have no specific model in mind. Second, they can be used as a diagnostic check of the suitability of a linear model or help us decide which form of nonlinear model might be appropriate. Third, they can be used for modeling and prediction, particularly as part of generalized additive models (Chapter 13).

5.6 | Power of tests in correlation and regression

Since H_0s about individual correlation and regression coefficients are tested with t tests, power calculations are relatively straightforward based on non-central t distributions (Neter *et al.* 1996; see also Chapters 3 and 7). In an *a priori* context, the question of interest is "How many observations do we need to be confident (at a specified level, i.e. power) that we will detect a regression slope of a certain size if it exists, given a preliminary estimate of σ_ε^2?" Equivalent questions can be phrased for correlation coefficients. As always with power analyses, the difficult part is determining what effect size, e.g. size of regression slope, is important (see Chapter 7).

5.7 | General issues and hints for analysis

5.7.1 General issues

- Estimating and testing correlations are straightforward for linear (straight-line) relationships. Use robust methods (e.g. non-parametric) if relationships are nonlinear but monotonic.
- Classical linear regression models fitted by OLS assume that X is a fixed variable (Model I). In biology, both Y and X are usually random (Model II) and alternative methods are available for estimating the slope. Even with X random, predictions and tests of hypotheses about the regression slope can be based on Model I analyses.
- The null hypothesis that the slope of the Model I regression equals zero can be tested with either a t test or an ANOVA F-ratio test. The conclusions will be identical and both are standard output from statistical software. These are also identical to the tests of the null hypotheses that the correlation coefficient equals zero and the slope of the RMA (Model II) regression equals zero.
- The standardized regression slope provides a measure of the slope of the linear relationship between the response and the predictor variable that is independent of their units.
- The assumptions of linear regression analysis (normality, homogeneity of variance, independence) apply to the error terms from the model and also to the response variable. Violations of these assumptions, especially homogeneity of variances and independence, can have important consequences for estimation and testing of the linear regression model.

- If transformations are ineffective or inapplicable, robust regression based on M-estimation or on ranks should be considered to deal with outliers and influential observations.
- Smoothing functions are very useful exploratory tools, suggesting the type of model that may be most appropriate for the data, and also for presentation, describing the relationship between two variables without being constrained by a specific model.

5.7.2 Hints for analysis

- Tests of null hypotheses for non-zero values of the correlation coefficient are tricky because of complex distribution of r; use procedures based on Fishers's z transformation.
- A scatterplot should always be the first step in any correlation or simple regression analysis. When used in conjunction with a smoothing function (e.g. Loess), scatterplots can reveal nonlinearity, unequal variances and outliers.
- As always when fitting linear models, use diagnostic plots to check assumptions and adequacy of model fit. For linear regression, plots of residuals against predicted values are valuable checks for homogeneity of residual variances. Checks for autocorrelation, especially if the predictor variable represents a time sequence, should also precede any formal analysis. Cook's D_i statistic (or DFITS$_i$) is a valuable measure of the influence each observation has on the fitted model.
- Transformations of either or both variables can greatly improve the fit of linear regression models to the data and reduce the influence of outliers. Try transforming the response variable to correct for non-normality and unequal variances and the predictor if variances are already roughly constant.
- Think carefully before using a no-intercept model. Forcing the model through the origin is rarely appropriate and renders measures of fit (e.g. r^2) difficult to interpret.

Chapter 6

Multiple and complex regression

In Chapter 5, we examined linear models with a single continuous predictor variable. In this chapter, we will discuss more complex models, including linear models with multiple predictor variables and models where one predictor interacts with itself in a polynomial term, and also nonlinear models. Note that this chapter will assume that you have read the previous chapter on bivariate relationships because many aspects of multiple regression are simply extensions from bivariate (simple) regression.

6.1 | Multiple linear regression analysis

A common extension of simple linear regression is the case where we have recorded more than one predictor variable. When all the predictor variables are continuous, the models are referred to as multiple regression models. When all the predictor variables are categorical (grouping variables), then we are dealing with analysis of variance (ANOVA) models (Chapters 8–11). The distinction between regression and ANOVA models is not always helpful as general linear models can include both continuous and categorical predictors (Chapter 12). Nonetheless, the terminology is entrenched in the applied statistics, and the biological, literature. We will demonstrate multiple regression with two published examples.

Relative abundance of C_3 and C_4 plants
Paruelo & Lauenroth (1996) analyzed the geographic distribution and the effects of climate variables on the relative abundance of a number of plant functional types (PFTs) including shrubs, forbs, succulents (e.g. cacti), C_3 grasses and C_4 grasses. The latter PFTs represent grasses that utilize the C from the atmosphere differently in photosynthesis and are expected to have different responses to CO_2 and climate change. They used data from 73 sites across temperate central North America and calculated the relative abundance of each PFT, based on cover, biomass and primary production, at each site. These relative abundance measures for each PFT were the response variables. The predictor variables recorded for each site included longitude and latitude (centesimal degrees), mean annual temperature (°C), mean annual precipitation (mm), the proportion of precipitation falling in winter between December and February, the proportion of precipitation falling in summer between June and August, and a categorical variable representing biome (one for grassland, two for shrubland). The analyses of these data are in Box 6.1.

Abundance of birds in forest patches
Understanding which aspects of habitat and human activity affect the biodiversity and abundance of organisms within remnant patches of forest is an important aim of modern conservation biology. Loyn (1987) was interested in what characteristics of habitat were related to the abundance and diversity of forest birds. He selected 56 forest patches in southeastern Victoria, Australia, and recorded the number of species and abundance of forest birds in each patch as two response variables. The predictor variables recorded for

Box 6.1 | Worked example of multiple linear regression: relative abundance of plant functional types

Paruelo & Lauenroth (1996) analyzed the geographic distribution and the effects of climate variables on the relative abundance of a number of plant functional types (PFTs) including shrubs, forbs, succulents (e.g. cacti), C_3 grasses and C_4 grasses. There were 73 sites across North America. The variables of interest are the relative abundance of C_3 plants, the latitude in centesimal degrees (LAT), the longitude in centesimal degrees (LONG), the mean annual precipitation in mm (MAP), the mean annual temperature in °C (MAT), the proportion of MAP that fell in June, July and August (JJAMAP) and the proportion of MAP that fell in December, January and February (DJFMAP). The relative abundance of C_3 plants was positively skewed and transformed to $\log_{10} + 0.1$ ($\log_{10}C_3$).

A correlation matrix between the predictor variables indicated that some predictors are strongly correlated.

	LAT	LONG	MAP	MAT	JJAMAP	DJFMAP
LAT	1.00					
LONG	0.097	1.000				
MAP	−0.247	−0.734	1.000			
MAT	−0.839	−0.213	0.355	1.000		
JJAMAP	0.074	−0.492	0.112	−0.081	1.000	
DJFMAP	−0.065	0.771	−0.405	0.001	−0.792	1.00

Note the high correlations between LAT and MAT, LONG and MAP, and JJAMAP and DJFMAP, suggesting that collinearity may be a problem with this analysis.

With six predictor variables, a linear model with all possible interactions would have 64 model terms (plus an intercept) including four-, five- and six-way interactions that are extremely difficult to interpret. As a first pass, we fitted an additive model:

$$(\log_{10}C_3)_i = \beta_0 + \beta_1(\text{LAT})_i + \beta_2(\text{LONG})_i + \beta_3(\text{MAP})_i + \beta_4(\text{MAT})_i + \beta_5(\text{JJAMAP})_i + \beta_6(\text{DJFMAP})_i + \varepsilon_i$$

Coefficient	Estimate	Standard error	Standardized coefficient	Tolerance	t	P
Intercept	−2.689	1.239	0		−2.170	0.034
LAT	0.043	0.010	0.703	0.285	4.375	<0.001
LONG	0.007	0.010	0.136	0.190	0.690	0.942
MAP	<0.001	<0.001	0.181	0.357	1.261	0.212
MAT	−0.001	0.012	−0.012	0.267	−0.073	0.942
JJAMAP	−0.834	0.475	−0.268	0.316	−1.755	0.084
DJFMAP	−0.962	0.716	−0.275	0.175	−1.343	0.184

It is clear that collinearity is a problem with tolerances for two of the predictors (LONG & DJFMAP) approaching 0.1.

Paruelo & Lauenroth (1996) separated the predictors into two groups for their analyses. One group included LAT and LONG and the other included MAP, MAT, JJAMAP and DJFMAP. We will focus on the relationship between log-transformed relative abundance of C_3 plants and latitude and longitude. We fitted a multiplicative model including an interaction term that measured how the relationship between C_3 plants and latitude could vary with longitude and vice versa:

$$(\log_{10}C_3)_i = \beta_0 + \beta_1(LAT)_i + \beta_2(LONG)_i + \beta_3(LAT \times LONG)_i + \varepsilon_i$$

Coefficient	Estimate	Standard error	Tolerance	t	P
Intercept	7.391	3.625		2.039	0.045
LAT	−0.191	0.091	0.003	−2.102	0.039
LONG	−0.093	0.035	0.015	−2.659	0.010
LAT × LONG	0.002	0.001	0.002	2.572	0.012

Note the very low tolerances indicating high correlations between the predictor variables and their interactions. An indication of the effect of collinearity is that if we omit the interaction and refit the model, the partial regression slope for latitude changes sign. We refitted the multiplicative model after centring both LAT and LONG.

Coefficient	Estimate	Standard error	Tolerance	t	P
Intercept	−0.553	0.027		20.130	<0.001
LAT	0.048	0.006	0.829	8.483	<0.001
LONG	−0.003	0.004	0.980	−0.597	0.552
LAT × LONG	0.002	0.001	0.820	2.572	0.012

Now the collinearity problem has disappeared. Diagnostic checks of the model did not reveal any outliers nor influential values. The boxplot of residuals was reasonably symmetrical and although there was some heterogeneity in spread of residuals when plotted against predicted values, and a 45° line representing sites with zero abundance of C_3 plants, this was not of a form that could be simply corrected (Figure 6.2).

The estimated partial regression slope for the interaction hasn't changed and we would reject the H_0 that there is no interactive effect of latitude and longitude on log-transformed relative abundance of C_3 plants. This interaction is evident in the DWLS smoother fitted to the scatterplot of relative abundance of C_3 plants against latitude and longitude (Figure 6.11). If further interpretation of this interaction is required, we would then calculate simple slopes for relative abundance of C_3 plants against latitude for specific values of longitude or vice versa. We will illustrate the simple slopes analysis with Loyn's (1987) data in Box 6.2.

Out of interest, we also ran the full model with all six predictors through both a forward and backward selection routine for stepwise multiple regression. For both methods, the significance level for entering and removing terms based on partial F statistics was set at 0.15.

The backward selection is as follows.

Coefficient	Estimate	Standard error	t	P
JJAMAP	−1.002	0.433	−2.314	0.024
DJFMAP	−1.005	0.486	−2.070	0.042
LAT	0.042	0.005	8.033	<0.001

The forward selection is as follows.

Coefficient	Estimate	Standard error	t	P
MAP	<0.001	<0.001	1.840	0.070
LAT	0.044	0.005	66.319	<0.001

Note the marked difference in the final model chosen by the two methods, with only latitude (LAT) in common.

each patch included area (ha), the number of years since the patch was isolated by clearing (years), the distance to the nearest patch (km), the distance to the nearest larger patch (km), an index of stock grazing history from 1 (light) to 5 (heavy), and mean altitude (m). The analyses of these data are in Box 6.2.

6.1.1 Multiple linear regression model

Consider a set of $i = 1$ to n observations where each observation was selected because of its specific X-values, i.e. the values of the p ($j = 2$ to p) predictor variables $X_1, X_2, \ldots X_j \ldots X_p$ were fixed by the investigator, whereas the Y-value for each observation was sampled from a population of possible Y-values. Note that the predictor variables are usually random in most biological research and we will discuss the implications of this in Section 6.1.17. The multiple linear regression model that we usually fit to the data is:

$$y_i = \beta_0 + \beta_1 x_{i1} + \beta_2 x_{i2} + \ldots + \beta_j x_{ij} + \ldots + \beta_p x_{ip} + \varepsilon_i \tag{6.1}$$

The details of the linear regression model, including estimation of its parameters, are provided in Box 6.3.

For Loyn's (1987) data, p equals six and a linear model with all predictors would be:

(bird abundance)$_i = \beta_0 + \beta_1$(patch area)$_i +$
β_2(years isolated)$_i + \beta_3$(nearest patch distance)$_i +$
β_4(nearest large patch distance)$_i +$
β_5(stock grazing)$_i + \beta_6$(altitude)$_i + \varepsilon_i$ (6.2)

Using the data from Paruelo & Lauenroth (1996), we might fit a model where p equals two to represent geographic pattern of C_3 grasses:

(relative abundance of C_3 grasses)$_i = \beta_0 +$
β_1(latitude)$_i + \beta_2$(longitude)$_i + \varepsilon_i$ (6.3)

A multiple regression model cannot be represented by a two-dimensional line as in simple regression and a multidimensional plane is needed (Figure 6.1). We can only graphically present such a model with two predictor variables although such graphs are rarely included in research publications.

Note that this is an additive model where all the explained variation in Y is due to the additive effects of the response variables. This model does not allow for interactions (multiplicative effects) between the predictor variables, although such interactions are possible (even likely) and will be discussed in Section 6.1.12.

We have the following in models 6.1 and 6.3.

y_i is the value of Y for the ith observation when the predictor variable X_1 equals x_{i1}, X_2 equals x_{i2}, X_j equals x_{ij}, etc.

$\beta_0, \beta_1, \beta_2, \beta_j$ etc. are population parameters, also termed regression coefficients, where

β_0 is the population intercept, e.g. the true mean value of the relative abundance of C_3 grasses when latitude and longitude equal zero.

β_1 is the population slope for Y on X_1 holding X_2, X_3, etc., constant. It measures the change in relative abundance of C_3 grasses for a one

Box 6.2 | Worked example of multiple linear regression: abundance of birds in forest patches

Loyn (1987) selected 56 forest patches in southeastern Victoria, Australia, and related the abundance of forest birds in each patch to six predictor variables: patch area (ha), distance to nearest patch (km), distance to nearest larger patch (km), grazing stock (1 to 5 indicating light to heavy), altitude (m) and years since isolation (years). Three of the predictor variables (patch area, distance to nearest patch or dist, distance to nearest larger patch or ldist) were highly skewed, producing observations with high leverage, so these variables were transformed to $\log_{10}$. A correlation matrix indicated some moderate correlations between predictors, especially between $\log_{10}$ dist and $\log_{10}$ ldist, $\log_{10}$ area and graze, and graze and years.

	$\log_{10}$ dist	$\log_{10}$ ldist	$\log_{10}$ area	Grazing	Altitude	Years
$\log_{10}$ dist	1.000					
$\log_{10}$ ldist	0.604	1.000				
$\log_{10}$ area	0.302	0.382	1.000			
Grazing	−0.143	−0.034	−0.559	1.000		
Altitude	−0.219	−0.274	0.275	−0.407	1.000	
Years	−0.020	0.161	−0.278	0.636	−0.233	1.000

As for the data set from Paruelo & Lauenroth (1996), a multiple linear regression model relating abundance of forest birds to all six predictor variables and their interactions would have 64 terms plus an intercept, and would be unwieldy to interpret. So an additive model was fitted:

$$(\text{bird abundance})_i = \beta_0 + \beta_1(\log_{10}\text{ area})_i + \beta_2(\log_{10}\text{ dist})_i + \beta_3(\log_{10}\text{ ldist})_i + \beta_4(\text{grazing})_i + \beta_5(\text{altitude})_i + \beta_6(\text{years})_i + \varepsilon_i$$

	Estimate	Standard error	Standardized coefficient	Tolerance	t	P
Intercept	20.789	8.285	0		2.509	0.015
$\log_{10}$ area	7.470	1.465	0.565	0.523	5.099	<0.001
$\log_{10}$ dist	−0.907	2.676	−0.035	0.604	−0.339	0.736
$\log_{10}$ ldist	−0.648	2.123	−0.035	0.498	−0.305	0.761
Grazing	−1.668	0.930	−0.229	0.396	−1.793	0.079
Altitude	0.020	0.024	0.079	0.681	0.814	0.419
Years	−0.074	0.045	−0.176	0.554	−1.634	0.109

Diagnostic checks of the model did not reveal any outliers or influential values. The response variable (bird abundance) was not skewed, the boxplot of residuals was reasonably symmetrical and although there was some heterogeneity of spread of residuals when plotted against predicted values, this was not of a form that could be simply corrected (Figure 6.3). The r^2 was 0.685, indicating that about 69% of the variation in bird abundance can be explained by this combination of predictors. Note that none of the tolerances were very low suggesting that despite some correlations among the predictors, collinearity may not be a serious issue for this data set. There was a significant positive partial regression slope for bird abundance against $\log_{10}$ area. No other partial regression slopes were significant.

Source	df	MS	F	P
Regression	6	723.513	17.754	<0.001
Residual	49	40.752		

The H_0 that all partial regression slopes equal zero was also rejected.

Now we will fit a second model to investigate possible interactions between predictor variables. A model with six predictors plus interactions is unwieldy so we will simplify the model first by omitting those predictors that contributed little to the original model ($\log_{10}$ dist, $\log_{10}$ ldist, altitude). The first two were correlated with each other and with $\log_{10}$ area anyway. Refitting the additive model with these three predictors omitted changed the estimated regression slopes of the remaining terms only slightly, suggesting that any bias in the estimates of the remaining predictors from omitting other predictors is small. This leaves us with a model with three predictors and their interactions:

$$\text{(bird abundance)}_i = \beta_0 + \beta_1(\log_{10}\text{ area})_i + \beta_2(\text{grazing})_i + \beta_3(\text{years})_i + \beta_4(\log_{10}\text{ area} \times \text{grazing})_i + \beta_5(\log_{10}\text{ area} \times \text{years})_i + \beta_6(\text{grazing} \times \text{years})_i + \beta_7(\log_{10}\text{ area} \times \text{grazing} \times \text{years})_i + \varepsilon_i$$

Tolerance values were unacceptably low (all <0.10) unless the predictor variables were centered so the model was based on centered predictors.

	Estimate	Standard error	Standardized coefficient	Tolerance	t	P
Intercept	22.750	1.152	0		19.755	<0.001
$\log_{10}$ area	8.128	1.540	0.615	0.373	5.277	<0.001
Grazing	−2.979	0.837	−0.408	0.386	−3.560	0.001
Years	0.032	0.057	0.076	0.280	0.565	0.574
$\log_{10}$ area × Grazing	2.926	0.932	0.333	0.450	3.141	0.003
$\log_{10}$ area × Years	−0.173	0.063	−0.305	0.411	−2.748	0.008
Grazing × Years	−0.101	0.035	−0.343	0.362	−2.901	0.006
$\log_{10}$ area × Grazing × Years	−0.011	0.034	−0.037	0.397	−0.329	0.743

The three-way interaction was not significant so we will focus on the two-way interactions. The $\log_{10}$ area × grazing term indicates how much the effect of grazing on bird density depends on $\log_{10}$ area. This interaction is significant, so we might want to look at simple effects of grazing on bird density for different values of $\log_{10}$ area. We chose mean $\log_{10}$ area (0.932) ± one standard deviation (0.120, 1.744). Because the three-way interaction was not significant, we simply set years since isolation to its mean value (33.25). We could also just have ignored years since isolation and calculated simple slopes as for a two predictor model and got similar patterns. The simple slopes of bird abundance against grazing for different $\log_{10}$ area values and mean of years since isolation were as follows.

Log$_{10}$ area	Simple slopes	Standard error	Standardized slope	t	P
0.120	−5.355	1.223	−0.734	−4.377	<0.001
0.932	−2.979	0.837	−0.408	−3.560	0.001
1.744	−0.603	1.024	−0.083	−0.589	0.558

As we predicted, the negative effect of grazing on bird abundance is stronger in small fragments and there is no relationship between bird abundance and grazing in the largest fragments.

Box 6.3 | **The multiple linear regression model and its parameters**

Consider a set of $i = 1$ to n observations where each observation was selected because of its specific X-values, i.e. the values of the p ($j = 2$ to p) predictor variables $X_1, X_2, ... X_j ... X_p$ were fixed by the investigator, whereas the Y-value for each observation was sampled from a population of possible Y-values. The multiple linear regression model that we usually fit to the data is:

$$y_i = \beta_0 + \beta_1 x_{i1} + \beta_2 x_{i2} + ... + \beta_j x_{ij} + ... + \beta_p x_{ip} + \varepsilon_i \tag{6.1}$$

In model 6.1 we have the following.

y_i is the value of Y for the ith observation when the predictor variable X_1 equals x_{i1}, X_2 equals x_{i2}, X_j equals x_{ij}, etc.

β_0 is the population intercept, the true mean value of Y when X_1 equals zero, X_2 equals zero, X_j equals zero, etc.

β_1 is the partial population regression slope for Y on X_1 holding X_2, X_3, etc., constant. It measures the change in Y per unit change in X_1 holding the value of all other X-variables constant.

β_2 is the partial population regression slope for Y on X_2 holding X_1, X_3, etc., constant. It measures the change in Y per unit change in X_2 holding the value of all other X-variables constant.

β_j is the partial population regression slope for Y on X_j holding X_1, X_2, etc., constant; it measures the change in Y per unit change in X_j holding the value of the other $p - 1$ X-variables constant.

ε_i is random or unexplained error associated with the ith observation. Each ε_i measures the difference between each observed y_i and the mean of y_i; the latter is the value of y_i predicted by the population regression model, which we never know. We assume that when the predictor variable X_1 equals x_{i1}, X_2 equals x_{i2}, X_j equals x_{ij}, etc., these error terms are normally distributed, their mean is zero ($E(\varepsilon_i)$ equals zero) and their variance is the same and is designated σ_ε^2. This is the assumption of homogeneity of variances. We also assume that these ε_i terms are independent of, and therefore uncorrelated with, each other. These assumptions (normality, homogeneity of variances and independence) also apply to the response variable Y when the predictor variable X_1 equals x_{i1}, X_2 equals x_{i2}, X_j equals x_{ij}, etc.

Fitting the multiple regression model to our data and obtaining estimates of the model parameters is an extension of the methods used for simple linear regression, although the computations are complex. We need to estimate the parameters (β_0, $\beta_1, \beta_2, ..., \beta_p$ and σ_ε^2) of the multiple linear regression model based on our random sample of n ($x_{i1}, x_{i2}, ..., x_{ip}, y_i$) observations. Once we have estimates of the parameters, we can determine the sample regression line:

$$\hat{y}_i = b_0 + b_1 x_{i1} + b_2 x_{i2} + ... + b_j x_{ij} + ... + b_p x_{ip}$$

where:

$\hat{y}_i$ is the value of y_i for $x_{i1}, x_{i2}, ..., x_{ij}, ..., x_{ip}$ predicted by the fitted regression line,
b_0 is the sample estimate of β_0, the Y-intercept,
$b_1, b_2, ..., b_j, ... b_p$ are the sample estimates of $\beta_1, \beta_2, ..., \beta_j, ..., \beta_p$, the partial regression slopes.

We can estimate these parameters using either (ordinary) least squares (OLS) or maximum likelihood (ML). If we assume normality, the OLS estimates of β_0, β_1, etc., are the same as the ML estimates. As with simple regression, we will focus on OLS estimation. The actual calculations for the OLS estimates of the model parameters involve solving a set of simultaneous normal equations, one for each parameter in the model, and are best represented with matrix algebra (Box 6.4).

The OLS estimates of $\beta_0, \beta_1, \beta_2$, etc., are the values that produce a sample regression line ($\hat{y}_i = b_0 + b_1 x_{i1} + b_2 x_{i2} + ... + b_j x_{ij} + ... + b_p x_{ip}$) that minimizes $\sum_{i=1}^{n}(y_i - \hat{y}_i)^2$. These are the sum of the squared deviations (SS) between each observed y_i and the value of y_i predicted by the sample regression line for each x_{ij}. Each ($y_i - \hat{y}_i$) is a residual from the fitted regression plane and represents the vertical distance between the regression plane and the Y-value for each observation (Figure 6.1). The OLS estimate of σ_ε^2 (the variance of the model error terms) is the sample variance of these residuals and is the Residual (or Error) Mean Square from the analysis of variance (Section 6.1.3).

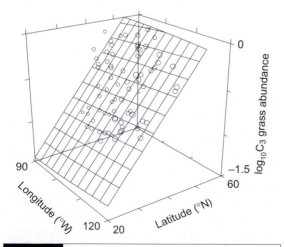

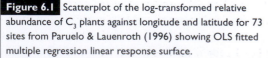

Figure 6.1 Scatterplot of the log-transformed relative abundance of C_3 plants against longitude and latitude for 73 sites from Paruelo & Lauenroth (1996) showing OLS fitted multiple regression linear response surface.

centesimal degree change in latitude, holding longitude constant.

β_2 is the population slope for Y on X_2 holding X_1, X_3, etc., constant. It measures the change in relative abundance of C_3 grasses for a one centesimal degree change in longitude, holding latitude constant.

β_j is the population slope for Y on X_j holding X_1, X_2, etc., constant; it measures the change in Y per unit change in X_j holding the value of the other $p - 1$ X-variables constant.

ε_i is random or unexplained error associated with the ith observation of relative abundance of C_3 grasses not explained by the model.

The slope parameters (β_1, $\beta_2, ..., \beta_j, ..., \beta_p$) are termed partial regression slopes (coefficients) because they measure the change in Y per unit change in a particular X holding the other $p-1$ X-variables constant. It is important to distinguish these partial regression slopes in multiple linear regression from the regression slope in simple linear regression. If we fit a simple regression model between Y and just one of the X-variables, then that slope is the change in Y per unit change in X, ignoring the other $p-1$ predictor variables we might have recorded plus any predictor variables we didn't measure. Again using the data from Paruelo & Lauenroth (1996), the partial regression slope of the relative abundance of C_3 grasses against longitude measures the change in relative abundance for a one unit (one centesimal degree) change in longitude, holding latitude constant. If we fitted a simple linear regression model for relative abundance of C_3 grasses against longitude, we completely ignore latitude and any other predictors we didn't record in the interpretation of the slope. Multiple regression models enable us to assess the relationship between the response variable and each of the predictors, adjusting for the remaining predictors.

6.1.2 Estimating model parameters

We estimate the parameters (β_0, β_1, β_2,..., β_p and σ_ε^2) of the multiple linear regression model, based on our random sample of n (x_{i1}, x_{i2},..., x_{ij},..., x_{ip}, y_i) observations, using OLS methods (Box 6.3). The fitted regression line is:

$$\hat{y}_i = b_0 + b_1 x_{i1} + b_2 x_{i2} + \ldots + b_j x_{ij} + \ldots + b_p x_{ip} \qquad (6.4)$$

where:

$\hat{y}_i$ is the value of relative abundance of C_3 grasses for x_{i1}, x_{i2},..., x_{ij},..., x_{ip} (e.g. a given combination of latitude and longitude) predicted by the fitted regression model,

b_0 is the sample estimate of β_0, the Y-intercept,

b_1, b_2,..., b_j,...b_p are the sample estimates of β_1, β_2,..., β_j,..., β_p, the partial regression slopes. We can also determine standardized partial regression slopes that are independent of the units in which the variables are measured (Section 6.1.6).

The OLS estimates of these parameters are the values that minimize the sum of squared deviations (SS) between each observed value of rel-ative abundance of C_3 grasses and the relative abundance of C_3 grasses predicted by the fitted regression model. This difference between each observed y_i and each predicted $\hat{y}_i$ is called a residual (e_i). We will use the residuals for checking the fit of the model to our data in Section 6.1.8.

The actual calculations for the OLS estimates of the model parameters involve solving a set of simultaneous normal equations (see Section 5.2.3), one for each parameter in the model, and are best represented with matrix algebra (Box 6.4). The computations are tedious but the estimates, and their standard errors, should be standard output from multiple linear regression routines in your statistical software. Confidence intervals for the parameters can also be calculated using the t distribution with $n-p$ df. New Y-values can be predicted from new values of any or all of the p X-variables by substituting the new X-values into the regression equation and calculating the predicted Y-value. As with simple regression, be careful about predicting from values of any of the X-variables outside the range of your data. Standard errors and prediction intervals for new Y-values can be determined (see Neter et al. 1996). Note that the confidence intervals for model parameters (slopes and intercept) and prediction intervals for new Y-values from new X-values depend on the number of observations and the number of predictors. This is because the divisor for the $MS_{Residual}$, and the df for the t distribution used for confidence intervals, is $n-(p+1)$. Therefore, for a given standard error, our confidence in predicted Y-values from our fitted model is reduced when we include more predictors.

6.1.3 Analysis of variance

Similar to simple linear regression models described in Chapter 5, we can partition the total variation in Y (SS_{Total}) into two additive components (Table 6.1). The first is the variation in Y explained by its linear relationship with X_1, X_2,..., X_p, termed $SS_{Regression}$. The second is the variation in Y not explained by the linear relationship with X_1, X_2,..., X_p, termed $SS_{Residual}$ and which is measured as the difference between each observed y_i and the Y-value predicted by the regression model ($\hat{y}_i$). These SS in Table 6.1 are identical to those in Table 5.1 for simple regression models. In fact, the

Box 6.4 | Matrix algebra approach to OLS estimation of multiple linear regression models and determination of leverage values

Consider an additive linear model with one response variable (Y) and p predictor variables ($X_1, X_2...X_p$) and a sample of n observations. The linear model will have $p + 1$ parameters, a slope term for each X-variable and an intercept. Let $\mathbf{Y}$ be a vector of observed Y-values with n rows, $\hat{\mathbf{Y}}$ be a vector of predicted Y-values with n rows and $\mathbf{X}$ be an $n \times (p + 1)$ matrix of the values of the X-variables (one X-variable per column) plus a column for the intercept. The linear model can be written as:

$$\mathbf{Y} = \beta\mathbf{X} + \varepsilon$$

where β is a vector of model parameters ($\beta_0, \beta_1,..., \beta_p$) with $p + 1$ rows and ε is a vector of error terms with n rows. The OLS estimate of β can be found by solving the normal equations:

$$\mathbf{X}'\mathbf{X}\mathbf{b} = \mathbf{X}'\mathbf{Y}$$

The OLS estimate of β then is:

$$\mathbf{b} = (\mathbf{X}'\mathbf{X})^{-1}(\mathbf{X}'\mathbf{Y})$$

where $\mathbf{b}$ is a vector of sample partial regression coefficients ($b_0, b_1,..., b_p$) with $p + 1$ rows. Note that $(\mathbf{X}'\mathbf{X})^{-1}$ is the inverse of $(\mathbf{X}'\mathbf{X})$ and is critical to the solution of the normal equations and hence the OLS estimates of the parameters. The calculation of this inverse is very sensitive to rounding errors, especially when there are many parameters, and also to correlations (linear dependencies – see Rawlings *et al.* 1998) among the X-variables, i.e. collinearity. Such correlations exaggerate the rounding errors problem and make estimates of the parameters unstable and their variances large (see Box 6.5).

The matrix containing the variances of, and the covariances between, the sample partial regression coefficients ($b_0, b_1,..., b_p$) is:

$$s_\mathbf{b}^2 = MS_{Residual}(\mathbf{X}'\mathbf{X})^{-1}$$

From the variances of the sample partial regression coefficients, we can calculate standard errors for each partial regression coefficient.

We can also create a matrix $\mathbf{H}$ whereby:

$$\mathbf{H} = \mathbf{X}(\mathbf{X}'\mathbf{X})^{-1}\mathbf{X}'$$

$\mathbf{H}$ is an $n \times n$ matrix, usually termed the hat matrix, whose n diagonal elements are leverage values (h_{ii}) for each observation (Neter *et al.* 1996). These leverage values measure how far an observation is from the means of the X-variables. We can then relate $\mathbf{Y}$ to $\hat{\mathbf{Y}}$ by:

$$\hat{\mathbf{Y}} = \mathbf{H}\mathbf{Y}$$

So the hat matrix transforms observed Y into predicted Y (Bollen & Jackman 1990).

Table 6.1 | Analysis of variance table for a multiple linear regression model with an intercept, p predictor variables and n observations

Source of variation	SS	df	MS
Regression	$\sum_{i=1}^{n}(\hat{y}_i - \bar{y})^2$	p	$\dfrac{\sum_{i=1}^{n}(\hat{y}_i - \bar{y})^2}{p}$
Residual	$\sum_{i=1}^{n}(y_i - \hat{y}_i)^2$	$n-p-1$	$\dfrac{\sum_{i=1}^{n}(y_i - \hat{y}_i)^2}{n-p-1}$
Total	$\sum_{i=1}^{n}(y_i - \bar{y})^2$	$n-1$	

partitioning of the SS_{Total} for the simple linear regression model is just a special case of the multiple regression model where p equals one, although the calculation of the SS for multiple regression models is more complex. These SS can be converted into variances (mean squares) by dividing by the appropriate degrees of freedom. For example, using the data from Paruelo & Lauenroth (1996) and the regression model 6.3, the SS_{Total} in relative abundance of C_3 grasses across the 73 sites is partitioned into the SS explained by the linear regression on latitude and longitude and that unexplained by this regression.

The expected values of these two mean squares are again just an extension of those we described for simple regression (Table 6.2). The expected value for $MS_{Residual}$ is σ_ε^2, the variance of the error terms (ε_i), and of y_i, which are assumed to be constant across each combination of $x_{i1}, x_{i2}, ..., x_{ij}$, etc. The expected value for $MS_{Regression}$ is more complex (Neter et al. 1996) but importantly it includes the square of each regression slope plus σ_ε^2.

6.1.4 Null hypotheses and model comparisons

The basic null hypothesis we can test when we fit a multiple linear regression model is that all the partial regression slopes equal zero, i.e. $H_0: \beta_1 = \beta_2 = ... = \beta_j = ... = 0$. For example, Paruelo &

Lauenroth (1996) might have tested the H_0 that the partial regression slopes for abundance of C_3 plants on latitude and longitude both equal zero. We test this H_0 with the ANOVA partitioning of the total variation in Y into its two components, that explained by the linear regression with X_1, X_2, etc., and the residual variation. If the H_0 is true, then $MS_{Regression}$ and $MS_{Residual}$ both estimate σ_ε^2 and their F-ratio should be one. If the H_0 is false, then at least one of the partial regression slopes does not equal zero and $MS_{Regression}$ estimates σ_ε^2 plus a positive term representing the partial regression slopes, so the F-ratio of $MS_{Regression}$ to $MS_{Residual}$ should be greater than one. So we can test this H_0 by comparing the F-ratio statistic to the appropriate F distribution, just as we did with simple linear regression in Chapter 5.

Irrespective of the outcome of this test, we would also be interested in testing null hypotheses about each partial regression coefficient, i.e. the H_0 that any β_j equals zero. We can use the process of comparing the fit of full and reduced models that we introduced in Chapter 5 to test these null hypotheses. Imagine we have a model with three predictor variables (X_1, X_2, X_3). The full model is:

$$y_i = \beta_0 + \beta_1 x_{i1} + \beta_2 x_{i2} + \beta_3 x_{i3} + \varepsilon_i \qquad (6.5)$$

Using the data from Loyn (1987), we might model the abundance of forest birds against patch area, years since isolation and grazing intensity:

$$(\text{bird abundance})_i = \beta_0 + \beta_1(\text{patch area})_i + \beta_2(\text{years isolated})_i + \beta_3(\text{stock grazing})_i + \varepsilon_i \qquad (6.6)$$

To test the H_0 that the partial regression slope for bird abundance against patch area holding years since isolation and grazing intensity constant (i.e. β_1) equals zero, we compare the fit of models 6.5 and 6.6 to the reduced models:

$$y_i = \beta_0 + \beta_2 x_{i2} + \beta_3 x_{i3} + \varepsilon_i \qquad (6.7)$$

$$(\text{bird abundance})_i = \beta_0 + \beta_2(\text{years isolated})_i + \beta_3(\text{stock grazing})_i + \varepsilon_i \qquad (6.8)$$

Models 6.7 and 6.8 assume the H_0 (β_1 equals zero) is true. If the explained variance ($SS_{Regression}$) of models 6.6 and 6.8 is not different, then there is no evidence to reject H_0; if there is an increase in explained variation for the full model compared to the reduced model, we have evidence suggesting the H_0 is false. We calculate the extra SS explained by including β_1 in the model:

$$SS_{Extra} = Full\ SS_{Regression} - Reduced\ SS_{Regression} \quad (6.9)$$

This SS_{Extra} is sometimes expressed as $SS_{Regression}(X_1|X_2,X_3)$, the increase in $SS_{Regression}$ when X_1 is added to a model already including X_2 and X_3, e.g. $SS_{Regression}$(patch area | years isolated, grazing stock). This is identical to measuring the drop in unexplained variation by omitting β_1 from the model:

$$SS_{Drop} = Reduced\ SS_{Residual} - Full\ SS_{Residual} \quad (6.10)$$

also expressed as $SS_{Residual}(X_1|X_2,X_3)$, the decrease in $SS_{Residual}$ when X_1 is added to a model already including X_2 and X_3. We convert the SS_{Extra} or SS_{Drop} into a MS by dividing by the df. There is one df in this case because we are testing a single regression parameter. In general, the df is the number of predictor variables in the full model minus the number of predictor variables in the reduced model. We can then use an F test, now termed a partial F test, to test the H_0 that a single partial regression slope equals zero:

$$F_{1,n-p} = \frac{MS_{Extra}}{Full\ MS_{Residual}} \quad (6.11)$$

For any predictor variable X_j, we can also test the H_0 that β_j equals zero with a t statistic with $(n-(p+1))$ df:

$$t = \frac{b_j}{s_{b_j}} \quad (6.12)$$

where s_{b_j} is the standard error of b_j (see Box 6.4). These t tests are standard multiple regression output from statistical software. Note that the F and t tests for a given H_0 are equivalent and F equals t^2. We prefer the F tests, however, because the model fitting procedure (comparing full and reduced models) can be used to test any subset of regression coefficients, not just a single coefficient. For example, we could calculate the $SS_{Regression}(X_2,X_3|X_1)$ to test the H_0 that β_2 equals β_3 equals zero. We just need to fit a full and a reduced (H_0 is true) model. In general, the full model will contain all the predictor variables and the reduced model omits those predictors that are specified in H_0 to be zero. In Section 6.1.15, we will

see that it is also possible to test partial regression coefficients in a sequential fashion, omitting those terms found to be not significantly different from zero from the model.

The H_0 that β_0 (population intercept) equals zero can also be tested, either with a t test or with an F test by comparing a full model with an intercept to a reduced model without. The test of zero intercept is usually of much less interest because it is testing a parameter using an estimate that is usually outside the range of our data (see Chapter 5).

6.1.5 Variance explained

The multiple r^2 is the proportion of the total variation in Y explained by the regression model:

$$r^2 = \frac{SS_{Regression}}{SS_{Total}} = 1 - \frac{SS_{Residual}}{SS_{Total}} = 1 - \frac{Full\ SS_{Residual}}{Reduced\ SS_{Residual}}$$

$$(6.13)$$

Here the reduced model is one with just an intercept and no predictor variables (i.e. $\beta_1 = \beta_2 = ... = \beta_j = ... = 0$). Interpretation of r^2 in multiple linear regression must be done carefully. Just like in simple regression, r^2 is not directly comparable between models based on different transformations (Anderson-Sprecher 1994; Chapter 5). Additionally, r^2 is not a useful measure of fit when comparing models with different numbers of, or combinations of, predictor variables (e.g. interaction terms, see Section 6.1.12). As more predictors are added to a model, r^2 cannot decrease so that models with more predictors will always appear to fit the data better. Comparing the fit of models with different numbers of predictors should use alternative measures (see Section 6.1.15).

6.1.6 Which predictors are important?

Once we have fitted our multiple linear regression model, we usually want to determine the relative importance of each predictor variable to the response variable. There are a number of related approaches for measuring relative importance of each predictor variable in multiple linear regression models.

Tests on partial regression slopes

The simplest way of assessing the relative importance of the predictors in a linear regression model is to use the F or t statistics, and their associated P values, from the tests of the null hypotheses that each β_j equals zero. These tests are straightforward to interpret but only tell us the probability of observing our sample observations or ones more extreme for these variables if the H_0 for a given predictor is true. Also, some statisticians (Neter et al. 1996, Rawlings et al. 1998) have argued that we are testing null hypotheses about a number of regression coefficients simultaneously from a single data set, so we should adjust the significance level for each test to limit the overall probability of at least one Type I error among all our tests to α. Such an adjustment will reduce the power of individual tests, and as we discussed in Chapter 3, seems unnecessarily harsh. If you deem such an adjustment necessary, however, one of the sequential Bonferroni procedures is appropriate.

Change in explained variation

The change in variation explained by the model with all predictors and the model with a specific predictor omitted is also a measure of importance of that predictor. This is basically comparing the fit of two models to the data; because the number of predictors differs between the two models, the choice of measure of fit is critical and will be discussed further when we consider model selection in Section 6.1.15. To measure the proportional reduction in the variation in Y when a predictor variable X_j is added to a model already including the other predictors (X_1 to X_p except X_j) is simply:

$$r_{X_j}^2 = \frac{SS_{Extra}}{Reduced\ SS_{Residual}} \tag{6.14}$$

where SS_{Extra} is the increase in $SS_{Regression}$, or the decrease in $SS_{Residual}$, when X_j is added to the model and Reduced $SS_{Residual}$ is unexplained SS from the model including all predictor variables except X_j. This $r_{X_j}^2$ is termed the coefficient of partial determination for X_j and its square root is the partial correlation coefficient between Y and X_j holding the other predictor variables constant (i.e. already including them in the model).

A related approach is hierarchical partitioning (Chevan & Sutherland 1991, Mac Nally 1996), which quantifies the independent correlation of each predictor variable with the response variable. It works by partitioning any measure of explained variance (e.g. r^2) into components measuring the independent contribution of each predictor. It is an important tool for multivariate inference, especially in multiple regression models, and we will describe it in more detail in Section 6.1.16.

Standardized partial regression slopes

The sizes of the individual regression slopes are difficult to compare if the predictor variables are measured in different units (see Chapter 5). We can calculate standardized regression slopes by regressing the standardized response variable against the standardized predictor variables, or alternatively, calculate for predictor X_j:

$$b_j^* = b_j \frac{s_{X_j}}{s_Y} \tag{6.15}$$

These standardized regression slopes are comparable independently of the scales on which the predictors are measured. Note that the regression model based on standardized variables doesn't include an intercept, because its OLS (and ML) estimate will always be zero. Note also that if the predictor variables are not correlated with each other, then the standardized regression slopes relating Y to each X_j are the same as the correlation coefficients relating Y to X_j.

For model 6.3, standardized regression slopes would not assist interpretation because both predictors (latitude and longitude) are in the same units (centesimal degrees). However, if we included mean annual temperature (°C) and mean annual precipitation (mm) in the model, then the magnitudes of the unstandardized regression slopes would not be comparable because of the different units, so standardization would help.

Bring (1994) suggested that the size of each standardized slope should relate to the reduction in explained variation when each predictor is omitted from the full model (see Equation 6.14). He argued that standardization should be based on partial standard deviations rather than ordinary standard deviations, so that the size of the b_j^* relates to the reduction in r^2 when that X_j is omitted from the model. The partial standard deviation of predictor variable j (X_j) is:

$$s_{X_j}^* = \frac{s_{X_j}}{\sqrt{VIF_j}} \sqrt{\frac{n-1}{n-p}} \tag{6.16}$$

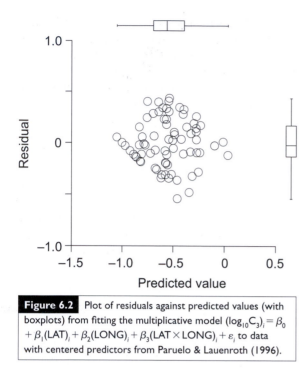

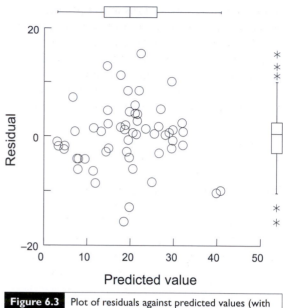
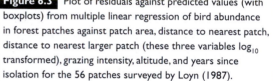

Figure 6.2 Plot of residuals against predicted values (with boxplots) from fitting the multiplicative model $(\log_{10} C_3)_i = \beta_0 + \beta_1 (\text{LAT})_i + \beta_2 (\text{LONG})_i + \beta_3 (\text{LAT} \times \text{LONG})_i + \varepsilon_i$ to data with centered predictors from Paruelo & Lauenroth (1996).

Figure 6.3 Plot of residuals against predicted values (with boxplots) from multiple linear regression of bird abundance in forest patches against patch area, distance to nearest patch, distance to nearest larger patch (these three variables $\log_{10}$ transformed), grazing intensity, altitude, and years since isolation for the 56 patches surveyed by Loyn (1987).

VIF is the variance inflation factor and will be defined in Section 6.1.11 when we examine the problem of multicollinearity. This partial standard deviation can then be incorporated in the formula for the standardized regression slope (Equation 6.15).

Regressions on standardized variables will produce coefficients (except for the intercept) that are the same as the standardized coefficients described above. The hypothesis tests on individual standardized coefficients will be identical to those on unstandardized coefficients. Standardization might be useful if the variables are on very different scales and the magnitude of coefficients for variables with small values may not indicate their relative importance in influencing the response variable. However, it is the predictor variables that are important here and standardizing the response variable may not be necessary and will make predicted values from the model more difficult to interpret. Regression models using standardized (or simply centered) predictors are very important for detecting and treating multicollinearity and interpreting interactions between predictors (Sections 6.1.11 and 6.1.12).

6.1.7 Assumptions of multiple regression

As with simple linear regression (Chapter 5), interval estimation and hypothesis tests of the parameters of the multiple linear regression model rely on a number of assumptions about the model error terms at each combination of $x_{i1}, x_{i2}, ..., x_{ip}$. We assume that the error terms, and therefore the Y-values, are normally distributed, they have constant variance and they are independent of each other. Checks of these assumptions are carried out as for simple linear regression (Chapter 5). Boxplots and probability plots of the residuals can be used to check for normality, plots of residuals against $\hat{y}_i$ can detect heterogeneity of variance (Section 6.1.9; Figure 6.2, Figure 6.3) and plots of residuals against each X_j can detect autocorrelation if X_j is a time sequence.

We also assume that each X is a fixed variable with the values x_{i1}, x_{i2}, etc., being constants that would not vary from sample to sample. This is unlikely in biological research with some or all of the predictors likely to be random variables and our observations actually coming from a multivariate distribution that we assume is normal.

Both of our examples illustrate this point: Paruelo & Lauenroth (1996) did not choose specific latitudes and longitudes for their sampling sites and Loyn (1987) did not choose forest patches with specifically chosen values of area, number of years since the patch was isolated by clearing, distance to the nearest patch, distance to the nearest larger patch, stock grazing history, or altitude. Our inferences are then conditional on the particular values of x_{i1}, x_{i2}, etc., that we have in our sample. Model II multiple regression when the predictor variables are random will be discussed in Section 6.1.17.

An additional assumption that affects multiple linear regression is that the predictor variables must be uncorrelated with each other. Violation of this assumption is called (multi)collinearity and is such an important issue for multiple regression that we will discuss it separately in Section 6.1.11.

Finally, the number of observations must exceed the number of predictor variables or else the matrix calculations (Box 6.4) will fail. Green (1991) proposed specific minimum ratios of observations to predictors, such as $p + 104$ observations for testing individual predictor variables, and these guidelines have become recommendations in some texts (*e.g.* Tabachnick & Fidell 1996). These numbers of observations are probably unrealistic for many biological and ecological research programs. Neter *et al.* (1996) are more lenient, recommending six to ten times the number of predictors for the number of observations. We can only suggest that researchers try to maximize the numbers of observations and if trade-offs in terms of time and cost are possible, reducing the numbers of variables to allow more observations is nearly always preferable to reducing the number of observations.

6.1.8 Regression diagnostics

Diagnostic checks of the assumptions underlying the fitting of linear models and estimating their parameters, and to warn of potential outliers and influential observations, are particularly important when there are multiple predictor variables. We are usually dealing with large data sets and scanning the raw data or simple bivariate scatterplots (see Section 6.1.9) that might have worked for simple regression models will rarely be adequate for checking the appropriateness of a multiple regression model. Fortunately, the same diagnostic checks we used for simple regression in Chapter 5 apply equally well for multiple regression. All are standard output from regression or linear model routines in good statistical software.

Leverage

Leverage measures how extreme each observation is from the means of all the X_j (the centroid of the p X-variables), so in contrast to simple regression, leverage in multiple regression takes into account all the predictors used in the model. Leverage values greater than $2(p/n)$ should be cause for concern, although such values would also be detected as influential by Cook's D_i.

Residuals

Residuals in multiple regression are interpreted in the same way as for simple regression, the difference between the observed and predicted Y-values for each observation ($y_i - \hat{y}_i$). These residuals can be standardized and studentized (see Chapter 5) and large residuals indicate outliers from the fitted model that could be influential.

Influence

Measures of how influential each observation is on the fitted model include Cook's D_i and DFITS$_i$ and these are as relevant for multiple regression as they were for simple regression (Chapter 5). Observations with a D_i greater than one are usually considered influential and such observations should be checked carefully.

6.1.9 Diagnostic graphics

As we emphasized for simple regression models, graphical techniques are often the most informative checks of assumptions and for the presence of outliers and influential values.

Scatterplots

Bivariate scatterplots between the X_js are important for detecting multicollinearity (see Section 6.1.11) and scatterplots between Y and each X_j, particularly in conjunction with smoothing functions, provide an indication of the nature of relationships being modeled. Scatterplot matrices

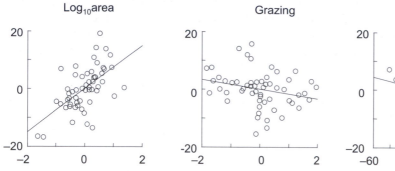

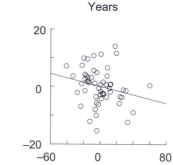

Figure 6.4 Partial regression plots for three of the predictors from a linear model relating bird abundance in forest patches to patch area, distance to nearest patch, distance to nearest larger patch (these three variables $\log_{10}$ transformed), grazing intensity, altitude, and years since isolation for the 56 patches surveyed by Loyn (1987). Vertical axis is residuals from OLS regression of bird abundance against all predictors except the one labelled, horizontal axis is residuals from OLS regression of labelled predictor against remaining predictors. See Section 6.1.9 for full analysis.

(SPLOMs; see Chapter 4) are the easiest way of displaying these bivariate relationships. However, scatterplots between Y and X_1, Y and X_2, etc., ignore the other predictor variables in the model and therefore do not represent the relationship we are modeling, i.e. the relationship between Y and X_j holding all other Xs constant.

A scatterplot that does show this relationship for each predictor variable is the added variable, or partial regression, plot, which is a plot between two sets of residuals. Let's say we are fitting a model of Y against p predictor variables and we want a scatterplot to show the relationship between Y and X_j, holding the other $p-1$ X-variables constant. The residuals for the vertical axis of the plot (e_{i1}) come from the OLS regression of Y against all p predictors except X_j. The residuals for the horizontal axis of the plot (e_{i2}) come from the OLS regression of X_j against all p predictors except X_j. This scatterplot of e_{i1} against e_{i2} shows the relationship between Y and X_j holding the other X-variables constant and will also show outliers that might influence the regression slope for X_j. If we fit an OLS regression of e_{i1} against e_{i2}, the fitted slope of this line is the partial regression slope of Y on X_j from the full regression model of Y on all p predictors.

Three partial regression plots are illustrated in Figure 6.4 from a model relating bird abundance in forest patches to patch area, distance to nearest patch, distance to nearest larger patch (these three variables $\log_{10}$ transformed), stock grazing, altitude, and years since isolation for the 56 patches surveyed by Loyn (1987). The partial regression plot for patch area (Figure 6.4, left) has the residuals from a model relating bird abundance to all predictors except patch area on the vertical axis and the residuals from a model relating patch area to the other predictors on the horizontal axis. Note the strong positive relationship for $\log_{10}$ area and the weak negative relationships for grazing and years since isolation. There was little pattern in the plots for the other three predictors. The slopes of the OLS regression lines fitted to these residual plots are the partial regression slopes from the multiple regression model relating bird abundance to these predictors.

Residual plots

There are numerous ways residuals from the fit of a multiple linear regression model can be plotted. A plot of residuals against $\hat{y}_i$, as we recommended for simple regression (Chapter 5), can detect heterogeneity of variance (wedge-shaped pattern) and outliers (Figure 6.2 and Figure 6.3). Plots of residuals against each X_j can detect outliers specific to that X_j, nonlinearity between Y and that X_j and can also detect autocorrelation if X_j is a time sequence. Finally, residuals can be plotted against predictors, or interactions between predictors, not included in the model to assess whether these predictors or their interactions might be important, even if they were deleted from the model based on other criteria (Neter *et al.* 1996).

6.1.10 Transformations

Our general comments on transformations from Chapter 4, and specifically for bivariate regression in Chapter 5, are just as relevant for multiple regression. Transformations of the response variable can remedy non-normality and heterogeneity of variance of error terms and transformations of one or more of the predictor variables might be necessary to deal with nonlinearity and influential observations due to high leverage. For example, the abundance of C_3 plants in the study by Paruelo & Lauenroth (1996) was transformed to logs to reduce strong skewness and three of the predictor variables in the study by Loyn (1987) were also log transformed to deal with observations with high leverage (Box 6.2). Transformations can also reduce the influence of interactions between predictors on the response variable, i.e. make an additive model a more appropriate fit than a multiplicative model (see Section 6.1.12).

6.1.11 Collinearity

One important issue in multiple linear regression analysis, and one that seems to be ignored by many biologists who fit multiple regression models to their data, is the impact of correlated predictor variables on the estimates of parameters and hypothesis tests. If the predictors are correlated, then the data are said to be affected by (multi)collinearity. Severe collinearity can have important, and detrimental, effects on the estimated regression parameters. Lack of collinearity is also very difficult to meet with real biological data, where predictor variables that might be incorporated into a multiple regression model are likely to be correlated with each other to some extent. In the data set from Loyn (1987), we might expect heavier grazing history the longer the forest patch has been isolated and lighter grazing history for bigger patches since domestic stock cannot easily access larger forest fragments (Box 6.2).

The calculations for multiple linear regression analysis involve matrix inversion (Box 6.4). Collinearity among the X-variables causes computational problems because it makes the determinant of the matrix of X-variables close to zero and matrix inversion basically involves dividing by the determinant. Dividing by a determinant that is close to zero results in values in the inverted matrix being very sensitive to small differences in the numbers in the original data matrix (Tabachnick & Fidell 1996), i.e. the inverted matrix is unstable. This means that estimates of parameters (particularly the partial regression slopes) are also unstable (see Philippi 1993). Small changes in the data or adding or deleting one of the predictor variables can change the estimated regression coefficients considerably, even changing their sign (Bowerman & O'Connell 1990).

A second effect of collinearity is that standard errors of the estimated regression slopes, and therefore confidence intervals for the model parameters, are inflated when some of the predictors are correlated (Box 6.5). Therefore, the overall regression equation might be significant, i.e. the test of the H_0 that all partial regression slopes equal zero is rejected, but none of the individual regression slopes are significantly different from zero. This reflects lack of power for individual tests on partial regression slopes because of the inflated standard errors for these slopes.

Note that as long as we are not extrapolating beyond the range of our predictor variables and we are making predictions from data with a similar pattern of collinearity as the data to which we fitted our model, collinearity doesn't necessarily prevent us from estimating a regression model that fits the data well and has good predictive power (Rawlings et al. 1998). It does, however, mean that we are not confident in our estimates of the model parameters. A different sample from the same population of observations, even using the same values of the predictor variables, might produce very different parameter estimates.

Detecting collinearity

Collinearity can be detected in a number of ways (e.g. Chaterjee & Price 1991, Neter et al. 1996, Philippi 1993) and we illustrate some of these in Box 6.1 and Box 6.2 with our example data sets. First, we should examine a matrix of correlation coefficients (and associated scatterplots) between the predictor variables and look for large correlations. A scatterplot matrix (SPLOM) is a very useful graphical method (Chapter 4) and, if the response variable is included, also indicates nonlinear relationships between the response variable and any of the predictor variables.

Box 6.5 | Collinearity

Here is a simple illustration of the effects of collinearity in a multiple regression model with one response variable (Y) and two predictor variables (X_1, X_2). Two artificial data sets were generated for the three variables from normal distributions. In the first data set, X_1 and X_2 are relatively uncorrelated ($r = 0.21$). A multiple linear regression model, including an intercept, was fitted to these data.

	Coefficient	Standard error	Tolerance	t	P
Intercept	−1.045	1.341		−0.779	0.447
Slope X_1	0.893	0.120	0.954	7.444	<0.001
Slope X_2	−0.002	0.112	0.954	−0.017	0.987

Note that tolerance is 0.95 indicating no collinearity problems and standard errors are small. The partial regression slope for Y on X_1 holding X_2 constant is significant.

For the second data set, the values of X_2 were re-arranged between observations (but the values, their mean and standard deviation were the same) so that they are highly correlated with X_1 ($r = 0.99$), which along with Y is unchanged. Again a multiple linear regression model, including an intercept, was fitted.

	Coefficient	Standard error	Tolerance	t	P
Intercept	0.678	1.371		0.495	0.627
Slope X_1	−0.461	0.681	0.024	−0.678	0.507
Slope X_2	1.277	0.634	0.024	2.013	0.060

Note that tolerance is now very low indicating severe collinearity. The standard error for the partial regression slope of Y against X_1 is much bigger than for the first data set and the test of the H_0 that this slope equals zero is now not significant, despite the values of Y and X_1 being identical to the first data set.

Now let's add a third predictor (X_3) that is correlated with both X_1 and X_2.

	Coefficient	Standard error	Tolerance	t	P
Intercept	−0.306	1.410		−0.217	0.831
Slope X_1	−0.267	0.652	0.023	−0.410	0.687
Slope X_2	0.495	0.746	0.015	0.664	0.516
Slope X_3	0.657	0.374	0.068	1.758	0.098

Note that the estimated regression coefficients for X_1 and X_2 have changed markedly upon the addition of X_3 to the model.

Second, we should check the tolerance value for each predictor variable. Tolerance for X_j is simply $1 - r^2$ from the OLS regression of X_j against the remaining $p - 1$ predictor variables. A low tolerance indicates that the predictor variable is correlated with one or more of the other predictors. An approximate guide is to worry about tolerance values less than 0.1. Tolerance is sometimes expressed as the variance inflation factor (VIF), which is simply the inverse of tolerance (and can also be calculated from the eigenvectors and eigenvalues derived from a PCA on the predictor variables – see Chapter 17); VIF values greater than ten suggest strong collinearity.

Third, we can extract the principal components from the correlation matrix among the predictor variables (see Chapter 17). Principal components with eigenvalues (i.e. explained variances) near zero indicate collinearity among the original predictor variables, because those components have little variability that is independent of the other components. Three statistics are commonly used to assess collinearity in this context. First, the condition index is the square root of the largest eigenvalue divided by each eigenvalue ($\sqrt{\lambda_{max}/\lambda}$). There will be a condition index for each principal component and values greater than 30 indicate collinearities that require attention (Belsley et al. 1980, Chaterjee & Price 1991). The second is the condition number, which is simply the largest condition index ($\sqrt{\lambda_{max}/\lambda_{min}}$). Third, Hocking (1996) proposed an indicator of collinearity that is simply λ_{min} and suggested values less than 0.5 indicated collinearity problems.

It is worth noting that examining eigenvalues from the correlation matrix of the predictor variables implicitly standardizes the predictors to zero mean and unit variance so they are on the same scale. In fact, most collinearity diagnostics give different results for unstandardized and standardized predictors and two of the solutions to collinearity described below are based on standardized predictor variables.

Dealing with collinearity

Numerous solutions to collinearity have been proposed. All result in estimated partial regression slopes that are likely to be more precise (smaller standard errors) but are no longer unbiased. The first approach is the simplest: omit predictor variables if they are highly correlated with other predictor variables that remain in the model. Multiple predictor variables that are really measuring similar biological entities (e.g. a set of morphological measurements that are highly correlated) clearly represent redundant information and little can be gained by including all such variables in a model. Unfortunately, omitting variables may bias estimates of parameters for those variables that are correlated with the omitted variable(s) but remain in the model. Estimated partial regression slopes can change considerably when some predictor variables are omitted or added. Nonetheless, retaining only one of a

number of highly correlated predictor variables that contain biologically and statistically redundant information is a sensible first step to dealing with collinearity.

The second approach is based on a principal components analysis (PCA) of the X-variables (see Chapter 17) and is termed principal components regression. The p principal components are extracted from the correlation matrix of the predictor variables and Y is regressed against these principal components, which are uncorrelated, rather than the individual predictor variables. Usually, components that contribute little to the total variance among the X-variables or that are not related to Y are deleted and the regression model of Y against the remaining components refitted. The regression coefficients for Y on the principal components are not that useful, however, because the components are often difficult to interpret as each is a linear combination of all p predictor variables. Therefore, we back-calculate the partial regression slopes on the original standardized variables from the partial regression slopes on the reduced number of principal components. The back-calculated regression slopes are standardized because the PCA is usually based on a correlation matrix of X-variables, so we don't have to worry about an intercept term. Because principal components regression requires an understanding of PCA, we will describe it in more detail in Chapter 17; see also Jackson (1991), Lafi & Kaneene (1992) and Rawlings et al. (1998).

Note that deciding which components to omit is critical for principal components regression. Simply deleting those with small eigenvalues (little relative contribution to the total variation in the X-variables) can be very misleading (Jackson 1991, Hadi & Ling 1998). The strength of the relationship of each component with Y must also be considered.

The third approach is ridge regression, another biased regression estimation technique that is somewhat controversial. A small biasing constant is added to the normal equations that are solved to estimate the standardized regression coefficients (Chaterjee & Price 1991, Neter et al. 1996). Adding this constant biases the estimated regression coefficients but also reduces their

Table 6.2 | Expected values of mean squares from analysis of variance for a multiple linear regression model with two predictor variables

Mean square	Expected value
$MS_{Regression}$	$\sigma_\varepsilon^2 + \dfrac{\beta_1^2 \sum_{i=1}^{n}(x_{i1} - \bar{x}_1)^2 + \beta_2^2 \sum_{i=1}^{n}(x_{i2} - \bar{x}_2) + 2\beta_1\beta_2 \sum_{i=1}^{n}(x_{i1} - \bar{x}_1)(x_{i2} - \bar{x}_2)}{2}$
$MS_{Residual}$	σ_ε^2

variability and hence their standard errors. The choice of the constant is critical. The smaller its value, the less bias in the estimated regression slopes (when the constant is zero, we have an OLS regression); the larger its value, the less collinearity (increasing the constant reduces the VIF). Usually a range of values is tried (say, increasing from 0.001) and a diagnostic graphic (the ridge trace) used to determine the smallest value of the constant that is the best compromise between reducing the variation in the estimated regression slopes and reducing their VIFs. Neter *et al.* (1996) provided a clear worked example.

Careful thought about the predictor variables to be included in a multiple linear regression model can reduce collinearity problems before any analysis. Do not include clearly redundant variables that are basically measuring similar biological entities. If the remaining predictor variables are correlated to an extent that might affect the estimates of the regression slopes, then we prefer principal components regression over ridge regression for two reasons. First, it is relatively straightforward to do with most statistical software that can handle multiple regression and PCA, although some hand calculation might be required (e.g. for standard errors). Second, PCA is also a useful check for collinearity so is often done anyway. The calculations required for ridge regression, in contrast, are complex and not straightforward in most statistical software.

6.1.12 Interactions in multiple regression

The multiple regression model we have been using so far is an additive one, i.e. the effects of the predictor variables on Y are additive. In many biological situations, however, we would anticipate interactions between the predictors (Aiken & West

1991, Jaccard *et al.* 1990) so that their effects on Y are multiplicative. Let's just consider the case with two predictors, X_1 and X_2. The additive multiple linear regression model is:

$$y_i = \beta_0 + \beta_1 x_{i1} + \beta_2 x_{i2} + \varepsilon_i \quad (6.17)$$

This assumes that the partial regression slope of Y on X_1 is independent of X_2 and vice-versa. The multiplicative model including an interaction is:

$$y_i = \beta_0 + \beta_1 x_{i1} + \beta_2 x_{i2} + \beta_3 x_{i1} x_{i2} + \varepsilon_i \quad (6.18)$$

The new term $(\beta_3 x_{i1} x_{i2})$ in model 6.18 represents the interactive effect of X_1 and X_2 on Y. It measures the dependence of the partial regression slope of Y against X_1 on the value of X_2 and the dependence of the partial regression slope of Y against X_2 on the value of X_1. The partial slope of the regression of Y against X_1 is no longer independent of X_2 and vice versa. Equivalently, the partial regression slope of Y against X_1 is different for each value of X_2.

Using the data from Paruelo & Lauenroth (1996), model 6.2 indicates that we expect no interaction between latitude and longitude in their effect on the relative abundance of C_3 plants. But what if we allow the relationship between C_3 plants and latitude to vary for different longitudes? Then we are dealing with an interaction between latitude and longitude and our model becomes:

(relative abundance of C_3 grasses)$_i = \beta_0 +$
β_1(latitude)$_i + \beta_2$(longitude)$_i +$
β_3(latitude)$_i \times$(longitude)$_i + \varepsilon_i \quad (6.19)$

One of the difficulties with including interaction terms in multiple regression models is that lower-order terms will usually be highly correlated with their interactions, *e.g.* X_1 and X_2 will be highly correlated with their interaction X_1X_2. This results in all the computational problems and inflated variances of estimated coefficients associated with collinearity (Section 6.1.11). One solution to this problem is to rescale the predictor variables by centering, i.e. subtracting their mean from each observation, so the interaction is then the product of the centered values (Aiken & West 1991, Neter *et al.* 1996; see Box 6.1 and Box 6.2). If X_1 and X_2 are centered then neither will be strongly correlated with their interaction. Predictors can also be standardized (subtract the mean from each observation and divide by the standard deviation) which has an identical affect in reducing collinearity.

When interaction terms are not included in the model, centering the predictor variables does not change the estimates of the regression slopes nor hypothesis tests that individual slopes equal zero. Standardizing the predictor variables does change the value of the regression slopes, but not their hypothesis tests because the standardization affects the coefficients and their standard errors equally. When interaction terms are included, centering does not affect the regression slope for the highest-order interaction term, nor the hypothesis test that the interaction equals zero. Standardization changes the value of the regression slope for the interaction but not the hypothesis test. Centering and standardization change all lower-order regression slopes and hypothesis tests that individual slopes equal zero but make them more interpretable in the presence of an interaction (see below). The method we will describe for further examining interaction terms using simple slopes is also unaffected by centering but is affected by standardizing predictor variables.

We support the recommendation of Aiken & West (1991) and others that multiple regression models with interaction terms should be fitted to data with centered predictor variables. Standardization might also be used if the variables have very different variances but note that calculation and tests of simple slopes must then be based on analyzing standardized variables but using the unstandardized regression coefficients (Aiken & West 1991).

Probing interactions

Even in the presence of an interaction, we can still interpret the partial regression slopes for other terms in model 6.18. The estimate of β_1 determined by the OLS fit of this regression model is actually the regression slope of Y on X_1 when X_2 is zero. If there is an interaction (β_3 does not equal zero), this slope will obviously change for other values of X_2; if there is not an interaction (β_3 equals zero), then this slope will be constant for all levels of X_2. In the presence of an interaction, the estimated slope for Y on X_1 when X_2 is zero is not very informative because zero is not usually within the range of our observations for any of the predictor variables. If the predictors are centered, however, then the estimate of β_1 is now the regression slope of Y on X_1 for the mean of X_2, a more useful piece of information. This is another reason why variables should be centered before fitting a multiple linear regression model with interaction terms.

However, if the fit of our model indicates that interactions between two or more predictors are important, we usually want to probe these interactions further to see how they are structured. Let's express our multiple regression model as relating the predicted y_i to two predictor variables and their interaction using sample estimates:

$$\hat{y}_i = b_0 + b_1 x_{i1} + b_2 x_{i2} + b_3 x_{i1} x_{i2} \tag{6.20}$$

This can be algebraically re-arranged to:

$$\hat{y}_i = (b_1 + b_3 x_{i2}) x_{i1} + (b_2 x_{i2} + b_0) \tag{6.21}$$

We now have $(b_1 + b_3 x_{i2})$, the simple slope of the regression of Y on X_1 for any particular value of X_2 (indicated as x_{i2}). We can then choose values of X_2 and calculate the estimated simple slope, for either plotting or significance testing. Cohen & Cohen (1983) and Aiken & West (1991) suggested using three different values of X_2: $\bar{x}_2$, $\bar{x}_2 + s$, $\bar{x}_2 - s$, where s is the sample standard deviation of X_2. We can calculate simple regression slopes by substituting these values of X_2 into the equation for the simple slope of Y on X_1.

The H_0 that the simple regression slope of Y on X_1 for a particular value of X_2 equals zero can also be tested. The standard error for the simple regression slope is:

$$\sqrt{s_{11}^2 + 2x_2 s_{13}^2 + x_2^2 s_{33}^2} \tag{6.22}$$

where s_{11}^2 and s_{33}^2 are the variances of b_1 and b_3 respectively, s_{13}^2 is the covariance between b_1 and b_3

and x_2 is the value of X_2 chosen. The variance and covariances are obtained from a covariance matrix of the regression coefficients, usually standard output for regression analyses with most software. Then the usual t test is applied (simple slope divided by standard error of simple slope). Fortunately, simple slope tests can be done easily with most statistical software (Aiken & West 1990, Darlington 1990). For example, we use the following steps to calculate the simple slope of Y on X_1 for a specific value of X_2, such as $\bar{x}_2 + s$.

1. Create a new variable (called the conditional value of X_2, say CVX_2), which is x_{i2} minus the specific value chosen.
2. Fit a multiple linear regression model for Y on X_1, CVX_2, X_1 by CVX_2.
3. The partial slope of Y on X_1 from this model is the simple slope of Y on X_1 for the specific value of X_2 chosen.
4. The statistical program then provides a standard error and t test.

This procedure can be followed for any conditional value. Note that we have calculated simple slopes for Y on X_1 at different values of X_2. Conversely, we could have easily calculated simple slopes for Y on X_2 at different values of X_1.

If we have three predictor variables, we can have three two-way interactions and one three-way interaction:

$$y_i = \beta_0 + \beta_1 x_{i1} + \beta_2 x_{i2} + \beta_3 x_{i3} + \beta_4 x_{i1} x_{i2} + \beta_5 x_{i1} x_{i3} + \beta_6 x_{i2} x_{i3} + \beta_7 x_{i1} x_{i2} x_{i3} + \varepsilon_i \quad (6.23)$$

In this model, β_7 is the regression slope for the three-way interaction between X_1, X_2 and X_3 and measures the dependence of the regression slope of Y on X_1 on the values of different combinations of both X_2 and X_3. Equivalently, the interaction is the dependence of the regression slope of Y on X_2 on values of different combinations of X_1 and X_3 and the dependence of the regression slope of Y on X_3 on values of different combinations of X_1 and X_2. If we focus on the first interpretation, we can determine simple regression equations for Y on X_1 at different combinations of X_2 and X_3 using sample estimates:

$$\hat{y}_i = (b_1 + b_4 x_{i2} + b_5 x_{i3} + b_7 x_{i2} x_{i3}) x_{i1} + (b_2 x_{i2} + b_3 x_{i3} + b_6 x_{i2} x_{i3} + b_0) \quad (6.24)$$

Now we have $(b_1 + b_4 x_{i2} + b_5 x_{i3} + b_7 x_{i2} x_{i3})$ as the simple slope for Y on X_1 for specific values of X_2 and X_3 together. Following the logic we used for models with two predictors, we can substitute values for X_2 and X_3 into this equation for the simple slope. Aiken & West (1991) suggested using $\bar{x}_2$ and $\bar{x}_3$ and the four combinations of $\bar{x}_2 \pm s_{x_2}$ and $\bar{x}_3 \pm s_{x_3}$. Simple slopes for Y on X_2 or X_3 can be calculated by just reordering the predictor variables in the model. Using the linear regression routine in statistical software, simple slopes, their standard errors and t tests for Y on X_1 at specific values of X_2 and X_3 can be calculated.

1. Create two new variables (called the conditional values of X_2 and X_3, say CVX_2 and CVX_3), which are x_{i2} and x_{i3} minus the specific values chosen.
2. For each combination of specific values of X_2 and X_3, fit a multiple linear regression model for Y on X_1, CVX_2, CVX_3, X_1 by CVX_2, X_1 by CVX_3, CVX_2 by CVX_3, and X_1 by CVX_2 by CVX_3.
3. The partial slope of Y on X_1 from this model is the simple slope of Y on X_1 for the chosen specific values of X_2 and X_3.

With three or more predictor variables, the number of interactions becomes large and they become more complex (three-way interactions and higher). Incorporating all possible interactions in models with numerous predictors becomes unwieldy and we would need a very large sample size because of the number of terms in the model. There are two ways we might decide which interactions to include in a linear regression model, especially if our sample size does not allow us to include them all. First, we can use our biological knowledge to predict likely interactions and only incorporate this subset. For the data from Loyn (1987), we might expect the relationship between bird density and grazing to vary with area (grazing effects more important in small fragments?) and years since isolation (grazing more important in new fragments?), but not with distance to any forest or larger fragments. Second, we can plot the residuals from an additive model against the possible interaction terms (new variables formed by simply multiplying the predictors) to see if any of these interactions are related to variation in the response variable.

There are two take-home messages from this section. First, we should consider interactions between continuous predictors in multiple linear regression model because such interactions may be common in biological data. Second, these interactions can be further explored and interpreted using relatively straightforward statistical techniques with most linear regression software.

6.1.13 Polynomial regression

Generally, curvilinear models fall into the class of nonlinear regression modeling (Section 6.4) because they are best fitted by models that are nonlinear in the parameters (e.g. power functions). There is one type of curvilinear model that can be fitted by OLS (i.e. it is still a linear model) and is widely used in biology, the polynomial regression.

Let's consider a model with one predictor variable (X_1). A second-order polynomial model is:

$$y_i = \beta_0 + \beta_1 x_{i1} + \beta_2 x_{i1}^2 + \varepsilon_i \qquad (6.25)$$

where β_1 is the linear coefficient and β_2 is the quadratic coefficient. Such models can be fitted by simply adding the x_{i1}^2 term to the right-hand side of the model, and they have a parabolic shape. Note that x_{i1}^2 is just an interaction term (i.e. x_{i1} by x_{i1}). There are two questions we might wish to ask with such a model (Kleinbaum *et al.* 1988). First, is the overall regression model significant? This is a test of the H_0 that β_1 equals β_2 equals zero and is done with the usual F test from the regression ANOVA. Second, is a second-order polynomial a better fit than a first-order model? We answer this with a partial F statistic, which tests whether the full model including X^2 is a better fit than the reduced model excluding X^2 using the principle of extra SS we described in Section 6.1.4:

$$F(X^2 | X) = \frac{(SS_{Extra} \text{ due to added } X^2)/1}{Full\ MS_{Residual}} \qquad (6.26)$$

where the SS_{Extra} is the difference between the $SS_{Regression}$ for the full model with the second-order polynomial term and the $SS_{Regression}$ for the reduced model with just the first-order term.

For example, Caley & Schluter (1997) examined the relationship between local and regional species diversity for a number of taxa and geographic regions at two spatial scales of sampling

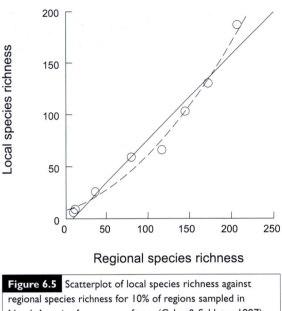

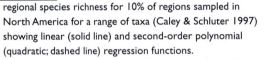

Figure 6.5 Scatterplot of local species richness against regional species richness for 10% of regions sampled in North America for a range of taxa (Caley & Schluter 1997) showing linear (solid line) and second-order polynomial (quadratic; dashed line) regression functions.

(1% of region and 10% of region). Regional species diversity was the predictor variable and local species diversity was the response variable and Caley & Schluter (1997) showed that adding a quadratic term to the model explained significantly more of the variance in local species diversity compared with a simple linear model (Box 6.6; Figure 6.5).

Polynomial regressions can be extended to third-order (cubic) models, which have a sigmoid shape:

$$y_i = \beta_0 + \beta_1 x_{i1} + \beta_2 x_{i1}^2 + \beta_3 x_{i1}^3 + \varepsilon_i \qquad (6.27)$$

Polynomial models can also contain higher orders (quartic, quintic, etc.) and more predictors. We have to be very careful about extrapolation beyond the range of our data with polynomial regression models. For example, a quadratic model will have a parabolic shape although our observations may only cover part of that function. Imagine fitting a quadratic model to the species area data in Figure 5.17. Predicting species number for larger clumps using this quadratic model would be misleading as theory suggests that species number would not then decline with increasing clump area.

Box 6.6 | Worked example of polynomial regression

We will use the data set from Caley & Schluter (1997), examining the regression of local species richness against regional species richness just for North America and at a sampling scale of 10% of the region. Although there was some evidence that both local and regional species richness were skewed, we will, like the original authors, analyze untransformed variables. Caley & Schluter (1997) forced their models through the origin, but because that makes interpretation difficult, we will include an intercept in the models. First, we will fit a second-order polynomial to the data:

$$(\text{local species richness})_i = \beta_0 + \beta_1(\text{regional species richness})_i + \beta_2(\text{regional species richness})_i^2 + \varepsilon_i$$

	Coefficient	Standard error	Tolerance	t	P
β_0	8.124	6.749		1.204	0.283
β_1	0.249	0.170	0.066	1.463	0.203
β_2	0.003	0.001	0.066	3.500	0.017

We would reject the H_0 that β_2 equals zero. Note that the tolerances are very low, indicating collinearity between regional species richness and (regional species richness)^2 as we would expect. This collinearity might affect the estimate and test of β_1 but won't affect the partitioning of the variance and the calculation of SS_{Extra} [(regional species richness)^2 | regional species richness], so we, like Caley & Schluter (1997) will continue the analysis with uncentered data.

The partitioning of the variation resulted in the following ANOVA.

Source	SS	df	MS	F	P
Regression	2.781×10^4	2	1.390×10^4	184.582	<0.001
Residual	376.620	5	75.324		

Note the $SS_{Regression}$ has two df because there are three parameters in the model. We would reject the H_0 that β_1 equals β_2 equals zero.

Now we fit a reduced model without the quadratic term:

$$(\text{local species richness})_i = \beta_0 + \beta_1(\text{regional species richness})_i + \varepsilon_i$$

Source	SS	df	MS	F	P
Regression	2.688×10^4	1	2.688×10^4	124.152	<0.001
Residual	1299.257	6	216.543		

The $SS_{Regression}$ from the full model is 2.781×10^4 and the $SS_{Regression}$ from the reduced model is 2.688×10^4. Therefore SS_{Extra} is 922.7 with one df and F [(regional species richness)^2 | regional species richness] equals 12.249 with $P < 0.018$. We would conclude that adding the second-order polynomial term to this model contributes significantly to explained variation in local species richness. It is apparent from Figure 6.5, despite the small sample size, that the second-order polynomial model provides a better visual fit than a simple linear model. Note that quadratic models were not better fits than linear for any of the other combinations of region (worldwide, Australia, North America) and spatial scale (1% and 10% of region).

Table 6.3	Dummy variable coding for grazing effect from Loyn (1987)			
Grazing intensity	$Grazing_1$	$Grazing_2$	$Grazing_3$	$Grazing_4$
Zero (reference category)	0	0	0	0
Low	1	0	0	0
Medium	0	1	0	0
High	0	0	1	0
Intense	0	0	0	1

Polynomial terms in these models will always be correlated with lower-order terms, so collinearity can be a problem, causing unstable estimates of the coefficients for the lower order terms and increasing their standard errors. Since the polynomial term is just an interaction, centring the predictors will reduce the degree of collinearity, without affecting the estimate and test of the slope for the highest-order term in the model nor the partitioning of the SS. However, the estimate of the slope for the lower-order terms will be different but also more reliable with smaller standard errors once collinearity has been reduced.

6.1.14 Indicator (dummy) variables

There are often situations when we would like to incorporate a categorical variable into our multiple regression modeling. For example, Loyn (1987) included a predictor variable indicating the historical intensity of grazing in each of his forest patches. This variable took values of 1, 2, 3, 4 or 5 and was treated as a continuous variable for the analysis. We could also treat this as a categorical variable, with five categories of grazing. While the values of this variable actually represent a quantitative scale (from low grazing intensity to high grazing intensity), many categorical variables will be qualitative. For example, Paruelo & Lauenroth (1996) included a categorical variable that separated sites into shrubland and grassland. To include categorical variables in a regression model, we must convert them to continuous variables called indicator or dummy variables. Commonly, dummy variables take only two values, zero or one, although other types of coding are possible.

In the example from Paruelo & Lauenroth (1996) where there are only two categories, we could code grasslands as zero and shrublands as one, although the authors used coding of one and two. As long as the interval is the same, the coding doesn't matter in this case. For Loyn's (1987) grazing history variable, there are five categories that we will call zero, low, medium, high, and intense grazing. The dummy variables would be as follows.

X_1 1 if low
      0 if not

X_2 1 if medium
      0 if not

X_3 1 if high
      0 if not

X_4 1 if intense
      0 if not

This defines all our categories (Table 6.3) and we would fit a linear model including each of these dummy variables as predictors. For a predictor variable with c categories, we only need $c - 1$ dummy variables. Interpreting the regression coefficients is a little tricky. The coefficients for X_1, X_2, X_3 and X_4 indicate how different the effects of low, medium, high and intense grazing respectively are compared to zero grazing, i.e. the coefficients for dummy variables measure the differential effects of each category compared to a reference category (in which all dummy variables equal zero). The choice of the reference category should be made prior to analysis. In this example, we used the zero grazing category ("control") as the reference category. An alternative method of coding dummy variables is using the deviation of each category mean from the overall mean, which is commonly used in analysis of variance models (see Chapter 8 onwards) and is termed effects coding.

Box 6.7 | Worked example of indicator (dummy) variables

We will consider a subset of the data from Loyn (1987) where abundance of forest birds is the response variable and grazing intensity (1 to 5 from least to greatest) and $\log_{10}$ patch area are the predictor variables. First, we treat grazing as a continuous variable and fit model 6.28.

Coefficient	Estimate	Standard error	t	P
Intercept	21.603	3.092	6.987	<0.001
Grazing	−2.854	0.713	−4.005	<0.001
$\log_{10}$ area	6.890	1.290	5.341	<0.001

Note that both the effects of grazing and $\log_{10}$ area are significant and the partial regression slope for grazing is negative, indicating that, holding patch area constant, there are fewer birds in patches with more intense grazing.

Now we will convert grazing into four dummy variables with no grazing (level 1) as the reference category (Table 6.3) and fit model 6.29.

	Estimate	Standard error	t	P
Intercept	15.716	2.767	5.679	<0.001
$Grazing_1$	0.383	2.912	0.131	0.896
$Grazing_2$	−0.189	2.549	−0.074	0.941
$Grazing_3$	−1.592	2.976	−0.535	0.595
$Grazing_4$	−11.894	2.931	−4.058	<0.001
$\log_{10}$ area	7.247	1.255	5.774	<0.001

The partial regression slopes for these dummy variables measure the difference in bird abundance between the grazing category represented by the dummy variable and the reference category for any specific level of $\log_{10}$ area. Note that only the effect of intense grazing (category: 5; dummy variable: $grazing_4$) is different from the no grazing category.

If our linear model only has categorical predictor variables ("factors"), then they are usually considered as classical analyses of variance models. Commonly, we have linear models with a mixture of categorical and continuous variables. The simplest case is one categorical predictor (converted to dummy variables) and one continuous predictor. For example, consider a subset of the data from Loyn (1987) where we will model the abundance of forest birds against grazing intensity (1 to 5 indicating no grazing to intense grazing) and patch area (transformed to $\log_{10}$ – see Box 6.7). Because the levels of grazing categories are quantitative, grazing intensity can be treated as a continuous variable with the following typical multiple regression model:

$$(\text{bird abundance})_i = \beta_0 + \beta_1(\text{grazing})_i + \beta_2(\log_{10}\text{area})_i + \varepsilon_i \tag{6.28}$$

Alternatively, we could consider grazing intensity as a categorical variable and we would create four dummy variables (Table 6.3) and include these in our model:

$$(\text{bird abundance})_i = \beta_0 + \beta_1(\text{grazing}_1)_i + \beta_2(\text{grazing}_2)_i + \beta_3(\text{grazing}_3)_i + \beta_4(\text{grazing}_4)_i + \beta_5(\log_{10}\text{area})_i + \varepsilon_i \tag{6.29}$$

This model can be envisaged as separate linear regression models between Y and $\log_{10}$ area for each level of the categorical predictor (grazing). The partial regression slope for each dummy variable measures the difference in the predicted value of Y between that category of grazing and the reference category (zero grazing) for any specific value of $\log_{10}$ area. Using analysis of covariance terminology (Chapter 12), each regression slope measures the difference in the adjusted mean of Y between that category and the reference category (Box 6.7). Interaction terms between the dummy variables and the continuous variable could also be included. These interactions measure how much the slopes of the regressions between Y and the $\log_{10}$ area differ between the levels of grazing. Most statistical software now automates the coding of categorical variables in regression analyses, although you should check what form of coding your software uses. Models that incorporate continuous and categorical predictors will also be considered as part of analysis of covariance in Chapter 12.

6.1.15 Finding the "best" regression model

In many uses of multiple regression, biologists want to find the smallest subset of predictors that provides the "best fit" to the observed data. There are two apparent reasons for this (Mac Nally 2000), related to the two main purposes of regression analysis – explanation and prediction. First, the "best" subset of predictors should include those that are most important in explaining the variation in the response variable. Second, other things being equal, the precision of predictions from our fitted model will be greater with fewer predictor variables in the model. Note that, as we said in the introduction to Chapter 5, biologists, especially ecologists, seem to rarely use their regression models for prediction and we agree with Mac Nally (2000) that biologists are usually searching for the "best" regression model to explain the response variable.

It is important to remember that there will rarely be, for any real data set, a single "best" subset of predictors, particularly if there are many predictors and they are in any way correlated with each other. There will usually be a few models, with different numbers of predictors, which provide similar fits to the observed data. The choice between these competing models will still need to be based on how well the models meet the assumptions, diagnostic considerations of outliers and other influential observations and biological knowledge of the variables retained.

Criteria for "best" model

Irrespective of which method is used for selecting which variables are included in the model (see below), some criterion must be used for deciding which is the "best" model. One characteristic of such a criterion is that it must protect against "overfitting", where the addition of extra predictor variables may suggest a better fit even when these variables actually add very little to the explanatory power. For example, r^2 cannot decrease as more predictor variables are added to the model even if those predictors contribute nothing to the ability of the model to predict or explain the response variable (Box 6.8). So r^2 is not suitable for comparing models with different numbers of predictors.

We are usually dealing with a range of models, with different numbers of predictors, but all are subsets of the full model with all predictors. We will use P to indicate all possible predictors, p is the number of predictors included in a specific model, n is the number of observations and we will assume that an intercept is always fitted. If the models are all additive, i.e. no interactions, the number of parameters is $p + 1$ (the number of predictors plus the intercept). When interactions are included, then p in the equations below should be the number of parameters (except the intercept) in the model, including both predictors and their interactions. We will describe four criteria for determining the fit of a model to the data (Table 6.4).

The first is the adjusted r^2 which takes into account the number of predictors in the model and, in contrast to the usual r^2, basically uses mean squares instead of sum of squares and can increase or decrease as new variables are added to the model. A larger value indicates a better fit. Using the $MS_{Residual}$ from the fit of the model is equivalent where a lower value indicates a better fit.

The second is Mallow's C_p, which works by comparing a specific reduced model to the full model with all P predictors included. For the full model with all P predictors, C_p will equal $P + 1$ (the number of parameters including the intercept). The choice of the best model using C_p has two components: C_p should be as small as possible and as close to p as possible.

Box 6.8 | Hierarchical partitioning and model selection.

The data from Loyn (1987) were used to compare model selection criteria. Only the best two models (based on the BIC) for each number of predictors are presented as well as the full model. The model with the lowest BIC is in bold.

No. predictors	Model	r^2	Adj r^2	C_p	AIC	Schwarz (BIC)
1	$\log_{10}$ area	0.548	0.539	18.4	224.39	228.45
1	grazing	0.466	0.456	31.1	223.71	237.76
2	**$\log_{10}$ area + grazing**	**0.653**	**0.640**	**4.0**	**211.59**	**217.67**
2	$\log_{10}$ area + years	0.643	0.630	5.4	213.06	219.14
3	$\log_{10}$ area + grazing + years	0.673	0.654	2.8	210.19	218.29
3	$\log_{10}$ area + grazing + $\log_{10}$ ldist	0.664	0.644	4.3	211.77	219.88
4	$\log_{10}$ area + grazing + years + altitude	0.682	0.657	3.4	210.60	220.73
4	$\log_{10}$ area + grazing + years + $\log_{10}$ ldist	0.679	0.654	3.9	211.15	221.28
5	$\log_{10}$ area + grazing + years + $\log_{10}$ ldist + $\log_{10}$ dist	0.681	0.649	5.1	212.89	225.05
5	$\log_{10}$ area + grazing + altitude + $\log_{10}$ ldist + $\log_{10}$ dist	0.668	0.635	5.1	215.11	227.27
6	$\log_{10}$ area + grazing + years + altitude + $\log_{10}$ ldist + $\log_{10}$ dist	0.685	0.646	7.0	214.14	228.32

The Schwarz criterion (BIC) selects a model with just two predictors ($\log_{10}$ area and grazing). In contrast, the AIC and Mallow's C_p selected a model that included these two predictors and years since isolation, and the adjusted r^2 selected a four-predictor model that added altitude to the previous three predictors. Note that the unadjusted r^2 is highest for the model with all predictors.

For these data, automated forward and backward selection procedures (the significance level for entering and removing terms based on partial F-ratio statistics was set at 0.15) produced the same final model including $\log_{10}$ area, grazing and years since isolation. The results from a hierarchical partitioning of r^2 from the model relating abundance of forest birds to all six predictor variables from Loyn (1987) are shown below.

	Independent	Joint	Total
$\log_{10}$ area	0.315	0.232	0.548
$\log_{10}$ dist	0.007	0.009	0.016
$\log_{10}$ ldist	0.014	<0.001	0.014
Altitude	0.057	0.092	0.149
Grazing	0.190	0.275	0.466
Years	0.101	0.152	0.253

Clearly, $\log_{10}$ area and grazing contribute the most to the explained variance in abundance of forest birds, both as independent effects and joint effects with other predictors, with some contribution also by years since isolation.

Table 6.4 | Criteria for selecting "best" fitting model in multiple linear regression. Formulae are for a specific model with p predictors included. Note that p excludes the intercept

Criterion	Formula
Adjusted r^2	$1 - \dfrac{SS_{Residual}/[n-(p+1)]}{SS_{Total}/(n-1)}$
Mallow's C_p	$\dfrac{\text{Reduced } SS_{Residual}}{\text{Full } MS_{Residual}} - [n - 2(p+1)]$
Akaike Information Criterion (AIC)	$n[\ln(SS_{Residual})] + 2(p+1) - n\ln(n)$
Schwarz Bayesian Information Criterion (BIC)	$n[\ln(SS_{Residual})] + (p+1)\ln(n) - n\ln(n)$

The remaining two measures are in the category of information criteria, introduced by Akaike (1978) and Schwarz (1978) to summarize the information in a model, accounting for both sample size and number of predictors (Table 6.4). Although these information criteria are usually based on likelihoods, they can be adapted for use with OLS since the estimates of parameters will be the same when assumptions hold. The first of these criteria is the Akaike information criterion (AIC), which tends to select the same models as Mallow's C_p as n increases and the $MS_{Residual}$ becomes a better estimate of σ_ε^2 (Christensen 1997; see Box 6.8). The Bayesian (or Schwarz) information criterion (BIC) is similar but adjusts for sample size and number of predictors differently. It more harshly penalizes models with a greater number of predictors than the AIC (Rawlings *et al.* 1998).

For both AIC and BIC, smaller values indicate better, more parsimonious, models (Box 6.8). We recommend the Schwarz criterion for determining the model that best fits the data with the fewest number of parameters (see also Mac Nally 2000). It is simple to calculate and can be applied to linear and generalized linear models (see Chapter 13).

Selection procedures

The most sensible approach to selecting a subset of important variables in a complex linear model is to compare all possible subsets. This procedure simply fits all the possible regression models (i.e. all possible combinations of predictors) and chooses the best one (or more than one) based on one of the criteria described above. Until relatively recently, automated fitting of all subsets was beyond the capabilities of most statistical software because of the large number of possible models. For example, with six predictors, there are 64 possible models! Consequently, stepwise procedures were developed that avoided fitting all possible models but selected predictor variables based on some specific criteria. There are three types of stepwise procedures, forward selection, backward selection and stepwise selection.

Forward selection starts off with a model with no predictors and then adds the one (we'll call X_a) with greatest F statistic (or t statistic or correlation coefficient) for the simple regression of Y against that predictor. If the H_0 that this slope equals zero is rejected, then a model with that variable is fitted. The next predictor (X_b) to be added is the one with the highest partial F statistic for X_b given that X_a is already in the model [$F(X_b|X_a)$]. If the H_0 that this partial slope equals zero is rejected, then the model with two predictors is refitted and a third predictor added based on $F(X_c|X_a,X_b)$. The process continues until a predictor with a non-significant partial regression slope is reached or all predictors are included.

Backward selection (elimination) is the opposite of forward selection, whereby all predictors are initially included and the one with the smallest and non-significant partial F statistic is dropped. The model is refitted and the next predictor with the smallest and non-significant partial F statistic is dropped. The process continues until there are no more predictors with non-significant partial F statistics or there are no predictors left.

Stepwise selection is basically a forward selection procedure where, at each stage of refitting the model, predictors can also be dropped using backward selection. Predictors added early in the process can be omitted later and vice versa.

For all three types of variable selection, the decision to add, drop or retain variables in the model is based on either a specified size of partial F statistics or significance levels. These are sometimes termed F-to-enter and F-to-remove and obviously, the values chosen will greatly influence which variables are added or removed from the model, especially in stepwise selection. Significance levels greater than 0.05, or small F statistics, are often recommended (and are default settings in stepwise selection routines of most regression software) because this will result in more predictors staying in the model and reduce the risk of omitting important variables (Bowerman & O'Connell 1990). However, as always, the choice of significance levels is arbitrary. Note that so many P values for tests of partial regression slopes are generated in variable selection procedures that these P values are difficult to interpret, due to the multiple testing problem (see Chapter 3) and lack of independence. Variable selection is not suited to the hypothesis testing framework.

It is difficult to recommend any variable selection procedure except all subsets. The logical and statistical problems with the forward, backward and stepwise procedures have been pointed out elsewhere (e.g. James & McCulloch 1990, Chaterjee & Price 1991, Neter *et al.* 1996). They all use somewhat arbitrary statistical rules (significance levels or the size of F statistics) for deciding which variables enter or leave the model and these rules do not consider the increased probability of Type I errors due to multiple testing. These approaches seem to be an abuse of the logic of testing *a priori* statistical hypotheses; statistical hypothesis testing and significance levels are ill-suited for exploratory data-snooping. Also, the forward, backward and stepwise approaches for

including and excluding variables can produce very different final models even from the same set of data (James & McCulloch 1990, Mac Nally 2000), particularly if there are many predictors. Additionally, simulation studies have shown that these stepwise procedures can produce a final model with a high r^2, even if there is really no relationship between the response and the predictor variables (Flack & Chang 1987, Rencher & Pun 1980). Finally, variable selection techniques are sensitive to collinearity between the predictors (Chaterjee & Price 1991). This is because collinearity will often result in large variances for some regression slopes that may result in those predictor variables being excluded from the model irrespective of their importance.

The all-subsets procedure is limited by the large number of models to be compared when there are many predictor variables, although most statistical software can now compare all subsets for reasonable numbers of predictors. It is difficult to envisage a data set in biology with too many variables for all subsets comparisons that is also not plagued by serious collinearity problems, which would invalidate any variable selection procedure.

If the number of observations is large enough, then we recommend using cross-validation techniques to check the validity of the final model. The simplest form of cross-validation is randomly to split the data set in two and fit the model with half the data set and then see how well the model predicts values of the response variable in the other half of the data set. Unfortunately, splitting the data for cross-validation is not always possible because of small sample sizes often encountered in biology.

In the end, however, the best argument against stepwise variable selection methods is that they do not necessarily answer sensible questions in the current age of powerful computers and sophisticated statistical software. If a regression model is required for explanation, then we wish to know which variables are important, and the criteria we described above, combined with hierarchical partitioning (Section 6.1.16), are the best approaches. If a model is required for prediction, with as few predictor variables as possible, then comparing all-subsets is feasible and probably the most sensible, although more complex procedures are possible (Mac Nally 2000). We conclude with a quote from James & McCulloch (1990, pp. 136–137): "Many authors have documented the folly of using stepwise procedures with any multivariate method. Clearly, stepwise regression is not able to select from a set of variables those that are most influential."

6.1.16 Hierarchical partitioning

Hierarchical partitioning is a method that has been around for some time but its utility for interpreting the importance of variables in linear models has only recently been appreciated in the statistical (Chevan & Sutherland 1991) and biological literature (Mac Nally 1996). Its purpose is to quantify the "independent" correlation of each predictor variable with the response variable. It works by measuring the improvement in the fit of all models with a particular predictor compared to the equivalent model without that predictor and the improvement in fit is averaged across all possible models with that predictor. We can use any of a number of measures of fit, but for linear models, it is convenient to use r^2.

Consider a model with a response variable (Y) and three predictor variables (X_1, X_2, X_3). There are 2^p possible models when there are p "independent" predictor variables, so here, there are 2^3 equals eight models. We can calculate r^2 for the eight possible models listed in Table 6.5. Note that there are four hierarchical levels of model complexity, representing the number of predictors in the model. Hierarchical partitioning splits the total r^2 for each predictor, i.e. the r^2 for the linear relationship between Y and each predictor by itself (as in Models 2, 3 and 4), into two additive components.

- The "independent" contributions of each predictor variable, which is a partitioning of the r^2 for the full model with all predictors (Model 8).
- The "joint" contributions of each predictor in conjunction with other predictors.

For the independent contributions, we calculate for each predictor variable the improvement in fit by adding that predictor to reduced models without that predictor at each hierarchical level.

Table 6.5 Eight possible models with one response variable and three predictor variables

Label	Model	Level of hierarchy
1	No predictors, r^2 equals zero	0
2	X_1	1
3	X_2	1
4	X_3	1
5	$X_1 + X_2$	2
6	$X_1 + X_3$	2
7	$X_2 + X_3$	2
8	$X_1 + X_2 + X_3$	3

For example, for X_1, we would compare the following r^2 values:

$r^2(X_1)$ vs $r^2(\text{Null})$

$r^2(X_1, X_2)$ vs $r^2(X_2)$

$r^2(X_1, X_3)$ vs $r^2(X_3)$

$r^2(X_1, X_2, X_3)$ vs $r^2(X_2, X_3)$

The differences in r^2 values are averaged within each hierarchical level (first order, second order, third order) and then averaged across the levels to produce the independent contribution of X_1 to the explained variance in Y. The same procedure is followed for the other predictor variables. These independent contributions of all the predictor variables represent a partitioning of the r^2 from the full model with all predictors included. For example, the sum of the independent contributions of $\log_{10}$ area, $\log_{10}$ dist, $\log_{10}$ ldist, altitude, grazing and years to forest bird abundance for the data from Loyn (1987) equals the r^2 from the fit of the full model with all these predictors (Box 6.8).

If the predictor variables are completely independent of (i.e. uncorrelated with) each other, then there will be no joint contributions and the sum of the r^2 for Models 2, 3 and 4 (Table 6.5) will equal the total r^2 from the full model. This latter r^2 can be unambiguously partitioned into the independent contributions of each predictor and the analysis would be complete. We know, however, that correlations between predictors nearly always occur within real data sets so the sum of the r^2 for Models 2, 3 and 4 will exceed the total r^2 from the full model because of the joint effects of predictors. These joint effects represent the variation in Y that is shared between two or more predictors. The joint effects for each predictor are calculated from the difference between the squared partial correlation for the model relating Y to that predictor and the average r^2 representing the independent contribution of that predictor already determined. This simply uses the additive nature of the independent and joint contributions of each predictor to the total r^2 for each predictor, as described above.

The sum of the average independent and average joint contribution to r^2 is the total contribution of each predictor variable to the variation in the response variable, measured by the r^2 for the model relating Y to each predictor. We might like to test the H_0 that this total contribution equals zero for each predictor. Unfortunately, hypothesis tests for r^2 are not straightforward, although Mac Nally (1996) suggested an expedient solution of using the appropriate critical value of the correlation coefficient ($\sqrt{r^2}$).

As Mac Nally (1996) has pointed out, hierarchical partitioning uses all possible models and averages the improvement in fit for each predictor variable, both independently and jointly, across all these models. Note that hierarchical partitioning does not produce a predictive model nor does it provide estimates of, and tests of null hypotheses about, parameters of the regression model. With anything more than a few predictors, hierarchical partitioning cannot be done manually and the algorithm of Chevan & Sutherland (1991) needs to be programmed.

Mac Nally (1996) illustrated the utility of hierarchical partitioning for a data set relating breeding passerine bird species richness to seven habitat variables. The two predictor variables retained by hierarchical partitioning were the same as those with significant bivariate correlations with the response variable but were quite different from those chosen by a full model multiple regression and variable selection (backwards and forwards) procedures (Box 6.8).

6.1.17 Other issues in multiple linear regression

Regression through the origin
We argued in Chapter 5 that forcing a regression model through the origin by omitting an intercept was rarely a sensible strategy. This is even more true for multiple regression because we would need to be sure that Y equals zero when all X_j equal zero. Even if this was the case, forcing our model through the origin will nearly always involve extrapolating beyond the range of our observed values for the predictor variables and measures of fit for no-intercept models are difficult to interpret.

Weighted least squares
Weighting each observation by a value related to the variance in y_i is one way of dealing with heterogeneity of variance although determining the appropriate weights is not straightforward (Chapter 5). As with simple linear regression, our preference is to transform Y and/or the X-variables if the heterogeneity of variance is due to skewed distributions of the variables, particularly if our understanding of the biology suggests a different scale of measurement is more appropriate for one or more of the variables. Alternatively, generalized linear models with an appropriate non-normal distribution of the error terms should be used (Chapter 13).

X random (Model II regression)
The extension of Model II bivariate regression techniques (Chapter 5) to the situation with multiple predictor variables was reviewed by McArdle (1988). To calculate the RMA equivalent estimates for each β_j, first produce a correlation matrix among all the variables (Y and all p X-variables). Then run a principal components analysis (see Chapter 17) on this correlation matrix and extract the eigenvector for the last component with the smallest eigenvalue (explained variance). The estimate of the regression slope for each predictor variable (X_j) is:

$$b_j = \frac{\alpha_j}{\alpha_Y} \tag{6.30}$$

where b_j is the regression slope for X_j, α_j is the coefficient for X_j and α_Y is the coefficient for Y from the eigenvector for the principal component with the smallest eigenvalue. McArdle (1988) refers to this method as the standard minor axis (SMA) and simply becomes the RMA method when p equals one. Note that these are standardized regression slopes, because they are based on a correlation matrix, so the regression model does not include an intercept.

The choice between OLS and SMA is not as straightforward as that between OLS and RMA for simple bivariate regression. McArdle's (1988) simulations suggested that if the error variance in X_j is greater than about half the error variance in Y, then SMA is better. However, the relative performance of OLS and SMA depended on the correlation between Y and X_j so definitive guidelines cannot be given.

Robust regression

When the underlying distribution of error terms may not be normal, especially if extreme observations (outliers) occur in the data that we cannot deal with via deletion or transformation, then the usual OLS procedure may not be reliable. One approach is to use robust fitting methods that are less sensitive to outliers. The methods described in Chapter 5, least absolute deviations, Huber M-estimation and non-parametric (rank-based) regression, all extend straightforwardly to multiple predictor variables. The major difficulty is that the computations and associated algorithms are complex (Birkes & Dodge 1993). Fortunately, robust regression procedures are now common components of good statistical software.

The randomization test of the H_0 that β_1 equals zero in simple linear regression can also be extended to multiple regression. We compare the observed partial regression slopes to a distribution of partial regression slopes determined by randomly allocating the y_i to observations but not altering the x_{i1}, x_{i2}, etc., for each observation (Manly 1997). Other randomization methods can be used, including using the residuals, although the different methods appear to give similar results (Manly 1997).

Missing data

It is common for biological data comprising two or more variables to have missing data. In data sets suited to multiple regression modeling, we may be missing values for some of the predictor variables or the response variable for some sampling units. It is important to distinguish missing values (no data) from zero values (data recorded but the value was zero) – see Chapter 4. If missing values for the response variable reflect a biological process, e.g. some organisms died during an experiment and therefore growth rate could not be measured, then analyzing the pattern of missing values in relation to the predictor variables may be informative. More commonly, we have missing values for our predictor variables, often due to random events such as equipment failure, incorrect data entry or data being subsequently lost. In these circumstances, most linear models software will omit the entire sampling unit from analysis, even if data are only missing for one of the variables. Alternatives to deletion when missing data occur, including imputing replacement values, will be discussed in Chapter 15.

Power of tests

The tests of whether individual partial regression coefficients equal zero are based on t statistics and therefore the determination of power of these tests is the same as for any simple t test that a single population parameter equals zero (Chapters 3 and 7). Our comments on power calculations for simple regression analyses (Chapter 5) apply similarly for multiple regression.

6.2 | Regression trees

An alternative to multiple linear regression analysis for developing descriptive and predictive models between a response variable and one or more predictor variables is regression tree analysis (Brieman et al. 1984, De'ath & Fabricius 2000). A "upside-down" tree is created where the root at the top contains all observations, which are divided into two branches at a node, then each branch is further split into two at subsequent nodes and so on. A branch that terminates without further branching is called a leaf.

Consider the data from Loyn (1987), where we have a continuous response variable (abundance of forest birds) and six predictor variables describing 56 forest patches, in this case all continuous.

All possible binary splits of the observations are assessed for each predictor variable. The first split is based on the predictor that results in two groups with the smallest within-group (residual) sums-of-squares for the response variable. Other measures of (lack of) fit can be used, including absolute deviations around the mean or median for a more robust measure of fit (see Chapter 5). These splitting criteria are different indices of impurity, a measure of heterogeneity of the groups at a split (De'ath & Fabricius 2000). This "recursive binary-partitioning" process is repeated within each of the two groups for all the predictors, again choosing the next split based on the predictor that results in the minimum residual SS within groups. Groups further along in the splitting process are more homogeneous than those higher up. The regression tree looks like a dendrogram from cluster analysis (Chapter 18), but is really a tree with the root (the undivided complete data set) at the top, branches with nodes for each division and leaves where branches terminate (terminal nodes).

Regression trees produce a predictive model. For any observation, a predicted value is the mean of the observations at a leaf, i.e. in a terminal group. Obviously, predicted values for observations in the one group (leaf) will be the same. This is in contrast to the usual linear model, which will have different predicted values for all observations unless they have identical values for all predictors. Because we have observed and predicted values, we can also calculate residuals for each observation and use these residuals as a diagnostic check for the appropriateness of the model and whether assumptions have been met. Normality of predictor variables is not a concern because only the rank order of a variable governs each split, although transformation of the response variable to alleviate variance heterogeneity may be important (De'ath & Fabricius 2000).

The splitting process (tree building) could continue until each leaf contains a single observation and for the Loyn (1987) data, we would have 56 terminal nodes. In this situation, the tree would predict the observed values of the response variable perfectly and explain all the variance in the response variable, the equivalent of fitting a saturated linear regression model (Section 6.1.4).

Usually, we want the best compromise between tree simplicity (few nodes) and explained variance in the response variable. In practice, therefore, *a priori* stopping criteria are used, such as a maximum number of nodes allowed, a minimum number of objects in each group or a minimum reduction in explained variance from adding more nodes. Different software for building trees will use different measures of fit and different default stopping rules so don't expect trees based on the same data built using different programs to be the same unless these criteria are set to be the same. Once the tree is built, using the stopping criteria, we can also "prune" or "shrink" trees to produce simpler models that achieve a better compromise between fit and simplicity, often using criteria similar to those used for model selection in standard multiple regression (Section 6.1.15). Alternatively, we can assess the predictive capabilities of different sized trees and choose the "best" tree as the one with the smallest prediction error, i.e. the model that provides the most accurate predictions.

De'ath & Fabricius (2000) argue strongly that the best approach for determining prediction error and thus appropriate tree size is using cross-validation (Section 6.1.15; De'ath & Fabricius 2000). One method for cross-validation is where the observations are divided randomly into two groups of a specified size, e.g. 10% and 90% of the observations, and the regression tree model is fitted to the larger group ("training group") to predict values in the smaller group ("validation group"). The difference between the observed and predicted values of the response variable in the smaller group is a measure of prediction error. Of interest is how much of the total variation in the observed values of the response variable is explained by the predicted values. Cross-validation is usually repeated many times, each with a new random allocation of observations to the groups of pre-defined size, i.e. in a randomization testing framework. Randomization testing can also be used to test whether the derived regression tree explains more of the variation in the response variable than we would expect by chance. Brieman *et al.* (1984) and De'ath & Fabricius (2000) provide more detail on cross-validation for regression trees.

Regression trees are often included in statistical software under the acronym CART (classification and regression tree analyses). The main distinction between classification and regression trees is that the former is based on categorical response variables and the latter on continuous response variables. Two common algorithms are AID (Automatic Interaction Detection) for regression trees and CHAID (Chi-squared Automatic Interaction Detection) for classification trees.

We will use two biological examples of regression tree analysis. The first comes from Rejwan *et al.* (1999), who used both standard multiple regression and regression trees to analyze the relationship between the density of nests of smallmouth bass (continuous response variable) and four predictor variables (wind/wave exposure, water temperature, shoreline reticulation and littoral-floor rugosity) for 36 sites in Lake Opeongo, Canada. There were nonlinear relationships between both exposure and littoral-floor rugosity and nest density. The standard multiple regression analysis showed that shoreline reticulation, temperature and (temperature)^2, and exposure were significant predictors, the final model explaining 47% of the variation in nest density between sites. However, cross-validation analysis showed that the model had little predictive power, with almost none of the variation in nest density in random samples of 10% of the sites predictable from the model fitted to the other 90% of the sites.

Their regression tree analysis split the sites based on a temperature cut-off of 17.05 °C into two initial groups of 28 and 8 sites, and then split the latter group into two groups of four sites each based on shoreline reticulation below and above 100m. This tree explained 58% of the variation in nest density and cross-validation analysis showed that the tree model had more predictive power and could explain about 20% of the variation nest density in random samples of 10% of sites.

The second example, illustrated in Box 6.9, uses the data set from Loyn (1987), who recorded the abundance of forest birds in 56 forest fragments and related this response variable to six predictors that described aspects of each patch (area, distance to nearest patch and nearest larger patch, stock grazing, altitude and years since iso-

lation) – see Box 6.2. We built a regression tree model for these data, after transforming area and the two distances to logs. The first split was between patches with grazing indices from one to four and those with a grazing index of five. This former group was further split into two groups with $\log_{10}$ area ± 1.176 (approx. 15 ha). The final tree is presented in Figure 6.6. This tree is a little different from the results of the multiple linear regression analysis of these data in Box 6.2. There, $\log_{10}$ area was a significant predictor, with grazing not significant ($P = 0.079$), although model selection and hierarchical partitioning both resulted in a model with $\log_{10}$ area and grazing as the two predictors (Box 6.8). The fit of the regression tree model was 0.699. The equivalent multiple linear regression model including just grazing and $\log_{10}$ area as predictors resulted in an r^2 of 0.653 so the regression tree model produced a slightly better fit.

This brief introduction might encourage you to explore these methods further. The standard reference is Brieman *et al.* (1984), and De'ath & Fabricius (2000) provide an excellent and up-dated overview with ecological applications.

6.3 | Path analysis and structural equation modeling

The linear model we fit for a multiple regression represents our best guess at causal relationships. The model is postulating that the predictor variables we have incorporated may have biological effects on our response variable. The multiple regression model is, however, a conveniently simple representation of potential causal pathways among our variables as it only considers direct effects of each predictor, adjusting for the others, on the response variable. We may hypothesize much more complex causal links between variables. For example, we may include indirect effects where one predictor affects a second predictor, which in turn affects the response variable, and we may have two or more response variables that can affect each other. The statistical technique we use to analyze models of potential causal relationships was first developed over 50 years ago by Wright (1920, 1934) and is called path analysis

Box 6.9 | Worked example of regression trees: abundance of birds in forest patches

A regression tree for the data from Loyn (1987) related the abundance of forest birds in 56 forest fragments to log area, log distance to nearest patch and nearest larger patch, grazing intensity, altitude and years since isolation. We used OLS as our measure of fit and set stopping criteria so that no split would result in less than five observations in a group, the maximum number of nodes was less than 20 (although this latter criterion turned out to be irrelevant) and the minimum proportional reduction in residual variance was 5%. The first node in the tree was between 43 habitat patches with grazing indices from one to four and the 13 patches with a grazing index of five (Figure 6.6). This former group was further split into two groups, 24 patches with $\log_{10}$ area less than 1.176 (approx. 15 ha) and 19 patches with $\log_{10}$ area greater than 1.176.

The fit of this tree model was 0.699. The plot of residuals from the tree model is shown in Figure 6.8(a) with four observations in the group of small patches with low grazing (less than five) standing out from the others and warranting checking and possibly re-running the analysis after their omission to evaluate their influence.

Out of interest, we refitted the tree with looser stopping criteria (smaller allowable reduction in residual variance) to see what subsequent splits in the data would have occurred (Figure 6.7). On one side of the tree, the 13 patches with a grazing index of five were further split by $\log_{10}$ dist. On the other side, the 24 small patches were further split by age (and then by $\log_{10}$ area and $\log_{10}$ dist) and the 19 larger patches were further split by $\log_{10}$ area again. The fit of the model was improved to 0.84 but the model is much more complex with additional variables, some repeated throughout the tree (e.g. $\log_{10}$ area) so the improvement in fit is at least partly a consequence of the increased number of predictors in the tree model. The residuals show a more even pattern, with no obvious outliers (Figure 6.8(b)).

Figure 6.6 Regression tree modeling bird abundance in forest patches against patch area, distance to nearest patch, distance to nearest larger patch (these three variables $\log_{10}$ transformed), grazing intensity, altitude, and years since isolation for the 56 patches surveyed by Loyn (1987). The criteria for each node are included, with left-hand branches indicating observations with values for that predictor below the cut-off and right-hand branches indicating observations with values for that predictor above the cut-off. The predicted value (mean) and number of observations for each leaf (terminal group) are also provided.

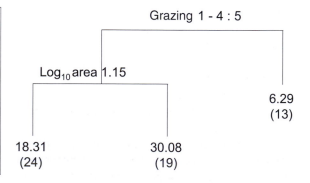

(see also Mitchell 1993 for a review). Path analysis was originally designed for simple multiple regression models and is now considered a subset of a more sophisticated collection of analytical tools called structural equation modeling (SEM), also called analysis of covariance (correlation) structure (Tabachnick & Fidell 1996). It is very important to remember that causality can only really be demonstrated by carefully designed and analyzed manipulative experiments, not by any specific statistical procedure. SEM and path analysis are basically analyses of correlations, although

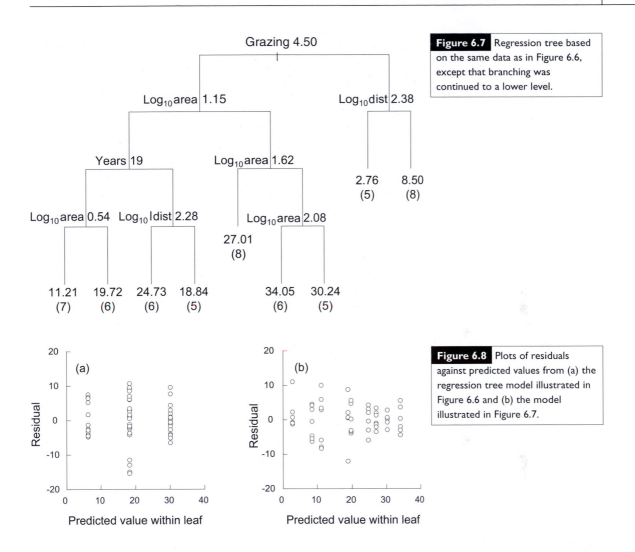

Figure 6.7 Regression tree based on the same data as in Figure 6.6, except that branching was continued to a lower level.

Figure 6.8 Plots of residuals against predicted values from (a) the regression tree model illustrated in Figure 6.6 and (b) the model illustrated in Figure 6.7.

they can be used to analyze experimental data (Smith *et al.* 1997), and simply test how well postulated causal pathways fit the observed data in a modeling context.

The fundamental component of SEM or path analysis is the *a priori* specification of one or more causal models, although most published applications of path analysis in biology do not seem to compare competing models. Let's consider a simple path diagram, based on the data from Loyn (1987), that relates the abundance of forest birds in isolated patches of remnant forest to a number of predictor variables (Figure 6.9). We will include three of these predictors ($\log_{10}$ patch area, years since isolation, grazing) and include all correlations among the predictors and all supposed causal links between each predictor and

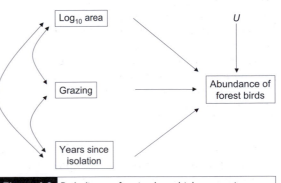

Figure 6.9 Path diagram for simple multiple regression model relating three predictor variables ($\log_{10}$ patch area, grazing, years since isolation) to one response variable (abundance of forest birds) using the data from Loyn (1987).

the response variable in our path diagram. Single-headed arrows represent supposed causal links between variables and double-headed arrows represent correlations between variables with no directional causality postulated. U represents unexplained causes (variables we have not measured) that might affect a response variable.

The process starts by specifying the model for each response variable. In our simple example, there is only one response variable and the model is a standardized multiple regression model without an intercept:

$$(\text{bird abundance})_i = \beta_1(\log_{10}\text{area})_i + \beta_2(\text{years})_i + \beta_3(\text{grazing})_i + \varepsilon_i \qquad (6.31)$$

Path analyses basically represent a restructuring of the correlations (or covariances) between all the variables under consideration (Mitchell 1993). The correlation (r_{jY}) between any predictor variable X_j and the response variable Y can be partitioned into two components: the direct and the indirect effects (Mitchell 1993). This partitioning simply represents the normal equations that we used for fitting the regression model using OLS (Box 6.3). The direct effect is measured by the standardized partial regression coefficient between Y and X_j, holding all other predictor variables constant. This direct effect is now the path coefficient relating Y to X_j. Path coefficients are identical to standardized regression coefficients if all correlations between predictor variables are included in our path diagram. The indirect effect is due to the correlations between X_j and the other predictors, which may in turn have direct effects on Y.

Mathematically, this decomposition of the correlations can be derived from the set of normal equations used for estimating the parameters of the multiple regression model (Petraitis *et al.* 1996). For example, for predictor variable one ($\log_{10}$ area):

$$r_{1Y} = b_1 + r_{12}b_2 + r_{13}b_3 \qquad (6.32)$$

where r represents simple correlations and b represents standardized partial regression coefficients.

For the Loyn (1987) data:

$$r_{\log_{10}\text{ area.abundance}} = b_{\log_{10}\text{ area.abundance}} + r_{\log_{10}\text{ area.years}}b_{\text{years.abundance}} + r_{\log_{10}\text{ area.grazing}}b_{\text{grazing.abundance}} \qquad (6.33)$$

The direct effect of $\log_{10}$ area on bird abundance is represented by the standardized regression slope. The indirect effect of $\log_{10}$ area on bird abundance via the former's correlation with years since isolation and with grazing is calculated from the sum of the last two terms in the right hand side of Equation 6.33 above. The correlations between years since isolation and bird abundance and between grazing and bird abundance can be similarly decomposed into direct and indirect effects. The path identified by U (unexplained effects) can be determined from $\sqrt{(1-r^2)}$ from the fit of the model for a given response variable (Mitchell 1993). The results are summarized in Box 6.10 and Figure 6.9.

Complex path models, with multiple response variables, are not as easily handled by the multiple regression approach to path analysis we have just described (Mitchell 1992). More sophisticated forms of structural equation modelling, such as those implemented in software based on CALIS (Covariance Analysis of Linear Structural equations; in SAS) and LISREL (Linear Structural Relations; in SPSS) algorithms, offer some advantages, especially in terms of model testing and comparison. These procedures estimate the path coefficients and the variances and covariances of the predictor variables simultaneously from the data using maximum likelihood, although other estimation methods (including OLS) are available (Tabachnick & Fidell 1996). A covariance matrix is then determined by combining these parameter estimates and this covariance matrix is compared to the actual covariance matrix based on the data to assess the fit of the model. Most software produces numerous measures of model fit, the AIC (see Section 6.1.15) being one of the preferred measures. As pointed out by Mitchell (1992) and Smith *et al.* (1997), such goodness-of-fit statistics can only be determined when there are more correlations between variables than there are coefficients being estimated, i.e. the model is over-identified. For example, we cannot test the fit of the path model in Figure 6.9 because we have estimated all the direct and indirect effects possible, i.e. there are no unestimated correlations. The number of unestimated correlations contributes to the df of the goodness-of-fit statistic (Mitchell 1993).

Box 6.10	Worked example of path analysis: abundance of birds in forest patches

We will use the data from Loyn (1987) to relate the abundance of forest birds in isolated patches of remnant forest to three predictor variables: $\log_{10}$ patch area, years since isolation, grazing (Figure 6.9). Our path model includes all correlations among the predictors and all supposed causal links between each predictor and the response variable. The path model outlined in Figure 6.9 was evaluated by calculating both direct and indirect effects of predictors on the response variable. The full correlation matrix was as follows.

	Abundance	$\log_{10}$ area	Years	Grazing
Abundance	1.000			
$\log_{10}$ area	0.740	1.000		
Years	−0.503	−0.278	1.000	
Grazing	−0.683	−0.559	0.636	1.000

The direct and indirect effects for $\log_{10}$ area were calculated from:

$$r_{\log_{10}\ area.abundance} = b_{\log_{10}\ area.abundance} + r_{\log_{10}\ area.years}b_{years.abundance} + r_{\log_{10}\ area.grazing}b_{grazing.abundance}$$

where $b_{\log_{10}\ area.abundance}$ is the direct effect of $\log_{10}$ area on abundance (the partial regression coefficient), $r_{\log_{10}\ area.years}b_{years.abundance}$ is the indirect effect of $\log_{10}$ area on abundance via years and $r_{\log_{10}\ area.grazing}b_{grazing.abundance}$ is the indirect effect of $\log_{10}$ area on abundance via grazing. Equivalent equations were used for the other predictors. Correlations between predictor variables were also calculated. The final results were as follows.

Predictor	Direct effects	Indirect effects	Total effects
$\log_{10}$ area	0.542	0.198	0.740
via years		0.542	
via grazing		0.146	
Years since isolation	−0.187	−0.317	−0.503
via $\log_{10}$ area		−0.151	
via grazing		−0.166	
Grazing	−0.261	−0.422	−0.683
via $\log_{10}$ area		−0.303	
via years		−0.119	

It is clear that the "effect" of $\log_{10}$ area on bird abundance is primarily a direct effect whereas the "effects" of grazing and years since isolation are primarily indirect through the other predictors. Our use of quotation marks around "effect" here emphasizes that this is simply a correlation analysis; attributing causality to any of these predictor variables can only be achieved by using manipulative experiments. The r^2 for this model is 0.673 so the coefficient of the path from U to bird abundance is 0.572.

These programs also allow for latent (unmeasured) variables, which are unfortunately termed factors in the SEM literature. Latent variables are not commonly included in path models in the biological literature, although Kingsolver & Schemske (1991) discussed the inclusion of unmeasured phenotypic factors in path analyses of selection in evolutionary studies. The difficulty with these sophisticated SEM programs is they are more complex to run. For example, LISREL requires that a number of matrices be specified, representing the variances, covariances and relationships between variables. Detailed comparisons of these different programs, including required input and interpretation of the output, are available in Tabachnick & Fidell (1996)

The limitations and assumptions of classical path analysis are the same as those for multiple regression. The error terms from the model are assumed to be normally distributed and independent and the variances should be similar for different combinations of the predictor variables. Path analysis will also be sensitive to outliers and influential observations, and missing observations will have to be addressed, either by replacement or deletion of an entire observation (see Chapters 4 and 15). Collinearity among the predictor variables can seriously distort both the accuracy and precision of the estimates of the path coefficients, as these are simply partial regression coefficients (Petraitis *et al.* 1996; Section 6.1.11). There is still debate over whether more sophisticated SEM techniques, such as those based on LISREL, are more robust to these issues (Petraitis *et al.* 1996, Pugusek & Grace 1998). Diagnostics, such as residual plots, should be an essential component of any path analysis. Irrespective of which method is used, all estimates of path coefficients are sensitive to which variables are included or which coefficients (correlation or path) are set to zero (Mitchell 1992, Petraitis *et al.* 1996). This is no different to multiple regression, where estimates of partial regression slopes are sensitive to which predictors are included or not.

Finally, we repeat our earlier caution that, although structural equation modeling analyzes postulated causal relationships, it cannot "confirm or disprove the existence of causal links" (Petraitis *et al.* 1996 p. 429). Such causal links can only be demonstrated by manipulative experiments. SEM and path analyses do allow complex linear models to be evaluated and path diagrams provide a useful graphical representation of the strengths of these relationships.

6.4 | Nonlinear models

When the relationship between Y and X is clearly curvilinear, there are a number of options. We have already discussed using a polynomial model (Section 6.1.13) or linearizing transformations of the variables (Section 6.1.10), but these are not always applicable. For example, the relationship between Y and X might be complex and cannot be approximated by a polynomial nor can it be linearized by transformations of the variables. The third option is to fit a model that is nonlinear in the parameters. For example, the relationship between number of species (S) and island area (A) can be represented by the power function:

$$S = \alpha A^\beta \tag{6.34}$$

where α and β are the parameters to be estimated (Loehle 1990) – see Box 6.11. This is a two parameter nonlinear model. A three parameter nonlinear model which is very useful for relating a binary variable (e.g. presence/absence, alive/dead) to an independent variable is the logistic model:

$$Y = \frac{\alpha}{1 + e^{(\beta - \delta X)}} \tag{6.35}$$

where α, β and δ are the parameters to be estimated. Ratkowsky (1990) has described a large range of multiparameter nonlinear models, both graphically and statistically, and some of their practical applications.

OLS or ML methods can be used for estimation in nonlinear regression modeling, as we have described for linear models. The OLS estimates of the parameters are the ones that minimize the sum of squared differences between the observed and fitted values and are determined by solving a set of simultaneous normal equations. Solving these equations is much trickier than in linear models and some sort of iterative search procedure is required, whereby different estimates are tried in a sequential fashion. Obviously, with two

Box 6.11 Worked example of nonlinear regression: species richness of macroinvertebrates in mussel clumps

As described in Chapter 5, Peake & Quinn (1993) collected 25 clumps of an intertidal mussel from a rocky shore at Phillip Island in Victoria. The relationship between the number of species (Y) per clump and clump area in m^2 (X) was examined. The scatterplot suggested a nonlinear relationship between number of species and clump area (Figure 5.17) and theory suggests that a power function might be appropriate:

$$species = \alpha(area)^{\beta}$$

This power function was fitted using a modified Gauss–Newton method (quasi-Newton). No starting values were provided. The algorithm took six iterations to converge on the following estimates, with their approximate standard errors.

Parameter	Estimate	Standard error	t	P
α	18.540	0.630	29.449	<0.001
β	0.334	0.035	9.532	<0.001

The $MS_{Residual}$ was 7.469. The fitted model was, therefore:

$$species = 18.540(area)^{0.334}$$

Note that the $MS_{Residual}$ for the nonlinear power function (7.469) is about half that for a linear model (14.133), indicating the former is a better fit to the data. The fitted model is shown in Figure 6.10(a) and the residual plot (Figure 6.10(b)) suggested no strong skewness in the response variable and there were no unusual outliers.

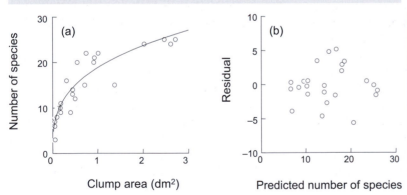

Figure 6.10 (a) Plot of number of species against mussel clump area from Peake & Quinn (1993) showing fitted nonlinear model: number of species $= 18.540 \times (area)^{0.334}$. (b) Plot of residuals against predicted values (with boxplots) from fitted nonlinear model in (a) fitted to number of species against mussel clump area from Peake & Quinn (1993).

or more parameters, the number of possible combinations of values for the parameters is essentially infinite so these searching procedures are sophisticated in that they only try values that improve the fit of the model (i.e. reduce the $SS_{Residual}$).

The most common method is the Gauss–Newton algorithm or some modification of it

(Myers 1990). Starting values of the parameters must be provided and these are our best guess of what the values of the parameters might be. The more complex the model, the more important it is for the starting values to be reasonably close to the real parameter values. Starting values may come from fits of the equivalent model to other, similar, data (e.g. from the published literature), theoretical considerations or, for relationships that can be linearized by transformation, back-transformed values from a linear model fitted to transformed data. The Gauss–Newton search method is complex, using partial derivatives from the starting values and X-values to fit an iterative series of essentially linear models and using OLS to estimate the parameters. The best estimates are reached when the sequential iterations converge, i.e. don't change the estimates by very much. Variances and standard errors for the parameter estimates can be determined; the calculations are tedious but most statistical software provides this information. Confidence intervals, and t tests for null hypotheses, about parameters can also be determined (Box 6.11).

There are a number of difficulties with nonlinear modeling. First, sometimes the iterative Gauss–Newton procedure won't converge or converges to estimates that are not the best possible ("local minimum"). Most statistical software use modified Gauss–Newton procedures, which help convergence, and choosing realistic starting values is very important. It is usually worth refitting nonlinear models with different starting values just to be sure the final model can be achieved consistently. Second, OLS works fine for linear models if the errors (residuals) are independent, normally distributed with constant variance; however, for nonlinear models, even when these assumptions are met, OLS estimators and their standard errors, and confidence intervals and hypothesis tests for the parameters, are only approximate (Myers 1990; Rawlings *et al.* 1998). We can be more certain of our estimates and confidence intervals if different combinations of search algorithms and starting values produce similar results. Finally, measuring the fit of nonlinear models to the data is tricky; r^2 cannot be easily interpreted because the usual SS_{Total} for the response variable cannot always be partitioned into two additive components ($SS_{Regression}$ and $SS_{Residual}$). Comparing different models, some of which might be nonlinear, can only be done with variables measured on the same scale (i.e. untransformed; see Chapter 5) and the $MS_{Residual}$ is probably the best criterion of fit.

Once a nonlinear model has been estimated, diagnostic evaluation of its appropriateness is essential. Residuals can be calculated in the usual manner and large values indicate outliers. Because OLS estimation is commonly used for nonlinear models, assumptions of normality, homogeneity of variance and independence of the error terms from the model are applicable. Boxplots of residuals and scatterplots of residuals against predicted values (Figure 6.10) can detect problems with these assumptions as described for linear models. Other estimation methods, such as maximum likelihood, might be more robust than OLS.

For simple nonlinear structures, transforming the variables to achieve linearity is usually recommended, particularly if the transformed variables can be easily interpreted because the transformed scale is a natural alternative scale of measurement for that variable. Note that the transformed model is not the same as the untransformed nonlinear model, in the same way that a t test on untransformed data is not testing the same H_0 as a t test on the same data transformed. Our parameter estimates from the transformed model cannot easily be interpreted in terms of the original nonlinear model, which may have the stronger theoretical basis.

6.5 | Smoothing and response surfaces

The linear plane representing the linear regression model of Y against X_1 and X_2 illustrated in Figure 6.1 is sometimes referred to as a response surface, a graphical representation of the relationship between a response variable and two predictors. Response surfaces obviously also exist when there are more than two predictors but we cannot display them graphically. Response surfaces, in this graphical context, are often used to display the model chosen as the best fit based on the model-fitting techniques we have already described. Additionally, exploring a range of response surfaces may help decide what sort of model is best to use and detect patterns we might have missed by being restricted to a specific model.

Model-based surfaces that are linear in parameters include linear and curvilinear relationships.

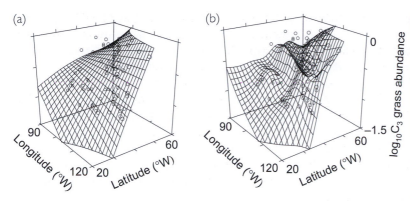

(a)

(b)

$\log_{10}C_3$ grass abundance

Figure 6.11 Response surfaces relating log-transformed relative abundance of C_3 plants to latitude and longitude for 73 sites in North America (Paruelo & Lauenroth 1996). (a) Quadratic model fitted, and (b) distance-weighted least squares (DWLS) fitted.

For example, polynomial models (quadratic, cubic, etc.) are often good approximations to more complex relationships and provide a more realistic representation of the relationship between Y and X_1 and X_2 than a simple linear model. Figure 6.11(a) shows a quadratic response surface, representing a model including linear and quadratic terms for both predictors as well as their interaction, fitted to the data from Paruelo & Lauenroth (1996). Note that compared with the first-order linear model in Figure 6.1, the quadratic model allows a hump-shaped response of log-transformed C_3 plant abundance to longitude for a given latitude. The choice of whether to use this response surface would depend on the results of fitting this model compared with a simpler first-order model.

Smoothing functions, like we discussed in Chapter 5, can sometimes also be applied to three-dimensional surfaces. While the Loess smoother cannot easily be extended to three dimensions, DWLS can and allows a flexible exploration of the nature of the relationship between Y and X_1 and X_2 unconstrained by a specific model. For the data from Paruelo & Lauenroth (1996), the DWLS surface (Figure 6.11(b)) suggests a potentially complex relationship between log transformed C_3 plant abundance and longitude in the northern, high latitude, sites, a pattern not revealed by the linear or polynomial models. Note that, like the bivariate case, parameters for these smoothing functions cannot be estimated because they are not model-based; they are exploratory only.

Response surfaces also have other uses. For example, comparing the fitted response surfaces for linear models with and without an interaction between two predictors can help interpret the nature of such an interaction. Again for the data from Paruelo & Lauenroth (1996), the DWLS smoothing function suggests that the relationship between log-transformed abundance of C_3 plants and latitude depends on longitude and vice versa (Figure 6.11(b)). Most statistical software can plot a range of model-based and smoothing response surfaces on three-dimensional scatterplots.

6.6 General issues and hints for analysis

6.6.1 General issues

- Multiple regression models are fitted in a similar fashion to simple regression models, with parameters estimated using OLS methods.
- The partial regression slopes in a multiple regression model measure the slope of the relationship between Y and each predictor, holding the other predictors constant. These relationships can be represented with partial regression plots.
- Comparisons of fit between full and reduced models, the latter representing the model when a particular H_0 is true, are an important method for testing null hypotheses about model parameters, or combinations of parameters, in complex models.
- Standardized partial regression slopes should be used if the predictors and the response variable are measured in different units.
- Collinearity, correlations between the predictor variables, can cause estimates of parameters to be unstable and have artificially large

variances. This reduces the power of tests on individual parameters.

- Interactions between predictors should be considered in multiple regression models and multiplicative models, based on centered predictors to avoid collinearity, should be fitted when appropriate.

- Hierarchical partitioning is strongly recommended for determining the relative independent and joint contribution of each predictor to the variation in the response variable.

- Regression trees provide an alternative to multiple linear models for exploring the relationships between response and predictor variables through successive binary splits of the data, although cross-validation is necessary for evaluation of predictive power and hypothesis testing.

- Path analysis can be a useful technique for graphically representing possible causal links between response and predictor variables, and also between predictor variables themselves.

- Nonlinear models can be fitted using OLS, although the estimation procedure is more complex. The trick is deciding *a priori* what the most appropriate theoretical model is.

6.6.2 Hints for analysis

- Multiple regression analyses are sensitive to outliers and influential values. Plots of residuals and Cook's D_i statistic are useful diagnostic checks.

- Information criteria, such as Akaike's (AIC) or Schwarz's (BIC) are the best criteria for distinguishing the fit of different models, although $MS_{Residual}$ is also applicable for regression models fitted using OLS.

- Avoid automated selection procedures (forward, backward, etc.) in model fitting. Their results are inconsistent and hard to interpret because of the large number of significance tests. For moderate numbers of predictors, compare the fit of all possible models.

- Use simple slopes for further interpretation of interactions between predictor variables in multiple regression models.

- Causality can only be demonstrated by careful research and experimentation, not by a particular statistical analysis. For example, path analysis is a method for summarizing correlation structures among variables and cannot show causality.

- Always examine scatterplots and correlations among your variables, to detect nonlinear relationships but also to detect collinearity among predictors. Tolerance (or the variance inflation factor) will also indicate collinearity. Choose which predictor variables to include in the final model carefully, avoiding variables that are highly correlated and measuring a similar quantity.

Chapter 7

Design and power analysis

7.1 | Sampling

Fundamental to any statistical analysis, including the regression models we described in the previous two chapters, is the design of the sampling regime. We are assuming that we can clearly define a population of interest, including its spatial and temporal boundaries, and that we have chosen an appropriate type and size of sampling unit. These units may be natural units (e.g. stones, organisms, and lakes) or artificially delineated units of space (e.g. plots or quadrats). Our aim is to design a sampling program that provides the most efficient (in terms of costs) and precise estimates of parameters of the population. It is important to remember that we are talking about a statistical population, all the possible sampling or experimental units about which we wish to make some inference. The term population has another meaning in biology, a group of organisms of the same species (Chapter 2), although this might also represent a statistical population of interest.

We will only provide a brief overview of some sampling designs. We recommend Levy & Lemeshow (1991), Manly (2001) and Thompson (1992), the latter two having more of a biological emphasis, as excellent references for more detail on the design of sampling programs and using them to estimate population parameters.

7.1.1 Sampling designs
Simple random sampling was introduced in Chapter 2 and is where all the possible sampling units in our population have an equal chance of being selected in a sample. Technically, random sampling should be done by giving all possible sampling units a number and then choosing which units are included in the sample using a random selection of numbers (e.g. from a random number generator). In practice, especially in field biology, this method is often difficult, because the sampling units do not represent natural distinct habitat units (e.g. they are quadrats or plots) and cannot be numbered in advance or because the sampling units are large (e.g. 20 m^2 plots) and the population covers a large area. In these circumstances, biologists often resort to "haphazard" sampling, where sampling units are chosen in a less formal manner. We are assuming that a haphazard sample has the same characteristics as a random sample.

The formulae provided in Chapter 2 for estimating population means and variances, standard errors of the estimates and confidence intervals for parameters assume simple random sampling. If the size of the total population of sampling units is finite, then there are correction factors that can be applied to the formulae for variances and standard errors, although many populations in biological research are essentially infinite.

You can't really go wrong with simple random sampling. Estimates of the parameters of the population, especially the mean, will be ML estimators and generally unbiased. The downside of simple random sampling is that it may be less efficient than other sampling designs, especially when there is identified heterogeneity in the population or we wish to estimate parameters at a range of spatial or temporal scales.

Other sampling designs take into account heterogeneity in the population from which we are sampling. Stratified sampling is where the population is divided into levels or strata that represent clearly defined groups of units within the population and we sample independently (and randomly) from each of those groups. For example, we may wish to estimate characteristics of a population of stones in a stream (our variable might be species richness of invertebrates). If the stones clearly fall into different habitat types, e.g. riffles, pools and backwaters, then we might take random samples of stones from each habitat (stratum) separately. Stratified sampling is likely to be more representative in this case than a simple random sample because it ensures that the major habitat types are included in the sample. Usually, the number of units sampled from each stratum is proportional to the total number of possible units in each stratum or the total size of each stratum (e.g. area). Estimating population means and variances from stratified sampling requires modification of the formulae provided in Chapter 2 for simple random sampling. If sampling within a stratum is random, the estimate of stratum population mean is as before but the estimate of the overall population mean is:

$$\bar{y}_{str} = \sum_{h=1}^{l} W_h \bar{y}_h \qquad (7.1)$$

where there are $h = 1$ to l strata, W_h is the proportion of total units in stratum h (often estimated from the proportion of total area in stratum h) and $\bar{y}_h$ is the sample mean for stratum h (Levy & Lemeshow 1991). If our sample size within each stratum is proportional to the number of possible units within each stratum, Equation (7.1) simplifies to:

$$\bar{y}_{str} = \frac{\sum_{h=1}^{l} \sum_{i=1}^{n_h} y_{hi}}{n} \qquad (7.2)$$

where there are $i = 1$ to n_h observations sampled within stratum h, y_{hi} is the ith observation from the hth stratum and n is the total sample size across all strata. The standard error of this mean is:

$$s_{\bar{y}_{str}} = \sqrt{\sum_{h=1}^{l} (W_h)^2 \frac{s_h^2}{n_h}} \qquad (7.3)$$

where s_h^2 is the sample variance for stratum h. Approximate confidence intervals can also be determined (Levy & Lemeshow 1991, Thompson 1992). When statistical models are fitted to data from stratified sampling designs, the strata should be included as a predictor variable in the model. The observations from the different strata cannot be simply pooled and considered a single random sample except maybe when we have evidence that the strata are not different in terms of our response variable, e.g. from a preliminary test between strata.

Cluster sampling also uses heterogeneity in the population to modify the basic random sampling design. Imagine we can identify primary sampling units (clusters) in a population, e.g. individual trees. For each primary unit (tree), we then record all secondary units, e.g. branches on each tree. Simple cluster sampling is where we record all secondary units within each primary unit. Two stage cluster sampling is where we take a random sample of secondary units within each primary unit. Three stage cluster sampling is where we take a random sample of tertiary units (e.g. leaves) within each secondary unit (e.g. branches) within each primary unit (e.g. trees). Simple random sampling is usually applied at each stage, although proportional sampling can also be used. These designs are used to estimate variation at a series of hierarchical (or nested) levels, often representing nested spatial scales and nested linear ANOVA models are often fitted to data from two or more stage cluster sampling designs (Section 9.1).

Systematic sampling is where we choose sampling units that are equally spaced, either spatially or temporally. For example, we might choose plots along a transect at 5 m intervals or we might choose weekly sampling dates. Systematic sampling is sometimes used when we wish to describe an environmental gradient and we want to know where changes in the environment occur. For example, we want to measure the gradient in species richness away from a point source of pollution. Simple random sampling away from the source might miss the crucial region where the species richness undergoes rapid change. Sampling at regular intervals is probably a better bet. Various methods exist for estimating means and variances from systematic sampling, although the estimates are biased unless certain conditions are met (Levy & Lemeshow 1991).

The big risk with systematic sampling is that the regular spacing may coincide with an unknown environmental gradient and so any inference to the whole population of possible sampling units would be biased (Manly 2001). This is probably more likely in field biology (e.g. ecology) where environmental gradients can occur at a range of different spatial and temporal scales.

Systematic sampling can have a single random starting point, where the first unit is chosen randomly and then the remainder evenly spaced. Alternatively, a cluster design could be used, where clusters are chosen at random and then systematic selection on secondary sampling units within each cluster is used.

Finally, we should briefly mention adaptive sampling. When a sampling program has a temporal component, which is often the case in biology, especially when sampling ecological phenomena or environmental impacts, then we might modify our sampling design on the basis of estimates of parameters early in the program. For example, we might change our sample size based on preliminary estimates of variance or we might even change to a stratified design if the initial simple random sampling indicates clear strata in the population that were not detected early on. Thompson (1992) provides an introduction to adaptive sampling but a more detailed text is Thompson & Seber (1995).

7.1.2 Size of sample

If we have idea of the level of variability between sampling units in our population, we can use this information to estimate the required sample size to be confident (e.g. 95% confident) that any sample mean will not be different from the true mean by more than a specified amount under repeated sampling. The calculations are simple, assuming we have sampled randomly and the Central Limit Theorem (Chapter 2) holds:

$$n \geq \frac{z^2 \sigma^2}{d^2} \tag{7.4}$$

where z is the value from a standard normal distribution for a given confidence level (z equals 1.96

for 95% confidence so z^2 approximately equals four – Manly 2001), σ^2 is the variance of the population (usually estimated with s^2 from some pilot sample or previous information) and d is the maximum allowable absolute difference between the estimated mean and the true population mean. Note that the estimation of sample sizes depends on the variance estimate from the pilot study matching the variance in the population when we sample.

7.2 | Experimental design

While our emphasis is on manipulative experiments, most of the principles we will outline below also apply to non-manipulative contrasts that we might make as part of sampling programs. General principles of experimental design are described in many standard statistical texts, and in great statistical detail in some very good, specialized books, such as Mead (1988) and Underwood (1997). Hairston (1989) and Resetarits & Fauth (1998) describe many examples of ecological experiments and evaluate their design.

The most important constraint on the unambiguous interpretation of an experiment is the problem of confounding. Confounding means that differences due to experimental treatments, i.e. the contrast specified in your hypothesis, cannot be separated from other factors that might be causing the observed differences. A simple, albeit trivial, example will illustrate the problem. Imagine you wished to test the effect of a particular hormone on some behavioral response of crayfish. You create two groups of crayfish, males and females, and inject the hormone into the male crayfish and leave the females as the control group. Even if other aspects of the design are OK (random sampling, controls, etc.), differences between the means of the two groups cannot be unambiguously attributed to effects of the hormone. The two groups are also different genders and this may also be, at least partly, determining the behavioral responses of the crayfish. In this example, the effects of hormone are confounded with the effects of gender. The obvious solution is to randomize the allocation of crayfish to treatments so that the two groups are just as

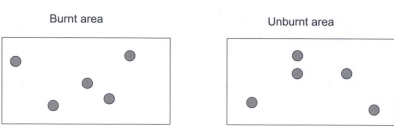

Figure 7.1 Example of an inappropriately replicated study on the effects of fire on soil invertebrates. Each area is sampled with five replicate soil cores.

Burnt area

Unburnt area

likely to have males and females. Unfortunately, possible confounding is rarely this obvious and confounding can sneak into an experimental design in many ways, especially through inappropriate replication, lack of proper controls and lack of randomized allocation of experimental units to treatments. These issues will be our focus in this chapter.

Sometimes, confounding is a deliberate part of experimental design. In particular, when we have too many treatment combinations for the number of available replicate units, we might confound some interactions so we can test main effects (Chapter 9). Designs with such deliberate confounding must be used with care, especially in biology where interactive effects are common and difficult to ignore.

7.2.1 Replication

Replication means having replicate observations at a spatial and temporal scale that matches the application of the experimental treatments. Replicates are essential because biological systems are inherently variable and this is particularly so for ecological systems. Linear model analyses of designed experiments usually rely on comparing the variation between treatment groups to the inherent variability between experimental units within each group. An estimate of this latter variability requires replicate units.

Replication at an appropriate scale also helps us avoid confounding treatment differences with other systematic differences between experimental units. For example, to test if there are effects of fish predation on the abundance of a species of bivalve on intertidal mudflats, we might set up a field experiment using fish exclusion cages and suitable cage controls (see Section 7.2.2 for discussion of controls) over plots (experimental units) on the mudflat. If we simply have a single exclusion plot and a single control plot, then the effects of our treatment (fish exclusion) are confounded

with inherent differences between the two plots related to their spatial location, such as tidal height, sediment composition, etc. With two or more replicate plots for each of the two treatments (exclusion and control), we can be much more confident in attributing differences between treatment and control plots to fish exclusion rather than inherent plot differences. Note that replication does *not* guarantee protection from confounding because it is still possible that, by chance, all our treatment plots are different from our control plots in some way besides access to fish. However, the risk of confounding is reduced by replication, especially when combined with randomized allocation of treatments to experimental units (Section 7.2.3).

While most biologists are well aware of the need for replication, we often mismatch the scale of those replicates relative to treatments being applied. Probably no other aspect of experimental design causes more problems for biologists (Hurlbert 1984). Imagine a study designed to test the effects of fire on the species richness of soil invertebrates. Fire is difficult to manipulate in the field, so investigators often make use of a natural wildfire. In our example, one burnt area might be located and compared to an unburnt area nearby. Within each area, replicate cores of soil are collected and the species richness of invertebrates determined for each core (Figure 7.1). The mean number of species of invertebrates between the two areas was compared with a *t* test, after verifying that the assumptions of normality and equal variances were met.

There is nothing wrong with the statistical test in this example. If the assumptions are met, a *t* test is appropriate for testing the H_0 that there is no difference in the mean number of invertebrate species between the two areas. The difficulty is that the soil cores are not the appropriate scale of replication for testing the effects of fire. The spatial unit to which fire was either applied or not applied was the whole area, and the measures of species richness from within the burned area measure the impact of the same fire. Therefore, there is only one replicate for each of the two treatments (burnt and unburnt). With only a single replicate area for each of our treatments, the effect of fire is completely confounded with inherent differences between the two areas that may also affect invertebrates, irrespective of fire. It is very difficult to draw conclusions about the effect of fire from this design; we can only conclude from our analysis that the two areas are different.

The replicate soil cores within each area simply represent subsamples. Subsampling of experimental units does not provide true replication, only pseudoreplication (*sensu* Hurlbert 1984). Pseudoreplication is a piece of jargon that has been adopted by many biologists and used to refer to a wide range of flawed experimental designs. In many cases, biologists using this term do not have a clear understanding of the problem with a particular design, and are using the phrase as a catch-all to describe different kinds of confounding. We will avoid the term, in part to encourage you to learn enough of experimental design to understand problem designs, but also because the term is a little ambiguous. The design is replicated, but the replication is at the wrong scale, with replicates that allow us to assess each area, and the differences between areas, but no replicates at the scale of the experimental manipulation.

Confounding as a result of inappropriate replication is not restricted to non-manipulative field studies. Say as marine biologists, we wished to test the effects of copper on the settlement of larvae of a species of marine invertebrate (e.g. a barnacle). We could set up two large aquaria in a laboratory and in each aquarium, lay out replicate substrata (e.g. Perspex panels) suitable for settling barnacle larvae. We dose the water in one aquarium with a copper solution and the other aquarium with a suitable inert control solution (e.g. seawater). We then add 1000 cyprid larvae to each aquarium and record the number of larvae settling onto each of the panels in each aquarium. The mean number of settled larvae between the two aquaria was compared with a *t* test.

We have the same problem with this experiment as with the fire study. The appropriate experimental units for testing the effects of copper are the aquaria, not individual panels within each aquarium. The effects of copper are completely confounded with other inherent differences between the two aquaria and panels are just subsamples. We emphasize that there is nothing wrong with the *t* test; it is just not testing a null hypothesis about copper effects, only one about differences between two aquaria. To properly test for the effects of copper (rather than just testing for differences between two aquaria), this experiment requires replicate treatment and control aquaria. Note that this experiment has other problems, particularly the lack of independence between the multiple larvae in one aquarium – barnacle cyprids are well known to be gregarious settlers.

As a final example, consider a study to investigate the effects of a sewage discharge on the biomass of phytoplankton in a coastal habitat. Ten randomly chosen water "samples[1]" are taken from the sea at a location next to the outfall and another ten water "samples" are taken from the sea at a location away (upcurrent) from the outfall. As you might have guessed, the appropriate units for testing the effects of sewage are locations, not individual volumes of water. With this design, the effect of sewage on phytoplankton biomass is completely confounded with other inherent differences between the two locations and the water "samples" are just subsamples.

How do we solve these problems? The best solution is to have replicates at the appropriate scale. We need replicate burnt and unburnt areas, replicate aquaria for each treatment, replicate locations along the coast with and without sewage outfalls. Such designs with correct replication provide the greatest protection against

---

1 Biologists and environmental scientists often use the term sample to describe a single experimental or sampling unit, e.g. a sample of mud from an estuary, a sample of water from a lake. In contrast, a statistical sample is a collection of one or more of these units ("samples") from some defined population. We will only use the term sample to represent a statistical sample, unless there are no obvious alternative words for a biological sample, as in this case.

confounding. In some cases, though, replication is either very difficult or impossible. For example, we might have an experiment in which constant temperature rooms are the experimental units, but because of their cost and availability within a research institution, only two or three are available. In the example looking at the effects of sewage outfalls, we usually only have a single outfall to assess, although there may be no limit to the availability of locations along the coast without outfalls. Experiments at very large spatial scales, such as ecosystem manipulations (Carpenter *et al.* 1995), often cannot have replication because replicate units simply don't exist in nature.

In situations where only one replicate unit is possible for each treatment, especially in a true manipulative experiment that is relatively short-term, one possibility is to run the experiment a number of times, each time switching the treatments between the experimental units. For example, run the copper experiment once, and then repeat it after reversing which aquarium is the treatment and which is the control. Repositioning the aquaria and repeating the experiment a number of times will reduce the likelihood that differences between aquaria will confound the effects of copper. Alternatively, we could try and measure all variables that could possibly influence settlement of barnacles and see if they vary between our aquaria – if not, then we are more confident that the only difference between aquaria is copper. Of course, we can never be sure that we have accounted for all the relevant variables, so this is far from an ideal solution.

For the sewage outfall example, the problem of confounding can be partly solved by taking samples at several places well away from the outfall, so we can at least assess the amount of variation between places. Ideally, however, we need samples from several outfalls and corresponding areas far away, but it is difficult to recommend the installation of multiple outfalls just for statistical convenience. A substantial literature has developed to try and make a conclusion about impacts of human activities when there is only one place at which a potential impact occurs. These designs are generally called Before-After-Control-Impact (BACI) designs (Green 1979,

Stewart-Oaten *et al.* 1986), and various suggestions include sampling through time to provide replication, sampling multiple control areas, etc. These designs have been contentious, and a critical evaluation of their pros and cons can be found in Keough & Mapstone (1995) and Downes *et al.* (2002).

The above examples illustrate spatial confounding, but confounding with time can also occur, although it is less common. Consider an experiment to test for the effects of floods on drifting insects in streams. We might set up six artificial stream channels with drift nets at the end – six stream channels are all we have available. We want to impose two treatments, high flow and normal flow, and we know from previous work that we will need a minimum of six replicates per treatment to detect the desired effect if it occurs (see Section 7.3 on power analyses). We could do the experiment at two times with six replicates of high flow at time one and six replicates of normal flow at time two. Unfortunately, the effects of flow would be completely confounded with differences between the two times. The appropriate design of this experiment would be to have three replicates of each treatment at each time, therefore becoming a two factor experiment (treatment and time). If we only have enough experimental units to have one replicate for each treatment, then we can use time as a blocking factor (see Chapter 10).

7.2.2 Controls

In most experimental situations, many factors that could influence the outcome of the experiment are not under our control and are allowed to vary naturally. Therefore, it is essential to know what would happen if the experimental manipulation had not been performed. This is the function of controls. An excellent example of the need for controls comes from Hairston (1980, see also 1989) who wished to test the hypothesis that two species of salamanders (*Plethodon jordani* and *P. glutinosus*) in the Great Smoky Mountains compete. He set up experiments where *P. glutinosus* was removed from plots. The population of *P. jordani* started increasing during the three years following *P. glutinosus* removal, but the population of *P. jordani* on control plots (with *P. glutinosus* not removed) showed an identical increase. Without the control plots, the increase in *P. jordani* might have been incorrectly attributed to *P. glutinosus* removal.

Simply deciding to have controls is not enough. The controls must also allow us to eliminate as many artifacts as possible introduced by our experimental procedure. For example, research in animal physiology often looks at the effects of a substance (e.g. some drug or hormone or toxin) on experimental animals, e.g. rats, or *in vitro* tissue preparations. The effects of the substance are assessed by comparing the response of animals injected with the substance to the response of control animals not injected. However, differences in the responses of the two groups of animals may be due to the injection procedure (handling effects, injury from needle etc.), not just the effect of the substance. The effects of the substance are confounded with differences in experimental procedure. Such an experiment would need control animals that are injected with some inert substance (e.g. saline solution), but which undergo the experimental procedure identically to the treatment animals; such a control is sometimes termed a procedural control. Then any difference between the groups can be more confidently attributed to the effect of the substance alone.

Ecological field experiments also offer challenges in designing appropriate controls (Hairston 1989, Underwood 1997). For example, to examine the effect of predatory fish on marine benthic communities, we might compare areas of substratum with fish exclusion cages to areas of substratum with no cages. However, the differences between two types of area may be due to effects of the cages other than excluding fish (e.g. shading, reduced water movement, presence of hard structure). The effects of fish exclusion are confounded with these other caging effects. We must use cage controls, e.g. cages that have larger gaps in the mesh that allow in fish but are otherwise as similar to the exclusion cages as possible. Then, any difference between treatments can be more confidently attributed to the effect of excluding fish alone. This is not a simple matter – if a major effect of cages is to alter water movement (and hence sedimentation), it may be difficult to leave big enough gaps for fish to enter at the same rate

as they enter uncaged areas, without changing flow rates. In many cases, the cage control will be physically intermediate between caged and uncaged areas. The marine ecological literature contains many examples of different kinds of cage controls, including the step of using cages to both enclose and exclude a particular predator.

Ecological experiments sometimes involve translocating organisms to different areas to test a specific hypothesis. For example, to test what determines the lower limit of intertidal gastropods on intertidal rocky shores, we might consider translocating gastropods to lower levels of the shore. If they die, it may be an effect of height on the shore or an effect of translocation procedure. Appropriate controls should include gastropods that are picked up and handled in exactly the same way as translocated animals except they are replaced at the original level. Additional controls could include gastropods at the original level that are not moved, as a test for the effects of handling by themselves. Controls for translocation experiments are tricky – see Chapman (1986) for a detailed evaluation.

7.2.3 Randomization

There are two aspects of randomization that are important in the design and analysis of experiment. The first concerns random sampling from clearly defined populations, as we discussed in Chapter 2 and in Section 7.1.1. It is essential that the experimental units within each of our treatments represent a random (or at least haphazard) sample from an appropriate population of experimental units. This ensures that our estimates of population parameters (means, treatment effects, mean squares) are unbiased and our statistical inferences (conclusions from the statistical test) are reliable.

For example, our experimental animals that received a substance in a treatment should represent a random sample of all possible animals that we could have given the substance and about which we wish to draw conclusions. Our caged plots in the marine example must be a random sample of all possible caged plots in that habitat – similarly for our control plots. We must clearly define our treatment (and control) populations when we design our experiment. The converse is

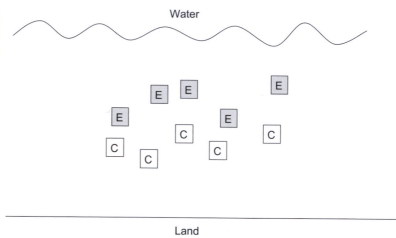

that we can only draw conclusions about the population from which we have taken a random sample. If our plots on a mud flat were scattered over a 20 m × 20 m area, then our conclusions only apply to that area; if we used a particular strain of rats, then we have only a conclusion about that genetic strain, and so on.

The second aspect of randomization concerns the allocation of treatments to experimental units or vice versa. One of the standard recommendations in experimental design is that the experimental units be randomly allocated to treatment groups. This means that no pattern of treatments across experimental units is subjectively included or excluded (Mead 1988) and should ensure that systematic differences between experimental units that might confound our interpretation of treatment effects are minimized (Hurlbert 1984, Underwood 1997). The crayfish example described at the beginning of Section 7.2 is an illustration, if somewhat contrived, of the problem.

An artificial example, analogous to one described by Underwood (1997), involves an experiment looking at the difference in growth rates of newly hatched garden snails fed either the flowers or the leaves of a particular type of plant. The flowers are only available for a short period of time, because the plant flowers soon after rain. When the flowers are available, we feed it to any snails that hatch over that period. Snails that hatch after the flowering period are given the leaves of the plant. The obvious problem here is that the two groups of snails may be inherently different because they hatched at different times. Snails that hatch earlier may be genetically different from snails that hatch later, have had different levels of yolk in their eggs, etc. Our results may

reflect the effect of diet, or they may reflect differences in the snails that hatch at different times, and these two sources of variation are confounded. Clearly, we should take all the snails that hatch over a given period, say the flowering period, and give some of them flowers and others leaves to eat.

The allocation of experimental units to treatments raises the difficult issue of randomization versus interspersion (Hurlbert 1984). Reconsider the experiment described earlier on the effects of fish predation on marine benthic communities. Say we randomly choose ten plots on an intertidal mudflat and we randomly allocate five of these as fish exclusion (E) plots and five as cage-control (C) plots. What do we do if, by chance, all the control plots end up higher on the shore than all the exclusion plots (Figure 7.2)? Such an arrangement would concern us because we really want our treatment and control plots to be interspersed to avoid confounding fish effects with spatial differences such as tidal height. The simplest solution if we end up with such a clumped pattern after an initial randomization is to re-randomize – any other pattern (except the complete reverse with all control plots lower on the shore) will incorporate some spatial interspersion of treatments and controls. However, we must decide *a priori* what degree of spatial clumping of treatments is unacceptable; re-randomizing until we get a particular pattern of interspersion is not really randomization at all.

Why not guarantee interspersion by arranging

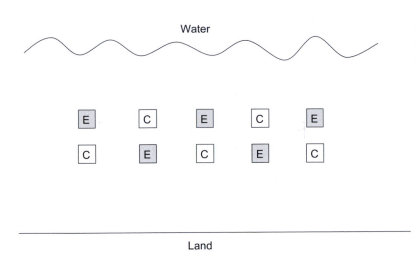

Figure 7.3 Regular positioning of ten plots on mudflat combined with systematic allocation of plots to two treatments – fish exclusion (E) and cage-control (C) – to guarantee interspersion.

our plots regularly spaced along the shore and alternating which is exclusion and which is control (Figure 7.3)? One problem with this design is that our plots within each group no longer represent a random sample of possible plots on this shore so it is difficult to decide what population of plots our inferences refer to. Also, it is possible that the regular spacing coincides with an unknown periodicity in one or more variables that could confound our interpretation of the effects of excluding fish. A compromise might be to randomly select plots on the shore but then ensure interspersion by alternating exclusions and controls. At least we have chosen our plots randomly to start with so the probability of our treatments coinciding with some unknown, but systematic, gradient along the shore won't change compared to a completely randomized design. There is still a problem, however; because, once we have allocated an E, the next plot must be a C, and it becomes more difficult to know what population our E and C plots refer to. This example has additional complications – our replicates will not be truly random, as we will have some minimal separation of replicates. We would not place plots on top of each other, and, as biologists, we have some feeling for the distance that we need to keep plots apart to ensure their independence. If the minimum separation distance is large, we may tend towards uniformly spaced replicates. In a field study, it is also possible that plots are easier to find when they are regular, or, for example if we are working on an intertidal mudflat, with plots not marked clearly, regular spacing of plots makes it easier for researchers and their assistants to avoid walking on one plot accidentally when moving across the area. The eventual positioning of replicates will be a combination of desired randomization, minimum spacing, and logistic considerations.

This issue of randomization versus interspersion illustrates one of the many grey areas in experimental design (and in philosophy – see debate between Urbach 1984 and Papineau 1994). Randomization does not guarantee avoidance of confounding but it certainly makes it less likely. With only a small number of experimental units, spatial clumping is possible and deliberate interspersion, but combined with random sampling, might be necessary. It is crucial that we recognize the potential problems associated with non-randomized designs.

7.2.4 Independence

Lack of independence between experimental units will make interpretation difficult and may invalidate some forms of statistical analysis. Animals and plants in the same experimental arena (cage, aquarium, zoo enclosure, etc.) may be exposed to a set of physical and biological conditions that are different from those experienced by organisms in other arenas. We may have a number of preparations of tissue from a single animal, and other such sets taken from other animals. The animals may differ from each other, so two tissue samples from the same animal might have more similar responses than two pieces of tissue chosen at random from different animals or plants. We will consider statistical problems arising from lack of independence in the appropriate chapters.

7.2.5 Reducing unexplained variance

One of the aims of any biological research project is to explain as much about the natural world as possible. Using linear models, we can estimate the amount of variation in our response variable that we have explained with our predictor variables. Good experimental design will include consideration of how to reduce the unexplained variation ($MS_{Residual}$) as much as possible. There are two broad strategies to achieve this.

- Including additional predictor variables in our analyses. We have discussed this in the context of multiple regression in Chapter 6 and will examine it further in the analysis of multifactor experiments in Chapter 9.
- Change the spatial structure of the design, particularly by incorporating one or more blocking variables. This will be discussed in Chapters 10 and 11.

7.3 | Power analysis

Recall from Chapter 3 that the complement to a Type II error is the concept of power – the long-run probability of detecting a given effect with our sample(s) if it actually occurs in the population(s). If β is the risk of making a Type II error, $1 - \beta$, or power, is the probability that we haven't made an error. More usefully, statistical power is a measure of our confidence that we would have detected an important effect if one existed.

This concept can be used in a range of situations. In designing an experiment or making an *a posteriori* assessment of the usefulness of an experiment, the important questions are as follows.

Supposing that there *is* a change of a particular size, what kind of sampling program would be needed to detect that change with reasonable certainty (or to estimate the magnitude of such a change)? Or, given a particular level of resources, what kind of change could we reasonably expect to detect? For *post hoc* assessment (of a non-significant result), we must ask, if our treatments really did have an effect (of a particular size), would we have detected that effect with our experimental design and analysis?

Power analysis is therefore a useful tool for designing an experiment, and it should (but will not, unfortunately, in many cases) also provide justification for publishing non-significant results.

An emerging body of the statistical and biological literature is concerned with questions of power. Here we provide a very broad overview of the uses of statistical power, but for detailed planning of specific experiments or programs, good general reviews are provided by Cohen (1988, 1992), Peterman (1990a,b), National Research Council (1990), Fairweather (1991), and Keough & Mapstone (1995). We will also return to power analysis as we begin to consider more complex designs later in this book.

To determine the power of an analysis, we need to specify the alternative hypothesis (H_A), or effect size, that we wish to detect. For most types of analyses (e.g. simple two group comparisons, ANOVA and regression models), power is proportional to the following.

- Effect size (ES) – how big a change is of interest. We are more likely to detect large effects.
- Sample size (n) – a given effect is easier to detect with a larger sample size.
- Variance (σ^2) between sampling or experimental units – it is harder to detect an effect if the population is more variable.
- Significance level (α) to be used. Power varies with α. As mentioned in Chapter 3, most biologists use a value of $\alpha = 0.05$.

More formally,

$$Power \propto \frac{ES\ \alpha\ \sqrt{n}}{\sigma} \tag{7.5}$$

Exactly how we link values of these parameters to power depends on the particular statistical test being used (hence the proportional sign in the equation). For individual cases, we construct a specific equation, usually using the relevant non-central statistical distribution[2], which in turn requires precise knowledge of the statistical test that will be used (see Box 7.1 and Figure 7.4).

---

2 A non-central distribution describes the distribution of our test statistic that would be expected if H_A, rather than H_0, is correct.

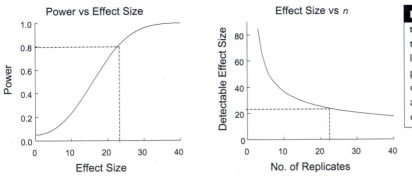

Figure 7.4 Power functions for the abalone example. The panel on the left is for $n = 24$, and the dashed lines indicate the solution for 80% power. The right panel shows detectable effect size vs sample size, and the dashed line shows the calculated effect size.

Box 7.1 | Simple example of power analysis

In an earlier project (Keough & King 1991), we were examining the effect of closing a range of shores to collection of abalone, through proclamation of two marine parks. The closure was contentious, denying both commercial and recreational divers the chance to collect, and, therefore, it was imperative to collect information to test whether the management strategy had worked. The assumption (untested) was that exploitation of abalone had reduced abundances. The intention was to survey a range of rocky headlands after a few years of protection, surveying areas where collection was still allowed and areas where it had been banned (there were no differences between these areas before proclamation of the marine parks). The important question was the feasibility of these surveys. The parameters of the power equation were estimated as follows:

- the test of management could be simplified to a t test, with a replicate observation being a rocky reef site (with some replicate observations within each reef, to get a better idea of its state),
- α was left at 0.05, and $1 - \beta$ set to 0.80, by convention, and
- σ was estimated by sending teams of divers out to sample a range of sites in the same way planned for the real monitoring. Those pilot surveys produced a mean density of abalone of 47.5 legal-sized animals per 50 m² area, with a standard deviation of 27.7. This latter value was used as an estimate of σ.

In the first case, let's calculate the number of observations (sites) required. Determining the effect size was very difficult, as little work had been done on these animals in the areas concerned, and was eventually calculated using a range of unconnected data sets. As a working assumption, recreational divers and poachers were assumed to take approximately as many animals as commercial divers. Commercial divers were required to file regular reports listing the mass of abalone taken, broken down into small reporting regions. An earlier paper (McShane & Smith 1990) had described size–frequency relationships for commercial catches of abalone, and length–weight relationships (McShane et al. 1988), so it was possible to convert a mass of abalone into an average number of animals taken per year from each reporting region. Another fisheries publication provided maps of major abalone reefs, giving their approximate areas. From these data, the number of animals taken could be converted into an approximate number per 50 m². In this case, the value for heavily fished areas (averaged over 6 years of diver returns) was

11.6 animals m^{-2}, or approximately 25% of the standing stock. Adding supposed recreational and poaching catches, these values become 23.2, and 50%, respectively.

The power calculations then become quite simple, and can be done using a range of software packages. For these values, the number of sites to be sampled is 24.

In the second case, if we are unhappy with the number of approximations made in calculating the effect size, we could construct a curve of MDES vs n (Figure 7.4)[3]. The relationship is also shown as a curve of power vs effect size for n equals 24, to illustrate the comparison with the first approach. Note that the solution for 80% power corresponds to an effect size of 23.

The important panel is the one for detectable effect size vs sample size, showing that small numbers of sites (less than seven) would require at least a doubling of the number of legal-sized abalone in the area for an effect to show up, whereas our best guess is that the change is more likely to be around 50%, and the dashed line shows that an effect size of 23 corresponds to $n = 24$. The curve also emphasizes the rapid returns resulting from an increase in sample size, if you start with a poorly replicated experiment – the detectable effect declines dramatically at low n values, but tapers off, indicating a region of diminishing return.

3 We constructed the curve shown on using the free software package Power Pack, written by Russell Lenth. His web site (www.divms.uiowa.edu/~rlenth/Power) includes several options for doing power calculations.

7.3.1 Using power to plan experiments (*a priori* power analysis)

There are two ways that power analysis can be used in the design of an experiment or sampling program.

Sample size calculation (power, σ, α, ES known)
The most common use of power analysis during the planning of an experiment is to decide how much replication is necessary. We can then decide whether it is feasible to use this many replicates. To do these calculations, we need to specify the effect size and have an estimate of σ. At the planning stage, you may not have a good idea of the variation you are likely to get, and need to get an estimate, either from previous studies or pilot work. The most difficult step will be specifying the effect size (Section 7.3.3).

Effect size (power, n, σ, known)
If external factors are likely to restrict the number of observations (sample size) to relatively low levels, the alternative approach is to calculate the constraints of the experiment – using this many observations, and with the likely background variability, what is the smallest change that we could expect confidently to identify? This situation is common when the sampling itself is expensive. For example:

- expensive laboratory analyses for trace chemicals,
- benthic marine sampling requiring large ships,
- if there are few laboratories capable of doing assays,
- if processing each observation takes a large amount of your time,
- experimental units are expensive, such as doing physiological work on small mammals, where the cost of each animal may be very restrictive, especially for students.

At either the planning stage, or after an experiment or sampling program has been completed, it is possible to calculate the size of change that could be or could have been detected. This has been termed "reverse power analysis" by Cohen (1988), and the effect size that we calculate has been labelled the Minimum Detectable Effect Size (MDES). We are asking, for a given level of background variability, sample size, and a desired certainty or power, how big would the change need to be before we would detect it as significant? Again, it is best to use this calculation beforehand, to decide if the work is worth doing, and although it might also be used afterwards to reassure readers that everything was done properly. Calculating the detectable effect may be a preferred solution when you are not comfortable with specifying an *a priori* effect size.

For example, from surveys of intertidal molluscs in protected and collected areas near Williamstown in Victoria, we found changes of 15–25% in the mean size of species that are collected by humans (Keough *et al.* 1993). Because these data came from surveys, rather than controlled experiments, we also measured sizes of a set of species that are not collected by humans in great numbers. To be confident that the patterns seen for collected species did not reflect a response to some unmeasured environmental variable, we analysed the non-collected species, and found no significant difference between sites with and without human access. For non-collected species to be an appropriate control, we need to be confident that we could have detected a pattern the same as that shown by collected species. We used power analysis to show that our sampling program would have detected a change as small as 10% for some of these species, i.e., if non-collected species changed as much as collected ones, we would have detected it (Keough *et al.* 1993).

Sequence for using power analysis to design experiments

The statistical design stage of any experiment or sampling program should include the following steps.

1. State clearly the patterns to be expected if no effect occurs, and the patterns expected if there are changes. In formal statistical terms, this corresponds to clear formulations of the null hypothesis and its alternative.

2. Identify the statistical model to be applied to the data, and state the desired power and the significance levels to be used.

3. Identify the assumptions of that statistical procedure. If possible, use existing or compara-

ble data as a rough guide to whether those assumptions are likely to be satisfied. Consider possible data transformations. If you expect to use transformed data, the effect size must be expressed on that transformed scale. For example, if you are interested in a doubling of numbers of a particular organism, and will analyze log-transformed data, your effect size will be 0.301 when converted to a $\log_{10}$ scale.

4. Obtain some pilot estimate of variation in the variable to be analyzed. In some cases, we require estimates of variation in space and time, while in other cases we may only be comparing in space or through time alone. In some ecological studies, estimating variation through time requires pre-existing data sets involving time periods of at least a few years. If there are no local data, some ballpark estimates may be obtained from the literature from other geographic regions. It is crucial that the estimate of variability must be based on same scales of space and time as your final data. There is no reason to expect that variation on one scale will be a good predictor of variation on a different scale.

If you have complex experimental designs (e.g. Chapters 9–11), you need to think about the variation that is used to test a particular hypothesis. If you have, for example, nested or split-plot designs, different hypotheses will be tested against different measures of variation, and you would need to do power analyses for each separate hypothesis. Importantly in this context, you must get an estimate of σ at the appropriate level.

5. The next step depends on whether your design will be limited by logistical constraints.

(a) If our aim is to design the best possible experiment, we should specify the effect size that we wish to detect – how large a change is of biological interest? The implication here is that detecting changes less than the specified amount has low priority. In practice, this decision is very difficult, but it is nevertheless critical. The effect size may be chosen from a range of sources, e.g. other studies of the same biological system, studies of other processes that you might wish to compare to the one you are investigating, etc. (Section 7.3.3). Using our desired ES, an estimate of σ and the specified value of α, it should then be possible to calculate the number of replicates needed to detect that effect size with power $1 - \beta$.

(b) If we have constraints on the size of our experiment or sampling program, we can use an estimate of σ, the chosen values of α and β and the upper limit to the number of observations possible to determine the Minimum Detectable Effect Size (MDES). It is often useful to calculate MDES values for a range of sampling efforts, and to represent the results as a plot of MDES versus sample size. This relationship can then be used to show how much return we would get for a big change in sampling effort, or the sample size necessary to reach a particular MDES value (see Peterman 1989).

7.3.2 *Post hoc* power calculation

If an experiment or sampling program has been completed, and a non-significant result has been obtained, *post hoc* power analysis can be used to calculate power to detect a specified effect, or to calculate the minimum detectable effect size for a given power. Calculating *post hoc* power requires that we define the effect size we wished to detect, given that we know n and have an estimate of σ. Obviously, once the experiment has been done, we have estimates of σ, e.g. from the $MS_{Residual}$ from a regression or ANOVA model, and we know how much replication we used. The effect size should be the size of change or effect that it is important for us to detect. It is obviously useful to demonstrate that our test had high power to detect a biologically important and pre-specified effect size (Thomas 1997). The downside is that if power is low, all that you have demonstrated is your inability to design a very good experiment, or, more charitably, your bad luck in having more variable data than expected! It is far more useful to use these calculations at the planning stage (Section 7.3.1; Underwood 1999). After an experiment, we would expect to use the calculations to satisfy ourselves that power is high enough, that our initial power calculations, often based on very rough estimates of variance, were correct.

Some statistical packages offer a flawed kind of *post hoc* power calculation, sometimes called "observed power" (Hoenig & Heisey 2001). In this approach, we use the existing analysis to estimate both the effect size and sample variance, and use those values in the power equation. For example, in a two-sample t test, we would use the difference between the two means as the effect size. This observed effect size is unlikely to match a difference that we decide independently is important. Perhaps most importantly, Hoenig & Heisey (2001) have demonstrated that observed power has a 1:1 relationship with the P value so higher P values mean lower power and calculation of observed power tells us nothing new (see also Thomas 1997). We emphasize again the importance of thinking carefully about the kinds of effects that you wish to detect in any experiment, and the value of making this and other decisions before you sample.

Post hoc power calculations can be used to convince reviewers and editors that our non-significant results are worth publishing. Despite the clear value of a confident retention of a null hypothesis (see Underwood 1990, 1999), it can still be difficult in practice to get such results published. We have already emphasized in Chapter 3 that any assessment of the literature can be seriously compromised by the "file-drawer problem". If non-significant results are less likely to be published, because of an active policy of editors and referees or lack of enthusiasm of the researchers, then unbiased syntheses of a particular discipline are not possible. Providing measures of observed effect size and showing you had good power to detect pre-specified effect sizes of biological interest will make non-significant results much more interpretable.

7.3.3 The effect size

The most difficult step of power analyses is deciding an effect size. Our aim is to identify an effect of experimental treatments that we consider important, and that, therefore, we would want to detect. How do we decide on an important effect? The decision is not statistical, but in most cases uses biological judgment by the research worker, who must understand the broad context of the study. In most pieces of research, the work is not self-contained, but our aim is to investigate a phenomenon and to compare that phenomenon to related ones. We might want to:

- compare results for our species to those for other species,
- compare the role of a particular biological process to other processes acting on a particular species or population, or
- contrast the physiological responses to a chemical, gas mixture, exercise regime, etc., to other such environmental changes.

In these cases, we should be guided by two questions. Can we identify a change in the response variable that is important for the organism, such as a change in a respiration parameter, blood pressure, etc., that would be likely to impair an organism's function, or a change in population density that would change the risk of local extinction? What were the levels of response observed in the related studies that we intend to compare to our own? These questions sound simple, but are in practice very difficult, especially in whole-organism biology, where we are often dealing with biological systems that are very poorly studied. In this case, we may not be able to predict critical levels of population depletion, changes in reproductive performance, etc., and will have very little information with which to make a decision. The available information gets richer as we move to sub-organismal measurements, where work is often done on broadly distributed species, standard laboratory organisms, or on systems that are relatively consistent across a wide range of animals or plants. In any case, we must decide what kind of change is important to us.

What if we can not identify an effect size about which we feel confident?

Quite often, we will not be able to select an effect size that we could defend easily. In this case, there are three options available.

1. Use an arbitrary value as a negotiating point. In many published ecological studies, including a range of environmental impact studies, an arbitrary change, usually of 50 or 100% (relative to a control group) in the abundance of a target species, has been used. These values seem to be accepted as being "large", and with the potential to be important. They are not necessarily biologically meaningful – a much smaller change may be important for some populations, while others that vary widely through time may routinely change by 50% or more between years or places. The major value of this approach is in environmental monitoring, where a sampling program may be the result of negotiation or arbitration between interested parties arguing for increases and decreases in the scope of the monitoring program.

2. Cohen (1988) proposed conventions of large, medium, and small effects. Rather than expressing an effect size as, for example, a difference between two means, he standardized the effect size by dividing by σ. For a simple case of comparing two groups, he suggested, based on a survey of the behavioral and psychological literature, values of 0.2, 0.5, and 0.8 for standardized differences (i.e., $(\bar{y}_a - \bar{y}_b)/\sigma$, for small, medium, and large). He acknowledged that these values are arbitrary, but argued that we use arbitrary conventions very often, and proposed this system as one for dealing with cases where there is no strong reason for a particular effect size. These values may or may not be appropriate for his field of research, but they are not necessarily appropriate for the range of biological situations that we deal with. A critical change in migration rates between geographically separated populations, for example, will be very different when we are investigating genetic differentiation between populations, compared to measuring ecologically important dispersal that produces metapopulations. Considerable exchange is necessary for ecological links, but very low rates of exchange are sufficient to prevent genetic separation. Any broad recommendation such as Cohen's must be tempered by sensible biological judgment.

3. A more useful approach may be the one we describe above, in which, rather than use a single effect size, we plot detectable effect size versus sampling effort or power versus effect size. In this case, we get an idea of the kinds of changes that we could detect with a given sampling regime, or, the confidence that we would have in detecting a range of effects. While we don't have a formal criterion for deciding whether to proceed, this approach is useful for giving an idea of the potential of the experiment.

Environmental monitoring – a special case

One common activity for biologists is to assess the effects of various human interventions in the natural environment, and, in this case, we are not always comparing our results to a broader literature, but collecting information to make decisions about the acceptability of a particular activity, in a particular region. The question, then, is whether the activity in question has an unacceptable impact. We need to decide how big a change in the response variable is unacceptable. In this case, we may get advice on the effect size from formal regulations (e.g. criteria for water quality, setting standards for human health or environmental "health"). There may also be occasions when the level at which the human population becomes concerned defines the target effect size. This level may be unrelated to biological criteria. For example, oiled seabirds washing up on beaches triggers public complaints, but the number of sick or dead animals may not result in a population decline. There will, however, be intense pressure to monitor charismatic megafauna, with an effect size determined by political considerations. In other monitoring situations, we may fall back on arbitrary values, using them as a negotiating point, as described above. Keough & Mapstone (1995, 1997) have described this process, and there is a good discussion of effect sizes in Osenberg *et al.* (1996).

7.3.4 Using power analyses

The importance of these power calculations is that the proposed experiment or sampling program can then be assessed, to decide whether the MDES, power, or sample size values are acceptable. For example, if the variable of interest is the areal extent of seagrass beds, and a given sampling program would detect only a thousand-fold reduction over ten years, it would be of little value. Such a reduction would be blindingly obvious without an expensive monitoring program, and public pressure would stimulate action before that time anyway.

If the results of the power analyses are acceptable because the MDES is small enough, or the recommended number of observations is within the budget of the study, we should proceed. If the solution is unacceptable, the experiment will not

be effective, and the level of replication should be increased. If you decide to go ahead with no increase in sample size, it is important that you are aware of the real limitations of the sampling. Proceeding with such a program amounts to a major gamble – if a real effect does occur, the chance of your actually detecting it may be very low – often less than 20%, rather than the commonly used 80%. That means that there is a high probability that you'll get a non-significant result that is really a non-result – a result in which you have little confidence, and your resources will have been wasted. You may be lucky, and the effect of your treatments may be much larger than the one you aimed to detect, but that result is unlikely.

How much should you gamble? Again, there's no simple answer, as we are dealing with a continuum, rather than a clear cut-off. If the power is 75%, you wouldn't be too worried about proceeding, but what of 70%? 50%? The decision will most often be the result of a suite of considerations. How exciting would a significant result be? How important is it that we get some information, even if it's not conclusive? Will some other people add to my data, so eventually we'll be able to get a clear answer to the hypothesis? Would an unpublishable non-significant result be a career impediment? The answer to the last question depends on who you are, what stage of your career you are at, how strong your scientific record is, and so on.

If you aren't willing to gamble, you have only a couple of options. The first is to look hard at the experimental design. Are there ways to make the experiment more efficient, so I need less time or money to deal with each replicate? Decreasing the resources needed for each experimental unit may allow you to increase the sample size. Alternatively, are there other variables that could be incorporated into the design that might reduce the background noise?

The second option, which is intermediate between a calculated gamble and rethinking the analysis, is the approach described in Chapter 3, in which we don't regard the rates of Type I and Type II errors as fixed. One conventional approach would be to use a less stringent criterion for statistical significance, i.e., increase α, producing an increase in power. This solution isn't satisfactory, as we would still be allowing the Type II error rate to fluctuate according to logistic constraints, and just fixing the Type I error rate at a new value. The solution proposed by Mapstone (1995) is that, when we must compromise an experimental design, we do so by preserving the relative sizes of the two errors. He suggests that, as part of the design phase, we have identified the desirable error rates, and those two rates should be chosen to reflect our perception of the importance of the two kinds of errors. He suggested that compromises should preserve those relative rates, so that if we proceed with a less than optimal experiment, we are more likely to make both kinds of decision errors. That approach has been detailed for environmental monitoring by Keough & Mapstone (1995, 1997), including a flow diagram to detail those authors' view of how a sampling program gets designed. This approach is sensible, but it is too soon to see if it will gain wide acceptance in the broader scientific literature.

Occasionally, the calculations may show that the MDES is much less than the desirable effect size, suggesting that the experimental/sampling program is more sensitive than expected. In this case, you could consider reducing the replication, with the possibility of using "spare" resources for further studies. Our experience suggests that this latter situation is uncommon.

While formal power analysis is part of the Neyman–Pearson approach (Chapter 3), and most often discussed as part of hypothesis testing, the general principles apply to other statistical tasks. When estimating the value of a particular parameter, we may wish to be certain that we produce an accurate estimate of that parameter (Section 7.1.2), and the confidence that we have in that estimate will be similar to power, depending on sampling effort, variability, etc. If our aim is to produce a confidence interval around an estimate, the procedures become even more similar – a confidence interval requires a statement about the level of confidence, e.g. 0.95, and depends also on sampling effort and variation. We must also make some decision about the distribution of our parameter, either by assigning a formal distribution (e.g. normal, Poisson), or by opting for a randomization procedure.

A priori power analysis should, we think, be a routine part of planning any experiment. Our initial power estimates may be quite crude, especially when we have a poor estimate of the variation present in our data. As we will see in later chapters, too, for complex designs, we may be faced with a large range of power curves, corresponding to different patterns among our treatments, and we will not be sure what pattern to expect. However, we will at least know whether "important" effects are likely to be detected, given our available resources. Having that knowledge makes us decide whether to reallocate our resources to maximize the power for our key hypotheses.

Perhaps the most valuable part of a priori power analysis is that, to do the calculations, we must specify the alternative hypothesis, and, most importantly, the statistical model that we will apply to the data. Specifying the model makes us think about the analysis before the data have been collected, a habit that we recommend strongly.

The final, important point is that power calculations, especially at the planning stage, are approximate. We usually use pilot estimates of variation that, if we do the appropriate calculations, tend to have alarmingly large confidence intervals, so our power estimates will also have considerable imprecision. If our target power value is 0.80, we should be looking for calculations that give power values in this region. Often, our sample sizes in biological work are quite small, and power values move in substantial increments, because the sample size, n, is an integer. In planning, we should not focus on whether power is 0.75, 0.80, etc., but on making sure we have enough samples to approach the desirable value, rather than giving values of 0.30 or 0.40.

7.4 | General issues and hints for analysis

7.4.1 General issues

- When thinking about experimental design, the need for appropriate controls is familiar to most researchers, but less attention is often paid to appropriate units of replication. It is crucial to identify, for a particular hypothesis, and set of experimental treatments, the experimental units to which these treatments are applied. These experimental units are the replicates for testing that hypothesis.

- In more complex designs, testing several hypotheses, the experimental units may occur at several temporal and spatial scales. Attention must be paid to identifying the appropriate amount of replication for each of these hypotheses.
- Power analysis, used when planning a sampling or experimental program, provides a means of determining whether our plan is feasible, or of deciding the resources that are necessary for a particular experiment.
- A power analysis can only be done when we have an estimate of the variation in the system under study. If the power analysis is done before sampling, we must obtain an estimate of variation on the same spatial and temporal scale as our planned experimental units.
- Power analysis also requires us to specify the statistical model that will be applied to the data – without this step, no calculations can be made. While we may be forced to make changes when the real data arrive, this step is useful in formalizing our experimental design.
- Power equations can be used to determine the number of replicates (at the planning stage), the change that could be detected (at planning or analysis stages), or the degree of confidence in the analysis (after a non-significant result).
- The most difficult task is almost always determining an important effect size, but doing so focuses our attention on what is biologically important, rather than just looking for statistical significance.

7.4.2 Hints for analysis

- At the planning stage, write out an analysis table and its associated statistical model, to be sure that you understand the design clearly. Identify the key hypothesis tests.
- Determine the effect size by thinking about what would be important biologically.
- Focus on using power analysis to determine appropriate sample sizes in the design stage. *Post hoc* power calculations can be useful for pre-specified effect sizes. Calculating observed power, the power to detect the observed effect, is pointless.
- The formal analysis of power for simple designs can now be done using a wide range of software packages.
- More complex analyses require an understanding of the calculation of non-centrality parameters. After making that calculation, non-central distribution functions are freely available for most common statistical distributions.

Chapter 8

Comparing groups or treatments – analysis of variance

The analysis of variance (ANOVA) is a general statistical technique for partitioning and analyzing the variation in a continuous response variable. We used ANOVA in Chapters 5 and 6 to partition the variation in a response variable into that explained by the linear regression with one or more continuous predictor variables and that unexplained by the regression model. In applied statistics, the term "analysis of variance" (ANOVA) is commonly used for the particular case of partitioning the variation in a response variable into that explained and that unexplained by one or more categorical predictors, called factors, usually in the context of designed experiments (Sokal & Rohlf 1995, Underwood 1997). The categories of each factor are the groups or experimental treatments and the focus is often comparing response variable means between groups. We emphasized in Chapter 5 that the statistical distinction between "classical regression" and "classical ANOVA" is artificial. Both involve the general technique of partitioning variation in a response variable (analysis of variance) and of fitting linear models to explain or predict values of the response variable. It turns out that ANOVA can also be used to test hypotheses about group (treatment) means.

The two main aims of classical ANOVA, therefore, are:

- to examine the relative contribution of different sources of variation (factors or combination of factors, i.e. the predictor variables) to the total amount of the variability in the response variable, and

- to test the null hypothesis (H_0) that population group or treatment means are equal.

8.1 | Single factor (one way) designs

A single factor or one way design deals with only a single factor or predictor, although that factor will comprise several levels or groups. Designs that can be analyzed with single factor ANOVA models are completely randomized (CR) designs, where there is no restriction on the random allocation of experimental or sampling units to factor levels. Designs that involve restricted randomization will be described in Chapters 10 and 11. We will use two recent examples from the literature to illustrate use of this analysis.

Diatom communities and heavy metals in rivers
Medley & Clements (1998) studied the response of diatom communities to heavy metals, especially zinc, in streams in the Rocky Mountain region of Colorado, USA. As part of their study, they sampled a number of stations (between four and seven) on six streams known to be polluted by heavy metals. At each station, they recorded a range of physico-chemical variables (pH, dissolved oxygen etc.), zinc concentration, and variables describing the diatom community (species richness, species diversity H′ and proportion of diatom cells that were the early-successional species, *Achanthes minutissima*). One of their analyses was to ignore streams and partition the 34 stations into four zinc-level categories: background (<20 μg l^{-1}, 8 stations), low ($21-50$ μg l^{-1}, 8 stations), medium

51–200 µg l^{-1}, 9 stations), and high (>200 µg l^{-1}, 9 stations) and test the null hypothesis that there were no differences in diatom species diversity between zinc-level groups, using stations as replicates. We will also use these data to test the null hypothesis that there are no differences in diatom species diversity between streams, again using stations as replicates. The full analyses of these data are in Box 8.1.

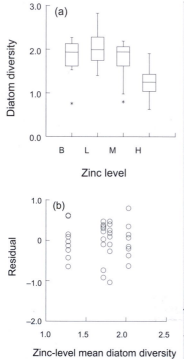

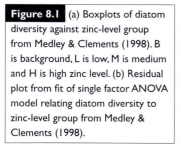

Figure 8.1 (a) Boxplots of diatom diversity against zinc-level group from Medley & Clements (1998). B is background, L is low, M is medium and H is high zinc level. (b) Residual plot from fit of single factor ANOVA model relating diatom diversity to zinc-level group from Medley & Clements (1998).

Box 8.1 | Worked example: diatom communities in metal-affected streams

Medley & Clements (1998) sampled a number of stations (between four and seven) on six streams known to be polluted by heavy metals in the Rocky Mountain region of Colorado, USA. They recorded zinc concentration, and species richness and species diversity of the diatom community and proportion of diatom cells that were the early-successional species, *Achanthes minutissima*.

Species diversity versus zinc-level group

The first analysis compares mean diatom species diversity (response variable) across the four zinc-level groups (categorical predictor variable), zinc level treated as a fixed factor. The H_0 was no difference in mean diatom species diversity between zinc-level groups. Boxplots of species diversity against group (Figure 8.1(a)) showed no obvious skewness; two sites with low species diversity were highlighted in the background and medium zinc groups as possible outliers. The results from an analysis of variance from fitting a linear model with zinc level as the predictor variable were as follows.

Source	SS	df	MS	F	P
Zinc level	2.567	3	0.856	3.939	0.018
Residual	6.516	30	0.217		
Total	9.083	33			

The residual plot from this model (Figure 8.1(b)) did not reveal any outliers or any unequal spread of the residuals, suggesting the assumptions of the ANOVA were appropriate. Additionally, Levene's test produced no evidence that the H_0 of no differences in variances of species diversity between the zinc-level groups should be rejected (Levene-mean: $F_{3,30} = 0.087$, $P = 0.967$; Levene-median: $F_{3,30} = 0.020$, $P = 0.996$).

Tukey's pairwise comparison of group means: mean differences with Tukey adjusted P values for each pairwise comparison in brackets.

	Background	Low	Medium	High
Background	0.000 (1.000)			
Low	0.235 (0.746)	0.000 (1.000)		
Medium	0.080 (0.985)	0.315 (0.515)	0.000 (1.000)	
High	0.520 (0.122)	0.755 (0.012)	0.440 (0.209)	0.000 (1.000)

The only H_0 to be rejected is that of no difference in diatom diversity between sites with low zinc and sites with high zinc.

We could also analyze these data with more robust methods, especially if we were concerned about underlying non-normality or outliers. To test the H_0 that there is no difference in the location of the distributions of diatom diversity between zinc levels, irrespective of the shape of these distributions, we would use the Kruskal–Wallis non-parametric test based on ranks sums.

Zinc level	Rank sum
Background	160.0
Low	183.0
Medium	166.5
High	85.5

The Kruskal–Wallis H-statistic equals 8.737. The probability of getting this value of one more extreme when the H_0 is true (testing with a chi-square distribution with 3 df) is 0.033, so we would reject the H_0.

We might also consider a randomization test, where we reallocate observations to the four groups at random many times to generate a distribution of a suitable test statistic. We used Manly's (1997) program RT, the percentage of total SS attributable to zinc levels (groups) as the statistic and used 1000 randomizations. The percentage of SS_{Total} accounted for by SS_{Groups} was 28.3% and the probability of getting this value or one more extreme if the H_0 of no effects of zinc level on diatom diversity was true was 0.023. Again, we would reject the H_0 at the 0.05 level.

Species diversity versus stream

The second analysis compared diatom species diversity across the streams. Streams are treated as a random factor, assuming these streams represent a random sample of all possible streams in this part of the Rocky Mountains. The H_0 then is that there is no added variance (above the variation between stations) due to differences in diatom species diversity between streams in this part of the Rocky Mountains.

Source	SS	df	MS	F	P
Stream	1.828	5	0.366	1.411	0.251
Residual	7.255	28	0.259		
Total	9.083	33			

The residual plot (Figure 8.2) indicates no variance heterogeneity, although the sample sizes within each stream are too small for useful boxplots. We used the ANOVA, ML and REML methods to estimate the two variance components (σ_ε^2 and σ_α^2). ML and REML estimates are tedious to calculate by hand so we used SPSS (Ver 9.0) to obtain these estimates. Confidence intervals (95%) are provided for σ_ε^2 only; unequal sample sizes preclude reliable confidence intervals for σ_α^2.

Method	Estimate of σ_ε^2	Estimate of σ_α^2
ANOVA	0.259 (0.159–0.452)	0.0189
ML	0.257	0.0099
REML	0.258	0.0205

Note that there is little difference in the estimates of σ_ε^2, although both ML and REML estimates will be biased. The estimates of σ_α^2 differ considerably between estimation methods, however. Based on Section 8.2.1, the REML estimate of 0.0205 is probably the most reliable. Most of the variance is due to differences between stations within streams rather than due to differences between all possible streams.

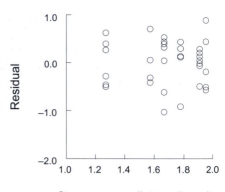

Figure 8.2 Residual plot from fit of single factor random effects ANOVA model relating diatom diversity to stream group from Medley & Clements (1998).

Settlement of invertebrate larvae

Keough & Raimondi (1995) were interested in the degree to which biofilms – films of diatoms, algal spores, bacteria, and other organic material – that develop on hard surfaces influence the settlement of invertebrate larvae. In an earlier paper, from southeastern Australia, Todd & Keough (1994) had manipulated these biofilms by covering experimental surfaces with fine mesh that excluded most larvae, but allowed diatoms, etc., to pass through. These nets were then removed to allow invertebrates to settle. Keough & Raimondi focused on the ability of larvae to respond to successional changes that occur in biofilms, and, because the earlier procedure was time-consuming, decided to test whether the films that developed in laboratory seawater systems had similar effects to those developing in the field. At the same time, they tested whether covering a surface with netting altered the biofilm (or at least its attractiveness to larvae). They used four experimental treatments: substrata that had been conditioned in sterile seawater, surfaces immersed in laboratory aquaria, surfaces in laboratory aquaria, but with fine mesh netting over the surface, and surfaces immersed in the field, and covered with identical netting. After one week for biofilms to develop, the experimental surfaces (11 cm × 11 cm pieces of Perspex (Plexiglas)) were placed in the field in a completely randomized array. They were left for one week, and then the newly settled invertebrates identified and counted. To control for small numbers of larvae passing through the netting during the conditioning period, they used an additional treatment, which was netted, and returned to the laboratory after one week and censused. The values of this treatment were used to adjust the numbers in the treatment that started in the field. The data for analysis then consisted of four treatments: sterile, lab films with net, lab films without net, and field films with net. We will use their data to test the null hypothesis that there are no differences in recruitment of one family of polychaete worms, the serpulids, and to specifically compare some combinations of treatments. The analyses of these data are in Box 8.2 and Box 8.4.

8.1.1 Types of predictor variables (factors)

There are two types of categorical predictor variables in linear models. The most common type is a fixed factor, where all the levels of the factor (i.e. all the groups or treatments) that are of interest are included in the analysis. We cannot extrapolate our statistical conclusions beyond these specific levels to other groups or treatments not in the study. If we repeated the study, we would usually use the same levels of the fixed factor again. Linear models based on fixed categorical predictor variables (fixed factors) are termed fixed effects models (or Model 1 ANOVAs). Fixed effect models are analogous to linear regression models where X is assumed to be fixed. The other type of factor is a random factor, where we are only using a random selection of all the possible levels (or groups) of the factor and we usually wish to make inferences about all the possible groups from our sample of groups. If we repeated the study, we would usually take another sample of groups from the population of possible groups. Linear models based on random categorical predictor variables (random factors) are termed random effects models (or Model 2 ANOVAs). Random effects models are analogous to linear regression models where X is random (Model II regression; see Chapter 5).

To illustrate the difference between these types of factors, the zinc-level groups created by Medley & Clements (1998) clearly represent a fixed factor. These groups were specifically chosen to match the USA EPA chronic criteria values for zinc and any further study would definitely use the same groupings. Any conclusions about differences in diatom communities between zinc levels are restricted to these specific groups. In contrast, we might consider the six streams used by Medley & Clements (1998) as a possible random sample from all metal-polluted streams in the southern Rocky Mountain ecoregion of Colorado and hence treat streams as a random factor. A new study might choose a different sample of streams from this region. Conclusions from our analysis could be extrapolated to all metal-polluted streams in this region.

We argue that the random (or at least haphazard) nature of the selection of groups for a random factor is important for valid interpretation of

Box 8.2 | Worked example: serpulid recruitment onto surfaces with different biofilms

Keough & Raimondi (1995) set up an experiment to examine the response of serpulid (polychaete worms) larvae to four types of biofilms on hard substrata in shallow marine waters. The four treatments were: sterile substrata, biofilms developed in the lab with a covering net, lab biofilms without a net, and biofilms developed in the field with a net. The substrata were left for one week, and then the newly settled worms identified and counted. To control for small numbers of larvae passing through the netting during the conditioning period, they used an additional treatment, which was netted, and returned to the laboratory after one week and censused. The values of this treatment were used to adjust the numbers in the treatment that started in the field.

We have not shown the initial data screening stages, but the response variable was log-transformed to improve skewed distributions. The H_0 was that there was no difference between treatments in the mean log-transformed number of serpulid recruits per substratum. The residual plot from the single factor model 8.3 with log-transformed numbers of serpulid recruits revealed a single outlier, but very similar spread of data between groups, suggesting that the assumptions were met. The similarity of data ranges is probably a more reliable guide to the reliability of the ANOVA than the formal identification of outliers from boxplots, when there are only seven observations per group.

The results from the analysis of variance were as follows.

Source	SS	df	MS	F	P
Biofilms	0.241	3	0.080	6.006	0.003
Residual	0.321	24	0.013		
Total	0.562	27			

We would reject the H_0 of no difference between treatments in the log numbers of serpulid recruits. In this particular example, however, we are more interested in the planned contrasts between specific treatments (Box 8.4).

the subsequent analysis. Selecting specific levels of a factor and then calling the factor random simply to allow extrapolation to some population of levels is inappropriate, just as would be selecting a specific set of observations from a population and calling that set a random sample.

Our conclusions for a fixed factor are restricted to those specific groups we used in the experiment or sampling program. For a random factor, we wish to draw conclusions about the population of groups from which we have randomly chosen a subset. Random factors in biology are often randomly chosen spatial units like sites or blocks. Time (e.g. months or years) is also some-

times considered a random factor but it is much more difficult to envisage a sequence of months (or years) being a random sample from a population of times to which we would wish to extrapolate.

Although the distinction between fixed and random factors does not affect the model fitting or calculations for subsequent hypothesis tests in a single factor model, the hypotheses being tested are fundamentally different for fixed and random factors. When we consider more complex experimental designs in later chapters, it will be clear that the distinction between fixed and random factors can also affect the calculation of the hypothesis tests.

8.1.2 Linear model for single factor analyses

Linear effects model

We introduced linear models in Chapters 5 and 6 for regression analysis. The structure of the linear model when the predictor variable is categorical is similar to those models, although there are two types of models we can fit (Box 8.3). Consider a data set consisting of p groups or treatments ($i = 1$ to p) and n replicates ($j = 1$ to n) within each group (Figure 8.1). From Medley & Clements (1998), p equals four zinc levels and n equals eight or nine stations. From Keough & Raimondi (1995), p equals four biofilm treatments and n equals seven substrata.

The linear effects model is:

$$y_{ij} = \mu + \alpha_i + \varepsilon_{ij} \tag{8.1}$$

The details of the linear single factor ANOVA model, including estimation of its parameters and means, are provided in Box 8.3 and Table 8.1. OLS means and their standard errors are standard output from linear models routines in statistical software.

From Medley & Clements (1998):

$$\text{(diatom species diversity)}_{ij} = \mu + \text{(effect of zinc level)}_i + {}_{ij} \tag{8.2}$$

From Keough & Raimondi (1995):

$$\text{(no. of serpulids)}_{ij} = \mu + \text{(effect of biofilm type)}_i + \varepsilon_{ij} \tag{8.3}$$

Box 8.3 | **Single factor ANOVA models, overparameterization and estimable functions**

Consider a data set consisting of p groups or treatments ($i = 1$ to p) and n replicates ($j = 1$ to n) within each group (Figure 8.4).

The linear effects model is:

$$y_{ij} = \mu + \alpha_i + \varepsilon_{ij}$$

In this model:

- y_{ij} is the jth replicate observation of the response variable from the ith group of factor A;
- μ is the overall population mean of the response variable (also termed the constant because it is constant for all observations);
- if the factor is fixed, α_i is the effect of ith group (the difference between each group mean and the overall mean $\mu_i - \mu$);
- if the factor is random, α_i represents a random variable with a mean of zero and a variance of σ_α^2, measuring the variance in mean values of the response variable across all the possible levels of the factor that could have been used;
- ε_{ij} is random or unexplained error associated with the jth replicate observation from the ith group. These error terms are assumed to be normally distributed at each factor level, with a mean of zero ($E(\varepsilon_{ij})$ equals zero) and a variance of σ_ε^2.

This model is structurally similar to the simple linear regression model described in Chapter 5. The overall mean replaces the intercept as the constant and the treatment or group effect replaces the slope as a measure of the effect of the predictor variable on the response variable. Like the regression model, model 8.1 has two components: the model ($\mu + \alpha_i$) and the error (ε_{ij}).

We can fit a linear model to data where the predictor variable is categorical in a form that is basically a multiple linear regression model with an intercept. The factor levels (groups) are converted to dummy variables (Chapter 6) and a multiple regression model is fitted of the form:

$$y_{ij} = \mu + \beta_1(\text{dummy}_1)_{ij} + \beta_2(\text{dummy}_2)_{ij} + \beta_3(\text{dummy}_3)_{ij} + \ldots + \beta_{p-1}(\text{dummy}_{p-1})_{ij} + \varepsilon_{ij}$$

Fitting this type of model is sometimes called dummy coding in statistical software. The basic results from estimation and hypothesis testing will be the same as when fitting the usual ANOVA models (effects or means models) except that estimates of group effects will often be coded to compare with a reference category so only $p-1$ effects will be presented in output from statistical software. You should always check which category your preferred software uses as its reference group when fitting a model of this type.

The linear effects model is what statisticians call "overparameterized" (Searle 1993) because the number of group means (p) is less than the number of parameters to be estimated ($\mu, \alpha_1 \ldots \alpha_p$). Not all parameters in the effects model can be estimated by OLS unless we impose some constraints because there is no unique solution to the set of normal equations (Searle 1993). The usual constraint, sometimes called a sum-to-zero constraint (Yandell 1997), a Σ-restriction (Searle 1993), or a side condition (Maxwell & Delaney 1990), is that the sum of the group effects equals zero, i.e. $\Sigma_{i=1}^{p} \alpha_i = 0$. This constraint is not particularly problematical for single factor designs, although similar constraints for some multifactor designs are controversial (Chapter 9). The sum-to-zero constraint is not the only way of allowing estimation of the overall mean and each of the α_i. We can also set one of the parameters, either μ or one of the α_i, to zero (set-to-zero constraint; Yandell 1997), although this approach is only really useful when one group is clearly a control or reference group (see also effects coding for linear models in Chapter 5).

An alternative single factor ANOVA model is the cell means model. It simply replaces $\mu + \alpha_i$ with μ_i and therefore uses group means instead of group effects (differences between group means and overall mean) for the model component:

$$y_{ij} = \mu_i + \varepsilon_{ij}$$

The cell means model is no longer overparameterized because the number of parameters in the model component is obviously the same as the number of group means. While fitting such a model makes little difference in the single factor case, and the basic ANOVA table and hypothesis tests will not change, the cell means model has some advantages in more complex designs with unequal sample sizes or completely missing cells (Milliken & Johnson 1984, Searle 1993; Chapter 9).

Some linear models statisticians (Hocking 1996, Searle 1993) regard the sum-to-zero constraint as an unnecessary complication that limits the practical and pedagogical use of the effects model and can cause much confusion in multifactor designs (Nelder & Lane 1995). The alternative approach is to focus on parameters or functions of parameters that are estimable. Estimable functions are "those functions of parameters which do not depend on the particular solution of the normal equations" (Yandell 1997, p. 111). Although all of the α_i are not estimable (at least, not without constraints), $(\mu + \alpha_i)$ is estimable for each group. If we equate the effects model with the cell means model:

$$y_{ij} = \mu + \alpha_i + \varepsilon_{ij} = \mu_i + \varepsilon_{ij}$$

we can see that each estimable function $(\mu + \alpha_i)$ is equivalent to the appropriate cell mean (μ_i), hence the emphasis that many statisticians place on the cell means model. In practice, it makes no difference for hypothesis testing whether we fit the cell means or effects model. The F-ratio statistic for testing the H_0 that $\mu_1 = \mu_2 = \ldots = \mu_i = \ldots = \mu$ is identical to that for testing the H_0 that all α_i equal zero.

We prefer the effects model for most analyses of experimental designs because, given the sum-to-zero constraints, it allows estimation of the effects of factors and their interactions (Chapter 9), allows combinations of continuous and categorical variables (e.g. analyses of covariance, Chapter 12) and is similar in structure to the multiple linear regression model. The basic features of the effects model for a single factor ANOVA are similar to those described for the linear regression model in Chapter 5. In particular, we must make certain assumptions about the error terms (ε_{ij}) from the model and these assumptions equally apply to the response variable.

1. For each group (factor level, i) used in the design, there is a population of Y-values (y_{ij}) and error terms (ε_{ij}) with a probability distribution. For interval estimation and hypothesis testing, we assume that the population of y_{ij} and therefore ε_{ij} at each factor level (i) has a normal distribution.

2. These populations of y_{ij} and therefore ε_{ij} at each factor level are assumed to have the same variance (σ_ε^2, sometimes simplified to σ^2 when there is no ambiguity). This is termed the homogeneity of variance assumption and can be formally expressed as $\sigma_1^2 = \sigma_2^2 = \ldots = \sigma_i^2 = \ldots = \sigma_\varepsilon^2$.

3. The y_{ij} and the ε_{ij} are independent of, and therefore uncorrelated with, each other within each factor level and across factor levels if the factor is fixed or, if the factor is random, once the factor levels have been chosen (Neter et al. 1996).

These assumptions and their implications are examined in more detail in Section 8.3.

There are three parameters to be estimated when fitting model 8.1: μ, α_i and σ_ε^2, the latter being the variance of the error terms, assumed to be constant across factor levels. Estimation of these parameters can be based on either OLS or ML and when certain assumptions hold (see Section 8.3), the estimates for μ and α_i are the same whereas the ML estimate of σ_ε^2 is slightly biased (see also Chapter 2). We will focus on OLS estimation, although ML is important for estimation of some parameters when sample sizes differ between groups (Section 8.2).

The OLS estimates of μ, μ_i and α_i are presented in Table 8.1. Note the estimate of α_i is simply the difference between the estimates of μ_i and μ. Therefore, the predicted or fitted values of the response variable from our model are:

$$\hat{y}_{ij} = \bar{y} + (\bar{y}_i - \bar{y}) = \bar{y}_i$$

So any predicted Y-value is simply predicted by the sample mean for that factor level.

In practice, we tend not to worry too much about the estimates of μ and α_i because we usually focus on estimates of group means and of differences or contrasts between group means for fixed factors (Section 8.6) and components of variance for random factors (Section 8.2). Standard errors for these group means are:

$$s_{\bar{y}_i} = \sqrt{\frac{MS_{Residual}}{n_i}}$$

and confidence intervals for μ_i can be constructed in the usual manner based on the t distribution.

The error terms (ε_{ij}) from the linear model can be estimated by the residuals, where a residual (e_{ij}) is simply the difference between each observed and predicted Y-value ($y_{ij} - \bar{y}_i$). Note that the sum of the residuals within each factor level equals zero ($\sum_{j=1}^{n} e_{ij} = 0$). The OLS estimate of σ_{ε}^2 is the sample variance of these residuals and is termed the Residual (or Error) Mean Square (Table 8.1); remember from Chapter 2 that a mean square is just a variance.

Box 8.4 | Worked example: planned comparisons of serpulid recruitment onto surfaces with different biofilms

The mean log number of serpulid recruits for each of the four biofilm treatments from Keough & Raimondi (1995) were (see also Figure 8.3) as follows.

Treatment	Field (F)	Netted lab (NL)	Sterile lab (SL)	Un-netted lab (UL)
Log mean number of serpulid recruits	2.117	2.185	1.939	2.136

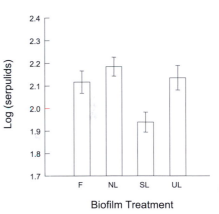

Figure 8.3 Plot of means and standard errors of log number of serpulid recruits for the four biofilm treatments used by Keough & Raimondi (1995). F denotes the treatment with biofilms developing in the field; NL, UL and SL indicates biofilms developed under laboratory conditions, with NL and UL being substrata in laboratory aquaria with (N) and without (U) nets, and SL substrata being immersed in sterile seawater.

A series of planned comparisons were done, each testing a hypothesis about the nature of the biofilms. The contrasts were done in sequence, with each comparison depending on the result of previous ones.

First, Keough & Raimondi (1995) tested whether the presence of a net over a surface affected recruitment, by comparing the netted and un-netted laboratory treatments. The H_0 is:

$$\mu_{NL} = \mu_{UL} \text{ or } \mu_{NL} - \mu_{UL} = 0$$

We use the latter expression to define the linear contrast equation:

$$(0)\bar{y}_F + (+1)\bar{y}_{NL} + (0)\bar{y}_{SL} + (-1)\bar{y}_{UL}$$

Note that this contrast specifically represents the H_0 and we use coefficients of zero to omit groups that are not part of the H_0. This linear contrast can be used to calculate the SS due to this comparison. The complete ANOVA table below indicates that we would not reject this H_0.

Second, the laboratory and field films were compared. Because the two kinds of laboratory-developed films did not differ, we can pool them, so the H_0 is:

$$(\mu_{NL} + \mu_{UL})/2 = \mu_F \text{ or } (\mu_{NL} + \mu_{UL})/2 - \mu_F = 0$$

The linear contrast equation is:

$$(+1)\bar{y}_F + (-0.5)\bar{y}_{NL} + (0)\bar{y}_{SL} + (-0.5)\bar{y}_{UL} \text{ or}$$

$$(+2)\bar{y}_F + (-1)\bar{y}_{NL} + (0)\bar{y}_{SL} + (-1)\bar{y}_{UL}$$

Note that the coefficients for the two lab treatments produce the average of those two groups, which is contrasted to the field treatment. The ANOVA table below indicates that we would not reject this H_0.

Finally, we compare the whole set of substrata with biofilms present, to the single, unfilmed treatment. The H_0 is:

$$(\mu_F + \mu_{NL} + \mu_{UL})/3 = \mu_{SL} \text{ or } (\mu_F + \mu_{NL} + \mu_{UL})/3 - \mu_{SL} = 0$$

The linear contrast equation is:

$$(+1)\bar{y}_F + (-0.33)\bar{y}_{NL} + (-0.33)\bar{y}_{SL} + (-0.33)\bar{y}_{UL} \text{ or}$$

$$(+3)\bar{y}_F + (-1)\bar{y}_{NL} + (-1)\bar{y}_{SL} + (-1)\bar{y}_{UL}$$

Now the coefficients for the three lab treatments represent the average of those three groups and is contrasted to the field treatment. We would reject this H_0.

Source	SS	df	MS	F	P
Biofilms	0.241	3	0.080	6.006	0.003
NL vs UL	0.008	1	0.008	0.635	0.433
F vs average (NL & UL)	0.008	1	0.008	0.644	0.423
SL vs average (F & NL & UL)	0.217	1	0.217	16.719	<0.001
Linear trend	0.079	1	0.079	6.096	0.021
Residual	0.321	24	0.013		
Total	0.562	27			

Note that as long as the coefficients sum to zero (i.e. $\sum_{i=1}^{P} n_i c_i = 0$) and represent the contrast of interest, the size of the coefficients is irrelevant, e.g. in the first example above, we could have used $1, -1, 0, 0$ or $0.5, -0.5, 0, 0$ or $100, -100, 0, 0$, the results would be identical. Note also that these comparisons are orthogonal. For example, for the first two comparisons, we can use the formal test of orthogonality $\sum_{i=1}^{P} c_{i1} c_{i2} = (0)(1) + (1)(-0.5) + (0)(0) + (-1)(-0.5) = 0 - 0.5 + 0 + 0.5 = 0$.

Although Keough & Raimondi did not ask this question, it could have been that the sterile water and the three biofilm treatments became monotonically richer as a cue for settlement. If so, a test for trend would have been appropriate, with the four treatments ranked SL, NL, UL, F and considered equally spaced. Using the information in Table 8.8, the contrast equation is:

$$(+3)\bar{y}_F + (-1)\bar{y}_{NL} + (-3)\bar{y}_{SL} + (+1)\bar{y}_{UL}$$

The results for this contrast are in the ANOVA table above and we would reject the H_0 and conclude that there is a trend, although inspection of the means (Figure 8.3) suggests that the trend is influenced by the low settlement of worms onto the unfilmed (SL) treatment. If we had decided to test for a quadratic trend, our coefficients would be of the form $1 -1 -1 1$, and, in the order in which our treatments are listed, the coefficients would be $1 -1 1 -1$. Such a trend is not of much interest here.

Table 8.1 Parameters, and their OLS estimates, from a single factor linear model with example calculations illustrated for diatom species diversity in different zinc-level groups from Medley & Clements (1998)

Parameter	Estimate	Medley & Clements (1998)
μ_i	$\bar{y}_i = \dfrac{\sum\limits_{j=1}^{n} y_{ij}}{n_i}$	Group mean ($\pm$SE) diversity: Background 1.797 $\pm$ 0.165 Low 2.033 $\pm$ 0.165 Medium 1.718 $\pm$ 0.155 High 1.278 $\pm$ 0.155
μ	$\bar{y} = \dfrac{\sum\limits_{i=1}^{p} \bar{y}_i}{p}$	Overall mean diversity: 1.694
$\alpha_i = \mu_i - \mu$	$\bar{y}_i - \bar{y}$	Background: 1.797 − 1.694 = 0.103 Low: 2.033 − 1.694 = 0.339 Medium: 1.718 − 1.694 = 0.024 High: 1.278 − 1.694 = −0.416
ε_{ij}	$e_{ij} = y_{ij} - \bar{y}_i$	Background: Obs 1: 2.270 − 1.797 = 0.473 Obs 2: 2.200 − 1.797 = 0.403 Obs 3: 1.890 − 1.797 = 0.093 Obs 4: 1.530 − 1.797 = −0.267 etc.
σ_ε^2	$MS_{Residual}$ $\dfrac{\sum\limits_{i=1}^{p}\sum\limits_{j=1}^{n}(y_{ij}-\bar{y}_i)^2}{\sum\limits_{i=1}^{n} n_i - p}$	$= [(0.473)^2 + (0.403)^2 + (0.093)^2 + \cdots]/[(8+8+9+9)-4]$

In models 8.1 and 8.2 we have the following.

y_{ij} is the jth replicate observation from the ith group, e.g. the diatom species diversity in the jth station from the ith zinc-level group.

μ is the overall population mean diatom species diversity across all possible stations from the four zinc-level groups.

If the factor is fixed, α_i is the effect of ith group (the difference between each group mean and the overall mean $\mu_i - \mu$), e.g. the effect of the ith zinc-level group on diatom species diversity, measured as the difference between the mean species diversity for the ith zinc level and the overall mean species diversity. If the factor is random, α_i represents a random variable with a mean of zero and a variance of σ_α^2, e.g. the

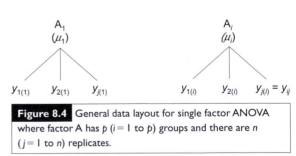

Figure 8.4 General data layout for single factor ANOVA where factor A has p ($i = 1$ to p) groups and there are n ($j = 1$ to n) replicates.

variance in the mean diatom species diversity per stream across all the possible streams in the southern Rocky Mountains that Medley & Clements (1998) could have used in their study.

ε_{ij} is random or unexplained error associated with the jth replicate observation from the ith group. For example, this measures

Table 8.2 | ANOVA table for single factor linear model showing partitioning of variation

Source of	SS	df	MS
Between groups	$\sum_{i=1}^{p} n_i(\bar{y}_i - \bar{y})^2$	$p-1$	$\dfrac{\sum_{i=1}^{p} n_i(\bar{y}_i - \bar{y})^2}{p-1}$
Residual	$\sum_{i=1}^{p}\sum_{j=1}^{n}(y_{ij} - \bar{y}_i)^2$	$\sum_{i=1}^{p} n_i - p$	$\dfrac{\sum_{i=1}^{p}\sum_{j=1}^{n}(y_{ij} - \bar{y}_i)^2}{\sum_{i=1}^{p} n_i - p}$
Total	$\sum_{i=1}^{p}\sum_{j=1}^{n}(y_{ij} - \bar{y})^2$	$\sum_{i=1}^{p} n_i - 1$	

the error associated with each replicate observation of diatom species diversity at any possible station within any of the four zinc levels.

For interval estimation and tests of hypotheses about model parameters, we must make certain assumptions about the error terms (ε_{ij}) from model 8.1 and these assumptions also apply to the response variable. First, the population of y_{ij} and therefore ε_{ij} at each factor level (i) has a normal distribution. We assume that there is a population of stations with normally distributed diatom species diversity for each zinc level. Second, these populations of y_{ij} and therefore ε_{ij} at each factor level are assumed to have the same variance (σ_ε^2, sometimes simplified to σ^2 when there is no ambiguity). We assume the variances in diatom species diversity among stations for each zinc level are equal. Finally, the y_{ij} and the ε_{ij} are independent of, and therefore uncorrelated with, each other within each factor level and across factor levels if the factor is fixed or, if the factor is random, once the factor levels have been chosen (Neter *et al.* 1996). In the study of Medley & Clements (1998), some stations were on the same stream so what happens upstream might influence what happens downstream, an issue of concern for all stream ecologists (see Downes *et al.* 2001). We will examine these assumptions and their implications in more detail in Section 8.3.

Predicted values and residuals

The Y-values predicted from the linear model are simply the sample means for the factor level containing the observed value:

$$\hat{y}_{ij} = \bar{y}_i \tag{8.4}$$

The error terms (ε_{ij}) from the linear model can be estimated by the residuals, where each residual (e_{ij}) is the difference between the observed and the predicted Y-value:

$$e_{ij} = y_{ij} - \bar{y}_i \tag{8.5}$$

For example, the residuals from the model relating diatom species diversity to zinc-level group are the differences between the observed species diversity at each station and the mean species diversity for the zinc level that station came from. As in regression analysis, residuals provide the basis of the OLS estimate of σ_ε^2 and they are valuable diagnostic tools for checking assumptions and fit of our model (Section 8.4).

8.1.3 Analysis of variance

As described in Chapters 5 and 6 for regression models, ANOVA partitions the total variation in the response variable into its components or sources. This partitioning of variation is expressed in the form of an ANOVA table (Table 8.2). We first describe the variation in Y as sums of squares (SS). The SS$_{\text{Total}}$ for Y is the sum of the squared differences between each y_{ij} and the overall mean $\bar{y}$. The degrees of freedom (df) is the

Table 8.3 | Imaginary data based on Medley & Clements (1998) showing diatom species diversity at eight stream stations in each of four zinc levels (background, low, medium, high) – see text for details. In (a), all the variation is residual and SS_{Groups} explains none of the variation in Y (no difference between group means). In (b), there is no residual variation and SS_{Groups} explains all the variation in Y

(a) Zinc level	B	L	M	H
	0.8	0.7	1.8	2.6
	0.9	1.7	2.1	0.6
	2.4	1.0	0.6	1.2
	1.4	1.4	1.1	1.3
	1.3	1.2	2.4	2.2
	1.8	2.4	1.2	0.9
	2.1	1.1	0.9	1.9
	1.0	2.2	1.6	1.0
Means	1.4625	1.4625	1.4625	1.4625

(b) Zinc level	B	L	M	H
	1.2	2.3	1.8	0.7
	1.2	2.3	1.8	0.7
	1.2	2.3	1.8	0.7
	1.2	2.3	1.8	0.7
	1.2	2.3	1.8	0.7
	1.2	2.3	1.8	0.7
	1.2	2.3	1.8	0.7
	1.2	2.3	1.8	0.7
Means	1.2	2.3	1.8	0.7

relevant group mean $\bar{y}_i$. This is a measure of how different the observations are within each group, summed across groups, and also how much of the total variation in Y is not explained by the difference between groups or treatments. The df associated with the $SS_{Residual}$ is the number of observations in each group minus one, summed across groups, which is equal to the sum of the sample sizes minus the number of groups.

These SS and df are additive:

$$SS_{Total} = SS_{Groups} + SS_{Residual}$$
$$df_{Total} = df_{Groups} + df_{Residual}$$

As pointed out in Chapter 5, the sum-of-squares (SS) is a measure of variation that is dependent on the number of observations that contribute to it. In contrast to the SS, the variance (mean square) is a measure of variability that does not depend on sample size because it is an average of the squared deviations (Chapter 2). We convert the SS into Mean Squares (MS) by dividing them by their df (Table 8.2).

A detailed description of the algebra behind this partitioning of the variation can be found in Underwood (1997). Note that there are re-expressions of the formulae in Table 8.2 that are much easier to use when doing the calculations by hand (Sokal & Rohlf 1995, Underwood 1981, 1997). In practice, however, statistical software will calculate the SS and MS by fitting and comparing linear models (Section 8.1.5).

The best way to appreciate the variation between groups and the residual variation is to look at two extreme imaginary data sets, based on species diversity of stream diatoms at different zinc levels (Medley & Clements 1998). The data in Table 8.3(a) show a situation in which all the variation is between observations within each group (residual) with no variation between groups (identical group means). In contrast, the data in Table 8.3(b) are where all the variation is between groups with no residual variation (all observations within each group are identical).

The mean squares from the ANOVA are sample variances and, as such, they estimate population parameters. Statisticians have determined the expected values of MS_{Groups} and $MS_{Residual}$, termed expected mean squares (EMS), i.e. the means of the probability distributions of these sample

total number of observations across all groups minus one. SS_{Total} can be partitioned into two additive components.

First is the variation due to the difference between group means, calculated as the difference between each $\bar{y}_i$ and the overall mean $\bar{y}$. This is a measure of how different the group means are and how much of the total variation in Y is explained by the difference between groups, or in an experimental context, the effect of the treatments. The df associated with the variation between group means is the number of groups minus one.

Second is the variation due to the difference between the observations within each group, calculated as the difference between each y_{ij} and

Table 8.4 | Expected mean squares for a single factor ANOVA

Source	Fixed factor (Model 1)	Random factor (Model 2)	F-ratio
MS_{Groups}	$\sigma_\varepsilon^2 + \sum_{i=1}^{p} n_i \dfrac{(\alpha_i)^2}{p-1}$	$\sigma_\varepsilon^2 + \dfrac{\left[\left(\sum_{i=1}^{p} n_i\right)^2 - \sum_{i=1}^{p} n_i^2\right]\sigma_\alpha^2}{\sum_{i=1}^{p} n_i(p-1)}$	$\dfrac{MS_{Groups}}{MS_{Residual}}$
	If equal n: $\sigma_\varepsilon^2 + n\sum_{i=1}^{p} \dfrac{(\alpha_i)^2}{p-1}$	If equal n: $\sigma_\varepsilon^2 + n\sigma_\alpha^2$	
$MS_{Residual}$	σ_ε^2	σ_ε^2	

variances or what population values these mean squares actually estimate (Table 8.4; see Underwood 1997 for a clear, biologically orientated, explanation).

The $MS_{Residual}$ estimates σ_ε^2, the pooled population variance of the error terms, and hence of the Y-values, within groups. Note that we must assume homogeneity of error variances across groups (homogeneity of variances assumption; see Sections 8.1.2 and 8.3) for this expectation to hold.

The MS_{Groups} estimates the pooled variance of the error terms across groups plus a component representing the squared effects of the chosen groups if the factor is fixed, or the variance between all possible groups if the factor is random (Table 8.4). Note that these EMS are subject to the important constraint that $\sum_{i=1}^{p}\alpha_i$ equals zero, i.e. the sum of the group effects equals zero. Without this constraint, we cannot get unbiased estimators of individual treatment effects (Box 8.3; Underwood 1997, Winer *et al.* 1991).

8.1.4 Null hypotheses

The null hypothesis tested in a single factor fixed effects ANOVA is usually one of no difference between group means:

$H_0: \mu_1 = \mu_2 = \ldots = \mu_i = \ldots = \mu$

We defined group effects (α_i) in Section 8.1.2 and Box 8.3 as $\mu_i - \mu$, the difference between the population mean of group i and the overall mean.

This is a measure of the effect of the ith group, or in an experimental context, the ith treatment. The null hypothesis can therefore also be expressed as no effects of groups or treatments, i.e. all treatment or group effects equal zero:

$H_0: \alpha_1 = \alpha_2 = \ldots = \alpha_i = \ldots = 0$

For a random effects ANOVA, the null hypothesis is that the variance between all possible groups equals zero:

$H_0: \sigma_\alpha^2 = 0$

The EMS from our ANOVA table (Table 8.4) allow us to determine F-ratios for testing these null hypotheses.

If the H_0 for a fixed factor is true, all α_i equal zero (no group effects). Therefore, both MS_{Groups} and $MS_{Residual}$ estimate σ_ε^2 and their ratio should be one. The ratio of two variances (or mean squares) is called an F-ratio (Chapter 2). If the H_0 is false, then at least one α_i will be different from zero. Therefore, MS_{Groups} has a larger expected value than $MS_{Residual}$ and their F-ratio will be greater than one. A central F distribution is a probability distribution of the F-ratio when the two sample variances come from populations with the same expected values. There are different central F distributions depending on the df of the two sample variances (see Figure 1.2). Therefore, we can use the appropriate probability distribution of F (defined by numerator and denominator df) to determine whether the probability of obtaining our sample F-ratio or one more extreme (the usual hypothesis testing logic; see Chapter 3), is less than some specified significance level (e.g. 0.05) and therefore whether we reject H_0 or not.

If the H_0 for a random factor is true, then σ_α^2 equals zero (no added variance due to groups) and both MS_{Groups} and $MS_{Residual}$ estimate σ_ε^2 so their F-ratio should be one. If the H_0 is false, then σ_α^2 will be greater than zero, MS_{Groups} will have a larger expected value than $MS_{Residual}$ and their F-ratio will be greater than one.

These F-ratio tests (usually abbreviated to F tests) of null hypotheses for fixed and random factors are illustrated for our worked examples in Box 8.1 and Box 8.2. The construction of the tests of null hypotheses is identical for fixed and random factors in the single factor ANOVA model, but these null hypotheses have very different interpretations. The H_0 for the fixed factor refers only to the groups used in the study whereas the H_0 for the random factor refers to all the possible groups that could have been used. It should also be clear now why the assumption of equal within group variances is so important. If σ_1^2 does not equal σ_2^2, etc., then $MS_{Residual}$ does not estimate a single population variance (σ_ε^2), and we cannot construct a reliable F-ratio for testing the H_0 of no group effects.

8.1.5 Comparing ANOVA models

The logic of fitting ANOVA models is the same as described in Chapters 5 and 6 for linear regression models. Either OLS or ML can be used, the fit being determined by explained variance or log-likelihoods respectively. We will use OLS in this chapter.

The full effects model containing all parameters is:

$$y_{ij} = \mu + \alpha_i + \varepsilon_{ij} \tag{8.1}$$

The reduced model when H_0 that all α_i equal zero is true is:

$$y_{ij} = \mu + \varepsilon_{ij} \tag{8.6}$$

Model 8.6 simply states that if there are no group effects, our best prediction for each observation is the overall mean, e.g. if there are no effects of zinc level on diatom species diversity, then our best predictor of species diversity at each station is the overall species diversity across all stations. The residual variation when the full model is fitted is the $SS_{Residual}$ from the ANOVA in Table 8.2. The residual variation when the reduced model is fitted is the SS_{Total} from the ANOVA in Table 8.2. The difference between the unexplained variation of the full model ($SS_{Residual}$) and the unexplained variation from the reduced model (SS_{Total}) is simply the SS_{Groups}. It measures how much more of the variation in Y is explained by the full model compared to the reduced model. It is, therefore, the relative magnitude of the MS_{Groups} that we use to evaluate the H_0 that there are no group effects. Although comparing full and reduced models is trivial for a single factor ANOVA, the model comparison approach has broad applicability for testing null hypotheses about particular parameters in more complex linear and generalized linear models.

8.1.6 Unequal sample sizes (unbalanced designs)

Unequal sample sizes within each group do not cause any computational difficulties, particularly when the ANOVA is considered as a general linear model as we have described. However, unequal sample sizes can cause other problems. First, the different group means will be estimated with different levels of precision and this can make interpretation difficult (Underwood 1997). Note that sample size is only one contributor to the precision of an estimate and some statisticians have suggested that experiments should be designed with different sample sizes depending on the inherent variability of the variable in each group or the relative importance of each group (Mead 1988). Second, the ANOVA F test is much less robust to violations of assumptions, particularly homogeneity of variances, if sample sizes differ (Section 8.3). The worst case is when larger variances are associated with smaller sample sizes. This is a very important reason to design experiments and sampling programs with equal sample sizes where possible. Third, estimation of group effects, particularly variance components, is much more difficult (see Section 8.2). Finally, power calculations for random effects models are difficult because when σ_ε^2 is greater than zero and sample sizes are unequal, then the F-ratio

$MS_{Groups}/MS_{Residual}$ does not follow an F distribution (Searle *et al.* 1992). For testing null hypotheses with fixed effects, unequal sample sizes are only really a worry if the analysis produces a result that is close to the critical level; you will not be confident enough that the P value is accurate for you to be comfortable interpreting the result of your analysis. If, however, the result is far from significant, or highly significant (e.g. $P < 0.001$), you may still be confident in your conclusions.

One solution to unequal sample sizes in single factor designs is deleting observations until all groups have the same n. We regard this practice as unnecessarily extreme; the linear models approach can deal with unequal sample sizes and biological studies often suffer from lack of power and deleting observations will exacerbate the situation, particularly if one group has a much lower sample size than others. Alternatively, we can substitute group means to replace missing observations. In such circumstances, the $df_{Residual}$ should be reduced by the number of substituted observations (Chapter 4). However, if there is no evidence that the assumption of homogeneity of variance is seriously compromised, and the difference in sample sizes is not large (which is usually the case as unequal sample sizes are often caused by one or two observations going missing), then we recommend simply fitting the linear ANOVA model. Nonetheless, we support the recommendation of Underwood (1997) that experimental and sampling programs in biology with unequal sample sizes should be avoided, at least by design.

8.2 | Factor effects

In linear regression, we could measure the "effect" of the predictor variable on the response variable in a number of ways, including the standardized regression slope or the proportion of variation in Y explained by the linear regression with X (e.g. r^2). These are measures of effect size (the "effects" of X on Y), although linear regression models are often fitted to non-experimental data so we are not implying any cause–effect relationship. In designs where the predictor variable is categorical, measuring effect size is of much more interest. One measure of group or treatment effects is the variance associated with the groups

over and above the residual variance. The proportion of total variance in the population(s) explained by the groups then can be expressed as (Smith 1982):

$$\eta^2 = \frac{\sigma_Y^2 - \sigma_\varepsilon^2}{\sigma_Y^2} = \frac{\sigma_\alpha^2}{\sigma_\varepsilon^2 + \sigma_\alpha^2} \tag{8.7}$$

where σ_ε^2 is the residual variance, σ_α^2 is the variance explained by the groups and σ_Y^2 is the total variance in the response variable. Our aim, then, is to estimate the parameter η^2. Petraitis (1998) termed indices like η^2 PEV (proportion of explained variance) measures. One measure of η^2 is r^2, defined here, as for linear regression models (Chapters 5 and 6), as the proportion of the total SS explained by the predictor variable (groups), i.e. SS_{Groups} / SS_{Total}. Unfortunately, r^2 is dependent on the sample size in each group and also tends to overestimate the true proportion of the total variance explained by group effects (Maxwell & Delaney 1990). We need to consider other PEV measures, noting that their calculation and interpretation depend on whether we are talking about fixed or random factors.

8.2.1 Random effects: variance components

Let's first look at random effects models because they are straightforward, at least when sample sizes are equal. In the random effects model, there are two components of variance (termed "variance components") of interest (Table 8.5). The true variance between replicate observations within each group, averaged across groups, is σ_ε^2 and is estimated by $MS_{Residual}$. The true variance between the means of all the possible groups we could have used in our study is σ_α^2 and is termed the added variance component due to groups. We can estimate this added variance explained by groups by equating the observed and expected values of the mean squares (Brown & Mosteller 1991, Searle *et al.* 1992; see Table 8.4 and Table 8.5). This method of estimating variance components is termed the ANOVA or expected mean square (EMS) method (also method of moments). There are no distributional assumptions underlying these point estimates unless confidence intervals are developed or null hypotheses tested.

Confidence intervals can be calculated for these variance components (Table 8.5; Brown &

Table 8.5 ANOVA estimates of variance components and confidence intervals for a single factor random effects model. For 95% confidence intervals, we use critical values of the χ^2 and F distributions at 0.975 for upper confidence intervals and 0.025 for lower confidence intervals (covers range of 0.95)

Variance component	ANOVA estimate	Confidence interval
σ_α^2	Unequal n: $$\dfrac{MS_{Groups} - MS_{Residual}}{\left(\sum n_i - \sum n_i^2 / \sum n_i\right)/(p-1)}$$ Equal n: $$\dfrac{MS_{Groups} - MS_{Residual}}{n}$$	Approximate for equal n only: $$\pm \dfrac{SS_{Groups}(1 - F_{p-1,p(n-1)}/F)}{n\chi_{p-1}^2}$$ where: F is F-ratio from ANOVA $F_{p-1,p(n-1)}$ is value from F distribution with $p-1$ and $p(n-1)$ df χ^2 is value from χ^2 distribution with $p-1$ df
σ_ε^2	$MS_{Residual}$	$$\pm \dfrac{SS_{Residual}}{\chi^2}$$ where: χ^2 is value from χ^2 distribution with $$\sum_{i=1}^{p} n_i - p \text{ df}$$
$\rho_I = \dfrac{\sigma_\alpha^2}{\sigma_\varepsilon^2 + \sigma_\alpha^2}$	Equal n: $$\dfrac{MS_{Groups} - MS_{Residual}}{MS_{Groups} + (n-1)MS_{Residual}}$$	Equal n: $$\pm \dfrac{F/F_{p-1,p(n-1)} - 1}{n + F/F_{p-1,p(n-1)} - 1}$$ where: F and $F_{p-1,p(n-1)}$ as defined above

Mosteller 1991, Burdick & Graybill 1992, Searle *et al.* 1992). The confidence intervals are based on the χ^2 distribution, or equivalently the F distribution ($\chi^2_{\alpha;df_1} = df_1 F_{\alpha;df_1,\infty}$), because variances are distributed as a chi-square. For 95% confidence intervals, we use critical values of the χ^2 or F distribution at 0.975 for upper confidence intervals and 0.0125 for lower confidence intervals (covers range of 0.95). These confidence intervals are interpreted as a 95% probability under repeated sampling that this interval includes the true population variance explained by the groups. Note that the confidence interval for σ_α^2 is only an approximation (Searle *et al.* 1992), although exact confidence intervals can be determined for various ratios of σ_α^2 to σ_ε^2 and $\sigma_\alpha^2 + \sigma_\varepsilon^2$. With unbalanced data, a confidence interval for σ_α^2 based on the ANOVA method is not possible, although approximations

are again available but tedious to calculate (Burdick & Graybill 1992, Searle *et al.* 1992).

Note that sometimes, MS_{Groups} will be less than $MS_{Residual}$ (and the F-ratio will be less than one), resulting in a negative estimate for σ_α^2. This is a problem, because variances obviously cannot be negative, by definition. The usual recommendation is to convert a negative variance component estimate to zero (Brown & Mosteller 1991). Hocking (1993) and Searle *et al.* (1992) argued that negative variance components suggest an inappropriate model has been applied or there may be serious outliers in the data and therefore that negative variance components might be a useful diagnostic tool.

An alternative approach is to use a method of variance component estimation that specifically excludes negative estimates (Searle *et al.* 1992). This is particularly important in multifactor unbalanced designs (Chapter 9; see also Underwood 1997). These alternatives include the following.

- Maximum likelihood estimation (MLE) that involves deriving ML equations and their iterative solutions, although the estimators are biased (remember from Chapter 2 that ML estimators for variances are biased).
- Restricted maximum likelihood estimation (REML) that is a modification of MLE that excludes μ (the only fixed parameter in the random effects model) from the likelihood function, partly to correct the bias in ML estimates.
- Minimum norm quadratic unbiased estimation (MINQUE), a method that requires solving linear equations and a priori "guesses" of the components to be used in the estimation procedure.

REML produces the same estimates as the ANOVA method for σ_α^2 in balanced designs whereas the ML estimate will be slightly biased. Both ML and REML also preclude negative variance estimates for σ_α^2. However, in contrast to the ANOVA method, likelihood methods must assume normality for point estimates and all methods assume normality for interval estimates and hypothesis testing. Searle et al. (1992) summarized the merits of the different methods for unbalanced data in the single factor model and recommended REML for estimating the added variance components due to groups (σ_α^2) and the ANOVA method for estimating the residual variance (σ_ε^2).

Ideally, estimated variance components should be provided with confidence intervals. It might be tempting for biologists working with few df to talk about an "important" factor effect based on a large estimated variance component despite a non-significant F statistic and P value. However, the confidence interval associated with the variance component is likely to include zero under such circumstances. Interpretation of variance components should only follow a rejection of the H_0 of no added variance.

To calculate the proportion of total variance due to the random factor, we simply substitute our estimators into $\sigma_\alpha^2/(\sigma_\varepsilon^2 + \sigma_\alpha^2)$, which is sometimes called the intraclass correlation (ρ_I).

8.2.2 Fixed effects

Now let's look at PEV measures for fixed factors, which are more problematical. In many cases, the effects are displayed most simply using the means for each group, but we may be interested in describing or estimating the pattern of effects across all groups. For a fixed factor, the effect of any group is α_i, the difference between that group mean and the overall mean $\mu_i - \mu$ and we can calculate the variance of these group effects $[\sum_{i=1}^{p}\alpha_i^2/(p-1)]$. This measures the true variance among the fixed population group means in the specific populations from which we have sampled. Brown & Mosteller (1991) pointed out that it is somewhat arbitrary whether we use p or $p-1$ in the denominator for this variance, although since we have used the entire population of groups (a fixed factor), dividing by p (the number of groups) may actually be more appropriate. If we use $p-1$, the estimate of this variance is identical to the estimate of the added variance component for a random effect (Table 8.5), although its interpretation is different.

Petraitis (1998) has discussed the limitations of trying to calculate the proportion of total variance in the response variable that is explained by the fixed groups. One approach (see Hays 1994) is termed omega squared (ω^2) and is the variance of the fixed group means (using p in the denominator) as a proportion of this variance plus the residual variance (Table 8.6). If we base the estimate of ω^2 in Table 8.6 with $p-1$ instead of p in the denominator, we end up with the proportion of total variance due to a random factor (the intraclass correlation). So the main computational difference between the PEV based on ω^2 (fixed factor) or ρ_I (random factor) is whether p or $p-1$ is used in the denominator for the variance between groups.

Another measure of group effects for a fixed factor was provided by Cohen (1988), based on his work on power analyses. He defined effect size (f) as the difference among means measured in units of the standard deviation between replicates within groups (Table 8.6; see also Kirk 1995). The formula looks complex but is basically measuring the ratio of the standard deviation between group means and the standard deviation between replicates within each group (Cohen 1992). In this

Table 8.6 Measures of explained group (or treatment) variance in a single factor fixed effects model illustrated for diatom species diversity in different zinc-level groups from Medley & Clements (1998)

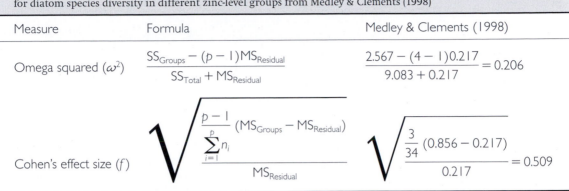

Measure	Formula	Medley & Clements (1998)
Omega squared (ω^2)	$\dfrac{SS_{Groups} - (p-1)MS_{Residual}}{SS_{Total} + MS_{Residual}}$	$\dfrac{2.567 - (4-1)0.217}{9.083 + 0.217} = 0.206$
Cohen's effect size (f)	$\sqrt{\dfrac{\dfrac{p-1}{p}(MS_{Groups} - MS_{Residual})}{\sum\limits_{i=1}^{p} n_i \quad MS_{Residual}}}$	$\sqrt{\dfrac{\dfrac{3}{34}(0.856 - 0.217)}{0.217}} = 0.509$

context, we are measuring the effect in the observed data. Cohen's effect size is more commonly used to set effect sizes, based on the alternative hypothesis, in power calculations (Section 8.9, Box 8.5). Note that ω^2 equals $f^2/(1+f^2)$ (Petraitis 1998).

Glass & Hakstian (1969), Underwood & Petraitis (1993) and Underwood (1997) have criticized measures of variance explained for fixed factors. They argued that the population "variance" of a set of fixed groups makes no sense and this measure cannot be compared to the average population variance between observations within groups, which is a true variance (see also Smith 1982). For instance, confidence intervals around estimates of explained between groups variance are silly for fixed factors because the sampling distribution would always be based on the same fixed groups. Also, these measures of proportion of variance explained by fixed groups are difficult to compare between different analyses. However, like Smith (1982), we recommend that PEV measures are useful descriptive summaries of explained variance for fixed factor ANOVA models, and recommend that using the method of equating mean squares to their expected values provides the simplest measure that is computationally equivalent to the variance component for a random effects model. We will discuss the issue of measuring explained variance for fixed and random factors in the context of multifactor ANOVA (Chapter 9).

It is important to realize that the interpretation of a fixed treatment variance and an added variance component for a random factor is very different (Underwood 1997). The former is an estimate of the variance between these particular group means in the specific population(s) being sampled. It is not an estimate of a variance of a larger population of groups. In contrast, the variance component for a random factor estimates the variance between the means of all the possible groups that could have been used in the analysis; this variance is due to the random sample of groups chosen and represents a real variance.

8.3 | Assumptions

The assumptions for interval estimation and hypothesis testing based on the single factor ANOVA model actually concern the residual or error terms (ε_{ij}) but can be equivalently expressed in terms of the response variable Y. These assumptions are similar to those for linear regression models (Chapters 5 and 6). Most textbooks state that the single factor ANOVA is robust to these assumptions, i.e. the F test and interval estimates of effects are reliable even if the assumptions are not met. However, this robustness is very difficult to quantify and is also very dependent on balanced sample sizes. The F test can become very unreliable when unequal sample sizes are combined with non-normal data with heterogeneous variances. We strongly recommend that the assumptions of the ANOVA be carefully checked before proceeding with the analysis.

Box 8.5 | Variation in formal implementations of power analysis

There are two possible sources for confusion when calculating power. First, effect sizes can be expressed differently. In some cases, the effect is described as the pattern of means, or, in the case of fixed effects, the α_i values. Other authors, e.g. Cohen (1988), combine the variation among means and an estimate of σ_ε^2, to produce a standardized effect.

For example, for a two sample t test, Cohen's effect size parameter is $d = (\mu_1 - \mu_2)/\sigma_\varepsilon$, and for a one factor ANOVA, his parameter f, is given by

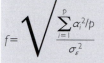

$$f = \sqrt{\frac{\sum_{i=1}^{p} \alpha_i^2/p}{\sigma_\varepsilon^2}}$$

which can then be estimated from the α_i values specified by the alternative hypothesis, and an estimate of residual variance.

In a similar way, the non-centrality parameter is most often expressed as λ, as defined in Equation 8.9. However, Searle (1971) defines the non-centrality parameter as $\lambda/2$, and sometimes non-centrality is defined as $\sqrt{\lambda/(p-1)}$, or as $\varphi = \sqrt{(\lambda/p)}$, with p being the number of groups.

If power is to be calculated using tabulated values, we find that most authors provide power values tabulated against φ (e.g. Kirk 1995, Winer et al. 1991), although Cohen (1988) provides very extensive tables of power against f and n. Note that $f = \varphi/\sqrt{n}$ This reflects a difference in philosophy, with the use of φ representing a standardization using the standard error of the mean, and f a standardization using σ_ε.

These different formulations are mathematically equivalent, but it is confusing initially to encounter different definitions of ostensibly the same parameter. It is essential that you check the formulation used by a particular author or piece of software. A good check is to use a standard example from one of the major texts, and run it through the new calculations. When the same answer is obtained, begin your own calculations.

8.3.1 Normality

We assume that the error terms, and the observations, within each group come from normally distributed populations, i.e. the ε_{ij}s are normally distributed within each group. If sample sizes and variances are similar, then the ANOVA tests are very robust to this assumption. Check for outliers, skewness and bimodality. We can check the normality assumption in a number of ways because we have replicate observations within each group (Chapter 4). Boxplots of observations or residuals (Section 8.4) within groups should be symmetrical. Means and variances from a normal distribution are independent so a plot of sample means against sample variances should show no relationship. Samples from skewed distributions will show a positive relationship between means and variances. Probability plots of the residuals are also informative (Chapter 4). There are some formal tests of normality (e.g. the Wilks & Shapiro tests; goodness-of-fit tests such as Kolmogorov–Smirnov), but we find graphical methods much more informative for checking assumptions before a linear models analysis (Chapter 4).

Because lack of normality is really only a serious problem for ANOVA models when it results in variance heterogeneity, we will consider solutions in Section 8.3.2.

8.3.2 Variance homogeneity

A very important assumption is that the variances of the error terms (and of the observations in the populations being sampled) should be approximately equal in each group. This is termed the assumption of homogeneity of variances. This is a more serious assumption than that of normality; unequal variances can seriously affect the ANOVA F test (reviewed by Coombs et al. 1996). Wilcox et al. (1986) showed by simulation that with four groups and n equal to eleven, a 4:1 ratio of largest to smallest standard deviation (i.e. a 16:1 ratio of variances) resulted in a Type I error rate of 0.109 for a nominal α of 0.05. With sample sizes of six, ten, 16 and 40 and the same standard deviation ratio (largest standard deviation associated with smallest sample size), the Type I error rate could reach 0.275. The situation is similar to that described for t tests in Chapter 3, where larger variances associated with smaller sample sizes result in increased Type I error rates and larger variances associated with larger sample sizes result in reduced power (Coombs et al. 1996). Unequal variances, particularly when associated with unequal sample sizes, can therefore be a problem for hypothesis tests in linear ANOVA models.

There are a number of useful checks of the homogeneity of variance assumption. Boxplots of observations within each group should have similar spread. The spread of residuals (see Section 8.4) should be similar when plotted against group means. There are formal tests of homogeneity of variance that test the H_0 that population variances are the same across groups (e.g. Bartlett's, Hartley's, Cochran's, Levene's tests; see Neter et al. 1996, Sokal & Rohlf 1995, Underwood 1997). We will discuss these in Section 8.8 when the research hypothesis of interest concerns group variances rather than group means. However, we suggest that such tests should not be used by themselves as preliminary checks before fitting an ANOVA model for three reasons. First, some of them are very sensitive to non-normality, especially positive skewness (Conover et al. 1981, Rivest 1986), a common trait of continuous biological variables. Second, we really want to know if the variances are similar enough for the ANOVA F test to still be reliable. Tests for homogeneity of variance simply test whether sample groups come from populations with equal variances. If the sample size is large, these tests could reject the H_0 of equal variances when the ANOVA F test would still be reliable. Conversely, and more importantly, if sample sizes are small, they might not reject the H_0 of equal variances when the ANOVA F test would be in trouble. Finally, tests of homogeneity of variances provide little information on the underlying cause of heterogeneous variances, and diagnostic techniques (e.g. residual plots) are still required to decide what corrective action is appropriate.

There are a number of solutions to variance heterogeneity when fitting ANOVA models. If the heterogeneity is related to an underlying positively skewed distribution of the response variable, and hence the error terms from the ANOVA model, then transformations of the response variable will be particularly useful (see Chapter 4). Alternatively, fitting generalized linear models that allow different distributions for model error terms (Chapter 13) can be effective for linear models with categorical predictors. Weighted least squares, as described for linear regression models in Chapter 5, can also be used and various robust test statistics have been developed for testing hypotheses about means when variances are unequal (see Section 8.5.1).

8.3.3 Independence

The error terms and the observations should be independent, i.e. each experimental or sampling unit is independent of each other experimental unit, both within and between groups. Underwood (1997) has provided a detailed examination of this assumption in the context of ANOVA in biology. He distinguished different types of non-independence (see also Kenny & Judd 1986).

• Positive correlation between replicates within groups, which results in an underestimation of the true σ_ε^2 and increased rate of Type I errors. Such correlation can be due, for example, to experimental organisms responding positively to each other (Underwood 1997) or sequential recording of experimental units through time (Edwards 1993).

Table 8.7	Residuals from single factor ANOVA model
Residual	$y_{ij} - \bar{y}_i$
Studentized residual	$\dfrac{y_{ij} - \bar{y}_i}{\sqrt{\dfrac{MS_{Residual}(n_i - 1)}{n_i}}}$

- Negative correlation between replicates within groups, which results in an overestimation of σ_ε^2 and increased rate of Type II errors.

Lack of independence can also occur between groups if the response of experimental units in one treatment group influences the response in other groups. For example, an experimental treatment that results in animals leaving experimental units may increase abundances on nearby controls. Additionally, if time is the grouping factor and the data are repeated observations on the same experimental or sampling units, then there will often be positive correlations between observations through time.

This assumption must usually be considered at the design stage. Note that we are not arguing that non-independent observations preclude statistical analysis. However, if standard linear models are to be used, it is important to ensure that experimental units are independent of each other, both within and between groups. Randomization at various stages of the design process can help provide independence, but can't guarantee it. For some specific designs, hypothesis tests for linear models can be adjusted conservatively to correct for increasing Type I error rates resulting from positive autocorrelations (Chapters 10 and 11), and these tests fall in the general category of unified mixed linear models (Laird & Ware 1982). Alternatively, the lack of independence (e.g. spatial correlations) can be incorporated into the design and the modeling (Legendre 1993, Ver Hoef & Cressie 1993). Generalized estimating equations (GEEs; see Chapter 13), as developed for handling correlated observations in regression models, may also be useful for ANOVA models because they can be applied to models with both continuous and categorical predictors (Ware & Liang 1996). Finally, measuring and testing hypotheses about spatial patterns, especially when we anticipate that sampling units closer together will be more correlated, are more suited to the fields of spatial statistics and geostatistics (see Koenig 1999, Manly 2001 and Rossi et al. 1992 for ecological perspectives).

8.4 | ANOVA diagnostics

The predictor variable (factor) in a single factor ANOVA model is categorical, so the range of available diagnostics to check the fit of the model and warn about influential observations is limited compared with linear regression models (Chapter 5). Leverage ("outliers" in the X-variable) has no useful meaning for a categorical predictor and Cook's D_i is also hard to interpret, partly because it is based on leverage. However, residuals are still a crucial part of checking any linear model (Box 8.1 and Box 8.2, Table 8.7). Studentized residuals, the residual divided by its standard deviation (Neter et al. 1996), are usually easier for comparison between different models because they have constant variance (Table 8.7). Plots of residuals or studentized residuals against predicted values (group means) are the most informative diagnostic tools for ANOVA models. The residuals should show equal spread across groups, indicating variance homogeneity. Increasing spread of residuals (a wedge shape) suggests a skewed (non-normal) distribution of Y in each group and unequal variances (Figure 8.5). These residual plots can also indicate autocorrelation, just as in regression analysis (Chapter 5).

Outliers can either be observations very different from the rest in a sample (Chapter 4) or observations with a large residual that are a long way from the fitted model compared with other observations (Chapter 5). Outliers will usually have undue influence on estimates of group effects (or variances) and the conclusions from the ANOVA F test. Such observations should always be checked. If they are not a mistake and cannot be corrected or deleted, then one solution is to fit the ANOVA model twice, with the outlier(s) omitted and with

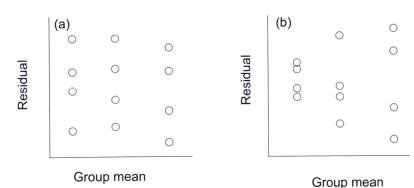

Figure 8.5 Diagrammatic residual plots for single factor ANOVA with three groups and n equals four: (a) similar variances, (b) variance increasing with mean, suggesting positively skewed distribution.

the outlier(s) included (Chapter 4). If there is little difference between the two analyses, it suggests that the outlier(s) are not influential. In the worst case, the outlier(s) may change the result between significant and non-significant. There is not much that you can do in this case, other than to describe both results, and discuss biological explanations for the outliers.

8.5 | Robust ANOVA

We have already pointed out that the F test in a single factor ANOVA is sensitive to large differences in within group variances, especially when sample sizes are unequal. This has led to the development of a number of alternative tests for differences between groups that are more robust to either heterogeneity of variances or outliers or both. We won't present formulae for these tests because, except for the rank versions, the computations are reasonably tedious and we figure biologists are unlikely to use these tests until they appear in statistical software. These robust tests fall into three categories.

8.5.1 Tests with heterogeneous variances
A number of procedures have been developed for testing equality of group means (and specific comparisons; Section 8.6) when variances are very different (Wilcox 1987a, 1993). One of the earliest was Welch's test (Day & Quinn 1989, Wilcox 1993), which uses adjusted degrees of freedom to protect against increased Type I errors under variance heterogeneity. Wilcox (1997) described a modification of Welch's test that extends Yuen's use of trimmed means to more than two groups (the

Yuen–Welch test). Other tests include the Brown–Forsythe test and James second order method (see review by Coombs et al. 1996). These tests generally have less power than the standard ANOVA F test and are relatively complicated to calculate. Wilcox (1993) described the Z test, which is an extension of his H test (Chapter 3) for two groups; it is based on M-estimators and bootstrap methods to determine critical values. Coombs et al. (1996) recommended this test for unequal variances and non-normal distributions and the James second-order method for normal distributions. These tests are not yet available in most statistical software. Our preference is to examine outlying values and, if appropriate, apply a sensible transformation of the data. This encourages researchers to explore their data and think carefully about the scale of measurement. Alternatively, if the underlying distribution of the observations and the residuals is known, and hence why a transformation might be effective, generalized linear modeling (GLM) can be applied (Chapter 13).

8.5.2 Rank-based ("non-parametric") tests
For non-normal distributions (but similar variances), methods based on ranks (Chapter 3) might be used. There are two broad types of rank-based tests for comparing more than two groups. First is the Kruskal–Wallis test, which is a rank-randomization test and an extension of the Mann–Whitney–Wilcoxon test described in Chapter 3 for comparing two groups. It tests the H_0 that there is no difference in the location of the distributions between groups or treatments and is based on ranking the pooled data, determining the rank sums within each group and calculating the H statistic that follows a χ^2 distribution with $(p-1)$ df (Hollander & Wolfe 1999, Sokal & Rohlf 1995). Although the Kruskal–Wallis test is non-parametric in the sense that it does not assume

that the underlying distribution is normal, it does assume that the shapes of the distributions are the same in the different groups (the only possible difference being one of location, as tested in the H_0). This implies that variances should be similar (Hollander & Wolfe 1999). Therefore, the Kruskal–Wallis test is not a recommended solution for testing under unequal variances. However, it is a useful approach for dealing with outliers that do not represent more general variance heterogeneity. The Kruskal–Wallis test is sometimes described as a "non-parametric ANOVA" but this is a little misleading; there is no partitioning of variance and the H_0 does not test means unless the distributions are symmetric.

In the rank transform (RT) method, we transform the data to ranks and then fit a parametric ANOVA model to the ranked data (Conover & Iman, 1981). This really is an "analysis of variance" because the RT approach can be viewed as just an extreme form of transformation resulting in an ANOVA on rank-transformed data. It turns out that, for a single factor design, an RT F test will produce the same result as the Kruskal–Wallis test (Neter *et al.* 1996), but it is a more general procedure and can potentially be used for complex ANOVAs (Chapter 9). The RT approach also does not deal with unequal variances; if the variances are unequal on the raw scale, the ranks may also have unequal variances. We would also need to conduct the usual model-checking diagnostics on the ranked data.

8.5.3 Randomization tests

We can also use a randomization test to test the H_0 of no difference between groups (Crowley 1992, Edgington 1995, Manly 1997; Chapter 3). The procedure randomly allocates observations (or even residuals) to groups (keeping the same sample sizes) many times to produce the distribution of a test statistic (e.g. F-ratio or SS_{Groups} or MS_{Groups}; see Manly 1997) under the H_0 of no group effects. If this H_0 is true, we would expect that all randomized allocations of observations to groups are equally likely. We simply compare our observed statistic to the randomized distribution of the statistic to determine the probability of getting our observed statistic, or one more extreme, by chance. Manly (1997) indicated, based on simula-

tions, that randomization of observations and residuals produced similar results. However, such a randomization test to compare group means may not be robust against unequal variances, as Crowley (1992) and Manly (1997) have both pointed out that the H_0 can be rejected because of different variances without any differences between the means. While the conclusions from a randomization test also cannot easily be extrapolated to a population of interest, in contrast to the traditional approaches, randomization tests don't rely on random sampling from populations and therefore will be useful when random sampling is not possible (Ludbrook & Dudley 1998).

8.6 | Specific comparisons of means

Very few aspects of applied statistics have created as much discussion and controversy as multiple comparisons, particularly comparisons of group means as part of ANOVAs (see reviews by Day & Quinn 1989, Hancock & Klockars 1996, Hochberg & Tamhane 1987). We discussed the issues related to multiple significance testing in Chapter 3. Much of the debate and development of techniques for dealing with this problem have arisen in the context of multiple comparisons of group means following ANOVA models. Two issues are of particular importance. The first is the general multiple testing problem and increased rate of Type I errors (Chapter 3). For example, if we have five groups in our design, we would need ten pairwise tests to compare all groups with each other. The probability of at least one Type I error among the family of ten tests, if each test is conducted at α equals 0.05 and the comparisons are independent of each other, is 0.40 (Table 3.1). Much of the discussion about specific group contrasts in ANOVA models has focused on the need to correct for this increase in family-wise Type I error rates and the best methods to achieve this correction.

The second issue is independence (the statistical term is orthogonality) of the contrasts. For example, say we have three groups with equal sample sizes and our sample mean for group A is greater than that for group B with group C having the smallest mean. If our pairwise tests reject the null hypotheses that group A and B have equal population means and that group B and C have equal population means, then the contrast of groups A and C is redundant. We know that the mean for group A is significantly greater than the mean for group C without needing to do the test. Ensuring a set of contrasts is independent (orthogonal) is important for two reasons. First, independent contrasts are straightforward to interpret because the information each contains is independent. Second, the family-wise Type I error rate can be easily calculated if necessary, using Equation 3.9; the family-wise Type I error rate cannot be easily calculated for non-independent contrasts.

As discussed in Chapter 3, traditional adjustments to significance levels to correct for multiple testing are very severe, restricting the family-wise Type I error rate to the same level as the comparison-wise level for each comparison (e.g. 0.05). It seems strange to us that we are willing to allocate a significance level of 0.05 for individual comparisons but as soon as we consider a family of comparisons, we constrain the probability of at least one Type I error to the same level (0.05). The cost of this very tight control of family-wise Type I error is that our individual comparisons have decreasing power as the number of comparisons in our family increases.

Our broad recommendation is that the default position should be no adjustment for multiple testing if the tests represent clearly defined and separate hypotheses (Chapter 3). The exception is when we are scanning all possible comparisons in an exploratory manner where the aim is to detect significant results from all possible tests that could be carried out on a data set. Under these circumstances, we agree with Stewart-Oaten (1995) that some protection against increasing Type I error rates should be considered and, when comparing all possible group means in an ANOVA design, the procedures outlined in Section 8.6.2 should be adopted. However, we also urge biologists not to be constrained to the convention of 0.05 as a significance level. A sensible balance between power and Type I error rate in situations where adjustments are made for multiple testing can also be achieved by setting family-wise Type I error rates at levels above 0.05.

8.6.1 Planned comparisons or contrasts

These are interesting and logical comparisons (often termed contrasts) of groups or combinations of groups, each comparison commonly using a single df. They are usually planned as part of the analysis strategy before the data are examined, i.e. the choice of contrasts is best not determined from inspection of the data (Day & Quinn 1989, Ramsey 1993, Sokal & Rohlf 1996). Many texts recommend that planned contrasts should be independent of each other, where the comparisons should contain independent or uncorrelated information and represent a non-overlapping partitioning of the SS_{Groups}. The number of independent comparisons cannot be more than the df_{groups} ($p - 1$). This means that the outcome of one comparison should not influence the outcome of another (see Maxwell & Delaney 1990 for examples) and the family-wise Type I error rate can be easily calculated (Chapter 3). Even the question of orthogonality is not without differences of opinion among statisticians, and some argue that the set of planned comparisons need not be orthogonal (e.g. Winer et al. 1991), and that it is more important to test all of the hypotheses of interest than to be constrained to an orthogonal set. We agree with Toothaker (1993) that orthogonality has been given too much emphasis in discussions of group comparisons with ANOVA models, especially in terms of error rates, and that it is more important to keep the number of contrasts small than worrying about their orthogonality.

There is some consensus in the literature that each planned contrast, especially when they are orthogonal, can be tested at the chosen comparison-wise significance level (e.g. equals 0.05), and no control over familywise Type I error rate is necessary (Day & Quinn 1989, Kirk 1995, Sokal & Rohlf 1995). We agree, although we place much less emphasis on the need for orthogonality. The arguments in favour of not adjusting significance levels are that the number of comparisons is small so the increase in family-wise Type I error rate will also be small and each comparison is of specific interest so power considerations are particularly important. Another argument is that contrasts represent independent hypotheses, so there is no multiple testing involved. This approach is not universally supported. For example, Ramsey (1993) argued that the family-wise error rate should be controlled in any multiple testing situation, although the power of individual tests in complex ANOVAs with numerous hypotheses (main effects and interactions) surely would be unacceptable with this strategy. Additionally, some statisticians have argued that adjustment is necessary only when non-orthogonal contrasts are included and Keppel (1991) proposed adjusting the significance level of only those comparisons that are not orthogonal – see Todd & Keough (1994) for an example of this approach.

The H_0 being tested is usually of the form $\mu_A = \mu_B$ (e.g. the mean of group A equals the mean of group B). The hypotheses can be more complicated, such as $(\mu_A + \mu_B)/2 = \mu_C$ (e.g. the average of the means of group A and group B equals the mean of group C); note that this comparison will still have one df because there are only two "groups", one being formed from a combination of two others. For example, Newman (1994) examined the effects of changing food levels on size and age at metamorphosis of tadpoles of a desert frog. He used small plastic containers as the experimental units, each with a single tadpole. There were four treatments: low food (one-quarter ration, n equals 5 containers), medium food (half-ration, n equals 8), high food (full ration, n equals 6), and food decreasing from high to low during the experiment (n equals 7). Single factor ANOVAs were used to test for no differences between the four treatments on size and age at metamorphosis. In addition to the overall effect of food level, Newman (1994) was particularly interested in the hypothesis that a deteriorating growth environment changes timing of metamorphosis compared to a constant good environment so he included a single planned contrast: decreasing food vs constant high food.

Another example is from Marshall & Keough (1994), who examined the effects of increasing intraspecific densities of two size classes (large and small) of the intertidal limpet *Cellana tramoserica* on mortality and biomass of large limpets. There were seven treatments (one large limpet per experimental enclosure, two large, three large, four large, one large and ten small, one large and 20 small, one large and 30 small), four replicate enclosures for each treatment and a single factor ANOVA was used to test for treatment effects. They included three specific contrasts to test for the effects of small limpets on large limpets: ten small vs ten small and one large, ten small vs ten small and two large, ten small vs ten small and three large.

In our worked example, Keough & Raimondi (1995) used three specific contrasts to identify effects of different kinds of biofilms on settlement of serpulid worms: lab netted vs lab un-netted, then, with a non-significant result, the average of the two lab films were compared to field biofilms, and, finally, if these did not differ, the average of all three filmed treatments were compared to the substrata that had been in sterile seawater (Box 8.4).

There are two ways of doing these planned comparisons, partitioning the between groups SS or using two group t tests.

Partitioning SS

The SS_{Groups} can be partitioned into the contribution due to each comparison. Each $SS_{Comparison}$ will have one df (we are only comparing two means or two combinations of means) and, therefore, the $SS_{Comparison}$ equals the $MS_{Comparison}$. The H_0 associated with each comparison is tested with an F-ratio ($MS_{Comparison}/MS_{Residual}$). This approach is simply an extension of the partitioning of the variation that formed the basis of the ANOVA and is illustrated in Box 8.4.

We need to define a linear combination of the p means representing the specific contrast of interest:

$$c_1\bar{y}_1 + \ldots + c_i\bar{y}_i + \ldots \text{etc.} \tag{8.8}$$

where c_i are coefficients, $\sum_{i=1}^{p} n_i c_i$ equals zero (this ensures a valid contrast) and $\bar{y}_i$ are treatment or group means. The details for working out these linear contrasts are provided for the worked example from Keough & Raimondi (1995) in Box 8.4. Note that the absolute values of the coefficients are not relevant as long as the coefficients sum to zero and represent the contrast of interest. We prefer to use integers for simplicity. We can also define orthogonality in terms of coefficients. Two comparisons, A and B, are independent (orthogonal) if $\sum_{i=1}^{p} c_{iA} c_{iB}$ equals zero, i.e. the sum of the products of their coefficients equals zero. It is often not intuitively obvious whether two comparisons are orthogonal, and the only way to be sure is to do these calculations. If comparisons are orthogonal, then the sum of the $SS_{Comparison}$ will not exceed SS_{Groups}. If comparisons are not orthogonal, then sum of $SS_{Comparison}$ can exceed available SS_{Groups}, indicating we are using the same information in more than one comparison.

t test

A t test can be used to compare groups A and B with the modification that

$$\sqrt{\left(\frac{1}{n_A} + \frac{1}{n_B}\right) MS_{Residual}}$$

is used as the standard error of the comparison. This standard error makes use of the better estimate of residual variance from the ANOVA (if the assumption of homogeneity of variance holds) and has more df than the usual t test which would just use the data from the two groups being compared.

Partitioning the SS and t test are functionally equivalent; the F-ratio will equal t^2 and the P values will be identical. Both approaches can handle unequal sample sizes and the t test approach can be adjusted for unequal variances (Chapter 3). We prefer the former because it is a natural extension of the ANOVA and the results are easy to present as part of the ANOVA table. Note that a significant ANOVA F test is not necessary before doing planned comparisons. Indeed, the ANOVA might only be done to provide the $MS_{Residual}$.

8.6.2 Unplanned pairwise comparisons

Now we will consider multiple testing situations, and specifically multiple comparisons of means, where control of family-wise Type I error rate might be warranted. There are two broad approaches to adjusting significance levels for multiple testing. The first is to use specific tests, often based on the F or q distributions. A more general method, which can be used for any family tests, is to adjust the P values (Chapter 3).

Unplanned pairwise comparisons, as the name suggests, compare all possible pairs of group means (i.e. each group to every other group) in a *post hoc* exploratory fashion to find out which

groups are different after a significant ANOVA F test. These multiple comparisons are clearly not independent (there are more than $p - 1$ comparisons), there are usually lots of them and they involve data snooping (searching for significant results, or picking winners (Day & Quinn 1989), from a large collection of tests). There seems to be a much stronger argument that, in these circumstances, some control of family-wise Type I error rate is warranted. The usual recommendation is that the significance level (α) for each test is reduced so the family-wise Type I error rate stays at that chosen (e.g. 0.05).

Underwood (1997) has argued that there has been too much focus on Type I error rates at the expense of power considerations in multiple comparisons. We agree, although controlling family-wise error rates to a known maximum is important. We do not support increasing power of individual comparisons by using procedures that allow a higher, but unknown, rate of Type I errors under some circumstances (e.g. SNK or Duncan's tests – see below). To increase power when doing all pairwise comparisons, we would prefer using a multiple comparison procedure that has a known upper limit to its family-wise error rate and then setting that rate (significance level) above 0.05.

There are many unplanned multiple comparison tests available and these are of two broad types. Simultaneous tests, such as Tukey's test, use the value of the test statistic based on the total number of groups in the analysis, irrespective of how many means are between any two being compared. These simultaneous tests also permit simultaneous confidence intervals on differences between means. Stepwise tests use different values of the test statistic for comparisons of means closer together and are generally more powerful, although their control of the family-wise Type I error rate is not always strict. Both types of test can handle unequal sample sizes, using minor modifications, e.g. harmonic means of sample sizes. Day and Quinn (1989) and Kirk (1995) provide detailed evaluation and formulae but brief comments are included below.

Tukey's HSD test

A simple and reliable multiple comparison is Tukey's (honestly significant differenced, or HSD) test, which compares each group mean with every other group mean in a pairwise manner and controls the family-wise Type I error rate to no more than the nominal level (e.g. 0.05). Tukey's HSD test is based on the studentized range statistic (q), which is a statistic used for multiple significance testing across a number of means. Its sampling distribution is defined by the number of means in the range being compared (i.e. the number of means between the two being compared after the means are arranged in order of magnitude) and the $df_{Residual}$. The q distribution is programmed into most statistical software and critical values can be found in many textbooks.

We illustrate the logic of Tukey's HSD test as an example of an unplanned multiple comparison test (see also Day & Quinn 1989 and Hays 1994 for clear descriptions):

- As we did for planned comparisons using a t test, calculate the standard error for the difference between two means from

$$\sqrt{\left(\frac{1}{n_A} + \frac{1}{n_B}\right) MS_{Residual}}$$

Using the harmonic mean of the sample sizes is sometimes called the Tukey–Kramer modification (Day & Quinn 1989) and reduces to $1/n$ for equal sample sizes.
- Determine appropriate value of (q) from the q distribution at the chosen significance level (for family-wise Type I error rate), using $df_{Residual}$ and the number of means being compared (i.e. the number of groups, a).
- Calculate the *HSD* (honestly significant difference, sometimes termed the minimum significant difference, *MSD*; Day & Quinn, 1989). The *HSD* is simply q times the standard error and is the smallest difference between two means that can be declared significant at the chosen family-wise significance level.
- Compare the observed difference between two sample means to the *HSD*. If the observed difference is larger, then we reject the H_0 that the respective population means are equal. Repeat this for all pairs of means.
- Presenting the results of multiple comparisons is not straightforward because the number of tests can be large. Two common approaches

are to join those means not significantly different with an underline (e.g. A B < C D) or to indicate groups not significantly different from each other with the same subscript or superscript in tables or figures.

Fisher's Protected Least Significant Difference test (LSD test)

This test is based on pairwise t tests using pooled within groups variance ($MS_{Residual}$) for the standard error, as described for planned comparisons (Section 8.6.1) and applied only if the original ANOVA F test is significant (hence "protected"). However, it does not control family-wise Type I error rate unless the true pattern among all groups is that there are no differences. It is not recommended for large numbers of unplanned comparisons (Day & Quinn 1989).

Duncan's Multiple Range test

This stepwise test based on the q statistic for comparing all pairs of means was historically popular. However, it does not control the family-wise Type I error rate at a known level (nor was it ever designed to!) and is not recommended for unplanned pairwise comparisons.

Student–Neuman–Keuls (SNK) test

This test is very popular, particularly with ecologists, because of the influence of Underwood's (1981) important review of ANOVA methods. It is a relatively powerful stepwise test based on the q statistic. Like the closely related Duncan's test, it can fail to control the family-wise Type I error rate to a known level under some circumstances when there are more than three means (specifically when there are four or more means and the true pattern is two or more different groups of two or more equal means). Although Underwood (1997) argued that the SNK test might actually be a good compromise between Type I error and per comparison power, we prefer other tests (Tukey's, Ryan's, Peritz's) because they provide *known* control of family-wise Type I error. Underwood (1997) provided formulae and a worked example of the SNK test.

Ryan's test

This is one of the most powerful stepwise multiple comparison procedures that provides control over the family-wise Type I error rate and is often referred to as the Ryan, Einot, Gabriel and Welsch (REGW) procedure. It can be used with either the q or the F-ratio statistic and it is the recommended multiple comparison test if software is available, but it is a little tedious to do by hand.

Peritz's test

This is basically an SNK test that switches to a REGW-type test in situations where the SNK cannot control Type I error, so it is a combined SNK and Ryan's test. It is probably too complicated for routine use.

Scheffe's test

This is a very conservative test, based on the F-ratio statistic, designed for testing comparisons suggested by the data. It is not restricted to pairwise comparisons, in contrast to Tukey's test, but is not very efficient for comparing all pairs of means.

Dunnett's test

This is a modified t test designed specifically for comparing each group to a control group. Under this scenario, there are fewer comparisons than when comparing all pairs of group means, so Dunnett's test is more powerful than other multiple comparison tests in this situation.

Robust pairwise multiple comparisons

Like the ANOVA F test, the multiple comparison tests described above assume normality and, more importantly, homogeneity of variances. Pairwise multiple comparison procedures based on ranks of the observations are available (Day & Quinn 1989) and there are also tests that are robust to unequal variances, including Dunnett's T3, Dunnett's C and Games–Howell tests (Day & Quinn 1989, Kirk 1995). They are best used in conjunction with robust ANOVA methods described in Section 8.5.

Tests based on adjusting P values

Multiple comparisons of group means are simply examples of multiple testing and therefore any of the P value adjustment methods described in Chapter 3 can be applied to either t or F tests (or the robust procedures) used to compare specific

groups. Sequential Bonferroni methods are particularly appropriate here.

8.6.3 Specific contrasts versus unplanned pairwise comparisons

A small number of planned contrasts is always a better approach than comparing all pairs of means with an unplanned multiple comparison procedure. In most cases, you probably have in mind some specific hypotheses about the groups and tests of these hypotheses are usually more powerful because there is less of an argument for adjusting error rates and they are nearly always more interpretable. They also encourage biologists to think about their hypotheses more carefully at the design stage. Unplanned comparisons are usually only done when the ANOVA F test indicates that there is a significant result to be found; then we often wish to go "data-snooping" to find which groups are different from which others.

As we have already discussed, the adjustment of Type I error rates for most standard unplanned multiple comparison procedures means that the power of individual comparisons can be weak, especially if there are lots of groups, and this can make the unplanned tests difficult to interpret. For example, an unplanned multiple comparison test (with family-wise adjustment), following a "marginally significant" ($0.01 < P < 0.05$) ANOVA F test may not reveal any differences between groups. Also, some unplanned multiple comparisons can produce ambiguous results, e.g. with three means in order smallest (A) to largest (C), the test might show $C > A$ but $A = B$ and $B = C$! Underwood (1997) has argued that no conclusions can be drawn from such a result because no alternative hypothesis can be unambiguously identified. We view the multiple comparison test as a set of different hypotheses and suggest that such a result allows us to reject the H_0 that A equals C, but no conclusion about whether B is different from A or C.

Finally, specific contrasts of groups are mainly relevant when the factor is fixed, and we are specifically interested in differences between group means. When the factor is random, we are more interested in the added variance component (Section 8.2.1) and not in specific differences between groups.

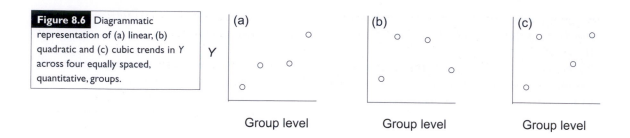

Figure 8.6 Diagrammatic representation of (a) linear, (b) quadratic and (c) cubic trends in Y across four equally spaced, quantitative, groups.

8.7 | Tests for trends

If the factor in an ANOVA is fixed and quantitative (i.e. the treatment levels have some numerical value), then tests for trends in the group means may be more informative than tests about whether there are specific differences between group means. Usually, we wish to test for a linear trend or some simple nonlinear (e.g. quadratic or cubic – see Chapter 6) trend. For example, Glitzenstein *et al.* (1995) studied the mortality of sandhill oak (*Quercus* spp.) across eight season-of-burn treatments (eight two-week periods during 1981/1982). They used a single factor ANOVA (season-of-burning, with seven df) but were more interested in trends in oak mortality through the eight seasons than specific differences between season means. They tested for linear and quadratic patterns in mortality across burn season. Marshall & Keough (1994) examined the effects of increasing intraspecific densities of two size classes (large and small) of the intertidal limpet *Cellana tramoserica* on mortality and biomass of large limpets. There were seven treatments (one large, two large, three large, four large, one large and ten small, one large and 20 small, one large and 30 small), four replicate enclosures for each treatment and a single factor ANOVA was used to test the overall H_0 of no treatment differences. Marshall & Keough (1994) also included a trend analysis to test for a linear relationship in mean mortality (or biomass) across the intra-size-class treatments (one, two, three, four large limpets per enclosure). We will illustrate a linear trend analysis with the data on serpulid recruitment from Keough & Raimondi (1995), where the equally spaced levels of biofilm represented an increasingly stronger cue for settlement (Box 8.4). Note that the factor is not really quantitative in this

example, but can be considered a rank order and therefore still suitable for testing trends.

The method of orthogonal polynomials fits polynomial equations to the group means using contrast coefficients, just as for planned contrasts between specific group means. A linear polynomial represents a straight-line relationship through the group means, a quadratic represents a U-shaped relationship with a single "change of direction" and the cubic represents a more complex pattern with two "changes of direction" (Figure 8.6; Kirk 1995). We don't provide computational details for fitting orthogonal polynomials to group means (see Kirk 1995, Maxwell & Delaney 1990, Winer *et al.* 1991) but the logic is similar to contrasts of means described in Section 8.6.1 and they are simple to do with most statistical software. The SS_{Groups} is partitioned up into SS_{Linear}, $SS_{Quadratic}$, SS_{Cubic}, etc., each with one df. The null hypothesis of no linear (or quadratic, etc.) trend is tested with F tests, using the $MS_{Residual}$. Our experience is that polynomials above cubic are difficult to interpret biologically and are rarely fitted in practice, even when there are enough df to do so. If the levels of the factor are equally spaced and sample sizes are equal, the coefficients for the contrasts equations for linear, quadratic, etc., trends can be found in Table 8.8; unequal sample sizes and/or spacing of factor levels are discussed below.

The rules for contrast coefficients still apply. The coefficients for each polynomial should sum to zero and we could multiply the coefficients for any contrast by a constant and still get the same result (e.g. $-30, -10, 10, 30$ is the same linear contrast as $-3, -1, 1, 3$). Successive polynomials (linear, quadratic, etc.) are independent (orthogonal) as long as the number of successive polynomials, starting with linear, doesn't exceed the df_{Groups}, i.e. if there are four groups, there are

Table 8.8 | Coefficients for linear, quadratic and cubic polynomials for between three and six equally spaced group levels. See Kirk (1995) or Winer *et al.* (1991) for more orders and levels

	X_1	X_2	X_3	X_4	X_5	X_6
Linear	−1	0	1			
	−3	−1	1	3		
	−2	−1	0	1	2	
	−5	−3	−1	1	3	5
Quadratic	1	−2	1			
	1	−1	−1	1		
	2	−1	−2	−1	2	
	5	−1	−4	−4	−1	5
Cubic	−1	3	−3	1		
	−1	2	0	−2	1	
	−5	7	4	−4	−7	5

three df and we can have three orthogonal polynomials: linear, quadratic, cubic.

When sample sizes are equal in all groups, the SS from fitting a linear contrast across the means using orthogonal polynomials will be the same as the $SS_{Regression}$ from fitting a linear regression model to the original observations. Note that the $SS_{Residual}$, and therefore the test of linearity, will be different in the two cases because the classical regression and ANOVA partitions of SS_{Total} are different. The $SS_{Residual}$ from fitting the ANOVA model will be smaller but also have fewer df, as only one df is used for the regression but $(p-1)$ is used for the groups. The difference in the two $SS_{Residual}$ (from the regression model and the ANOVA model) is termed "lack-of-fit" (Neter *et al.* 1996), representing the variation not explained by a linear fit but possibly explained by nonlinear (quadratic, etc.) components.

The SS from fitting a quadratic contrast across the means will be the same as the SS_{Extra} from fitting a quadratic regression model over a linear regression model to the original observations (Chapter 6). So the quadratic polynomial is testing whether there is a quadratic relationship between the response variable and the factor over and above a linear relationship, the cubic polynomial is testing whether there is a cubic relationship over and above a linear or quadratic relationship,

and so on. Sometimes, the remaining SS after SS_{Linear} is extracted from SS_{Groups} is used to test for departures from linearity (Kirk 1995).

When sample sizes are unequal or the spacing between factor levels is unequal, contrast coefficients can be determined by solving simultaneous equations (Kirk 1995) and good statistical software will provide these coefficients. Alternatively, we could simply fit a hierarchical series of polynomial regression models, testing the linear model over the intercept-only model, the quadratic model over the linear model, etc. (Chapter 6). Unfortunately, the equality of the SS due to a particular contrast between group means and the SS due to adding that additional polynomial in a regression model fitted to the original observations breaks down when sample sizes are different (Maxwell & Delaney 1990) so the two approaches will produce different (although usually not markedly) results. We prefer using the contrast coefficients and treating the test for a linear trend as a planned contrast between group means.

8.8 | Testing equality of group variances

It may sometimes be of more biological interest to test for differences in group variances, rather than group means, when we expect that experimental treatments would affect the variance in our response variable. Tests on group variances may also be a useful component of diagnostic checks of the adequacy of the ANOVA model and the assumption of homogeneity of variance (Section 8.3).

Traditional tests for the H_0 of equal population variances between groups include Bartlett's test, which is based on logarithms of the group variances and uses a χ^2 statistic, Hartley's F_{max} test, which is based on an F-ratio of the largest to the smallest variance, and Cochran's test, which is the ratio of the largest variance to the sum of the variances. Unfortunately, Conover *et al.* (1981) and Rivest (1986) have shown that all these tests are very sensitive to non-normality. Given the prevalence of skewness in biological data, this lack of robustness is a serious concern and these tests cannot be recommended for routine use.

Alternative tests recommended by Conover *et al.* (1981) basically calculate new (pseudo)observations that represent changes in the variance and then analyze these pseudo-observations (Ozaydin *et al.* 1999). Levene's test is based on absolute deviations of each observation from its respective group mean or median (i.e. absolute residuals) and is simply an *F* test based on using these absolute deviations in a single factor ANOVA. The H_0 is that the means of the absolute deviations are equal between groups. Although Levene's test is robust to non-normality of the original variable (Conover *et al.* 1981), the pseudo-observations are not necessarily normal nor will their variances be equal (assumptions of the *F* test). Suggested solutions have been to use robust methods for single factor ANOVAs to analyze the pseudo-observations (see Section 8.5), such as ranking them (Conover *et al.* 1981) and then modifying the ranks with score functions (Fligner & Killeen 1976) or even using a randomization test, although we have not seen this recommended.

8.9 | Power of single factor ANOVA

The *F*-ratio statistic, under the H_0 of equal group means, follows a central *F* distribution (see Chapter 1). When the H_0 is false, the *F*-ratio statistic follows a non-central *F* distribution. The exact shape of this distribution depends on df_{Groups}, $df_{Residual}$ and on how different the true population means are under H_A. This difference is summarized by the non-centrality parameter (λ), which is defined as:

$$\lambda = \frac{\sum_{i=1}^{p} \alpha_i^2}{\sigma_\varepsilon^2/n} = \frac{n\sum_{i=1}^{p} \alpha_i^2}{\sigma_\varepsilon^2} \quad (8.9)$$

To determine the power of a single factor ANOVA, we need to calculate λ (or $\phi = \sqrt{(\lambda/p)}$). This requires us to specify the alternative hypothesis (H_A) and to know (or guess) the residual variation. Remember the general formula relating power and effect size that we used in Chapter 7:

$$\text{Power} \propto \frac{ES\sqrt{n}}{\sigma} \quad (7.5)$$

The non-centrality parameter λ incorporates the effect size [group effects (α_i) squared] and the

within group standard deviation σ. We can then calculate power by referring to power charts (e.g. Neter *et al.* 1996, Kirk 1995), which relate power to λ or ϕ for different df (i.e. *n*). Alternatively, we can use software designed for the purpose. It is important to note, however, that the formal calculations can vary between different texts and software packages (Box 8.5).

These calculations can be used to:

- determine the power of an experiment *post hoc*, usually after a non-significant result,
- determine the minimum detectable effect size for an experiment *post hoc*, and
- calculate sample size required to detect a certain effect size when planning an experiment.

An example of power calculations is included in Box 8.6 and Underwood (1981, 1997) has also provided worked biological examples. These power calculations are straightforward for two groups but become more difficult with more than two groups. When there are only two groups, the effect size is simply related to the difference between the two means. However, when we have more than two groups, the H_A could, for example, have the groups equally spaced or two the same and one different. These different patterns of means will lead to different values of λ, and, hence, power. The difficulty of specifying H_A becomes greater as the number of groups increases, unless we have a very specific H_A that details a particular arrangement of our groups (e.g. a linear trend across groups).

If the number of groups is not too large, one option is to calculate the power for a range of arrangements of treatments. For example, we can calculate the power characteristics for four different arrangements of groups for a given difference in means (between the largest and smallest), such as groups equally spaced, one group different from all others (which are equal), and so on. An example of such power curves are plotted in Figure 8.7 where for a given effect size you can easily see the range of power values. Note that there is little difference for very large or very small differences between the largest and smallest group means. For planning experiments, it may be enough to know the range of power values

Box 8.6 | Worked example: power analysis for serpulid recruitment onto surfaces with different biofilms

Two of the other response variables in the study of recruitment by Keough & Raimondi (1995), the number of spirorbid worms, and bryozoans in the genus *Bugula*, showed no differences between any of the filming treatments, so power becomes an issue. For the spirorbids, the analysis of variance was as follows.

Source	SS	df	MS	F	P
Biofilms	0.296	3	0.099	1.624	0.210
Residual	1.458	24	0.061		
Total	1.754	27			

The mean for the unfilmed (SL) treatment was 0.273. We can use this information to look at the power of the test for this species.

If we define the effect size as an increase in settlement of 50% over the value for unfilmed surfaces, our ES = 0.137.

First, let's look at the overall power of the test. Suppose that we wanted to detect any effect of biofilms, in which case, the SL treatment would have a value of 0.273, and the other three would be 0.41. The grand mean would be 0.375, giving estimates of α_i of $-0.102, 0.034, 0.034$, and 0.034. For these values, $\sum_{i=1}^{p} \alpha_i^2 = 0.014$, and, from the table above, our estimate of σ_ε^2 is 0.061. Using Equation 8.9, $\lambda = (7 \times 0.014)/0.061 = 1.614$, and substituting this value into any software that calculates power, using $df_{Groups} = 3$ and $df_{Residual} = 24$, we get power of 0.143. Remember, power is the probability of statistically detecting this effect size if it occurred. This experiment had little chance of detecting an increase in settlement of 50% above the value for unfilmed surfaces.

To see how our specification of H_A affects power, let's look at the power for a pattern that is one of the hardest to detect using an overall F test, a gradual trend from largest to smallest mean. Using the example here, the four means would be 0.271, 0.319, 0.364, and 0.410. Then, the power is 0.117. These differences don't seem very large, mainly because the overall power is so low for this group of polychaetes. For comparison, we can look at the data for the bryozoans. Here, the mean for the sterile treatment is 0.820, and the $MS_{Residual}$ is 0.063. For these bryozoans, our general H_A would produce means of 0.82, 1.23, 1.23, and 1.23 for our four treatments. The non-centrality parameter, λ, is 14.01, giving power of 0.84, so we would feel confident that our non-significant result for this group of animals really represents an effect of less than 50%. If we calculate for the general trend case, the four hypothetical means would be 0.82, 0.96, 1.09, and 1.23, $\lambda = 10.38$, and power is 0.70, a drop of 15%.

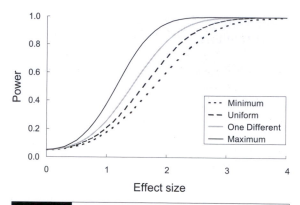

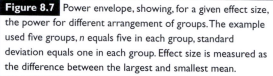

Figure 8.7 Power envelope, showing, for a given effect size, the power for different arrangement of groups. The example used five groups, *n* equals five in each group, standard deviation equals one in each group. Effect size is measured as the difference between the largest and smallest mean.

for a given effect, and to make decisions around one particular arrangement of groups, taking into account where that arrangement fits on the power spectrum.

8.10 | General issues and hints for analysis

8.10.1 General issues

- General experimental design principles, especially randomization and choice of appropriate controls, are nearly always important when designing studies for the application of single factor ANOVA models.
- Estimates of explained variance have different interpretations for fixed and random factors. Added variance component for a random factor is straightforward with equal sample sizes and confidence intervals should be used. Explained variance for a fixed factor is also useful as a descriptor but cannot be easily compared for different models and data sets and must be interpreted carefully.
- Be aware that some alternatives that may be suggested as an option when ANOVA assumptions are violated are rarely assumption free. For example, the rank-based non-parametric methods don't assume normality, but have an

assumption equivalent to the homogeneity of variances.

- We recommend planned comparisons (contrasts) rather than unplanned multiple comparisons. In most cases, you are not interested in comparing all possible groups, but can identify particular questions that are of greater interest.
- Power calculations are relatively simple for single factor models. However, once the number of groups is greater than two, you must think hard about the kind of differences between groups that is of interest to you. Different alternative patterns of means have different power characteristics.
- A problem for inexperienced biologists is that many of the decisions (how normal should the data be?, etc.) involve an informed judgment about where a particular data set fits along a continuum from assumptions being satisfied completely to major violations. There is no unambiguous division, but, in many cases, it doesn't matter because the *P* values will be far from any grey zone.

8.10.2 Hints for analysis

- Aim for equal sample sizes. The linear model calculations can easily handle unequal samples, but the analysis is more sensitive to the underlying assumptions and parameter estimates and hypothesis tests will be more reliable if sample sizes are equal.
- Homogeneity of variances is an important assumption. ANOVA is robust to small and moderate violations (especially with equal sample sizes), but big differences (e.g. many-fold differences between largest and smallest variances) will alter the Type I error rate of the *F* test.
- Examine homogeneity of variances with exploratory graphical methods, e.g. look at the spread of boxplots, plot group variances or standard deviations against group means, or plot residuals against group means and look for patterns. We don't recommend formal tests of equal group variances as a preliminary check before an ANOVA.
- Transformations will be effective when the

error terms, and the observations, have positively skewed distributions. For biological data, the most likely effective transformations are log and square (or fourth) root. Although ANOVA models are robust to violations of non-normality, such normalizing transformations will usually make variances more similar between groups.

- For moderate violations of normality and homogeneity of variances, we recommend proceeding with the analysis, but being cautious about results that are marginally significant or non-significant. Otherwise we recommend using generalized linear models when the underlying distribution of the response variable can be determined, or one of the robust tests.

- Use planned contrasts wherever possible for testing specific differences between groups. If unplanned comparisons must be used, Ryan's (REGW) or Tukey's tests are recommended, the latter if simultaneous confidence intervals are required.

Chapter 9

Multifactor analysis of variance

In Chapter 8, we examined designs with a single factor where the appropriate linear model had a single categorical predictor variable. Commonly in biology, however, we design studies with more than one factor and there are two main reasons why we might include additional factors. First, to try and reduce the unexplained (or residual) variation in our response variable, similarly to multiple regression (Chapter 6). Second, to examine the interactions between factors, i.e. whether the effect of a particular factor on the response variable is dependent on another factor. In this chapter, we will examine two types of multifactor design, nested and factorial, and describe the appropriate linear models for their analysis. The emphasis is on completely randomized (CR) designs, following from Chapter 8, where the experimental units are randomly allocated to factor groups or combinations of factor groups.

9.1 | Nested (hierarchical) designs

A common extension of the single factor design, and the single factor ANOVA linear model, is when additional factors are included that are nested within the main factor of interest. An example based on a manipulative experiment comes from Quinn & Keough (1993) who examined the effect of different enclosure (fence) sizes on growth of the rocky intertidal limpet *Cellana tramoserica*. Part of that experiment used two enclosure sizes (1225 cm^2 and 4900 cm^2), with five replicate enclosures nested within each size and four or five replicate

limpets from each enclosure. The response variable was limpet shell height. These nested designs can also be part of sampling programs. For example, Caselle & Warner (1996) looked at recruitment densities of a coral reef fish at five sites on the north shore of the US Virgin Islands, with six random transects within each site and replicate observations of density of recruits along each transect.

Both these examples are two factor nested (or hierarchical) designs, where the levels (categories) of the nested factor are different within each level of the main factor. Quinn & Keough (1993) used enclosure size as the main factor, replicate enclosures within enclosure size as the nested factor and replicate limpets from each enclosure as the residual. Caselle & Warner (1996) used sites as the main factor, transects within each site as the nested factor and replicate observations of fish density as the residual.

The characteristic feature of nested designs that distinguish them from other multifactor designs is that the categories of the nested factor(s) within each level of the main factor are different. The main factor can be fixed or random whereas the nested factor(s) is(are) usually random in biology, often representing levels of subsampling or replication in a spatial or temporal hierarchy. In the example from Quinn & Keough (1993), the enclosures are replicates for the enclosure size treatments, the individual limpets are replicates for the enclosures. However, fixed nested factors can also occur. Bellgrove *et al.* (1997), studying the abundance of algal propagules along exposed rocky coastlines, collected volumes of water from an intertidal shore at different dates within two seasons. The dates within each season were chosen specifically to correspond to the start and end of other experiments (i.e. they were not randomly chosen and so represent a fixed factor) but they were clearly different dates in each of the two seasons (so date was a nested, fixed, factor). Caselle & Warner (1996) also analyzed temporal variation in recruitment of reef fish and chose specific (fixed) months (from the time of the year when the fish recruited) nested within each of two years.

Grazing by sea urchins

To illustrate the formal analysis of nested designs, we will use a recent example from the marine ecological literature. Andrew & Underwood (1993) studied the effects of sea urchin grazing on a shallow subtidal reef in New South Wales, Australia. They set up four urchin density treatments (0% original, 33% original, 66% original, 100% original), with four patches (3–4 m^2) of reef for each treatment and five quadrats from each patch. The response variable was percentage cover of filamentous algae in each quadrat. The complete analysis of these data is in Box 9.1.

Box 9.1 | Worked example of nested ANOVA: grazing by sea urchins

Andrew & Underwood (1993) manipulated the density of sea urchins in the shallow subtidal region of a site near Sydney to test the effects on the percentage cover of filamentous algae. There were four urchin treatments (no urchins, 33% of original density, 66% of original density and 100% of orginal density). The treatments were replicated in four distinct patches (3–4 m^2) per treatment and percentage cover of filamentous algae (response variable) was measured in five random quadrats per patch. This is a nested design with treatment (fixed factor), patch nested within treatment (random factor) and quadrats as the residual.

Null hypotheses

No difference in the mean amount of filamentous algae between the four sea urchin density treatments.

No difference in the mean amount of filamentous algae between all possible patches in any of the treatments.

ANOVA

There were large differences in within-cell variances. Even the variances among patch means within treatments varied, with very low variance among control patch means. These data are percentages, although an arcsin$\sqrt{}$ had no effect in improving variance homogeneity, nor did a log transformation. Like Andrew & Underwood (1993), we analyzed untransformed data, relying on the robustness of tests in balanced ANOVA designs.

Source of variation	df	MS	F	P	Var. comp.
Treatment	3	4809.71	2.72	0.091	(151.98)
Patches (treatment)	12	1770.16	5.93	<0.001	294.31
Residual	64	298.60			298.60

There was significant variation between the replicate patches within each treatment but there was no significant difference in amount of filamentous algae between treatments. The very low variances between observations within control patches and between control patch means would cause us concern about the reliability of this analysis. However, when the control group is omitted, the test comparing treatments results in a P value of 0.397. Any treatment effect might be due to the low means of, or the low variance between, control patches compared to the rest, although this analysis cannot separate effects on means from effects on variances. A robust Welch test comparing the four treatment groups, based on patch means, also did not find any significant differences.

The variance in algal cover due to patches was very similar to that due to quadrats within patches. Because the design was balanced, ANOVA, ML and REML all gave identical estimates of components of variance for the random nested factor and the residual. If we equate the mean squares to their expected values and calculate the "variance" component for the fixed treatment effects, we can see that less of the total variation in algal cover was explained by the fixed density effects than by the random patch and quadrat terms.

A one factor ANOVA comparing the four treatments with patch means as replicates produces an identical F test for the main effect (note that the MS values are smaller, by a factor of five, the number of quadrats, but the F-ratios are identical).

Source of variation	df	MS	F	P
Treatment	3	961.9	2.72	0.091
Residual	12	354.0		

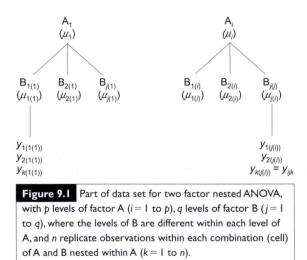

Figure 9.1 Part of data set for two factor nested ANOVA, with p levels of factor A ($i = 1$ to p), q levels of factor B ($j = 1$ to q), where the levels of B are different within each level of A, and n replicate observations within each combination (cell) of A and B nested within A ($k = 1$ to n).

9.1.1 Linear models for nested analyses

Linear effects model

Complex designs can be represented with factor relationship diagrams (Bergerud 1996). Let us consider the two factor nested design, shown in Figure 9.1 and illustrated with the specific example from Andrew & Underwood (1993) in Table 9.1. The main factor A (sea urchin density treatment) has p equals four groups ($i = 1$ to p), the nested factor B (patch) has q equals four groups within each level of A ($j = 1$ to q) and there are n equals five replicate quadrats ($k = 1$ to n) within each combination of A and B categories (patch and density treatment). Note that the groups (levels) of factor B, the patches, are different within each level of A (sea urchin density), so any patch within 0% original density cannot be the same as any patch within 33% original density and so on. Clearly, the same applies to replicate quadrats that are different within each combination of density and patch. Analysis of designs with unequal numbers of levels of B within each level of A, and of replicate observations within each level of B will be discussed in Section 9.1.4.

The mean for each level of A is μ_i (the average of the means for all possible levels of B within each level of A) and the mean for each level of B within each level of A is $\mu_{j(i)}$ (Table 9.1). Note the subscripting, where $j(i)$ represents the jth level of factor B within the ith level of factor A.

Table 9.1 | Data structure and sample means for percentage cover of algae from Andrew & Underwood (1993). Factor A was four densities of sea urchins (100%, 66%, 33% and 0% of natural density), factor B was four patches of reef nested within each density treatment and there were n equals five replicate quadrats within each patch within each density

Factor A (A_i)	Density	Density mean $\bar{y}_i$ est μ_i	Factor B ($B_{j(i)}$)	Patch	Patch mean $\bar{y}_{j(i)}$ est $\mu_{j(i)}$
A_1	0%	39.2	$B_{1(1)}$	1	34.2
			$B_{2(1)}$	2	62.0
			$B_{3(1)}$	3	2.2
			$B_{4(1)}$	4	58.4
A_2	33%	19.0	$B_{1(2)}$	5	2.6
			$B_{2(2)}$	6	0.0
			$B_{3(2)}$	7	37.6
			$B_{4(2)}$	8	35.8
A_3	66%	21.6	$B_{1(3)}$	9	28.4
			$B_{2(3}$	10	36.8
			$B_{3(3)}$	11	1.0
			$B_{4(3}$	12	20.0
A_4	100%	1.3	$B_{1(4)}$	13	1.6
			$B_{2(4)}$	14	0.0
			$B_{3(4)}$	15	1.0
			$B_{4(4)}$	16	2.6

The linear (effects) model used to analyze this nested design is:

$$y_{ijk} = \mu + \alpha_i + \beta_{j(i)} + \varepsilon_{ijk} \qquad (9.1)$$

The details of the nested linear ANOVA model, including estimation of its parameters and means, are provided in Box 9.2 and Table 9.2. OLS means and their standard errors are standard output from linear models routines in statistical software and can handle unequal sample sizes.

The model used by Andrew & Underwood (1993) was:

$$\text{(\% cover algae)}_{ijk} = \mu + \text{(sea urchin density)}_i + \text{(patch within sea urchin density)}_{j(i)} + \varepsilon_{ijk} \qquad (9.2)$$

In models 9.1 and 9.2 we have the following.

y_{ijk} is the percentage cover of algae in the kth replicate quadrat from the jth patch within the ith density.

μ is the (constant) mean percentage cover of algae over all possible quadrats in all possible patches in the four sea urchin density treatments.

In this study, sea urchin density is a fixed factor, so α_i is the effect of the ith density, which is the difference between the mean algal cover for the ith sea urchin density treatment and the overall mean algal cover for all the sea urchin density treatments.

Factor B is nearly always random in biology so $\beta_{j(i)}$ is a random variable with a mean of zero and a variance of σ_β^2, measuring the variance among all patches that could have been chosen within each of the four sea urchin density treatments.

ε_{ijk} is residual or unexplained error associated with the kth quadrat within the jth patch within the ith density. This term measures the error associated with each replicate observation (quadrat) of algal cover within each patch within each sea urchin density treatment. The variance of these error terms is σ_ε^2.

The model used by Caselle & Warner (1996) was:

$$\text{(recruit densities)}_{ijk} = \mu + \text{(site)}_i + \text{(transect within site)}_{j(i)} + \varepsilon_{ijk} \qquad (9.3)$$

Table 9.2 OLS estimates of cell and marginal means, with standard errors, in a two factor linear model with equal sample sizes per cell

	Population mean	Sample mean	Standard error
Cell mean	μ_{ij}	$\dfrac{\sum\limits_{k=1}^{n} y_{ijk}}{n}$	$\sqrt{\dfrac{MS_{Residual}}{n}}$
Nested design			
Factor A mean	μ_i	$\dfrac{\sum\limits_{j=1}^{q} \bar{y}_{j(i)}}{q}$	$\sqrt{\dfrac{MS_{B(A)}}{qn}}$
Crossed design			
Factor A mean	μ_i	$\dfrac{\sum\limits_{j=1}^{q} \bar{y}_{ij}}{q}$	$\sqrt{\dfrac{MS_{Residual}}{qn}}$
Factor B mean	μ_i	$\dfrac{\sum\limits_{i=1}^{p} \bar{y}_{ij}}{p}$	$\sqrt{\dfrac{MS_{Residual}}{pn}}$

Box 9.2 | The nested ANOVA model and its parameters

The main factor A has p groups ($i = 1$ to p), the nested factor B has q groups within each level of A ($j = 1$ to q) and there are n_i replicates ($k = 1$ to n_i) within each combination of A and B categories. Assume the number of levels of B in each level of A is the same and the number of replicates (n) in each combination of A and B is the same. There are a total of pq cells in this nested design with n replicate observations in each cell. The mean for each level of A is μ_i (the average of the means for all possible levels of B within each level of A) and the mean for each level of B within each level of A is $\mu_{j(i)}$. Note the subscripting, where $j(i)$ represents the jth level of factor B within the ith level of factor A. The linear (effects) model used to analyze this nested design is:

$$y_{ijk} = \mu + \alpha_i + \beta_{j(i)} + \varepsilon_{ijk} \tag{9.1}$$

In model 9.1 we have the following:

y_{ijk} is the kth replicate observation from the jth group of factor B within the ith group of factor A.

μ is the overall (constant) mean of the response variable.

If factor A is fixed, α_i is the effect of the ith group which is the difference between each A group mean and the overall mean $\mu_i - \mu$. If factor A is random, α_i represents a random variable with a mean of zero and a variance of σ_α^2, measuring the variance in mean values of the response variable across all the possible levels of factor A that could have been used. Factor B is nearly always random in biology so $\beta_{j(i)}$ is a random variable with a mean of zero and a variance of σ_β^2, measuring the variance in mean values of the response variable across all the possible levels of factor B that could have been used within each level of factor A.

ε_{ijk} is residual or unexplained error associated with the kth replicate within the jth level of B within the ith level of A. These error terms are assumed to be normally distributed at each combination of A and B, with a mean of zero ($E(\varepsilon_{ij}) = 0$) and a variance of σ_ε^2.

Model 9.1 is overparameterized (see Box 8.1) because the number of cell means is less than the number of model parameters to be estimated ($\mu, \alpha_1 \ldots \alpha_p, \beta_{1(1)} \ldots \beta_{q(p)}$). In the usual situation of factor A being fixed and factor B being random, estimation of the parameters of the effects model 9.1 can still be achieved using the sum-to-zero constraint $\sum_{i=1}^{P} \alpha_i = 0$, as outlined in Box 8.1. Alternatively, a simpler means model could be fitted:

$y_{ijk} = \mu_{ij} + \varepsilon_{ijk}$

where μ_{ij} is the mean of the response variable for each combination of A and B (each cell). Cell means models don't offer many advantages for nested designs but do become important when we consider missing cells designs in Section 9.2.6.

OLS estimates of the parameters of the nested linear model 9.1 follow the procedures outlined for a single factor model in Chapter 8 with the added complication of two of more factor effects. When the nested factors are random, the means of levels of factor A are estimated from the average of the cell means in each level of A. With different sample sizes within each cell, this results in unweighted means for factor A groups (Table 9.2). OLS standard errors of means in nested designs are calculated using the mean square in the denominator of F-ratio statistic used for testing the H_0 that the means are equal. With A fixed and B(A) random, then $MS_{B(A)}$ will be used for standard errors for factor A means (Table 9.2).

The estimate of the effect of any level of factor A ($\alpha_i = \mu_i - \mu$) is simply the difference between the sample marginal mean for that group and the overall mean:

$\bar{y}_i - \bar{y}$

Factor B is usually random, so $\beta_{j(i)}$ is a random variable with a mean of 0 and a variance of σ_β^2 and it is this variance which is of interest, the variance in mean values of the response variable between all the possible levels of factor B that could have been used within each level of factor A. This is estimated as a variance component (Section 9.1.6).

Imagine that Cassele & Warner (1996) had chosen sites at random from a population of possible sites on the north shore of the US Virgin Islands. Then factor A is random and α_i has a mean of zero and a variance of σ_α^2, measuring the variance in the mean number of fish recruits per transect across all the possible sites that could have used in their study.

Predicted values and residuals

The predicted or fitted values of the response variable from model (9.1) are:

Any predicted Y-value is predicted by the sample mean for the cell (level of B within each level of A) that contains the Y-value. For example, the predicted percentage cover of algae for quadrat one in patch one for the zero density treatment is the sample mean for patch one for the zero density treatment.

The error terms (ε_{ijk}) from the linear model can be estimated by the residuals, where a residual (e_{ijk}) is simply the difference between each observed and predicted Y-value:

$$\hat{y}_{ijk} = \bar{y} + (\bar{y}_i - \bar{y}) + (\bar{y}_{j(i)} - \bar{y}_i) = \bar{y}_{j(i)} \qquad (9.4)$$

$$e_{ijk} = y_{ijk} - \bar{y}_{j(i)} \qquad (9.5)$$

Table 9.3 ANOVA table for two factor nested linear model with factor A (p levels), factor B (q levels) nested within A, and n replicates within each combination of A and B

Source	SS	df	MS
A	$nq \sum_{i=1}^{p} (\bar{y}_i - \bar{y})^2$	$p - 1$	$\dfrac{SS_A}{p-1}$
B(A)	$n \sum_{i=1}^{p} \sum_{j=1}^{q} (\bar{y}_{j(i)} - \bar{y}_i)^2$	$p(q-1)$	$\dfrac{SS_{B(A)}}{p(q-1)}$
Residual	$\sum_{i=1}^{p} \sum_{j=1}^{q} \sum_{k=1}^{n} (y_{ijk} - \bar{y}_{j(i)})^2$	$pq(n-1)$	$\dfrac{SS_{Residual}}{pq(n-1)}$
Total	$\sum_{i=1}^{p} \sum_{j=1}^{q} \sum_{k=1}^{n} (y_{ijk} - \bar{y})^2$	$pqn - 1$	

For example, the residuals from the model relating algal cover to sea urchin density and patch nested within density are the differences between the observed algal cover on each quadrat and the mean algal cover for the patch and density combination (cell) that contained that quadrat. Note that the sum of the residuals within each cell ($\sum_{k=1}^{n} e_{ijk}$) equals zero. As for all linear models, residuals provide the basis of the OLS estimate of σ_ε^2 and they are valuable diagnostic tools for checking assumptions and fit of our model (Section 9.1.7). The OLS estimate of σ_ε^2 is the sample variance of these residuals and is termed the Residual (or Error) Mean Square and is determined as part of the partitioning of the total variation in the response variable described in the next section.

9.1.2 Analysis of variance

The partitioning of the variation in the response variable Y proceeds in a similar manner to that for a single factor model described in Chapter 8. The SS_{Total} in Y can be partitioned into its additive components as illustrated for balanced designs in Table 9.3. These formulae are not really used in practice (and are for balanced designs only), as we estimate the ANOVA terms and test relevant hypotheses by comparing the fit of general linear models (Section 9.1.5). Nonetheless, the formulae in Table 9.3 illustrate the logic behind the partitioning of the total variation in Y.

SS_A measures the sum of squared differences

between each A mean and the overall mean, e.g. sum of squared differences between the mean percentage cover of algae for each density treatment and the overall mean percentage cover of algae.

$SS_{B(A)}$ measures the sum of squared differences between each B mean (i.e. cell mean) and the mean of the appropriate level of A, summed across the levels of A, e.g. the sum of squared differences between the mean percentage cover of algae for each patch and the mean percentage cover of algae for the density treatment containing that patch, summed over all density treatments.

$SS_{Residual}$ measures the sum of squared differences between each replicate observation and the appropriate B mean within each cell, summed across all cells, e.g. the sum of squared differences between the percentage cover of algae in each quadrat and the mean percentage cover of algae for the patch containing that quadrat, summed over all patches in all density treatments.

These SS are divided by the appropriate df to produce mean squares (MS or variances). The df_A is simply the number of A levels minus one [$p - 1$], the df_B is the number of B levels within each A level minus one summed over the A levels [$p(q-1)$] and the $df_{Residual}$ is the number of observations in each cell minus one summed over all cells [$pq(n-1)$].

Statisticians have determined what population values these sample mean squares estimate,

Table 9.4 Expected mean squares and F-ratios for tests of null hypotheses for two factor nested ANOVA model

| Source | A fixed, B random | | A fixed, B fixed | |
	Expected mean square	F-ratio	Expected mean square	F-ratio
A	$\sigma_\varepsilon^2 + n\sigma_\beta^2 + nq\dfrac{\sum_{i=1}^{p}\alpha_i^2}{p-1}$	$\dfrac{MS_A}{MS_{B(A)}}$	$\sigma_\varepsilon^2 + nq\dfrac{\sum_{i=1}^{p}\alpha_i^2}{p-1}$	$\dfrac{MS_A}{MS_{Residual}}$
B(A)	$\sigma_\varepsilon^2 + n\sigma_\beta^2$	$\dfrac{MS_{B(A)}}{MS_{Residual}}$	$\sigma_\varepsilon^2 + n\dfrac{\sum_{i=1}^{p}\sum_{j=1}^{q}\beta_{j(i)}^2}{p(q-1)}$	$\dfrac{MS_{B(A)}}{MS_{Residual}}$
Residual	σ_ε^2	σ_ε^2		

i.e. what their expected values are, if the assumption of homogeneity of variance (see Section 9.1.7) holds (Table 9.4). In the usual situation of factor A being fixed and factor B random, the $MS_{Residual}$ estimates σ_ε^2 (the variance in the error terms in each cell, pooled across cells), $MS_{B(A)}$ estimates σ_ε^2 plus added variance due to the effects of factor B and MS_A estimates the sum of both these components plus the added effect of fixed levels of factor A.

9.1.3 Null hypotheses

There are two null hypotheses that we test in a two factor nested model, the test for no effects of A and the test for no effects of B nested within A. The expected values of the MS (Table 9.4) provide the logic for testing these null hypotheses, analogous to the single factor model (Chapter 8).

Factor A

$H_0(A)$: $\mu_1 = \mu_2 = \ldots = \mu_i = \mu$, i.e. no difference between the means for factor A. This is equivalent to $H_0(A)$: $\alpha_1 = \alpha_2 = \ldots = \alpha_i = 0$, i.e. no effect of any level of factor A. In the Andrew & Underwood (1993) example, this null hypothesis is that there is no difference in the mean percentage algal cover between urchin densities. This H_0 is essentially that for a single factor model, using the means for each patch (B level) as replicate observations for the test of urchin density (A level).

If A is random, then $H_0(A)$ is σ_α^2 equals zero, i.e. no added variance due to differences between all the possible levels of A.

Factor B

$H_0(B)$: σ_β^2 equals zero if factor B is random, i.e. no added variance due to differences between all the possible levels of B with any level of A. In the Andrew & Underwood (1993) example, this H_0 is that there is no added variation due to differences in mean percentage algal cover between patches within any urchin density treatment.

In the rarer case of B being a fixed factor, then $H_0(B)$ is $\mu_{1(1)} = \mu_{2(1)} = \ldots = \mu_{j(i)} = \ldots = \mu$, i.e. no difference between the means of the specifically chosen levels of B within any level of factor A. This H_0 when B is fixed is equivalent to H_0: $\beta_{1(1)} = \beta_{2(1)} = \ldots = \beta_{j(i)} = 0$, i.e. no effect of any of the specifically chosen levels of factor B within any level of factor A. This is a pooled test of differences between the levels of B for each level of A and the H_0 is false if the mean values for the levels of B are different from each other within one or more of the levels of A.

F-ratios

The F-ratios for testing these H_0s are provided in Table 9.4. If $H_0(A)$ that there is no effect of factor A is true, then all α_is equal zero and MS_A and $MS_{B(A)}$ both estimate $\sigma_\varepsilon^2 + n\sigma_\beta^2$ so their ratio (F-ratio) should be less than or equal to one. If $H_0(B)$ that there is no added variance due to differences between the possible levels of factor B within each level A is true, then all β_j equal zero (and therefore $n\sigma_\beta^2$ equals zero) and $MS_{B(A)}$ and $MS_{Residual}$ both estimate σ_ε^2 so their ratio (F-ratio) should be one.

These F-ratios follow an F distribution under

homogeneity of variance and normality assumptions (Section 9.1.7) with one exception. If B is random and the number of replicate observations within each level of B varies, then the F-ratio of $MS_{B(A)}$ and $MS_{Residual}$ does not follow an F distribution when σ_β^2 is greater than zero because $MS_{B(A)}$ is not distributed as a multiple of a χ^2 distribution (Searle *et al.* 1992, see Chapter 8). This also affects estimates of variance components (Chapter 8) and power calculations (Section 9.1.10) for unbalanced nested models. Fortunately, the F-ratio of $MS_{B(A)}$ and $MS_{Residual}$ does follow an F distribution when σ_β^2 equals zero, so the F-ratio test of the H_0 for B(A) with unbalanced data is unaffected.

When B is a random factor, $MS_{B(A)}$ provides the denominator for the F-ratio for the test of A, i.e. the units of replication for testing the effects of A are the means of B. This has important considerations for the power of the test for factor A (Section 9.1.10) and the design of experiments based on nested models. When B is fixed, the expected MS for A does not include a component for B so the F-ratio for testing A uses $MS_{Residual}$ as the denominator. If A is random, the F-ratios are the same as if A is fixed. Note that some statistical software assumes all factors are fixed so will not, by default, provide the correct F tests for nested ANOVAs when the nested factors are random. This problem was pointed out by Ouborg & van Groenendael (1996), who correctly criticized the paper of Heschel & Paige (1995) for incorrectly using the $MS_{Residual}$ instead of $MS_{B(A)}$ in their nested ANOVAs comparing populations of the scarlet gilia (a species of plant), with random seed families nested within populations, and replicates within each seed family (see also response by Paige & Heschel 1996).

9.1.4 Unequal sample sizes (unbalanced designs)

Unequal sample sizes can occur in nested designs in two ways. First, there can be unequal numbers of observations within each cell (unequal n_{ij}). Second, there can be unequal numbers of levels of the nested factor(s) within each level of the higher factor. Neither case is different to unequal sample sizes for single factor ANOVA models and neither causes any computational difficulties. However, as for all linear models fitted by OLS, tests of hypoth-

eses using F-ratios are more sensitive to violations of the assumptions (normality, homogeneity of variances) when sample sizes are unequal (see Chapter 8). Additionally, estimation of variance components for random nested factors is difficult with unequal sample sizes (Chapter 8). When the test for factor A is based on different numbers of B means within each A level, the analysis could be based on a missing cells design and the cell means model used (Kirk 1995; see also Chapter 8). However, as there are no interactions involved, this seems an unnecessary complication.

9.1.5 Comparing ANOVA models

The relative importance of different terms in the linear model for a nested design can be measured, and tests of hypotheses about these terms can also be done, by comparing full and reduced models as described in Section 8.1.5. For example, to test the H_0 that σ_β^2 equals zero, we would compare the fit of the full model (9.1) to a reduced model that omits the B(A) term:

$$y_{ijk} = \mu + \alpha_i + \varepsilon_{ijk} \tag{9.6}$$

Using the example from Andrew & Underwood (1993), we would compare the fit of model 9.2 to the reduced model:

$$(\text{% cover algae})_{ijk} = \mu + (\text{sea urchin density})_i + \varepsilon_{ijk} \tag{9.7}$$

The difference in fit of these two models is simply the difference in their $SS_{Residual}$. This difference can be converted to a mean square by dividing by the difference in the $df_{Residual}$. The H_0 of no difference in fit of the two models (i.e. σ_β^2 equals zero; no added variance due to all the possible levels of factor B within each level of factor A) can be tested with an F test using $MS_{Residual}$ of the full model as the denominator. This is, of course, the identical test to that carried out as part of the nested ANOVA.

9.1.6 Factor effects in nested models

The estimation of the effect of the main fixed factor in these nested models is described in Box 9.2, although biologists usually examine fixed factors with planned contrasts or unplanned pairwise comparisons. The estimation of components of variance for random factors in nested models follows the procedures outlined in Chapter 8 for single factor models. The sample mean squares are equated to their expected values (the ANOVA approach) and the added variance due to the nested factors and the residual can be estimated (Table 9.5). The individual variance components for nested models with two or more nested factors are straightforward extensions of those for two factor models once the expected mean squares are known (Table 9.6). Note that these estimates of variance components for random nested factors are only valid for equal sample sizes within each level of the random factor. If the design is unbalanced, estimation of variance components and derivation of confidence intervals is more difficult (Searle *et al.* 1992), although Burdick & Graybill (1992) provide formulae. In general, the REML approach dicussed in Section 8.2 is considered more reliable than the ANOVA method for estimating variance components of random factors above the residual (Searle *et al.* 1992).

Table 9.5 Estimates of variance components (using ANOVA approach) for two factor nested design with B(A) random

Source	Estimated variance component
A	$\dfrac{MS_A - MS_{B(A)}}{nq}$ *
B(A)	$\dfrac{MS_{B(A)} - MS_{Residual}}{n}$
Residual	$MS_{Residual}$

Note:
*This represents variance between population means of specific levels of A if factor A is fixed and a true added variance component if A is random.

Table 9.6 (a) Estimates of variance components (using ANOVA approach) for three factor nested design with factors A (*p* levels), B within A (*q* levels) and C within B within A (*r* levels) random and *n* replicates within each cell. (b) Illustration of variance components for nested design from Downes *et al.* (1993) – see Section 9.1.6 for details

(a)

Source	Expected mean square	Estimated variance component	F-ratio
A	$\sigma_\varepsilon^2 + n\sigma_\gamma^2 + nr\sigma_\beta^2 + nrq\sigma_\alpha^2$	$\dfrac{MS_A - MS_{B(A)}}{nrq}$	$\dfrac{MS_A}{MS_{B(A)}}$
B(A)	$\sigma_\varepsilon^2 + n\sigma_\gamma^2 + nr\sigma_\beta^2$	$\dfrac{MS_{B(A)} - MS_{C(B(A))}}{nr}$	$\dfrac{MS_{B(A)}}{MS_{C(B(A))}}$
C(B(A))	$\sigma_\varepsilon^2 + n\sigma_\gamma^2$	$\dfrac{MS_{C(B(A))} - MS_{Residual}}{n}$	$\dfrac{MS_{C(B(A))}}{MS_{Residual}}$
Residual	σ_ε^2	$MS_{Residual}$	

(b)

Source	df	MS	Estimated variance component	% of total variance
Site	2	36188.34	−691.94*	0
Riffle	3	56946.62	2991.15	28
Group	24	12074.12	2103.87	19
Stone (residual)	60	5762.52	5762.52	53

Note:
*Negative variance component converted to zero.

Confidence intervals for σ_ε^2 are calculated in the same way as for single factor designs and work for both balanced and unbalanced designs (Table 8.5). Confidence intervals on the remaining variance components can also be calculated, with approximations based on unweighted SS for unbalanced designs, although the formulae are somewhat tedious (Burdick & Graybill 1992). Note that for a nested model with A fixed and B random, the test of the H_0 that σ_β^2 equals zero is still reliable; it is only when σ_β^2 is greater than zero that the F-ratio of $MS_{B(A)}/MS_{Residual}$ no longer follows an F distribution, and estimation of a non-zero variance component is difficult.

These nested designs are commonly used to partition the variation in a response variable among levels of a spatial or temporal hierarchy and we are often interested in calculating the relative contribution of random nested terms to the total variation in Y. For example, Downes *et al.* (1993) examined spatial variation in the distribution of invertebrates living on stones in a stream. They used three randomly chosen sites (covering about 1.5 km of stream), two riffles (shallow, fast-flowing, stony areas) at each site, five groups of stones from each riffle and three stones from each group and wished to test the relative contribution of each of the spatial scales to the variation in total density of invertebrates. The components of variance for each of the random factors can be estimated using an appropriate method (ANOVA for balanced designs, REML or ML for unbalanced designs) and the percentage contribution of each random term to the total variance of the random terms can be calculated (Table 9.5).

In the common situation of a fixed main factor with one or more random nested factors, we can also partition the total variance using the ANOVA approach for both the fixed and nested random factors (Table 9.5). It is very important to remember that the interpretation of the true variance components for B(A) and Residual is quite different from the variance between fixed treatment effects for A, as we discussed in Chapter 8. Nonetheless, partitioning the total variation in a response variable between that explained by the fixed factor and one or more nested random factors is a useful interpretative tool.

9.1.7 Assumptions for nested models

The assumptions of normality and homogeneity of within-cell variances apply to hypothesis tests in nested ANOVA models and they are checked using the same techniques (boxplots, mean vs variance plots and residuals vs mean plots) already described in Chapters 4 and 8. Traditionally, the observations within each cell (combination of main and nested factors) in the data set are used to check the assumptions. However, because the test of the main effect of A is based on the means of the levels of B when B is random, the normality and homogeneity of variance assumptions for the test of factor A apply to these means rather than within cell observations. You may, therefore, need to look at the assumptions separately for each hypothesis that uses a different denominator to make up the F-ratio. Transformations are applicable as usual (Chapter 4) but we know of no accepted non-parametric or robust (at least to unequal variances) tests specifically for nested designs. Any approach would require the main effect of A to be tested using the nested factor means as observations with one of the robust single factor tests described in Chapter 8. For non-normal data, the RT (rank transform, see Section 9.2.9) approach may also be useful, particularly when outliers are present. Of course, generalized linear models (GLMs; see Chapter 13) would also be applicable when the underlying distribution of the response variable is not normal but known to fit one from the exponential family suited to GLMs.

In many cases, it is the higher levels in the hierarchy that are of most interest. We would expect, from the Central Limit Theorem, that normality will be satisfied for all levels other than the lowest one in the hierarchy, because we are effectively working with means at higher levels. Means are more likely to be normally distributed, regardless of the underlying distribution of the observations.

The assumption of independence is also relevant for nested ANOVA models. The observations within each cell (e.g. level of B with A) are commonly measured at small spatial scales, such as quadrats within patches (Andrew & Underwood 1993). We need to design our study to ensure that these observations are independent of each other within each level of B.

9.1.8 Specific comparisons for nested designs

The logic and mechanics of planned and unplanned comparisons are the same as for single factor ANOVA models (Chapter 8) with two exceptions. First, we are usually only interested in comparisons between levels of factor A if it is fixed. The nested factors are commonly random so specific comparisons of levels of these factors within each level of the higher factor are rarely relevant. Second, we must use the appropriate standard error for comparisons of means of the fixed factor. The standard error for contrasts between A means should be based on $MS_{B(A)}$ if B is random, just as for the F test for factor A in the ANOVA model (see Table 9.4).

9.1.9 More complex designs

These designs can be extended to three or more nested factors (Table 9.6(a)) and are often used when there are multiple levels of subsampling, e.g. plants within treatments, pieces of tissue within each plant, sections cut from each piece of tissue, cells measured from each section. We have already described the study of Downes *et al.* (1993) who used three sites along a river, two riffles (shallow stony areas) at each site, with five groups of three stones within each riffle to examine hierarchical spatial variation in the distribution of stream invertebrates (Table 9.6(b)). Their linear model incorporated site, riffle nested within site, group nested within riffle within site and replicate stones within group within riffle within site:

(density)$_{ijkl} = \mu + $ (site)$_i +$
(riffle within site)$_{j(i)} +$
(group within riffle within site)$_{k(j(i))} + \varepsilon_{ijkl}$ (9.8)

Another example is from Abrams *et al.* (1994), who examined variation in leaf structural parameters across three sites (xeric, mesic, wet-mesic) in Pennsylvania, with five or six different species at each site, six sapling trees of each species and replicate leaves from each tree. Their linear model incorporated site, species nested within site, tree nested within species within site and replicate measurements within tree within species within site:

(leaf structure)$_{ijkl} = \mu + $ (site)$_i +$
(species within site)$_{j(i)} +$
(trees within species within site)$_{k(j(i))} + \varepsilon_{ijkl}$ (9.9)

Both Abrams *et al.* (1994) and Downes *et al.* (1993) calculated variance components for each factor (Table 9.6(b)). Since all nested factors were random in these studies, the F-ratio for the null hypothesis for each term in the model used the term immediately below as the denominator.

9.1.10 Design and power

If the main (highest) factor in a nested design is fixed, we could use formal power analysis based on specified and negotiated effect sizes (Chapters 7 and 8) to determine the number of groups nested within that main factor that we need to detect a particular treatment effect. If the nested factor B is random, then the power of the test for A will depend on the level of replication of B, and on the amount of variation among levels of B. For example, based on the experiment of Andrew & Underwood (1993) manipulating sea urchin densities, we would specify the desired effect size between density treatments and use an estimate of the variance between patches within each treatment to determine the number of patches required to achieve a given power. This simply becomes a single factor design using patch means so the methods outlined in Chapter 8 are appropriate.

This has implications for the design of nested experimental and sampling programs. The higher level "units" in nested designs are often increasingly costly, either because they are more expensive (e.g. whole animals vs pieces of tissue) or take longer to record (large spatial areas vs small quadrats). It is then tempting to take more replicates at lower levels in the design hierarchy. It is very important to realize that to increase the power of the test for fixed main effects, we need to increase the number of levels of the random factor immediately below the fixed factor. For example, Andrew & Underwood (1993) could improve the power of the test for differences in algal cover among sea urchin densities more by increasing the number of patches per treatment rather than the number of quadrats per patch. Nonetheless, smaller-scale noise as part of the apparent variation in factor B can still be important. From the expected mean squares for a two factor nested design (Table 9.4), we see that the $MS_{B(A)}$ includes two components, small-scale variation (σ_ε^2) and

Box 9.3 | Calculations for optimal allocation of subsampling resources for two factor nested design based on Andrew & Underwood (1993)

Using the data from Andrew & Underwood (1993) as a pilot study and based on costs of 5 min to record a quadrat within a patch and 23 min to set up and work a patch (excluding quadrat recording time), we can estimate the optimal number of quadrats per patch:

$$n = \sqrt{\frac{C_{B(A)}s^2_{C(B(A))}}{C_{C(B(A))}s^2_{B(A)}}} = \sqrt{\frac{23 \times 298.60}{5 \times 1770.16}} = 0.88$$

Therefore, we would use a single quadrat per patch. If we set the total cost per density treatment at 4 h (240 min), we can determine the optimal number of patches per treatment if we have one quadrat per patch:

$$C_A = qC_{B(A)} + nqC_{C(B(A))}$$
$$240 = q \times 23 + 1 \times q \times 5$$
$$q = 8.57$$

The optimal experiment design would have nine patches per density treatment and one quadrat per patch.

---

the true variance between B groups ($n\sigma_\beta^2$). As we increase our subsampling effort (i.e. raise n), MS_B becomes increasingly dominated by σ_β^2. Therefore, while subsampling at levels below B has no direct effect on the power of the test of A, if there is considerable small-scale variation, then taking some replicates at lower levels will provide better variance estimates, and improve power.

At lower levels of nested designs, power is much less an issue, as degrees of freedom generally increase from top to bottom of hierarchical designs. Increases in replication at higher levels of the hierarchy will have cascading effects on power at lower levels. However, it must be remembered that formal power calculations would need to be done separately for each level, i.e., for each hypothesis of interest.

Note that power of tests of particular terms in a model may be increased by pooling non-significant terms with their error term, thus creating a pooled residual term with more degrees of freedom for tests of other terms. Issues and guidelines for pooling terms in multifactor ANOVA models will be discussed in Section 9.3.

Another important aspect of the design of studies that use a series of nested random factors is the allocation of limited resources to multiple spatial or temporal scales of sampling. For example, imagine we were following up the study of Andrew & Underwood (1993) who set up four sea urchin density treatment with four replicate patches within each treatment and five replicate quadrats within each patch. The number of treatments is obviously fixed, but in the new study, how should we allocate our sampling effort to the two different spatial levels in this design? Given limited resources, do we use more patches within each treatment, or more quadrats within each patch?

There are two criteria we use to decide on this relative allocation. First is the precision of the means for each level of the design or, conversely, the variance of these means. Second is the cost, in terms of money and/or time, of sampling each level in the design. We will illustrate the calculations for determining this relative allocation of resources for the study by Andrew & Underwood (1993) – see Box 9.3. This is a two factor nested design with p levels of A (density treatment), q levels of B (patches) nested within A (B(A)) and n replicate observations (quadrats) within each combination of density treatment and patch (C(B(A)), i.e. the Residual). Sokal & Rohlf (1995) illustrate the calculations for a three factor design. We use the variance components for each random term in the model to estimate the variance associated with each term in the model separately from the other components of variation (Section 9.1.6). The costs (C) must also be determined, preferably from our pilot study where costs can be estimated empirically. The cost for each quadrat is simply the time and/or money required to place the quadrat and estimate the percentage cover of algae, say five minutes. The cost for each patch would be the time taken to move all the gear to each patch (20 minutes) and the time taken to move between quadrats in each patch (three minutes) but NOT the time taken to process a quadrat.

A number of textbooks (Snedecor & Cochran 1989, Sokal & Rohlf 1995, Underwood 1997) provide equations for relating costs and variances to determine the optimum number of replicates at each level of sampling (and see Andrew & Mapstone 1987). In a two factor design, the optimum number of replicates (e.g. quadrats) in each level of B (e.g. each patch) is:

$$n = \sqrt{\frac{C_{B(A)}s^2_{C(B(A))}}{C_{C(B(A))}s^2_{B(A)}}} \qquad (9.10)$$

where C is the cost for the appropriate level and s^2 is the estimate of the variance, i.e. the mean square. Note that if the costs of recording a single quadrat are the same as the costs of setting up a new patch, then the sample size is just based on the ratio of the two variance components. Based on the variances and the costs listed above, the optimal number of quadrats per patch is 0.88, i.e. one (Box 9.3).

The number of patches (q) for each density treatment can be determined in two ways based on either the desired variance of the mean for each site (s_A^2) or the fixed total cost of sampling a site (C_A):

$$s_A{}^2 = \frac{ns^2_{B(A)} + s^2_{C(B(A))}}{nq} \qquad (9.11)$$

$$C_A = qC_{B(A)} + nqC_{C(B(A))} \qquad (9.12)$$

In the first case, we fix the desired level of precision for the mean of each site (s_A^2) and, using our values for n and the estimated variance components for quadrats and patches, solve for q. In the second case, we fix the total available cost for sampling each density and, again using our values for n and the estimated variance components for quadrats and patches, solve for q. In practice, having a fixed total cost, in time or money, is likely so the latter approach might be used more often. If we set the total cost for setting up each density treatment as four hours (240 minutes), then the number of patches would be 8.6, i.e. nine (Box 9.3). So based on these estimates, the most efficient design would be one quadrat per patch and nine quadrats per treatment. Note that these costs are guesses on our part so we are not suggesting that there was anything wrong with the design used by Andrew & Underwood (1993).

Keough & Mapstone (1995) made a number of sensible recommendations for deriving and using these values for sample size at each level of subsampling. First, the calculated sample sizes depend on the quality of the pilot data, particularly the variance estimates, and how well the variances in the subsequent main study will match those from the pilot study. It is important, therefore, that the pilot study is done in similar locations and at a similar time (e.g. season) to the main study. It is also important to check that these variance estimates still hold once the main research has started and adjust the sample sizes if necessary. It is much easier to reduce sample size during an ongoing research program than to increase them, so the initial sample sizes should be generous. Second, the sample size values will usually not be integers so they should be rounded up to the nearest integer. Finally, the calculations may recommend sample sizes of less than one, because the variance at that level is so small or the costs so cheap. However, some level of replication is necessary for sensible inference and, remembering that pilot studies may underestimate the true variance, we recommend that more than one replicate at any level should always be used.

9.2 | Factorial designs

An alternative multifactor linear model is used when our design incorporates two or more factors that are crossed with each other. The term crossed indicates that all combinations of the factors are

Table 9.7 | Illustration of marginal and cell means for a two factor factorial ANOVA design. Data from Quinn (1988) where factor A is limpet density, factor B is season and the response variable is number of egg masses per limpet in three replicate enclosures per cell

	B_1	B_2	B_j	Marginal means A
A_1	μ_{11}	μ_{12}	μ_{1j}	$\mu_{i=1}$
A_2	μ_{21}	μ_{22}	μ_{2j}	$\mu_{i=2}$
A_i	μ_{i1}	μ_{i2}	μ_{ij}	μ_i
Marginal means B	$\mu_{j=1}$	$\mu_{j=2}$	μ_j	Grand mean μ

Factor A (A_i)	Factor B (B_j) Season	B_1 Spring	B_2 Summer	Factor A marginal means
	Density			
A_1	8	$\bar{y}_{11} = 2.417$	$\bar{y}_{12} = 1.833$	$\bar{y}_{i=1} = 2.125$
A_2	15	$\bar{y}_{21} = 2.177$	$\bar{y}_{22} = 1.178$	$\bar{y}_{i=2} = 1.677$
A_3	30	$\bar{y}_{31} = 1.565$	$\bar{y}_{32} = 0.811$	$\bar{y}_{i=3} = 1.188$
A_4	45	$\bar{y}_{41} = 1.200$	$\bar{y}_{42} = 0.593$	$\bar{y}_{i=4} = 0.896$
Factor B marginal means		$\bar{y}_{j=1} = 1.840$	$\bar{y}_{j=2} = 1.104$	$\bar{y} = 1.472$

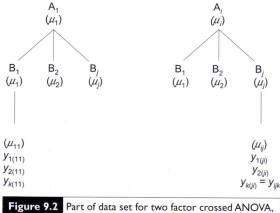

Figure 9.2 Part of data set for two factor crossed ANOVA, with p levels of factor A ($i = 1$ to p), q levels of factor B ($j = 1$ to q), where the levels of B are the same and crossed with each level of A, and n replicate observations within each combination (cell) of A and B ($k = 1$ to n).

included in the design and that every level (group) of each factor occurs in combination with every level of the other factors. Such designs are also termed factorial. This pattern is in contrast to nested designs, where the levels of the nested factor are different within each level of the main factor. We will first consider factorial (crossed) designs with two factors, where every level of one factor occurs at every level of the other factor and both factors are of equal importance – see Figure 9.2 and Table 9.7.

Factorial designs are most often used for manipulative experiments. For example, Poulson & Platt (1996) examined the effects of light micro-environment (three levels: beneath canopy, single treefall gap, multiple treefall gap) and seedling height class (three levels: 1–2 m small, 2–4 m medium, 4–8 m large) on the difference in growth between sugar maple and beech saplings (the response variable was the difference in growth of paired seedlings of each species). There were five replicate seedling pairs for each of the nine micro-environment–height combinations. Another example comes from Maret & Collins (1996), who set up an experiment to test the effects of invertebrate food level and the presence or absence of tadpoles on variation in size among larval salamanders. There were two factors: two levels of ration of invertebrate prey (low and high amounts of brine shrimp per day) and two levels of tadpole supplementation (with and without). There were originally eight replicate aquaria in each of the four cells, although some aquaria were omitted from analysis because one or more salamander larvae died. The response variable was mean snout–vent length of salamanders in each aquarium.

In these two examples, both factors in the design are fixed, i.e. all possible levels of interest for the two factors have been used in the study and our inference is restricted to these levels. These are analyzed with fixed effects linear models, also termed Model 1 analyses of variance.

Factorial designs can include random factors that are often randomly chosen spatial or temporal units. Designs that include only random factors are analyzed with random effects models, termed Model 2 analyses of variance, although these are unusual in biology. One example is from Kause *et al.* (1999), who examined phenotypic plasticity in the foraging behavior of sawfly larvae with an experiment that used six species of sawflies and 20 individual mountain birch trees that represented a range of leaf qualities for the herbivorous sawfly larvae. There were between four and six larvae per tree and species combination and the response variable was an aspect of foraging behavior (e.g. number of meals, relative consumption rate etc.). Both sawfly species and individual tree were random factors as they were a sample from all possible herbivorous sawflies and all possible trees.

Designs with a combination of fixed and random factors are analyzed with mixed linear models, also termed Model 3 analyses of variance. Including a random factor in a multifactor design is important in biology, because it allows us to generalize the effects of a fixed factor to the population of spatial or temporal units (Beck 1997). For example, Brunet (1996) tested the effects of position on an inflorescence and randomly chosen plants on fruit and seed production of a perennial herb. This was a two factor design with flower position as the fixed factor and individual plant as the random factor. A second example comes from Twombly (1996), who randomly assigned copepod nauplii from 15 sibships to one of four food treatments (high constant food and high switched to low at three different naupliar stages); there were four replicate dishes (each containing two nauplii) per factor combination and the response variable was age at metamorphosis. Food treatment was a fixed factor and sibship was a random factor.

Factorial designs can include three or more factors (Section 9.2.12), although we will illustrate the principles based on two factor designs. Factorial designs allow us to measure two different sorts of factor effects.

1. The main effect of each factor is the effect of each factor independent of (pooling over) the other factors.

2. The interaction between factors is a measure of how the effects of one factor depend on the level of one or more additional factors. The absence of an interaction means that the combined effect of two or more factors is predictable by just adding their individual effects together. The presence of an interaction indicates a synergistic or antagonistic effect of the two factors.

We can only measure interaction effects in factorial (crossed) designs. In nested designs where factor B is nested within factor A, different levels of B are used in each level of A so any interaction between A and B cannot be assessed. When all possible combinations of the two (or more) factors are used in factorial designs they are called complete factorials. Sometimes this is logistically impossible because the experiment would be too big and/or costly, so a subset of factor combinations is used and the design is termed a fractional factorial. Such designs are more difficult to analyze because not all interactions can be measured – see Section 9.2.12.

Fecundity of limpets: effects of season and adult density

Our first worked example of a factorial ANOVA design and analysis is from Quinn (1988). He examined the effects of season (two levels, winter/spring and summer/autumn) and adult density (four levels, 8, 15, 30 and 45 animals per $225 \, cm^2$) on the production of egg masses by rocky intertidal pulmonate limpets (*Siphonaria diemenensis*). Limpets (approx. 10 mm shell length) were enclosed in $225 \, cm^2$ stainless steel mesh enclosures attached to the rocky platform. There were eight treatment combinations (four densities at each of two seasons) and three replicate enclosures per treatment combination. Note that all four densities were used in both seasons, hence a factorial or crossed design. One of the important questions being asked with this experiment was whether the effect of density on number of egg masses per limpet depended on season. Quinn (1988) predicted that the density effect would be greater in summer/autumn, when algal food was scarce, than in winter/spring, when algal food was more abundant.

Quinn (1988) described another experiment looking at the same species of limpet lower on the shore. Here the limpets were bigger (15–20 mm shell length) and there was much less seasonal variation in the availability of algal food, algal cover being high all year round. The same two factors were used for this experiment but only three densities were included: 6, 12 and 24 limpets per 225 cm². So there were six treatment combinations (three densities at each of two seasons) and three replicate enclosures per treatment combination. The analyses of both experiments are in Box 9.4.

Oysters, limpets and mangrove forests
Our second example is from Minchinton & Ross (1999), who examined the distribution of oysters, and their suitability as habitat for limpets in a

---

Box 9.4 | Worked example of two factor fixed effects ANOVA

Quinn (1988) examined the effects of season (winter/spring and summer/autumn) and adult density (8, 15, 30 and 45 animals per 225 cm² enclosure) on the production of egg masses by intertidal pulmonate limpets (*Siphonaria diemenensis*). There were three replicate enclosures per treatment combination and the response variable was the number of egg masses per limpet in each enclosure.

The null hypotheses were as follows.

No difference between mean number of egg masses laid in each season, pooling densities.
No difference in mean number of egg masses laid at each density, pooling seasons.
No interaction between season and density, i.e. the effect of density on mean numbers of egg masses laid is independent of season and vice versa.

Source	df	MS	F	P
Density	3	1.76	9.67	0.001
Linear	1	5.02	27.58	<0.001
Quadratic	1	0.24	1.29	0.272
Season	1	3.25	17.84	0.001
Density × season	3	0.06	0.30	0.824
Residual	16	0.18		

There were no outliers and the residual plot (Figure 9.4(a)) did not suggest problems with assumptions. There was no evidence of an interaction ($P = 0.824$, see Figure 9.5(a)). There were significant effects of season (more egg masses in winter/spring than summer/autumn) and density. The main effect of density was further analyzed with orthogonal polynomials (see Chapter 8 and Section 9.2.10). There was a significant negative linear trend in egg mass production with density but no quadratic trend.

Quinn (1988) did a similar experiment at a lower level of the same shore where the limpets were larger. Different densities were used (6, 12, 24) but the same two seasons with three replicate enclosures per treatment combination. The null hypotheses were the same as above, except that there were only three densities. Again, the residual plot did not suggest any problem with variance heterogeneity (Figure 9.4(b)).

Source	df	MS	F	P
Density	2	2.00	13.98	0.001
Season	1	17.15	119.85	<0.001
Density × season	2	0.85	5.91	0.016
Density 6 vs 12 & 24 × season	1	1.53	10.66	0.007
Linear density × season	1	1.44	10.07	0.008
Residual	12	0.14		

There was a significant interaction between density and season ($P = 0.016$, Figure 9.5(b)). Treatment–contrast interaction tests showed that the comparison between control density and increased density varied between seasons and the linear trend in density was also significantly different between seasons. We also tested simple main effects of density separately for each season.

Source	df	MS	F	P
Winter density	2	0.17	1.21	0.331
Summer density	2	2.67	18.69	<0.001
Residual	12	0.14		

The effect of density was only significant in summer, not in winter. Note that the original $MS_{Residual}$ was used for both tests.

temperate mangrove forest. They chose two sites about 600 m apart and at each site recorded the density of oysters in four zones running up the shore: seaward zone without mangrove trees, seaward zone with mangrove trees, middle zone with trees, and a landward zone at the upper levels. In each of the eight combinations of site and zone, they used five quadrats to sample oysters (response variable) on the forest floor. An additional study examined the distribution of limpets on oysters on bent mangrove tree trunks. They used two sites, three zones (obviously the seaward zone without trees was not included) and two orientations of mangrove trunk (upper facing canopy and lower facing forest floor). This was a three factor sampling design with five quadrats in each of the 12 cells and densities of limpets per oyster surface as the response variable. For both designs, site was a random factor, representing all possible sites within the mangrove forest, and zone and orientation were fixed factors. The analyses of these data are in Box 9.5.

9.2.1 Linear models for factorial designs

In the sections that follow, we will describe two factor designs and their associated linear models.

Designs with more than two factors will be examined in Section 9.2.12. A two factor factorial design is illustrated in Figure 9.2 with a factor relationship diagram. Factor A has p groups ($i = 1$ to p), factor B has q groups ($j = 1$ to q) crossed with each level of A and there are n_i replicates ($k = 1$ to n_i) within each combination of A and B categories, i.e. each cell. Note that every level of factor B is crossed with every level of factor A and vice versa. For the moment, assume the number of replicate observations (n) in each combination of A and B is the same. Unequal sample sizes will be discussed in Section 9.2.6. There will be a total of pq cells in this factorial design with n replicate observations in each cell. From Quinn (1988), p was four limpet density treatments (factor A), q was two seasons (factor B) and n was three enclosures within each cell. From Minchinton & Ross (1999), p was four zones (factor A), q was two sites (factor B) and n was five quadrats within each cell.

We need to distinguish between two types of means in multifactor crossed designs (Table 9.7).

- Marginal means are the means for the levels of one factor pooling over the levels of the

Box 9.5 | Worked example of two factor mixed effects ANOVA

Minchinton & Ross (1999) examined the distribution of oysters, and their suitability as habitat for limpets in a temperate mangrove forest. There were two factors: randomly chosen sites (two sites about 600 m apart) and fixed zones (four levels running up the shore: seaward zone without mangrove trees, seaward zone with mangrove trees, middle zone with trees, and a landward zone at the upper levels). In each of the eight combinations of site and zone, they used five quadrats to sample limpets on oyster shells (response variable) on the forest floor. There was a strong relationship between cell means and cell variances (Figure 9.6), indicating that number of limpets was positively skewed. After transformation to square roots ($\times 100$, representing limpets per 100 oyster shells), much of the mean–variance relationship was removed, indicating that the distribution of the response variable was more symmetrical. Like Minchinton & Ross (1999), we analyzed the transformed variable.

The null hypotheses were as follows.

No difference in the mean square root number of limpets per quadrat between zones, pooling across all possible sites.

No difference in the mean square root number of limpets per quadrat between all possible sites, pooling across zones.

No interaction between zone and site, i.e. the effect of zone on the mean square root number of limpets per quadrat is independent of all possible sites that could have been used and vice versa.

The two factor mixed model ANOVA tested the fixed effect of zone against the interaction term, with only 3 and 3 df, because site was random.

Source	df	MS	F	P	Variance component	%
Zone	3	13.08	1.24	0.433	(0.25)	
Site	1	6.37	1.84	0.184	0.15	2.90
Zone × site	3	10.59	3.06	0.042	1.43	28.36
Residual	32	3.46			3.46	68.74

The H_0 of no interaction between zone and site was rejected, indicating that the effect of zone was not consistent between sites in this mangrove forest. This is clear in Figure 9.7 where site A has fewest limpets in the middle zone whereas site B has the most limpets in this zone. Most of the variance in limpet densities was unexplained, although the interaction explained nearly ten times more than the main effect of site.

Note that the F-ratio for zone would have been 3.78 with 3 and 32 df ($P = 0.020$) if site had been considered fixed, resulting in rejection of the H_0 of no effect of zone. We would be more confident of a zone effect for just the two sites used (site fixed), than a zone effect for all possible sites we could have used (site random).

second factor, so the marginal mean A_1 is the mean for the first level of A pooling over the levels of B. For example, the marginal mean for density eight from Quinn (1988) is the mean number of egg masses per limpet from all possible enclosures with eight limpets, pooling both seasons. The marginal mean for each level of A is μ_i and the marginal mean for each level of B is μ_j.

- Cell means are the means of the observations within each combination of A and B. For example, the mean number of egg masses per limpet from enclosures within each

density–season combination. The cell means for each combination of A and B are μ_{ij}.

Model 1 – both factors fixed

The linear ANOVA model for a factorial design with two fixed factors is an extension of the model used for single factor designs in Chapter 8. The two factor effects model is:

$$y_{ijk} = \mu + \alpha_i + \beta_j + (\alpha\beta)_{ij} + \varepsilon_{ijk} \qquad (9.13)$$

Statistical details of the crossed ANOVA model, including estimation of its parameters, are provided in Box 9.6.

Box 9.6 | **The fixed effects factorial ANOVA model and its parameters**

The linear ANOVA models for a factorial design with two fixed factors are extensions of the models used for single factor designs in Chapter 8. The effects model is:

$$y_{ijk} = \mu + \alpha_i + \beta_j + (\alpha\beta)_{ij} + \varepsilon_{ijk}$$

In model 9.13:

y_{ijk} is the kth replicate observation from the combination of the ith level of factor A and jth level of factor B, i.e. cell ij.

μ is the overall (constant) population mean of the response variable.

α_i is effect of ith level factor A, pooling the levels of factor B. This is the main effect of factor A, the effect of A pooling (independent of) factor B, and is defined as the difference between each A marginal mean and the overall mean $(\mu_i - \mu)$.

β_j is effect of jth level of factor B, pooling the levels of factor A, which is the difference between each B marginal mean and the overall mean. This is the main effect of factor B, the effect of B pooling (independent of) factor A, and is defined as the difference between each B marginal mean and the overall mean $(\mu_j - \mu)$.

$(\alpha\beta)_{ij}$ is the effect of the interaction of the ith level of A and the jth level of B and is defined as $(\mu_{ij} - \mu_i - \mu_j + \mu)$. Interactions measure whether the effect of one factor depends on the levels of the other factor and vice versa. This can also be viewed as measuring whether the effects of one factor are independent of the other second factor.

ε_{ijk} is random or unexplained error associated with the kth replicate observation from the combination of the ith level of factor A and jth level of factor B. These error terms are assumed to be normally distributed at each combination of factor levels, with a mean of zero $[E(\varepsilon_{ij}) = 0]$ and a variance of σ_ε^2.

This fixed effects model is overparameterized because the number of means (combinations of factors plus overall mean) is less than the number of model parameters to be estimated ($\mu, \alpha_1, \alpha_2, ..., \beta_1, \beta_2, ..., (\alpha\beta)_{11}, (\alpha\beta)_{12}, ...$). Overcoming this problem so we can estimate model parameters requires a series of "sum-to-zero" constraints:

$$\sum_{i=1}^{p} \alpha_i = 0, \sum_{j=1}^{q} \beta_j = 0, \sum_{i=1}^{p} (\alpha\beta)_{ij} = 0, \sum_{j=1}^{q} (\alpha\beta)_{ij} = 0.$$

These constraints appear formidable but simply imply that the sum of the effects of factor A, pooling B, and the sum of the effects of factor B, pooling A, are both zero. Additionally, the sum of the interaction effects for each level A and for each level of B are also zero. These constraints are necessary for fitting effects models, although such constraints have been criticized (Chapter 8), and further technical discussion of this issue can be found in Hocking (1996), Searle (1993) and Yandell (1997).

An alternative to imposing constraints on the effects model is to fit a much simpler means model:

$$y_{ijk} = \mu_{ij} + \varepsilon_{ijk}$$

where μ_{ij} is the mean of cell ij and ε_{ijk} is random or unexplained variation. The means model basically treats the analysis as a large single factor ANOVA comparing all cells and tests specific hypotheses about interactions and main effects. The means model estimates A and B means by averaging the cell means across rows or columns (Searle 1993), so it has certain advantages for unbalanced designs by ignoring the sample sizes completely. Means models are mainly useful for missing cells designs (see Section 9.2.6).

Estimating the parameters of the factorial linear model 9.13 follows the methods outlined for a single factor model in Chapter 8 and nested models in Box 9.2 with the added complication of estimating interaction effects. Cell means (μ_{ij}) for each combination of A and B are estimated from the sample mean of the observations in each cell, based on the sample size of the particular cell if sample sizes are unequal.

The factor level (marginal) mean for each level of A pooling levels of B is simply the mean of the sample means for each cell at level i of factor A, averaged across the levels of B (Table 9.2). An analogous calculation can be done for factor B means. These are unweighted means and ignore any difference in sample sizes between cells.

An alternative approach is to calculate a weighted marginal mean, which averages the observations for each level of A taking into account different n_{ij} within each cell. If we have a fully balanced design (all n_{ij} equal), then the unweighted and weighted estimates of factor level means will obviously be the same. If we have unequal numbers of observations per cell (some n_{ij} different), then the estimates will be different. In unbalanced crossed designs, only Type III SS are based on unweighted marginal means and therefore only F-ratio statistics based on Type III SS test hypotheses about unweighted marginal means (Section 9.2.6). Our preference for unbalanced designs is to estimate and test hypotheses about unweighted means.

Standard errors for these means are based on the mean squares used in the denominator of the appropriate F test of the H_0 that the population means are equal (Table 9.11). Note that the OLS standard error for a specific mean will be different from that calculated if we treat the observations producing that mean as a single sample and calculate the standard error as described in Chapter 2. The former uses a pooled variance estimate for the whole data set whereas the latter only uses the variance of the observations producing the mean.

The estimates of α_i ($\mu_i - \mu$) and β_j ($\mu_j - \mu$) are the differences between the mean of each A level or each B level and the overall mean, $\bar{y}_i - \bar{y}$ and $\bar{y}_j - \bar{y}$ respectively. Interaction effects measure how much the effect of one factor depends on the level of the other factor and vice versa. If there was no interaction between the two factors, we would expect the cell means to be represented by the sum of the overall mean and the main effects:

$$\mu_{ij} = \mu + \alpha_i + \beta_j$$

Therefore, the effect of the interaction between the ith level of A and jth level of B $(\alpha\beta)_{ij}$ can be defined as the difference between the ijth cell mean and its value we would expect if there was no interaction:

$$\alpha\beta_{ij} = \mu_{ij} - \mu_i - \mu_j + \mu$$

which is estimated by:

$$\bar{y}_{ij} - \bar{y}_i - \bar{y}_j + \bar{y}$$

This represents those effects not due to the overall mean and the main effects.

Note that in practice biologists rarely calculate the estimated factor or interaction effects, instead focusing on contrasts of marginal or cell means. The exception is when we have random factors in our model and estimating variance components is often of interest.

Using the example from Quinn (1988):

(no. egg masses per limpet)$_{ijk}$ = μ +
(effect of density)$_i$ + (effect of season)$_j$ +
(interaction between density and season)$_{ij}$ +
ε_{ijk}

(9.14)

In models 9.13 and 9.14 we have the following:

y_{ijk} is the number of egg masses per limpet from the kth replicate enclosure from the combination of the ith density and jth season, i.e. cell ij.

μ is the overall (constant) population mean number of egg masses per limpet from all possible enclosures in the eight density–season combinations.

α_i is the main effect of ith density on the number of egg masses per limpet, pooling (independent of) seasons.

β_j is the main effect of jth season on the number of egg masses per limpet, pooling (independent of) densities.

$(\alpha\beta)_{ij}$ is the effect on the number of egg masses per limpet of the interaction of the ith

density and jth season. This interaction measures whether the effect of density on number of egg masses per limpet depends on season and vice versa, also whether the effect of density is independent of the effect of season.

ε_{ijk} is random or unexplained error associated with the kth replicate enclosure from the combination of the ith level of density and jth level of season. This measures the random error associated with the number of egg masses per limpet in each enclosure and the existence of this error is why replicates within each cell produce different values for the response variable.

Model 2 – both factors random

These designs are relatively uncommon in biological research (but see Kause et al. (1999) for a recent example) so we will not examine them in detail – see Neter et al. (1996).

Model 3 – one factor fixed and one random

The linear model for a factorial design with one fixed and one random factor is the same as outlined in 9.13 although the interpretation of the terms is different. Using the example from Minchinton & Ross (1999):

(density of oysters)$_{ijk} = \mu +$
(effect of intertidal zone)$_i +$
(effect of randomly chosen site)$_j +$
(interaction between zone and site)$_{ij} + \varepsilon_{ijk}$ (9.15)

In models 9.13 and 9.15 we find the following.

y_{ijk} is the density of oysters from the kth quadrat from the combination of the ith zone and jth site.

μ is the overall (constant) population mean density of oysters.

α_i is effect of the ith zone on the density of oysters, pooling all possible sites.

β_j is a random variable with a mean of zero and a variance of σ_β^2, measuring the variance in mean density of oysters across all possible sites that could have been used, pooling zones.

$(\alpha\beta)_{ij}$ is a random variable with a mean of zero and a variance of $\sigma_{\alpha\beta}^2$ measuring the variance of the interaction between zone and site across all possible sites that could have been used. Biologically, this interaction term measures whether the zone effect is consistent across all possible randomly chosen sites.

ε_{ijk} is random or unexplained error associated with the kth replicate quadrat from the combination of the ith level of zone and jth level of site. This measures the random error associated with the density of oysters in each quadrat.

Predicted values and residuals

If we replace the parameters in our model by their OLS estimates (Box 9.6), it turns out that the predicted or fitted values of the response variable from our linear model (9.13) are:

$$\hat{y}_{ijk} = \bar{y} + (\bar{y}_i - \bar{y}) + (\bar{y}_j - \bar{y}) + (\bar{y}_{ij} - \bar{y}_i - \bar{y}_j + \bar{y}) = \bar{y}_{ij} \quad (9.16)$$

So any predicted Y-value is predicted by the sample mean for the cell that contains the Y-value. For example, the predicted number of egg masses per limpet for enclosure one in spring for the density of eight limpets is the sample cell mean for spring for the density of eight limpets.

The error terms (ε_{ijk}) from the linear model can be estimated by the residuals, where a residual

(e_{ijk}) is simply the difference between each observed and predicted Y-value:

$$e_{ijk} = y_{ijk} - \bar{y}_{ij} \quad (9.17)$$

For example, the residuals from the model relating number of egg masses per limpet to limpet density, season and their interaction are the differences between the observed number of egg masses per limpet in each enclosure and the mean number of egg masses per limpet from the enclosures within each limpet density and season combination that contained that enclosure. Note that the sum of the residuals within each cell ($\sum_{k=1}^{n} e_{ijk}$) equals zero. As in all linear models, residuals provide the basis of the OLS estimate of σ_ε^2 and they are valuable diagnostic tools for checking assumptions and fit of our model (Section 9.2.8). The OLS estimate of σ_ε^2 is the sample variance of these residuals and is termed the Residual (or Error) mean square and is calculated as part of the partitioning of the total variation in the response variable described in the next section.

9.2.2 Analysis of variance

The ANOVA table for a two factor factorial design with equal sample sizes per cell is shown in Table 9.8. The SS_A measures the sum of squared differences between each A marginal mean and the overall mean; the SS_B measures the sum of squared differences between each B marginal mean and the overall mean; the SS_{AB} measures the sum of squared differences for a particular contrast involving cell means, marginal means and the overall mean; $SS_{Residual}$ measures the difference between each replicate observation and the appropriate cell mean, summed across all cells. These SS represent an additive partitioning of the total SS in the response variable:

$$SS_{Total} = SS_A + SS_B + SS_{AB} + SS_{Residual} \quad (9.18)$$

In unbalanced designs (unequal n), there is no simple additive partitioning of the SS_{Total}, which causes some difficulties in the ANOVA. There are three different ways of determining the SS that represent very different philosophies for handling unequal sample sizes and we will discuss these in Section 9.2.6.

The degrees of freedom are calculated as usual (the number of components making up the

Table 9.8 | ANOVA table for two factor crossed model

Source	SS	df	MS
A	$nq \sum_{i=1}^{p} (\bar{y}_i - \bar{y})^2$	$p - 1$	$\dfrac{SS_A}{p - 1}$
B	$np \sum_{j=1}^{q} (\bar{y}_j - \bar{y})^2$	$q - 1$	$\dfrac{SS_B}{q - 1}$
AB	$n \sum_{i=1}^{p} \sum_{j=1}^{q} (\bar{y}_{ij} - \bar{y}_i - \bar{y}_j + \bar{y})^2$	$(p-1)(q-1)$	$\dfrac{SS_{AB}}{(p-1)(q-1)}$
Residual	$\sum_{i=1}^{p} \sum_{j=1}^{q} \sum_{k=1}^{n} (y_{ijk} - \bar{y}_{ij})^2$	$pq(n-1)$	$\dfrac{SS_{Residual}}{(pq(n-1)}$
Total	$\sum_{i=1}^{p} \sum_{j=1}^{q} \sum_{k=1}^{n} (y_{ijk} - \bar{y})^2$	$pqn - 1$	

Table 9.9 | Expected mean squares for a two factor crossed ANOVA model with both factors fixed (Model 1) or random (Model 2)

	A, B fixed	A, B random
MS_A	$\sigma_\varepsilon^2 + nq \dfrac{\sum_{i=1}^{p} \alpha_i^2}{p - 1}$	$\sigma_\varepsilon^2 + n\sigma_{\alpha\beta}^2 + nq\sigma_\alpha^2$
MS_B	$\sigma_\varepsilon^2 + np \dfrac{\sum_{j=1}^{q} \beta_j^2}{q - 1}$	$\sigma_\varepsilon^2 + n\sigma_{\alpha\beta}^2 + np\sigma_\beta^2$
MS_{AB}	$\sigma_\varepsilon^2 + n \dfrac{\sum_{i=1}^{p} \sum_{j=1}^{q} (\alpha\beta)_{ij}^2}{(p-1)(q-1)}$	$\sigma_\varepsilon^2 + n\sigma_{\alpha\beta}^2$
$MS_{Residual}$	σ_ε^2	σ_ε^2

variance minus one), with the df_{AB} being a product of the df_A and df_B.

The SS are divided by the df to produce mean squares (MS or variances) as we have done previously for single factor and nested ANOVA models. Statisticians have determined what population values these sample mean squares estimate, i.e. what their expected values are, if the assumption of homogeneity of variance holds (Table 9.9, Table 9.10). For all three models (fixed effects, random

effects and mixed effects), the $MS_{Residual}$ estimates σ_ε^2 (the variation in the error terms in each cell, pooled across all cells). The expected values for MS_A, MS_B and MS_{AB} depend critically on whether the factors are fixed or random. When both factors A and B are fixed, the mean squares estimate the residual variance plus a measure of the fixed factor or interaction effects. When both factors are random, MS_{AB} estimates the residual variance plus the added variance due to the interaction

Table 9.10 Expected mean squares for a two versions of a two factor crossed mixed ANOVA model (Model 3: A fixed, B random): restricted version imposes constraints on interaction terms and unrestricted imposes no such constraints

	Restricted version	Unrestricted version
MS_A	$\sigma_\varepsilon^2 + n\sigma_{\alpha\beta}^2 + nq\dfrac{\sum_{i=1}^{p}\alpha_i^2}{p-1}$	$\sigma_\varepsilon^2 + n\sigma_{\alpha\beta}^2 + nq\dfrac{\sum_{i=1}^{p}\alpha_i^2}{p-1}$
MS_B	$\sigma_\varepsilon^2 + np\sigma_\beta^2$	$\sigma_\varepsilon^2 + n\sigma_{\alpha\beta}^2 + np\sigma_\beta^2$
MS_{AB}	$\sigma_\varepsilon^2 + n\sigma_{\alpha\beta}^2$	$\sigma_\varepsilon^2 + n\sigma_{\alpha\beta}^2$
$MS_{Residual}$	σ_ε^2	σ_ε^2

terms, the mean squares for the main effects estimate the residual variance plus the added variance due to the interaction terms plus the added variance due to the random main effect of the relevant factor.

Things get even messier when we have a mixed model (A fixed, B random). The two alternative approaches for mixed models for factorial ANOVAs described in Box 9.7 produce different expected mean squares (Table 9.10), and the choice between the two versions of the mixed model has created much discussion in the statistical literature (Box 9.7). We recommend Model I, which results in MS_{AB} estimating the residual variance plus the added variance due to the interaction terms, MS_B estimating the residual variance plus the added variance due to the random main effect of B and MS_A estimating the residual variance plus the added variance due to the interaction terms plus the fixed factor A effects. The expectation for the mean square of the fixed factor in a two factor mixed model includes three components: the residual variance, the interaction variance and fixed factor effects.

As we will see in the next section, the different approaches to determining expected mean squares in ANOVA models have critical implications for the construction of hypothesis tests. The expected values for mean squares in three factor random and mixed models are even more complicated but following the Model I approach, the same general principles apply. Expected mean

squares for fixed factors and their interactions will include terms for variance due to higher order random interactions (Table 9.10). Many texts provide algorithms for calculating expected mean squares for any number and combination of fixed and random factors (e.g. Neter *et al.* 1996, Underwood 1997, Winer *et al.* 1991).

9.2.3 Null hypotheses

There are three general H_0s we can test in a two factor factorial ANOVA. The first two are tests of main effects and the third is the test of the interaction. The specific null hypotheses being tested in a factorial linear model depend on whether the factors are fixed or random (see Box 9.8 for terminology).

Fixed effects models

FACTOR A

$H_0(A)$: $\mu_1 = \mu_2 = ... = \mu_i = ... = \mu_p$. This H_0 states there is no difference between the marginal means for factor A pooling over the levels of factor B (Table 9.7). For example, no difference in the mean number of egg masses per limpet for each level of density, pooling over the two seasons (Quinn 1988). This is equivalent to $H_0(A)$: $\alpha_1 = \alpha_2 = ... = \alpha_i = 0$, i.e. no effect of any level of factor A pooling over the levels of factor B. For example, no effect of any of the four densities on the mean number of egg masses per limpet, pooling the two seasons.

Box 9.7 | The mixed factorial model and the mixed models controversy

Return to model 9.13 for a factorial design with two factors:

$$y_{ijk} = \mu + \alpha_i + \beta_j + (\alpha\beta)_{ij} + \varepsilon_{ijk}$$

When one of the factors, such as B, is random then two modifications occur. First, β_j is a random variable with a mean of zero and, most importantly, a variance of σ_β^2 measuring the variance in mean values of the response variable across all the possible levels of factor B that could have been used. Second, $(\alpha\beta)_{ij}$ is a random variable with a mean of zero and a variance of $\sigma_{\alpha\beta}^2$ (well, strictly $[(p-1)/p]\sigma_{\alpha\beta}^2$ to simplify the expected values of the mean squares – see Neter et al. 1996) measuring the variance across all the possible interaction terms. This interaction term measures whether the fixed effect of A is consistent across all possible randomly chosen levels of B.

To estimate the parameters of this model, we impose two sum-to-zero constraints. The first implies that the sum of the effects of the fixed factor A, pooling B, is zero and is the same as we used for the fixed effects model.

$$\sum_{i=1}^{p} \alpha_i = 0$$

The second implies that the sum of the interaction effects across the levels of A is also zero:

$$\sum_{i=1}^{p} (\alpha\beta)_{ij} = 0$$

This constraint also defines a covariance between pairs of interaction terms within each level of factor B, i.e. any two interaction terms will not be independent within each level of B. Using the Minchinton & Ross (1999) example, this model allows for the limpet densities per quadrat within a site to be positively or negatively correlated. The version of the mixed model that imposes this constraint originates with Scheffé (1959) and is termed the restricted (or Σ-restricted) model (Neter et al. 1996, Searle et al. 1992), also Model I in Ayres & Thomas (1990) and the constrained parameters (CP) model (Voss 1999), and is the version most commonly presented in linear models texts.

An alternative model (Model II) is one that does not impose any restrictions on the interaction terms and is termed, not surprisingly, the unrestricted model or the unconstrained parameters model (Voss 1999). This model implies that any two interaction terms are independent, within each level of A and B, and is recommended by a number of influential authors, including Hocking (1996), Milliken & Johnson (1984) and Searle et al. (1992). Using the Minchinton & Ross (1999) example, this model assumes that the covariance of limpet densities per quadrat within a site is the same for each pair of zones.

The two approaches for mixed models result in different expected mean squares (Table 9.10). Model I results in MS_{AB} estimating the residual variance plus the added variance due to the interaction terms, MS_B estimating the residual variance plus the added variance due to the random main effect of B and MS_A estimating the residual variance plus the added variance due to the interaction terms plus the fixed factor A effects. The alternative approach (Model II) results in a different expectation for MS_B, which now estimates the residual variance plus the variance due to the interaction and the variance due to the random main effect of B. Note that the difference in the two approaches is only in the expectation for the mean square for the random factor, not the fixed factor or the interaction.

The expected mean squares in Table 9.10 indicate that the test of the random factor B will be different under the two models because the expectation of MS_B changes. Under the unrestricted Model II, B should be tested against the MS_{AB}, in contrast to Model I where it is tested against the $MS_{Residual}$. Which version of the mixed model is most appropriate for testing main effects of factor B has been an issue of considerable debate among statisticians (Hocking 1985, Schwarz 1993, Searle et al. 1992, Voss 1999) and among biologists (Ayres & Thomas 1990, Fry 1992), although the discussion will be difficult for most biologists to appreciate as it involves a reasonably high level of statistical detail. Ayres & Thomas (1990) argued that the covariance assumptions behind Model II (i.e. independent interaction effects) need to be carefully assessed before it could be applied (but see also Fry 1992). It is difficult to determine, in most cases, whether biological data are likely to meet the assumption of completely independent interaction terms.

Voss (1999) proposed that the test for factor B based on Model I is correct no matter which of the two alternative formulations for expected mean squares are used for the mixed model. He argued that the H_0 for no main effects of factor B in Model II is actually that $\sigma_{\alpha\beta}^2 = \sigma_{\beta}^2 = 0$ which results in the same F-ratio test as in Model I. Voss (1999) claimed that this effectively resolved the controversy over expected mean squares for random factors in mixed models and their subsequent hypothesis tests.

In a more radical approach, Nelder & Lane (1995) proposed that usual sum-to-zero constraints imposed when using overparameterized effects models (Box 9.6) are unnecessary and pointed out that if we don't apply such constraints, the expected mean squares for factors A and B both include the effect of the interaction. Indeed, the expected mean squares, and F-ratios for hypothesis tests, for each term become basically identical for all combinations of fixed and random factors. Under this model for expected mean squares, which is not conventional, testing fixed main effects is relevant even in the presence of interactions because we are testing for the effect of the fixed factor over and above the interaction. Expected mean squares and appropriate hypothesis tests in factorial ANOVA models are obviously still a topic of research and debate among statisticians.

FACTOR B

$H_0(B)$: $\mu_1 = \mu_2 = \ldots = \mu_j = \ldots = \mu_q$. This H_0 states there is no difference between the marginal means for factor B pooling over the levels of factor A (Table 9.7). For example, no difference in the mean number of egg masses per limpet for each level of season, pooling over the four densities (Quinn 1988). This is equivalent to $H_0(B)$: $\beta_1 = \beta_2 = \ldots = \beta_j = 0$, i.e. no effect of any level of factor B pooling over the levels of factor A. For example, no effect of either of the two seasons on the mean number of egg masses per limpet, pooling the four densities.

INTERACTION BETWEEN A AND B

$H_0(AB)$: $\mu_{ij} - \mu_i - \mu_j + \mu = 0$ for all levels of A and all levels of B. This is testing that there are no effects in addition to the overall mean and the main effects. For example, there are no effects on the mean number of egg masses per limpet besides

Table 9.11 | *F*-ratios used for testing main effects and interactions in a two factor ANOVA model for different combinations of fixed and random factors

Source	A and B fixed	A and B random	A fixed, B random Restricted version	A fixed, B random Unrestricted version
A	$\dfrac{MS_A}{MS_{Residual}}$	$\dfrac{MS_A}{MS_{AB}}$	$\dfrac{MS_A}{MS_{AB}}$	$\dfrac{MS_A}{MS_{AB}}$
B	$\dfrac{MS_B}{MS_{Residual}}$	$\dfrac{MS_B}{MS_{AB}}$	$\dfrac{MS_B}{MS_{Residual}}$	$\dfrac{MS_B}{MS_{AB}}$
AB	$\dfrac{MS_{AB}}{MS_{Residual}}$	$\dfrac{MS_{AB}}{MS_{Residual}}$	$\dfrac{MS_{AB}}{MS_{Residual}}$	$\dfrac{MS_{AB}}{MS_{Residual}}$

Box 9.8 | **Terminology used for identifying fixed and random effects in expected mean squares**

- D_p, D_q and D_r reflect the terminology presented in Winer *et al.* (1991) for fixed and random factors. $D_p = 1 - p/P$, where p is the number of levels of factor A, and P is the possible number of levels. q and r denote the levels of factors B and C, respectively. If A is a fixed factor, then the p levels represent all possible levels, so $p = P$ and $D_p = 0$. If A is random, the p levels are assumed to be a (very small) sample of a population of possible levels, and $p/P = 0$, so $D_p = 1$.
- n represents the number of replicates at each combination of A, B and C.
- Terms associated with factors A, B and C are denoted by Greek letters α, β and γ, respectively.
- σ_α^2 refers to an added variance component when factor A is random and to the variance between fixed A group means ($\sum_{i=1}^p \alpha_i^2/(p-1)$) when factor A is fixed. Similar definitions apply for other terms.

---

the main effects of density and season (Quinn 1988). This is equivalent to $H_0(AB)$: $(\alpha\beta)_{ij} = 0$, i.e. no interaction between factor A and factor B; the effect of A is the same at all levels of B and the effect of B is the same at all levels of A. For example, the effect of density on the mean number of egg masses per limpet is the same in both seasons and the effect of season on the mean number of egg masses per limpet is the same for all four densities.

F-RATIOS

We can test these H_0s by seeing which of our mean squares have the same expected value when the H_0 is true (Table 9.9). The *F*-ratios for testing these H_0s are provided in Table 9.11. It is clear that MS_A and

$MS_{Residual}$ have the same expected value when there is no effect of factor A so these two mean squares are used in an *F*-ratio to test the $H_0(A)$. MS_B and $MS_{Residual}$ have the same expected value when there is no effect of factor B so these two mean squares are used in an *F*-ratio to test the $H_0(B)$. Finally, MS_{AB} and $MS_{Residual}$ have the same expected value when there is no effect of the interaction between A and B so these two mean squares are used in an *F*-ratio to test the $H_0(AB)$.

The degrees of freedom associated with these *F*-ratios are simply the df associated with the two terms. For example, the df for the *F*-ratio testing the interaction H_0 are $(p-1)(q-1)$ and $pq(n-1)$. The *F*-ratios are compared to an *F* distribution and conclusions about whether to reject or not reject the H_0 are drawn in the usual manner. The worked example from Quinn (1988) in Box 9.4 illustrates these tests for a fixed effects model.

Random effects models

With random factors, our focus is on tests of added variance components, rather than differences between the means of the chosen groups.

FACTOR A

$H_0(A)$: $\sigma_\alpha^2 = 0$, i.e. no added variance due to all possible levels of factor A that could have been used. For example, there is no added variance in the number of meals eaten by sawfly larvae due to all possible species of sawflies that Kause et al. (1999) could have used.

FACTOR B

$H_0(B)$: $\sigma_\beta^2 = 0$, i.e. no added variance due to all possible levels of factor B that could have been used. For example, there is no added variance in the number of meals eaten by sawfly larvae due to all possible trees that Kause et al. (1999) could have used.

INTERACTION BETWEEN A AND B

$H_0(AB)$: $\sigma_{\alpha\beta}^2 = 0$, i.e. no added variance due to any of the interaction effects between all possible levels of factor A and factor B that could have been used. For example, there is no added variance in the number of meals eaten by sawfly larvae due to any interaction between all possible species of sawflies and all possible trees that Kause et al. (1999) could have used in their study.

F-RATIOS

We can again test these H_0s by seeing which of our mean squares have the same expected value when the H_0 is true (Table 9.9, Table 9.11). The F-ratio for $H_0(A)$ uses MS_A and MS_{AB}, because the expected value for MS_A includes the interaction variance. The F-ratio for $H_0(B)$ uses MS_B and MS_{AB}, because the expected value for MS_B also includes the interaction variance. The F-ratio for $H_0(AB)$ uses MS_{AB} and $MS_{Residual}$ as in the fixed effects model.

Mixed effects models

The null hypotheses for main effects in a mixed model are basically the same as those in fixed and random effects models, for fixed and random

factors respectively. Let us assume that factor A is fixed and factor B is random and that we are using the traditional Model I values of the expected mean squares, i.e. imposing constraints on the interaction terms (Box 9.7).

FACTOR A (FIXED)

H_0: $\mu_1 = \mu_2 = \ldots = \mu_i = \ldots = \mu_p$. This H_0 states there is no difference between the marginal means for Factor A pooling over the levels of factor B. For example, no difference in the mean density of oysters per quadrat for each zone, pooling over all possible randomly chosen sites (Minchinton & Ross 1999). This is equivalent to H_0: $\alpha_1 = \alpha_2 = \ldots = \alpha_i = 0$, i.e. no effect of any level of factor A pooling over the levels of factor B. For example, no effect of any of the four zones on mean density of oysters per quadrat, pooling all possible sites.

FACTOR B (RANDOM)

H_0: $\sigma_\beta^2 = 0$, i.e. no added variance due to all possible levels of factor B that could have been used. For example, there is no added variance in the density of oysters per quadrat due to all possible sites that Minchinton & Ross (1999) could have used, pooling the four zones.

INTERACTION BETWEEN A AND B

The null hypothesis for the interaction term, which is considered a random variable even though it is an interaction between a fixed effect and a random variable, is H_0: $\sigma_{\alpha\beta}^2 = 0$, i.e. no added variance due to any of the interaction effects between the fixed levels of factor A and all possible levels of factor B that could have been used. When either factor is random, then the interaction is random because it represents a subset (depending on the levels of the random factor chosen) of all the possible interactions (Underwood 1997). For the Minchinton & Ross (1999) study, this H_0 is that there is no added variance in the density of oysters per quadrat due to any interaction between the fixed zones and all possible sites that could have been used.

F-RATIOS

We again test these H_0s by seeing which of our mean squares have the same expected value when the H_0 is true (Table 9.10). The F-ratios for

Table 9.12 | Main effects and interaction effects as sets of contrasts among marginal and cell means

(a)

	B_1	B_2	B_3	A marginal means
A_1	μ_{11}	μ_{12}	μ_{13}	μ_{A1}
A_2	μ_{21}	μ_{22}	μ_{23}	μ_{A2}
A_3	μ_{31}	μ_{32}	μ_{33}	μ_{A3}
B marginal means	μ_{B1}	μ_{B2}	μ_{B3}	

(b) H_0: no effects of A

Set 1	Set 2	Set 3
$H_0: \mu_{A1} - \mu_{A2} = 0$	$H_0: \mu_{A1} - \mu_{A2} = 0$	$H_0: \mu_{A1} - \mu_{A3} = 0$
$H_0: \mu_{A2} - \mu_{A3} = 0$	$H_0: \mu_{A1} - \mu_{A3} = 0$	$H_0: \mu_{A2} - \mu_{A3} = 0$

(c) H_0: no interaction effects

Effect of A same at each level of B		Effect of B same at each level of A	
Set 1	Set 2	Set 1	Set 2
$\mu_{11} - \mu_{21} - \mu_{12} + \mu_{22} = 0$	$\mu_{11} - \mu_{21} - \mu_{12} + \mu_{22} = 0$	$\mu_{11} - \mu_{12} - \mu_{21} + \mu_{22} = 0$	$\mu_{11} - \mu_{12} - \mu_{21} + \mu_{22} = 0$
$\mu_{12} - \mu_{22} - \mu_{13} + \mu_{23} = 0$	$\mu_{11} - \mu_{21} - \mu_{13} + \mu_{23} = 0$	$\mu_{21} - \mu_{22} - \mu_{31} + \mu_{32} = 0$	$\mu_{11} - \mu_{12} - \mu_{31} + \mu_{32} = 0$
$\mu_{21} - \mu_{31} - \mu_{22} + \mu_{32} = 0$	$\mu_{11} - \mu_{31} - \mu_{12} + \mu_{32} = 0$	$\mu_{12} - \mu_{13} - \mu_{22} + \mu_{23} = 0$	$\mu_{11} - \mu_{13} - \mu_{21} + \mu_{23} = 0$
$\mu_{22} - \mu_{32} - \mu_{23} + \mu_{33} = 0$	$\mu_{11} - \mu_{31} - \mu_{13} + \mu_{33} = 0$	$\mu_{22} - \mu_{23} - \mu_{32} + \mu_{33} = 0$	$\mu_{11} - \mu_{13} - \mu_{31} + \mu_{33} = 0$

testing these H_0s are provided in Table 9.11. It is clear that MS_A and MS_{AB} have the same expected value when there is no effect of factor A so these two mean squares are used in an F-ratio to test the $H_0(A)$. In contrast, the F-ratio for the $H_0(B)$ of no effect of the random factor B uses MS_B and $MS_{Residual}$. Finally, the F-ratio for the $H_0(AB)$ of no effect of the interaction between A and B uses MS_{AB} and $MS_{Residual}$ as in the fixed and random effects models.

9.2.4 What are main effects and interactions really measuring?

Fixed effects models

Main effects and interactions can be considered as a set of orthogonal (independent) contrasts between marginal means or cell means (Table 9.12(a)). The SS_A is simply the sum of the SS for two independent contrasts among the A marginal means. With three levels of A, the two contrasts in

any of the three sets in Table 9.12(b) make up the main effect of A. Similar contrasts can be generated for factor B. Remember from Chapter 8 that the number of independent contrasts possible will be the number of df for that factor. Contrasts between cell means can be determined for interaction effects. For example, if we consider the interaction as the effect of A at each level of B, then one set of four independent contrasts would include the difference between A_1 and A_2 at B_1 and B_2 at B_2 and B_3, and the difference between A_2 and A_3 at B_1 and B_2 and at B_2 and B_3, as indicated in the first column of Table 9.12(c). The sum of the SS for these contrasts will be SS_{AB}. There are other sets of independent interaction contrasts, for both the effect of A at each level of B and the effect of B at each level of A. The sum of the SS for the contrasts within any of these sets will be SS_{AB}. Milliken & Johnson (1984) provide clear examples and formulae for determining these contrasts. Understanding these contrasts is important when

Table 9.13 Illustration of interactions for an artifical two factor design with two levels of each factor.

(a)

	B_1	B_2	Marginal A means	$\beta\,(\mu_2-\mu_1)$
A_1	5	12.5	8.75	7.5
A_2	10	17.5	13.75	7.5
Marginal B means	7.5	15	11.25	
$\alpha\,(\mu_2-\mu_1)$	5	5		

(b)

	B_1	B_2	Marginal A means	$\beta\,(\mu_2-\mu_1)$	$\beta\,(\log\mu_2-\log\mu_1)$
A_1	5 (0.699)	10 (1.000)	7.5	5	0.301
A_2	10 (1.000)	20 (1.301)	15	10	0.301
Marginal B means	7.5	15	11.25		
$\alpha\,(\mu_2-\mu_1)$	5	10			
$\alpha\,(\log\mu_2-\log\mu_1)$	0.301	0.301			

(c)

	B_1	B_2	Marginal A means	$\beta\,(\mu_2-\mu_1)$	$\beta\,(\log\mu_2-\log\mu_1)$
A_1	5 (0.699)	20 (1.301)	12.5	15	0.602
A_2	10 (1.000)	10 (1.000)	10	0	0.000
Marginal B means	7.5	15	11.25		
$\alpha\,(\mu_2-\mu_1)$	5	-10			
$\alpha\,(\log\mu_2-\log\mu_1)$	0.301	-0.301			

Note:
Middle entries are cell means with $\log_{10}$ values in parentheses. Marginal means are also provided. (a) No interaction (all $(\alpha\beta)_{ij}=0$) where the effect of A is the same at each level of B and vice versa. (b) Simple interaction (all $(\alpha\beta)_{ij}=\pm1.25$) where the effect of A is greater at B_2 compared to B_1 and the effect of B is greater at A_2 compared to A_1. Note interaction effects removed by log transformation (all $(\alpha\beta)_{ij}=0$). (c) More complex interaction (all $(\alpha\beta)_{ij}=\pm3.75$) where the effect of A is in the opposite direction at B_2 compared to B_1 and there is no effect of B at A_2 but a strong effect at A_1. Note interaction not removed by log transformation.

we are dealing with designs with missing cells (Section 9.2.6). Note that with unbalanced designs (unequal sample sizes), the sum of the contrasts won't add to the SS for the relevant factor or interaction (Section 9.2.6).

Let's look at the meaning of the interaction term in more detail, by comparing three possible configurations of cell means in a design with two levels of two fixed factors (Table 9.13). In the first example (Table 9.13(a)), there are effects of A and B (both sets of marginal means differ) but no interaction between the two factors. The effect of A is the same at each level of B (a change by five units) and the effect of B is the same at each level of A (a change by 7.5 units). All the $(\mu_{ij}-\mu_i-\mu_j+\mu)$ equal zero, indicating no interaction. No interaction indicates the effects of factor A and factor B are additive and independent of each other, i.e. the response variable can be predicted by just the two main effects.

In the second example (Table 9.13(b)), there are also effects of both A and B as both sets of marginal means differ. More importantly, there is an interaction between the two factors. The effect of A is different at each level of B (five unit change at B_1 and ten unit change at B_2) and the effect of B is different at each level of A, although the effects are consistently in the same direction. The differences

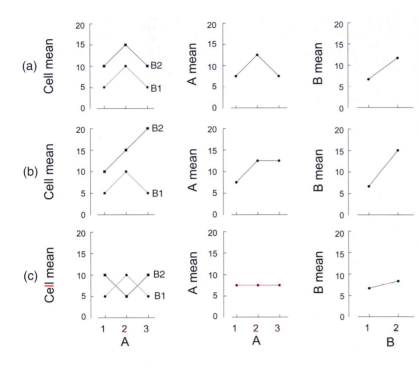

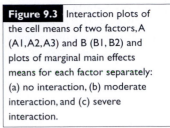

Figure 9.3 Interaction plots of the cell means of two factors, A (A1, A2, A3) and B (B1, B2) and plots of marginal main effects means for each factor separately: (a) no interaction, (b) moderate interaction, and (c) severe interaction.

second factor. The main effect of a given factor (comparison of marginal means) pools over the levels of the other factor, which is not appropriate if the effects of the two factors are not independent. Figure 9.3 shows a range of interactions between two factors; note that interactions can be moderate (B2 greater than B1 for all levels of A but relative size of difference varies) or severe (B2 greater than B1 for A1 and A3 but this difference is reversed for A2). Underwood (1981, 1997) provided clear examples of how large interactions can result in misleading interpretation of non-significant main effects in an ecological context. He showed how a strong interaction could result in non-significant main effects when the main effects were actually strong, they were just not consistent across the levels of the other factor.

This suggests that there should be a sequence of hypothesis tests for fixed effects factorial ANOVAs. Most textbooks recommend testing the H_0 of no interaction first. If this test is not significant, then tests of main effects can proceed. If the interaction is significant, then tests of main effects will be difficult to interpret. Neter *et al.* (1996) suggested a modification of this strategy. They argued that interactions can still be significant without precluding interpretation of main effects and recommended seeing if interactions are "important" before deciding whether main effects can be examined, although defining important interactions is subjective. One of the arguments for still interpreting main effects in the presence of an interaction is that it is difficult to envisage a significant interaction producing

between marginal means do not simply reflect the effects of each factor. All the $(\mu_{ij} - \mu_i - \mu_j + \mu)$ equal ± 1.25, indicating an interaction.

In the third example (Table 9.13(c)), there is a more complex interaction. Note that the marginal means indicate only a small effect of A (minus 2.5 units from A_1 to A_2). It is clear from the cell means, however, that there is actually an opposite effect of A at each level of B (plus five unit change at B_1 and minus ten unit change at B_2). A similar result occurs for B. The marginal means suggest a strong effect (plus 7.5 units from B_1 to B_2), whereas the cell means show only a strong effect of B at A_1 and no effect at A_2. Neither set of marginal means represents a consistent effect for each factor. All the $(\mu_{ij} - \mu_i - \mu_j + \mu)$ equal ± 3.75, indicating a stronger interaction than the previous example. In both Table 9.13(b) and (c), the interaction indicates the effects of factor A and factor B are multiplicative, i.e. the response variable cannot be predicted by just the two main effects.

If there are interactions then interpretation of main effects becomes more difficult. Remember that an interaction is telling us that the main effects are not independent of each other, i.e. the effect of one factor depends on the levels of the significant main effects where no real effects exist. Indeed, the examples in Underwood (1981, 1997) illustrated misleading non-significant main effects in the presence of an interaction.

We generally agree with the traditional approach that says that main effects may be difficult to interpret in the presence of statistically significant interactions when all factors are fixed and we recommend that examining the nature of the interaction is the most sensible strategy when it is clearly significant. Significant main effects may still be of interest despite an interaction but common sense must be used. Non-significant main effects in the presence of interactions won't have much meaning. In fact, interactions are often of as much biological interest as the main effects. For example, in the study of Quinn (1988), the interaction between density and season was of most interest because it would reflect changing effects of intraspecific competition when food availability changes. Interactions should not just be treated as a nuisance in factorial ANOVA models. They presumably are of considerable interest, which is why a factorial design has been used, and they nearly always offer important biological insights. There are numerous techniques for further exploring the nature of interactions in the context of factorial ANOVAs (Section 9.2.10).

Random effects models

Because the expected values of the mean squares for factors A and B both include the variance among interaction terms, the H_0s for the main effects are actually testing for a non-zero variance component over and above any random interaction effects. Therefore, the presence of an interaction does not cause problems for interpreting tests of main effects. Nonetheless, the tests of main effects will be less powerful in the presence of an interaction because the denominator of the F-ratio (MS_{AB}) will increase relatively more than the numerator (MS_A or MS_B). So strong interactions between the random factors will make main effects difficult to detect.

Mixed effects models

Irrespective of which version we use for a mixed model (Box 9.7, Table 9.10), the expected mean square for the fixed factor includes the variance component for the interaction term. Therefore, the test for the fixed factor actually tests for the effects of the fixed factor *over and above* the variation due to the interaction and the residual. So when one factor is random, the test of the fixed main effect is potentially interpretable even in the presence of an interaction. This is actually the justification for being able to test main treatment effects in a simple randomized blocks design even though there is no test for a block–treatment interaction, as long as the blocks factor is random (Chapter 10). Applying the Model I version of the mixed model, the tests of the random factor and the random interaction term will both use $MS_{Residual}$ as the denominator for the F-ratio. If we use the alternative Model II version of the mixed model, the test for the random factor changes – see discussion in Box 9.7.

Sometimes we might have a random factor with only a few levels, e.g. for practical/logistic reasons, we can only sample two or three randomly chosen sites. This causes problems because the interaction term used to test the fixed factor will not have many degrees of freedom and the test of the fixed effect may not be very powerful. This makes sense because our ability to generalize to a population of levels of a random factor should depend on how well we have sampled this population, i.e. how many levels of the random factor we use. This also explains why, when one factor is random, it is the F test of the fixed factor that changes. Rather than concluding whether there is an effect of the fixed factor, pooling only over the specific levels of another fixed factor, we wish to conclude whether there is a general effect of the fixed factor, pooling over all the possible levels of a random factor. We might expect such a test to be less powerful and to use a different error term.

To illustrate, consider the study by Losos (1995) who examined the survivorship of seedlings two species of palms in a coastal tropical forest in Peru. Along two randomly located transects, she defined four different successional zones running from the beach into the forest: early-seral near the beach, mid-seral and then late-seral further into the forest, and a zone dominated by a broad-leaved monocot, *Heliconia*, that may occur anywhere along the sequence. She transplanted seedlings into five plots within each zone and

Table 9.14 Two factor mixed model ANOVA from Losos (1995), where successional zone is a fixed factor and transect is a random factor. The effect of successional zone is tested against the successional zone by transect interaction with 3 and 3 df

Source	df	MS	F	P
Successional zone	3	0.060	0.31	0.819
Transect	1	0.045	3.10	0.041
Successional zone × transect	3	0.191	13.33	<0.001
Residual	30	0.014		

transect combination. A two factor model was used to analyze survivorship, with successional zone as a fixed factor and transect as a random factor (Table 9.14). The effect of successional zone, the main effect of interest, is tested against the interaction with only three and three df. In this example, the interaction was strongly significant, indicating spatial variation in the effect of successional zone on seedling survivorship. She could not reject the H_0 of no effects of successional zone over and above any variance due to the interaction.

This emphasizes an important design principle in factorial ANOVAs. When a random factor is included, it nearly always represents replication that affects the power of the test for the fixed factor (Section 9.2.13). If we cannot include many levels of the random factor, we need to decide whether we would be better to restrict our study to a single level of the random factor (e.g. a single site) but be much more confident of whether there are fixed factor effects.

9.2.5 Comparing ANOVA models

The methods we have described in Chapter 8 and Section 9.1.5 for comparing the fit of full and reduced models to test whether a particular model parameter equals zero are just as appropriate to factorial models. For example, to test the H_0 that $(\alpha\beta)_{ij}$ equals zero, i.e. no interaction in a fixed effects model, we can compare the fit of the full model:

$$y_{ijk} = \mu + \alpha_i + \beta_j + (\alpha\beta)_{ij} + \varepsilon_{ijk} \qquad (9.13)$$

to the fit of the reduced model that omits the term specified in the H_0:

$$y_{ijk} = \mu + \alpha_i + \beta_j + \varepsilon_{ijk} \qquad (9.19)$$

Using the example from Quinn (1988), we compare the full model:

(no. egg masses per limpet)$_{ijk}$ = μ + (effect of season)$_i$ + (effect of density)$_j$ + (interaction between season and density)$_{ij}$ + ε_{ijk} (9.14)

to the reduced model:

(no. egg masses per limpet)$_{ijk}$ = μ + (effect of season)$_i$ + (effect of density)$_j$ + ε_{ijk} (9.20)

Thus, we compare the fits of additive (no interaction) and multiplicative (with interaction) models (9.13 and 9.19). The difference in fit of these two models is simply the difference in their $SS_{Residual}$. This difference can be converted to a mean square by dividing by the difference in the $df_{Residual}$. The H_0 of no difference in fit of the two models (i.e. $(\alpha\beta)_{ij}$ equals zero; no interactive effects between the two factors) can be tested with an F test using $MS_{Residual}$ of the full model as the denominator. With equal sample sizes per cell, this model comparison test will produce the same result as the traditional ANOVA test. With unequal sample sizes, this equality does not hold. In practice, most statistical software uses comparison of general linear models to determine SS and MS, and test hypotheses, about specific terms in ANOVA models. This approach, in contrast to the formulae in Table 9.8, generalizes to unbalanced designs and designs with more factors, including crossed and nested, and combinations of categorical and continuous variables.

9.2.6 Unbalanced designs

Studies involving categorical predictor variables should usually be designed with equal sample sizes for two main reasons. First, hypothesis tests are much more robust to the assumptions of normality and variance homogeneity (Chapter 8, Section 9.2.8) when sample sizes are equal. Second, estimation of variance components for random effects is more difficult with unequal sample sizes. However, it is common in biology to end up with unequal sample sizes, even if the

Table 9.15 | Types I, II and III SS for unbalanced two factor data

(a)

Source	df	Type I	Type II	Type III
Factor A (treatment)	1	347.145	281.077	282.752
Factor B (time)	2	2 884.336	2 884.336	2 869.265
A×B	2	131.912	131.912	131.912
Residual	23	234.400	234.400	234.400

(b)

Source	df	Type I	Type II	Type III
Factor A (location)	3	17 781.391	21 804.379	49 201.833
Factor B (functional group)	1	4 442.202	4 442.202	6 919.109
A×B	3	67 782.672	67 782.672	67 782.672
Residual	49	59 088.060	59 088.060	59 088.060

Notes:
(a) From Hall et al. (2000), where there are six cells with sample sizes of five in all cells except one that has only four observations. (b) From Reich et al. (1999), where there are eight cells with sample sizes of two, two, three, three, five, six, 15, and 21. In this example, the F-ratio test for functional group was only significant for Type III SS ($P = 0.020$) but not for Type I or II SS ($P = 0.061$).

study was originally designed with equal numbers of observations per cell. If the inequality of sample sizes is thought to be causally related to the factors, then it is probably useful to analyze the effect of the factors on the final number of replicates in each cell as a contingency table: see Shaw & Mitchell-Olds 1993 and Chapter 14. In many cases, unequal sample sizes are caused by random loss of observations or by practical constraints limiting the number of observations in some cells but not others. Besides the robustness issue, unequal sample sizes in factorial ANOVAs means that there is no simple additive partitioning of the SS_{Total} into components due to main effects and interactions and the formulae in Table 9.8 no longer apply. Also, the determination of expected values of mean squares can be difficult, especially when there are random factors.

Unbalanced multifactor designs are sometimes termed non-orthogonal. There are two levels of sample size imbalance in factorial ANOVAs. The first is when there are observations in every cell but the numbers of observations vary. The second, and more difficult, situation is when there are one or more cells with no observations.

Unequal sample sizes

A common situation in biology is where the sample sizes are unequal but all cells in the design have at least one observation. Again, we will focus on a two factor model, with two examples. Hall et al. (2000) did an experiment that examined the effects of nutrients (N and P) on the macroinvertebrate assemblages colonizing small artificial habitat units submersed in a shallow subtidal region in SE Australia. These artificial habitat units were loosely rolled sheets of porous cloth. The two factors were nutrients (two levels: control and added nutrients) and time (three levels: two, four and six months after deployment) and the response variable was species richness of macroinvertebrates. Five replicate units were collected from each treatment after each time period, except that one unit was lost on collection so one cell (control after six months) had only four replicates. The response variable is log numbers of individuals of macroinvertebrates per habitat unit. The analyses of these data are in Table 9.15(a).

Reich et al. (1999) examined the generality of traits of leaves from different species across a range of ecosystems and geographic regions. They sampled a number of species from different functional groups (three levels: forb, shrub, tree) and from different study sites and related ecosystems (six levels: Colorado–alpine tundra, North Carolina–humid temperate forest, New Mexico–desert grassland/woodland and pinyon–juniper woodland, South Carolina–warm temperate/subtropical forest, Venezuela–tropical rain forest, Wisconsin–cold temperate forest and prairie and alkaline fen/bog). To avoid completely missing cells, we will use a subset of their data, omitting Colorado and North Carolina and only using shrubs and trees. The response variable was specific leaf surface area, there were eight cells (four sites and two functional groups) and sample sizes (number of species) ranged from two to 21 per cell. The analyses of these data are in Table 9.15(b).

There are three different ways of calculating the SS for the main effects and the interaction when cell sizes vary, termed Types I, II and III SS. They all provide the same values of SS for the residual and interaction terms. The former is simply the sum of squared deviations between each observation and the overall mean, obtained from the $SS_{Residual}$ when the full model (with both main effects and an interaction) is fitted. The latter is based on the comparison of the fit of a full model with the fit of a reduced model without the interaction term.

The real difference between the methods for calculating SS with unbalanced designs is for the main effects and relates to the way that marginal means are calculated. The most common method is to use Type III SS that are based on unweighted marginal means and therefore are not influenced by the sample size in each cell (Table 9.15). In a model comparison framework, Type III SS for each main effect are calculated from the comparison of fitting the full model to the model without the main effect of interest. For example, to determine the SS_A, we compare the fit of the full model:

$$y_{ijk} = \mu + \alpha_i + \beta_j + (\alpha\beta)_{ij} + \varepsilon_{ijk} \tag{9.13}$$

$$\text{(no. species)}_{ijk} = \mu + \text{(nutrient)}_i + \text{(time)}_j + \text{(nutrient} \times \text{time)}_{ij} + \varepsilon_{ijk} \tag{9.21}$$

to the fit of the reduced model:

$$y_{ijk} = \mu + \beta_j + (\alpha\beta)_{ij} + \varepsilon_{ijk} \tag{9.22}$$

$$\text{(no. species)}_{ijk} = \mu + \text{(time)}_j + \text{(nutrient} \times \text{time)}_{ij} + \varepsilon_{ijk} \tag{9.23}$$

Many authorities on linear models recommended Type III SS for unbalanced multifactor ANOVAs (e.g. Maxwell & Delaney 1990, Milliken & Johnson 1984, Searle 1993, Yandell 1997), a recommendation for ecologists supported by Shaw & Mitchell-Olds (1993). This recommendation is because tests of main effect hypotheses using Type III SS are based on unweighted means, rather than means that depend on the sample size within specific cells. Searle (1993) pointed out that Type III SS were the equivalent of his preferred SS developed using the cell means model, although we argue that the effects model is conceptually easier for biologists to understand because the traditional main effects and interaction terms are explicit.

Type I SS are determined from the improvement in fit gained by adding each term to the model in a hierarchical sequence. For example, SS_A is determined by comparing the fit of the models:

$$y_{ijk} = \mu + \alpha_i + \varepsilon_{ijk} \tag{9.24}$$

$$\text{(no. species)}_{ijk} = \mu + \text{(nutrient)}_i + \varepsilon_{ijk} \tag{9.25}$$

to the models:

$$y_{ijk} = \mu + \varepsilon_{ijk} \tag{9.26}$$

$$\text{(no. species)}_{ijk} = \mu + \varepsilon_{ijk} \tag{9.27}$$

The additional SS explained by models 9.24 and 9.25 is the Type I SS_A. SS_B are determined by comparing the fit of the next two models in the sequence:

$$y_{ijk} = \mu + \alpha_i + \beta_j + \varepsilon_{ijk} \tag{9.28}$$

$$\text{(no. species)}_{ijk} = \mu + \text{(nutrient)}_i + \text{(time)}_j + \varepsilon_{ijk} \tag{9.29}$$

versus

$$y_{ijk} = \mu + \alpha_i + \varepsilon_{ijk} \tag{9.24}$$

$$\text{(no. species)}_{ijk} = \mu + \text{(nutrient)}_i + \varepsilon_{ijk} \tag{9.25}$$

It is clear from Table 9.15 that SS_A are quite different for Type I and Type III methods, not surprising given the different pairs of models being compared. Unfortunately, there are two downsides of Type I SS. First is that the order of terms is important. The SS due to factor B will be different if it enters the model after factor A compared with before factor A. Second, Type I SS use marginal means weighted by sample sizes and hence test hypotheses weighted by sample sizes. Most biologists would probably prefer their hypotheses to be independent of the cell sample sizes.

Type II SS are also developed from sequential model fitting. Now, however, the contribution of each term is assessed by comparing a model with that term to a model without it, but including all other terms at the same or lower level. To determine the SS_A, we compare the fit of:

$$y_{ijk} = \mu + \alpha_i + \beta_j + \varepsilon_{ijk} \quad (9.28)$$

$$(\text{no. species})_{ijk} = \mu + (\text{treatment})_i + (\text{time})_j + \varepsilon_{ijk} \quad (9.29)$$

to

$$y_{ijk} = \mu + \beta_j + \varepsilon_{ijk} \quad (9.30)$$

$$(\text{no. species})_{ijk} = \mu + (\text{time})_j + \varepsilon_{ijk} \quad (9.31)$$

The additional SS explained by models 9.28 and 9.29 is the Type II SS_A. Type II SS are not dependent on the order of terms in the model but still test hypotheses of marginal means weighted by cell sample sizes. The main difference between Type II and Type III SS is that the Type III model comparison for main effects includes the interaction terms whereas the Type II model comparison doesn't.

In the example from Hall *et al.* (2000), the imbalance in the design does not affect conclusions from the *F* tests – both main effects and the interaction are significant for all three types of SS and model comparisons. However, the degree of imbalance is minor in this case. The different SS used to analyze the data from Reich *et al.* (1999) resulted in different conclusions for the hypothesis test of the main effect of location, where the *P* value based on Type III SS was 0.020 compared to 0.061 for Type I and II SS.

We prefer Type III SS for unbalanced (but not missing cells) designs, but this is still an issue of considerable debate in the statistical and ecological literature. For example, Nelder & Lane (1995) argued strongly in favor of Type I SS and recommended that hypothesis testing in linear models be based on a hierarchical series of models. They saw no role for Type III SS at all. Stewart-Oaten (1995) proposed that Type III SS are only useful for testing interactions. He argued that if interactions are absent, then test main effects with Type II SS

and if interactions are present, then main effects would not be tested anyway. However, Maxwell & Delaney (1990) pointed out that this approach depends on the power of our initial test for an interaction and suggested that Type III SS are more broadly applicable.

It is very important to remember that this whole debate becomes irrelevant when factorial designs are balanced because Type I, II and III SS are identical. Therefore, we agree strongly with Underwood (1997) that unequal sample sizes should be avoided, at least by design. As Underwood (1997) pointed out, there is unlikely to be a logical reason for estimating different cell means or marginal means with different levels of precision and unequal sample sizes make variance component estimation very difficult. However, as discussed in Chapters 4 and 8, we don't recommend deleting observations to make cell sizes equal. This will reduce power, which is rarely adequate in biological experiments anyway, and the model comparison approach can easily deal with unequal sample sizes as long as we are aware of which hypotheses the different approaches are testing and we are careful about checking the assumptions of the analysis.

Missing cells

The extreme form of unequal sample sizes is where there are no observations for one or more of the cells in a multifactor ANOVA. Such data are very difficult to analyze because not all marginal and cell means can be estimated and therefore not all main effects and interactions can be tested. Type III SS based on the effects models and unweighted marginal means for main effects are inappropriate in this situation. There is no single correct analysis for missing cells designs and different approaches test different hypotheses, all of which might be of interest. The basic approach is to consider tests of main effects and interactions as sets of contrasts between marginal means and cell means respectively (Section 9.2.2). We will use two examples to illustrate analyses of factorial designs with missing cells. The first is a modification of the data from Hall *et al.* (2000) we used above, where instead of having a single habitat unit missing from the control treatment after six months, we have lost all of the observations from that cell (Table 9.16(a)). The second example is

Table 9.16 Analyses of two factor ANOVA design modified from Hall *et al.* (2000) with a single missing cell. (a) Design structure, (b) cell means model with tests for main effects and interactions, with contrasts for the effect of time, (c) Type III SS test of interaction of treatment by time, and (d) subset analyses, omitting 6 months and omitting controls

(a)

	2 months	4 months	6 months
Control	μ_{C2}	μ_{C4}	
Added nutrients	μ_{N2}	μ_{N4}	μ_{N6}

(b)

Source	SS	df	MS	F	P
Cells	32.013	4	8.003	93.17	<0.001
Treatment:					
Control vs nutrient added for (2 and 4) months $(\mu_{C2}+\mu_{C4}=\mu_{N2}+\mu_{N4})$	1.063	1	1.063	12.38	0.002
Time:	34.991	3	11.664	135.62	<0.001
2 vs 4 marginal means $(\mu_{C2}+\mu_{N2}=\mu_{C4}+\mu_{N4})$	13.441	1	13.441	156.47	<0.001
2 vs 6 for nutrient added $(\mu_{N2}=\mu_{N6})$	19.720	1	19.720	229.57	<0.001
4 vs 6 for nutrient added $(\mu_{N4}=\mu_{N6})$	1.830	1	1.830	21.30	<0.001
Treatment × time:					
Control vs nutrient added at 2 months vs 4 months $(\mu_{C2}-\mu_{N2}-\mu_{C4}+\mu_{N4})$	0.491	1	0.491	5.72	0.027
Residual	1.718	20	0.086		

(c)

	SS_{Full}	df_{Full}	$SS_{Reduced}$	$df_{Reduced}$	Difference	$F_{1,20}$	P
Model	32.013	4	31.522	3	0.491	5.71	0.027
Residual	1.718	20	2.209	21			

(d)

	Omitting 6 months				Omitting controls			
	df	MS	F	P	df	MS	F	P
Treatment	1	1.063	12.53	0.003				
Time	1	13.441	158.34	<0.001	2	10.362	118.39	<0.001
Treatment × time	1	0.491	5.79	0.029				
Residual	16	0.085			12	0.088		

from Reynolds *et al.* (1997), who studied competition between three species of grassland plants. They identified patches dominated by each of the species, cleared a plot in each patch and seeded it with either the original species or one of the other species. Not all species–patch combinations were possible (Table 9.17(a)), so this was a design with three missing cells out of the nine possible combinations. The response variables were percentages of soil water, shoot $\delta^{13}C$ and nitrate accumulated on ion-exchange resin bags.

The best strategy is to fit a cell means model (Box 9.6), basically a single factor model for all the cells, and then test relevant contrasts based on

Table 9.17 | Missing cells design and analysis from Reynolds *et al.* (1997). Seeds of each of the three species were planted into patches already dominated by one of the species. Only six of the nine species–patch combinations were possible. (a) Design structure, (b) ANOVA with tests of possible contrasts

(a)

	Patch		
	1:	2:	3:
Species	*Plantago*	*Lasthenia*	*Calycadenia*
1: *Plantago*	μ_{11}	μ_{12}	μ_{13}
2: *Lasthenia*	μ_{21}	μ_{22}	
3: *Calycadenia*			μ_{33}

(b)

Source	df
Species	2
$\mu_{13} = \mu_{33}$	1
$\mu_{11} + \mu_{12} = \mu_{21} + \mu_{22}$	1
Patch	2
$\mu_{11} = \mu_{13}$	1
$\mu_{12} + \mu_{22} = \mu_{11} + \mu_{21}$	1
Species × patch	1
$\mu_{11} - \mu_{12} - \mu_{21} + \mu_{22}$	1

cell means. The residual from that means model is used for all subsequent tests when the factors are fixed. To test the interaction effects, we need to determine which interaction contrasts are estimable, where an estimable contrast is one that doesn't rely on the missing cells. For the modified artificial habitat data from Hall *et al.* (2000), there is only one interaction contrast that is estimable $(\mu_{C2} - \mu_{N2} - \mu_{C4} + \mu_{N4})$, the effect of nutrients at two and four months, which was significant (Table 9.16(b)). There was also only one estimable interaction contrast in the plant competition data (Table 9.17(b)). If there are more than two levels of both factors, and depending on the pattern of missing cells, there may be more than one estimable interaction contrast and sums of non-estimable contrasts might also be estimable (Searle 1993). We could also use Type III SS to compare the fit of the full effects model to the fit of the reduced model; from Hall *et al.* (2000), this

is the comparison of models 9.13 and 9.21 versus models 9.28 and 9.29. This F-ratio is testing the H_0 that all the estimable interaction contrasts are zero, and since there is only one estimable interaction contrast, this test is the same as obtained from the contrast as part of the cell means model. The point is that the F test based on Type III SS_{AB} does not test that all interactions between A and B are zero but only some subset that depends on the pattern of missing cells.

What about main effects? The recommended approach is to determine a set of contrasts of marginal means (for the part of the data set without missing cells) or cell means that test sensible hypotheses based on the available data. This is where the cell means model is very important. For the time factor in Hall *et al.*'s (2000) artificial habitat example, we can contrast two and four months using marginal means (H_0: $\mu_2 = \mu_4$) because all cells have observations. We can contrast two and six months and four and six months, but only using cell means for nutrient added treatments (Table 9.16(c)). For the plant competition example (Table 9.17(b)), Reynolds *et al.* (1997) contrasted the cell means for *Plantago* and *Calycadenia* for *Calycadenia* patches only (one df) and also measured the main effect of species from the analysis of the *Plantago* and *Lasthenia* combinations as a subset (one df). The combination of these two effects produced the final $SS_{Species}$ with two df. The SS_{Patch} was determined with a comparable set of contrasts. In all these cases, the residual from the cell means model was used as the denominator for all F tests.

Note that these analyses do not represent orthogonal partitioning of the SS_{Total}, because these designs are extreme examples of imbalance and we have already pointed out that there is no simple partitioning of the SS in unbalanced designs. We should also mention Type IV SS that are produced by the SAS statistical software package. When there are no missing cells, Type IV SS are the same as Type III SS. When there are missing cells, Type IV SS are calculated for all the estimable contrasts as described above, although SAS selects a subset of these (see Milliken & Johnson 1984 for details). Searle (1993) and Yandell (1997) have argued strongly that the default Type IV SS may not be useful for many missing cells designs. It is clearly a more sensible strategy to carefully think about what subset of hypotheses are of most interest from all those that can be tested when there are missing cells.

Another approach to missing cells designs is to analyze subsets of the data set with observations in all cells (Table 9.16(c)). In the artificial habitat example, we could delete all data from six months and fit a two factor model to the remaining data for two levels of time (two and four months) and two treatments (control and nutrients added). The SS_{AB} for this subset analysis is the same as the Type III SS from the full data set because the only estimable interaction contrast is the one from this subset (Table 9.16(c)). The first contrast of the time effect in the cell means analysis is also the main effect of time from an analysis of the subset of the data omitting six months. The other subset with observations in all cells is using added nutrient data only for all three times, although that becomes a single factor analysis. When both factors have more than two levels, and there is at least one missing cell, there may be more than one subset suitable for a factorial model. On the other hand, if there is a complex pattern of missing cells (disconnected data, *sensu* Searle 1993, Yandell 1997), then the subsets might be quite small compared to full data set, i.e. most of the rows and columns may need be to deleted to form an analyzable subset of the data.

In summary, the analysis of missing cells factorial designs will involve a combination of analyzing balanced subsets of the data, especially for interactions, and sensible contrasts of cell means for examining components of main effects. We have only discussed fixed factor models here. The tests of relevant contrasts in mixed models with missing cells are really messy because of the difficulty of calculating an appropriate error term.

9.2.7 Factor effects

When the factors are fixed (i.e. Model 1), we might wish to estimate the variance between the group means in the specific populations from which we have sampled. For factor A, this is $\sum_{i=1}^{p}\alpha_i^2/(p-1)$, where α_i is the difference between each group mean and the overall mean ($\mu_i-\mu$). Following Brown & Mosteller (1991), we can equate the mean squares to their expected values (the ANOVA

approach) to obtain an estimate of this variance of the population group means (Table 9.18). Analogous calculations work for the other fixed effects (B and the interaction A×B) and we simply determine the proportion that each contributes to the total variance (the sum of the variance components plus the residual). An alternative for fixed factor effects is to calculate ω^2 (Hays 1994) as a measure of strength of association between the response variable and the fixed factor (see Chapter 8). This is similar to the EMS measure above except we are estimating $\sum_{i=1}^{p}\alpha_i^2/p$ instead of $\sum_{i=1}^{p}\alpha_i^2/(p-1)$, so the two measures are related by the ratio $(p-1)/p$. The formula for ω^2 given in many texts (Hays 1994, Kirk 1995) automatically determines the percentage of the total variance explained (a PEV measure, *sensu* Petraitis 1998; see Chapter 8). For fixed factor A in a two factor ANOVA:

$$\omega_A^2=\frac{SS_A-(p-1)MS_{Residual}}{MS_{Residual}+SS_{Total}}\qquad(9.32)$$

The difference between the estimate of ω^2 and the estimate based on equating the mean squares to their expected values decreases as the number of levels of the fixed factor increases because the difference between $p-1$ and p decreases.

For a random effects model (Model 2), we wish to estimate the added variance component (the variance between the means for all possible groups) for A (σ_α^2), B (σ_β^2) and the interaction ($\sigma_{\alpha\beta}^2$). Again, we can use the ANOVA approach to estimate these variance components (Brown & Mosteller 1991, Searle *et al.* 1992) and calculate each as a proportion of the total (sum of the components plus the residual). These are equivalent calculations to those described above for fixed factors.

We emphasized in Chapter 8 that the "variance" components for fixed and random factors are interpreted differently. For a fixed factor, we are estimating the variance between group means from the specific populations we have used and the difference between the true population mean and our estimate is sampling error at the level of the replicate observations (i.e. we have used all possible groups but have sampled observations from those groups). For a random factor, we are estimating the variance between all possible

Table 9.18 ANOVA estimates of variance components for balanced two factor ANOVA model with different combinations of fixed and random factors

A, B fixed:

Source	Expected mean square	Estimated variance component
A	$\sigma_\varepsilon^2 + nq\dfrac{\sum_{i=1}^{p}\alpha_i^2}{p-1}$	$\dfrac{MS_A - MS_{Residual}}{nq}$ *
B	$\sigma_\varepsilon^2 + np\dfrac{\sum_{j=1}^{q}\beta_j^2}{q-1}$	$\dfrac{MS_B - MS_{Residual}}{np}$ *
AB	$\sigma_\varepsilon^2 + n\dfrac{\sum_{i=1}^{p}\sum_{j=1}^{q}(\alpha\beta)_{ij}^2}{(p-1)(q-1)}$	$\dfrac{MS_{AB} - MS_{Residual}}{n}$ *
Residual	σ_ε^2	$MS_{Residual}$

A, B random:

Source	Expected mean square	Estimated variance component
A	$\sigma_\varepsilon^2 + n\sigma_{\alpha\beta}^2 + nq\sigma_\alpha^2$	$\dfrac{MS_A - MS_{AB}}{nq}$
B	$\sigma_\varepsilon^2 + n\sigma_{\alpha\beta}^2 + np\sigma_\beta^2$	$\dfrac{MS_B - MS_{AB}}{np}$
AB	$\sigma_\varepsilon^2 + n\sigma_{\alpha\beta}^2$	$\dfrac{MS_{AB} - MS_{Residual}}{n}$
Residual	σ_ε^2	$MS_{Residual}$

A fixed, B random:

Source	Expected mean square	Estimated variance component
A	$\sigma_\varepsilon^2 + n\sigma_{\alpha\beta}^2 + nq\dfrac{\sum_{i=1}^{p}\alpha_i^2}{p-1}$	$\dfrac{MS_A - MS_{AB}}{nq}$ *
B	$\sigma_\varepsilon^2 + np\sigma_\beta^2$	$\dfrac{MS_B - MS_{Residual}}{np}$
AB	$\sigma_\varepsilon^2 + n\sigma_{\alpha\beta}^2$	$\dfrac{MS_{AB} - MS_{Residual}}{n}$
Residual	σ_ε^2	$MS_{Residual}$

Note:
Note that the "variance component" for fixed effects (*) represents the variance between the fixed group population means.

group means and the difference between the true population variance and our estimate is sampling error at the level of groups (i.e. we have used only a sample of all the possible groups).

For mixed models, there are two approaches. The most correct method is to calculate true variance components only for the random effects in the model and determine the proportion each contributes to the total (including the residual) of the random variation in the response variable. This approach formally recognizes that the "variance" between the fixed group means is not really comparable to the added variance due to random effects. The second method (Brown & Mosteller 1991) takes a more pragmatic line and doesn't distinguish between fixed and random effects in that the equivalent of variance components are calculated for both. The argument here is that the calculations are identical for both types of effects (using the expected mean square (ANOVA) approach) and we are simply trying to apportion the total variation in the response variable amongst all the model terms in a comparable way. The different interpretations of estimates of variance between fixed group means and true added variance components still must be recognized. Any measure of proportion of explained variance for multifactor models must be treated cautiously. These measures are obviously dependent on other terms in the model (Underwood & Petraitis 1993, Underwood 1997) and are difficult to compare between analyses.

The ANOVA approach to true variance component estimation relies on equal sample sizes. When sample sizes are different, there is no straightforward solution to estimating variance components of random factors. Searle et al. (1992) discussed a number of modifications of the EMS (ANOVA) method, including Hendersons's Methods I, II, and III, and using cell means, but could not make definitive recommendations about which is best. They preferred maximum likelihood (ML) and restricted maximum likelihood (REML) methods of estimation for unbalanced data and these were discussed in Chapter 8. They did point out that the major limitation of these methods of estimation is their complexity and the shortage of available software.

9.2.8 Assumptions

Fortunately, the assumptions of factorial ANOVA models are basically the same as we have already discussed for single factor and multifactor nested models. The assumptions of normality and homogeneity of within-cell variances for the error terms from the model and the observations apply to hypothesis tests in factorial ANOVA models. We can check these assumptions for the observations within each cell using the same techniques (boxplots, mean vs variance plots and residuals vs cell mean plots) already described in Chapters 4 and 8.

Formal tests of homogeneity of within-cell variances, as described in Chapter 8, can be applied to factorial designs. Levene's test is probably the best and also works well when based on randomized residuals (Manly 1997). Nonetheless, our reservations outlined in Chapter 8 about using these tests in isolation from more informative diagnostic checks still hold. When the research hypotheses of interest actually concern main effects and interaction effects on variances, rather than means, modifications of the tests based on pseudo-observations (e.g. absolute residuals) described in Chapter 8 can be used (Ozaydin et al. 1999).

The assumption of independence is also relevant for factorial ANOVA models and the observations within each cell should be independent of each other. Problems arise if we repeatedly measure experimental or sampling units through time (see Chapters 10 and 11) or we design our experiment so that the response of some units affects the responses of others (Chapter 7).

Transformations of the response variable deserve special mention for factorial ANOVA models. Transformations of variables with skewed distributions can greatly improve normality and homogeneity of within-cell variances (Chapters 4 and 8) and should be considered when these assumptions are not met. Transformations can also affect the interpretation of interaction terms, although the effect depends on the nature of the interaction (Sokal & Rohlf 1995).

In Table 9.13(a), the effects are additive and there is no interaction between factors A and B. The difference between the two levels of A is the same at each level of B and vice versa. In Table 9.13(b), the effects of factors A and B are clearly multiplicative and, on the raw scale, there is clearly an interaction. The difference between the two levels of A is not the same at each level of B and vice versa. However, if we log transform the cell means, this interaction effect disappears and an additive model without an interaction term would now be appropriate. After transformation, the percentage change from A_1 to A_2 is the same for both levels of B. In Table 9.13(c), the interaction is more complex, where the effects of the two levels of A are reversed for each level of B. A log transformation does not change the nature of the interaction term very much.

So a log transformation (other power transformations can also alter interaction strengths) will make effects that are multiplicative on the raw scale additive on the transformed scale (Emerson 1991, Kirk 1995, Neter *et al.* 1996, Sokal & Rohlf 1995). The decision whether to transform data before fitting multifactor ANOVA models then also depends on whether the biological interaction you are measuring is best represented on the transformed scale. An additive model after transformation is simpler but may miss multiplicative effects that represent important biological interactions. If, on the other hand, multiplicative effects are not considered biologically important interactions (i.e. only different relative percentage changes in one factor at each level of the other factor are relevant), then a log transformation to produce an additive model might be appropriate.

9.2.9 Robust factorial ANOVAs

There are few accepted robust factorial ANOVA techniques. One common approach is to use a rank transform (RT) method, whereby the data are converted to ranks and the usual ANOVA is applied to the ranks. Although this method may be useful for tests of main effects, it is inappropriate for testing interactions (McKean & Vidmar 1994, Seaman *et al.* 1994, Thompson 1991a,b) because of the nonlinear nature of rank-transformed data. The recently proposed aligned rank procedure of Salter & Fawcett (1993) may be more useful. As discussed in Chapters 3 and 8, the RT approach may not provide protection against unequal variances but can help in dealing with outliers.

The Wilcox Z test (Chapter 8) is robust to unequal variances and could be applied to

factorial designs by analyzing all the cells as a one factor design, with appropriate contrasts (like a cell means model). Of course, generalized linear models (GLMs; see Chapter 13) would also be applicable when the underlying distribution of the response variable is not normal but is known to be one from the exponential family.

Randomization tests for factorial ANOVAs have been described by Edgington (1995) and Manly (1997). With both main effects and interactions involved, there are a number of different ways to randomize observations (or residuals). Observations can be randomized across all cells and either F-ratios or mean squares for main effects and interactions used as test statistics. Randomizing residuals across all cells and using F-ratios can also be used. Edgington (1995) has suggested that true randomization tests for interactions are not possible and recommended restricted randomization for testing main effects, whereby observations are randomized between groups for one factor, controlling for the other factor. Manly (1997) summarizes these and other approaches and concludes from simulations (see also Gonzalez & Manly 1998) that when based on F-ratios, all methods gave similar results for testing main effects and interactions, and these were similar to the classical ANOVA tests.

9.2.10 Specific comparisons on main effects

If there are no strong interactions, interpreting main effects is relatively straightforward and involves tests of marginal means, e.g. the means of factor A pooling over the levels of B and vice versa. The tests of null hypotheses of no effect of A or no effect of B can include planned contrasts and/or trend analyses or be followed by unplanned multiple comparisons, as described in Chapter 8. For example, Poulson & Platt (1996) analyzed the difference in growth between sugar maple and beech saplings (the difference was the response variable) with a two factor ANOVA model. The factors were light microenvironment (three levels: beneath canopy, single treefall gap, multiple treefall gap) and height class (three levels: small, medium, large) and they incorporated two planned contrasts for each of the main effects, although for one response variable, the interaction was significant.

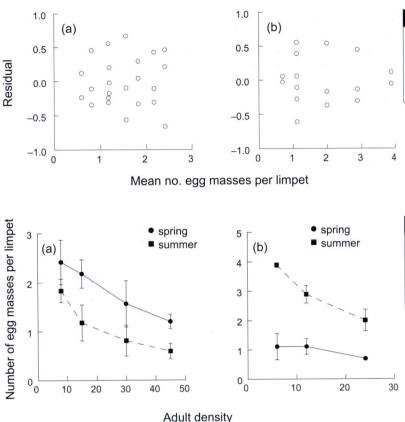

Figure 9.4 Residual plots from two factor ANOVA models for data on effects of density and season on egg mass production by *Siphonaria* limpets (Quinn 1988). (a) High shore limpets, (b) low shore limpets.

Figure 9.5 Plots of cell means and standard errors for data on effects of density and season on egg mass production by *Siphonaria* limpets (Quinn 1988). (a) High shore limpets, (b) low shore limpets.

also Table 9.13; Underwood 1997 provided a similar example and detailed explanation). In Figure 9.3(a), there is no interaction between the two factors (lines parallel) and the main effects (marginal mean plots) are straightforward to interpret. When there is a moderate interaction (Figure 9.3(b)), the marginal mean plots (and therefore tests of main effects) can become misleading. The marginal mean plot for A suggests A2 and A3 are similar whereas they are clearly different at each level of B. With complex interactions (Figure 9.3(c)), comparisons of marginal means can be completely uninterpretable. For example, the marginal mean plot for A suggests no effect when there are obvious effects at each level of B, they are just opposite.

The interaction plot for the data on the effects of adult density and season on egg production of *Siphonaria* limpets from Quinn (1988) shows no evidence of an interaction for high shore limpets but some interaction for low shore limpets (the difference between seasons is greater at density six than 12 or 24) – see Figure 9.4 and Figure 9.5. Such interaction graphs are helpful ways of understanding interactions but are necessarily subjective.

The only tricky part of contrasts or pairwise comparisons on main effect means is to ensure that the correct error term is used if the model contains random factors. In such situations, the error term for fixed factors, and therefore any contrasts on the means of those factors, is usually an interaction term rather than the $MS_{Residual}$.

9.2.11 Interpreting interactions

The presence of an interaction between two factors is often of considerable biological interest and nearly always deserves further analysis.

Exploring interactions

Plotting cell means with the response variable on the vertical axis, the levels of one factor on the horizontal axis and lines joining the means within levels of the other factor (see Figure 9.3) is sometimes called an interaction plot. An interaction is indicated by deviation of the lines from parallel. We illustrate the effects of interactions on interpretation of main effects in Figure 9.3 (see

Table 9.19 (a) Final output from data sweeping of a two factor ANOVA design. Top left value is overall mean, factor A and factor B effects are in row and column borders and interaction effects are in remaining cells. (b) Example of data sweeping from Quinn (1988) showing effects of season, density and interaction on number of egg masses produced per limpet. Note that the season effects are the strongest and the interaction effects are similar to, or less than, the density effects

(a)

		B_1	B_2	etc.
	$\bar{y}$	$\bar{y}_j - \bar{y}\ (j=1)$	$\bar{y}_j - \bar{y}\ (j=2)$	
A_1	$\bar{y}_i - \bar{y}\ (i=1)$	$\bar{y}_{ij} - \bar{y}_i - \bar{y}_j + \bar{y}\ (i=1, j=1)$	$\bar{y}_{ij} - \bar{y}_i - \bar{y}_j + \bar{y}\ (i=1, j=2)$	
A_2	$\bar{y}_i - \bar{y}\ (i=2)$	$\bar{y}_{ij} - \bar{y}_i - \bar{y}_j + \bar{y}\ (i=2, j=1)$	$\bar{y}_{ij} - \bar{y}_i - \bar{y}_j + \bar{y}\ (i=2, j=2)$	
etc.				

(b)

		Density 6	Density 12	Density 24
	1.948	0.551	0.051	−0.601
Spring	−0.967	−0.413	0.087	0.324
Summer	0.976	0.413	−0.087	−0.324

Another descriptive approach is to decompose the ANOVA into a table representing the main effects and interaction effects. The general technique of splitting up the data into effects and residuals is termed sweeping (Schmid 1991) and is described for a two factor ANOVA, using the data on the effects of adult density and season on egg production of low shore *Siphonaria* limpets from Quinn (1988) as an example, in Table 9.19. The border row and column show the main effects and the central entries show the interaction effects for each cell. The season effects were stronger than the density and interaction effects, the relatively small interaction effects matching the conclusions from the ANOVA and interaction plot for these data (Box 9.4) that there is a statistically significant interaction but it does not swamp main effects.

Unplanned multiple comparison

An unplanned multiple comparison test (e.g. Tukey test) on all cell means involved in the interaction can be done (Underwood 1997). Unfortunately, there will often be many means involved and multiple comparison tests can produce ambiguous results when there are lots of groups (Chapter 8). We do not recommend this approach unless the ANOVA is exploratory and no sensible contrasts can be determined.

Simple main effects

Simple main effects test the H_0 of no effect of factor A at each level of B separately and/or no effect of factor B at each level of A separately. As an example, Stehman & Meredith (1995) described an experiment based on Radwan et al. (1992) who examined the effects of nitrogen (two levels: present and absent) and phosphorus (four levels: 0, 100, 300, 500 kg ha^{-1}) on growth and foliar nutrient concentrations of Douglas fir trees. This experiment would be analyzed as a two factor factorial ANOVA. Testing simple main effects might involve comparing the four P levels separately for N present and N absent or comparing N present

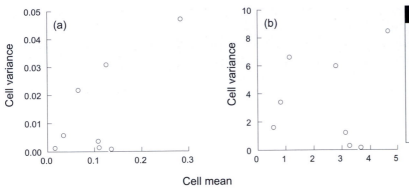

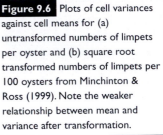

Figure 9.6 Plots of cell variances against cell means for (a) untransformed numbers of limpets per oyster and (b) square root transformed numbers of limpets per 100 oysters from Minchinton & Ross (1999). Note the weaker relationship between mean and variance after transformation.

and absent for each P level separately. The experiment examining the effect of density and season on egg mass production by limpets (Quinn 1988) showed a significant density by season interaction for low shore limpets (Box 9.4). A sensible test of simple main effects would test the density effects for each season separately.

Simple main effects don't really examine the interaction, just separate effects of one factor for each level of the other factor. In many cases, we might only wish to examine simple main effects for one of the factors. This might be particularly true if one factor is random. A significant interaction between the fixed and random factor suggests the effect of the fixed factor varies spatially or temporally and we would usually examine the simple main effects for the fixed factor at each level of the random factor separately. To illustrate from Minchinton & Ross (1999), we would test the simple main effects of intertidal zone on the density of oysters on mangrove trees for each randomly chosen site separately. When both factors are fixed, then we might want to test simple main effects for both factors. If there are many levels of one or both factors, then testing all simple main effects involves a lot of non-independent single factor ANOVAs. These are exploratory analyses looking for significant results among a collection of tests, so some correction (e.g. Bonferroni-type) to significance levels to adjust for multiple testing probably should be used (see Chapter 3).

Simple main effects tests are basically single factor ANOVAs at each level of the other factor but they are best considered as a set of particular contrasts and part of the original two factor ANOVA. The simple main effects for factor A at each level of B partition the SS and df for A and AB; simple

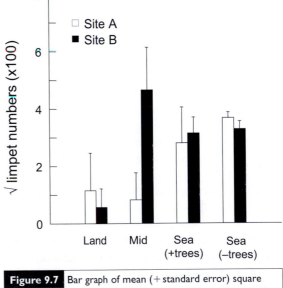

Figure 9.7 Bar graph of mean (+ standard error) square root transformed numbers of limpets per 100 oysters for different zones and sites from Minchinton & Ross (1999).

main effects for B at each level of A partition the SS and df for B and AB. When both factors are fixed, tests of simple main effects should use the original $MS_{Residual}$ as the denominator of their F tests, because we have already decided that is our best estimate of the residual variance in our data. Simply splitting the original data and testing across the levels of A for any specific level of B with a single factor ANOVA will result in an F test with a different denominator term with different df and different power characteristics than the tests in the original two factor ANOVA. This seems inappropriate so make sure the $MS_{Residual}$ from the original factorial ANOVA is used as the error term for simple main effect tests in Model 1 ANOVAs.

When one factor (say, B) is random (Model 3), then the main effect of A was tested against the AB interaction and the interaction was tested against the residual so there is no single denominator for tests of simple main effects of A from a partition of $(SS_A + SS_{AB})$. Under these circumstances, one approach might be to calculate a new pooled error term:

$$\frac{SS_A + SS_{AB}}{(p-1) + (p-1)(q-1)} \qquad (9.33)$$

This is based on the strategy recommended by Kirk (1995) and Maxwell & Delaney (1990) for partly nested models where we have both fixed and random factors (Chapter 11). We can use this pooled error term as the denominator for simple main effect tests for factor A, although tests will only be approximate.

Keep in mind also that planned contrasts and trend analyses and unplanned comparisons can be incorporated into tests of simple main effects of fixed factors. Underwood (1997) recommended simple main effects tests to interpret interactions, although he did not use this term. He also focused on multiple comparisons, recommending SNK (or Ryan's) tests to compare the A means at each level of B separately, rather than considering the F tests for the simple main effects.

Treatment–contrast and contrast–contrast interactions

Treatment–contrast interactions partition the interaction term by testing contrasts (e.g. group 1 versus group 2) and trends (e.g. linear, quadratic) in one factor against the levels of the second factor. We test whether a particular contrast of groups of one factor interacts with the second factor. In the study by Stehman & Meredith (1995) examining the effects of nitrogen and phosphorus on growth and foliar nutrient concentrations of Douglas fir trees, a number of treatment–contrast interactions make sense. First, is the difference between no P (control) and the average of P_{100}, P_{300}, P_{500} consistent for treatments with N present and N absent? Second, are the linear or quadratic trends across P the same for N present and N absent? In the example for low shore limpets from Quinn (1988), we could test whether the contrast of natural density (six limpets) with increased density (12 and 24 limpets) interacts

with season, i.e. whether this contrast was consistent between season (Box 9.4). Alternatively, we can test whether the linear trend in density interacts with season (Box 9.4).

Contrast–contrast interactions are a particular case of treatment–contrast interactions and test the interaction between contrasts or trends in one factor and contrast or trends in the second factor. For example, Corti et al. (1997) set up a factorial experiment to test the effects of hydroperiod and predation on macroinvertebrate communities in ponds on the Mississippi River floodplain. The two factors were pond (four levels: two permanently wet ponds, two temporary ponds which dried occasionally) and predator access (three levels: all access, small-fish access, no access). The design was actually slightly more complicated as there were also repeated measurements on dates (see Chapter 12) but we can just consider it a two factor analysis for the moment. They used a number of contrast–contrast interaction tests to interpret significant pond by predator interactions. For example, did the contrast between pond one and pond two (comparing the two temporary ponds) interact with the contrast of all access versus combined no access and small-fish access treatments? Did the temporary versus permanent pond contrast (ponds one and two vs three and four) interact with the contrast of all access versus combined no access and small-fish access treatments?

Both types of contrast were used by Mills & Bever (1998), who examined the effects of plant species (four levels: four species of perennial plants) and strain of pathogenic oomycete of the genus *Pythium* (six levels: control and five strains) on plant mass. Their design also included a block effect (see Chapter 10) but we can just consider the factorial component (plant species crossed with *Pythium* strain) here (Table 9.20). They included a treatment–contrast interaction test (does the effect of plant species interact with the contrast between the control and the average of the five *Pythium* strains?) and numerous contrast–contrast interaction tests (e.g. does the contrast between any two of the plant species interact with the contrast between the control and the average of the five *Pythium* strains?).

Kirk (1995) has provided computational formulae for developing such tests but they can usually be obtained from linear models routines in

Table 9.20 | Part of ANOVA table from Mills & Bever (1998) for experiment testing effects of four plant species (An = *Anthoxanthum*, Da = *Danthonia*, Pa = *Panicum*, Pl = *Plantago*) and six pathogenic oomycete treatments (control and five strains of *Pythium*) on plant mass and root:shoot ratios

Source	df
Block	1
Plant spp.	3
Treatment	5
Contol vs average *Pythium*	1
Among *Pythium*	4
Plant spp. × Treatment	15
Plant spp. × Contol vs average *Pythium*	3
An-Da × Contol vs average *Pythium*	1
An-Pa × Contol vs average *Pythium*	1
An-Pl × Contol vs average *Pythium*	1
Da-Pa × Contol vs average *Pythium*	1
Da-Pl × Contol vs average *Pythium*	1
Pa-Pl × Contol vs average *Pythium*	1
Residual	167

Note:
Specific comparisons for treatment main effect were control treatment versus average of the five *Pythium* strains and among the *Pythium* strains. Interaction contrasts were plant species by control treatment versus average of the five *Pythium* strains ("treatment–contrast interaction") and the difference between all pairs of plant species by control treatment versus average of the five *Pythium* strains ("contrast–contrast interaction").

statistical software that allows flexible coding of contrasts.

9.2.12 More complex designs

The two factor ANOVA model can be extended to handle more complex designs in three ways (i) three or more factor factorial designs, (ii) fractional factorial designs, and (iii) combinations of crossed and nested factors.

Complex factorial designs

Extending linear models to three or more factors is relatively straightforward, except for interpreting complex interactions. As an example, Ayres & Scriber (1994) studied climatic adaptation in caterpillars and tested the effects of sex (male, female), population (Michigan, Alaskan) and laboratory temperature (12°, 18°, 24°, 30°C) on mass of pupae produced. The three factor ANOVA model included a three factor interaction (is the interaction between temperature and population consistent for males and females?), three two factor interactions (e.g. is the difference between temperatures the same for both sexes, pooling populations?) and three main effects (e.g. is there a difference between sexes, pooling population and temperature?). Note that the three factor interaction is symmetrical – "is the interaction between temperature and population consistent for males and females?", "is the interaction between sex and population consistent across the four temperatures?", etc.

We can estimate factor effects, as either fixed factor "variances" or variance components for random factors, using modifications of the approaches described in Section 9.2.7. We can compare the relative contribution of the different main effects and interactions by equating the mean squares to their expected values as described in Section 9.2.7. Keep in mind the fundamentally different interpretation of variance components for random factors and the "variance" among fixed treatment effects. Note that when two or more random factors are included, calculation of variance components is difficult (see below).

The strategies for exploring complex interactions follow those outlined in Section 9.2.11. The equivalent of simple main effects are simple interaction effects, where the A×B interaction is examined at each level of C or the A×C interaction is examined at each level of B, etc. These simple interaction tests could then be followed by simple main effects. One difficulty is that the number of significance tests can quickly become very large when exploring complex interactions like this and some sort of Bonferroni correction to the significance levels of the tests to control the Type I error rate might be needed (Chapter 3).

If fixed and random factors are combined in these complex factorial designs, then the expected mean squares must be determined beforehand (Table 9.21) because including one or more random factors can mean that some tests will use interaction terms rather than the

Table 9.21 | Expected mean squares for three factor ANOVA model (after Winer *et al.* 1991). Factor A has *p* levels, B has *q* levels and C has *r* levels with *n* replicates in each cell

Source	General expected mean square
A	$\sigma_\varepsilon^2 + nD_qD_r\sigma_{\alpha\beta\gamma}^2 + nqD_r\sigma_{\alpha\gamma}^2 + nrD_q\sigma_{\alpha\beta}^2 + nqr\sigma_\alpha^2$
B	$\sigma_\varepsilon^2 + nD_pD_r\sigma_{\alpha\beta\gamma}^2 + npD_r\sigma_{\beta\gamma}^2 + nrD_p\sigma_{\alpha\beta}^2 + npr\sigma_\beta^2$
C	$\sigma_\varepsilon^2 + nD_pD_q\sigma_{\alpha\beta\gamma}^2 + npD_q\sigma_{\beta\gamma}^2 + nqD_p\sigma_{\alpha\gamma}^2 + npq\sigma_\gamma^2$
AB	$\sigma_\varepsilon^2 + nD_r\sigma_{\alpha\beta\gamma}^2 + nr\sigma_{\alpha\beta}^2$
AC	$\sigma_\varepsilon^2 + nD_q\sigma_{\alpha\beta\gamma}^2 + nq\sigma_{\alpha\gamma}^2$
BC	$\sigma_\varepsilon^2 + nD_p\sigma_{\alpha\beta\gamma}^2 + np\sigma_{\beta\gamma}^2$
ABC	$\sigma_\varepsilon^2 + n\sigma_{\alpha\beta\gamma}^2$
Residual	σ_ε^2

Note:
Coding used for expected mean squares outlined in Box 9.8.

$MS_{Residual}$ as the denominator for their *F*-ratio. This can result in reduced df and less power than anticipated for some tests. For example, as part of their study of limpets on oyster shells in mangrove forests, Minchinton & Ross (1999) used two randomly chosen sites, three zones (seaward zone with mangrove trees, middle zone with trees, and a landward zone at the upper levels) and two orientations of mangrove trunk (upper facing canopy and lower facing forest floor). There were five quadrats in each of the twelve cells and the response variable was densities of limpets per oyster surface. Although there were 48 df for the residual, the test of the interaction between the fixed factors (Zone by Orientation) used the three factor interaction with only two df as the denominator. The tests of the fixed main effects (Zone, Orientation) used the respective two factor interactions with the random factor (Zone by Site, Orientation by Site) as denominators with only two and one df respectively. To increase the power of these tests, the number of levels of the random factor (in this example, sites) needs to be increased, rather than the number of replicate observations in each cell (quadrats).

If two or three of the three factors are random (e.g. A, B and C random; see Table 9.22), then there will be no appropriate *F*-ratio tests for some terms

in the model, i.e. under the H_0, there will be no other mean square with the same expected value as the term being tested. For example, in a three factor fully crossed design where all three factors are random, there are no appropriate *F*-ratios for testing for any of the main effects. There are two solutions to this problem.

1. Quasi *F*-ratios must be calculated by combining mean squares until a suitable numerator and denominator combination is found that tests the hypothesis of interest (Blackwell *et al.* 1991). For factor A in a three factor random effects model, there are two possible quasi *F*-ratios:

$$F = MS_A / (MS_{AB} + MS_{AC} - MS_{ABC}) \qquad (9.34)$$

$$F = (MS_A + MS_{ABC}) / (MS_{AB} + MS_{AC}) \qquad (9.35)$$

The second of these is more useful, as the first method can lead to negative *F*-ratios, which should not, by definition, occur. The degrees of freedom are also complex, and formulae are provided by Winer *et al.* (1991).

2. Alternatively, if we are primarily interested in the random factors, we can calculate confidence intervals for the variance components and see if those confidence intervals include zero (Burdick 1994).

Table 9.22 | Expected mean squares (EMS) and denominator for *F*-ratio test of H_0 that effect of each term equals zero for three factor crossed ANOVA model. Factor A has *p* levels, B has *q* levels, C has *r* levels with *n* replicates per cell. (a) Model 1 (all factors fixed) and Model 2 (all factors random). (b) One possible Model 3 (factors A and B fixed, factor C random) illustrated with example from Minchinton & Ross (1999) – see Section 9.2.12 for details

(a)

Source	A, B, C fixed EMS	Denominator	A, B, C random EMS	Denominator
A	$\sigma_\varepsilon^2 + nqr\sigma_\alpha^2$	$MS_{Residual}$	$\sigma_\varepsilon^2 + n\sigma_{\alpha\beta\gamma}^2 + nq\sigma_{\alpha\gamma}^2 + nr\sigma_{\alpha\beta}^2 + nqr\sigma_\alpha^2$	Quasi (?)
B	$\sigma_\varepsilon^2 + npr\sigma_\beta^2$	$MS_{Residual}$	$\sigma_\varepsilon^2 + n\sigma_{\alpha\beta\gamma}^2 + np\sigma_{\beta\gamma}^2 + nr\sigma_{\alpha\beta}^2 + npr\sigma_\beta^2$	Quasi (?)
C	$\sigma_\varepsilon^2 + npq\sigma_\gamma^2$	$MS_{Residual}$	$\sigma_\varepsilon^2 + n\sigma_{\alpha\beta\gamma}^2 + np\sigma_{\beta\gamma}^2 + nq\sigma_{\alpha\gamma}^2 + npq\sigma_\gamma^2$	Quasi (?)
AB	$\sigma_\varepsilon^2 + nr\sigma_{\alpha\beta}^2$	$MS_{Residual}$	$\sigma_\varepsilon^2 + n\sigma_{\alpha\beta\gamma}^2 + nr\sigma_{\alpha\beta}^2$	MS_{ABC}
AC	$\sigma_\varepsilon^2 + nq\sigma_{\alpha\gamma}^2$	$MS_{Residual}$	$\sigma_\varepsilon^2 + n\sigma_{\alpha\beta\gamma}^2 + nq\sigma_{\alpha\gamma}^2$	MS_{ABC}
BC	$\sigma_\varepsilon^2 + np\sigma_{\beta\gamma}^2$	$MS_{Residual}$	$\sigma_\varepsilon^2 + n\sigma_{\alpha\beta\gamma}^2 + np\sigma_{\beta\gamma}^2$	MS_{ABC}
ABC	$\sigma_\varepsilon^2 + n\sigma_{\alpha\beta\gamma}^2$	$MS_{Residual}$	$\sigma_\varepsilon^2 + n\sigma_{\alpha\beta\gamma}^2$	$MS_{Residual}$
Residual	σ_ε^2		σ_ε^2	

(b)

Source	Minchinton & Ross (1999)	EMS	Denominator
A	Zone	$\sigma_\varepsilon^2 + nq\sigma_{\alpha\gamma}^2 + nqr\sigma_\alpha^2$	MS_{AC}
B	Orientation	$\sigma_\varepsilon^2 + np\sigma_{\beta\gamma}^2 + npr\sigma_\beta^2$	MS_{BC}
C	Site	$\sigma_\varepsilon^2 + npq\sigma_\gamma^2$	$MS_{Residual}$
AB	Zone × orientation	$\sigma_\varepsilon^2 + n\sigma_{\alpha\beta\gamma}^2 + nr\sigma_{\alpha\beta}^2$	MS_{ABC}
AC	Zone × site	$\sigma_\varepsilon^2 + nq\sigma_{\alpha\gamma}^2$	$MS_{Residual}$
BC	Orientation × site	$\sigma_\varepsilon^2 + np\sigma_{\beta\gamma}^2$	$MS_{Residual}$
ABC	Zone × orientation × site	$\sigma_\varepsilon^2 + n\sigma_{\alpha\beta\gamma}^2$	$MS_{Residual}$
Residual		σ_ε^2	

Unfortunately, quasi *F*-ratios do not follow an *F* distribution under the H_0 and quasi-*F* tests are approximate at best (Burdick 1994). The problem becomes almost intractable if multiple random factors are combined with an unbalanced design. Our experience is that multifactor designs with more than one random factor are not common in biology, so we don't come across this situation often.

Fractional factorial designs

Sometimes we might wish to explore the effects of a number of factors but the number of combinations of factor levels is so large that the experiment is logistically impossible because it would require too many replicate units. Fractional factorial designs are often used in these situations, especially when we have a large number of factors, each with two levels. The terminology in the literature identifies this as a 2^p design where *p* is the number of two level factors. If we had four factors (*p* equals four), then the number of model terms for a fully factorial design would be 16 and the total number of experimental units required would be 16 times the number of replicates per cell. When much fewer experimental units are available and the main purpose of the experiment is to screen for important effects, a fractional factorial design might be used. There are two ways in which the required number of units can be reduced. First, the design is nearly always unreplicated, so there is only one replicate unit within each of the cells used. By definition, this means that there is no estimate of the σ_ε^2 so some higher order interaction terms must be used as the residual for hypothesis tests. Second, the logical basis of these designs is the assumption that most of the important effects will be main effects or simple (e.g. two factor) interactions, and complex interactions will be relatively unimportant. The experiment is conducted using a subset of cells that allows estimation of main effects and simple interactions but confounds these with higher order interactions that are assumed to be trivial.

The combination of factor levels to be used is tricky to determine but, fortunately, most statistical software now includes experimental design modules that generate fractional factorial design structures. This software often includes methods such as Plackett–Burman and Taguchi designs, which set up fractional factorial designs in ways that try to minimize confounding of main effects and simple interactions.

A recent biological example of such a design comes from Dufour & Berland (1999), who studied the effects of a variety of different nutrients and other compounds on primary productivity in seawater collected from near atolls and from ocean sites. Part of their experiment involved eight factors (nutrients N, P, and Si; trace metals Fe, Mo and Mn; combination of B12, biotin and thiamine vitamins; ethylene diamine tetra-acetic acid EDTA) each with two levels. This is a 2^8 factorial experiment. They only had 16 experimental units (test tubes on board ship) so they used a fractional factorial design that allowed tests of main effects, five of the six two factor interactions and two of the four three factor interactions.

It is difficult to recommend these designs for routine use in biological research. We know that interactions between factors are of considerable biological importance and it is difficult to decide *a priori* in most situations which interactions are less likely than others. Possibly such designs have a role in tightly controlled laboratory experiments where previous experience suggests that higher order interactions are not important. However, the main application of these designs will continue to be in industrial settings where additivity between factor combinations is a realistic expectation. Good references include Cochran & Cox (1957), Kirk (1995) and Neter *et al.* (1996).

Mixed factorial and nested designs

Designs that combine both nested and factorial factors are common in biology. One design is where one or more factors, usually random, are nested within two or more crossed factors. For example, Twombly (1996) used a clever experiment to examine the effects of food concentration for different sibships (eggs from the same female at a given time) on the development of the freshwater copepod *Mesocyclops edax*. There were four food treatments, a fixed factor: constant high food during development, switch from high food to low food at naupliar stage three, the same switch at stage four, and also at stage five. There were 15 sibships, which represented a random sample of possible sibships. For each combination of food treatment and sibship, four replicate Petri dishes were used and there were two individual nauplii in each dish. Two response variables were recorded: age at metamorphosis and size at metamorphosis. The analyses are presented in Table 9.23 and had treatment and sibship as main effects. Because sibship was random, the food treatment effect was tested against the food treatment by sibship interaction. Dishes were nested within the combinations of treatment and sibship and this factor was the denominator for tests of sibship and the food treatment by sibship interaction. For age at metamorphosis, individual nauplii provided the residual term and the linear model was:

(age at metamorphosis)$_{ijkl} = \mu +$
(food treatment)$_i +$ (sibship)$_j +$
(food treatment $\times$ sibship)$_{ij} +$
(dish within food treatment and sibship)$_{k(ij)} +$
ε_{ijkl} (9.36)

For size at metamorphosis, replicate measurements were taken on each individual nauplius so the effect of individuals nested within dishes nested within each treatment and sibship combination could also be tested against the residual term, the variation between replicate measurements. This linear model was:

Table 9.23 | ANOVA table for experiment from Twombly (1996) examining the effects of treatment (fixed factor) and sibship (random factor) on age at metamorphosis and size at metamorphosis of copepods, with randomly chosen dishes for each combination of treatment and sibship for age and randomly chosen individual copepods from each randomly chosen dish for size

Age at metamorphosis		
Source	Denominator	df
Treatment	Treatment × Sibship	3, 42
Sibship	Dish (Treatment × Sibship)	14, 153
Treatment × Sibship	Dish (Treatment × Sibship)	42, 153
Dish (Treatment × Sibship)	Residual	153, 166
Residual		

Size at metamorphosis		
Source	Denominator	df
Treatment	Treatment × Sibship	3, 42
Sibship	Dish (Treatment × Sibship)	14, 10
Treatment × Sibship	Dish (Treatment × Sibship)	42, 101
Dish (Treatment × Sibship)	Individual (Dish (Treatment × Sibship))	101, 141
Individual (Dish (Treatment × Sibship))	Residual	141, 698
Residual		

$$
\begin{aligned}
(\text{size at metamorphosis})_{ijklm} = \mu\ + \\
(\text{food treatment})_i + (\text{sibship})_j + \\
(\text{food treatment} \times \text{sibship})_{ij}\ + \\
(\text{dish within food treatment and sibship})_{k(ij)}\ + \\
(\text{individual within dish within food} \\
\text{treatment and sibship})_{l(k(ij))} + \varepsilon_{ijklm} \quad (9.37)
\end{aligned}
$$

Note that both models could be simplified to a two factor ANOVA model by simply using means for each dish as replicates within each treatment and sibship combination. We would end up with the same SS and F tests as in the factorial part of the complete analyses. Note also that individuals within each dish (and replicate measurements on each individual) simply contribute to the dish means but make no real contribution to the df for tests of main effects or their interaction. Power for the tests of sibship and the treatment by sibship interaction could only be improved by increasing the number of dishes and for the test of treatment by increasing the number of sibships.

Some designs require models with more complex mixtures of nested and crossed factors. For example, factor B might be nested within factor

A but crossed with factor C. These partly nested linear models will be examined in Chapter 12.

9.2.13 Power and design in factorial ANOVA

For factorial designs, power calculations are simplest for designs in which all factors are fixed. Power for tests of main effects can be done using the principles described in the previous chapter, effectively treating each main effect as a one factor design. Power tests for interaction terms are more difficult, mainly because it is harder to specify an appropriate form of the effect size. Just as different patterns of means lead to different non-centrality parameters in one factor designs, combining two or more factors generates a large number of treatment combinations, and a great diversity of non-centrality parameters. Calculating the non-centrality parameter (and hence, power) is not difficult, but specifying exactly which pattern of means would be expected under some alternative hypothesis is far more difficult. Despite the difficulty specifying effects, the fixed effect factorial models have the advantage that power for all effects is increased by increasing the number of replicates in each treatment combination, and any such steps that are taken to increase the power of a test on particular main effects will also improve power of tests of interactions. As for nested designs, interaction tests often have more degrees of freedom than corresponding main effects, so power may be more of a problem for tests of main effects.

We have already emphasized the increased complexity that can arise when random factors are included in factorial designs (see also Underwood 1997). Fixed factors and their interactions are often tested against interactions with random factors and the power of these tests will depend on the number of levels of the random factor. In the case of a two factor mixed model design, the power of tests of the random factor and the interaction will be improved by increasing the number of replicates within each combination, but the test of the fixed factor will not be improved much by this tactic. Extra care needs to be taken when designing studies that include random factors, and separate power calculations may need to be done for the fixed and random factors.

9.3 | Pooling in multifactor designs

In multifactor ANOVAs with random factors, some main effects and interactions are not tested against the term with the greatest df (the Residual term). For example, in a two factor design with A fixed and B random, A is tested against B(A) if B is nested or against the AB interaction if B is crossed; in neither case is the Residual used for the test of A. What if B(A) or AB, which are tested against the Residual, are not statistically significant? Could we pool B(A) and the Residual, or AB and the Residual, to provide a test for A with more df and therefore more power?

Recommendations about whether to pool one or more non-significant sources of variation with the Residual in multifactor ANOVAs have been varied (Janky 2000). Most textbooks adopt a "sometime-pool" strategy where pooling under certain conditions is supported. The risk in pooling a nonsignificant result is that we may have made a Type II error, i.e. not rejected the H_0 that the source of variation equals zero when, in

fact, it is false. For this reason, Underwood (1997) supported Winer et al. (1991) in suggesting that the test for the source of variation to be pooled with the Residual be done at α equals 0.25 to protect against a Type II error. Hays (1994) suggested an even more conservative approach with α equals 0.50, which corresponds to an F-ratio of about one, although he recommended using α equals 0.25 in practice. Sokal & Rohlf (1995) also used conservative αs (0.25, 0.50) in their pooling guidelines. We also recommend that, before pooling, any test of the H_0 that the pooled term is not different from the Residual should use a conservative α of at least 0.25.

Is there a potential cost to pooling? The main risk is that pooling terms that really do have different expected means squares will result in biased F-ratios for other terms that use this pooled error term. Using the pooled term as the denominator for subsequent F-ratios means those F-ratios may not necessarily follow an F distribution if H_0 is true. Also, we may have designed our experiment by carefully considering power required to detect a certain effect size and chosen our sample size accordingly (Chapter 7); if we then change our error term by pooling, our original design strategy and sample size may no longer be relevant. There is also some concern in the literature that a preliminary test to determine whether to pool or not may affect the power of any subsequent test (Hines 1996, Janky 2000, Kirk 1995).

Hines (1996) and Janky (2000) have recently reviewed strategies for pooling terms in ANOVA designs. Hines (1996) argued that pooling is only beneficial if another term in the ANOVA is significant after pooling but not before. We do not agree that pooling can only be beneficial if it changes the result of another test in the ANOVA. A particular term may still be non-significant after pooling, but because of greater df for the test, the probability of a Type II error is less for a given effect size than without pooling. Janky (2000) studied the effects of pooling various error terms in a partly nested model (see Chapter 12) and showed that the supposed power advantages of pooling were not always realized. Our view is that for designs with random factors, the power of tests of fixed factors can be improved by pooling nominal denominator terms of F-ratios with lower terms in the model. This is particularly true in field biology where the units of the random factor (either nested or crossed) are often expensive to obtain and our designs are restricted to only a few levels. However, we recommend a "sometime-pool" strategy based on a conservative test of the term to be pooled.

9.4 | Relationship between factorial and nested designs

The sources of variation used in the partitioning of the total variability in the response variable depend on the experimental design. The partitioning of the nested designs we have just discussed can be related to the partitioning for a fully factorial design. For example, consider the comparison of a two factor nested (A, B within A) and a two factor factorial design. SS_A and $SS_{Residual}$ are the same in both analyses, whereas $SS_{B(A)}$ from the nested model equals SS_B plus SS_{AB} from the factorial model.

Similar equalities exist for more complex ANOVA models. For a three factor design, SS_A and $SS_{Residual}$ are again the same in both analyses, $SS_{B(A)}$ equals SS_B plus SS_{AB}, and $SS_{C(B(A))}$ equals SS_C plus SS_{AC} plus SS_{BC} plus SS_{ABC}. Nested and factorial ANOVAs are just different ways of partitioning the variability. These equalities allow nested ANOVAs to be done with software that only analyses factorial designs (Kirk 1995) but such equalities only hold for fully balanced designs.

9.5 | General issues and hints for analysis

9.5.1 General issues

- Nested designs usually include levels of random subsampling nested within higher levels. Tests at each level are the equivalent of single factor ANOVAs using the group means from the level below as observations.
- We recommend Type III SS for unbalanced factorial designs because they are based on unweighted marginal means.
- If you have missing cells, you need to use cell means models and test a restricted set of hypotheses about main effects and interactions. These analyses are difficult and should be done in consultation with an experienced linear models statistician.
- Interactions are nearly always biologically important and can be further analyzed in a number of ways, including tests of simple main effects, treatment–contrast and contrast–contrast interaction tests, and less formally by cell mean plots and data sweeping.
- Rank-based tests for factorial designs should be avoided because they do not reliably detect interaction effects.
- Avoid fractional factorial designs as they must assume that certain complex interactions are negligible.
- Nested factors can be included as subsampling in factorial designs and the analyses are straightforward, although the random nested term will become the denominator for F tests of main effects and interactions.
- Pooling two terms in a multifactor design can increase the power of some tests. However, test the equality of the two terms to be pooled with a conservative significance level, e.g. 0.25.

9.5.2 Hints for analysis

- Make sure that when testing the H_0 for factor A in a nested design that you use the B(A) term for the denominator of the F test if B is random. Your favorite software may default to testing all terms against the residual.
- To increase power of the test for factor A in a two or more factor nested design, you need to increase the number of levels of B within each level of A. Increasing the number of levels of lower factors won't help much.
- When including random factors in factorial designs, ensure that you have worked out the expected mean squares and you know which terms are used as denominators for F tests of fixed factors and interactions. You may not have as many df as you think and might need to increase the number of levels of the random factor, which basically forms part of the replication in these designs.
- When testing simple main effects and treatment–contrast or contrast–contrast interaction tests, make sure you use the appropriate term as the denominator of the F test. When all factors are fixed, this will be the $MS_{Residual}$ from fitting the orginal factorial ANOVA model.

Chapter 10

Randomized blocks and simple repeated measures: unreplicated two factor designs

In Chapter 9, we described the analyses of completely randomized (CR) designs where the factors were either crossed with, or nested in, others. There are several other experimental designs that have special analytical requirements, and are used very commonly in the biological sciences. These include unreplicated factorial designs and designs that combine crossed (factorial) and nested arrangements. We deal with these two groups of designs in the next two chapters. In most cases, the main aim of these designs is to reduce the unexplained variation ($MS_{Residual}$) compared to a CR design. Such designs can be more efficient than CR designs, i.e., they offer more precise estimates of parameters and more powerful tests of the null hypotheses of interest, with no increase in the overall resources needed for the experiment. In contrast to CR designs, however, they involve restricted randomization of factor levels to experimental units and usually have additional assumptions. We will consider the simplest of these designs in this chapter.

We also recommend that biologists distinguish between the physical design (or structure) of an experiment and the linear model used to analyze it. The same model can be applied to a number of different experimental designs and we find some of the literature on these analyses confusing because the label used for the design is often interchanged with the label used for the analysis.

10.1 | Unreplicated two factor experimental designs

A class of experimental designs commonly used in biology is based on a two factor crossed (factorial) design with a single observation in each cell. A completely randomized version of this design, where one experimental unit is allocated randomly to each combination of the two factors, and both factors are of equal interest, is rarely used in biology. This is because interactions between the two factors are likely to be of some interest in such settings and interactions cannot easily be detected without replication in each cell. Such experimental designs might only be useful in exploratory experiments where interactions are unlikely, such as industrial settings (Milliken & Johnson 1984). The linear model for a two factor crossed ANOVA with one observation per cell can, however, be used to analyze two types of experimental design that are very common in biological research – randomized complete blocks (RCB) and simple repeated measures (RM) designs. Although the physical structure of these types of experiments is different, Kirk (1995), Mead (1988) and others have emphasized, as we do in this chapter, that the appropriate null hypotheses and linear models are identical.

10.1.1 Randomized complete block (RCB) designs

These are experimental or sampling designs where one factor is a "blocking" variable and the other factor is the main treatment factor of interest. The

Completely Randomized

Randomized Block

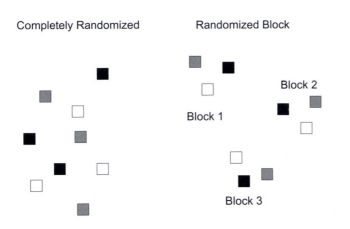

Block 2

Block 1

Block 3

Figure 10.1 Spatial layout of an experiment with three treatments (three levels of treatment factor) and three experimental units for each treatment, contrasting a completely randomized design and a randomized blocks design.

basic principle of blocking in experimental design is to group experimental units together into blocks (which are usually units of space or time) and then each level of the treatment factor(s) is applied to one experimental unit in each block (Figure 10.1). Such designs are used when we suspect that the background environment is patchy enough to increase the variation in the response variable substantially. If experimental units are placed randomly through space (or time), we may get such high levels of background variation as to obscure any effects of the factor of interest. If we group the experimental units into "blocks" that have similar background conditions (e.g. because they are closer together in space or time), we might be able to explain some of the total variation in the response variable by differences between blocks and thus reduce the residual (unexplained) variation. This will permit more precise estimates of parameters and more powerful tests of treatments. Although blocks are commonly spatial groupings, blocks may also represent experimental units matched by physical or biological characteristics that do not have to be grouped in space or time, e.g. using organisms of similar size or age, plots of ground with similar soil characteristics.

Randomized block designs are common in the biological literature.

- Robles *et al.* (1995) examined the effect of increased mussel (*Mytilus* spp.) recruitment on seastar numbers on a rocky shore. There were two treatments: 30 − 40 l of *Mytilus* (0.5–3.5 cm long) added, no *Mytilus* added. Four matched

pairs of mussel beds were chosen, each pair representing a block. Treatments were assigned randomly to mussel beds (experimental units) within a pair (block).

- Faeth (1992) applied one of four leaf damage treatments to four branches within eight randomly chosen trees of an evergreen oak. Trees were blocks and leaf damage was the treatment. Each damage treatment was represented once (on a single branch, the experimental unit) in each block.
- Evans & England (1996) applied one of three artificial honeydew treatments (honeydew followed by water ten days later, water followed by honeydew, water followed by water as control) to three plots in each of ten rows (30 plots in total) in a cultivated alfalfa field. The treatment was type of honeydew application and each row of three plots was a block, with ten blocks in total; a plot was the experimental unit. This experiment also included two repeated measurements, although we can ignore these for the purposes of this chapter and imagine analyzing either of them two times, or the difference between them, as the response variable in a RCB design.

It is apparent from these examples that blocks can be established in two ways (see also Newman *et al.* 1997). First, experimental units may be grouped into blocks at a spatial scale chosen by the investigator as part of the experimental design. The success of RCB designs then depends on establishing blocks at a scale that explains some of the variation in the response variable. Evans & England (1996) used plots (experimental units) in rows (blocks) and the spatial scale of plots within rows and between rows was determined by the investigators. Second, experimental units may be fixed in time or space and blocks are naturally occurring groups of such units and their scale is not under control of the investigator. Faeth (1992) used branches (experimental units) on trees (blocks) and the spatial scale of neither was under the investigator's control.

In RCB designs, factor levels are randomly applied to separate experimental units within each block. This design was originally developed for agricultural experiments where blocks are often paddocks (or fields) that are subdivided for the application of factor levels. RCB designs also extend logically to split-plot experiments (Chapter 11), where another set of factor levels is applied to the whole blocks in addition to the treatments within blocks. Note that the RCB design can also be compared to an equivalent-sized single factor design (factor equals treatments) in which the residual is split into variation due to blocks, representing an attempt to control "nuisance" variables related to the scale of block-

ing, and the remainder. RCB designs involve a restriction on randomization, in contrast to a CR two factor design (Hicks & Turner 1999). Randomization for the RCB design is restricted to experimental units within each block whereas for a CR two factor crossed design with one observation per cell, randomized allocation of experimental units is to all combinations of the two factors, i.e. randomization across both factors.

Mites and domatia on leaves

Walter & O'Dowd (1992) were interested in testing the hypothesis that leaves of the shrub *Viburnum tinus* with domatia (small shelters at the juncture of veins on leaves) have more mites than leaves without domatia. Fourteen paired leaves (blocks) on a shrub of *V. tinus* were randomly chosen and one leaf in each pair had its domatia shaved while the other remained as a control; the number of mites was recorded on each leaf (experimental unit) after two weeks. The analyses of this experiment are in Box 10.1.

Box 10.1 | **Worked example of randomized complete block analysis: mites on leaves**

Walter & O'Dowd (1992) examined the role of domatia (small shelters at the juncture of veins on leaves) in determining the numbers of mites on leaves of plant species with domatia. They did an experiment using 14 pairs of leaves (randomly chosen) with one leaf in each pair with shaved domatia and the other as a control (normal domatia). The response variable was total number of mites per leaf, which Walter & O'Dowd (1992) transformed to $\log_e(0.5 + (mite \times 10))$, ostensibly to improve normality and homogeneity of variances between treatments, the 0.5 added because of zeros although multiplication by ten seemed unnecessary. The data were analyzed using model 10.1, the factors being block and treatment and the response variable being $\log_e(0.5 + (mite \times 10))$.

The main H_0 of interest was that there was no effect of shaving domatia on the mean $\log_e(0.5 + (mite \times 10))$ per leaf, pooling across all possible blocks.

Source	SS	df	MS	F	P
Treatment	31.341	1	31.341	11.315	0.005
Block (leaf pair)	23.058	13	1.774	0.640	0.784
Residual	36.007	13	2.770		

The ANOVA showed that the H_0 of no effect of domatia shaving, averaging over leaf pairs, should be rejected with significantly fewer mites on leaves without domatia (Figure 10.4(a)). There were no effects of blocks although given the random blocks (leaf pairs), this test is only possible if we assume no treatment by block interaction (hence the shading in the ANOVA table). We could have achieved the same test for treatment by running a "repeated measures" analysis, with block (pair) as subject and treatment as the repeated measures factor. There would be no adjusted univariate or multivariate output because there are only two treatment levels.

We also checked for the possibility of an interaction by plotting the log-transformed number of mites for each leaf against block, separating the two treatments (an "interaction" plot: Figure 10.4(a)). The number of mites on leaves without domatia was consistently less than the number on leaves with domatia for all blocks except leaf pair 3. Tukey's test for additivity did not reveal any evidence of a strong interaction:

$$MS_{non-add} = 0.0136, MS_{Remainder} = 2.917, F_{1,18} = 0.012, P = 0.914.$$

Interestingly, for untransformed data, $F_{non-add(1,18)} = 41.98, P < 0.001$, suggesting a strong block by treatment interaction. Clearly, a log transformation improved additivity, as it often does, although the difference in strength of the interaction between transformed and untransformed data is not obvious from the interaction plots (Figure 10.4(a,b)).

The plot of residuals against comparison values from a median polish clearly shows outlying values from leaf pair number 3 at the bottom left and top right of the plot (Figure 10.5(a)). This is the leaf pair that shows the opposite pattern of treatments compared with the other leaf pairs. Note that there appear fewer points than the total number of observations (28) because some observations have identical values for both axes. The plot of residuals against predicted values from the fit of the model based on means (the standard ANOVA; Figure 10.5(b)) also shows the observations from leaf pair 3 as unusual (those with residuals near 3 and -3), although not as clearly as the median-based plot. Neither plot shows any consistent pattern indicating there is no strong interaction between block (leaf pair) and treatment.

10.1.2 Repeated measures (RM) designs

This is another experimental design based on an unreplicated two factor crossed ANOVA design where factor levels are applied to whole experimental units, called subjects, or where experimental units are recorded repeatedly through time. For example, Blake et al. (1994) made twice-yearly bird counts of 500 m segments from ten transects in forested areas in each of Michigan and Wisconsin. The segments in each transect were separated from each other by 50 m and were treated as the experimental units in the study – some segments were omitted (because they were logged or because they were recorded at the end of an observation period when bird numbers had declined) leaving 53 segments in Wisconsin and 51 in Michigan. Separate analyses were done for each state; segments were the subjects and time was the repeated measures factor.

In repeated measures designs, treatments are applied sequentially to the whole subject, which is the equivalent of the block in RCB designs. The RM design was originally developed for psychological and/or behavioral experiments where the block or subject was usually a person. Two different terms are sometimes used for these simple RM designs (Kirk 1995).

1. Subjects × treatments designs, in which the order of factor levels is randomized for each subject. The repeated measures factor is a set of treatments that can be ordered independently of time, e.g. a set of drugs applied to experimental animals.

2. Subjects × trials designs, in which the order of factor levels cannot be randomized. The repeated measures factor is actually time, as in the example from Blake *et al.* (1994).

There are specific difficulties associated with repeated measures experiments (Neter *et al.* 1996), especially when the factor involves experimental treatments applied by the investigator (e.g. drugs given to experimental animals). The first is the problem of carryover effects, where the effect of one treatment may be affected by the preceding treatment in the sequence. This can only be solved by ensuring that the time interval between treatments is long enough to allow recovery of the "subjects". The second problem is the order or sequence effect, where measurements early in a sequence may be different from those later in a sequence, irrespective of treatment. This problem can be alleviated by randomizing the order in which a subject receives each treatment (e.g. randomizing the order in which each animal receives each drug). In many biological experiments, especially in ecology, the factor of interest is commonly time and carryover effects are not so relevant and order or sequence effects are implicit in the hypothesis being tested, e.g. differences between weeks, seasons or years. Note the absence of carryover effects does not imply absence of correlations between successive treatments in a repeated measures sequence. Repeated observations on the same subject will always be correlated to some extent and the nature of these correlations is the main determinant of the analysis strategy for these designs (see Section 10.2).

The distinction between the structure of RCB and RM designs is important. The former allocates levels of the factor of interest (treatments) randomly to different experimental units within blocks; the latter applies the treatments successively to whole blocks, commonly termed subjects, although the order of treatments can be randomized.

Burning and frog numbers in catchments

Driscoll & Roberts (1997) examined the effects of fuel-reduction burning on the abundance of a species of frog in Western Australia. They used six drainages within a catchment, which represent the subjects. In each drainage, they had a matched burnt site and control (unburnt) site and the response variable for the experiment was the difference in the number of calling male frogs between the burnt and control site in each drainage. Note that the analysis of this study could have included the burnt and control sites as an additional factor, although we will analyze the data in the way Driscoll & Roberts (1997) did, using the burnt–control difference within each drainage at each time as the response variable. This variable was recorded three times (repeated measures factor): pre-burn (1992) and two post-burn times (1993, 1994). The analyses of these data are in Box 10.2.

Box 10.2 | Worked example of simple repeated measures analysis: frogs in burnt/unburnt catchments

Driscoll & Roberts (1997) examined the effects of fuel-reduction burning on the abundance of a species of frog in Western Australia. They used six drainages within a catchment, which represent the subjects or blocks. In each drainage, they had a matched burnt site and control (unburnt) site and the response variable for the experiment was the difference in the number of calling male frogs between the burnt and control site in each drainage. This variable was recorded three times (repeated measurements) – pre-burn (1992) and two times post-burn (1993, 1994). This is a classical repeated measures (subjects by trials) design.

The main H_0 of interest was that there was no difference between years in the mean difference in the number of calling male frogs between burnt and unburnt catchments.

The results from the ANOVA are as follows.

Source	df	GG–df	HF–df	MS	F	P	GG–P	HF–P
Years	2	1.42	1.83	184.722	9.660	0.005	0.0130	0.006
Residual	10	7.12	9.15	19.122				

The following are as published in Driscoll & Roberts (1997).

Source	SS	df	MS	F	P
Year	369.44	2	184.72	9.66	0.005
Block (drainage)	955.61	5	191.12	9.99	0.001
Residual	191.22	10	19.12		

Greenhouse–Geisser epsilon $= 0.712$, Huynh–Feldt epsilon $= 0.915$. Note that the Greenhouse–Geisser epsilon estimate is more conservative than the Huynh–Feldt estimate and the former results in a more severe correction of the df and a more conservative test. Although both epsilon estimates are less than one, the conclusions from the univariate ANOVA are unchanged irrespective of whether adjusted or unadjusted df and P values are used. We agree with the conclusion of Driscoll & Roberts (1997), that the H_0 of no difference between years should be rejected. The test of block (drainage) is only valid if we assume no year by block interaction. This test indicates significant variation between drainages.

We also included a planned contrast of the pre-burn year versus the two post-burn years, using a separate error term just for this contrast:

$F_{1,5} = 29.72, P = 0.003$, indicating that the post-burn years are significantly different from the pre-burn year in the burnt–control differences in the number of calling frogs.

MANOVA results:

Pillai Trace $= 0.873$ with 2, 4 df, $F = 13.69, P = 0.016$.

Mauchly sphericity test, $W = 0.5959$, chi-square approx. $= 2.0709$ (2 df), $P = 0.355$; Mauchly's test does not reject the H_0 of sphericity but is sensitive to non-normality.

We used some graphical checks and Tukey's test for non-additivity to see if an interaction was present. First, an "interaction" plot where blocks are along the horizontal axis and different lines/symbols represent the different years (Figure 10.6(a)). Note there is a change in the rankings of years 2 and 3 for blocks 5 and 6 but no evidence of any strong interaction. We also plotted residuals against predicted values and residuals against comparison values for the fitted additive model based on means, i.e. the standard ANOVA (Figure 10.6(b)). There is no curvilinear pattern in the first plot and no pattern at all in the second plot, suggesting that there is no strong interaction between years and blocks. The results of Tukey's test for non-additivity (see Box 10.5) were $F_{non-add} = 0.026/21.244 = 0.001$ with 1 and 9 df, $P = 0.974$, again no evidence of an interaction.

We also tested the H_0 that there was no linear trend in burnt–unburnt differences in frog numbers through the years.

Source	df	MS	F	P
Year	1	352.083	15.122	0.012
Residual	5	23.283		

Note that the error term used is different from the $MS_{Residual}$ in the original ANOVA; this is because we used a separate error term in case sphericity was not met. There is a significant linear trend from 1992 to 1994, with the difference between the burnt and control sites changing from negative to increasing positive. A quadratic trend test is also possible (years has two df) but is difficult to justify fitting a quadratic trend through three means.

Table 10.1 Data layout for a RCB design with p levels of factor A (treatments $i = 1$ to p) and q levels of factor B (blocks $j = 1$ to q) and n equals one in each cell

	A 1	A 2	A 3	A i	Block marginal means
Block 1	y_{11}	y_{21}	y_{31}	y_{i1}	$\bar{y}_{j=1}$
Block 2	y_{12}	y_{22}	y_{32}	y_{i2}	$\bar{y}_{j=2}$
Block 3	y_{13}	y_{23}	y_{33}	y_{i3}	$\bar{y}_{j=3}$
Block j	y_{1j}	y_{2j}	y_{3j}	y_{ij}	$\bar{y}_j$
A marginal means	$\bar{y}_{i=1}$	$\bar{y}_{i=2}$	$\bar{y}_{i=3}$	$\bar{y}_i$	Overall mean $\bar{y}$

Note:
From Walter & O'Dowd (1992), treatments (factor A) are leaves with domatia and shaved domatia, blocks are leaf pairs, individual leaves are the experimental units and the response variable is number of mites per leaf. For the simple RM design from Driscoll & Roberts (1997), treatments (factor A) are year (1992, 1993, 1994), blocks (i.e. subjects) are drainages, which are also the experimental units, and the response variable is difference in number of frogs between burnt and unburnt sites.

10.2 | Analyzing RCB and RM designs

10.2.1 Linear models for RCB and RM analyses

Linear effects model
Consider the RCB design from Walter & O'Dowd (1992) with factor A (domatia treatment) having $i = 1$ to p being groups ($p = 2$, shaved and unshaved domatia) and factor B (leaf pairs) having $j = 1$ to q blocks ($q = 14$ leaf pairs) – see Table 10.1 and Figure 10.2. The linear model we fit to these data is an additive effects model, in which the response variable in each cell represents an additive combination of factor A (treatments) and block effects and

we assume no interaction between treatments and blocks:

$$y_{ij} = \mu + \alpha_i + \beta_j + \varepsilon_{ij} \tag{10.1}$$

Details of this linear model, including estimation of its parameters and means, are provided in Box 10.3.

Using the example from Walter & O'Dowd (1992):

$$(\text{mite number})_{ij} = \mu + (\text{domatia treatment})_i + (\text{leaf pair})_j + \varepsilon_{ij} \tag{10.2}$$

From Driscoll & Roberts (1997):

$$(\text{burnt vs unburnt difference in frog numbers})_{ij} = \mu + (\text{year})_i + (\text{catchment})_j + \varepsilon_{ij} \tag{10.3}$$

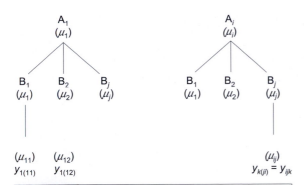

Figure 10.2 General data layout for randomized complete block ANOVA where factor A has p ($i = 1$ to p) groups and there are q ($j = 1$ to q) blocks and a single observation within each cell.

In models 10.1 and 10.2:

y_{ij} is the number of mites per leaf from the ith domatia treatment and the jth leaf pair (block).

μ is the overall (constant) mean number of mites per leaf for all combinations of domatia treatment and leaf pair (block).

If factor A is fixed, α_i is the main effect of the ith domatia treatment (removing domatia or leaving domatia) on the number of mites per leaf, pooling leaf pairs (blocks). If factor A is random, then α_i is a random variable with a variance (σ_α^2) measuring the variance in the number of mites per leaf among all possible groups that could have been used.

Box 10.3 | The randomized complete block (or simple repeated measures) linear model and its parameters

Consider a RCB design with factor A ($i = 1$ to p) being treatments and factor B ($j = 1$ to q) being blocks. Each observation is y_{ij} (the value in each cell), the marginal treatment means pooling blocks are $\bar{y}_i$ and the marginal block means pooling treatments are $\bar{y}_j$ (Table 10.1). Such data structures, where we have two factors and a single observation in each cell, are sometimes referred to as two-way tables (Emerson & Hoaglin 1983). Contingency tables of frequencies (Chapter 14) are another example of a two-way table.

The linear model we usually fit to these data is an additive effects model, in which the response variable in each cell represents an additive combination of factor A (treatments) and block effects and we assume no interaction between treatments and blocks:

$$y_{ij} = \mu + \alpha_i + \beta_j + \varepsilon_{ij}$$

In model 10.1 we find the following.

y_{ij} is the value of the response variable from the ith level of factor A and the jth block.

μ is the (constant) overall population mean of the response variable.

If factor A is fixed, α_i is effect of ith level of factor A ($\mu_i - \mu$) pooling over blocks. If factor A is random, α_i represents a random variable with a mean of zero and a variance of σ_α^2, measuring the variance in mean values of the response variable across all the possible levels of factor A that could have been used.

If blocks are fixed, β_j is the effect of the jth block ($\mu_j - \mu$) pooling over levels of factor A. If blocks are random, which is more common, β_j represents a random variable with a mean of zero and a variance of σ_β^2, measuring the variance in mean values of the response variable across all the possible blocks that could have been used.

ε_{ij} is random or unexplained error associated with the observation at each combination of the ith level of factor A and jth level of factor B and is measured as $y_{ij} - \mu_i - \mu_j + \mu$. This is the error in the value of the response variable within each treatment–block combination that is not due to the treatment or block. These error terms are assumed to be normally distributed at each combination of factor A level and block, with a mean of zero $[E(\varepsilon_{ij}) = 0]$ and a variance of σ_ε^2.

This model is overparameterized (see Box 8.1) so to estimate model parameters, we impose the usual restrictions that $\sum_{i=1}^{p} \alpha_i = 0$ if factor A is fixed and $\sum_{j=1}^{q} \beta_j = 0$ if blocks are fixed. Alternatively, we can fit a cell means model:

$$y_{ij} = \mu_{ij} + \varepsilon_{ij}$$

where μ_{ij} is the population mean for each cell and ε_{ij} is the error term associated with the observation in each cell, which we assume are normally distributed with a mean of zero and a variance of σ_ε^2. The cell means model is particularly useful when dealing with missing observations (Section 10.9).

In practice, we fit the additive effects model when analyzing RCB or simple RM designs. However, this model does not allow for an interaction between factor A (treatments) and blocks. In biological experiments, especially field experiments where blocks are spatial units, interactions between treatments and blocks are likely and we can conceptualize an alternative non-additive model that allows for an interaction between treatments and blocks:

$$y_{ij} = \mu + \alpha_i + \beta_j + [(\alpha\beta)_{ij}] + \varepsilon_{ij}$$

where μ, α_i, β_j, and ε_{ij} are defined as previously and $(\alpha\beta)_{ij}$ is the interaction between treatments and blocks. Note that the interaction term is in parentheses, because although we include it in this model, we can never estimate this term separately from the residual because we only have n equals one in each treatment–block combination. The RCB or simple RM experimental design does not permit us to separately estimate the interaction term and the error term associated with individual observations with each treatment–block combination. As Gates (1995) has pointed out, the residual or error term in a RCB design actually estimates three components: (i) block by treatment interaction, (ii) within block variability between experimental units, and potentially (iii) within experimental unit sampling variation. The important issue is that these different components cannot be distinguished because we only have one experimental unit for each treatment in each block. Although a formal test of the H_0 of no interaction is not possible, we can check for interactions in a less formal manner using graphical methods and use Tukey's test for non-additivity to detect some types of interactions (Section 10.3.2).

Conceptualizing the model in the non-additive form does have a practical use. We can include the interaction term when determining the expected mean squares for our analysis of variance and therefore assess what effect the presence of an interaction will have on the choice of F-ratios for testing both treatment and block effects.

Estimating the parameters of the factorial linear model 10.1 follows the procedures outlined for a single factor model in Chapter 8, and for nested and factorial models in Chapter 9. Consider a RCB or simple RM design, with the usual configuration of Factor A fixed and blocks/subjects random. The estimate of each cell mean μ_{ij} is simply the single observation within each cell. Estimates of the marginal means μ_i and μ_j are also straightforward. The marginal means for factor A are estimated from the observations for that level of factor A averaged across the blocks and vice versa for the marginal means for blocks. The estimate of μ is the average of all the observations, or the average of the A marginal means or the average of the B marginal means. Standard errors for these means are based on the estimate of the variance of the error terms σ_ε^2, the $MS_{Residual}$ (see Box 9.6).

The estimate of α_i is the difference between the mean of each A level and the overall mean. Interaction effects measure how much the effect of one factor depends on the level of the other factor and vice versa. If there is no interaction between the two factors, we would expect the cell means to be represented by the sum of the overall mean and the main effects:

$$\mu_{ij} = \mu_i + \mu_j - \mu$$

Therefore, the effect of the interaction between the ith level of A and jth block $(\alpha\beta)_{ij}$ can be defined as the difference between the ijth cell mean and its value we would expect if there was no interaction. This represents those effects not due to the overall mean and the main effects.

Note that in practice we don't calculate the estimated factor or interaction effects, usually focusing on contrasts of marginal or cell means (Section 10.6).

If factor B is fixed, β_j is the main effect of the specific leaf pairs (blocks) on the number of mites per leaf, pooling domatia treatments. If factor B is random, then β_j is a random variable with a variance (σ_β^2) measuring the variance in the number of mites per leaf among all possible leaf pairs (blocks) that could have been used.

ε_{ij} is random or unexplained error associated with the number of mites per leaf at each combination of the ith domatia treatment and jth leaf pair (block). This error has at least two components (Box 10.3). First, the true error due to random variability between replicate observations in the populations within each combination of treatment and block. Second, the error due to any interaction between treatment and block. With only a single observation in each block for each treatment, we cannot separately estimate these two sources of error.

Predicted values and residuals
If we replace the parameters in model 10.1 by their OLS estimates (Box 10.3), it turns out that the predicted or fitted values of the response variable from our linear model are:

$$\hat{y}_{ij} = \bar{y} + (\bar{y}_i - \bar{y}) + (\bar{y}_j - \bar{y}) = \bar{y}_i + \bar{y}_j - \bar{y} \qquad (10.4)$$

So any predicted Y-value is predicted by the marginal domatia treatment mean, the marginal leaf pair (block) mean and the overall mean. For example, the predicted number of mites per leaf for the domatia shaved treatment in leaf pair one is the marginal mean for the domatia shaved treatment (pooling leaf pairs) plus the marginal mean for leaf pair one (pooling domatia treatments) minus the overall mean number of mites per leaf.

The error terms (ε_{ijk}) from the linear model can be estimated by the residuals, where a residual (e_{ijk}) is simply the difference between each observed and predicted Y-value:

$$e_{ij} = y_{ij} - \hat{y}_{ij} = y_{ij} - \bar{y}_i - \bar{y}_j + \bar{y} \qquad (10.5)$$

For example, the residuals from the model relating number of mites per leaf to domatia treatment and leaf pair are the differences between the observed number of mites per leaf and the marginal mean for the domatia treatment (pooling leaf pairs) minus the marginal mean for leaf pair (pooling domatia treatments) plus the overall mean number of mites per leaf. These residuals actually estimate the effect of the interaction between blocks and treatments for each cell although this cannot be distinguished from the variation associated with each observation

Table 10.2 | ANOVA table for RCB design

Source	SS	df	MS
A (treatments)	$q\sum_{i=1}^{p}(\bar{y}_i-\bar{y})^2$	$p-1$	$\dfrac{SS_A}{p-1}$
B (blocks)	$p\sum_{j=1}^{q}(\bar{y}_j-\bar{y})^2$	$q-1$	$\dfrac{SS_B}{q-1}$
Residual	$\sum_{i=1}^{p}\sum_{j=1}^{q}(\bar{y}_{ij}-\bar{y}_i-\bar{y}_j+\bar{y})^2$	$(p-1)(q-1)$	$\dfrac{SS_{Residual}}{(p-1)(q-1)}$
Total	$\sum_{i=1}^{p}\sum_{j=1}^{q}(y_{ij}-\bar{y})^2$	$pq-1$	

Table 10.3 | The comparison of completely randomized and randomized block ANOVAs for the general case with p treatments and q experimental units per treatment and the example from Walter & O'Dowd (1992) with two treatments and either 14 replicates per treatment (completely randomized) or 14 blocks (block design)

Source	Randomized block		Completely randomized	
	general df	specific df	general df	specific df
Treatments	$p-1$	1	$p-1$	1
Blocks	$q-1$	13		
Residual	$(p-1)(q-1)$	13	$p(q-1)$	26
Total	$pq-1$	27	$pq-1$	27

within each cell (because n equals one for each treatment–block combination). As in all linear models, residuals provide the basis of the OLS estimate of σ_ε^2 and they are valuable diagnostic tools for checking assumptions and fit of our model (Section 10.4).

10.2.2 Analysis of variance

The classical partitioning of variation from a least squares fit of the additive effects model for a RCB or simple RM design is shown in Table 10.2. The SS are based on marginal means (Table 10.1) as for any factorial ANOVA model (see Chapter 9). SS_A measures the sum of squared differences between each treatment marginal mean and the overall mean; the SS_B measures the sum of squared differences between each block marginal mean and the overall mean; the $SS_{Residual}$ measures the sum of squared differences for a particular contrast

involving cell means, marginal means and the overall mean, i.e. the interaction between treatments and blocks. The mean squares (MS) are determined by dividing the SS by their df.

The comparison between the ANOVAs for a RCB design, where experimental units are grouped into blocks, and the equivalent sized single factor CR design, where the allocation of treatments to experimental units is randomized, is shown in Table 10.3. Note that the RCB design has fewer df for the residual than the single factor CR design. The residual term in the CR design has been simply split into blocks and "residual" components. We are making a trade-off in that we are accepting fewer df in the residual term of the RCB, in expectation that the SS and MS will be lower, and more than compensate for the loss of df in terms of the power of the test of treatments (Section 10.7).

Table 10.4 Structure of ANOVA table for "classical" repeated measures design. Note that this ANOVA is identical to a randomized blocks ANOVA, where subjects are blocks

Source	General df	Specific df
Between "subjects" (drainages)	$q - 1$	5
Within "subjects" (drainages)	$q(p - 1)$	12
Treatments (years)	$p - 1$	2
Residual	$(q - 1)(p - 1)$	10
Total	$pq - 1$	17

Note:
The specific example is from Driscoll & Roberts (1997) with three treatments (years) and six subjects.

For the analysis of a classical RM design, the ANOVA table is sometimes presented slightly differently compared with the analysis of a classical RCB design, to distinguish sources variation between subjects (i.e. blocks) and sources of variation within subjects – see Table 10.4. This ANOVA table is actually the same as for the usual RCB design except that within and between subjects (or blocks) sources of variation have been made explicit. The same linear model is used to analyze RCB and simple RM designs, an additive two factor ANOVA model.

The expected mean squares (EMS) for different combinations of fixed and random factors are given in Table 10.5. Note that we can derive these EMS is two ways. First, assuming there is no A by blocks interaction and fitting the standard additive model 10.1. Second, by including the possibility of an A by blocks interaction with a non-additive model (Box 10.3). In practice, we cannot really fit a non-additive model because we cannot estimate the interaction term separately from the true error. The non-additive form of the EMS, however, does allow us to evaluate the effect of an interaction on the relevant *F*-ratios for testing the null hypotheses.

The EMS for the non-additive model where factor A is fixed and blocks are random is based on the classical approach for mixed models (one factor fixed and one random) as outlined in Chapter 9. The interaction is considered a random effect and the interaction effects sum to zero across the levels of the fixed factor (McLean *et al.* 1991). The alternative formulation of EMS only changes the expected value of the mean square for the random block effect anyway, although the interpretation of the blocks term in these ANOVAs still creates considerable debate among statisticians (Samuels *et al.* 1991 and subsequent comments in same issue). Note that the EMS for the non-additive model are identical to those derived for the two factor crossed model described in Chapter 9.

10.2.3 Null hypotheses

There are two null hypotheses of interest in RCB (or simple RM) designs. The most important is the test for treatment effects, but the test of block effects might also be of some interest. The statistical tests of these null hypotheses depend on the expected mean squares (EMS) which in turn depend on whether we consider an interaction likely and whether the factors (treatments and blocks) are considered fixed or random. The most common situation in biological experiments is where block or subject is a random factor (the blocks used in the experiment are a random sample from a larger population of blocks and we wish to generalize our results to this population of blocks) and factor A ("treatment") is fixed, although other combinations are possible.

Factor A (fixed)
$H_0(A): \mu_1 = \mu_2 = ... = \mu_i = ... = \mu_p$. This H_0 states that there is no difference between the factor A marginal means, pooling blocks. Using the experiment from Walter & O'Dowd (1992), the H_0 is no difference between the mean number of mites per leaf for the two domatia treatments, pooling leaf pairs (blocks).

This is equivalent to:

$H_0: \alpha_1 = \alpha_2 = ... = \alpha_i = 0$, i.e. no effect of any level of factor A and therefore all treatment effects equal zero. For this example, there is no effect of domatia treatment on the mean number of mites per leaf (Walter & O'Dowd 1992).

Blocks (random)

$H_0(B)$: $\sigma_\beta^2 = 0$, i.e. no added variance due to all possible blocks that could have been used. From Walter & O'Dowd (1992), the H_0 is that there is no added variance due to all possible leaf pairs that could have been used.

F-ratios

We can test these null hypotheses by seeing which of our mean squares have the same expected value when the H_0 is true. The F-ratio from these mean squares will follow an F distribution if certain assumptions (see Section 10.4) hold. It is clear from Table 10.5 that MS_A and $MS_{Residual}$ have the same expected value when there is no effect of factor A so these two mean squares are used in an F-ratio to test the H_0. Note that when there are only two levels of factor A (treatments), the F test for treatments in a RCB or RM design is equivalent to a paired t test (Chapter 3) of the H_0 that the mean of the paired treatment differences equals zero.

There is no test for block effects if we allow for an interaction between treatments and blocks when blocks are random because there is no MS that has the same expected value as MS_{Blocks} when H_0 is true (the $MS_{Residual}$ has two components, rather than just σ_ε^2). As we pointed out in the previous section, the hypotheses being tested about block effects depend on which version of the EMS we use for mixed models (Chapter 9) and is an issue of debate among statisticians (Samuels et al. 1991).

For other combinations of fixed and random factors/blocks, tests of null hypotheses depend on whether we are willing to assume an underlying additive (no treatment by block interaction) model or not. For example, if both factor A (treatments) and blocks are fixed, there is no test for either unless we assume an underlying additive model. If factor A is random (H_0: $\sigma_\alpha^2 = 0$) but blocks are fixed (an unusual combination in practice), there is also no test for A unless we assume an additive model.

The complete ANOVAs and interpretation of the studies from Walter & O'Dowd (1992) and Driscoll & Roberts (1997) are presented in Box 10.1 and Box 10.2 respectively. These are both mixed models with blocks (or subjects) random, so the tests for blocks are only valid if there is no A by blocks interaction.

10.2.4 Comparing ANOVA models

The SS, df and MS for each term in the classical ANOVA (Table 10.2) can also be derived from comparing the fit of a full and a reduced linear model, where the reduced model simply omits the parameter specified to be zero in the H_0 – see Box 10.4. The approach of comparing linear models also offers strategies for handling missing values (Section 10.9) whereas the formulae in Table 10.2 are only applicable when there are no missing values. We use SS (and MS) to measure the fit of the different models, although likelihoods could also be used with the likelihood ratio replacing the F-ratio for testing whether the reduced model fits significantly worse than the full model (Chapter 13).

10.3 | Interactions in RCB and RM models

10.3.1 Importance of treatment by block interactions

If we do assume an underlying additive model, with its associated expected mean squares, then the H_0 for factor A is that there is no effect of treatments in any block (Newman et al. 1997). The additive model also allows a test of the block effects, although these are usually not of much interest in practice except for determining the efficiency of blocking compared to a CR design – see Section 10.7. Also, assuming an additive model allows a test of factor A and blocks if both are fixed; neither is testable in the presence of an interaction using the non-additive model. How realistic is the additive (no interaction) model for biological experiments?

Newman et al. (1997) argued that if blocks are spatial units defined by the investigator, then we might consider them simply large, randomly chosen, experimental units, and hence treatment by block interactions are unlikely. In contrast, others (e.g. Mead 1988, Underwood 1997) have argued that factor A by block interactions are quite likely in biological experiments, particularly for field experiments where experience suggests that treatment effects may vary spatially. Newman et al. (1997) suggested that interactions are more likely when blocks are naturally occurring units (e.g. organisms, genotypes) than when the scale of blocks is chosen by the investigator.

Table 10.5 Expected mean squares (EMS) for additive and non-additive models for a RCB design. There are p levels of factor A (treatments) and q blocks

Additive model

Source	A fixed, blocks fixed — EMS	F-ratio	A fixed, blocks random — EMS	F-ratio	A random, blocks fixed — EMS	F-ratio	A random, blocks random — EMS	F-ratio
A	$\sigma_\varepsilon^2 + q\dfrac{\sum_{i=1}^{p}\alpha_i^2}{p-1}$		$\sigma_\varepsilon^2 + q\dfrac{\sum_{i=1}^{p}\alpha_i^2}{p-1}$	$\dfrac{MS_A}{MS_{Residual}}$	$\sigma_\varepsilon^2 + q\sigma_\alpha^2$	$\dfrac{MS_A}{MS_{Residual}}$	$\sigma_\varepsilon^2 + q\sigma_\alpha^2$	$\dfrac{MS_A}{MS_{Residual}}$
Blocks	$\sigma_\varepsilon^2 + p\dfrac{\sum_{j=1}^{q}\beta_j^2}{q-1}$		$\sigma_\varepsilon^2 + p\sigma_\beta^2$	$\dfrac{MS_{Blocks}}{MS_{Residual}}$	$\sigma_\varepsilon^2 + p\dfrac{\sum_{j=1}^{q}\beta_j^2}{q-1}$		$\sigma_\varepsilon^2 + p\sigma_\beta^2$	$\dfrac{MS_{Blocks}}{MS_{Residual}}$
Residual	σ_ε^2		σ_ε^2		σ_ε^2		σ_ε^2	

Non-additive model

Source	A fixed, blocks fixed — EMS	F-ratio	A fixed, blocks random — EMS	F-ratio	A random, blocks fixed — EMS	F-ratio	A random, blocks random — EMS	F-ratio
A	$\sigma_\varepsilon^2 + q\dfrac{\sum_{i=1}^{p}\alpha_i^2}{p-1}$	No test	$\sigma_\varepsilon^2 + \sigma_{\alpha\beta}^2 + q\dfrac{\sum_{i=1}^{p}\alpha_i^2}{p-1}$	$\dfrac{MS_A}{MS_{Residual}}$	$\sigma_\varepsilon^2 + q\sigma_\alpha^2$	No test	$\sigma_\varepsilon^2 + \sigma_{\alpha\beta}^2 + q\sigma_\alpha^2$	$\dfrac{MS_A}{MS_{Residual}}$
Blocks	$\sigma_\varepsilon^2 + p\dfrac{\sum_{j=1}^{q}\beta_j^2}{q-1}$	No test	$\sigma_\varepsilon^2 + q\sigma_\beta^2$	No test	$\sigma_\varepsilon^2 + \sigma_{\alpha\beta}^2 + p\dfrac{\sum_{j=1}^{q}\beta_j^2}{q-1}$	$\dfrac{MS_{Blocks}}{MS_{Residual}}$	$\sigma_\varepsilon^2 + \sigma_{\alpha\beta}^2 + p\sigma_\beta^2$	$\dfrac{MS_{Blocks}}{MS_{Residual}}$
Residual	$\sigma_\varepsilon^2 + \dfrac{\sum_{i=1}^{p}\sum_{j=1}^{q}(\alpha\beta)_{ij}^2}{(p-1)(q-1)}$		$\sigma_\varepsilon^2 + \sigma_{\alpha\beta}^2$		$\sigma_\varepsilon^2 + \sigma_{\alpha\beta}^2$		$\sigma_\varepsilon^2 + \sigma_{\alpha\beta}^2$	

Box 10.4 | Fitting general linear models to test factor A in RCB design from Walter & O'Dowd (1992)

Full model fitted:

$(\text{Log mite number})_{ij} = \mu + (\text{treatment})_i + (\text{block})_j + \varepsilon_{ij}$

	SS	df	MS
Explained	54.399	14	3.886
Unexplained	36.007	13	2.770
$r^2 = 0.602$			

Reduced model fitted:

$(\text{Log mite number})_{ij} = \mu + (\text{block})_j + \varepsilon_{ij}$

	SS	df	MS
Explained	23.058	13	1.774
Unexplained	67.348	14	4.811
$r^2 = 0.255$			

Difference in fit of two models:

Full SS$_{\text{Explained}}$ (54.399) − Reduced SS$_{\text{Explained}}$ (23.058) = 31.341 with 1 df
MS$_A$ = 31.341, which is MS$_A$ from randomized block ANOVA (see Box 10.1).

Test of A:

$F = \text{MS}_A / \text{Full MS}_{\text{Residual}} = 31.341 / 2.770$ with 1,13 df = 11.32, $P = 0.005$.

Fortunately, the test for treatments (MS$_A$/MS$_{\text{Residual}}$) is statistically valid for a mixed model (A fixed, blocks random), whether we assume an additive model or not. If we allow for an interaction between A and block by using the expected mean squares from the non-additive model (Table 10.5), both MS$_A$ and MS$_{\text{Residual}}$ include $\sigma_\varepsilon^2 + \sigma_{\alpha\beta}^2$ in their expectations, the variance due to random differences between observations within each cell and the variance due to the interaction between treatments and blocks. With only n equals one per cell, we cannot separately estimate these two variances. These expected mean squares suggest that the test for factor A is really for the presence of an effect of treatments over and above the interaction between A and blocks (which still might exist, even if we cannot measure it in our unreplicated RCB or RM experiment) and true error variation. Bergerud (1996) suggested that treatment effects over and above interaction

effects would occur when the treatment rankings are consistent for each block, even if the actual differences between treatments change from block to block (a treatment by block interaction). The treatment by block interaction is only statistically critical when blocks are fixed, in which case there is no test of treatments unless we assume the A by block interaction is zero (Kirk 1995, Neter *et al.* 1996).

Even if we allow for an underlying non-additive model when determining our EMS and constructing our F-ratios for the mixed model case, the presence of A by block interactions can result in two other difficulties when interpreting the treatment effects. First, if there is an interaction, then the MS$_{\text{Residual}}$, whose expected value contains $\sigma_\varepsilon^2 + \sigma_{\alpha\beta}^2$, will increase proportionally more than MS$_A$, whose expected value also includes treatment effects. The F-ratio for A will therefore have relatively less power in the presence of an

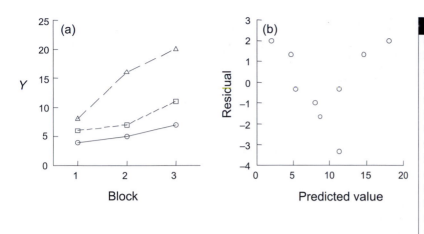

Figure 10.3 Illustration of detection of treatment by block interaction with (a) interaction plot and (b) residual plot – artificial data. Note that the difference between treatments is much greater for blocks 2 and 3 compared to block 1 but there is change in direction of treatment effects – no crossing over in interaction plot. There is clear evidence of a curvilinear relationship in the residual plot where the residuals change from positive to negative and back to positive as the predicted values increase.

interaction. Second, if the interaction is very strong, then there can be a logical difficulty with the interpretation of main effects, as discussed in Chapter 9 and by Underwood (1997). Complex interactions, where the effects of treatments are strong but in different directions between blocks, can result in a non-significant main effect of A averaging over blocks. Meaningful interpretation of such a non-significant main effect is difficult. However, interpretation of significant main effects can still be valid in the presence of an interaction (see Chapter 9). A significant main effect indicates that, averaging over blocks, there is a treatment effect even if the magnitude of that effect varies from block to block.

We recommend that you should check for A by block interactions in analyses of RCB and RM designs. Interpretation of main effects in the non-additive model may need to be constrained if strong interactions are present; the additive model, which may be necessary if blocks are fixed, relies on the absence of interactions.

10.3.2 Checks for interaction in unreplicated designs

With only one replicate experimental unit in every treatment–block combination, there is no formal test for an interaction. However, there are three ways in which an interaction between A and blocks might be detected. The first two are graphical and the third is a test for a particular type of interaction. We illustrate all three methods for the two worked examples in Box 10.1 and Box 10.2.

Cell "mean" plots

We discussed plots of cell means to interpret interactions for factorial designs in Chapter 9. These are simply plots (usually line graphs) of cell means, where the levels of one factor are used to define groups along the horizontal axis, the vertical axis is the value of the response variable and the different levels of the second factor are represented by different symbols (joined by lines). We can use the same plots for RCB or RM designs, except that the horizontal axis represents blocks or subjects and we plot the single values within each treatment–block combination (Figure 10.3(a)). Note that we still refer to population means for each cell (treatment–block combination) although we only estimate those means with n equals one in each cell in a RCB (RM) design. As with CR factorial designs, the lines should be roughly parallel if there is no interaction.

Residual plots

Another way to detect interactions is to examine the residuals. An interaction would be suggested if the pattern of the residuals changed markedly from block to block (Neter et al. 1996). Two graphical diagnostic techniques using residuals have been described in the statistical literature for showing interactions in RCB (RM) designs:

1. A plot of residuals against predicted values, the typical residual plot we have used extensively for assessing the adequacy of linear models in earlier chapters, is important in checking homogeneity of variance and the presence of

outliers and can also detect some types of interaction. A curvilinear relationship in this plot, where the residuals change from positive to negative and back to positive again as the predicted values increase, indicates a particular sort of block by treatment interaction (Neter *et al.* 1996), where the relative magnitudes of the treatment effects differ between blocks but not the direction of the effects (i.e. no crossing over in interaction plot) – see Figure 10.3(b). This is the sort of interaction that can often be removed by transformation (Box *et al.* 1978). In contrast, complex interactions where the direction of treatment effects changes between blocks are not easily detected with residual plots.

2. A plot of residuals against estimated comparison values (Emerson & Hoaglin 1983), where each comparison value is $(\alpha_i \beta_j)/\mu$ for each cell ij from the fit of the additive model 10.1. The estimates of μ, α_i and β_j are described in Box 10.3. Any consistent pattern suggests the presence of an interaction. Emerson & Hoaglin (1983) argued that this plot is particularly useful for determining the strength of an interaction already suggested by the first residual plot or a cell means plot and helps choose a transformation that might restore additivity. If the slope of the best-fit line on this plot is k, then a power transformation using a power of $1 - k$ will be effective. Emerson & Hoaglin (1983) also recommended using robust estimates of effects for calculating comparison values, such as those

from a median polish (see Section 10.5), to distinguish systematic non-additivity from the effects of just one or two unusual values.

Tukey's test for (non-)additivity
Tukey (1949) developed a test to detect one particular type of interaction in unreplicated factorial designs. Tukey's test for additivity can be viewed as a test of the curvilinear relationship between the residuals and the predicted values from the original linear model (Box *et al.* 1978), the relationship we were trying to detect with the residual plot described above. It is also a specific contrast–contrast test on the interaction (Hays 1994, Kirk 1995) where the contrast coefficients are $(\bar{y}_i - \bar{y})$ and $(\bar{y}_j - \bar{y})$. Kirk (1995) pointed out that Tukey's test for additivity is best at detecting relatively simple interactions which involve different magnitudes of treatment effects for each block but not different directions of the treatment effects (i.e. lines in interaction plot are not parallel but do not cross). He also suggested that a liberal significance level should be used ($\alpha = 0.10$ or 0.25) to reduce the risk of a Type II error (not detecting a real interaction), a recommendation we support.

The computational details are provided in Box 10.5 and illustrated using the data from Driscoll & Roberts (1997). Basically the $SS_{Residual}$ is split into that due to the specific type of non-additivity described above and that remaining. This $SS_{non-add}$ is a single df component from the original $SS_{Residual}$ and the remaining $(q - 1)(p - 1) - 1$ df

---

Box 10.5 | **Tukey's test for (non-)additivity, illustrated for data from Driscoll & Roberts (1997)**

Recall the non-additive linear model from Box 10.3 for the RCB/RM design:

$$y_{ij} = \mu + \alpha_i + \beta_j + [(\alpha\beta)_{ij}] + \varepsilon_{ij}$$

We can redefine $(\alpha\beta)_{ij}$ as $D\alpha_i\beta_j$ where D is a second-order polynomial function of α_i and β_j and represents the multiplicative relationship between factor A and blocks (Neter *et al.* 1996, Sokal & Rohlf 1995). The value of D is, using the terminology of Neter *et al.* (1996):

$$D = \frac{\sum_{i=1}^{p}\sum_{j=1}^{q}\alpha_i\beta_j y_{ij}}{\sum_{i=1}^{p}\alpha_i^2 \sum_{j=1}^{q}\beta_j^2}$$

where α_i and β_j are the effects of factor A and blocks respectively, as defined in Box 10.3. We replace these parameters by their sample estimates to obtain the estimated value of D:

$$\hat{D} = \frac{\sum_{i=1}^{p}\sum_{j=1}^{q}(\bar{y}_i - \bar{y})(\bar{y}_j - \bar{y})y_{ij}}{\sum_{i=1}^{p}(\bar{y}_i - \bar{y})^2\sum_{j=1}^{q}(\bar{y}_j - \bar{y})^2}$$

The SS for this specific form of non-additivity is $\sum_{i=1}^{p}\sum_{j=1}^{q}D^2\alpha_i^2\beta_j^2$ and this is estimated by:

$$\sum_{i=1}^{p}\sum_{j=1}^{q}\hat{D}^2(\bar{y}_i - \bar{y})^2(\bar{y}_j - \bar{y})^2$$

which equals:

$$\frac{\left[\sum_{i=1}^{p}\sum_{j=1}^{q}(\bar{y}_i - \bar{y})(\bar{y}_j - \bar{y})y_{ij}\right]^2}{\sum_{i=1}^{j}(\bar{y}_i - \bar{y})^2\sum_{j=1}^{q}(\bar{y}_j - \bar{y})^2}$$

To illustrate from Driscoll & Roberts (1997), here are the raw data and marginal means.

Block	1992	1993	1994	Block means
logging	4	17	18	13.00
angove	−10	−1	8	−1.00
newpipe	−15	−10	1	−8.00
oldquinE	−14	−11	−2	−9.00
newquinW	−4	6	0	0.67
newquinE	0	5	1	2.00
Year means	−6.50	1.00	4.33	−0.389

Using the equation above:

$$[\Sigma\Sigma(\bar{y}_i - \bar{y})(\bar{y}_j - \bar{y})y_{ij}]^2 = [(13-(-0.389))(-6.50-(-0.389))(4) + (-1-(-0.389))(-6.5-(-0.389))(-10) + \cdots + (2-(-0.389))(4.33-(-0.389))(1)]^2 = 510.34$$

$$\Sigma(\bar{y}_i - \bar{y})^2\Sigma(\bar{y}_j - \bar{y})^2 = (61.54)(318.53) = 19\,602.34$$

$$SS_{non-add} = 510.34/19602.34 = 0.026 \text{ with 1 df}$$

$$MS_{non-add} = 0.026$$

$$SS_{Remainder} = SS_{Total} - SS_A - SS_B - SS_{non-add} = 1516.278 - 369.444 - 955.611 - 0.026 = 191.197 \text{ with 9 df,}$$

$$MS_{Remainder} = 191.197/9 = 21.244$$

$$F_{non-add} = 0.026 / 21.244 = 0.001 \text{ with 1 and 9 df, } P = 0.974.$$

No evidence of strong interaction between blocks and years, even using a liberal α of 0.25.

component represents other sorts of interaction and the variation between experimental units ($SS_{Remainder}$). These SS are converted to MS and an F-ratio constructed which is $MS_{non-add}$ / $MS_{Remainder}$; this F-ratio follows an F distribution and the H_0 of no interaction can be tested in the usual manner.

Additivity and transformations

If evidence of an interaction is detected, there is an argument that we should try and reduce the effect of such an interaction, as this will increase the power and interpretability of the test for treatments. Presumably, a factor A by block interaction is not important to us biologically or else we would have replicated each treatment–block combination as a generalized RCB design (see Section 10.12). If the non-additivity is due to the scale on which the response variable is measured and therefore a multiplicative relationship between the response variable and treatments and blocks, then a transformation to a different scale of measurement (e.g. logs) may remove the interaction and make the relationship additive (Chapter 9). This is the type of non-additivity Tukey's test and residual plots are likely to detect, so a significant result from Tukey's test would suggest a transformation will reduce the extent of the interaction.

10.4 | Assumptions

10.4.1 Normality, independence of errors

We have already discussed the "assumption" of no factor A by block interaction, pointing out that the presence of an interaction does not invalidate the test for treatments if block is a random factor. In addition, the usual assumption that experimental units are randomly sampled from a population of experimental units is still important. We also assume, as usual, that the residuals are normally distributed and have constant variance within treatments across blocks (homogeneity of variance assumption). Plots of residuals, both within treatments and against predicted values, are interpreted in the same way as described in Chapters 8 and 9; watch out for wedge-shaped patterns suggesting an underlying skewed distribution. If the RCB or RM design is a mixed model with random blocks, the common scenario in biology, then the homogeneity of variance

assumption can be incorporated into a more general assumption about variances and covariances (Section 10.4.2). Outliers from the fitted model are as important to detect for RCB (RM) designs as for CR designs. Observations with large residuals can be identified from residual plots and most statistical software will warn of outliers when the model is fitted.

Even in RCB designs and RM designs, we assume that the residuals are independent of each other, even though the observations within a block or subject are not (Kirk 1995). This is because we assume that block effects are independent of residual effects, an assumption which is justified by the random allocation of levels of factor A to experimental units within a block (Brownie et al. 1993) or the random order of treatment application within a subject. Spatial heterogeneity between experimental units within blocks can be modeled as part of the analysis (Brownie et al. 1993), which may increase the precision of treatment means and the power of tests of treatment effects. Note that even though we acknowledge that observations from experimental units within a block are possibly correlated, sensible interpretation of biological experiments usually relies on the experimental units within blocks being far enough apart so that the effect of one treatment doesn't affect any other experimental unit, e.g. animals crawling off one experimental unit in response to a treatment and onto another. Similarly, in repeated measures designs, carryover effects must be explicitly avoided (by randomizing order of treatments and/or leaving a long enough gap between treatments) or be explicitly incorporated into the design and the hypotheses (see Kirk 1995).

10.4.2 Variances and covariances – sphericity

We have already indicated that in two factor linear models where one factor is random, the observations from the same level of the random factor are correlated with each other (Chapter 9). This correlation is exacerbated in RCB designs, because the experimental units in a block are often located close together, and in RM designs, because we have repeated observations on the same subject. This implies that the observations within a block, i.e. the observations from different treatments within a block (or within a subject in the repeated

Box 10.6 | Illustration of compound symmetry and sphericity assumptions using data from Driscoll & Roberts (1997)

Compound symmetry assumption:

$\sigma^2_{11} = \sigma^2_{22} = \sigma^2_{33}$ and $\sigma_{21} = \sigma_{31} = \sigma_{32}$, i.e. treatments variances are equal and treatment covariances are equal.

	General covariance matrix			Specific covariance matrix		
	Year 1	Year 2	Year 3	Year 1	Year 2	Year 3
Year 1	σ^2_{11}			59.90		
Year 2	σ^2_{21}	σ^2_{22}		79.40	113.20	
Year 3	σ^2_{31}	σ^2_{32}	σ^2_{33}	34.80	57.80	56.27

Estimates from data suggest difference between variances and between covariances.

Sphericity assumption:

$\sigma^2_{1-2} = \sigma^2_{1-3} = \sigma^2_{2-3}$, i.e. variances of differences between treatments are equal.

	Year 1	Year 2	Year 3	Year 1–2	Year 1–3	Year 2–3
Block 1	4	17	18	−13	−14	−1
Block 2	−10	−1	8	−9	−18	−9
Block 3	−15	−10	1	−5	−16	−11
Block 4	−14	−11	−2	−3	−12	−9
Block 5	−4	6	0	−10	−4	6
Block 6	0	5	1	−5	−1	4
s^2				14.30	46.57	53.87

The estimates of the variances of the treatment differences vary, with the variance of the year 1 minus year 2 difference considerably smaller than the other two differences, a strong indication that sphericity is not met.

measures context) are not independent of each other (Kirk 1995). Therefore, we not only have to be concerned about variances in these analyses but also about covariances (correlations). These variances and covariances can be expressed in the form of a variance–covariance matrix (see Chapter 15) whose diagonal matrix contains the variances between observations within each treatment and the other entries are the covariances between treatments (i.e. the covariances between observations from different treatments).

There are two conditions that must be met for the F-ratio for factor A to follow an F distribution when we fit a two factor mixed ANOVA model to data from a RCB or simple RM design. Not only do the variances have to be the same across treatments (the usual homogeneity of variance assumption) but the covariances (i.e. the correlations between treatments within each block or subject) also have to be the same. If the variances are all equal and the covariances are all equal, i.e. the correlations between all pairs of treatments are equal, then the variance–covariance matrix shows compound symmetry. This is a *sufficient* condition for the F-ratio to follow an F distribution but it is too restrictive an assumption, i.e. it is not a *necessary* condition. The F-ratio for factor A in the analyses of mixed model RCB and RM designs will follow an F distribution if the variance–covariance matrix shows a pattern known as sphericity. Put simply, the sphericity condition is that the variances of the differences between values of the response variable are the same for all pairs of treatments (see Box 10.6). The sphericity assumption is much less restrictive than compound symmetry because it does not require equality of variances and equality of covariances. Note that compound symmetry is simply one form of sphericity; a variance–covariance matrix which shows compound symmetry also shows sphericity by definition. If the sphericity assumption is not met, then the F test for treatments in RCB and RM designs can be liberal, i.e. the actual Type I error rate can exceed the nominal rate we set with our *a priori* significance level (Boik 1979, Box 1954). The F test is not very robust to this assumption.

There is no reason to expect the variances of the differences between pairs of treatments to be very different in classical RCB designs because the treatments are randomly allocated to different experimental units within each block. Think of this in terms of treatment correlations – the correlation between treatments one and two should not be very different from the correlation between treatments two and three if the experimental units are randomly arranged in each block and each experimental unit is randomly allocated to a treatment. In contrast, the sphericity assumption is less likely to hold for RM designs because observations for repeated measurements closer together in time will probably be more correlated than for repeated measurements further apart in time. If the order in which the treatments are applied to each experimental unit (subject) is randomized (treatments × subjects designs), then correlations between treatments might still be similar. However, in subjects by trials designs where the treatments are times (or time intervals), we would expect quite different correlations between times closer together compared to those further apart.

Note that the assumption of compound symmetry, or the more realistic assumption of sphericity, of the variance–covariance matrix only applies to mixed model RCB and RM analyses. If both factor A and blocks (or subjects) are fixed, then the linear model implies that observations are uncorrelated within treatments and within blocks (or subjects). This is probably why few textbooks (but see Kirk 1995, Neter *et al.* 1996) discuss any requirement for specific patterns of variances and covariances for RCB designs – such designs are usually presented with fixed blocks (e.g.

Hocking 1996). In contrast, RM designs are nearly always presented with subjects as random and hence the pattern of variances and covariances receives considerable attention. Note also that if there are only two treatments, then sphericity is not relevant because the variance–covariance matrix is actually a vector (only two variances and a single covariance).

There are two broad approaches for dealing with violations of the assumption of sphericity, adjusting univariate F tests to make them more conservative or using a multivariate test that does not assume sphericity.

Adjusting univariate F tests

The degree to which the variance–covariance matrix departs from compound symmetry and sphericity is measured by the epsilon (ε) parameter (Winer *et al.* 1991, Keselman & Keselman 1993, Kirk 1995). When sphericity is met, ε equals one; the further ε is from one, the more the sphericity assumption is violated. An estimate of ε can be determined from the sample variance–covariance matrix and is termed the Greenhouse–Geisser epsilon ($\hat{\varepsilon}$); it is complex to calculate, requiring some matrix gymnastics. The df for the F test for factor A can then be adjusted downwards based on the value of $\hat{\varepsilon}$:

$$\text{df}_{\text{adj}} = (p-1)\hat{\varepsilon} \text{ and } (p-1)(q-1)\hat{\varepsilon} \tag{10.6}$$

and the F test based on these adjusted df approximately follows an F distribution even when sphericity is not met. Unfortunately, the Greenhouse–Geisser estimate of ε can be conservatively biased when ε is close to 0.75 (Collier *et al.* 1967; see also Keselman & Keselman 1993, Winer *et al.* 1991), i.e. the adjustment to the df is too severe, making the test too conservative. An alternative estimate of ε is the Huynh–Feldt epsilon, although this can exceed one and therefore might be too liberal. Both estimates of ε and adjustments to df are standard output from most statistical software and we recommend the Greenhouse–Geisser adjustment because the true value of ε is never known so it is difficult to decide when to use the Huynh–Feldt version.

Note that a simpler version of the Greenhouse–Geisser adjustment is to set $\hat{\varepsilon}$ to its smallest value, which depends on the number of treatment

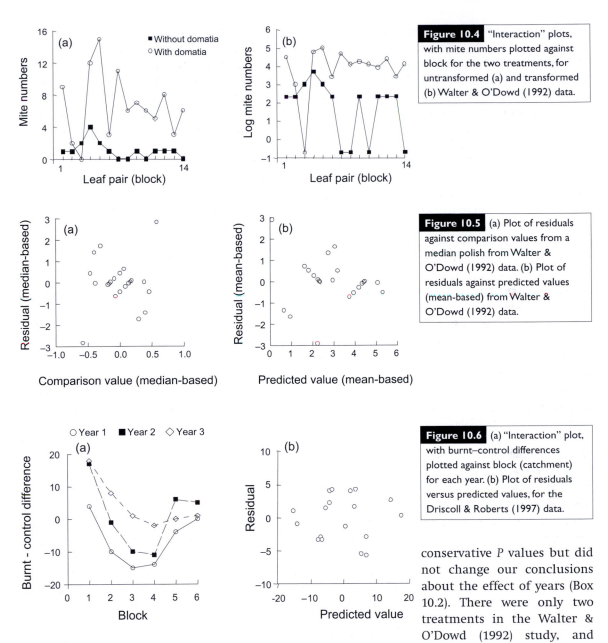

Figure 10.4 "Interaction" plots, with mite numbers plotted against block for the two treatments, for untransformed (a) and transformed (b) Walter & O'Dowd (1992) data.

Figure 10.5 (a) Plot of residuals against comparison values from a median polish from Walter & O'Dowd (1992) data. (b) Plot of residuals against predicted values (mean-based) from Walter & O'Dowd (1992) data.

Figure 10.6 (a) "Interaction" plot, with burnt–control differences plotted against block (catchment) for each year. (b) Plot of residuals versus predicted values, for the Driscoll & Roberts (1997) data.

groups (p) and equals $1/(p-1)$ – see Kirk (1995). This saves having to calculate $\hat{\varepsilon}$ but will obviously be conservative (it sets $\hat{\varepsilon}$ to the minimum value irrespective of the actual value of ε) and is unnecessary since most statistical software will calculate $\hat{\varepsilon}$.

In the Driscoll & Roberts (1997) example, the Greenhouse–Geisser epsilon was 0.71 and the Huynh–Feldt epsilon was 0.92, supporting the argument that the former is a more conservative estimate of ε. The adjusted df produced more conservative P values but did not change our conclusions about the effect of years (Box 10.2). There were only two treatments in the Walter & O'Dowd (1992) study, and therefore only one covariance, so the sphericity assumption was not relevant.

Multivariate tests

Another approach to dealing with the sphericity assumption is to use a procedure that does not require this assumption. We could use the differences between pairs of treatments (e.g. between pairs of times) as multiple response variables in a multivariate ANOVA (MANOVA; see Chapter 16). If there are p treatments (e.g. times), then only $p-1$

differences need to be used. The H_0 is that the population mean of the differences for all pairs of treatments equals zero. Because we are testing two or more population means simultaneously (e.g. with p equals three, there are two differences), we are really testing whether the $p-1$ differences have a population mean vector equal to zero (Keselman & Keselman 1993). Any of the test statistics used in MANOVA are applicable here but as discussed in Chapter 16, we recommend the Pillai trace statistic.

The MANOVA approach does not assume sphericity of the variance–covariance matrix but does assume multivariate normality, which is always difficult to check. It also requires more subjects or blocks than treatments, otherwise the MANOVA will encounter computational difficulties. In the Driscoll & Roberts (1997) example, the P value from the MANOVA testing whether the population mean differences between all pairings of the three years equals zero was 0.016, leading us to the same conclusion as for the adjusted univariate analysis (Box 10.2).

10.4.3 Recommended strategy

Formal tests of sphericity include Mauchley's test, which is very sensitive to deviations from multivariate normality and is not recommended (Keselman & Keselman 1993), and the "locally best invariant test", which is tedious to calculate (Kirk 1995). We suggest, like others (Keselman & Keselman 1993, Winer *et al.* 1991), that it is probably safer to assume that this assumption is not met and use adjusted univariate *F*-ratios or the multivariate approach (see Looney & Stanley 1989, Manly 1992, Potvin *et al.* 1990, von Ende 1993). Which is the best approach? As usual in applied statistics, that depends on the nature of the data. Looney & Stanley (1989) suggested using both approaches (most statistical packages automatically provide both analyses); if either the adjusted univariate or the multivariate indicates a significant result, reject the H_0. If neither indicate a significant result, do not reject H_0. Most statistical software routinely outputs all three approaches (unadjusted univariate, adjusted univariate, multivariate).

10.5 | Robust RCB and RM analyses

The only commonly used robust alternatives to the analyses we have described in this chapter are to transform the observations to ranks and then do the usual parametric analysis on the ranked data. The ranking can be done in two ways.

- Rank the data separately within each block (or subject) and then use the usual *F* test for factor A described earlier in this chapter. Note that this test is equivalent to the Friedman test (Hollander & Wolfe 1999), which also ranks the observations within each group but compares its test statistic to a chi-square distribution. The Friedman test is an extension of the Kruskal–Wallis test described in Chapter 8 for single factor ANOVA models.
- Alternatively, the data could be ranked over the entire data set as described for rank-transform (RT) procedures in CR designs (Chapters 8 and 9) and the usual *F* test for treatments applied to the ranked data (see Maxwell & Delaney 1990).

All of our previous comments about rank-based analyses (see Chapters 3 and 8) apply here, particularly that these tests do not assume normality but do not necessarily solve problems about variances and covariances (Maxwell & Delaney 1990) and can be inefficient when there are many ties (Neter *et al.* 1996). Rank-based tests do not deal with interactions very well (Chapter 9) so it is difficult to predict what effect block by treatment interactions will have on the analysis.

An alternative approach is to estimate the effects of the linear model in a robust manner, i.e. obtain estimates of the factor A and block (or subject) effects that are not sensitive (i.e. are resistant) to outliers. Emerson & Hoaglin (1983) and Emerson & Wong (1985) proposed a technique called a median polish, which uses the medians to fit an additive model of the form:

$$y_{ij} = m + \alpha_i + \beta_j + \varepsilon_{ij} \tag{10.7}$$

where m is the overall median and α_i, β_j and ε_{ij} are factor A effects, block effects and residuals estimated using marginal medians instead of marginal means. Median polish determines these effects in an iterative fashion, calculating the row effects, then the column effects, then recalculating the row effects, etc. The computations are a little tedious (see Emerson & Hoaglin 1983; MINITAB™ also provides median polish) but the results are useful for detecting some forms of non-additivity, by using comparison values calculated from the median polish (Section 10.3.2), and also for providing more robust detection of outliers.

Randomization tests are also possible by generating the distribution of an appropriate test statistic by randomly reallocating observations to treatment–block combinations, as we described for factorial designs in Chapter 9 (Manly 1997).

Finally, if the response variable being analyzed has a known distribution that fits an exponential form, then generalized linear modeling procedures can be used (Chapter 13). GLMs measure the fit of models with maximum likelihood techniques, allow a variety of underlying distributions, such as Poisson, binomial, lognormal, etc., and tests of hypotheses about model parameters use likelihood ratios.

10.6 | Specific comparisons

Planned contrasts and unplanned multiple comparisons between factor A levels in RCB (or RM) designs depend on whether the sphericity assumption is met, because these tests usually rely on a single error term, the $MS_{Residual}$. We argued in Section 10.4.2 that for classical RCB designs, where treatments are randomly allocated to independent experimental units within blocks, the sphericity assumption is less likely to be violated. The usual contrasts and pairwise comparison procedures described in Chapters 8 and 9 can be used; $MS_{Residual}$ would be used as the error term for calculating the standard errors of these comparisons. For RM designs, the variances and covariances are less likely to conform to sphericity (and adjusted df cannot easily be calculated for specific comparisons) so we agree with Kirk (1995) that separate denominators should be used for each pairwise (or more complex) comparison. Keselman & Keselman (1993) proposed pairwise t tests with separate error terms based on the two

levels being compared. For example, to compare groups 1 and 2 for factor A:

$$t = \frac{\bar{y}_1 - \bar{y}_2}{\sqrt{\dfrac{s_1^2 + s_2^2 - 2s_{12}}{q}}} \qquad (10.8)$$

where s_1^2 and s_2^2 are the sample variances for groups 1 and 2, s_{12} is the sample covariance between groups 1 and 2 and q is the number of subjects or blocks. Note that this is simply a paired t test (see Chapter 3) comparing the means of the two groups. The SS_A can also be partitioned into SS for each comparison, as described in Chapter 8 and the two groups compared with an F test. Not all statistical software provides separate denominators for these F-ratio tests of each contrast, so we illustrate the calculations of separate error terms for the Driscoll & Roberts (1997) data in Box 10.7. The calculated F-ratio statistic will be the same as the t statistic. For unplanned pairwise comparisons where control over the familywise Type I error rate is required, a Bonferroni-type correction (see Chapter 3) can be applied.

Trends (linear, quadratic, etc.) across levels of factor A can also be tested using the methods outlined in Chapter 8; these tests are often default output from some statistical software if the data are coded as repeated measures. The only difference in testing for trends between a RCB (or RM) design and a CR design is which denominator to use for the F-ratio (Kirk 1995). As for other contrasts described above, separate error terms for each trend test should be used if sphericity might not hold. Note that Winer et al. (1991) also suggested using a separate denominator for each trend (linear, quadratic, etc.), although their tests for each trend component are only slightly more conservative than those based on the $MS_{Residual}$ and we prefer the approach of Kirk (1995).

10.7 | Efficiency of blocking (to block or not to block?)

The decision to include a blocking factor in an experimental design depends on two questions.

• Are experimental units in blocks more similar to each other than to other experimental units

Box 10.7 | Calculation of separate error term for contrasts in RCB/RM analyses (see Kirk 1995), using the data of Driscoll & Roberts (1997)

First, calculate the relevant contrast (trend or otherwise) for each block/subject, e.g. the linear trend for block 1:

$\psi = (-1)4 + (0)17 + (1)18 = 14$, where $-1, 0$ and 1 are the contrast coefficients (c_i) for a linear trend through three equally spaced levels (see Table 8.8).

Second:

(i) sum the trend values across blocks/subjects ($\Sigma\psi$) = 65
(ii) sum the squared trend values across blocks/subjects ($\Sigma\psi^2$) = 937
(iii) sum the squared contrast coefficients (Σc_i^2) = 2

$$SS_{Residual(linear)} = \frac{\sum_{j=1}^{q}\psi^2 - \dfrac{\left(\sum_{j=1}^{q}\psi\right)^2}{q}}{\sum_{i=1}^{p} c_i^2} = [(937) - (65)^2/6]/2 = 116.42 \text{ with } q - 1 = 5 \text{ df.}$$

$$MS_{Residual(linear)} = SS_{Residual(linear)}/q - 1 = 116.42/5 = 23.28$$

in different blocks? If so, then the blocking factor will explain some of the residual variation, resulting in a smaller $MS_{Residual}$ and a more powerful test of factor A.

- Does the reduction in $MS_{Residual}$ compensate for the loss of df in the ANOVA?

In most cases, the answer to the second question is unknown unless good pilot data are available, so a decision to block is made primarily on the likely extent of between-block variation.

After an RCB experiment, we might also wish to know whether using blocks was a better experimental design than a CR experiment without any blocking, in terms of precision of estimates of treatment effect and power of the tests for factor A. Lentner et al. (1989) argued that a measure of relative efficiency (RE) should be used to compare an RCB design to a CR design, where RE is defined as the ratio of the variance of the treatment comparison of the CR experiment to the variance of the treatment comparison in the RCB experiment. Larger REs indicate that the RCB design produced a more precise (lower variance) estimate of treatment effects compared with the CR design. Based on the work of Yates and Kempthorne, they

defined an estimate of this relative efficiency (ERE) for a RCB design compared with a CR design:

$$ERE = \frac{(q-1)MS_{Block} + q(p-1)MS_{Residual}}{(pq-1)MS_{Residual}} \qquad (10.9)$$

Lentner et al. (1989) also noted that ERE is monotonically related to the ratio of $MS_{Blocks}/MS_{Residual}$, even though that F-ratio is inappropriate for testing blocks in the non-additive model, so either ERE or the F-ratio could be used. If either is greater than one then an RCB design is more efficient than a CR design where the number of replicates per treatment is equal to the number of blocks. In the Walter & O'Dowd (1992) example, the F-ratio for blocks is less than one so the RCB design probably did not offer more efficiency than a CR design in this case. The F-ratio for subjects (blocks) was much greater than one in the Driscoll & Roberts (1997) example, although it is difficult to envisage how such an RM design could have been set up as a CR design, so the efficiency of blocking is not so relevant.

10.8 | Time as a blocking factor

In all the examples we have so far used in this chapter, the blocks have been spatial units, locations in space. There are occasions where you only have a small number of experimental units and can only afford to have a single replicate of each treatment in an experiment (experimental units might be very large or very expensive). One option in these situations might be to repeat the unreplicated experiment a number of times. The experiment can then be analyzed as an RCB design with time as a blocking factor. One problem with using time as blocks is deciding whether time is a random factor. If we run the experiment over three successive weeks, for example, it's difficult to imagine from what population of times these three are a random sample. Under these circumstances, time might be treated as a fixed factor, which restricts us to using the additive model and therefore assuming no factor A by block interactions. Alternatively, we could argue that we have a random sample of at least a month or two, so time is random, and we are no worse off in our generalization – doing the experiment as a completely randomized one factor design would take only one week, and we couldn't generalize that result to any other time, anyway.

One particular design that uses time as a blocking factor is a crossover design, described in Section 10.11.4.

10.9 | Analysis of unbalanced RCB designs

Missing observations are potentially a big problem for RCB and RM designs because a single missing observation is, in effect, a missing cell. The equations in Table 10.2 are not appropriate when there are missing observations. The simplest approach to missing observations in RCB (RM) designs is to omit the whole block or subject that has the missing value(s). This is the default approach for most statistical software if data are arranged, and the analysis done, as a classical "repeated measures" ANOVA (Section 10.13). Of course, this removes non-missing observations from the block/subject with the missing observation, which is wasteful of data and reduces the power of the test for factor A.

It turns out that we can analyze unreplicated two factor designs with missing observations as long as (i) there are not too many missing values and (ii) there are no treatment by block interactions. Note that we are assuming that the observations are missing randomly. Cells may also be missing by design, because the number of available experimental units is less than the number of treatment–block combinations and hence an incomplete block design should be considered (see Section 10.11.2). There are two broad analytical approaches (Box 10.8 and Chapter 4): substitute a replacement observation or compare the fit of full and reduced linear models.

If we assume additivity, then we can predict a value for any cell using Equation 10.4. Snedecor & Cochran (1989) and Sokal & Rohlf (1995) proposed a more complex method for estimating a missing value based on treatment and block totals. Both methods use the available information from the same treatment and block in estimating the missing value and produce very similar estimated values. One df should be subtracted from the residual for each substituted value. Snedecor & Cochran (1989) indicated that the SS_A (and SS_{Blocks}; see Sokal & Rohlf 1995) is slightly biased upwards and recommended a correction, although it does not make much difference in practice. Note that any procedure for estimating a missing value in an unreplicated factorial design must assume that there are no treatment by block interactions.

Alternatively, we can use the comparison of linear models approach where SS_A and SS_{Blocks} are determined by comparing the fit of a full model versus the relevant reduced model (Section 10.2.4; Box 10.4). This is the default approach for most statistical software when the data are arranged, and the analysis done, as a classical RCB design and is termed the "regression" approach by Neter et al. 1996. Note that the SS are no longer orthogonal, i.e. the SS for A, blocks and residual do not add to the total SS. Generally, substituting a new value as described above and comparing full and reduced additive models will result in very similar tests for the effects of treatments (Box 10.8).

Box 10.8 | Analyzing RCB designs with a missing observation

Based on Driscoll & Roberts (1997) with one observation (newpipe in 1993) missing.

Raw data and marginal means:

Block	1992	1993	1994	Block means
logging	4	17	18	13.00
angove	−10	−1	8	−1.00
newpipe	−15		1	−7.00
oldquinE	−14	−11	−2	−9.00
newquinW	−4	6	0	0.67
newquinE	0	5	1	2.00
Year means	−6.50	3.20	4.33	0.18

To estimate the missing observation, we use Equation 10.4 to estimate the predicted value for any cell, in this case the cell with the missing observation:

$$\hat{y}_{ij} = \bar{y}_i + \bar{y}_j - \bar{y}$$

$$3.20 + (−7.00) − 0.18 = −3.98$$

This is very similar to the new value (−3.90) from the method of Snedecor & Cochran (1989) and Sokal & Rohlf (1995). We can then substitute this value for the missing observation and fit the ANOVA model as usual for this design, subtracting one df from the residual. Note that the actual value was −10, suggesting that simply predicting the missing observation assuming additivity is not ideal in this case, even though there was not strong evidence for an interaction between blocks and years.

The results of the three different approaches for dealing with this missing observation are presented below. Note the $MS_{Residual}$ is the same when we substitute a new value and when we compare full and reduced models and the tests of factor A (year) are very similar (see Neter et al. 1996).

Source	Omit block 3				Substitute new value				Model comparison approach			
	df	MS	F	P	df	MS	F	P	df	MS	F	P
Year	2	136.067	7.044	0.017	2	195.097	10.295	0.005	2	192.058	10.135	0.005
Block (drainage)	4	186.767			5	174.808			5	166.217		
Residual	8	19.317			9	18.950			9	18.950		

Since we are fitting a full model with no interaction term, the results from this linear models analysis will be similar to fitting the cell means model (Box 10.3) and using specific contrasts to test the subset of hypotheses for A and blocks using only those cells with data. The model we use is a restricted means model because it assumes that all treatment by block interactions are zero. Kirk (1995) illustrates using cell means models to analyze RCB designs with missing values.

This approach of comparing full and reduced effects models can only be used because the full model is an additive one with no interaction terms. In replicated factorial designs with missing cells, interactions are presumably potentially important and we cannot use a comparison of full and reduced models that include interaction terms in these circumstances (Chapter 9). Instead, the cell means approach and a subset of testable hypotheses about interactions and main effects must be used.

What is the best way of dealing with missing values in RCB or simple RM designs? The conservative approach is omitting the incomplete block or subject; it is simple, doesn't assume additivity, and is probably reasonable if the number of remaining blocks/subjects is not too small. However, the strength of inference about the effects of treatments across blocks will be reduced because we are using fewer blocks. In many cases, each block/subject may represent such an effort so that you are unwilling to discard the data from other treatments in the problem block/subject; alternatively, the number of blocks/subjects may be small and omitting one block could reduce the size of the experiment by an appreciable amount. In this case, there is no simple recommendation for which of the two alternatives (substitution, effects model comparisons) is best, although they will usually produce similar results. Both approaches assume no treatment by block interaction. Therefore, if you must analyze a design with missing observations, it is particularly important that checks for factor A by block interactions using the available data are done (Section 10.3.2). There is a downside to the model comparison approach, especially if the experiment really is a RM design where meeting the assumption of sphericity is likely to be a problem. Most software will not provide adjusted univariate or multivariate tests when general linear models are fitted (Section 10.13). This is actually a serious problem because, like other ANOVAs, the unbalanced RCB or RM ANOVAs are more sensitive to assumptions (especially sphericity) than a balanced design (Berk 1987). We can only suggest checking sphericity after omitting the block or subject with the missing value (using repeated measures coding in your statistical

software) before fitting the additive linear model to the whole data set.

We illustrate the analysis of RCB or simple RM designs with a missing observation by analyzing the Driscoll & Roberts (1997) data with the observation from the second year and the third block missing (Box 10.8). In this example, there are few blocks (only six) and omitting an entire block changes the ANOVA markedly compared to substituting a new value determined from the available data for block 3 and year 2 or simply comparing the fit of appropriate full and reduced additive linear models to the unbalanced data.

10.10 | Power of RCB or simple RM designs

The power of RCB or simple RM designs is determined similarly to a CR single factor design (see Chapter 8) except that the sample size is the number of blocks or subjects and the residual variation will probably be smaller than for a CR design. The non-centrality parameter is defined as:

$$\lambda = \sqrt{\frac{\sum_{i=1}^{p} \alpha_i^2}{\sigma_\varepsilon^2/q}} \tag{10.10}$$

which can also be expressed as:

$$\phi = \sqrt{\frac{\lambda}{p}} \tag{10.11}$$

Whether Equation 10.10 or Equation 10.11 is used depends on whether we are using power tables or curves (see Neter et al. 1996) or power analysis software. Ideally, we would use a pilot study to provide an estimate of σ_ε^2 (the residual variance) and then determine the number of blocks (q) required to detect a treatment effect of a given size, i.e. use power analysis for determining sample size required in the design phase of the experiment, although post hoc calculations of power can be carried out in the same manner as described for a CR design. Note that using power calculations to determine the number of blocks or subjects required in a RCB or RM experiment probably only makes sense when blocks are considered random; if blocks are fixed, then their number is also fixed.

10.11 | More complex block designs

10.11.1 Factorial randomized block designs

Block designs can also be extended to include factorial experiments, where all combinations of two or more factors are included in each block (Kirk 1995). For example, Brunkow & Collins (1996) did a field enclosure experiment that examined the effects of two factors (density and variance in initial size) on various response variables (growth, dry mass, stage of metamorphosis) for larval salamanders. This was a factorial design arranged in three spatial blocks with one replicate of each combination of density and initial variation in size in each block. A second example is from Wagner & Wise (1996), who set up a factorial experiment examining the effects of density (three levels: zero, low and high) and predator reduction (two levels: control and predator reduction) on growth rates of wolf spiderlings. One replicate of each combination of density and predator reduction was located in each of four spatial blocks.

The non-additive linear model, which includes block by factor interaction terms, for the factorial RCB design with two factors (A and C) replicated at a number of blocks (B) is:

$$y_{ijk} = \mu + \alpha_i + \gamma_k + \alpha\gamma_{ik} + \beta_j + \alpha\beta_{ij} + \gamma\beta_{kj} + \alpha\gamma\beta_{ijk} + \varepsilon_{ijk} \quad (10.12)$$

where α_i is the effect of factor A, γ_j is the effect of factor C, $\alpha\gamma_{ij}$ is the interaction between factors A and C, β_k is the effect of blocks, $\alpha\beta_{ik}$, $\gamma\beta_{jk}$, and $\alpha\gamma\beta_{ijk}$ are the interactions between A, C, AC and blocks and ε_{ijk} is the residual term independent of blocks. This is Model 1 of Newman *et al.* (1997). As with all unreplicated RCB designs, we cannot estimate the residual separately from at least one interaction term, in this case the $\alpha\gamma\beta_{ijk}$ interaction.

The ANOVA table based on this non-additive model with expected mean squares is shown in Table 10.6. If blocks (B) are considered random and the other factors (A and C) are fixed (the common

situation with biological experiments), then each term of interest in the model (A, C, AC) is tested against its interaction with blocks and there are no tests for blocks or its interactions. If blocks and either A or C are random, then some terms will have no appropriate *F* test, e.g. if blocks and C are random, there will be no other MS in the model with same expected value as MS_A if the H_0 of no effect of A is true. If blocks and both A and C are random, then there are no tests for either A or C. In these circumstances, we must rely on quasi *F*-ratios as outlined in Chapter 9 or else assume an additive model. If blocks are fixed, then there are no tests for the other factors in the non-additive model so we must assume no interactions with blocks and fit an additive model as described below.

The linear model 10.12 is the equivalent of a two factor repeated measures design where both factors are "within subjects" (Keppel 1991). We argue that terms such as "factorial randomized block" and "factorial within subjects repeated measures", while useful for describing the physical structure of the experiment, actually obscure the fundamental underlying linear model, which in this case is simply an unreplicated three factor, crossed, ANOVA model (Chapter 9). The EMS provided by Kirk (1995) for a factorial RCB with blocks random are identical to those provided by Winer *et al.* (1991) for a three factor ANOVA with one factor (blocks) random.

An alternative approach is to fit an additive model:

$$y_{ijk} = \mu + \alpha_i + \gamma_k + \alpha\gamma_{ik} + \beta_j + \varepsilon_{ijk} \quad (10.13)$$

which is Model 2 of Newman *et al.* (1997) and the one which users of factorial RCB designs often fit (e.g. Brunkow & Collins 1996, Wagner & Wise 1996). This model combines the block by A, C and A×C interactions (i.e., the three residual terms in Table 10.6) into a single residual term (Table 10.7). Although the use of this pooled error term increases the degrees of freedom in the denominators used to construct the F-ratios, and therefore increases the power of individual tests of A, C and A×C, there are costs. First, as the additive model implies, we have to assume that there are no interactions with blocks; this assumption is very difficult to test and, for biological experiments, might not be true in some situations

Table 10.6 | ANOVA table for a factorial randomized complete block design with factors A (p levels) and C (r levels) being fixed and B (q blocks) random

Source	Wagner & Wise (1996)	df	Expected mean square	Test (A, C fixed, blocks random)
B = Block	Block	$q-1$	$\sigma^2_\varepsilon + D_p D_r \sigma^2_{\alpha\gamma\beta} + D_p p r \sigma^2_{\gamma\beta} + D_p r \sigma^2_{\alpha\beta} + p r \sigma^2_\beta$	No test
A	Density	$p-1$	$\sigma^2_\varepsilon + D_q D_r \sigma^2_{\alpha\gamma\beta} + D_q r \sigma^2_{\alpha\beta} + D_r r \sigma^2_{\alpha\beta} + p r \sigma^2_\alpha$	$\dfrac{MS_A}{MS_{AB}}$
A × B = Residual 1	Density × Block	$(p-1)(q-1)$	$\sigma^2_\varepsilon + D_r \sigma^2_{\alpha\gamma\beta} + r \sigma^2_{\alpha\beta}$	No test
C	Predators	$r-1$	$\sigma^2_\varepsilon + D_q D_p \sigma^2_{\alpha\gamma\beta} + D_p q \sigma^2_{\alpha\gamma} + D_q p \sigma^2_{\gamma\beta} + p q r \sigma^2_\gamma$	$\dfrac{MS_C}{MS_{CB}}$
C × B = Residual 2	Predators × Block	$(r-1)(q-1)$	$\sigma^2_\varepsilon + D_p \sigma^2_{\alpha\gamma\beta} + p \sigma^2_{\gamma\beta}$	No test
A × C	Density × Predators	$(p-1)(r-1)$	$\sigma^2_\varepsilon + D_q \sigma^2_{\alpha\gamma\beta} + q \sigma^2_{\alpha\gamma}$	$\dfrac{MS_{AC}}{MS_{ACB}}$
A × C × B = Residual 3	Density × Predators × Block	$(p-1)(r-1)(q-1)$	$\sigma^2_\varepsilon + \sigma^2_{\alpha\gamma\beta}$	No test

Note:
There is only one replicate of each AC combination in each block (B). Components for fixed and random factors in expected mean squares are represented as "variances" – see Box 9.8.

Table 10.7 | ANOVA for factorial randomized complete block design from Table 10.6 assuming that all block by factor interactions (A × block, C × block, A × C × block) are zero and are pooled into residual

Source	Wagner & Wise (1996)	df	Expected mean square	Test (A, C fixed)
B = Block	Block	$q-1$	$\sigma_\varepsilon^2 + pr\sigma_\beta^2$	$\dfrac{MS_{Block}}{MS_{Residual}}$
A	Density	$p-1$	$\sigma_\varepsilon^2 + qD_r\sigma_{a\gamma}^2 + qr\sigma_\alpha^2$	$\dfrac{MS_A}{MS_{Residual}}$
C	Predators	$r-1$	$\sigma_\varepsilon^2 + qD_p\sigma_{a\gamma}^2 + qp\sigma_\gamma^2$	$\dfrac{MS_C}{MS_{Residual}}$
A × C	Density × Predators	$(p-1)(r-1)$	$\sigma_\varepsilon^2 + q\sigma_{a\gamma}^2$	$\dfrac{MS_{AC}}{MS_{Residual}}$
Residual	Residual	$(q-1)(pr-1)$	σ_ε^2	

Note:
Components for fixed and random factors in expected mean squares are represented as "variances" – see Box 9.8.

(Section 10.3.1). Second, the pooled residual term requires a restrictive omnibus sphericity condition (Kirk 1995), which also cannot easily be checked. We recommend that the non-additive model and separate error terms should be used.

Our earlier comments about using time as a blocking factor also apply to factorial randomized blocks. Factorial experiments are more costly than single factor experiments because of the larger number of combinations of the factors and it may not be possible to have enough experimental units to replicate such an experiment. Repeating the experiment through time and using time as a blocking variable is a useful option.

10.11.12 Incomplete block designs
Very occasionally, we may have an experimental design where we would like to block the treatments but the number of experimental units in each block is less than the number of treatments so we cannot have every treatment represented in each block. Under these circumstances, the trick is to allocate treatments to blocks so that relevant hypotheses can be tested although some interactions have to be assumed to be zero. The simplest arrangement is a balanced design where every pair of treatments occurs once (and only once) in

one of the blocks. These designs can be arranged using randomized blocks or Latin squares and can also be unbalanced so that not every pair of treatments occurs in any block. The definitive reference is Cochran & Cox (1957) but Kirk (1995) and Mead (1988) also describe these designs.

Of course, some (including us) might argue that if there is such a mismatch between the available experimental units and number of treatment combinations, then reducing the number of treatments in the experiment is a more realistic solution. This is especially so in biology where treatment by block interactions are quite possible. The one exception might be where the design can be set up as a square arrangement with two blocking factors, as we will describe next.

10.11.13 Latin square designs
Sometimes we want to include two blocking factors in our design to further reduce the unexplained variation in our response variable. If the allocation of treatment levels to all combinations of blocking factors can be randomized, we could simply treat the combinations of the two blocking factors as levels of a single, combined, blocking factor and use the usual model for an RCB design. However, if we are willing to restrict the number of levels of each of the two blocking factors to be

```
A  B  C        C  B  A        B  C  A
B  C  A        A  C  B        A  B  C
C  A  B        B  A  C        C  A  B
```

```
A  B  C  D     B  A  D  C     D  B  C  A
B  C  D  A     C  D  A  B     A  D  B  C
C  D  A  B     D  C  B  A     C  A  D  B
D  A  B  C     A  B  C  D     B  C  A  D
```

Figure 10.7 Three possible random arrangements for 3×3 (three treatments: A, B, C) and 4×4 (four treatments: A, B, C, D) Latin squares.

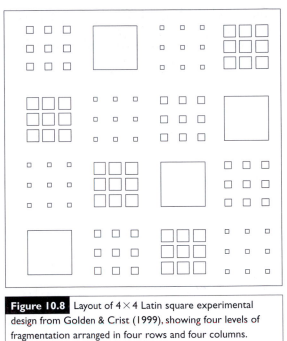

Figure 10.8 Layout of 4×4 Latin square experimental design from Golden & Crist (1999), showing four levels of fragmentation arranged in four rows and four columns.

the same as the number of treatment levels, we can also use a Latin square design. As the name suggests, Latin squares consider the experimental design as a square with equal numbers of rows and columns. One blocking factor is allocated to rows and the other to columns and there is a single experimental unit for each combination of row and column, i.e. cell. Latin square designs can be 2×2, 3×3, 4×4, etc. Treatments are allocated randomly to cells, with the restriction that each treatment is represented once in each row and in each column. By definition, the number of levels of factor A must be the same as the number of rows and the number of columns. Latin square designs are basically an extreme example of an incomplete block design, where the number of treatments represented in each block (row–column combination) is one!

There are many possible random arrangements of allocating treatments to cells in Latin square designs (Figure 10.7). For example, there are 12 possible arrangements for a 3×3 square and 576 arrangements for a 4×4 square. For a particular experiment, we simply select at random one of the possible arrangements of the appropriate size. Statistical software often include modules for the design of experiments that generate Latin square arrangements.

Traditionally, Latin square designs were used when the rows and columns represented a physical spatial arrangement of experimental units in the field. For example, Golden & Crist (1999) examined the effects of habitat fragmentation on old-field canopy insects using a 120×150 m field

(comprising goldenrod and wild carrot as dominant flora) in Ohio. They had four treatments (levels of factor A) set up by mowing: unfragmented, slightly fragmented (3 m² subplots separated by 2 m mown strips), moderately fragmented (2 m² subplots separated by 3.5 m mown strips) and heavily fragmented (1 m² subplots separated by 5 m mown strips). They created 16 plots (each 13×13 m) in four rows and four columns and allocated treatments in a four by four Latin square design, i.e. each treatment was represented once in each row and each column (Figure 10.8). Basically, this design is blocking treatments (fragmentation) against two blocking factors, rows and columns.

Latin square designs can also be used when the blocking factors do not really represent physical rows and columns. For example, Cochran & Cox (1957) describe an experiment where rows are five weeks, columns are the five days of the week, and each of five treatments was allocated to each combination of week and day in the usual manner.

Consider a Latin square design with factor A ($i = 1$ to p) being treatments, factor B ($j = 1$ to p) being rows and factor C ($k = 1$ to p) being columns. Each observation is y_{ijk} (the value in each cell), the marginal treatment means pooling rows and columns are $\bar{y}_i$, the marginal row means pooling treatments and columns are $\bar{y}_j$ and the marginal column means pooling treatments and rows are $\bar{y}_k$.

The linear model used for a Latin square design is:

$$y_{ijk} = \mu + \alpha_i + \beta_j + \gamma_k + \varepsilon_{ijk} \qquad (10.14)$$

From Golden & Crist (1999):

$$(\text{species richness of insects})_{ijk} = \mu + (\text{fragmentation})_i + (\text{rows})_j + (\text{columns})_k + \varepsilon_{ijk} \qquad (10.15)$$

In models 10.14 and 10.15 we find the following.

μ is the overall (constant) population mean, e.g. the overall mean number of insect species per leaf for all combinations of fragmentation treatment, row and column (i.e. all cells).

If factor A is fixed, α_i is effect of ith level of factor A $(\mu_i - \mu)$ pooling over rows and columns, e.g. the effect of fragmentation on the number of species of insects, pooling rows and columns. If factor A is random, α_i represents a random variable with a mean of zero and a variance of σ_α^2, measuring the variance in mean values of the response variable across all the possible levels of factor A that could have been used.

If rows are fixed, β_j is the effect of the jth row $(\mu_j - \mu)$ pooling over levels of factor A and columns, e.g. the effect of the different rows on the number of species of insects, pooling fragmentation treatments and columns. If rows are random, β_j represents a random variable with a mean of zero and a variance of σ_β^2, measuring the variance in mean values of the response variable across all the possible rows that could have been used.

If columns are fixed, γ_k is the effect of the kth column $(\mu_k - \mu)$ pooling over levels of factor A and rows, e.g. the effect of the different columns on the number of species of insects, pooling fragmentation treatments and rows. If columns are random, γ_k represents a random variable with a mean of zero and a variance of σ_γ^2, measuring the variance in mean values of the response variable across all the possible columns that could have been used.

ε_{ijk} is random or unexplained error associated with the observation at each combination of the ith level of factor A and jth row and kth column. For example, this measures the random error associated with the number of species of insects in each combination of fragmentation treatment, row and column. These error terms are assumed to be normally distributed in each cell, with a mean of zero $(E(\varepsilon_{ijk}) = 0)$ and a variance of σ_ε^2.

Note that model 10.14 is an additive model with no interaction terms. The total number of experimental units is simply the total number of row and column combinations (p^2) with a single level of factor A allocated to each combination. With a Latin square design, it is not possible to estimate any interaction terms and therefore we cannot fit a non-additive model.

The ANOVA from fitting model 10.14 is presented in Table 10.8. The SS for factor A, rows and columns are calculated from the respective marginal means as usual. The $SS_{Residual}$ is simply the difference between these SS and SS_{Total}. With only one observation per cell in Latin square designs, we have no real estimate of σ_ε^2 unless we assume that all interactions between A, rows and columns are zero. Sometimes, the $SS_{Residual}$ is termed $SS_{Remainder}$ (Neter et al. 1996). The test for factor A simply uses the $MS_{Residual}$ as the denominator.

Factor A would usually be fixed in most biological applications. If we have a true physical Latin square where the rows and columns are spatial arrangements within that square, then they may be considered fixed because it is difficult to imagine from what populations of rows and columns they could be a random sample. If rows and columns are not spatial arrangements within a real square, then either might be considered random. The F test of factor A is the same no matter what combination of fixed and random factors we have in a Latin square design, although the H_0 and its interpretation will be different.

Latin square designs are quite restrictive in their application. They require that the number of levels of factor A equal the number of levels of the two blocking factors, rows and columns, although Mead (1988) describes alternative rectangular designs where only the number of rows or

Table 10.8 ANOVA table for standard Latin square design, where the number of levels of factor A (p) equals the number of rows (p) equals the number of columns (p). Factor A, rows and columns are fixed although their components in expected mean squares are represented as "variances"

Source	df	MS	MS	Expected mean square	F	P
Factor A (fragmentation)	$(p-1)$	$\dfrac{p\sum\limits_{i=1}^{p}(\bar{y}_i - \bar{y})^2}{p-1}$	104.56	$\sigma_\varepsilon^2 + p\sigma_\alpha^2$	5.13	0.043
Row	$(p-1)$	$\dfrac{p\sum\limits_{j=1}^{p}(\bar{y}_j - \bar{y})^2}{p-1}$	75.22	$\sigma_\varepsilon^2 + p\sigma_\beta^2$	3.69	0.081
Column	$(p-1)$	$\dfrac{p\sum\limits_{k=1}^{p}(\bar{y}_k - \bar{y})^2}{p-1}$	233.73	$\sigma_\varepsilon^2 + p\sigma_\gamma^2$	11.46	0.007
Residual	$(p-1)(p-2)$	$\dfrac{\sum\limits_{j=1}^{q}\sum\limits_{k=1}^{q}(y_{ijk} - \bar{y}_j - \bar{y}_k - \bar{y}_i + 2\bar{y})^2}{(p-1)(p-2)}$	20.40	σ_ε^2		
Total	(p^2-1)					

Note:
The example is from Golden & Crist (1999). July species richness data only.

columns matches the number of treatments. Additionally, the number of df for the residual is often small. For example, a 3×3 design will have only two df for the residual and 4×4 design will have only six df. In these circumstances, we might wish to also replicate at the level of squares so we have multiple Latin squares (Mead 1988). Probably the most serious restriction on the application of Latin square designs in biology is that there should be no interactions between treatments, rows or columns. While we can use Tukey's test for non-additivity (Section 10.3.2; Box 10.5) to check for some forms of interaction (Kirk 1995), it is difficult to imagine that, in field experiments, treatments would not interact with spatial rows or columns. If there are interactions, then the test of factor A is biased in a messy way (Kirk 1995). Finally, like all ANOVAs based on unreplicated factorial models, missing values cause real difficulties for Latin square analyses and our comments in Section 10.8 apply.

Latin square designs can become more complex than the standard design described here. For example, Graeco-Latin square designs allow for three blocking factors by superimposing two standard Latin squares (Cochran & Cox 1957, Kirk 1995, Mead 1988). The restrictions discussed above for standard Latin squares apply even more so for these complex extensions.

10.11.4 Crossover designs

An experimental design that combines attributes of Latin squares and repeated measures designs is the crossover design, often used in experiments that apply multiple treatments to individual organisms. In its simplest form, the crossover design can be considered as a Latin square where subjects are one blocking factor (e.g. rows) and time periods are a second blocking factor (e.g. columns) and treatments are applied to each combination of subject and period using one of the Latin square randomizations. Consider the study of Feinsinger *et al.* (1991) who examined competition between three species of forest understory plants in Central America. They set up an experiment to examine the effects of four treatments (relative densities of one species, either *Besleria* or *Palicourea*, and a second species *Cephaelia*: 10:10, 90:10, 10:90, 50:50) on response variables such as

rate of hummingbird probes per flower or number of pollen tubes per style or number of seeds matured per flower. They had four time periods (either four or six days depending on the species) and used four focal plants (of either *Besleria* or *Palicourea*), which were the subjects, with a Latin square design as illustrated in Table 10.9. Actually, their experiment was more complicated because they replicated each square at three separate spatial blocks, but their basic unit was a single block (or square).

One of the characteristics of crossover designs is that different subjects receive the treatments in a different sequence, hence the value of the Latin square approach where each subject receives each treatment once but in a different order. So the effect of subjects (e.g. focal plants) in crossover designs is also an effect of sequence of treatments. Under some patterns of sequences across subjects, we may be able to separate out the effects of sequence from what are termed carryover effects. These are interaction effects between period and treatment and represent the effects of a preceding treatment independent of sequence. The pattern of treatment allocations must be a Latin square where every treatment follows or precedes every other treatment the same number of times because we can then measure carryover effects for all pairs of treatments without confounding with sequence. Not all randomization patterns for allocation of treatments to squares do this, but the pattern used by Feinsinger *et al.* (1991) did. For other patterns, sequence and carryover effects are confounded and cannot be separated. Note that when there are only two treatments (and two periods), the sequence and carryover effects are by definition the same. Really only simple carryover effects from the preceding treatment can be detected, rather than carryover effects from the preceding two or more treatments, unless we have a very large design.

Some details of the analysis of crossover designs can be found in experimental design texts like Cochran & Cox (1957), Crowder & Hand (1990), Mead (1988), Neter *et al.* (1996) and Yandell (1997), with a standard reference being Ratkowsky *et al.* (1993). We don't provide details on calculating the SS but the basic analysis from Feinsinger *et al.* (1991) is presented in Table 10.9. Basically the

Table 10.9 (a) Design of the crossover experiment from Feinsinger *et al.* (1991). Relative density treatments are indicated as A, B, C and D. Each square was replicated in three spatial blocks. (b) Analysis of crossover experiment from Feinsinger *et al.* (1991)

(a)

Time period	Focal plant			
	I	II	III	IV
1	A	B	C	D
2	B	D	A	C
3	C	A	D	B
4	D	C	B	A

(b)

Source	Single block (i.e. square) df	Replicated blocks (i.e. squares) df
Blocks		$(q-1) = 2$
Focal plants, i.e. sequence (within blocks)	$(p-1) = 3$	$(q(p-1)) = 9$
Periods	$(p-1) = 3$	$(p-1) = 3$
Periods × Blocks		$(p-1)(q-1) = 6$
Treatments, i.e. relative density	$(p-1) = 3$	$(p-1) = 3$
Treatments × Blocks		$(p-1)(q-1) = 6$
Carryover	$(p-1) = 3$	$(p-1) = 3$
Residual	rest $= 3$	rest $= 15$
Total	$(p^2-1) = 15$	$(qp^2-1) = 47$

Note:
First df column is from analysis of single block (square), second df is full analysis from three replicate blocks. There are $p = 4$ focal plants, $p = 4$ periods and $p = 4$ treatments in each block (square) and $q = 3$ blocks.

SS_{Total} is partitioned into $SS_{Treatments}$, SS_{Period} and $SS_{Sequence}$ based on marginal means, with the remainder forming the residual. This is the equivalent analysis from a Latin square design (Table 10.8). Feinsinger *et al.* (1991) could also measure carryover effects as a separate source of variation from the residual because their pattern of allocation of treatments to period and subject combinations had every treatment followed by every other treatment once. The number of carryover effects is the same as the number of treatments, as they are measuring the effect of each treatment on the one in the following period. If the rest period between treatments within a subject is long enough, there should be no carryover effects and Feinsinger *et al.* (1991) did not find any significant carryover effects in their study. Note that the correlations between repeated measures on the same subject, that require special consideration in the analyses of RM designs (Section 10.4.2), are assumed to be incorporated into the carryover effect (Yandell 1997).

Feinsinger *et al.* (1991) also replicated their basic Latin square in three spatial blocks, so their full design was a replicated Latin square (Yandell 1997) and the analysis included the block effect and interactions between blocks and treatments, periods and sequences. Because the squares are replicated spatially (blocks), then periods are crossed with squares. If the squares are replicated through time, then the periods would be different for each square and periods would be nested within square (or block). In these analyses, all terms are tested against residual unless there are replicate subjects for each sequence, e.g. replicate focal plants for each sequence of treatments. Then there would also be a subjects within-sequence term that would be used for testing the sequence effect. In the example from Feinsinger *et al.* (1991), there was only one subject (focal plant) per sequence so there was no subject within-sequence term.

The limitations of these designs are the same as Latin square designs, primarily the assumed lack of interactions between treatments, periods and subjects and the few df for the residual, especially when carryover effects are separated out as a source of variation. Also, there are the usual difficulties of handling missing observations and the requirement that the number of treatments needs to match the number of subjects or periods. These designs are most commonly used in research on the responses of animals to different treatments where the number of animals is very restricted and both repeated measures on animals and through multiple time periods are needed.

10.12 | Generalized randomized block designs

As we have emphasized, RCB designs are simply analyzed as unreplicated factorial ANOVAs. If replicates are possible within each combination of block and treatment, then we have a generalized randomized block design (GRB) whose advantages over the usual randomized block design include:

  1. no need for any assumption of additivity,
  2. separation of interaction effects from residual which may result in smaller $MS_{Residual}$ and more powerful test of treatments (Potvin 1993), and
  3. better handling of missing values.

A GRB design that includes replicate experimental units for each treatment within each block is analyzed with a standard two factor linear model as described in Chapter 9 with a test for the factor A by block interaction. Note that randomization (random allocation of experimental units to treatments) is still restricted to n experimental units within each block, compared with a CR factorial design in which experimental units would be randomly allocated to each combination of the two factors. It is important that the "replicates" for a GRB design be at the appropriate scale, otherwise the usual factorial linear model is not applicable (Bergerud 1996). We must replicate the experimental units to which the levels of factor A are applied within each block, e.g. we must replicate leaves with and without domatia in each block in the example from Walter & O'Dowd (1992). If we simply subsample from each unreplicated treatment–block combination, e.g. we measure the size of individual mites in each combination of block (leaf pair) and treatment (with or without domatia), we can not use a two factor ANOVA model. We actually have a subsampled randomized block ANOVA where the analysis is as described in Table 10.10 for our fictitious modification of the Walter & O'Dowd (1992) experiment. Here, the non-existent true replicates for the two factor ANOVA model (replicate leaves for each treatment–block combination) are included in the ANOVA table to illustrate that the subsampled mites are not the appropriate replicates for testing any of the higher terms in the model (Bergerud 1996) – this is just a more complicated example of "pseudoreplication" (Hurlbert 1984; see also Chapter 7). Like Bergerud (1996), we suspect that many biologists mistake subsampling for true replication and would incorrectly analyze this design in Table 10.10 as a completely randomized two factor ANOVA.

10.13 | RCB and RM designs and statistical software

Most statistical software distinguishes between RCB and RM designs in the way the data need to be coded. For an RCB design, each row in the data file represents an individual experimental unit, i.e. a treatment–block combination, and the data for the response variable are in a single column. The columns in the data file will be as follows.

Table 10.10 ANOVA table for a subsampled randomized block design, modifying Walter & O'Dowd (1992) so that 10 mites were sampled from each treatment–block combination, i.e. each single leaf for each treatment within each block

Source	df	Expected mean square
Treatment A	$p - 1 = 1$	$\sigma_\varepsilon^2 + \sigma_{\gamma(\alpha\beta)}^2 + \sigma_{\alpha\beta}^2 + \sigma_\alpha^2$
Block B	$q - 1 = 13$	$\sigma_\varepsilon^2 + \sigma_{\gamma(\alpha\beta)}^2 + \sigma_\beta^2$
Treatment × block (A × B)	$(p - 1)(q - 1) = 13$	$\sigma_\varepsilon^2 + \sigma_{\gamma(\alpha\beta)}^2 + \sigma_{\alpha\beta}^2$
Leaves (treatment and block) C(AB)	$pq(r - 1) = 0$	$\sigma_\varepsilon^2 + \sigma_{\gamma(\alpha\beta)}^2$
Mites (leaves (treatment and block)) D(C(AB))	$pqr(n - 1) = 252$	σ_ε^2

Note:
For simplicity, expected mean squares are provided without multipliers and components for both fixed and random terms are indicated as variances – see Box 9.8. Note that the leaves nested within each treatment–block combination are included in the ANOVA table although their df equal zero because there is still only one replicate leaf for each treatment in each block.

Factor A	Block or subject	Response variable
Shaved	1	9
Unshaved	1	1
etc.		

The analysis then uses a linear model statement that includes a constant (grand mean), factor A and blocks (but no interaction). Output is standard ANOVA but usually with no adjusted univariate or multivariate tests.

For an RM design, each row represents a block or subject and the response variables for each treatment (e.g. time) are in separate columns. The columns in the data file will be as follows.

Block or subject	A_1 (Shaved)	A_2 (Control)
1	9	1
etc.		

The analysis uses software-specific repeated measures commands or menu options. Output is usually standard repeated measures ANOVA with unadjusted and adjusted univariate tests and multivariate tests, and also trend contrasts across treatment means.

Why the difference? It is probably due to most textbooks distinguishing the two types of designs, particularly the influence of statistical texts focusing on psychological and educational research, such as Winer *et al.* (1991). The point is that it doesn't matter which way you set the data file up, the analyses will be identical. It depends on whether you want an estimate of epsilon, measuring whether the variances and covariances meet the sphericity assumption and the extended output of adjusted univariate tests or multivariate tests – if so, use the repeated measures set-up.

10.14 General issues and hints for analysis

10.14.1 General issues

- Randomized complete block (RCB) and simple repeated measures (RM) designs are both analyzed using a linear model for a two factor ANOVA with *n* equals one in each cell.
- The test for factor A is $MS_A / MS_{Residual}$ whether there is an interaction between treatments and blocks/subjects or not.
- If treatment by block or subject interactions exist, then the power of the test for factor A is reduced and, if the interaction is strong, non-significant treatment effects are difficult to interpret.

- Blocks should normally be a random factor, otherwise there is no test for treatments unless we assume no treatment by block interaction.
- Violation of the sphericity assumption can seriously affect the univariate F tests and either adjusted univariate or multivariate tests of treatment effects should be used, especially in repeated measures situations.
- Factorial RCB designs are analyzed equivalently to factorial "within subjects" designs in repeated measures terminology, using the linear model for a three factor unreplicated factorial ANOVA. Each fixed main effect and interaction term should be tested against their interaction with block if blocks are random.

10.14.2 Hints for analysis

- For most statistical software, you should consider creating two data files, one coded for an unreplicated two factor crossed linear model analysis and one coded for classical repeated measures design. The basic ANOVA output will be the same, but other aspects of the output will differ and both contain useful information.
- Even though treatment by block interactions does not preclude assessment of treatment effects, it is worth running checks for interactions. If interactions are present, significant main effects interpretation is an effect of treatment over and above the interaction between treatment and blocks. It would also suggest that a generalized (i.e. replicated) RCB design should be considered if the experiment is repeated.
- Transforming lognormal data to logs or count data to a power (e.g. square or fourth root) can greatly improve additivity and should be used if the absence of treatment by block interactions is important for the analysis or interpretation.
- Cell mean plots are the simplest way of detecting treatment by block/subject interactions, although various residual plots can be also be helpful; a formal test for simple interactions is Tukey's single df test for additivity.
- Use separate denominators for F tests of contrasts between, or trends through, treatments.
- With missing values, either omit the block/subject with missing value if the number of blocks is large, or else estimate the missing value from marginal and overall means or use the model comparison approach as part of fitting the relevant linear models.

Chapter 11

Split-plot and repeated measures designs: partly nested analyses of variance

In Chapter 9, we described multifactor ANOVA models that can involve crossed or nested factors, or a combination of both, and in Chapter 10, we introduced designs that incorporate either blocks or repeated measures. One particular class of experimental designs with both crossed and nested factors, and either blocks or repeated measures, includes split-plot designs (from an agricultural origin), and repeated measures designs (from psychology). These designs can be complex but are particularly common in biological research, so we have devoted a chapter to their analysis. We will use the term partly nested or partly hierarchical for the linear model we fit with these designs, and the least ambiguous name for these designs might also be partly nested. One of the important messages from this chapter is that these repeated measures and split-plot designs are basically analyzed with the same linear model, something that is often unappreciated by biologists, although some textbooks do emphasize the equivalence in models (e.g. Kirk 1995, Mead 1988). In its simplest form, this design has three factors: A and C are crossed, and B is nested within A but crossed with C, although the possible extensions of this design are almost limitless.

11.1 | Partly nested designs

11.1.1 Split-plot designs

Split-plot designs were originally used in agricultural experiments and represent a randomized complete block (RCB) design, with one or more factors applied to experimental units within each block. A second factor (or set of factors) is then applied to whole blocks, with replicate blocks for each level of this factor. Note that the terms blocks and plots are interchangeable in the context of these designs.

There are many examples of classical split-plot designs in the biological literature. First we will consider a fictitious extension of the RCB experiment we described in Chapter 10 from Walter & O'Dowd (1992), examining the role of domatia (small cavities on the leaf surface where mites can live) in determining the number of mites on leaves from species with domatia. They set up pairs of leaves (blocks) on a tree where one leaf in each pair was a control and the other leaf had its domatia removed. The treatment factor was applied to experimental units (leaves) within each block (leaf pair). If we now include additional plant species (those that have domatia), we now have a second factor applied at the scale of whole blocks, i.e. a block will be one or other of the species. This new experiment has blocks as the scale of replication for comparisons of species and leaves within blocks as the scale of replication for comparisons of treatments.

As another example, consider the experiment from Wissinger et al. (1996) who studied the effects of competition and water regime (hydroperiod) on the ecology of two species of larval caddisflies (*Asynarchus nigriculus* and *Limnephilus externus*) in ponds (Figure 11.1). The experiment was set up as a RCB design, with a block (i.e. plot) being a single pond, chosen for having some consistency in environmental conditions. Within each pond, they set

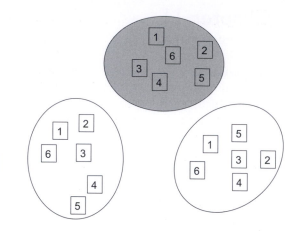

Figure 11.1 Diagrammatic representation of the split-plot experiment from Wissinger *et al.* (1996). There are four ponds (only two shown here) in each of two hydroperiods (permanent and autumnal, represented by different shading), the between plots factor. Within each pond, there were six cages, each containing one level of the within plots factor, competition treatment.

up six wood frame cages in the littoral zone and applied one of six competition treatments (low density *Asynarchus*, low density *Limnephilus*, high density *Asynarchus*, high density *Limnephilus*, high density both species, control with no caddis-flies) to each cage within each pond. The role of hydroperiod (permanent or autumnal) was investigated by having four ponds in each category. The response variables were body mass and survival of each species analyzed separately, so there were only three density treatments (those containing the same species). So there are two factors: hydroperiod was "applied" (non-experimentally) to whole ponds (plots) and is termed the between plots factor and density treatment was applied to cages within plots and is termed the within plots factor. Split-plot designs are characterized by having factors applied to experimental units at different, usually spatial, scales.

There are a number of practical design issues for this experiment.

- The experimental design that would be simplest to analyze would be to have whole ponds that are subjected to levels of both factors, hydroperiod and density treatment, forming a completely randomized (CR) factorial arrangement of two hydroperiods by six density treatments with *n* ponds per cell. Ponds are large units and we would expect considerable variability between them, resulting in large residual variance.
- It is often difficult to install cages, especially large ones. For example, covering whole ponds with cages to maintain experimental densities

would be very expensive to set up and probably require an immense amount of labour. We may find that we cannot physically deal with the required size of cages in the time available to set the experiment up, because the research grant has dried up, or we've exhausted the supply of eager volunteers in earlier experiments. We would also need a lot more ponds. The current design uses eight ponds, whereas a completely randomized design with even only two ponds per density and hydroperiod combination would need 24. That many ponds may simply not exist.

- The split-plot design chosen allows us to group our density treatments within ponds, minimizing spatial variation in environmental characteristics, and giving us a clearer test of the effects of density. It also reduces the size of cages. We have, however, linked together groups of cages, and changed our statistical model dramatically compared to the CR design. If anything happens to a pond (e.g. it dries up at the wrong time, or gets an algal bloom), we would be forced to discard all cages in that pond. If we'd used a CR design, we would lose just a single replicate in a cell.

As another example, Leonard *et al.* (1999) tested the prediction that flow had strong effects on the abundances of mussels and barnacles in an estuary but that these effects might vary with tidal height. They had a number of general design options for testing this prediction.

- They could have sampled a range of sites in the estuary. In the simplest case, they could sample replicate sites within combinations of flow regime and tidal height (i.e. a completely randomized factorial design, with two factors, flow regime and tidal height). This approach would require a large number of sites, and it may be difficult to find enough in the estuary.

• It is likely that sites of a given flow regime vary widely, and the researchers would require many replicate sites to get adequate power. They might get less variability if they sampled a given site at different tidal heights, because they could get more similar physical habitats, and make a better test of the effect of height (although the variation between sites will still be a problem for assessing the effects of flow).

Leonard *et al.* (1999) used a split-plot design: plots were sites and they "applied" six tidal heights (from 0.0 to 3.6 m above mean low water) within each site, and each site falls into one of two flow regimes, high and low flow. In analyzing this design, we need to keep the six height observations for each site together, so that we can compare their differences.

Split-plot designs can also be used when the plots or blocks do not obviously represent spatial units of replication. For example, Westly (1993) set up a split-plot experiment to examine the effects of inflorescence bud removal on asexual investment in the Jerusalem artichoke (*Helianthus tuberosus*). There were four populations of *H. tuberosus*, five genotypes (genotypes were actually tubers from single individuals) nested within each population and two treatments (normal flowering and inflorescence removed) applied to different tubers from each genotype. Genotypes were plots, population was the between plots factor and treatment was the within plots factor.

We will illustrate the analysis of split-plot designs in this chapter with a recent example from our own work on disturbances on rocky shores.

Effects of trampling on intertidal algae populations

These data come from a long-term experiment examining the impact of humans on the fauna and flora of rocky shores in southern Australia (Keough & Quinn 1998), and the full analysis is in Box 11.1. In this experiment, we were interested in disturbances caused by pedestrians, and whether a pattern of summer disturbance and autumn–winter–spring recovery results in a series of small disturbance–recovery cycles, or whether repeated disturbances eventually cause a major impact. We manipulated disturbance by trampling on marked intertidal areas each summer, using four different disturbance levels, which were the number of pedestrian passages. To determine the variability in results, we did the experiment on three different rock platforms, separated by hundreds to thousands of meters. On a smaller scale, at each site, we had two experimental plots, separated by tens of meters, and each plot contained eight experimental strips. This arrangement corresponds to a nested design, with sites (i.e. platforms), plots within sites, and strips within each plot.

Box 11.1 | Worked example of split-plot design: effects of trampling on intertidal limpet populations

Keough & Quinn (1998) examined the effect of pedestrian traffic (trampling) on the abundance of macroalgae and gastropods on rocky intertidal shores. They used three sites, representing different rock platforms separated by hundreds to thousands of meters. Within each site, there were two experimental plots separated by tens of meters and four levels of trampling intensity (0, 5, 10, 25 pedestrian passages per low tide on 6–8 days each summer) were allocated to each of two strips within each plot in each site. The response variable is the number of limpets per 0.25 m^2 quadrat per strip. With only two replicates of each plot–trampling combination, it is not worth producing boxplots, and the number of limpets did not vary widely, with numbers generally less than ten, and no extreme values. We did not transform the response variable, a decision that seems reasonable, as the model fitted the data very well (Keough & Quinn 1998, their Table 3). Model 11.2 was fitted, and includes a term for plots within sites × trampling, because we had replicate strips for each trampling treatment in every plot.

In this design, sites and plots are random factors, so you need to be sure that you use correct F-ratios (Table 11.3). You might need to recalculate the sites, trampling, and sites × trampling F-ratios from the default statistical output if your statistical software does not allow you to specify fixed and random factors.

The specific null hypotheses of interest were as follows.

No difference between sites in the mean number of limpets per strip, pooling trampling treatments.
No difference between trampling treatments in the mean number of limpets per strip, pooling sites.
No interaction between site and trampling treatment on the mean number of limpets per strip, i.e. the effect of trampling on the mean number of limpets per strip was the same at the three sites.

Because we had replicate strips for each trampling treatment within each plot at each site, we could also test two additional null hypotheses.

No added variance in mean number of limpets per strip due to all possible plots within each site.
No interaction between trampling treatment and all possible plots within each site on the mean number of limpets per strip, i.e. the effect of trampling on the mean the number of limpets per strip was the same on all possible plots within each site.

The final ANOVA table is shown below.

Source	SS	df	MS	F	P	Denominator
Sites	8.719	2	4.359	0.521	0.639	Plots(sites)
Plots(sites)	25.094	3	8.365	5.214	0.006	Residual
Trampling	18.354	3	6.118	5.071	0.044	Site × trampling
Site × trampling	7.240	6	1.207	0.485	0.805	Plots(sites) × trampling
Plots(sites) × trampling	22.406	9	2.490	1.552	0.187	Residual
Residual	38.500	24	1.604			

We would conclude that there is a significant main effect of trampling, and that the effect of trampling on the number of limpets does not vary between sites or plots. There is also significant spatial variation at the scale of plots. The number of limpets rose with the intensity of trampling and Figure 11.3(a) shows similar increases at all three platforms (with data averaged across plots). Trampling appears to benefit limpets! This effect occurred because the species most affected by trampling is a brown alga, *Hormosira banksii*, which forms dense mats on these rock platforms. Dense mats provide a poor habitat for the herbivorous limpets, with little food, so the destruction of these mats generates new, usable habitat for limpets. At the level of plots, we found wide variation in overall abundance of limpets (averaged across trampling levels) (Figure 11.3(b)). The plots with higher numbers were on different platforms (sites), as were those with low numbers, accounting for significant variation among plots, but not sites.

Within each plot, the eight strips were allocated randomly to one of the four trampling levels, with two replicates of each trampling level. With the same disturbance levels applied to all plots and sites, the factor trampling is orthogonal to sites and plots. The data used in this example are from a census of the number of limpets in each strip after three years of trampling.

11.1.2 Repeated measures designs

A simple repeated measures design, where the responses of a number of experimental units (or subjects) are recorded for a number of trials (or times), was discussed in detail in Chapter 10 and was also termed a subject by trials design. A modification of this design is a groups by trials design where the basic repeated measures design is modified to include a treatment structure between subjects, i.e. the subjects are randomly allocated to treatment groups in addition to their responses being recorded on a number of trials or times. Just as the linear model used for a subjects by trials repeated measures designs was the same as that used for a RCB design (an unreplicated two factor ANOVA model), groups by trials repeated measures designs can be analyzed in the same way as classical split-plot designs (with a partly nested ANOVA model). The term "plot" is replaced by "subject", and we simply have "between subjects" and "within subjects" effects in the same way as we had between and within plot effects. In biology and ecology, the "subjects" are experimental or sampling units (animals, plants, quadrats, etc.) and the trials are usually sequential times (von Ende 1993).

The term "repeated measures" has actually been used in a confusing manner in the literature. It really refers to repeated observations made on individual units (e.g. subjects, plots), either sequentially through time or under some treatment structure that is applied sequentially throughout time. Repeated measurements on experimental units can occur in any type of design. For example, a randomized block or split-plot design can have repeated measurements on each experimental unit within each block or plot (Gumpertz & Brownie 1993). The linear models used for repeated measures and split-plot designs are identical. The only complications are in the way the data are coded for computer analysis and which assumptions are applicable.

As an example of a group by trials repeated measures design, Schwartz et al. (1995) studied the effects of four temperatures (10°, 20°, 30°, 40 °C) on the dark respiration rate of five species of tree (four species of Torrea and one species of Taxus). Assume that it was desirable to have around five replicates to compare the five tree species, there are not large numbers of plants available, and individual plants were also likely to have different temperature profiles (leading to possibly reduced power). What are the design options for this experiment?

- Five replicate plants per cell, by four temperatures by five species means the experiment would require 100 plants. We would analyze this experiment with a CR two-factor design (factors: species and temperature).
- One temperature profile per plant, so each plant would be used four times for the four temperatures, and only 20 plants are required (five for each species).

The second is a sensible option, to reduce the number of plants used and cut costs (and, if an experiment required sacrificing animals, reducing the number of animals killed). If we choose this option, we don't have a set of independent measurements for each temperature, but a group of five at one temperature, then another group of five for the same set of plants at the next temperature, and so on. Our analysis therefore needs to maintain the relationships between the measurements. Schwartz et al. (1995) used this repeated measures design with five or six plants of each species and each plant was subjected to the four temperatures. Individual plants were subjects, species was the between subjects factor and temperature was the within subjects factor. You can see the similarity to the diagrammatic representation of the pond experiment (Wissinger et al. 1996): the "plots" are individual plants (in repeated measures designs, these are termed "subjects"), the hydroperiod treatment corresponds to species, and the density treatments correspond to the temperatures. This experiment has one "between subjects" factor (species) and one "within subjects" factor (temperature).

In this example, the within subjects factor is a series of treatments (temperatures) applied sequentially through time. Repeated measures designs are often used when the within subjects factor does not represent different treatments but just a time sequence of interest. For example, Gange (1995) measured aphid abundance on twenty individual trees of two species of alder on twenty consecutive dates between May and September. The response variable was aphid abundance, the between subjects factor was tree species and the within subjects factor was date.

We will illustrate the analysis of groups by trials repeated measures designs with an example from a postgraduate project on physiology of amphibians.

Responses of cane toads to hypoxia

Mullens (1993) investigated the ways that cane toads (*Bufo marinus*) respond to conditions of hypoxia. Toads, the subjects, show two different kinds of breathing patterns, lung or buccal, and this breathing pattern was the between subjects factor. The second factor was O_2 concentration, which had eight levels (0, 5, 10, 15, 20, 30, 40, 50%), and was applied within subjects (toads). Various aspects of breathing rate were measured in each trial. The full analysis of this example is in Box 11.2.

Box 11.2 | **Worked example of groups by trials repeated measures design: responses of cane toads to hypoxia**

Mullens (1993) investigated how the breathing rates of cane toads (*Bufo marinus*) respond to conditions of hypoxia. Toads, the subjects, show two different kinds of breathing patterns, lung or buccal, and this breathing pattern was the between subjects factor. The second factor was O_2 concentration, which had eight levels (0, 5, 10, 15, 20, 30, 40, 50%), and was applied within subjects (toads). The response variable was the frequency of buccal breathing and was transformed to square roots to reduce positive skewness (based on boxplots of the data for each O_2 concentration) and improve variance homogeneity (based on residual plots).

The specific null hypotheses of interest were as follows.

No difference between breathing types in the mean square root rate of breathing, pooling O_2 levels.
No difference between O_2 levels in the mean square root rate of breathing, pooling breathing types.
No interaction between breathing type and O_2 level on the mean square root rate of breathing, i.e. the effect of O_2 level on the mean square root rate of breathing was the same for both breathing types.

With no replicates within each combination of breathing type, toad and O_2 level, we could not test hypotheses about the random factor toads within breathing type or O_2 levels by toads within breathing type.

The data were initially coded in classical split-plot form, where toads were plots, and the model in Equation 11.3 was fitted. Because there is only one replicate observation for each toad for each O_2 concentration, this model is fully saturated, i.e. it fits the data perfectly because all sources of variation have been accounted for. The output from your statistical software usually won't include F tests or P values. You might just need to specify each effect in the model and its appropriate denominator to get these. In this example, breathing type and oxygen are clearly fixed factors, but toad is random, so breathing type is tested against toad within breathing type and the interaction between breathing type and O_2 level is tested against the toad within breathing type by O_2 level interaction. We could also achieve these latter tests by fitting a model without the toad within breathing type by O_2 level interaction, which would then become the residual term. Note that many statistical programs assume all factors are fixed and default to using this as the denominator for all tests, which is incorrect if B(A) is random.

Source	SS	df	MS	F	P
Breathing type	39.921	1	39.921	5.762	0.027
Toad(breathing type)	131.634	19	6.928		
O_2 level	25.748	7	3.678	4.884	<0.001
Breathing type × O_2 level	56.372	7	8.053	10.693	<0.001
Toad(Breathing type) × O_2 level	100.166	133	0.753		

We would conclude that there is a significant difference between toads with the different breathing types, but this depends on O_2 level (significant breathing type × O_2 level interaction).

We then re-analyzed the data after recoding them as a "repeated measures" design. For most software, we get even more extensive output.

BETWEEN SUBJECTS

Source	SS	df	MS	F	P
Breathing type	39.921	1	39.921	5.762	0.027
Residual	131.634	19	6.928		

Note:
This residual is actually toads nested within breathing type.

WITHIN SUBJECTS

Source	SS	df	MS	F	P	GG P	HF P
O_2 level	25.748	7	3.678	4.884	<0.001	0.004	0.002
Breathing type × O_2 level	56.372	7	8.053	10.693	<0.001	<0.001	<0.001
Residual	100.166	133	0.753				

Note:
This residual is actually toads within breathing type by O_2 level.

Greenhouse–Geisser epsilon:	0.428
Huynh–Feldt epsilon:	0.544

The "between subjects" and "within-subjects" parts of the ANOVA are distinguished and B(A), in this example toads within breathing type, is assumed to be random and all other factors fixed. The ANOVA output is, however, identical to the partly nested ANOVA above. Estimates of ε are also provided – the Greenhouse–Geisser is more conservative than the Huynh–Feldt estimate and neither is close to one, suggesting that the sphericity assumption is not met. Because both estimates of epsilon are less than 0.75, the Greenhouse–Geisser adjustment is preferred. Our conclusions would not be affected by these more conservative tests; there is a significant interaction between O_2 and breathing type. Both main effects are also significant, although it is more sensible to base further interpretation on the interaction. It is clear from Figure 11.4 that breathing rate decreases with increasing O_2 level for buccal breathing toads but increases with O_2 level for lung breathing toads.

Because of the interaction, simple main effects tests for O_2 level at each breathing type separately might be of interest. We adjust the df for these tests based on the Greenhouse–Geisser estimate of epsilon.

BUCCAL:

Source	SS	df	MS	F	P	GG df	GG P
O_2 level	75.433	7	10.776	14.311	<0.001	2.997	<0.001
Residual	100.166	133	0.753			56.951	

LUNG:

Source	SS	df	MS	F	P	GG df	GG P
O_2 level	19.907	7	2.844	3.777	0.001	2.997	0.015
Residual	100.166	133	0.753			56.951	

There is a significant effect of O_2 level for both breathing types, although the effect seems stronger for buccal breathing toads than lung breathing toads.

For most statistical software, "repeated measures" output will include polynomial trend analyses. With eight O_2 levels, up to seventh order polynomials could be examined, although we will just look at the first three. The interaction test of these polynomials is testing whether the trend (linear, quadratic, etc.) through O_2 level differs between breathing types; the main effect test is examining whether there is a trend through O_2 level pooling breathing types.

Polynomial Test of Order 1 (Linear)

Source	SS	df	MS	F	P
O_2 level	17.010	1	17.010	8.255	0.010
Breathing type $\times$ O_2 level	40.065	1	40.065	19.444	<0.001
Residual	39.149	19	2.060		

Polynomial Test of Order 2 (Quadratic)

Source	SS	df	MS	F	P
O_2 level	5.007	1	5.007	6.967	0.016
Breathing type $\times$ O_2 level	12.326	1	12.326	17.150	0.001
Residual	13.655	19	0.719		

Polynomial Test of Order 3 (Cubic)

Source	SS	df	MS	F	P
O_2 level	1.747	1	1.747	3.263	0.087
Breathing type $\times$ O_2 level	1.784	1	1.784	3.331	0.084
Residual	10.174	19	0.535		

Both linear and quadratic trends are different between the two breathing types; there is no evidence of a cubic trend. It is clear from Figure 11.4 that the linear trends are in different directions for the two breathing types. Note that separate error terms are used for each trend test, a requirement if there is a chance that sphericity of variances and covariances does not hold.

Finally, we get the multivariate tests of the within-subjects hypotheses.

O_2 level		Hypoth. df	Error df	F	P
Wilks' Lambda	0.115	7	13	14.277	<0.001
Pillai Trace	0.885	7	13	14.277	<0.001
Hotelling–Lawley Trace	7.688	7	13	14.277	<0.001

Breathing type $\times O_2$ level		Hypoth. df	Error df	F	P
Wilks' Lambda	0.325	7	13	3.853	0.017
Pillai Trace	0.675	7	13	3.853	0.017
Hotelling–Lawley Trace	2.075	7	13	3.853	0.017

The conclusions from the Pillai statistic agree with the univariate analysis – a significant interaction between O_2 level and breathing type.

11.1.3 Reasons for using these designs

The examples above demonstrate the two major reasons for using split-plot or repeated measures designs. First, if our experimental or sampling units (organisms, ponds, sites) are expensive or otherwise difficult to obtain, we might consider applying a number of treatments to each (or to subunits within each) or recording each through time. Second, if we expect lots of variation between these units, and are worried that this variation might obscure effects of our treatments, we can attempt to remove this variation by taking a biological "unit" and applying different treatments to it – sampling different parts of the same pond, applying a range of oxygen concentrations, etc. The basic difference between a split-plot and a group by trials repeated measures design is that the former allocates the within plots treatments to subunits within each plot whereas the latter allocates the within subjects treatments sequentially to each subject.

11.2 | Analyzing partly nested designs

We will first describe the analyses for a standard partly nested design that has three factors. One (the plots or subjects) is nested within the second, but both of these factors are crossed (orthogonal, factorial) with the third (Figure 11.2). In the split-plot example from Wissinger et al. (1996), we have hydroperiod (A), ponds within hydroperiods ((B(A)), and density treatment (C). In the repeated measures example from Schwartz et al. (1995), we have species (A), plants within each species ((B(A)), and temperature (C). In both examples, we have every combination of A and C (hydroperiod and density or species and temperature), so A and C form a factorial design. B and C are also factorial because every pond gets all density treatments and every plant gets all temperature treatments.

We could also have replicate observations from each combination of B and C (run each plant twice at each temperature, have replicate cages for each density treatment within each pond, etc.). As we will see below, in most cases, it makes little difference to how we test the effects of A and C.

We will describe the linear model and the various forms of analysis using split-plot terminology; keep in mind, however, that the plots are simply replaced by subjects in repeated measures designs. Components for fixed and random factors in expected mean squares are represented as "variances"; remember the different interpretations of variation between means of fixed treatment

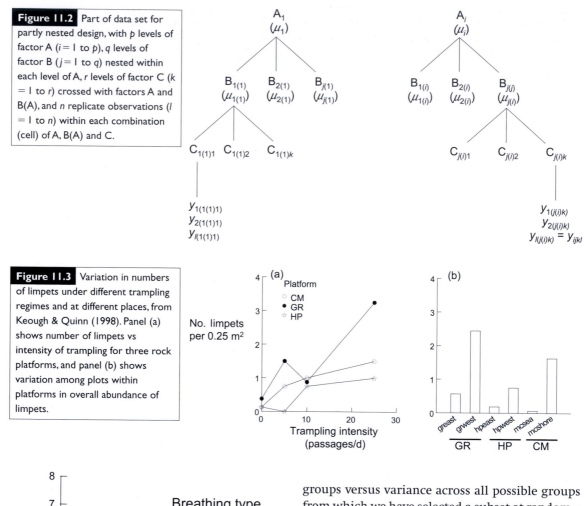

Figure 11.2 Part of data set for partly nested design, with p levels of factor A ($i = 1$ to p), q levels of factor B ($j = 1$ to q) nested within each level of A, r levels of factor C ($k = 1$ to r) crossed with factors A and B(A), and n replicate observations ($l = 1$ to n) within each combination (cell) of A, B(A) and C.

Figure 11.3 Variation in numbers of limpets under different trampling regimes and at different places, from Keough & Quinn (1998). Panel (a) shows number of limpets vs intensity of trampling for three rock platforms, and panel (b) shows variation among plots within platforms in overall abundance of limpets.

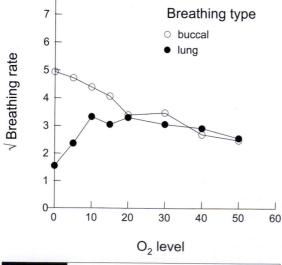

Figure 11.4 Mean square root transformed rate of buccal breathing for lung and buccal breathing toads for eight levels of O_2 concentration from Mullens (1993).

groups versus variance across all possible groups from which we have selected a subset at random – see Box 9.8.

11.2.1 Linear models for partly nested analyses

Linear effects model

Consider a design with p levels of factor A ($i = 1$ to p), q levels of factor B (plots or subjects) nested within each level of A ($j = 1$ to q) and r levels of factor C ($k = 1$ to r), crossed with both A and B (Table 11.1). From Keough & Quinn (1998), p equals three (the number of sites), q equals two (the number of plots) and r equals four (trampling treatments). From Mullens (1993), p equals two (the different breathing types), q equals eight or 13 (the number of toads of each breathing type) and r equals eight (O_2 levels). For completeness, we will describe the model with replicate observations

Table 11.1 | Marginal means for a partly nested design with i levels of factor A, j levels of factor B within each level of factor A and k levels of factor C crossed with both A and B

		C_1	C_2	C_k	B marginal means	A marginal means
A_1	$B_{1(1)}$	y_{111}	y_{112}	y_{11k}	$\bar{y}_{j=1(1)}$	
	$B_{2(1)}$	y_{121}	y_{122}	y_{12k}	$\bar{y}_{j=2(1)}$	$\bar{y}_{i=1}$
	$B_{j(1)}$	y_{1j1}	y_{1j2}	y_{1jk}	$\bar{y}_{j(1)}$	
A_2	$B_{j(2)}$	y_{2j1}	y_{2j2}	y_{2jk}	$\bar{y}_{j(2)}$	$\bar{y}_{i=2}$
A_i	$B_{j(i)}$	y_{ij1}	y_{ij2}	y_{ijk}	$\bar{y}_{j(i)}$	$\bar{y}_i$
C marginal means		$\bar{y}_{k=1}$	$\bar{y}_{k=2}$	$\bar{y}_k$		

($l = 1$ to n) within each combination of A, B and C, e.g. Keough & Quinn (1998) had replicate observations (strips) within each site, plot and treatment combination. Usually, however, there is only a single observation (e.g. a single toad) of each level of C in each plot/subject.

The formal linear model for a split-plot design is:

$$y_{ijkl} = \mu + \alpha_i + \beta_{j(i)} + \gamma_k + \alpha\gamma_{ik} + \beta\gamma_{j(i)k} + \varepsilon_{ijkl} \qquad (11.1)$$

Details of this linear model, including estimation of its parameters, are provided in Box 11.3.

From Keough & Quinn (1998):

(number of limpets)$_{ijkl} = \mu + $ (site)$_i + $ (plot within site)$_{j(i)} + $ (trampling)$_k + $ (interaction between site and trampling)$_{ik} + $ (interaction between plot within site and trampling)$_{j(i)k} + \varepsilon_{ijkl}$ (11.2)

From Mullens (1993):

(breathing rate)$_{ijkl} = \mu + $ (breathing type)$_i + $ (toad within breathing type)$_{j(i)} + $ (O_2 level)$_k + $ (interaction between breathing type and O_2 level)$_{ik} + $ (interaction between toad within breathing type and O_2 level)$_{j(i)k} + \varepsilon_{ijkl}$ (11.3)

In models 11.1 and 11.2 we have the following.

y_{ijkl} is the number of limpets in the lth strip in the kth level of trampling treatment for the jth plot at the ith site. Commonly in these designs, n equals one, although Keough & Quinn (1998) had n equals two.

μ is the overall (constant) population mean number of limpets per strip for all levels of trampling in all plots across all sites.

Factor A is fixed, so α_i is the effect of ith site on the number of limpets per strip, pooling over these designs, $l = 1$, but our two worked examples in this chapter include one in which $l = 2$ (Box 11.1) and one with $l = 1$ (Box 11.2).

μ is the overall (constant) population mean of the response variable.

If factor A is fixed, α_i is the effect of ith level of factor A ($\mu_i - \mu$), pooling over factor C. If factor A is random, α_i is a random variable with a mean of zero and a variance of σ_α^2, measuring the variance in mean values of the response variable across all possible levels of factor A that could have been used.

Plots or subjects are nearly always random so $\beta_{j(i)}$ is a random variable with a mean of zero and a variance of σ_β^2, measuring the variance in mean values of the response variable across all possible plots or subjects that could have been used within any level of A.

If factor C is fixed, γ_k is the effect of the kth level of factor C ($\mu_k - \mu$), pooling over factor A. If factor C is random, γ_k is a random variable with a mean of zero and a variance of σ_γ^2, measuring the variance in mean values of the response variable across all possible levels of factor C that could have been used.

If factors A and C are both fixed, $\alpha\gamma_{ik}$ is the effect of the interaction between the ith level of A and kth level of C. If either factor is random, then $\alpha\gamma_{ik}$ is a random variable with a mean of zero and a variance of $\sigma_{\alpha\gamma}^2$, measuring the variance across all the possible interaction terms between the fixed levels (if A is fixed) or all possible levels (if A is random) of factor A and the fixed levels (if C is fixed) or all possible levels (if C is random) of factor C.

Because plots/subjects are nearly always random, the interaction between factor C and plots/subjects $\beta\gamma_{j(i)k}$ is a random variable with a mean of zero and a variance of $\sigma_{\beta\gamma}^2$, measuring the variance across all the possible interaction terms between all the possible plots/subjects within any level of A and the fixed levels (if C is fixed) or all possible levels (if C is random) of factor C.

ε_{ijkl} is random or unexplained error associated with the lth observation in the kth level of factor C for the jth plot/subject in the ith level of factor A. These error terms are assumed to be normally distributed in each combination of A, B and C with a mean of zero and a variance of σ_ε^2. Note that classical split-plot and repeated measures designs usually do not have replication for each combination of plot and factor C ($n = 1$) so ε_{ijkl} usually cannot be separately estimated.

This effects model is overparameterized (Box 8.3) so the usual sum-to-zero constraints are imposed on the fixed effects. We can also use a cell means model (Kirk 1995) which may be useful when there are missing observations (Section 11.6).

Estimating the parameters of the partly nested model follows the procedures outlined in the previous three chapters for single factor, multifactor and randomized block models. The cell means (μ_{ijk}) are estimated by means of the observations in each cell, although there is often only a single observation for each A, B and C combination. The marginal means are shown in Table 11.1 and represent averages across the appropriate cell means (or single observations). Standard errors for these means must be based on the appropriate variance estimate (mean square), the one that is used as the denominator of the F-ratio for testing the H_0 that the means are equal (see Boxes 9.2 and 9.6).

plots and trampling treatment. If factor A was random, e.g. sites were chosen at random along the shore, then α_i is a random variable with a mean of zero and a variance of σ_α^2, measuring the variance in mean number of limpets across all possible sites that could have been used.

Plots are random so $\beta_{j(i)}$ is a random variable with a mean of zero and a variance of σ_β^2, measuring the variance in mean number of limpets across all possible plots that could have been used within any site, pooling trampling treatments.

Factor C is fixed, so γ_k is the effect of the kth level of trampling treatment, pooling over plots and sites. If factor C was random, e.g. trampling levels were chosen at random from the possible trampling levels that could have been used, then γ_k is a random variable with a mean of zero and a variance of σ_γ^2, measuring the variance in mean number of limpets across possible levels of trampling that could have been used.

Factors A and C are both fixed, so $\alpha\gamma_{ik}$ is the effect of the interaction between the ith site and kth trampling treatment. This interaction measures whether the effect of trampling is consistent at all sites used. If one factor is random, e.g. random sites, then $\alpha\gamma_{ik}$ is a random variable with a mean of zero and a variance of $\sigma_{\alpha\gamma}^2$, measuring the variance of all the possible interaction terms between all possible sites and the fixed trampling levels. This interaction would measure whether the effect of trampling was consistent across all possible sites.

Because plots are random, the interaction between trampling treatment and plots [$\beta\gamma_{j(i)k}$] is a random variable with a mean of zero and a variance of $\sigma_{\beta\gamma}^2$, measuring the variance of all the possible interaction terms between all the possible plots within any site and the fixed trampling treatments. This measures the variation in effects of trampling at the spatial scale of plots.

ε_{ijkl} is random or unexplained error associated with the lth strip in the kth trampling treatment for the jth plot at the ith site. This is the error associated with each strip that is not due to trampling treatment, plot or site. Note that classical split-plot and repeated measures designs usually do not have replication for each

combination of plot and factor C (n equals one) so ε_{ijkl} usually cannot be separately estimated from $\sigma_{\beta\gamma}^2$.

Predicted values and residuals
If we replace the parameters in our model by their OLS estimates (Box 11.3), it turns out that the predicted or fitted values of the response variable from our linear model 11.1 are:

$$\hat{y}_{ijkl} = \bar{y}_{ijk} \tag{11.4}$$

The error terms from model 11.1 can be estimated by the residuals, the difference between each observed and predicted value. In most applications of split-plot and groups by trials repeated measures designs, there is only a single observation per cell and these residuals all equal zero. In these circumstances, we cannot directly estimate σ_ε^2, the variance of the error terms, unless we assume that $\sigma_{\beta\gamma}^2$, the variance due to the B(A)$\times$C interaction, equals zero. Not being able to estimate σ_ε^2 does not, however, compromise our tests of the main hypotheses of interest, those of A, C and A$\times$C, the argument being similar to that used for analyses of RCB and simple repeated measures designs in Chapter 10 (see Section 11.2.3).

11.2.2 Analysis of variance
The partitioning of variance from the OLS fit of the linear model 11.1 is shown in Table 11.2. We do not provide computational details for sums-of-squares (SS) for each term in this ANOVA – see Winer *et al.* (1991) and Kirk (1995) for the classical formulae. In practice, however, we assume that you have access to statistical software with a general linear modeling routine when dealing with these complex designs. The SS for each source of variation are calculated by comparing the fit of the full model with the fit of an appropriate reduced model (the model including all terms except the one we wish to test in our H$_0$), as we described in Chapters 8, 9 and 10 for simpler ANOVA models. The general expected values of the mean squares are also provided in Table 11.2(a), as well as those for the usual case of factors A and C being fixed and factor B (plots or subjects) being random.

This ANOVA is more complicated than those from previous chapters but not really that difficult

Table 11.2 | (a) Classical split-plot or repeated measures design with general expected mean squares and those for the specific case of A and C fixed, but B (plots or subjects) random, showing *F*-ratios used to test all hypotheses. For explanation of the conversion of the general model to particular combinations of fixed and random factors, see Box 9.8. (b) ANOVA for split-plot design from Wissinger *et al.* (1996), where hydroperiod and treatment are fixed factors, ponds is random and nested within hydroperiod, and from repeated measures design from Gange (1995), where species and date are fixed factor; trees is random and nested within species

(a)

Source	df	General expected mean square (EMS)	EMS (A, C fixed, B random)	Test (A, C fixed, B random)
Between plots/subjects				
A	$p-1$	$\sigma_\varepsilon^2 + nD_q D_r \sigma_{\beta\gamma}^2 + nqD_r \sigma_{\alpha\gamma}^2 + nrD_q \sigma_\beta^2 + nqr\sigma_\alpha^2$	$\sigma_\varepsilon^2 + nr\sigma_\beta^2 + nqr\sigma_\alpha^2$	$MS_A/MS_{B(A)}$
B(A)	$p(q-1)$	$\sigma_\varepsilon^2 + nD_r\sigma_{\beta\gamma}^2 + nr\sigma_\beta^2$	$\sigma_\varepsilon^2 + nr\sigma_\beta^2$	$MS_{B(A)}/MS_{Residual}$
Within plots/subjects				
C	$r-1$	$\sigma_\varepsilon^2 + nD_q\sigma_{\beta\gamma}^2 + nqD_p\sigma_{\alpha\gamma}^2 + npq\sigma_\gamma^2$	$\sigma_\varepsilon^2 + n\sigma_{\beta\gamma}^2 + npq\sigma_\gamma^2$	$MS_C/MS_{B(A)C}$
A×C	$(p-1)(r-1)$	$\sigma_\varepsilon^2 + nD_q\sigma_{\beta\gamma}^2 + nq\sigma_{\alpha\gamma}^2$	$\sigma_\varepsilon^2 + n\sigma_{\beta\gamma}^2 + nq\sigma_{\alpha\gamma}^2$	$MS_{AC}/MS_{B(A)C}$
B(A)×C	$p(q-1)(r-1)$	$\sigma_\varepsilon^2 + n\sigma_{\beta\gamma}^2$	$\sigma_\varepsilon^2 + n\sigma_{\beta\gamma}^2$	$MS_{B(A)C}/MS_{Residual}$
Residual	$pqr(n-1)$	σ_ε^2	σ_ε^2	

(b)

Source	df	Source	df
Between plots (i.e. ponds)		*Between subjects (i.e. trees)*	
Hydroperiod	1	Species	1
Ponds within hydroperiod	6	Trees within species	38
Within plots (i.e ponds)		*Within subjects (i.e. trees)*	
Treatment	2	Date	19
Hydroperiod × treatment	2	Species × date	19
Ponds within hydroperiod × treatment	12	Trees within species × date	799

– let's look at the different components. The between plots/subjects section is just a single factor ANOVA on the mean values for each plot/subject (i.e. averaging over the levels of factor C) and the plots/subjects within A (i.e. factor B) term is the equivalent of the residual term in this single factor ANOVA. The within plots/subjects section is just a number of RCB (or simple repeated measures) designs, one for each level of A. The effects of factor C and the A×C interaction are interpreted in the same way as for a two factor crossed ANOVA (Chapter 9). The C × plots within A [i.e. C×B(A)] term represents the pooled error terms from the p randomized block designs which comprise the within plots/subjects component of the analysis, i.e. for each level of A, we have a C by plots RCB design (Kirk 1995).

These ANOVA tables are illustrated in Table 11.2(b) for some of the examples we described in Section 11.1. The first is the split-plot design from Wissinger et al. (1996) where the between plots factor was hydroperiod, the within plots factor was density treatment and the plots were ponds nested within each hydroperiod. The second was the groups by trials repeated measures design from Gange (1995) where the between-subjects factor was tree type, the within-subjects factor was date, the subjects were individual trees and the response variable was aphid abundance. The ANOVA tables for our two worked examples are also provided in Box 11.1 and Box 11.2.

11.2.3 Null hypotheses

There are three null hypotheses of primary interest when we fit the partly nested model 11.1.

Factor A (fixed)

H_0: $\mu_1 = \mu_2 = \ldots = \mu_i$. This H_0 states that there is no difference between the factor A marginal means, pooling levels of factor C. For example, no difference in the mean number of limpets per strip between sites, pooling the trampling treatments.

This is equivalent to:

H_0: $\alpha_1 = \alpha_2 = \ldots = \alpha_i = 0$, i.e. no effect of any level of factor A. For example, no effect of site on the mean number of limpets per strip, pooling the trampling treatments.

Factor C (fixed)

H_0: $\mu_1 = \mu_2 = \ldots = \mu_k$. This H_0 states that there is no difference between the factor C marginal means, pooling levels of factor A. For example, no difference in the mean number of limpets per strip between trampling treatments, pooling sites.

This is equivalent to:

H_0: $\gamma_1 = \gamma_2 = \ldots = \gamma_k = 0$, i.e. no effect of any level of factor C. For example, no effect of trampling treatment on the mean number of limpets per strip, pooling sites.

A×C interaction (fixed)

H_0: $\mu_{ijk} - \mu_i - \mu_k + \mu = 0$, which is the same as $(\alpha\gamma)_{ik} = 0$. This H_0 states that there are no interactions between A and C, e.g. the effect of site on the mean number of limpets per strip is the same for all trampling treatments and the effect of trampling treatment on the mean number of limpets per strip is the same for all sites.

The modifications of these H_0s for random factors are straightforward as described in Chapters 9 and 10.

Two other null hypotheses might also be tested in some circumstances.

Factor B(A) (random)

H_0: $\sigma_\beta^2 = 0$, i.e. the variance in mean values of the response variable across all possible plots or subjects that could have been used within any level of A equals zero. For example, no variance in the mean number of limpets per strip between plots in either site, pooling trampling treatments.

B(A)×C interaction (random)

H_0: $\sigma_{\beta\gamma}^2 = 0$, i.e. the variance across all the possible interaction terms between all the possible plots/subjects within any level of A and the fixed levels (if C is fixed) or all possible levels (if C is random) of factor C equals zero. For example, no variance in the mean number of limpets per strip across all the possible interaction terms between plots within each site and trampling treatment.

F-ratios

The F-ratios for testing these null hypotheses are based on the expected values of the relevant mean squares (Table 11.2(a)). When factors A and C are both fixed, the F test for factor A uses a different denominator [$MS_{B(A)}$] than those for factor C and $A \times C$ [$MS_{CB(A)}$]. This is typical for designs with both fixed and random factors and is apparent in all these partly nested designs because the plots/subjects term is nearly always random. In the classical split-plot or repeated measures design with n equals one observation for each cell, the B(A) and $C \times B(A)$ terms cannot be tested. The implications of not being able to test the $C \times B(A)$ are analogous to the implications of having no test for a block by treatment interaction in a RCB design (Chapter 10). This makes sense given that the $C \times B(A)$ interaction comprises the pooled residual terms from the p RCB designs and each of these residual terms includes the plot/subject by treatment interaction. The first implication is that if B is random, then a strong $C \times B(A)$ interaction will reduce the power of the tests of C and $A \times C$, although these tests are still valid because the expected mean squares of both C and $A \times C$ include the variance component due to $C \times B(A)$. This is not the case if B is fixed, where $C \times B(A)$ is an inappropriate error term for testing C and $A \times C$ (see below). The second implication is that the use of $C \times B(A)$ as an error term for C and $A \times C$ can be invalid if the observations within each plot/subject are correlated, which is almost certainly the case for repeated measures designs. For the $C \times B(A)$ to be used as an error term, we must make certain assumptions about the covariances of the observations (Section 11.3).

With replicate observations in each cell, the B(A) and $C \times B(A)$ terms can be tested against the residual. Note, however, that using many replicate observations within each cell, e.g. multiple measurements on toads or multiple strips within plots, may not be providing a much better test of the terms that you really care about. The B(A) term is rarely of much interest, and you probably don't care much if factor C has a different effect across levels of B, i.e. a $C \times B(A)$ interaction. The effort expended in sampling at this lowest level may not be producing a more powerful statistical test of any of the biologically interesting effects, only increasing the cost of the design in terms of time and/or money. When there is no replication within plots, Underwood (1997) argued that tests of the main effects of C and the $A \times C$ interaction

can only be done if we assume there is no $C \times B(A)$ interaction, i.e. the effects of C do not vary from plot to plot. However, it is clear from Table 11.2(a) that the expected mean squares for C and the $A \times C$ interaction include the variance due to $C \times B(A)$ interaction, so the F test for C and $A \times C$ is testing for these effects over and above the variation due to the $C \times B(A)$ interaction and any residual variation. Therefore, we can interpret a significant effect of C or the $A \times C$ interaction even if the effects of C do vary for different levels B(A), which is similar to the argument we made in Chapter 10 for RCB designs when the blocks factor was random. A non-significant C or $A \times C$ interaction is more difficult to interpret in the presence of a $C \times B(A)$ interaction, but interpreting non-significant tests is always problematical.

As you can see from Table 11.2(a), the effects of A, C and the $A \times C$ interaction are all tested against other terms in the analysis, all featuring effects of B within A. Because you cannot control the number of levels of A or C when they are fixed factors, the only way to increase the power of these tests is to increase the degrees of freedom. This can only be achieved by using more levels of B (more plots or subjects, e.g. more toads, more plots, etc.), i.e. increasing q.

The expected mean squares and appropriate F tests for other combinations of fixed and random factors are presented in Table 11.3. When A, C and plots/subjects (i.e. B) are all fixed (Table 11.3), you can see that all terms are tested using the $MS_{Residual}$ as the denominator. Note that you must have replicate observations in each cell if plots (B) are fixed because $MS_{CB(A)}$ is not an appropriate denominator here unless you are very sure that the $C \times B(A)$ interaction is negligible. In almost every case that we deal with, factor B will be random so this design is unlikely for biological experiments. If factors A and plots/subjects are random, but C is fixed, the tests are straightforward (Table 11.3), but note that again, they use different combinations of denominators for F tests for the various hypotheses. Problems occur when plots/subjects and factor C are random (Table 11.3). It does not matter whether A is fixed or random in this case. The difficulty is that the main effect of factor A (which will almost always be of central interest) cannot be tested directly, because there is no

Table 11.3 | ANOVA tables with expected mean squares (EMS) for partly nested models, showing F-ratios used to test all hypotheses

Source	df	A, B, C fixed		A, B random, C fixed		A fixed, B, C random	
		EMS	Test	EMS	Test	EMS	Test
A	$p-1$	$\sigma_\varepsilon^2 + npr\sigma_\alpha^2$	$MS_A/MS_{Residual}$	$\sigma_\varepsilon^2 + nr\sigma_\beta^2 + nqr\sigma_\alpha^2$	$MS_A/MS_{B(A)}$	$\sigma_\varepsilon^2 + n\sigma_{\beta\gamma}^2 + nq\sigma_{\alpha\gamma}^2 + nr\sigma_\beta^2 + nqr\sigma_\alpha^2$	No test
B(A)	$p(q-1)$	$\sigma_\varepsilon^2 + nr\sigma_\beta^2$	$MS_{B(A)}/MS_{Residual}$	$\sigma_\varepsilon^2 + nr\sigma_\beta^2$	$MS_{B(A)}/MS_{Residual}$	$\sigma_\varepsilon^2 + n\sigma_{\beta\gamma}^2 + nr\sigma_\beta^2$	$MS_{B(A)}/MS_{B(A)C}$
C	$r-1$	$\sigma_\varepsilon^2 + npq\sigma_\gamma^2$	$MS_C/MS_{Residual}$	$\sigma_\varepsilon^2 + n\sigma_{\beta\gamma}^2 + nq\sigma_{\alpha\gamma}^2 + npq\sigma_\gamma^2$	MS_C/MS_{AC}	$\sigma_\varepsilon^2 + n\sigma_{\beta\gamma}^2 + npq\sigma_\gamma^2$	$MS_C/MS_{B(A)C}$
A×C	$(p-1)(r-1)$	$\sigma_\varepsilon^2 + nq\sigma_{\alpha\gamma}^2$	$MS_{AC}/MS_{Residual}$	$\sigma_\varepsilon^2 + n\sigma_{\beta\gamma}^2 + nq\sigma_{\alpha\gamma}^2$	$MS_{AC}/MS_{B(A)C}$	$\sigma_\varepsilon^2 + n\sigma_{\beta\gamma}^2 + nq\sigma_{\alpha\gamma}^2$	$MS_{AC}/MS_{B(A)C}$
B(A)×C	$p(q-1)(r-1)$	$\sigma_\varepsilon^2 + n\sigma_{\beta\gamma}^2$	$MS_{B(A)C}/MS_{Residual}$	$\sigma_\varepsilon^2 + n\sigma_{\beta\gamma}^2$	$MS_{B(A)C}/MS_{Residual}$	$\sigma_\varepsilon^2 + n\sigma_{\beta\gamma}^2$	$MS_{B(A)C}/MS_{Residual}$
Residual	$pqr(n-1)$	σ_ε^2		σ_ε^2		σ_ε^2	

appropriate denominator. The only option is to use quasi F-ratios, which are combinations of mean squares that produce an approximate test of your hypothesis (see Chapter 9). Winer *et al.* (1991) discussed this option in detail, but you should be aware that the resulting F tests are only approximate and not necessarily robust, and you probably should avoid this situation if possible.

11.2.4 Comparing ANOVA models
The SS, df and MS for each term in the partly nested model 11.1 can be derived from comparing the fit of a full and a reduced model, where the reduced model omits the parameter specified to be zero in the H_0. This is the same principle we have described in Chapters 9 and 10 for other multifactor models.

11.3 | Assumptions

Irrespective of whether it is for a split-plot design or a groups by trials repeated measures design, the partly nested ANOVA model 11.1 has a number of assumptions that need to be assessed. Additionally, we should always check for outliers from our fitted model. A useful first step is to examine the residuals from the fit of the model. If we only have n equals one within each combination of A, B and C, then we should omit the $B(A) \times C$ term, otherwise the model is saturated (a perfect fit) and all the residuals are zero. These residuals will indicate any obvious outliers and also indicate any strong skewness in the data. Generally, however, the assumptions, and their assessment, in these analyses are considered separately for the between plots/subjects and within plots/subjects components.

11.3.1 Between plots/subjects
The test of factor A assumes normality and homogeneity of variance and the comments about these assumptions in Chapters 8 and 9 apply here. Note that, for the usual case of B random and A and C fixed, these assumptions apply to the levels of A (pooled across C) with the mean of Y in each level of B(A) as a replicate observation. It is often useful to create a new variable that is the average across the levels of C and then use that variable in

boxplots for each level of A or to examine residuals from the fit of a single factor ANOVA model with p groups to that variable.

11.3.2 Within plots/subjects and multisample sphericity
The tests for any terms including within-plots/subjects factors(s), i.e. tests of C and $A \times C$, have the assumption of sphericity of variances and covariance, as did RCB and simple repeated measures designs (Chapter 9). Unless this assumption holds, then the $B(A) \times C$ term is an inappropriate denominator for the test of C and $A \times C$. Remember that these partly nested designs can be envisaged as a series of RCB (factor C by blocks, plots or subjects) experiments, one for each level of factor A, so the assumption is now multisample sphericity. Not only must the variance–covariance matrices be the same for each level of factor A, they must each show sphericity, which means that the variances of the differences between the levels of the repeated factor must be the same.

In classical repeated measures designs, the levels of the within-subjects factor (C) can usually be applied in random order to each subject (Winer *et al.* 1991). Similarly, in classical split-plot designs, the levels of the within-plot factor (C) should be randomly allocated to experimental units (subplots) within each plot. Under these randomization conditions, there is no reason for the sphericity assumption not to hold; in fact, the sphericity assumption is often not discussed when general statistics texts describe split-plot designs. In contrast, the sphericity assumption is unlikely to hold in repeated measures designs when subjects are recorded through time because the differences between times closer together are likely to be less variable (i.e. more similar) than times further apart. If sphericity is not met, the F-ratio statistics for within subjects effects (C and $A \times C$) will be inflated, increasing the risk of a Type I error above the nominal level (e.g. 0.05) – see Keselman & Keselman (1993), Keselman *et al.* (1995) and Rasmussen (1989). There is no easy test for the null hypothesis that the variance–covariance matrices conform to multisample sphericity. Kirk (1995) recommended the W test and provided critical values, although we suggest it is safer to assume that multisample sphericity is not met in

Table 11.4 Degrees of freedom for within-plots or -subjects components of partly nested ANOVA

Source	df	Adjusted df
Within plots/subjects		
C	$(r-1)$	$(r-1)\hat{\varepsilon}$
A×C	$(p-1)(r-1)$	$(p-1)(r-1)\hat{\varepsilon}$
B(A)×C	$p(q-1)(r-1)$	$p(q-1)(r-1)\hat{\varepsilon}$

Note:
Adjustment based on estimate of ε indicating how far variance–covariance matrix is from sphericity.

repeated measures type designs and use one or more of the following analytical strategies.

Adjusted univariate *F*-ratio tests

As described in Chapter 10 for RCB and simple repeated measures designs, we can make the *F* tests more conservative using adjusted df. An index of sphericity is the population parameter ε, which can be estimated by the epsilon statistic ($\hat{\varepsilon}$). Two methods of estimating ε were described in Chapter 10, the Greenhouse–Geisser (G–G) estimate or the Huynh–Feldt (H–F) estimate (Winer *et al.* 1991, Yandell 1997). These sample $\hat{\varepsilon}$s can be used to adjust the df for within plots/subjects tests downwards to make the tests more conservative, since non-sphericity increases the risk of Type I error. The adjustment is simple, being the original df multiplied by $\hat{\varepsilon}$, although the new df will not be integers (Table 11.4). If ε is greater than 0.75, the correction based on the Huynh–Feldt $\hat{\varepsilon}$ is better, when ε is less than 0.75, the correction based on the Greenhouse–Geisser $\hat{\varepsilon}$ is better (Keselman & Kesleman 1993). These adjusted tests are standard output from most statistical software.

Multivariate tests

An alternative solution to the sphericity assumption is to treat the levels of the within-subjects or within-plots factor (i.e. the repeated measures factor) as multiple response variables in a multivariate analysis of variance (MANOVA in Chapter 16; see also Keselman & Keselman 1993, Looney & Stanley 1989, Kirk 1995, Tabachnick & Fidell 1996). The MANOVA actually uses the difference between

successive repeated measurements (i.e. times) for each subject or plot as response variables and tests the null hypothesis that the difference scores have a population centroid (multivariate mean) equal to zero. The MANOVA approach can be useful for these designs because it doesn't assume sphericity of variances and covariances, although it does have all the usual MANOVA assumptions (Chapter 16; Johnson & Field 1993) and has fewer degrees of freedom. Also, if the *n* is less than the number of differences between successive repeated measurements (i.e. less than the number of levels of the within-plots or -subjects factor minus one), then the MANOVA approach cannot be used. As discussed in Chapter 16, the Pillai trace statistic is recommended for these multivariate tests.

Profile analysis

Another approach is to summarize the responses for each plot/subject as a single value and then use these values in a single factor ANOVA model comparing the levels of A. The between plots/subjects part of the partly nested univariate ANOVA does this by summarizing the responses of each plot/subject as an average across the levels of C. If factor C is quantitative, e.g. time, we can also summarize the responses of each plot/subject as a trend or response curve, such as a linear, quadratic, etc., and analyze the coefficients of these trends in separate one factor ANOVAs (Meredith & Stehman 1991). This provides a test of whether such trends (linear, quadratic, etc.) vary across factor A, i.e. a test of a treatment–contrast interaction (Chapter 9). Such tests are usually default output from statistical software and will be discussed in Section 11.5.2.

Which strategy is the best?

As we pointed out in Chapter 10 for RCB and simple repeated measures designs, neither the epsilon-adjusted univariate nor the multivariate approach is always more powerful, unless sphericity is met, when the traditional partly nested univariate analysis is clearly preferred. Looney & Stanley (1989) recommended using both approaches and rejecting the within-subjects null hypotheses if either the adjusted univariate or multivariate tests are significant. Kirk (1995) recommended a preliminary test for multisample sphericity and using the adjusted univariate tests if the sphericity test is significant; however, his preliminary test is not straightforward and not available in statistical software. We suggest that preliminary tests for sphericity are of limited value and support the Looney & Stanley (1989) approach and the use of profile analyses if factor C is quantitative.

11.4 | Robust partly nested analyses

As for other linear model analyses, the RT (rank transform) procedure has been proposed as a general method for overcoming problems of non-normality and possibly other assumptions of the partly nested analyses of variance (see discussion in Thompson 1991b). We reiterate our comments from Chapters 9 and 10. The rank transformation is nonlinear in nature (Akritas 1991) and therefore cannot effectively deal with interactions; indeed, a significant main effect may be indicated when it is simply due to an undetected interaction (Thompson 1991b). As the A×C interaction is often of considerable interest in the designs discussed in this chapter, the RT procedure seems inappropriate. RT procedures are also inappropriate for nested factors (Thompson 1991b), which are important in the models used to analyze split-plot and groups by trials repeated measures designs. Also, as discussed in Chapter 10 for analyses of RCB designs, a rank transformation can also change the nature of variances and covariances, making the assumption of sphericity less tenable (Akritas 1991). Although Thompson (1991b) has developed a general rank-based multivariate test statistic that is applicable to repeated measures designs, its usefulness is restricted to situations where there are no interactions.

We could also fit the models in this chapter using generalized linear models (GLMs), that allow a range of different error distributions of which normal is just one (Chapter 13). Maximum likelihood techniques are used for fitting the models and estimating the parameters and likelihood ratios are used for hypothesis tests of these parameters. Care must be taken in the choice of full and reduced models for such complex analyses because some models won't make much

biological or statistical sense, e.g. a model that includes B(A) but not A. Note that GLM analyses are still sensitive to the specification of the error distribution so model diagnostics are very important, just as they are for linear models. Chapter 13 includes a more detailed discussion of GLMs.

11.5 | Specific comparisons

11.5.1 Main effects

Planned contrasts for the between-plots/subjects main effect are done in the same way as described in Chapter 8 and simply average across the within-plots/subjects factor levels for each experimental unit. Planned contrasts for the within-plots/subjects main effect assume multisample sphericity if the usual B(A)×C term is to be used as the denominator. The two alternatives are to adjust the df for these contrasts using the G–G or H–F estimates of ε (Section 11.3.2) or use separate error terms, e.g. $C_{contrast} \times B(A)$, for each contrast (Kirk 1995). These error terms are calculated similarly to those for analyses RCB (or simple repeated measures) designs described in Chapter 10, except that the contrasts are calculated across the levels of factor A; Kirk (1995) provides computational details but good statistical software will calculate these separate error terms. They basically represent a separate F-ratio testing for differences in the levels of C within each level of A. Keselman & Keselman (1993) suggested an approximate paired t test with separate error terms based on the two groups being compared, called the KKS test, similar to that described in Chapter 10, although Satterthwaite's adjusted df are used.

Unplanned comparisons for between-plots/subjects factors are done in the same way as described in Chapter 8, and simply average across the within-plots/subjects factor levels for each experimental unit or subject. The usual unplanned multiple comparison procedures may not be reliable for within-plot/subjects factors because the means are probably correlated to some extent, particularly for repeated measures designs. Keselman & Keselman (1993) described some new stepwise multiple comparison procedures for within-subjects/plots factors. The simplest approach might be to contrast the specific levels of C applying a Bonferroni-type adjustment of significance levels for multiple testing if required (Chapter 3). Note that these contrasts between levels of C will use the $B(A) \times C$ term as the denominator and therefore assume multisample sphericity; adjusted df should be used based on G–G or H–F estimates of ε.

11.5.2 Interactions

In partly nested ANOVA models, the main interaction of interest is between A and C and represents an interaction between a between-plots/subjects factor and a within-plots/subjects factor. This interaction can be explored with "interaction" plots of means, where we might have the levels of factor C along the horizontal axis, the response variable along the vertical axis and each point represents the mean of factor A levels across plots/subjects within each A level. Deviations from parallel lines indicate some interaction between A and C.

Tests of simple main effects can also be done as described in Chapter 9, the only difficulty for the designs in this chapter is choosing the appropriate denominator for the F tests (Kirk 1995, Maxwell & Delaney 1990). In Chapter 9, we pointed out that for a two factor crossed (A, B, A×B) linear model, the SS for simple main effect tests for factor A represent partitioning of the SS_A and SS_{AB}, whereas the simple main effects tests for B represent partitioning of the SS_B and SS_{AB}. In contrast to the two factor completely randomized design, however, the test of the A term in a partly nested model with A and C fixed and B (plots/subjects) random uses a different denominator than the tests of the C and A×C interaction terms. So what denominators do we use for the simple main effects tests in a partly nested model?

The simple effects tests for C at each level of A separately, e.g. the effect of O_2 level for each breathing type separately in the Mullens (1993) example, are relatively straightforward because both C (O_2 level) and A×C (breathing type × O_2 level) use the same denominator – C×B(A). Note that if multisample sphericity does not hold, then these tests should be based on adjusted degrees of freedom using the G–G or H–F estimates of ε (Section 11.3.2). Alternatively, separate denominators should be used for each simple effect, the equivalent to calculating a simple repeated measures ANOVA

testing C within each level of A separately (Chapter 10).

For the simple effects tests for A at each level of C separately, e.g. the effect of breathing type for each O_2 level separately, Kirk (1995) and Maxwell & Delaney (1990) recommended using a denominator that represents the average of the B(A) and $B(A) \times C$ terms. This is sometimes called the within-cells error term:

$$\frac{SS_{B(A)} + SS_{B(A) \times C}}{p(q-1) + p(q-1)(r-1)} \tag{11.5}$$

Tests using the error term in expression 11.5 might be biased, especially if the two terms contributing to the pooled term are very different.

11.5.3 Profile (i.e. trend) analysis

A useful approach, which can be used in conjunction with any experimental design where at least one factor is quantitative, is to look for trends across levels of the quantitative factor (Chapter 8). For designs in this chapter, the common approach is to test for trends across the levels of factor C (the within plots/subjects factor) if C is quantitative (e.g. time, O_2 level). The simplest trends to examine are those of a polynomial form, such as linear, quadratic, cubic, etc. (see Chapter 8). Tabachnick & Fidell (1996) provide an excellent description of these methods for repeated measures designs, and therefore for partly nested models in general.

The number of polynomial contrasts that can be calculated is one less than the number of levels of the relevant factor. For example, if there were six levels of factor C, you could test for linear (X), quadratic (X^2), cubic (X^3), quartic (X^4) and quintic (X^5) polynomials, although it is often difficult to attach biological meaning to trends more complex than cubic. It is important to remember that these trend tests depend on the metric (spacing) of levels of the quantitative factor(s), as discussed in Chapter 8, and that most statistical software assumes equal spacing by default. The tests of these polynomials are statistically orthogonal (independent) of each other because each is tested using a separate component of df_C and MS_C (or A×C if trends are tested as part of the interaction), with separate components of the $df_{CB(A)}$ and $MS_{CB(A)}$ for the denominators of each trend F test.

Testing for trends as part of analyses of classical repeated measures designs is often termed profile analysis (Tabachnick & Fidell 1996). As with tests of trends in completely randomized factorial designs discussed in Chapter 9, there are two types of tests of interest in profile analysis:

- Main effect trends, usually across the within-plots/subjects factor C pooling the levels of factor A. For example, is there a linear trend in breathing rate of toads across oxygen concentrations, pooling the two breathing types? Is there a quadratic trend? A cubic trend? Trends could also be examined across factor A as part of the between-plots/subjects part of the analysis.
- Treatment–contrast interactions for examining the A × C interaction term. Here we compare trends of the same form (e.g. linear) across C between different levels of factor A. For example, is the linear trend in breathing rate of toads across oxygen concentrations the same for the two breathing types? Is the quadratic trend the same? These tests are often described as tests of parallelism (Tabachnick & Fidell 1996), since testing whether the linear trends are the same across level of A is clearly a test of whether the trends are parallel.

We do not provide computational details for calculating these trend tests because there is nothing additional to the information we included in Chapter 9 and these trend tests are usually default output from statistical software if the data are coded, and analysis run, as a classical repeated measures design. Note that some software will automatically test each trend MS against a separate error term so that multisample sphericity is not assumed. Alternatively, the B(A) × C term could be used, with adjustments to the df based on the G–G or H–F estimates of $\hat{\varepsilon}$. Growth curve analysis can also be useful for ecophysiological studies and involves comparisons of nonlinear regressions of a more complicated form than simple polynomials (Potvin et al. 1990).

An example of these trend analyses was provided by Sharpe & Keough (1998), who examined temporal trends in chlorophyll-a and in the density of herbivorous snails following the removal of dominant grazers from the intertidal zone of a rocky shore. The removal treatments were the between-subjects/plots factor, and time was the repeated factor. Individual boulders were the plots/subjects, so different boulders received different removal treatments. They recorded chlorophyll-a from randomly selected areas on each boulder, and censused a range of herbivores once a month. They contrasted the linear temporal trend in abundance of each species (as a measure of recolonization rate) between particular combinations of treatments. We also illustrate these trend analyses in the worked examples in Box 11.2 and Box 11.4.

11.6 | Analysis of unbalanced partly nested designs

Unequal sample sizes can arise in partly nested (split-plot or repeated measures) designs in two ways. First, the number of plots or subjects in each level of the between plots factor might vary. Since the between-plots tests average over the within-plots factors, this type of unequal sample size is no different to unequal sample sizes in the usual factorial ANOVAs described in Chapter 9, and our recommendations are the same. Remember that checking assumptions becomes much more important when sample sizes are unequal and that even tests of within-plots/subjects factors can be more sensitive to assumptions (e.g. sphericity) when the between-plots/subjects part of the design is unbalanced (Keselman & Keselman 1993). Second, when we have no replication within each cell (the classical split-plot or repeated measures design), then missing observations equate to missing cells. If you have a reasonable number of plots/subjects, then a simple approach is to delete the plot(s) or subject(s) with the missing observations; this causes problems if sample sizes (number of plots or subjects) are small because the between-subjects/plots part of the analysis may become severely unbalanced. Basically, most statistical software will use this approach by default if the data are set up for a classical repeated measures analysis. If you don't have many plots/subjects but lots of levels of the within-subjects/plots factor(s), then it might be better to omit the level of factor C (or the combination of levels if you have more than one within-subjects/plots factor) with the missing observations. This approach changes the null hypotheses being tested, of course, but if the hypotheses are general ones about trends through time and you have a long time sequence, then omitting one or two times may not have much effect.

An alternative solution is to simply fit the partly nested linear model (Berk 1987) and compare this full model with appropriate reduced models for specific hypotheses, as described in Chapter 10 for RCB designs. Unfortunately, the F tests are more sensitive to the sphericity assumption when observations are missing and most statistical software doesn't provide epsilon estimates, nor adjusted univariate tests, when the analysis is run this way, so be careful. As we recommended in Chapter 10 for RCB and simple repeated measures designs, a practical strategy may be to delete the subject(s)/plot(s) with the missing observation(s), running the analysis as a classical repeated measures design to check sphericity and then only fit a partly nested linear model to the data with all subjects/plots if that assumption is tenable. This is messy but there are not many practical options when dealing with missing observations in these designs.

More complicated solutions are provided by Berk (1987), who suggested ML and REML estimation procedures that weight the observations, by Kirk (1995), who described using the cell means model and testing a subset of hypotheses using contrasts, and by Rovine & Delaney (1990). All these methods will be difficult for practicing biologists, at least until they are standard components of statistical software.

11.7 | Power for partly nested designs

As expected, power calculations become more complicated with these complex designs, with the possibility of separate power calculations for a series of main effects, and interactions. We can divide these tests into those involving only between-plot/subject terms, only within-plot/subject terms, and interactions between the two groups. For between-subjects factors, power calculations are similar to those described for Chapters 8 and 9. They are routine when main effects are of interest, and they can be made easier by recoding the data file as means, averaging across the repeated or within-plots factor levels. For the more complex within-subjects/plots effects, the power calculations can be done, with two important steps. First, specifying an effect size can be very difficult, as for all complex interactions. Second, in computing power for a particular effect, we must identify the denominator used to test that effect, and use that MS to generate the variance estimate needed to calculate power.

One special case in which the power calculation is relatively simple is the family of BACI (Before-After-Control-Impact) designs used in environmental monitoring. The test for an environmental impact is an interaction between Before-After and Control-Impact, tested using, for example, changes Before-After at replicate locations within Control and Impact categories. In the original formulation of this design, with two locations (C and I), two periods (B and A), and multiple sampling times within each period, we could use a partly nested analysis, with periods, times within periods, and samples at C and I at each time. An impact would be revealed as a change in the difference between C and I, from the Before to the After period. Stewart-Oaten et al. (1986) pointed out that this design can be analyzed as a t test, simply by calculating the difference, C-I, and comparing that difference between periods. As a consequence, rather than formulating an effect size based on the interaction, we can specify an effect size as the divergence or convergence of these C-I differences. More complex formulations of this design (e.g. Downes et al. 2002, Keough & Mapstone 1997) can also be simplified in this way, because the interaction of interest is between the main between- and within-plots factors, and each of them has only two levels.

11.8 | More complex designs

So far we have considered partly nested designs involving one between-subjects/plots factor (A), one within-subjects/plots factor (C) and one factor representing subjects/plots (B). These experimental designs can be extended to include more than one between-subjects/plots factor and/or more than one within-subjects/plots factor.

11.8.1 Additional between-plots/subjects factors

There is nothing difficult about additional between-subjects/plots factors, because this part of the analysis is just an ANOVA on the average of the response variable for each plot/subject. For example, a four factor design might have two between-subjects/plots factors (A and C), one within-subjects/plots factor (D), and factor B representing plots nested within A and C. For example, McGoldrick & Mac Nally (1998) studied the impact of eucalypt flowering on the dynamics of bird communities in forests of southeastern Australia. They had eight sites (i.e. plots) arranged in a two factor crossed design with factor A being habitat (two levels: dominated by ironbark eucalypts vs dominated by stringybark eucalypts) and factor B being region (two levels: north of Great Dividing Range and south of Great Dividing Range) with two sites within each combination. Each site was censused monthly for twelve months, so month was the within-plots/subjects factor. The response variables included flowering index, density of nectarivorous birds, species richness of nectarivorous birds etc. The analysis for this example is in Box 11.4, where we analyze the density of nectarivorous birds, transformed to logs after adding one to each observation to account for zero values.

Box 11.4 | Impact of flowering on forest bird communities

As described in Section 11.8.1, McGoldrick & Mac Nally (1998) studied the impact of eucalypt flowering on the dynamics of bird communities in forests of S.E. Australia. They used a partly nested design with two between-plots/subject factors (habitat and region) with two sites within each combination. Each site was censused monthly for twelve months, so time was the within-plots/subjects factor. The response variable we will analyze is natural log transformed (density of nectarivorous birds + 1).

The specific null hypotheses of interest were as follows.

No difference between habitats in the mean $\log_e$ (density of nectarivorous birds + 1), pooling regions and months.

No difference between regions in the mean $\log_e$ (density of nectarivorous birds + 1), pooling habitat and months.

No interaction between habitat and region on the mean $\log_e$ (density of nectarivorous birds + 1), pooling months. Rephrased, the effect of habitat on the mean $\log_e$ (density of nectarivorous birds + 1) was the same for both regions and vice versa, pooling months.

No difference between months in the mean $\log_e$ (density of nectarivorous birds + 1), pooling habitats and regions.

No interactions between habitat and month, region and month, or habitat and region and month on the mean $\log_e$ (density of nectarivorous birds + 1). Re-phrased, the effect of habitat, pooling regions, was the same in all months, the effect of region, pooling habitats, was the same in all months, and the interaction between habitat and region was the same in all months.

With no replicates within each combination of habitat, region, site and month, we could not test hypotheses about the random factor sites within habitat and region or months by sites within habitat and region.

Between plots/subjects

Source	SS	df	MS	F	P
Habitat	88.313	1	88.313	48.975	0.002
Region	0.106	1	0.106	0.059	0.821
Habitat × region	1.334	1	1.334	0.740	0.438
Site(habitat, region)	7.213	4	1.803		

Within plots/subjects

Source	SS	df	MS	F	P	GG
Month	48.676	11	4.425	5.941	<0.001	0.019
Habitat × month	75.152	11	6.559	8.806	<0.001	<0.006
Region × month	11.436	11	1.040	1.396	0.209	0.299
Habitat × region × month	3.858	11	0.351	0.471	0.911	0.665
Site(habitat, region) × month	32.774	44	0.745			

Greenhouse–Geisser epsilon:	0.2104
Huynh–Feldt epsilon:	0.8907

Our analysis agrees with that published by McGoldrick & Mac Nally (1998), although they did not present adjusted tests for within-plots/subjects tests. The adjusted df did not change our conclusions. The month effect varied between habitats and there were neither effects of region nor any interactions between habitat and region or region and month. Note that the epsilon estimates differ greatly and for the three factor interaction, the adjusted test is more liberal than the unadjusted tests.

Linear trends:

Source	SS	df	MS	F	P
Time	16.056	1	16.056	12.231	0.025
Habitat × month	24.532	1	24.532	18.689	0.012
Region × month	3.028	1	3.028	2.307	0.203
Habitat × region × month	0.717	1	0.717	0.546	0.501
Site(habitat, region) × month	5.251	4	1.313		

Quadratic trends:

Source	SS	df	MS	F	P
Time	13.099	1	13.099	8.897	0.041
Habitat × month	17.935	1	17.935	12.182	0.025
Region × month	1.574	1	1.574	1.069	0.360
Habitat × region × month	0.822	1	0.822	0.558	0.496
Site(habitat, region) × month	5.889	4	1.472		

Cubic trends:

Source	SS	df	MS	F	P
Time	1.696	1	1.696	2.943	0.161
Habitat × month	22.695	1	22.695	39.375	0.003
Region × month	1.401	1	1.401	2.432	0.194
Habitat × region × month	0.167	1	0.167	0.290	0.619
Site(habitat, region) × month	2.306	4	0.576		

The trend analyses indicate that any linear, quadratic or cubic trends through time differ between the two habitats. It is clear from Figure 11.5 that there is little change through time in stringybark habitats but marked declines from the austral autumn and winter through to spring and summer for ironbark habitat.

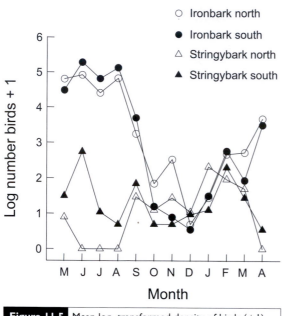

Figure 11.5 Mean log$_e$ transformed density of birds (+1) for two habitats (ironbark and stringybark forests) and two regions (north and south) for twelve months from McGoldrick & Mac Nally (1998).

The appropriate linear model for a split-plot or repeated measures design with two crossed between-plots/subjects factors is:

$$y_{ijklm} = \mu + \alpha_i + \gamma_k + \alpha\gamma_{ik} + \beta_{j(ik)} + \delta_l + \alpha\delta_{il} + \gamma\delta_{kl} + \alpha\gamma\delta_{ikl} + \beta\delta_{j(ik)l} + \varepsilon_{ijklm} \quad (11.6)$$

From McGoldrick & Mac Nally (1998):

(log density of nectarivorous birds plus one)$_{ijklm}$ = μ + (habitat)$_i$ + (region)$_k$ + (interaction between habitat and region)$_{ik}$ + (site within habitat and region)$_{j(ik)}$ + (month)$_l$ + (interaction between habitat and month)$_{il}$ + (interaction between region and month)$_{kl}$ + (interaction between habitat, region and month)$_{ikl}$ + (interaction between site within habitat and region and month)$_{j(ik)l}$ + ε_{ijklm} \quad (11.7)

In models 11.6 and 11.7 we find the following.

μ is the overall (constant) population mean log density of nectarivorous birds plus one.

α_i is the effect of the ith level of the first between plots factor A (effect of habitat), pooling regions and months.

γ_k is the effect of the kth level of the second

between plots factor C (effect of region), pooling habitats and months.

$\alpha\gamma_{ik}$ is the effect of the interaction between the ith level of A and kth level of C (interaction between habitat and region), pooling months.

$\beta_{j(ik)}$ is the effect of the jth plot (factor B, site) within the ikth combination A and C.

δ_l is the effect of the lth level of the within-plots factor D (effect of month).

$\alpha\delta_{il}$ is the effect of the two way interaction between the ith level of A and the lth level of D (interaction between habitat and month).

$\gamma\delta_{kl}$ is the effect of the two way interaction between the kth level of C and the lth level of D (interaction between region and month).

$\alpha\gamma\delta_{ikl}$ is the effect of the three way interaction between the ith level of A, the kth level of C and the lth level of D (interaction between habitat and region and month).

$\beta\delta_{j(ik)l}$ is the effect of the interaction between the jth plot (factor B) within the ikth combination A and C and the lth level of D (interaction between site (within habitat and region) and month).

ε_{ijklm} is the error term. Note that ε_{ijklm} cannot be estimated separately from $\beta\delta_{j(ik)l}$ in this model unless there is replication within each cell, which is unusual. By recording the same sites once at each time, McGoldrick & Mac Nally (1998) did not have replicates within each combination of habitat, region and month and so could not estimate ε_{ijklm}.

The general expected mean squares are in Table 11.5, as well as those for the common case whereby A, C and D are fixed and B (plots or subjects) is random. The between-plots/subjects terms are tested against MS$_{B(AC)}$ and the within-plots/subjects terms are tested against MS$_{DB(AC)}$. Error terms for other combinations can be determined from the expected mean squares and are provided in Table 11.5 following the rules in Box 9.8 – see also Kirk (1995) and Winer et al. (1991).

To further illustrate this design, consider the study of Morris (1996) who examined factors affecting the density of rodents in the Rocky Mountains of the USA. He had nine locations, with two habitats (xeric and mesic) at each location (i.e. a 9 × 2 factorial design), with two replicate grids

Table 11.5 ANOVA table for partly nested design with two crossed between-plots factors and one within-plots factor

Source	df	General expected mean square (EMS)	EMS (A, C, D fixed; B random)	Test
Between plots/subjects				
A	$(p-1)$	$\sigma^2_\varepsilon + D_qD_t\sigma^2_{\beta\delta} + qD_t\sigma^2_{\alpha\gamma\delta} + qrD_t\sigma^2_{\alpha\delta} + tD_q\sigma^2_\beta + qtD_r\sigma^2_{\alpha\gamma} + qrt\sigma^2_\alpha$	$\sigma^2_\varepsilon + t\sigma^2_\beta + qrt\sigma^2_\alpha$	$MS_A/MS_{B(AC)}$
C	$(r-1)$	$\sigma^2_\varepsilon + D_qD_t\sigma^2_{\beta\delta} + qD_pD_t\sigma^2_{\alpha\gamma\delta} + pqD_t\sigma^2_{\gamma\delta} + tD_q\sigma^2_\beta + qtD_p\sigma^2_{\alpha\gamma} + pqt\sigma^2_\gamma$	$\sigma^2_\varepsilon + t\sigma^2_\beta + pqt\sigma^2_\gamma$	$MS_C/MS_{B(AC)}$
A×C	$(p-1)(r-1)$	$\sigma^2_\varepsilon + D_qD_t\sigma^2_{\beta\delta} + qD_t\sigma^2_{\alpha\gamma\delta} + tD_q\sigma^2_\beta + qt\sigma^2_{\alpha\gamma}$	$\sigma^2_\varepsilon + t\sigma^2_\beta + qt\sigma^2_{\alpha\gamma}$	$MS_{AC}/MS_{B(AC)}$
B(AC)	$pr(q-1)$	$\sigma^2_\varepsilon + D_t\sigma^2_{\beta\delta} + t\sigma^2_\beta$	$\sigma^2_\varepsilon + t\sigma^2_\beta$	No test
Within plots/subjects				
D	$(t-1)$	$\sigma^2_\varepsilon + D_q\sigma^2_{\beta\delta} + qD_pD_r\sigma^2_{\alpha\gamma\delta} + pqD_r\sigma^2_{\gamma\delta} + qrD_p\sigma^2_{\alpha\delta} + pqr\sigma^2_\delta$	$\sigma^2_\varepsilon + \sigma^2_{\beta\delta} + pqr\sigma^2_\delta$	$MS_D/MS_{B(AC)D}$
A×D	$(p-1)(t-1)$	$\sigma^2_\varepsilon + D_q\sigma^2_{\beta\delta} + qD_r\sigma^2_{\alpha\gamma\delta} + qr\sigma^2_{\alpha\delta}$	$\sigma^2_\varepsilon + \sigma^2_{\beta\delta} + qr\sigma^2_{\alpha\delta}$	$MS_{AD}/MS_{B(AC)D}$
C×D	$(r-1)(t-1)$	$\sigma^2_\varepsilon + D_q\sigma^2_{\beta\delta} + qD_p\sigma^2_{\alpha\gamma\delta} + pq\sigma^2_{\gamma\delta}$	$\sigma^2_\varepsilon + \sigma^2_{\beta\delta} + pq\sigma^2_{\gamma\delta}$	$MS_{BD}/MS_{B(AC)D}$
A×C×D	$(p-1)(r-1)(t-1)$	$\sigma^2_\varepsilon + D_q\sigma^2_{\beta\delta} + q\sigma^2_{\alpha\gamma\delta}$	$\sigma^2_\varepsilon + \sigma^2_{\beta\delta} + q\sigma^2_{\alpha\gamma\delta}$	$MS_{ABD}/MS_{B(AC)D}$
B(AC)×D	$(t-1)pr(q-1)$	$\sigma^2_\varepsilon + \sigma^2_{\beta\delta}$	$\sigma^2_\varepsilon + \sigma^2_{\beta\delta}$	No test

Note:
Expected mean squares are provided for the general case (see Box 9.8) and for the usual case of A, C and D fixed with B (plots or subjects) random. There is only one observation within each combination of A, B, C and D.

Table 11.6 | ANOVA table for partly nested design from Morris (1996) with two crossed between-plots factors (habitat and location, both fixed), one within-plots factor (time, fixed) and grids as random plots. There is only one observation within each combination of A, B, C and D

Source	Source	df	F-ratio denominator
Between plots/subjects	*Between grids*		
A	Habitat	1	Grid (habitat, location)
C	Location	8	Grid (habitat, location)
A×C	Habitat × location	8	Grid (habitat, location)
B(AC)	Grid (habitat, location)	18	
Within plots/subjects	*Within grids*		
D	Time	2	Grid (habitat, location) × time
A×D	Habitat × time	2	Grid (habitat, location) × time
C×D	Location × time	16	Grid (habitat, location) × time
A×C×D	Habitat × location × time	16	Grid (habitat, location) × time
B(AC)×D	Grid (habitat, location) × time	36	

for each combination of location and habitat. Grids were thus the plots or subjects and location and habitat were the between plots/subjects factors. He sampled each grid at three times (early, mid, late summer), so sampling time was the within plots/subjects factor. The ANOVA for this study is in Table 11.6, illustrating the appropriate error terms for each effect in the model, based on all factors except grids (i.e. plots) being fixed.

A more complicated version of this design was used by Letourneau & Dyer (1998), who examined the effects of top predators (beetle larvae present or absent), soil type (nutrient rich or poor) and light level (high or low) on colony size of an ant species on seedlings planted in three replicate pots (i.e. plots) in a three factor crossed design. Each pot was recorded on five occasions over 18 months, with time as the within-plots/subjects factor. The ANOVA for this study is in Table 11.7 with error terms based on all factors except plots being fixed.

A further modification of the between-plots/subjects part of the design is where A (the between plots factor) and plots are arranged as a RCB design (Table 11.8). The appropriate linear model for this design is:

$$y_{ijkl} = \mu + \alpha_i + \beta_j + \alpha\beta_{ij} + \gamma_k + \alpha\gamma_{ik} + \beta\gamma_{jk} + \alpha\beta\gamma_{ijk} + \varepsilon_{ijkl} \quad (11.8)$$

In model 11.8:

μ is the overall (constant) population mean,
α_i is the effect of factor A,
γ_k is the effect of factor C,
$\alpha\gamma_{ik}$ is the interaction between factors A and C,
β_j is the effect of plots/subjects (i.e. blocks),
$\alpha\beta_{ij}$, $\beta\gamma_{jk}$, and $\alpha\beta\gamma_{ijk}$ are the interactions between A, C, A×C and plots/subjects, and
ε_{ijkl} is the error effect. Note that ε_{ijkl} cannot be estimated separately from $\alpha\beta\gamma_{ijk}$ in this model unless there is replication within each cell, which is unusual.

This is basically a three factor unreplicated ANOVA, identical to a factorial RCB design (Chapter 10). If A and C are fixed and B (plots/subjects or blocks) is random, then A is tested against A×B (plot), as in all RCB designs, C is tested against C×B and A×C is tested against A×B×C (Table 11.8). There are no tests for plot/subject (i.e. block) or its interactions with A and C, unless quasi F-ratios are used.

Aguiar & Sala (1997) used such an analysis in their investigation of seed movement in the Patagonia steppe. They had three sites recorded on three dates and they measured seed availability in four microsites (bare ground, grass, shrub,

Table 11.7 | ANOVA table for partly nested design from Letourneau & Dyer (1998) with three crossed between-plots factors (predators, light level, soil; all fixed), one within-plots factor (time, fixed) and plots as random plots

Source	Source	df	F-ratio denominator
Between plots/subjects	*Between plots*		
A	Predators	1	Plot (predators, soil, light)
C	Soil	1	Plot (predators, soil, light)
D	Light	1	Plot (predators, soil, light)
A × C	Predators × soil	1	Plot (predators, soil, light)
A × D	Predators × light	1	Plot (predators, soil, light)
C × D	Soil × light	1	Plot (predators, soil, light)
A × C × D	Predators × soil × light	1	Plot (predators, soil, light)
B(ACD)	Plot (predators, soil, light)	16	
Within plots/subjects	*Within plots*		
E	Time	4	Plot (predators, soil, light) × time
A × E	Predators × time	4	Plot (predators, soil, light) × time
C × E	Soil × time	4	Plot (predators, soil, light) × time
D × E	Light × time	4	Plot (predators, soil, light) × time
A × C × E	Predators × soil × time	4	Plot (predators, soil, light) × time
A × D × E	Predators × light × time	4	Plot (predators, soil, light) × time
C × D × E	Soil × light × time	4	Plot (predators, soil, light) × time
A × C × D × E	Predators × soil × light × time	4	Plot (predators, soil, light) × time
B(ACD) × E	Plot (predators, soil, light) × time	64	

litter) in each site on each date. Site and date were between plots factors (although there was only one "plot" for each combination of site and date) and microsite was a within plot factor (Table 11.9). Although not stated in their paper, they treated site as a random block effect and assumed there was no site by date interaction since they tested the random site effect against this interaction term. A second example comes from Evans & England (1996) who looked at the effect of artificial honeydew on the numbers of adult weevil parasitoids on alfalfa plants. They had three treatments (early application of artificial honeydew followed by water, early application of water followed by artificial honeydew, two applications of water only), each allocated to one of three "subplots" in each of ten rows (plots or blocks). The numbers of parasitoids were recorded from each subplot on two separate dates about ten days apart. The ANOVA for this design is also in Table 11.9 and Evans & England (1996) fitted an additive model with no treatment × row interactions, allowing tests for row (i.e. plots) and row × date.

11.8.2 Additional within-plots/subjects factors

Extra within-plots/subjects factors can also be included in these designs, although this complicates the analysis because multiple denominators now must be used for the F tests for the within-subjects/plots terms. With one between-plots factor (A), two within-plots factors (C and D) and plots (factor B) nested within A, the appropriate linear model is:

$$y_{ijklm} = \mu + \alpha_i + \beta_{j(i)} + \gamma_k + \alpha\gamma_{ik} + \beta\gamma_{j(i)k} + \delta_l + \alpha\delta_{il} + \beta\delta_{j(i)l} + \gamma\delta_{kl} + \alpha\gamma\delta_{ikl} + \beta\gamma\delta_{j(i)kl} + \varepsilon_{ijklm} \quad (11.9)$$

In model 11.9:

μ is the overall (constant) population mean,

α_i is the effect of ith level of factor A (the between-plots factor),

$\beta_{j(i)}$ is the effect of the jth plot (factor B) within the ith level of factor A,

γ_k is the effect of the kth level of factor C (the first within-plots factor),

Table 11.8 ANOVA table for partly nested design with a RCB between-plots component (A fixed and B = blocks random) and within-plots factor C fixed. The fitted model is non-additive, including A×Blocks interactions. An additive model means that all the $(\alpha\beta)$ terms would disappear from the EMS, allowing tests for B (blocks) and B (blocks)×C

Source	df	General expected mean square (EMS)	EMS (A, C fixed, B random)	Test
Between plots/subjects				
A	$(p-1)$	$\sigma_\varepsilon^2 + D_q D_p D_r \sigma_{\alpha\beta\gamma}^2 + D_r \sigma_{\alpha\gamma}^2 + D_q r \sigma_{\alpha\beta}^2 + qr\sigma_\alpha^2$	$\sigma_\varepsilon^2 + r\sigma_{\alpha\beta}^2 + qr\sigma_\alpha^2$	MS_A / MS_{AB}
B (block)	$(q-1)$	$\sigma_\varepsilon^2 + D_p D_r \sigma_{\alpha\beta\gamma}^2 + D_r p \sigma_{\beta\gamma}^2 + D_p r \sigma_{\alpha\beta}^2 + pr\sigma_\beta^2$	$\sigma_\varepsilon^2 + r\sigma_{\alpha\beta}^2 + pr\sigma_\beta^2$	No test
A×B	$(p-1)(q-1)$	$\sigma_\varepsilon^2 + D_r \sigma_{\alpha\beta\gamma}^2 + r\sigma_{\alpha\beta}^2$	$\sigma_\varepsilon^2 + r\sigma_{\alpha\beta}^2$	No test
Within plots/subjects				
C	$(r-1)$	$\sigma_\varepsilon^2 + D_q D_p \sigma_{\alpha\beta\gamma}^2 + D_p q \sigma_{\alpha\gamma}^2 + D_q p \sigma_{\beta\gamma}^2 + pqr\sigma_\gamma^2$	$\sigma_\varepsilon^2 + p\sigma_{\beta\gamma}^2 + pqr\sigma_\gamma^2$	MS_C / MS_{BC}
A×C	$(p-1)(r-1)$	$\sigma_\varepsilon^2 + D_q \sigma_{\alpha\beta\gamma}^2 + q\sigma_{\alpha\gamma}^2$	$\sigma_\varepsilon^2 + \sigma_{\alpha\beta\gamma}^2 + q\sigma_{\alpha\gamma}^2$	MS_{AC} / MS_{ABC}
B×C	$(q-1)(r-1)$	$\sigma_\varepsilon^2 + D_p \sigma_{\alpha\beta\gamma}^2 + p\sigma_{\beta\gamma}^2$	$\sigma_\varepsilon^2 + p\sigma_{\beta\gamma}^2$	No test
A×B×C	$(p-1)(q-1)(r-1)$	$\sigma_\varepsilon^2 + \sigma_{\alpha\beta\gamma}^2$	$\sigma_\varepsilon^2 + \sigma_{\alpha\beta\gamma}^2$	No test

Table 11.9 ANOVA table for partly nested designs with a RCB between-plots component

Aguiar & Sala (1997)			Evans & England (1996)		
Source	df	F-ratio denominator	Source	df	F-ratio denominator
Between plots/subjects			*Between plots/subjects*		
Date	2	Residual (site × date)	Treatment	2	Residual
Site (= block)	2		Row (= block)	9	Residual
Residual (date × site)	4		Residual	18	
Within plots/subjects			*Within plots/subjects*		
Microsite	3	Date × microsite	Date	1	Treatment × row × date
Date × microsite	6	Date × site × microsite	Treatment × date	2	Treatment × row × date
Site × microsite	6		Row × date	9	Treatment × row × date
Date × site × microsite	12		Treatment × row × date	18	

Note:

The example from Aguiar & Sala (1997) has date (fixed) and site (a random blocking factor) as between-plots (blocks) factors and microsite (fixed) as a within-plots (blocks) factor. There is only one observation for each site and date combination and the four microsites were located within each plot (block). The example from Evans & England (1996) has treatment (fixed) and row (a random blocking factor) as between-plots (blocks) factors and date as a within-plots (blocks) factor. Evans & England (1996) fitted an additive model assuming no treatment × row and no treatment × row × date interactions, allowing tests for row and row × date. There is only one observation for each treatment and row combination and each combination was recorded on two dates.

$\alpha\gamma_{ik}$ is the effect of the two way interaction between the ith level of A and kth level of C (i.e. A×C interaction),

$\beta\gamma_{j(i)k}$ is the interaction between the kth level of C and the jth plot (B) within the ith level of A (B within A×C interaction),

δ_l is the effect of the lth level of factor D (the second within-plots factor),

$\alpha\delta_{il}$ is the effect of the two way interaction between the ith level of A and the lth level of D (A×D interaction),

$\beta\delta_{j(i)l}$ is the interaction between the lth level of D and the jth plot (B) within the ith level of A (B within A×D interaction),

$\gamma\delta_{kl}$ is the effect of the two way interaction between the kth level of C and the lth level of D (C×D interaction),

$\alpha\gamma\delta_{ikl}$ is the effect of the three way interaction between the ith level of A, the kth level of C and the lth level of D (A×C×D interaction),

$\beta\gamma\delta_{j(i)kl}$ is the effect of the interaction between the kth level of C and the lth level of D and jth plot (B) within the ith level of A (B within A×C×D interaction), and

ε_{ijklm} is the error effect. Note that ε_{ijklm} cannot be estimated separately from $\beta\gamma\delta_{j(i)kl}$ in this model unless there is replication within each cell, which is unusual.

The general expected mean squares, and those when factors A, C and D are fixed and plots/subjects random, are provided in Table 11.10. Note that when A, C and D are fixed, C and A×C are tested against C×plots within A, D and A×D against D×plots within A and C×D and A×C×D against C×D×plots within A.

These designs are sometimes termed split-split-plot designs because we can have a main between-plots factor and two within-plots factors, one applied to sub-plots within each plot and one applied to sub-sub-plots within each sub-plot. More commonly, however, these experimental designs include a single within-plots factor with repeated measurements through time or two within-subjects time factors. For example, we mention the following.

- Vasquez (1996) looked at the effect of illumination (two fixed levels: bright and dark) and seed distribution (two fixed levels:

dispersed and clumped) on seed consumption in experimental arenas for three species of rodents. Species was the between-subjects factor and there were approximately 17 individuals/subjects for each species. Each individual was tested under each illumination level and each seed distribution in a crossed arrangement (four combinations), so illumination and seed distribution were separate within subjects factors (Table 11.11).
- Green (1997) studied the effects of land crabs on recruitment of rainforest seedlings on Christmas Island. He used two habitats (understory and gap) in the rainforest as the between-plots factor with seven paired plots in understory habitat and three paired plots in gap habitat. These pairs were the "plots" or "subjects". One plot (i.e. "sub-plot") in each pair allowed access to crabs and one (sub)plot excluded crabs, so exclusion was one within-plots factor. Additionally, each plot and (sub)plot was recorded monthly for 23 months (although only 22 months were analyzed) so time was a second within-plots factor. This example includes a factor whose levels are allocated to (sub)plots within plots (pairs) plus a factor representing the whole plots recorded through time (Table 11.11).

Other designs can be termed doubly repeated measures designs because the within-plots factors both represent repeated measurements through time. Meserve et al. (1996) set up an experiment to examine the effect of predation on the survivorship of degus, a species of rodent. One factor was predation (two fixed levels: predators excluded using fencing and netting and control), with four plots within each level. The number of rodents alive was recorded on each plot at six monthly censuses over four years – year (four fixed levels) and month (six fixed levels) were within-plots factors and were crossed (Table 11.11). In all these examples, there were four different denominators used for testing hypotheses in the ANOVA.

11.8.3 Additional between-plots/subjects and within-plots/subjects factors

These partly nested analyses of variance can be applied to a variety of complex split-plot (repeated

Table 11.10 ANOVA with expected mean squares for partly nested design with one between-plots factor (A), plots/subjects (B) and two crossed within-plots factors (C and D). There is only a single observation within each combination of A, B, C and D

Source	df	EMS general	EMS (A, C, D fixed, B random)	Test
Between plots/subjects				
A	$(p-1)$	$\sigma^2_\varepsilon + D_q D_r D_t \sigma^2_{\beta\gamma\delta} + qD_q D_t \sigma^2_{\alpha\gamma\delta} + rD_q D_t \sigma^2_{\beta\delta} + qrD_t \sigma^2_{\alpha\delta} + tD_q D_r \sigma^2_{\beta\gamma} + qtD_r \sigma^2_{\alpha\gamma} + rtD_q \sigma^2_{\beta} + qrt\sigma^2_{\alpha}$	$\sigma^2_\varepsilon + rt\sigma^2_{\beta} + qrt\sigma^2_{\alpha}$	$MS_A / MS_{B(A)}$
B(A)	$p(q-1)$	$\sigma^2_\varepsilon + D_q D_t \sigma^2_{\beta\gamma\delta} + rD_t \sigma^2_{\beta\delta} + tD_r \sigma^2_{\beta\gamma} + rt\sigma^2_{\beta}$	$\sigma^2_\varepsilon + rt\sigma^2_{\beta}$	No test
Within plots/subjects				
C	$(r-1)$	$\sigma^2_\varepsilon + D_q D_t \sigma^2_{\beta\gamma\delta} + qD_p D_t \sigma^2_{\alpha\gamma\delta} + pqD_t \sigma^2_{\gamma\delta} + tD_q \sigma^2_{\beta\gamma} + qtD_p \sigma^2_{\alpha\gamma} + pqt\sigma^2_{\gamma}$	$\sigma^2_\varepsilon + t\sigma^2_{\beta\gamma} + pqt\sigma^2_{\gamma}$	$MS_C / MS_{B(A)C}$
A×C	$(p-1)(r-1)$	$\sigma^2_\varepsilon + D_q D_t \sigma^2_{\beta\gamma\delta} + qD_p D_t \sigma^2_{\alpha\gamma\delta} + tD_q \sigma^2_{\beta\gamma} + qt\sigma^2_{\alpha\gamma}$	$\sigma^2_\varepsilon + t\sigma^2_{\beta\gamma} + qt\sigma^2_{\alpha\gamma}$	$MS_{AC} / MS_{B(A)C}$
B(A)×C	$p(q-1)(r-1)$	$\sigma^2_\varepsilon + D_t \sigma^2_{\beta\gamma\delta} + t\sigma^2_{\beta\gamma}$	$\sigma^2_\varepsilon + t\sigma^2_{\beta\gamma}$	No test
D	$(t-1)$	$\sigma^2_\varepsilon + D_q D_r \sigma^2_{\beta\gamma\delta} + qD_p D_r \sigma^2_{\alpha\gamma\delta} + pqD_r \sigma^2_{\gamma\delta} + rD_q \sigma^2_{\beta\delta} + qrD_p \sigma^2_{\alpha\delta} + pqr\sigma^2_{\delta}$	$\sigma^2_\varepsilon + r\sigma^2_{\beta\delta} + pqr\sigma^2_{\delta}$	$MS_D / MS_{B(A)D}$
A×D	$(p-1)(t-1)$	$\sigma^2_\varepsilon + D_q D_r \sigma^2_{\beta\gamma\delta} + qD_p D_r \sigma^2_{\alpha\gamma\delta} + rD_q \sigma^2_{\beta\delta} + qr\sigma^2_{\alpha\delta}$	$\sigma^2_\varepsilon + r\sigma^2_{\beta\delta} + qr\sigma^2_{\alpha\delta}$	$MS_{AD} / MS_{B(A)D}$
B(A)×D	$p(q-1)(t-1)$	$\sigma^2_\varepsilon + D_r \sigma^2_{\beta\gamma\delta} + r\sigma^2_{\beta\delta}$	$\sigma^2_\varepsilon + r\sigma^2_{\beta\delta}$	No test
C×D	$(r-1)(t-1)$	$\sigma^2_\varepsilon + D_q \sigma^2_{\beta\gamma\delta} + qD_p \sigma^2_{\alpha\gamma\delta} + pq\sigma^2_{\gamma\delta}$	$\sigma^2_\varepsilon + \sigma^2_{\beta\gamma\delta} + pq\sigma^2_{\gamma\delta}$	$MS_{CD} / MS_{B(A)CD}$
A×C×D	$(p-1)(r-1)(t-1)$	$\sigma^2_\varepsilon + D_q \sigma^2_{\beta\gamma\delta} + q\sigma^2_{\alpha\gamma\delta}$	$\sigma^2_\varepsilon + \sigma^2_{\beta\gamma\delta} + q\sigma^2_{\alpha\gamma\delta}$	$MS_{ACD} / MS_{B(A)CD}$
B(A)×C×D	$p(q-1)(r-1)(t-1)$	$\sigma^2_\varepsilon + \sigma^2_{\beta\gamma\delta}$	$\sigma^2_\varepsilon + \sigma^2_{\beta\gamma\delta}$	No test

Table 11.11 Examples of partly nested designs from the literature with one between-plots factor and two crossed within-plots (subjects) factors. There is only a single observation within each combination of A, B, C and D. See Section 11.8.2 for more details of specific examples

General source	F-ratio denominator	Meserve et al. (1996) Source	df	Vasquez (1996) Source	df	Green et al. (1997) Source	df
Between plots/subjects							
A	B(A)	Predation	1	Species	1	Habitat	2
B(A)		Plots(predation)	6	Subject(species)	6	Pairs(habitat)	48
Within plots/subjects							
C	B(A)×C	Year	3	Illumination	3	Exclusion	1
A×C	B(A)×C	Year×predation	3	Illumination×species	3	Exclusion×habitat	2
B(A)×C		Plots(predation)×year	18	Subject(species)×illumination	18	Pairs(habitat)×exclusion	48
D	B(A)×D	Month	5	Distribution	5	Time	1
A×D	B(A)×D	Month×predation	5	Distribution×species	5	Time×habitat	2
B(A)×D		Plots(predation)×month	30	Subject(species)×distribution	30	Pairs(habitat)×time	48
C×D	B(A)×C×D	Year×month	15	Illumination×distribution	15	Exclusion×time	1
A×C×D	B(A)×C×D	Year×month×predation	15	Illumination×distribution×species	15	Exclusion×time×habitat	2
B(A)×C×D		Plots(predation)×year×month	90	Subject(species)×illumination×distribution	90	Pairs(habitat)×exclusion×time	48

measures) experimental designs that include multiple between-plots/subjects factors and multiple within-subjects/plots factors. We will use the study of Gough & Grace (1998) on the effects of herbivores and productivity levels on plant species densities to illustrate such a complex design. They chose two freshwater marshes on a river near the Louisiana/Mississippi border in eastern USA. In each marsh, they established eight fenced areas (plots), to exclude herbivores like rabbit, muskrat, etc., and eight unfenced areas. So the between plots component of the design had two fixed factors (marsh and fence) in a crossed arrangement with replicate areas (i.e. plots). There were three sub-plots within each fenced or unfenced area and each sub-plot received one of three nutrient enrichment treatments (no addition, nutrient addition, and natural soil addition). So enrichment was the first within-plots factor. Additionally, each sub-plot was also censused seven times over two years, so time was a second within-plots factor. All factors were considered fixed except for area (i.e. plot). The resulting ANOVA model (Table 11.12) had 19 terms and four different denominators for testing hypotheses.

11.8.4 General comments about complex designs

Gumpertz & Brownie (1993) discussed split-plot designs that include repeated measures (usually multiple times) in some detail. They recommended using trend analyses to examine patterns in the repeated factor and its interactions with the other factors in the design (Section 11.5.3). They also recommended against analyzing such designs as univariate split-split-plot designs, i.e. using the partly nested models we have described, because of the assumption of sphericity of variance–covariance matrices across times, and preferred a multivariate approach. We agree that the sphericity assumption may be important but instead recommend epsilon-adjusted univariate tests in addition to the multivariate tests. Winer *et al.* (1991) and Kirk (1995) provide details of these complex designs and approaches to analyses; they also provide general formula for determining EMS for any combination of fixed and random factors. Kirk's (1995) unique terminology adapts well to these designs.

11.9 | Partly nested designs and statistical software

Data files for these partly nested analyses can be set up in two ways. First, we could create a file for a classical "split-plot analysis" with each factor in a separate column (Table 11.13). A partly nested linear model is then fitted and most software requires that all terms are specified in the model and each term specifically tested against the appropriate denominator. Only unadjusted univariate tests are usually provided but this approach provides great flexibility in structuring the model and choosing denominators for F tests. Second, the data can be coded for a "repeated measures analysis", with between-subjects factors coded as usual but the different levels of the within-subjects factors are in individual columns (Table 11.13). If you have replicate observations within each cell, it can be difficult to code the data file for "repeated measures" analysis and you must either just use cell means or switch to the "split-plot" set up. Software using the "repeated measures" approach nearly always assumes B(A) is random and all other factors are fixed but provides additional output, including estimates of ε (for multisample sphericity), adjusted and unadjusted univariate tests, multivariate tests, and polynomial trend analyses; it also explicitly distinguishes "between-subjects" and "within-subjects" components of the ANOVA. Note that the unadjusted univariate tests will be identical to those provided by the first analysis. The important point is that although the two univariate analyses are functionally identical, the alternative analyses (adjusted univariate, MANOVA) and automatic extras (profile analyses) will often only be provided when the data are coded for a classical repeated measures design, not for a split-plot. The profile analyses can usually also be obtained by including contrasts as part of a split-plot analysis.

Table 11.12 | ANOVA table from complex partly design from Gough & Grace (1998) with two crossed and fixed between-plots/subjects factors and two crossed and fixed within-plots/subjects factors – see Section 11.8.3

Source	df	F-ratio denominator
Between plots		
A	1	Plots (marsh, fence)
B	1	Plots (marsh, fence)
A × B	1	Plots (marsh, fence)
C(AB)	28	
Within plots		
D	2	Plots (marsh, fence) × enrichment
A × D	2	Plots (marsh, fence) × enrichment
B × D	2	Plots (marsh, fence) × enrichment
A × B × D	2	Plots (marsh, fence) × enrichment
C(AB) × D	56	
E	6	Plots (marsh, fence) × time
A × E	6	Plots (marsh, fence) × time
B × E	6	Plots (marsh, fence) × time
A × B × E	6	Plots (marsh, fence) × time
C(AB) × E	168	
D × E	12	Plots (marsh, fence) × enrichment × time
A × D × E	12	Plots (marsh, fence) × enrichment × time
B × D × E	12	Plots (marsh, fence) × enrichment × time
A × B × D × E	12	Plots (marsh, fence) × enrichment × time
C(AB) × D × E	336	

Table 11.13 | Data coding for unreplicated "split-plot" analysis and for unreplicated "repeated measures" analysis

Data file for "split-plot" analysis

Factor A	Plots/subjects (B)	Factor C	Y
1	1	1	y_{111}
1	1	2	y_{112}
1	2	1	y_{121}
1	2	2	y_{122}
2	3	1	y_{231}
i	j	k	y_{ijk}

Data file for "repeated measures" analysis

Factor A	Plots/subjects (B)	C_1	C_k
1	1	y_{111}	y_{11k}
1	2	y_{121}	y_{12k}
1	3	y_{231}	y_{23k}
i	j	y_{ij1}	y_{ijk}

11.10 | General issues and hints for analysis

11.10.1 General issues

- Partly nested designs are very commonly used in biology, as ways to use resources more economically – save money, kill fewer organisms, etc. There is a cost to this rationalization, as the statistical models have more assumptions than completely randomized factorial designs.
- Although they are treated differently in many textbooks, unreplicated partly nested, split-plot and repeated measures ("groups × trials") designs are analyzed with an identical linear model. For repeated measures designs, this model is usually described with a larger set of assumptions, which imposes more restrictions on the analysis. We recommend that, because the two designs (split-plot and repeated measures) require identical models, you should examine the larger set of assumptions for all partly nested designs.
- Unreplicated partly nested designs, i.e. those with only a single observation of each level of

C for each plot/subject within each level of A, prevent you from testing one higher-order interaction or require that you assume that interaction to be zero, depending on the exact design. In the usual situation of all factors being fixed except B (i.e. plots or subjects), this does not preclude tests of the fixed factors or their interactions.
- These designs can include additional factors, both between-plots/subject and within-plots/subjects. Once the model is decided, the analysis is straightforward except that care must be taken to determine the correct F-ratios depending on which factors are fixed and which are random.

11.10.2 Hints for individual analyses

- These designs are complex, and generally have mixtures of fixed and random factors. As a first step, before doing the experiment, write out the linear model, the ANOVA table, and include details of the F-ratios.
- The different designs will change the df, and hence the power, of many of your tests of hypotheses. Before doing the experiment, look at all of the relevant degrees of freedom, and decide whether this arrangement of your experimental units and resources will give you the best compromise between power and cost.
- The assumption of normality is less a problem for the between-plots/subjects factors, as those analyses effectively use means of other data, allowing the Central Limit Theorem to be invoked.
- Tests of the between-plots/subjects factors assume homogeneity of between-group variances.
- The assumption of sphericity is important for the tests of within-plots/subjects factors and incorporates the homogeneity of variance assumption for this component of the analysis. Examine the various measures of the validity of this assumption (particularly the Greenhouse–Geiser and Huynh–Feldt estimates of ε), and, if $\hat{\varepsilon}$ values are low, use the conservative corrections to the F tests or the MANOVA approach. There is no agreed-upon test for the assumption of multisample sphericity.

- If the design is unreplicated, consider coding the data file up as repeated measures, allowing you to routinely get the $\hat{\varepsilon}$ values, corrected univariate F-ratios, and the multivariate equivalents. We follow Looney & Stanley (1989), and suggest you look for a significant result in either the univariate or multivariate analyses.

Chapter 12

Analyses of covariance

In Chapter 10, we described a technique for reducing the residual or unexplained variation in an experiment by grouping experimental units into spatial or temporal blocks. Another approach to reducing the residual variation is to measure one or more concomitant continuous variables for each experimental unit along with the response variable. These concomitant variables, or covariates, are usually considered as continuous predictor variables, with the one or more factors being categorical predictors. A linear models analysis of this design is sometimes called an analysis of covariance (ANCOVA), where the effect of the covariate on the response variable is removed from the unexplained variability by regression analysis. The final ANCOVA tests the difference between factor level means, adjusted for the effect of the covariate.

Another use of ANCOVA is to compare the slopes and/or intercepts of two or more regression lines, although this use is less common. We will cover basic methods for ANCOVA in this chapter, but also pay particular attention to complex designs and situations with regression slopes that are heterogeneous between the factor levels (see also Figure 12.1).

12.1 | Single factor analysis of covariance (ANCOVA)

The simplest ANCOVA design is one analogous to a single factor ANOVA where we have a single categorical predictor variable (factor). In addition to a single continuous response variable, we also record the value of a continuous covariate from each experimental or sampling unit. Some examples from the biological literature include the following.

- Tollrian (1995) studied the effect of a chemical cue (kairomone) released by predators (midge larva *Chaoborus*) on morphology of the aquatic cladoceran *Daphnia*. The response variable was body mass of *Daphnia*, the factor was kairomone treatment (two levels: presence, resulting in neckteeth-induced morphs, and absent, resulting in typical morphs) and the covariate was body length. If body length explains some of the variation in body mass, a more powerful test of kairomone treatment will be obtained.

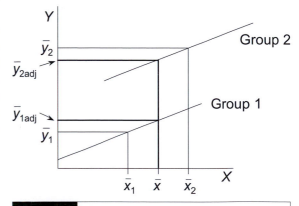

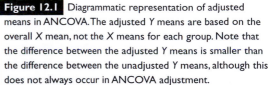

Figure 12.1 Diagrammatic representation of adjusted means in ANCOVA. The adjusted Y means are based on the overall X mean, not the X means for each group. Note that the difference between the adjusted Y means is smaller than the difference between the unadjusted Y means, although this does not always occur in ANCOVA adjustment.

- Mothershead & Marquis (2000) looked at the effects of increased leaf damage (two levels: natural herbivore damage, artificially increased damage mimicking increased herbivory) on floral traits of flowers of the perennial herb *Oenothera macrocarpa* in Missouri, USA. The response variables were corolla diameter and floral tube length, changes in which would result in changes in pollinator preference and efficiency. They used flower order (successive seasonal flowering) as a covariate to help explain some of the variation in floral traits and provide a more powerful test of damage effects.

We illustrate ANCOVA with two examples from the biological literature.

Sex and fruitfly longevity

Partridge & Farquhar (1981) examined the effect of number and type of mating partners on longevity (response variable) of fruitflies. There was a single factor (partner type) with five treatments: one virgin female per day, eight virgin females per day, a control group with one newly inseminated female per day, a control group with eight newly inseminated females per day, a control group with no females. Also, the thorax length of each individual fly was recorded as a covariate. If thorax length explains some of the variation in longevity, then the test of the effect of partner type on longevity adjusted for thorax length will be more powerful. The analysis of these data is presented in Box 12.1.

Shrinking in sea urchins

Constable (1993) studied the role of sutures (joins between plates in the test) in the shrinking of the test of the sea urchin *Heliocidaris erythrogramma*. He compared widths of inter-radial sutures (mm), the response variable, between urchins kept under high and low food regimes and an initial sample, the factor with three groups, with body volume (ml, cube root transformed) as the covariate. The analysis of these data is presented in Box 12.2.

Box 12.1 | Worked example of ANCOVA: sex and fruitfly longevity

Partridge & Farquhar (1981) studied the effect of number of mating partners on longevity of fruitflies. There were five treatments: one virgin female per day, eight virgin females per day, a control group with one newly inseminated female per day, a control group with eight newly inseminated females per day, a control group with no females. Also, the thorax length of each individual fly was recorded as a covariate. If thorax length explains some of the variation in longevity, then the test of the effect of treatments on longevity adjusted for thorax length will be more powerful. The raw data were extracted by reading from Figure 2 in the original paper (see also description and discussion in Hanley & Shapiro 1994). Our general H_0 was that there was no effect of partner treatment on longevity of male fruitflies, adjusting for thorax length.

An ANCOVA model relating longevity to treatment group with thorax length as a covariate (model 12.2) was fitted and the model residuals examined. The plot of residuals against predicted longevity showed evidence of heterogeneous variances (Figure 12.2(a)). The model was refitted with $\log_{10}$ transformation of longevity. The residual plot was much improved with consistent variances for different levels of the covariate (Figure 12.2(b)). There was no indication that the treatments affected thorax length (ANOVA on thorax length: $F_{4,120} = 1.26$, $P = 0.289$).

The specific H_0 was that there was no effect of partner treatment on $\log_{10}$ longevity of male fruitflies, adjusting for thorax length.

The ANCOVA from the fit of the model based on $\log_{10}$ longevity against treatment group with thorax length as a covariate is as follows.

Source	df	MS	F	P
Treatment	4	0.196	27.97	<0.001
Thorax	1	1.017	145.44	<0.001
Residual	119	0.007		

There was a significant difference between adjusted treatment means. The pooled within-groups regression coefficient was 1.194. The $MS_{Residual}$ for an ANOVA on $\log_{10}$ longevity (without thorax as covariate) was 0.015 with 120 df, so including a covariate has reduced the unexplained variation by around 50%.

Adjusted and unadjusted OLS treatment means were as follows.

Treatment	Adjusted mean	Unadjusted mean
1	1.808	1.789
2	1.771	1.789
3	1.794	1.799
4	1.717	1.737
5	1.589	1.564

The standard errors were 0.017 for adjusted means and 0.025 for unadjusted means. Note that the covariance adjustment reduced the mean $\log_{10}$ longevity of treatment one relative to treatments two and three.

The test for homogeneity of within-groups regression slopes was done by fitting a model that related $\log_{10}$ longevity to treatment group, thorax length and the interaction between treatment group and thorax length, the latter term testing the H_0 of equal slopes.

Source	df	MS	F	P
Treatment × thorax length	4	0.011	1.56	0.189
Residual	115	0.007		

The null hypothesis of equal within-group regression slopes was not rejected and it is clear from Figure 12.3 that there was little evidence for non-parallel slopes.

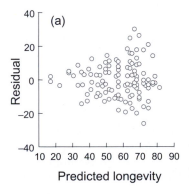

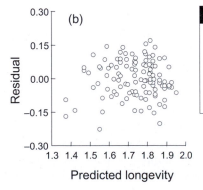

Figure 12.2 Plots of residuals versus predicted values of the response variable from ANCOVA models fitted to data from Partridge & Farquar (1981). (a) Untransformed longevity and (b) $\log_{10}$-transformed longevity.

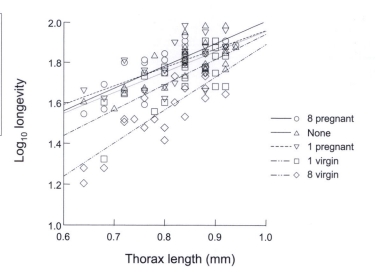

Figure 12.3 Scatterplots with linear regression lines of $\log_{10}$ longevity (days) against thorax length (mm) for male fruitflies under each of the five partner treatment groups. The number and type of female partners for each treatment group are indicated in the legend.

Legend:
——○ 8 pregnant
—— △ None
----▽ 1 pregnant
—·—□ 1 virgin
—··—◇ 8 virgin

Box 12.2 | Worked example of ANCOVA: shrinking in sea urchins

Constable (1993) studied the role of sutures in the shrinking of the test of the sea urchin *Heliocidaris erythrogramma*. He compared widths of inter-radial sutures (mm) between urchins kept under high and low food regimes and an initial sample (one factor with three groups) with body volume (ml, cube root transformed) as the covariate and $n = 24$ urchins in each group. There was a significant interaction between the factor and the covariate ($F_{2,66} = 4.701, P = 0.012$), indicating heterogeneous slopes (Figure 12.4). Constable (1993) used the Wilcox modification of the Johnson–Neyman procedure (Box 12.4) to determine over which values of body volume the groups were significantly different.

> Initial > Low food for cube root volume > 2.95
> High food > Initial for cube root volume > 1.81
> High food > Low food for cube root volume > 2.07

So initial suture width was greater than low food suture width for body volumes greater than 2.95, high food suture width was greater than initial for volumes greater than 1.81 and high food suture width was greater than low food suture width for volumes greater than 2.07.

12.1.1 Linear models for analysis of covariance

Linear effects model

So far, we have focused on linear models where all the predictors are continuous (classical regression analyses in Chapters 5 and 6) or categorical (classical analyses of variance in Chapters 8–11). In Chapter 6, we explained how a linear model could include both categorical (factors) and continuous (covariates) predictors. Now consider a data set where factor A is a fixed categorical predictor variable with p groups ($i = 1$ to p), X is a continuous predictor variable and we have a continuous response variable Y, with both Y and X recorded for each experimental or sampling unit within each group. In the example from Partridge & Farquhar (1981), factor A is partner

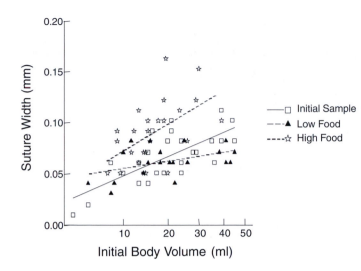

Figure 12.4 Scatterplots with linear regression lines of suture width against cube root transformed body volume for sea urchins under each of the three food level groups. Treatment groups: low food, high food and initial sample.

type ($p = 5$), X is thorax length, the response variable Y is longevity and each experimental unit is a fruitfly. In Constable's (1993) study, factor A is food regime ($p = 3$), X is body volume, Y is suture width with individual urchins as the experimental units.

The ANCOVA model is a linear model with one continuous predictor (covariate) and one categorical predictor (factor) but where we focus on the effects of the factor levels, adjusted for the covariate. The ANCOVA model is best considered as an "ANOVA" model with a covariate included, rather than a "regression" model with a categorical predictor.

The usual form of the ANCOVA model is:

$$y_{ij} = \mu + \alpha_i + \beta(x_{ij} - \bar{x}) + \varepsilon_{ij} \qquad (12.1)$$

The details of the linear ANCOVA model, including estimation of its parameters and means, are provided in Box 12.3. Note that if there is no relationship between the response variable and the covariate, i.e. $\beta = 0$, then model 12.1 simply becomes the single factor ANOVA model described in Chapter 8. If there are no effects of the treatments, i.e. all $\alpha_i = 0$, then model 12.1 becomes a simple linear regression model described in Chapter 5. These reduced models will be discussed further in Section 12.1.4.

Box 12.3 | The linear ANCOVA model and its parameters

Consider a data set with n observations ($j = 1$ to n) where factor A is a categorical predictor variable with p groups ($i = 1$ to p), X is a continuous predictor variable and we have a continuous response variable Y, with both Y and X recorded for each experimental or sampling unit within each group. Based on the Constable (1993) example, we could code factor A as two dummy variables (Chapter 6), so that X_1 equals 1 for high food and 0 for otherwise and X_2 equals 1 for low food and 0 for otherwise, and call the covariate X_3. The (multiple) linear (regression) model we could fit to these data, explicitly ignoring the group structure is:

$$y_j = \beta_0 + \beta_1 x_{j1} + \beta_2 x_{j2} + \beta_3 x_{j3} + \varepsilon_j$$

From Constable (1993):

$$(\text{suture width})_j = \beta_0 + \beta_1(\text{high food vs initial})_j + \beta_2(\text{low food vs initial})_j + \beta_3(\text{body volume})_j + \varepsilon_j$$

In these two models we have the following.

y_j is the jth replicate observation of the response variable, e.g. the suture width for the jth urchin.

β_0 is the intercept of the linear model, the mean of Y when X_1, X_2, and $X_3 = 0$, e.g. the suture width for an urchin with zero body volume in the initial sample.

β_1 is the partial regression slope for X_1, e.g. the regression slope relating suture width to the difference between high food and initial sample groups, holding the difference between low food and initial sample groups, and body volume, constant.

β_2 is the partial regression slope for X_2, e.g. the regression slope relating suture width to the difference between low food and initial sample groups, holding the difference between high food and initial sample groups, and body volume, constant.

β_3 is the partial regression slope for X_3, e.g. the regression slope relating suture width to body volume, holding the difference between high food and initial sample groups, and low food and initial sample groups, constant.

ε_j is random or unexplained error associated with the jth replicate observation.

The interpretations here are those of a standard multiple regression with one continuous and one categorical predictor (Chapter 6). No specific adjustment is made to the values of the response variable or the means of the response variable for each group, although the interpretation of each regression coefficient is based on holding the other predictors constant.

The usual form of the ANCOVA model is:

$$y_{ij} = \mu + \alpha_i + \beta(x_{ij} - \bar{x}) + \varepsilon_{ij}$$

In this model we have the following.

y_{ij} is the value of the response variable for jth observation in the ith level of factor A.

μ is the overall (constant) mean value of the response variable.

α_i is effect of ith level factor A, defined as the difference between each A mean and the overall mean $(\mu_i - \mu)$.

β is a combined regression coefficient representing the pooling of the regression slopes of Y on X within each group. A basic assumption is that the regression slopes within each group are the same, otherwise pooling them to produce β can result in interpretation of factor effects that are misleading.

x_{ij} is the covariate value for the jth replicate observation from the ith level of factor A.

$\bar{x}$ is the mean value of the covariate.

ε_{ij} is random or unexplained error associated with the jth replicate observation from the ith level of factor A, representing the component of the response variable not explained by the effects of the factor or the relationship with the covariate. These error terms are assumed to be normally distributed at each level of factor A, with a mean of zero $[E(\varepsilon_{ij}) = 0]$ and a variance of σ_ε^2.

This model is overparameterized so, when factor A is fixed, then the usual constraint $\sum_{i=1}^p \alpha_i = 0$ applies, so that parameters in the effects model can be estimated.

Note that we have centered the X-values, by subtracting the mean. If we don't, the model is:

$$y_{ij} = \mu + \alpha_i + \beta x_{ij} + \varepsilon_{ij}$$

and μ is now a population intercept (for $X = 0$) rather than an overall population mean of Y. It doesn't matter for the partitioning of variance and testing hypotheses which version we use, although the first is most common in the literature.

The focus in the usual ANOVA models is on estimating group or cell means. In ANCOVA models, we wish to estimate group means adjusted for the effects of the covariate, i.e. adjusted means. These are the means of the adjusted values of the response variable defined in expression 12.7. For group i, the adjusted mean represents the mean value of the response variable if the mean value of the covariate for that group equals the overall mean value for the covariate:

$$\mu_{i(adjusted)} = \mu_i - \beta(\bar{x}_i - \bar{x})$$

This is estimated by:

$$\mu_{i(adj)} = \bar{y}_i - b(\bar{x}_i - \bar{x})$$

The standard error of the adjusted mean is:

$$s_{\bar{y}_{i(adjusted)}} = \sqrt{MS_{Residual}\left(\frac{1}{n_i} + \frac{(\bar{x}_i - \bar{x})^2}{SS_{Residual(X)}}\right)}$$

where $MS_{Residual}$ is from the ANCOVA partitioning of variation (Table 12.1) and $SS_{Residual(X)}$ is from an ANOVA on the covariate.

We may also wish to estimate β, the pooled within-groups regression coefficient relating Y to X. Unfortunately in terms of computation, this is neither the estimate of the regression slope of Y on X pooling all observations, as pointed out above, nor is it a simple average of the within-group regression slope estimates. Fortunately, the general linear model routine in most statistical software will provide this estimate (b) and its standard error (s_b), although the former can be calculated from:

$$b = \frac{\sum_{i=1}^{p}\sum_{j=1}^{n}(x_{ij} - \bar{x}_i)(y_{ij} - \bar{y}_i)}{SS_{Residual(X)}}$$

where the numerator is the sum, across groups, of the covariance between Y and X within each group.

From Partridge & Farquhar (1981):

$(longevity)_{ij}$ = overall mean + $(partner\ treatment)_i + \beta[(thorax\ length)_{ij} - (mean\ thorax\ length)] + \varepsilon_{ij}$ \hfill (12.2)

From Constable (1993):

$(suture\ width)_{ij}$ = overall mean + $(food\ treatment)_i + \beta[(body\ volume)_{ij} - (mean\ body\ volume)] + \varepsilon_{ij}$ \hfill (12.3)

In models 12.1 and 12.3 we have the following:

y_{ij} is the value of suture width for the jth urchin in the ith food treatment.

μ is the overall (constant) mean value of suture width.

α_i is effect of ith food treatment on suture width. This effect is defined as the difference between each food treatment mean and the overall mean ($\mu_i - \mu$).

Table 12.1 ANOVA table for single factor ANCOVA based on factor A being fixed and response variable adjusted for the effects of the covariate

Source of variation	df	Mean square	Expected mean square	F-ratio
Factor A (adjusted)	$(p-1)$	$\dfrac{SS_{A(adjusted)}}{(p-1)}$	$\sigma_\varepsilon^2 + \dfrac{n\sum\limits_{i=1}^{n}\alpha_i^2}{p-1}$	$\dfrac{MS_{A(adjusted)}}{MS_{Residual(adjusted)}}$
Residual (adjusted)	$p(n-1)-1$	$\dfrac{SS_{Residual(adjusted)}}{p(n-1)-1}$	σ_ε^2	
Total (adjusted)	$pn-2$			

β is a combined regression coefficient representing the pooling of the regression slopes relating suture width to body volume within each food treatment group. A basic assumption is that the regression slopes within each group are the same, otherwise pooling them to produce β can result in interpretations of factor effects that are misleading.

x_{ij} is the value of body volume for the jth urchin from the ith food level group.

ε_{ij} is random or unexplained error associated with the jth urchin in the ith food level group not explained by the food treatment or the body volume.

Although our model includes both effects of a categorical predictor (α_i) on the response variable and the slope (β) of a regression line relating a continuous predictor to the response variable, the interpretation of the parameters is familiar. We measure the effects of treatments (factor A) adjusting for the covariate, i.e. holding it constant. The ANCOVA can therefore be considered as an ANOVA on data adjusted by the regression slope of Y on the covariate X. Each adjusted observation (the value of an observation "corrected" for the effects of the covariate) can be expressed as:

$$y_{ij(adj)} = y_{ij} - \beta(x_{ij} - \bar{x}) = \mu + \alpha_i + \varepsilon_{ij} \quad (12.4)$$

These adjusted observations are also the residuals from the fit of a regression model of Y on X (Winer et al. 1991). In model 12.4, α_i is effect of ith level factor A, adjusted for the effects of the covariate $(\mu_{i(adj)} - \mu_{(adj)})$. Substituting the OLS estimate of the pooled within-groups regression slope, we obtain:

$$y_{ij(adj)} = y_{ij} - b(x_{ij} - \bar{x}) \quad (12.5)$$

Each adjusted value is the value of Y for an observation in any group adjusted (centered) to the mean value of the covariate. For example, the suture width of an urchin is adjusted for the effects of the covariate X by subtracting a term that represents a shift, using the regression of suture width on body volume, of the body volume for that urchin to the mean body volume of all urchins in the experiment:

$$(\text{suture width})_{ij(adj)} = (\text{suture width})_{ij} - b[(\text{body volume})_{ij} - (\text{mean body volume})] \quad (12.6)$$

The focus in the usual ANOVA models is on estimating group or cell means. In ANCOVA models, we wish to estimate group means adjusted for the effects of the covariate, i.e. adjusted group means. These are the means of the adjusted values of the response variable defined in Equation 12.4 and, for group i, represent the mean value of the response variable if the mean value of the covariate for that group equals the overall mean value for the covariate:

$$\mu_{i(adjusted)} = \mu_i - \beta(\bar{x}_i - \bar{x}) \quad (12.7)$$

This is estimated by:

$$\bar{y}_{i(adj)} = \bar{y}_i - b(\bar{x}_i - \bar{x}) \quad (12.8)$$

From Constable (1993):

$$(\text{mean suture width})_{i(adj)} = (\text{mean suture width})_i - b[(\text{mean body volume})_i - (\text{overall mean body volume})] \quad (12.9)$$

Details on estimating adjusted means and their standard errors are provided in Box 12.3.

Table 12.2 | Analyses of variance from Partridge & Farquhar (1981) for $\log_{10}$ longevity of fruitflies for different partner treatments, showing ANOVA on Y ($\log_{10}$ longevity), regression of Y ($\log_{10}$ longevity) on covariate X (thorax length) and ANCOVA on Y ($\log_{10}$ longevity) adjusting for covariate X (thorax length). The SS_{Total} and df_{Total} for ANCOVA sum $SS_{Treatment}$ and $SS_{Residual}$ for data adjusted for effects of covariate

Source	ANOVA Y		Regression Y on X		ANCOVA Y	
	SS	df	SS	df	SS	df
Treatment	0.977	4			0.783	4
Regression on thorax length			1.212	1	1.017	1
Residual	1.850	120	1.615	123	0.833	119
Total	2.827	124	2.827	124	1.615	123

Predicted values and residuals

In practice, the ANCOVA model fitted is that in Equation 12.4 where a single factor ANOVA model is fitted to observations adjusted for the effects of the covariate. The predicted values from this model are based on the regression adjustment and the treatment group:

$$\hat{y}_{ij} = \bar{y}_i - b(\bar{x}_i - \bar{x}_{ij}) \tag{12.10}$$

These predicted values are different for each observation within each group, in contrast to the ANOVA model where the predicted values within each group were the same, i.e. the group mean. The residuals from the fitted ANCOVA model are the differences between each observed Y-value and the predicted Y-value:

$$e_{ij} = y_{ij} - \hat{y}_{ij} = y_{ij} - \bar{y}_i + b(\bar{x}_i - x_{ij}) \tag{12.11}$$

These residuals in Equation 12.11 incorporate the effects of both the continuous covariate and the categorical factor. As for all linear models, residuals provide the basis of the OLS estimate of σ_ε^2 and they are valuable diagnostic tools for checking assumptions and fit of our model.

12.1.2 Analysis of (co)variance

The $SS_{Total(adj)}$ from the ANCOVA is simply the SS_{Total} from an ANOVA on Y less the $SS_{Regression}$ from a linear regression of Y on X, the latter representing the adjustment to the Y-values based on the relationship between Y and X. This $SS_{Total(adj)}$ can be partitioned into that due to the difference between adjusted A group means ($SS_{A(adj)}$) and that not explained by factor A ($SS_{Residual(adj)}$). The $df_{A(adj)}$ is the number of groups minus one and the $df_{Residual(adj)}$ is the total

number of observations minus the number of groups minus one for the regression of Y on the covariate. These sum to the $df_{Total(adj)}$, the total number of observations minus two (one for the regression of Y on the covariate). The mean squares are the SS divided by the df as usual and the expected values of these mean squares are identical to those from a single factor ANOVA (Chapter 8), except that the analysis is based on Y-values adjusted for the covariate.

The relationship between the analyses of variance from fitting a single factor ANOVA model to unadjusted Y-values, a simple regression model fitted to unadjusted Y-values against the covariate, and the ANCOVA model fitted to adjusted Y-values is illustrated for the data from Partridge & Farquhar (1981) in Table 12.2. The $SS_{Total(adj)}$ represents the total variation in unadjusted Y (SS_{Total} from the ANOVA on Y) less that explained by the regression of unadjusted Y on X across the whole data set ($SS_{Regression}$ from regression analysis on complete data set). The unexplained variation in unadjusted Y ($SS_{Residual}$ from ANOVA on Y) is split into the variation due to the pooled within-groups regression of Y on X (SS for the covariate from ANCOVA) and the variation in adjusted Y not explained by the treatment groups ($SS_{Residual(adj)}$ from ANCOVA). Note that the $SS_{Regression}$ from the whole data set is not the same as the SS for the covariate from the ANCOVA because the latter is the variation explained by the pooled within-groups regression.

12.1.3 Null hypotheses

The H_0 for a single factor ANCOVA with a single covariate is based on adjusted means and adjusted treatment effects, i.e. means and effects of A adjusted for the covariate:

$$H_0: \mu_{1(adj)} = \mu_{2(adj)} = \ldots = \mu_{i(adj)} = \ldots = \mu_{(adj)}$$
$$H_0: \alpha_{1(adj)} = \alpha_{2(adj)} = \ldots = \alpha_{i(adj)} = \ldots = 0$$

The adjusted means are simply group (treatment) means of the adjusted observations. They are also the mean values of Y in each group when the covariate is adjusted to equal $\bar{x}$, using the estimate of pooled within-groups regression slope of Y on X (β). Because of the assumption that the slopes of the individual within-group regression lines are the same (see Section 12.3), the differences between adjusted means are the same as the differences between adjusted Y-values for any value of X. When $X = 0$, we are dealing with Y intercepts for regression models with the common pooled within-groups regression slope fitted to the population of observations in each group. Any test of equality of adjusted population group means is also a test of equality of population group intercepts.

The expected values of the mean squares for the ANCOVA in Table 12.1 indicate that the test of the H_0 of no difference between adjusted group means uses an F-ratio of $MS_{A(adjusted)}$ to $MS_{Residual(adjusted)}$. This F-ratio is compared to an F distribution with $(p-1)$ and $p(n-1) - 1$ df in the usual manner.

12.1.4 Comparing ANCOVA models

We can also test the H_0 of no effects of factor A using full and reduced models. The full model 12.1 is:

$$y_{ij} = \mu + \alpha_i + \beta(x_{ij} - \bar{x}) + \varepsilon_{ij} \qquad (12.11)$$

The reduced model is a simple linear regression model based on no group effects (H_0: all α_is equal zero):

$$y_{ij} = \mu + \beta(x_{ij} - \bar{x})\varepsilon_{ij} \qquad (12.12)$$

Here, β is the regression slope of Y on X for all groups combined. The SS_{Total} from the ANCOVA (i.e. $SS_{Total(adjusted)}$) is simply the $SS_{Residual}$ from the full model and $SS_{Residual(adjusted)}$ is simply the $SS_{Residual}$ from the reduced model, analogous to the model fitting procedure described in previous chapters.

We could also compare the full model 12.1

with a reduced ANOVA model ignoring the covariate:

$$y_{ij} = \mu + \alpha_i + \varepsilon_{ij} \qquad (12.13)$$

This tests the null hypothesis that pooled within-groups regression slope between Y and X equals zero. If this H_0 is true, then we would expect the covariate not to contribute to explaining the variation in Y and $SS_{Residual}$ from the ANOVA model would be the same as that from the ANCOVA model. Note that model 12.13 is fitted to unadjusted observations so is not the same as model 12.4.

12.2 | Assumptions of ANCOVA

The assumptions for ANCOVA include those for regression models (Chapter 5) and ANOVA models (Chapter 8). The error terms from our fitted ANCOVA model should be normally distributed, they should have similar variances between groups and they should be independent. Note that these error terms are the errors from the linear regression of Y on X (model 12.1) and from the ANOVA model fitted to the adjusted observations (model 12.4). We use the residuals in 12.11 to check these assumptions. Because our ANCOVA model has a regression component, these residuals will be different for observations within each group as well as between groups. Plots of residuals against adjusted group means are the best check of the assumption of homogeneous variances. Transformations of Y will often help if the heterogeneous variances are due to skewed distributions of Y within each group and generalized linear models (Chapter 13) are also applicable.

Because the ANCOVA is a linear model with both categorical and continuous predictors, some other assumptions are discussed below. A fundamental assumption underlying the application of the ANCOVA model and calculation of adjusted group means, that the within-group regression slopes relating Y to X are equal, will be examined in Section 12.3.

12.2.1 Linearity

The relationship between Y and X in each group should be linear. As always, scatterplots are a good way of checking this assumption and transformations should be used where appropriate. Specific forms of nonlinearity between Y and the covariate may be dealt with by including a polynomial term as an extra covariate (Maxwell *et al.* 1993; see also Section 12.7.1). These analyses will not be straightforward because there will probably be collinearity between the covariate and its polynomial term (see Chapter 6). Also, the test of homogeneity of within-groups regression slopes is more complex because there are at least two slopes for each group, one for X and one for each polynomial term.

12.2.2 Covariate values similar across groups

ANCOVA also assumes that the covariate has the same distribution, especially the range of covariate values, for all groups. This assumption is basically one of no collinearity between the continuous and categorical predictors in the model. We are assuming that the covariate is independent of the treatment groups, i.e. the covariate values do not depend on the groups. This assumption means in practice that you should avoid situations in which there is a range of covariate values that is present in one group, but absent from others. The problem is that the adjustment procedure would involve extrapolation of the regression between Y and X beyond the range of X values in some groups. Note that a correlation between the covariate and the factor is not the same as an interaction between the covariate and the factor on the response variable. The latter is about homogeneity of within-group regression slopes and will be considered in Section 12.3.

There is no hard and fast rule about what constitutes too little overlap of covariate values between groups, but if the covariate means are not significantly different between groups (from a single factor ANOVA on the covariate), then the ANCOVA is probably reliable. If you have problems with this assumption, the only solution is to omit observations within groups that have unusually high or low covariate values.

The other important implication of this assumption is that ANCOVA models should not be used as a correction for different values of the covariate in each group of an experiment. For example, if the initial body sizes of animals are different between treatments at the start of a growth experiment, then using initial size as a covariate to "adjust" for this difference is inappropriate.

12.2.3 Fixed covariate (X)

The covariate X is assumed to be a fixed variable with no error associated with it. This is the standard fixed X assumption of linear regression (Chapter 5). This assumption is almost never valid for ANCOVA in biological settings because the covariate is usually a random variable, just like the response variable. As we pointed out in Chapter 5, X being a random variable in regression analysis usually results in underestimation of the true regression slope. If the assumptions about homogeneity of variance, range of covariate values and parallel slopes hold, there is no reason to suspect that the underestimation of the true pooled within-groups regression coefficient between Y and X will vary between treatments. Therefore, tests of significance should still be reliable. We know of no extension of the Model II regression approach (Chapter 5) to ANCOVA.

12.3 | Homogeneous slopes

The comparison of adjusted means relies on the slopes of the regressions of Y on X being the same between groups, i.e. homogeneity (equality) of slopes. The adjustment of the Y-values to produce adjusted group means and effects is based on a pooled within-groups regression coefficient. This pooled slope must be a reasonable representation of the individual slopes, which will only be true if the individual slopes are similar, i.e. the individual regression lines are parallel.

12.3.1 Testing for homogeneous within-group regression slopes

The H_0 of equal within group regression slopes ($\beta_1 = \beta_2 = \beta_i = \beta$) is tested by examining whether the interaction between the categorical predictor (factor A) and the continuous predictor (covariate) equals zero, i.e. no interaction. We have already examined interactions between continuous predictors (Chapter 6) and between categorical predictors (Chapters 9 to 11). An interaction between a categorical and a continuous predictor is interpreted as a change in the slope of the regression line of Y on X for different levels of the factor (i.e. different groups). No interaction indicates that the regression coefficients (slopes) are the same in the different groups. This assumption is tested by comparing the fit of a full model with a factor by covariate interaction term to a reduced model with no interaction term. The formal model terminology for interactions between covariate and factors is tedious so we will illustrate the models for the data from Constable (1993). The full model is:

$$\begin{aligned}(\text{suture width})_{ij} &= \text{overall mean} + \\ (\text{food level})_i &+ (\text{body volume})_{ij} + \\ (\text{food level} &\times \text{body volume})_{ij} + \varepsilon_{ij}\end{aligned} \quad (12.14)$$

The reduced model, assuming homogeneous regression slopes between groups, is:

$$\begin{aligned}(\text{suture width})_{ij} &= \text{overall mean} + \\ (\text{food level})_i &+ (\text{body volume})_{ij} + \varepsilon_{ij}\end{aligned} \quad (12.15)$$

In practical terms, heterogeneous slopes cause problems for interpreting our data. If the regression lines in the different groups are not parallel, and you are trying to decide if their adjusted means or intercepts differ, your answer depends on where along the range of X-values you do the comparison. For some X-values, the adjusted means or intercepts will be closer together than for others.

Maxwell et al. (1993) suggested that homogeneity of slopes should not be thought of as merely an assumption. While main effects are difficult to interpret in the presence of interactions, interactions between factors and covariates usually represent effects of considerable biological interest. Differences between the slopes of the regression lines indicate that the treatments affect the relationship between Y and the covariate and explaining this might be as important as interpreting differences between adjusted means.

There is one important problem that often occurs, especially with data like morphometrics. If your factor has many levels, or you have large numbers of observations in each group, or the linear regression model of Y on X fits the data in

each group very well (i.e. r^2 is very high), you may have a very sensitive test of the H_0 of no interaction. You may find yourself rejecting H_0, even though a scatterplot suggests the regression lines are almost parallel. This is always a difficulty when using formal significance tests for checking assumptions before a linear model analysis. We suggest plotting the lines to see how different they look and to examine the individual regression slopes. If they seem parallel, consider doing the ANCOVA anyway or else simply use the Wilcox procedure described below for heterogeneous slopes.

12.3.2 Dealing with heterogeneous within-group regression slopes

When slopes are clearly heterogeneous, there are a number of possible approaches, which depend on the questions of interest. First, if the slopes themselves are of primary interest, you can contrast slopes across treatment combinations. This is like using treatment–contrast interactions to examine the Y by covariate interaction (Chapter 9). Second, if the treatment (group) effects are the main interest, Huitema (1980) recommended a test called the Wilcox procedure (Wilcox 1987b), which is a modification of the original Johnson–Neyman technique (Box 12.4; see also Maxwell et al. 1993). This test compares groups in a pairwise fashion, and identifies ranges of the covariate for which the group means are significantly different, and ranges for which there are no differences. It is analogous to a test for simple main effects in a factorial ANOVA (Maxwell et al. 1993; Chapter 9), asking for what values of the covariate are the treatments significantly different. It is essentially an unplanned comparison technique, which, with the Wilcox modification, adjusts probability levels to take account of the number of tests. We recommend comparing only a few pairs of treatments, treating them as essentially planned contrasts where possible. Constable (1993) described the application of the Wilcox procedure to compare treatments in sea urchins (see Box 12.2).

A related approach is to choose certain values of covariate and compare groups at those specific values, e.g. using the mean of X or the value of X for which the distance between regression lines has the most precision (Maxwell et al. 1993, Rogosa 1980).

Box 12.4 | **Computations for the Wilcox modification of the Johnson–Neyman procedure for testing over which ranges of the covariate are the group means different**

Significantly different slopes in an analysis of covariance indicates that the relationship between the response variable and the covariate differs between treatments. The differences between the regressions may be examined by plotting the 95% confidence bands around each line, and seeing whether these bands overlap. However, the interpretation of these differences is difficult, because the relative effects of the treatments become obscure when the distributions of values about each line begin to overlap. Generally, it is interesting to know the range of the covariate over which the treatments differ. This is analogous to tests of simple main effects (i.e. means) in a multi-factorial analysis of variance when there is a significant interaction, e.g. identifiying the levels of factor B for which there is an effect of treatment A (see Huitema 1980 for a discussion).

One procedure for making such a comparison determines the lower and upper limits of the covariate (X_{lower} and X_{upper}) between which we are 95% certain that two treatments under consideration are *not* significantly different, i.e. region over which the lines cross. Johnson & Neyman (1936; J–N) originally designed a procedure for comparing two treatments at single values of the covariate. Huitema (1980) and Wilcox (1987b) have suggested ways of controlling experiment-wise Type I error rates for simultaneous comparisons of two treatments at more than one region of the covariate (i.e. defining regions of significant differences), as well as for controlling error rates for simultaneous comparisons of more than two treatments. Huitema's (1980) method simply exchanges the F-ratio in the original J–N formulae with a modified Bonferroni F-ratio, which acccounts for the total number of comparisons to be made between treatments (see Huitema 1980, pp. 292–293). Wilcox (1987b) developed formulae similar to the J–N technique, but based on the Tukey–Kramer simultaneous multiple comparisons procedure and Studentized range distribution, rather than on the F distribution. In these formulae, he accounts for unequal variances, allows simultaneous determination of the lower and upper limits of the regions of non-significance between all pairs of treatments and the subsequent generalizations, as well as controlling the potential effects of differences between the range of the covariate in the treatments. Wilcox (1987b) also developed a statistic, 'h' (table included in his paper) to help control the error rates due to repeated comparisons of both intercepts and slopes of all treatment regressions. For comparisons of treatments with very large sample sizes or large differences in sample sizes, h should be substituted by $\sqrt{(2SMM)}$, where SMM, the Studentized Maximum Modulus, is read from the table in Rohlf & Sokal (1969).

The Wilcox (J–N) procedure is computationally tedious but there is a computer program (WILCOX.EXE), written by Andrew Constable from the Antarctic Division (Australia), to do the analysis and it is available from our website. It requires some of the standard ANCOVA output from statistical software.

The procedure adopted here comprises the comparisons for unequal variances of Wilcox (1987b, p. 91), which we have called the "Wilcox comparisons". To compare two groups, j and k:

$$X_{upper} = -B - \sqrt{(B^2 - 4AC)}/2A$$
$$X_{lower} = -B + \sqrt{(B^2 - 4AC)}/2A$$

where

$$A = (b_{1j} - b_{1k})^2 - \left(\frac{h^2}{2}\right)\left(\frac{MS_{Residual(j)}}{SS_{\bar{x}_j}} + \frac{MS_{Residual(k)}}{SS_{\bar{x}_k}}\right)$$

$$B = 2(b_{1j} - b_{1k})(b_{0j} - b_{0k}) + h^2\left(MS_{Residual(j)}\frac{\bar{x}_j}{SS_{\bar{x}_j}} - MS_{Residual(k)}\frac{\bar{x}_j}{SS_{\bar{x}_k}}\right)$$

$$C = (b_{0j} - b_{0k})^2 - E - \left(\frac{h^2}{2}\right)\left(MS_{Residual(j)}\frac{\bar{x}_j^2}{SS_{\bar{x}_j}} + MS_{Residual(k)}\frac{\bar{x}_k^2}{SS_{\bar{x}_k}}\right)$$

and

$$E = \left(\frac{h^2}{2}\right)\left(\frac{MS_{Residual(j)}}{n_j} + \frac{MS_{Residual(k)}}{n_k}\right)$$

with

b_{0j}, b_{0k} the intercepts of the regressions for groups j and k
b_{1j}, b_{1k} the slopes of the regressions for groups j and k
$MS_{Residual(j)}, MS_{Residual(k)}$ the residual mean squares from the regression within each group
$\bar{x}_j, \bar{x}_k$ the mean values of the covariate in each group
$SS_{\bar{x}_j}, SS_{\bar{x}_k}$ the sums of squares for the means of each covariate in each group
n_j, n_k sample sizes in each group
$h, h_{\alpha, J, df}$ read from Table 1 in Wilcox (1987b)
and
α significance level (usually 0.05)
J number of groups for factor A
df degrees of freedom for the comparison between j and k based on the Satterthwaite and Welch adjustment (Chapter 3).

12.3.3 Comparing regression lines

We mentioned at the start of this chapter that ANCOVA can also be used as a way of comparing regression lines between groups. The comparison of regression slopes across groups, a test for parallelism, uses the methods described in the previous section, testing the factor group by covariate interaction term. If the within-group regression slopes are different, then there is usually no interest in comparing intercepts because the difference between intercepts is not maintained for other values of X. If the regression lines are found to be not significantly different from parallel, then a pooled within-group regression slope is used to "force" the lines to be parallel and the differences between intercepts represent differences for any value of X. So the test comparing intercepts is simply the test comparing adjusted means

(Section 12.1.3) once a pooled within-groups regression slope has been fitted.

12.4 | Robust ANCOVA

There has been a surprising amount of theoretical work on robust alternatives to ANCOVA, just about all based on ranks (see review in Maxwell *et al.* 1993). Such robust methods may be required if there is non-normality in the response variable (Y) or nonlinearity in the relationship between Y and the covariate. Puri & Sen's (1969) test, one of the first, ranks Y and X separately then calculates a special test statistic. Alternatively, a simple rank transform (RT) approach could be used whereby the usual ANCOVA is done on rank transformed data (both Y and X). Olejnik & Algina (1987) indicated that the different rank transform tests in ANCOVA generally perform similarly but their results showed that only when the parametric assumptions were seriously compromised did the parametric ANCOVA do badly. The rank transform approaches are probably most useful when inexplicable outliers are present or when the relationship between Y and X is nonlinear, effectively requiring a non-parametric regression. Given the concerns expressed in Chapter 9 about the ability of rank transform tests to detect interactions in ANOVA designs, their ability to pick up heterogeneity of slopes in ANCOVA designs must also be in doubt.

Randomization tests could also be used if we consider the ANCOVA model as a multiple regression and do multiple randomizations of experimental or sampling units to groups (as in a single factor ANOVA design – see Chapter 8), keeping the pairing between Y and the covariate (Manly 1997).

12.5 | Unequal sample sizes (unbalanced designs)

There are no specific difficulties associated with ANCOVAs with unequal sample sizes between groups beyond what we have already discussed in Chapter 8 for single factor ANOVAs. We have to be more careful about checking assumptions with unequal sample sizes and if our design has two or more factors as well as a covariate, we recommend using Type III SS (see Chapter 9).

12.6 | Specific comparisons of adjusted means

12.6.1 Planned contrasts
Contrasts among adjusted means can be done with a t test:

$$t = \frac{c_1 \bar{y}_{1(adjusted)} + c_2 \bar{y}_{2(adjusted)} + \cdots}{\sqrt{MS_{Residual}\left[c_1^2/n_1 + c_2^2/n_2 + \cdots + \frac{(c_1\bar{x}_1 + c_2\bar{x}_2 + \cdots)^2}{SS_{Residual(X)}}\right]}}$$
(12.16)

This daunting equation is simply the usual t test for a contrast in a standard ANOVA except it takes

into account the covariate means and the covariate residual variation. The c_is are the contrast coefficients, $MS_{Residual}$ is from the ANCOVA and $SS_{Residual(X)}$ is from an ANOVA on the covariate. There will be an equivalent F test ($F = t^2$) that can be partitioned from the $SS_{A(adjusted)}$. Note that most statistical software will provide adjusted means as output from fitting an ANCOVA model and also allow contrasts on adjusted means as part of the general linear models routines.

12.6.2 Unplanned comparisons
To do unplanned multiple comparisons of adjusted means, use either the Bryant–Paulson–Tukey (B–P–T) test or the Conditional Tukey–Kramer test (Day & Quinn 1989, p. 461). The latter test is simpler, because it uses the usual q distribution. The B–P–T test uses special tables (Kirk 1995). Both can be used as stepwise Ryan's tests. As a general rule, however, we recommend that you avoid unplanned multiple comparisons and try and plan a small number of sensible contrasts wherever possible. Most statistical software won't do either multiple comparison test, so an alternative is to do all pairwise contrasts based on the t tests in Equation 12.16 with a Bonferroni-style adjustment of significance levels to correct for multiple testing (Chapter 3).

12.7 | More complex designs

Single factor ANCOVA models are relatively straightforward, but things get more complicated with multiple factors and/or multiple covariates. The adjustment procedure is just an extension of the single factor design, but the test of homogeneity of slopes is much trickier. Each broad type of design will be considered separately in this section.

12.7.1 Designs with two or more covariates
In designs with multiple covariates, the regression component of the ANCOVA becomes a multiple regression. The adjustment for a design with one factor and two covariates (X and Z) is:

$$\bar{y}_{i(adjusted)} = y_{ij} - b_{YX}(x_{ij} - \bar{x}) - b_{YZ}(z_{ij} - \bar{z})$$
(12.17)

Table 12.3 Factorial ANCOVA with factor A (p levels), factor B (q levels) and covariate

Source	Morse & Bazzaz (1994)	df	Morse & Bazzaz (1994)
A	Temperature	$(p-1)$	2
B	CO_2	$(q-1)$	1
A × B	Temperature × CO_2	$(p-1)(q-1)$	2
Covariate	*Biomass*	1	1
Residual	Residual	$pq(n-1)-1$	231

Note:

Example is from Morse & Bazzaz (1994), who had unequal numbers of plants within each cell. The covariate term does not contribute to the $SS_{Total(adjusted)}$.

where b_{YX} is the estimate of the pooled within-groups regression slope relating Y to X (β_{YX}) and b_{YZ} is the estimate of the pooled within-groups regression slope relating Y to Z (β_{YZ}). The analysis is then done on these adjusted values in a similar manner to when there is a single covariate. We must be very careful about collinearity problems, particularly correlations between the two covariates. Two highly correlated covariates provide redundant information so won't help in reducing the residual variation much anyway. Additionally, if either of the covariates are different between the groups, the adjustment requires extrapolation of either the Y on X or Y on Z regression lines.

For most statistical software, we simply include the multiple covariates when we fit our linear ANCOVA model. Checking homogeneity of within-group regression slopes is more difficult. Essentially the assumption is about parallelism of a series of planes (or higher-dimensional spaces!), rather than simple lines. We suggest that you check the homogeneity of slopes for each covariate separately, by testing the interactions between the factor and each covariate.

12.7.2 Factorial designs

Factorial designs that include one or more covariates measured on each experimental or sampling unit are common. For example, Morse & Bazzaz (1994) did an experiment to test the effects of three temperature regimes and two levels of CO_2 on the number of nodes (an estimate of developmental age) of individuals of two species of annual plants (*Abutilon theophrasti*, a C_3 plant, and *Amaranthus retroflexus*, a C_4 plant). Each species was

analyzed separately with a factorial linear model with replicate plants in each cell. Because the number of nodes might be affected by size independently of age, the aboveground biomass (i.e. size) was also used as a covariate for these analyses.

The ANCOVA model for this design is based on adjusting the Y-values using a within-cells regression slope pooled across all the combinations of factors A and B (the pq cells):

$$y_{ijk(adj)} = y_{ijk} - b(x_{ijk} - \bar{x}) \tag{12.18}$$

This adjustment is based on the estimate (b) of the pooled within-cells regression slope (β). The analysis then uses these adjusted values in a two factor crossed ANOVA (Table 12.3). For most software, the model fitted is the usual two factor crossed ANOVA model including a covariate term.

Maxwell *et al.* (1993) point out that the effects of the two factors in crossed ANCOVAs are not orthogonal, i.e. we have the same difficulty partitioning the $SS_{Total(adj)}$ as we do trying to partition the SS_{Total} in a crossed ANOVA design with unequal sample sizes (Chapter 9). Our recommendation for Type III SS in unbalanced factorial models also applies to factorial ANCOVAs, even when the sample sizes are equal. When random factors are included in these models, the denominators of the F tests for the fixed factors will change, as described in Chapter 9.

Since the adjustment in Equation 12.18 is based on the pooled within-cells regression slope, the test for homogeneity of slopes in these factorial designs should compare the regression slopes across all pq cells. For a two factor (A and B) with

Source	Leonard et al. (1999)	df	Leonard et al. (1999)	Denominator
A	Predation	$p-1$	1	B(A)
B(A)	Site(Predation)	$p(q-1)$	4	Residual
Covariate	*Length*	1	1	*Residual*
Residual	Residual	$pq(n-1)-1$	204	

Table 12.4 Nested ANCOVA with fixed factor A (p levels), random factor B (q levels) nested within A and covariate

Note:
Example is from Leonard et al. (1999) who had unequal numbers of mussels within each site within each predation level. Denominator for F test of H_0 for each term provided. The covariate term does not contribute to the $SS_{Total(adjusted)}$.

one covariate (X) design, the following model would be fitted:

$$y_{ijk} = \mu + \alpha_i + \beta_j + (\alpha\beta)_{ij} + X + \alpha_i X + \beta_j X + (\alpha\beta)_{ij} X + \varepsilon_{ijk} \quad (12.19)$$

Note that β_j here refers to the effect of factor B, not the regression slope for the covariate. The regression slopes are implied by the covariate term X and its interactions in the model. Model 12.19 will result in three heterogeneity of slopes terms: $A \times X$, $B \times X$ and $A \times B \times X$. Huitema (1980) recommended that these terms be combined and tested against the $MS_{Residual}$ from this model. This tests for any variation between slopes across all cells. This is the same test that we would get if we fitted a model that considered the factor combinations as levels of a single factor (a cell means model) and tested the factor by covariate interaction term.

Tests of main effects in factorial designs pool across the levels of the other factor(s), so it might be more appropriate to do separate tests for homogeneity of slopes for each effect based on adjusted means. So we would test homogeneity of slopes for the $A \times B$ interaction (test $A \times B \times X$ against the Residual), test for homogeneity of slopes for the A main effect (test $A \times X$ against Residual) and again for the B main effect (test $B \times X$ against Residual). We have not seen this approach discussed in the literature, although we suggest a version of it for nested designs in Section 12.7.3.

If the H_0 of equal slopes is rejected, you can then test simple main effects with separate ANCOVAs or examine the interaction between the factors and the covariates in more detail. Either

way, the Wilcox (J–N) procedure will again play an important role. As before, we recommend doing only a small number of possible comparisons, as planned contrasts. If the homogeneity of slopes test is not significant, then those interaction terms involving the covariate can be omitted and the model refitted – this then is a standard ANCOVA model.

12.7.3 Nested designs with one covariate

Nested designs can also include covariates. For example, Leonard et al. (1999) examined attachment strength of intertidal mussels at sites with either high levels of crab predation or low levels of crab predation. The prediction was that attachment strength would be greater at sites where predation was important. This was a nested design, with factor A being high vs low predation, there were three sites (factor B) nested within each predation level and attachment strength (Y) was measured on randomly chosen mussels. Because attachment strength might also be related to mussel size (larger mussels have stronger attachments), shell length was recorded for each mussel as a covariate (X).

The ANCOVA model for this design is based on adjusting the Y-values using a pooled within-cells regression slope. This adjustment is the same as used for a factorial design, based on the estimate (b) of the pooled within-cells regression slope (β) – see Equation 12.18 in previous section.

The nested ANCOVA then uses these adjusted values (Table 12.4). The model fitted is the usual nested ANOVA model including the covariate term.

Testing for homogeneity of regression slopes tests can be done in two ways. First, we can test for any differences in slopes of the regression models for Y on X across all cells. This test is done by fitting the following model:

$$y_{ijk} = \mu + \alpha_i + \beta_{j(i)} + X + \alpha_i X + \beta_{j(i)} X + \varepsilon_{ijk} \qquad (12.20)$$

This model includes the $A \times X$ and the $B(A) \times X$ interactions and we would combine these into a single test of homogeneity of within-cells regression slopes.

The second approach acknowledges that factor B is usually random in these designs and A is then tested against B(A). This suggests that we might do a separate test of homogeneity of slopes among the levels of A, using the $B(A) \times X$ interaction terms as the error ($A \times X$ against $B(A) \times X$). The question that we are now asking is, "Is there significant variation in slopes between levels of A, relative to variation in slopes between the levels of B within levels of A?" This seems to be the approach taken by Leonard et al. (1999), who tested the Predation $\times$ Length interaction against either the Site(Predation) or the Site(Predation) $\times$ Length term. We suggest the latter denominator is more appropriate, especially when the question focuses on adjusted A level means. There will be some cases where you explicitly want to compare slopes across all cells in a nested design, and then the pooled test of homogeneity of regression slopes is applicable.

12.7.4 Partly nested models with one covariate

In split-plot and groups by trials repeated measures designs (Chapter 11), there are two ways a covariate can be included. First, separate measures for the covariate are taken for each sub-plot within each plot or for each subject at each time or within-subjects group. In the example from Mullens (1993) described in Chapter 11, blood pressure might be measured as a covariate for each toad each time breathing rate is recorded. Second, a single covariate measure is associated with each plot or with each subject, irrespective of sub-plot or level of within subjects factor. Again from Mullens (1993), body size or basal breathing rate might be used as a covariate and there would be only a single value for each toad, as this would

not vary with O_2 level. Krupnick & Weis (1999) used this second type of partly nested ANCOVA to analyze their experiments on the effect of florivory on plant success. They had a repeated measures design with individual plants of the perennial shrub *Isomeris arborea* as the subjects. The between-subjects factor was three insecticide treatments (protected from herbivory by insecticide spraying, exposed to herbivory but sprayed with water control, exposed to herbivory without spray). The within-subjects factor was date as each plant was recorded on numerous occassions in each of three years – separate analyses were done for each year (Table 12.5). The response variable was fruit production but because this might also be affected by plant size, the number of branches on each plant was recorded as a covariate. This covariate did not vary for each plant during the experiment.

In the more general first scenario, there are regressions of Y on X at two levels – between plots or subjects, and within plots or subjects. The second situation is just a special case of the first where the covariate measure is the same for every observation on each subject or plot. In this situation, there is only a between-subject or plot regression, so only the between-subjects means are adjusted in practice. In the first case, the adjustment is done for between-subjects effects (A) and within-subjects effects (C and $A \times C$).

The ANCOVA adjustment for the first case is (Kirk 1995):

$$y_{ijk(adj)} = y_{ijk} - b_{\text{Between}}(\bar{x}_i - \bar{x}) - b_{\text{Within}}(x_{ijk} - \bar{x}_i) \qquad (12.21)$$

where b_{Between} is the estimate of the pooled within A groups (i.e. between plots/subjects) regression slope (β_{Between}) and b_{Within} is the estimate of the pooled within C groups (i.e. within plots/subjects) regression slope (β_{Within}). When the covariate has a single value for each plot or subject, then the second component of the adjustment in 12.21 simply becomes zero. The analysis then uses these adjusted values in a partly nested ANOVA (Table 12.5). The model fitted is the usual partly nested model including the covariate term.

Testing homogeneity of slopes in these designs is tricky and rarely discussed in textbooks. Even a recent review of ANCOVAs for split-plot designs (Federer & Meredith 1992) did not describe testing

Table 12.5 | Partly nested ANCOVA with factor A (p levels) and factor B (plots/subjects with q levels) nested within A, factor C (r levels) as within-plots/subjects factor and a covariate measured on each plot/subject

Source	Krupnick & Weis (1999)	df	Krupnick & Weis (1999)
Between plots/subjects			
A	Treatment	$(p-1)$	2
Covariate (X)	No. branches	1	1
B(A)	Plants within treatment	$p(q-1)-1$	26
Within plots/subjects			
C	Date	$(r-1)$	25
A×C	Treatment × date	$(p-1)(r-1)$	50
C×X	Date × no. branches	$(r-1)$	25
B(A)×C	Plants within treatment × date	$p(q-1)(r-1)-1$	650

Note:
Example is for 1992 fruit production in *Isomeris arborea* from Krupnick & Weis (1999) – their Table 2. Factor A was insecticide treatment, plots/subjects were plants, factor C was date and the covariate was number of branches on each plant.

for homogeneity of slopes, although their paper emphasized estimation, not hypothesis testing. For the general case with separate covariate measures for each sub-plot or each subject at each level of the within-subjects factor, a model that includes all factor by covariate interactions is fitted:

$$y_{ijkl} = \mu + \alpha_i + \beta_{j(i)} + \gamma_k + (\alpha\gamma)_{ik} + \beta\gamma_{j(i)k} + X + \\ \alpha_i X + \beta_{j(i)} X + \gamma_k X + (\alpha\gamma)_{ik} X + \varepsilon_{ijkl} \quad (12.22)$$

Note that l usually equals one in these designs so each observation is actually y_{ijk}. In such a design, we cannot separately estimate $\beta\gamma_{j(i)k}$ and ε_{ijkl} nor can we separately estimate the covariate by factor interaction terms $\beta_{j(i)}$ by X and $(\alpha\gamma)_{ik}$ by X. We suggest testing homogeneity of slopes for A, C and A×C separately using the appropriate error terms, i.e. A×X against B(A), C×X and A×C×X against B(A)×C. For the case where we have only single covariate measure for each plot or subject, homogeneity of slopes is only relevant across levels of A, so only the interaction of A×X would be included in the model and tested against the B(A) term. This approach was used by Krupnick & Weis (1999) who tested for an interaction between insecticide treatment (the between-subjects factor) and number of branches (covariate).

Note that if the covariate measures are different for each sub-plot or level of the within-

subjects factor, your data file will need to be coded for a classical split-plot analysis (Chapter 11), even if you have a repeated measures design. Note also that the number of terms in these models, including all the interactions with the covariate, can get large and this can cause computational problems when the number of observations (especially plots/subjects within A) is relatively small.

12.8 | General issues and hints for analysis

12.8.1 General issues

- Including one or more covariates can reduce the unexplained variation in ANOVA designs and increase precision of estimates of group means and power of tests.
- The basic ANCOVA tests null hypotheses about adjusted means and factor effects, where the linear relationship between the covariate and the response variable (Y) is taken into account. These means are adjusted to the overall mean value for the covariate by the relationship between Y and the covariate.
- Since a pooled within-groups regression slope is used for the adjustment, the assumption of homogeneous slopes across groups is very important for interpreting ANCOVA models

and should always be checked. The Johnson–Neyman (J–N) procedure is applicable for simple designs if this assumption is not met.

- Contrasts and unplanned multiple comparisons between adjusted means require different methods than for unadjusted means, taking into account the linear relationship with the covariate.
- Covariates can be included in more complex ANOVA models (nested, factorial, and partly nested), the major difficulty being deriving tests for homogeneity of slopes.

12.8.2 Hints for analysis

- Most common statistical software offers ANCOVA as a menu option, but in most of them, you will be fitting an ANCOVA model that assumes homogeneity of slopes. To fit a model testing for heterogeneous slopes, you will generally need to specify the model fully through the general linear models option.
- Homogeneity of within-group regression slopes is tested by including factor by covariate interaction terms in a preliminary model. In complex models, homogeneity of slopes can be checked by combining all factor by covariate terms into a single interaction term that is tested or by treating the design as a single factor means model and testing the single factor by covariate term. Alternatively, homogeneity of slopes may be better tested separately for each component of the analysis, e.g. homogeneity of slopes for main effects separately.
- If slopes are heterogeneous, the comparison of adjusted means using the Johnson–Neyman (J–N) procedure is not available as part of most statistical software, and must be computed manually (Box 12.4) or with the program WILCOX.
- Assumptions such as normality, homogeneity of variances and linearity are best examined with graphical techniques such as residual plots and scatterplots.

Chapter 13

Generalized linear models and logistic regression

So far, most of the analyses we have described have been based around linear models that assume normally distributed populations of the response variable and of the error terms from the fitted models. Most linear models are robust to this assumption, although the extent of this robustness is hard to gauge, and transformations can be used to overcome problems with non-normal error terms. There are situations where transformations are not effective in making errors normal (e.g. when the response variable is categorical) and, in any case, it might be better to model the actual data rather than data that are transformed to meet assumptions. What we need is a technique for modeling that allows other types of distributions besides normal. Such a technique was introduced by Nelder & Wedderburn (1972) and further developed by McCullough & Nelder (1989) and is called generalized linear modeling (GLM). In this chapter, we will examine two common applications of GLMs: logistic regression, used when the response variable is binary, and Poisson regression, when the response variable represents counts. In the next chapter, we will describe log-linear models when both response and predictor variables are categorical and usually arranged in the form of a contingency table.

13.1 | Generalized linear models

Generalized linear models (GLMs) have a number of characteristics that make them more generally applicable than the general linear models we have considered so far. One of the most important is that least squares estimation no longer applies and maximum likelihood methods must be used (Chapter 2).

A GLM consists of three components. First is the random component, which is the response variable and its probability distribution (Chapter 1). The probability distribution must be from the exponential family of distributions, which includes normal, binomial, Poisson, gamma and negative binomial. If Y is a continuous variable, its probability distribution might be normal; if Y is binary (e.g. alive or dead), the probability distribution might be binomial; if Y represents counts, then the probability distribution might be Poisson. Probability distributions from the exponential family can be defined by the natural parameter, a function of the mean, and the dispersion parameter, a function of the variance that is required to produce standard errors for estimates of the mean (Hilbe 1993). For distributions like binomial and Poisson, the variance is related to the mean and the dispersion parameter is set to one. For distributions like normal and gamma, the dispersion parameter is estimated separately from the mean and is sometimes called a nuisance parameter.

Second is the systematic component, which represents the predictors (X variables) in the model. These predictors might be continuous and/or categorical and interactions between predictors, and polynomial functions of predictors, can also be included.

Third is the link function, which links the random and the systematic component. It actually links the expected value of Y to the predictors by the function:

$$g(\mu) = \beta_0 + \beta_1 X_1 + \beta_2 X_2 + \cdots \qquad (13.1)$$

where $g(\mu)$ is the link function and β_0, β_1, etc., are parameters to be estimated. Three common link functions include the following.

1. Identity link, which is $g(\mu) = \mu$, and models the mean or expected value of Y. This is used in standard linear models.

2. Log link, which is $g(\mu) = \log(\mu)$, and models the log of the mean. This is used for count data (that cannot be negative) in log-linear models (Chapter 14).

3. Logit link, which is $g(\mu) = \log[\mu/(1 - \mu)]$, and is used for binary data and logistic regression (Section 13.2).

GLMs are considered parametric models because a probability distribution is specified for the response variable and therefore for the error terms from the model. A more flexible alternative is to use quasi-likelihood models that estimate the dispersion parameter from the data rather than constraining it to the value implied by a specific probability distribution, such as one for a binomial and Poisson. Quasi-likelihood models are particularly useful when our response variable has a binomial or Poisson distribution but is over or under dispersed, i.e. the probability distribution has a dispersion parameter different from one and therefore a variance greater or less than expected from the mean.

GLMs are linear models because the response variable is described by a linear combination of predictors (Box 5.1). Fitting GLMs and maximum likelihood estimation of their parameters is based on an iterative reweighted least squares algorithm called the Newton–Raphson algorithm. Linear regression models (Chapters 5 and 6) can be viewed as a GLM, where the random component is a normal distribution of the response variable and the link function is the identity link so that the expected value (the mean of Y) is modeled. The OLS estimates of model parameters from the usual linear regression will be very similar to the ML estimates from the GLM fit.

Readable introductions to GLMs can be found in, among others, Agresti (1996), Christensen (1997), Dobson (1990), and Myers & Montgomery (1997).

13.2 | Logistic regression

One very important application of GLMs in biology is to model response variables that are binary (e.g. presence/absence, alive/dead). The predictors can be either continuous and/or categorical. For example, Beck (1995) related two response variables, the probability of survival (survived or didn't survive) and the probability of burrowing (burrowed or didn't burrow), to carapace width for stone crabs (*Menippe* spp.). Matlack (1994) examined the relationship between the presence/absence of individual species of forest shrubs (response variables) against a number of continuous predictors, such as stand area, stand age, distance to nearest woodland, etc. In both examples, logistic regression was required because of the binary nature of the response variable.

13.2.1 Simple logistic regression
We will first consider the case of a single continuous predictor, analogous to the usual linear regression model (Chapter 5). When the response variable is binary (i.e. categorical with two levels, zero or one), we actually model $\pi(x)$, the probability that Y equals one for a given value of X. The usual model we fit to such data is the logistic regression model, a nonlinear model with a sigmoidal shape (Figure 13.1). The change in the probability that Y equals one for a given change in X is greatest for values of X near the middle of its range, rather than for values at the extremes. The error terms from the logistic model are not normally distributed; because the response variable is binary, the error terms have a binomial distribution. This suggests that ordinary least squares (OLS) estimation is not appropriate and maximum likelihood (ML) estimation of model parameters is necessary. In this section, we will examine a situation with one binary response variable (Y), which can take values of zero or one, and one continuous predictor (X).

Lizards on islands
Polis *et al.* (1998) studied the factors that control spider populations on islands in the Gulf of

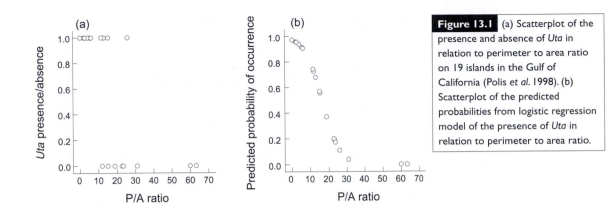

Figure 13.1 (a) Scatterplot of the presence and absence of *Uta* in relation to perimeter to area ratio on 19 islands in the Gulf of California (Polis *et al.* 1998). (b) Scatterplot of the predicted probabilities from logistic regression model of the presence of *Uta* in relation to perimeter to area ratio.

California. Potential predators included lizards of the genus *Uta* and scorpions (*Centruroides exilicauda*). We will use their data to model the presence/absence of lizards against the ratio of perimeter to area for each island. The analysis of these data is presented in Box 13.1.

Logistic model and parameters

The logistic model is:

$$\pi(x) = \frac{e^{\beta_0 + \beta_1 x}}{1 + e^{\beta_0 + \beta_1 x}} \qquad (13.2)$$

where β_0 and β_1 are parameters to be estimated. For the Polis *et al.* (1998) example, $\pi(x)$ is the probability that $y_i = 1$ (i.e. *Uta* is present) for a given x_i (P/A ratio). As we will see shortly, β_0 is the constant (intercept) and β_1 is the regression coefficient (slope), which measures the rate of change in $\pi(x)$ for a given change in X. This model can be fitted with nonlinear modeling techniques (Chapter 6) to estimate β_0 and β_1 but the modeling process is tedious and the output from software unhelpful.

An alternative approach is to transform $\pi(x)$ so that the logistic model closely resembles a familiar linear model. First, we calculate odds that an event occurs (e.g. $y_i = 1$ or *Uta* is present), which is the probability that an event occurs relative to its converse, i.e. the probability that $y_i = 1$ relative to the probability that $y_i = 0$:

$$\frac{\pi(x)}{1 - \pi(x)} \qquad (13.3)$$

If the odds are >1, then the probability that $y_i = 1$ is greater than the probability that $y_i = 0$; if the odds are <1, then the converse is true. Then we take the natural log of the odds that $y_i = 1$:

$$\ln\left[\frac{\pi(x)}{1 - \pi(x)}\right] \qquad (13.4)$$

This is the logit transformation or link function, that we will term $g(x)$, and which can be modeled against our predictor much more easily as:

$$g(x) = \beta_0 + \beta_1 x_i \qquad (13.5)$$

For the example from Polis *et al.* (1998):

$$g(x) = \beta_0 + \beta_1 (\text{P/A ratio})_i \qquad (13.6)$$

In model 13.6, $g(x)$ is the natural log (i.e. logit) of the odds that *Uta* is present on an island relative

---

Box 13.1 | **Worked example of logistic regression: presence/absence of lizards on islands**

Polis *et al.* (1998) studied the factors that control spider populations on islands in the Gulf of California. We will use part of their data to model the presence/absence of lizards (*Uta*) against the ratio of perimeter to area (P/A, as a measure of input of marine detritus) for 19 islands in the Gulf of California. We modeled the presence of *Uta* (binary) against P/A as:

$$g(x) = \beta_0 + \beta_1 (P/A \text{ ratio})_i$$

where $g(x)$ is the natural log of the odds of *Uta* occurring on an island. *Uta* occurred on ten of the 19 islands and the data are plotted in Figure 13.1(a). The H_0 of main interest was that there was no relationship between the presence of *Uta* (i.e. the odds that *Uta* occurred relative to not occurred) and the P/A ratio of an island. This is the H_0 that $\beta_1 = 0$.

The maximum likelihood estimates of the model parameters were as follows.

Parameter	Estimate	ASE	Wald statistic	P
β_0	3.606	1.695	2.127	0.033
β_1	−0.2196	0.101	−2.184	0.029

Note that the Wald statistic is significant so we would reject the H_0 that $\beta_1 = 0$. The odds ratio for P/A was estimated as 0.803 with 95%CI from 0.978 to 0.659. For a one unit increase in P/A, an island has a 0.803 chance of having *Uta* compared to not have *Uta*, a decrease in the odds of having *Uta* of approximately 20%. The plot of predicted probabilities from this model is shown in Figure 13.1(b), clearly showing the logistic relationship.

The other way to test the fit of the model, and therefore test the H_0 that $\beta_1 = 0$, is to compare the fit of the full model ($g(x) = \beta_0 + \beta_1 x_i$) to the reduced model ($g(x) = \beta_0$).

Full model log-likelihood = −7.110
Reduced model (constant only) log-likelihood = −13.143
$G^2 = -2$(difference in log-likelihoods) = 12.066, df = 1, $P = 0.001$. This is also the difference in deviance of the full and reduced models. This test also results in us rejecting the H_0 that $\beta_1 = 0$. Note that the Wald test seems more conservative (larger P value).

Goodness of fit statistics were calculated to assess the fit of the model. The Hosmer–Lemeshow statistic was more conservative than either Pearson χ^2 or G^2 and was not significant. Along with the low values for Pearson χ^2 or G^2, there was no evidence for lack of fit of the model. The logistic analogue of r^2 indicated that about 46% of the uncertainty in the presence of *Uta* on islands could be explained by P/A ratio.

Statistic	Value	df	P
Hosmer–Lemeshow ($\hat{C}$)	2.257	5	0.813
Pearson χ^2	15.333	17	0.572
Deviance (G^2)	14.221	17	0.651
r_L^2	0.459		

Analysis of diagnostics showed that two islands, Cerraja and Mitlan, were more influential than the rest on the outcome of the model fitting. They had the largest Pearson and deviance residuals and also unusually large values for the logistic regression equivalent of Cook's measure of influence, Hosmer & Lemeshow's (1989) $\Delta\beta$. However, our conclusion for the test of whether $\beta_1 = 0$ based on the G^2 statistic (deviance) was not changed if either of these two observations were omitted.

to being absent. We now have a familiar linear model, although the interpretation of the coefficients is a little different (see below). The logit transformation does two important things. First, $g(x)$ now ranges between $-\infty$ and $+\infty$ whereas $\pi(x)$ is constrained to between zero and one. Linear models are much more appropriate when the response variable can take any real value. Second, the binomial distribution of errors is now modeled.

The logistic regression model is a GLM. The random component is Y with a binomial probability distribution; the systematic component is the continuous predictor X; and the link function that links the expected value of Y to the predictor(s) is a logit link.

Now we use maximum likelihood (ML) techniques to estimate the parameters β_0 and β_1 from logistic model 13.5 by maximizing the likelihood function L:

$$L = \prod_{i=1}^{n} \pi(x_i)^{y_i}[1 - \pi(x_i)]^{1-y_i} \quad (13.7)$$

It is mathematically much easier to maximize the log-likelihood function $\ln(L)$ (Chapter 2). ML estimation is an iterative process requiring appropriate statistical software that will also provide standard errors of the ML estimates of β_0 and β_1. These standard errors are asymptotic because they are based on a normal distribution of the parameter estimates that is only true for large sample sizes. Confidence intervals for the parameters can also be calculated from the product of the asymptotic standard error and the standard normal z distribution. Both the standard errors and confidence intervals should be considered approximate.

We earlier defined the odds of an event occurring, which is the probability an event occurs relative to its converse, i.e. the probability that $y_i = 1$ relative to the probability that $y_i = 0$ or the probability that Uta occurs on an island relative to it not occurring. Our logistic regression model is that the natural log of the odds equals the constant (β_0) plus the product of the regression coefficient (β_1) and x_i:

$$\ln\left[\frac{\pi(x)}{1 - \pi(x)}\right] = \beta_0 + \beta_1 x_i \quad (13.8)$$

We can compare the value of the log of the odds

$$\ln\left[\frac{\pi(x)}{1 - \pi(x)}\right]$$

for $X = x_i$ and $X = x_i + 1$, i.e. for the predicted Y-values in a logistic regression model for X-values one unit apart. For the Polis et al. (1998) data, this is comparing the log of the odds of Uta occurring on an island for P/A ratios that differ by one unit. The ratio of these two odds is called the odds ratio and it is a measure of how the odds of Uta occurring change with a change in P/A ratio. Some simple arithmetic produces:

$$\text{odds ratio} = e^{\beta_1} \quad (13.9)$$

This is telling us that β_1 represents the change in the odds of an outcome for an increase in one unit of X. For the Polis et al. (1998) data, the estimated logistic regression coefficient (b_1) is an estimate of how much the odds of Uta occurring on an island (compared to not occurring) would change for an increase in P/A ratio of one unit. A positive value of b_1 indicates that the odds would increase and a negative value indicates the odds would decrease.

The constant, β_0, is the value of $g(x)$ when $x_i = 0$ and represents the intercept of the logistic regression model; its interpretation is similar to the intercept of the linear regression model (Chapter 5) and it is usually of less biological interest.

Null hypotheses and model fitting

The H_0 of main interest when fitting a simple logistic regression model is that $\beta_1 = 0$, i.e. there is no relationship between the binary response variable and the predictor variable. In the Polis et al. (1998) study, the H_0 is that there is no relationship between the presence/absence of Uta and the P/A ratio of an island. Equivalently, the H_0 is that the log of the odds of Uta occurring on an island relative to not occurring is independent of the P/A ratio of the island.

There are two common ways of testing this H_0. The first is to calculate the Wald statistic, a ML version of a t test, which is the parameter estimate divided by the standard error of the parameter estimate:

$$\frac{b_1}{s_{b_1}} \quad (13.10)$$

Note that the standard error (s_{b_1}) is asymptotic (often written as ASE), which means the distribution of b_1 approaches normality for large sample sizes, so the standard error should be considered approximate for small sample sizes. The Wald statistic is sometimes called the Wald t (or t ratio) statistic because of its similarity to a t statistic (Chapter 3). The Wald statistic is traditionally compared to the standard normal z distribution (Agresti 1996, Neter *et al.* 1996).

The Wald statistic is most reliable when sample sizes are large so an alternative hypothesis testing strategy that is more robust to small sample sizes and provides a link to measuring the fit of GLMs would be attractive. The approach is similar to that described for OLS regression models in Chapters 5 and 6 where we compare full and reduced models, except that we use log-likelihood as a measure of fit rather than least squares. To test the H_0 that $\beta_1 = 0$ for a simple logistic regression model with a single predictor, we compare the fit (the log-likelihood) of the full model:

$$g(x) = \beta_0 + \beta_1 x_i \qquad (13.5)$$

to the fit of the reduced model:

$$g(x) = \beta_0 \qquad (13.11)$$

To compare likelihoods, we use a likelihood ratio statistic (Λ), which is the ratio of the log-likelihood of reduced model to the log-likelihood of full model. Remember from Chapter 2 that larger log-likelihoods mean a better fit, so if Λ is near one, then β_1 contributes little to the fit of the full model whereas if Λ is less than one, then β_1 does contribute to the fit of the full model. To test the H_0, we need the sampling distribution of Λ when H_0 is true. The sampling distribution of Λ is messy so instead we calculate a G^2 statistic:

$$G^2 = -2\ln(\Lambda) \qquad (13.12)$$

This is also called the likelihood ratio χ^2 statistic. Sokal & Rohlf (1995) called it the G statistic. It can be simplified to:

$$G^2 = -2(\text{log-likelihood reduced} - \text{log-likelihood full}) \qquad (13.13)$$

If H_0 ($\beta_1 = 0$) is true and certain assumptions hold (Section 13.2.4), the sampling distribution of G^2 is

very close to a χ^2 distribution with one df.

Therefore, we can test H_0 that $\beta_1 = 0$ with either the Wald test or with G^2 test comparing the fit of reduced and full models. In contrast to least squares model fitting (Chapter 5), where the t test and the F test for testing $\beta_1 = 0$ are identical for a simple linear regression, the Wald and G^2 tests are not the same in logistic regression. The Wald test tends to be less reliable and lacks power for smaller sample sizes and the likelihood ratio statistic is recommended (Agresti 1996, Hosmer & Lemeshow 1989).

The G^2 statistic is also termed the deviance when the likelihood ratio is the likelihood of a specific model divided by the likelihood of the saturated model. The deviance therefore is:

$$-2(\text{log-likelihood specific model} - \text{log-likelihood saturated model}) \qquad (13.14)$$

The saturated model is a model that explains all the variation in the data. In regression models, the saturated model is one with as many parameters as there are observations, like a linear regression through two points (Hosmer & Lemeshow 1989). Note that the full model [$g(x) = \beta_0 + \beta_1 x_i$] is not a saturated model, as it does not fit the data perfectly. In a simple logistic regression with two parameters (β_0 and β_1), we can compare the deviance of the full and reduced models, i.e. the G^2 statistics for each model compared to a saturated model. The difference between the deviances tells us whether or not the two models fit the data differently. We do not actually fit a saturated model in practice because the log-likelihood of the saturated model is always zero (the maximum value of a log-likelihood because the model is a perfect fit), so the deviance for a given model is simply the log-likelihood of that model. Therefore, the difference in deviances equals:

$$-2(\text{log-likelihood reduced} - \text{log-likelihood full}) \qquad (13.15)$$

This is simply the G^2 statistic we calculated earlier. The likelihood ratio χ^2 statistic (G^2) therefore equals the difference in deviance of the two models. This concept becomes much more important when we have models with numerous parameters (i.e. multiple predictors) and therefore we have lots of possible reduced models (Section 13.2.2).

The other reason the deviance is a useful quantity is because it is the GLM analogue of $SS_{Residual}$, i.e. it measures the unexplained variation for a given model and therefore is a measure of goodness-of-fit (Section 13.2.5). In the same way that we could create analysis of variance tables for linear models by partitioning the variability, we can create an analysis of deviance table for GLMs. Such a partitioning of deviance is very useful for GLMs with numerous parameters, especially complex contingency tables (Chapter 14).

13.2.2 Multiple logistic regression

Logistic regression can be easily extended to situations with multiple predictor variables. The model fitting procedure is just an extension of the log-likelihood approach described in the previous section. For example, Wiser et al. (1998) studied the invasion of mountain beech forests in New Zealand by the exotic perennial herb *Hieracium lepidulum*. They modeled the probability of the exotic occurring on approximately 250 plots in relation to a number of predictor variables measured for each plot, including richness of plant species, the percentage of total species in the tall herb guild, the distance to the nearest non-alpine open land, other physical variables such as annual potential solar radiation, elevation, etc., and chemical characteristics of the soil (Ca, K, Mg, P, pH, N and C:N). Hansson et al. (2000) modeled the probability of predation by avian predators on artificial eggs in nests of the Great Reed Warbler in Sweden. Their predictor variables included experimental period (early and late in year) and attractiveness of the territory in which nest occurred, as well as the interaction between these two variables. Our worked example will be taken from a study of the ecology of fragmentation in urban landscapes.

Fragmentation and native rodents

Bolger et al. (1997) recorded the number of species of native rodents (except *Microtus californicus*) on 25 canyon fragments in southern California. These fragments have been isolated by urbanization. We will use their data to model the presence/absence of any species of native rodent in a fragment against three predictor variables: distance (meters) of fragment to nearest source canyon, age (years) since the fragment was isolated by urbanization, and percentage of fragment area covered in shrubs. The analysis of these data is presented in Box 13.2.

Box 13.2 | Worked example of logistic regression: presence/absence of rodents in habitat fragments

Using the data from Bolger et al. (1997), we will model the presence/absence of any species of native rodent (except *Microtus californicus*) against three predictor variables: distance (meters) to nearest source canyon (X_1), age (years) since fragment was isolated by urbanization (X_2), and percentage of fragment area covered in shrubs (X_3):

$$g(x) = \beta_0 + \beta_1 (\text{distance})_i + \beta_2 (\text{age})_i + \beta_3 (\% \text{ shrub})_i$$

where $g(x)$ is the natural log of the odds of a species of native rodent occurring in a fragment. The scatterplots of the presence of rodents against each predictor are shown in Figure 13.2. The H_0s of main interest were that there was no relationship between the presence of native rodents (i.e. the odds that native rodents occurred relative to not occurred) and each of the predictor variables, holding the others constant. These H_0s are that $\beta_1 = 0, \beta_2 = 0$ and $\beta_3 = 0$.

The maximum likelihood estimates and tests of the parameters were as follows.

Parameter	Estimate	ASE	Wald statistic	P
β_0	−5.910	3.113	−1.899	0.058
β_1	0.000	0.001	0.399	0.690
β_2	0.025	0.038	0.664	0.570
β_3	0.096	0.041	2.361	0.018

The odds ratios were as follows.

Predictor	Distance	Age	Percentage shrub cover
Odds ratio	1.000	1.025	1.101
95% CI	0.999–1.002	0.952–1.104	1.016–1.192

Model comparisons include the following.
  Log-likelihood of full model: −9.679.

Reduced model	H_0	Log-likelihood	G^2	P
$\beta_0 + \beta_2(\text{age})_i + \beta_3(\text{\% shrub})_i$	$\beta_1(\text{distance}) = 0$	−9.757	0.156	0.693
$\beta_0 + \beta_1(\text{distance})_i + \beta_3(\text{\% shrub})_i$	$\beta_2(\text{age}) = 0$	−9.901	0.444	0.505
$\beta_0 + \beta_1(\text{distance})_i + \beta_2(\text{age})_i$	$\beta_3(\text{\% shrub}) = 0$	−14.458	9.558	0.002

The conclusions from the Wald test and from the G^2 tests from the model fitting procedure agree. Only the effect of percentage shrub cover on the probability of rodents being present, holding age and distance from nearest source canyon constant, is significant. The odds ratio for percentage shrub cover was estimated as 1.101 and the 95% CI do not include one; for a 1% increase in shrub cover, a fragment has a 1.101 more chance of having a rodent than not, so even though the effect is significant, the effect size is small. The odds ratios for the other two predictors clearly include one, indicating that increases in those predictors do not increase the probability of a rodent being present in a fragment.

Goodness of fit statistics were calculated to assess the fit of the model. The Hosmer–Lemeshow statistic was not significant indicating no evidence for lack of fit of the model.

Statistic	Value	df	P
Hosmer–Lemeshow ($\hat{C}$)	6.972	6	0.323
Pearson χ^2	20.823	21	0.470
Deviance (G^2)	19.358	21	0.562
r_L^2	0.441		

The model diagnostics suggested that the only fragment that might be influential on the results of the model fitting was Spruce, with a dfbeta ($\Delta\beta$) and Pearson and deviance residuals much greater than the other observations. Unfortunately, we could not get the algorithm to converge on ML estimates when this observation was deleted, so we could not specifically examine its influence on the estimated regression coefficients.

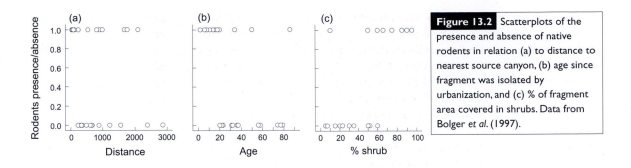

Figure 13.2 Scatterplots of the presence and absence of native rodents in relation (a) to distance to nearest source canyon, (b) age since fragment was isolated by urbanization, and (c) % of fragment area covered in shrubs. Data from Bolger *et al.* (1997).

Logistic model and parameters

The general multiple logistic regression model for p predictors is:

$$g(x) = \beta_0 + \beta_1 x_{i1} + \beta_2 x_{i2} + \ldots + \beta_p x_{ip} \qquad (13.16)$$

For the Bolger *et al.* (1997) data:

$$g(x) = \beta_0 + \beta_1(\text{distance})_i + \beta_2(\text{age})_i + \\ \beta_3(\% \text{ shrub})_i \qquad (13.17)$$

In models 13.16 and 13.17 we find the following.

$g(x)$ is the natural log of the odds ratio of $y_i = 1$ versus $y_i = 0$, i.e. the log of the odds of a species of native rodent occurring relative to not occurring in a fragment.

β_0 is the intercept or constant, i.e. the log of the odds of a species of native rodent occurring relative to not occurring in a fragment when all predictors equal zero.

β_1 is the partial regression coefficient for X_1, holding the remaining predictors constant, i.e. the change in the log of the odds of a species of native rodent occurring relative to not occurring in a fragment for a single unit increase in distance to nearest source canyon, holding canyon age and percentage shrub cover constant.

β_2 is the partial regression coefficient for X_2, holding the remaining predictors constant, i.e. the change in the log of the odds of a species of native rodent occurring relative to not occurring in a fragment for a single unit increase in canyon age, holding distance to nearest source canyon and percentage shrub cover constant.

β_3 is the partial regression coefficient for X_3, holding the remaining predictors constant, i.e. the change in the log of the odds of a species of native rodent occurring relative to not occurring in a fragment for a single unit increase in percentage shrub cover, holding distance to nearest source canyon and canyon age constant.

Just like in multiple linear regression models, we can firstly test the significance of the overall regression model by comparing the log-likelihood of the full model (13.16 and 13.17) to the log-likelihood of the reduced model (constant, or β_0, only). We calculate a G^2 statistic [-2(log-likelihood reduced $-$ log-likelihood full)] to test the H_0 that at least one of the regression coefficients equals zero.

To test individual coefficients, we can calculate Wald statistics, each one being the estimated regression coefficient divided by standard error of estimated coefficient. These Wald statistics are the equivalent of t tests for partial regression coefficients in multiple linear regression (Chapter 6) and can be compared to the standard normal (z) distribution. Our reservations about Wald tests (lack of power with small sample sizes) described in Section 13.2.1 apply equally here.

A better approach is to fit a series of reduced models and compare their fit to the full model. To test H_0 that β_1 (distance) $= 0$, we compare the fit of the full model:

$$g(x) = \beta_0 + \beta_1(\text{distance})_i + \beta_2(\text{age})_i + \\ \beta_3(\% \text{ shrub})_i \qquad (13.17)$$

to the fit of a reduced model based on H_0 being true:

$$g(x) = \beta_0 + \beta_2(\text{age})_i + \beta_3(\% \text{ shrub})_i \qquad (13.18)$$

with the G^2 statistic:

$$-2(\text{log-likelihood reduced} - \\ \text{log-likelihood full}) \qquad (13.15)$$

If the G^2 test is significant, we know that the inclusion of distance as a predictor makes the full model a better fit to our data than the reduced model and therefore H_0 is rejected. We can do a similar model comparison test for the other predictors.

The difference between the full and reduced models is also the difference in the deviances of the two models. Remember that the deviance is a measure of the unexplained variability after fitting a model so comparing deviances is just like comparing $SS_{Residuals}$ for linear models. Neter *et al.* (1996) called this the partial deviance and we can present the results of a multiple logistic regression as an analysis of deviance table.

Other aspects of multiple linear regression described in Chapter 6 also apply to multiple logistic regression. In particular, including interactions between predictors and polynomial terms might have great biological relevance and these terms can be tested by comparing the fit of full model to the appropriate reduced models.

13.2.3 Categorical predictors

Categorical predictor variables can be incorporated in the logistic modeling process by converting them to dummy variables (Chapter 5). Logistic regression routines in most statistical software will do this automatically. We described two sorts of coding for turning categorical predictors into continuous dummy variables for OLS regression in Chapter 5. It is important that you know which method your statistical software is using, as the interpretation of the coefficients and odds ratios is not the same for the two methods. Most programs use reference cell coding where one group of a categorical predictor is used as a reference and the effects of the other groups are relative to that reference group. Alternatively, effects coding could be used, where each group logit is compared to the overall logit (Hosmer & Lemeshow 1989).

A model with a binary response variable and one or more categorical predictors is usually termed a logit model (Agresti 1990, 1996), to distinguish it from classical logistic regression. If all the predictors are categorical, then log-linear modeling (Chapter 14) is a more sensible procedure because the data are in the form of a contingency table. However, log-linear modeling does not automatically distinguish one of the variables

as a response variable. For different log-linear models, there are equivalent logit models that identify a response variable (see Agresti 1996, p. 165; Chapter 14).

13.2.4 Assumptions of logistic regression

Like all GLMs, logistic regression assumes that the probability distribution for the response variable, and hence for the error terms from the fitted model, is adequately described by the random component chosen. For logistic regression, we assume that the binomial distribution is appropriate, which is likely for binary data. The reliability of the model estimation also depends on the logistic model being appropriate and checking the adequacy of the model is important (Section 13.2.5).

When there are two or more predictors in the model, then absence of strong collinearity (strong correlations between the predictors) is as important for logistic regression models as it was for OLS regression models (Chapter 6). While not necessarily reducing the predictive value of the model, collinearity will inflate the standard errors of the estimates of the model coefficients and can produce unreliable results (Hosmer & Lemeshow 1989, Menard 1995, Tabachnick & Fidell 1996). Most logistic regression routines in statistical software do not always provide automatic collinearity diagnostics, but examining a correlation matrix between the continuous predictors or a contingency table analysis for categorical predictors will indicate if there are correlations/associations between predictors. Tolerance, the r^2 of a regression model of a particular variable as the response variable against the remaining variables as predictors, can also be calculated for each predictor by simply fitting the model as a usual OLS linear regression model. Because tolerance only involves the predictor variables, its calculation is not affected by the binary nature of the response variable.

13.2.5 Goodness-of-fit and residuals

Checking the adequacy of the regression model is just as important for logistic models as for general linear models. One simple and important diagnostic tool for checking whether our model is adequate is to examine the goodness-of-fit. As with linear models fitted by least squares, the fit of a logistic model is determined by how similar the observed Y-values are to the expected or predicted Y-values. The predicted probabilities that $y_i = 1$ for given x_i are:

$$\hat{\pi}(x) = \frac{e^{b_0 + b_1 x}}{1 + e^{b_0 + b_1 x}} \tag{13.19}$$

In model 13.19, b_0 and b_1 are the estimated coefficients of the logistic regression model. A measure of fit of a particular model is the difference between the observed and fitted values, i.e. the residuals. Residuals in GLMs are similar to those for linear models, the difference between the observed probability that $y_i = 1$ and the predicted (from the logistic regression model) probability that $y_i = 1$.

There are two well-known statistics for assessing the goodness-of-fit of a logistic regression model. These statistics can be used to test that the observed data came from a population in which the fitted logistic regression model is true. The first is the Pearson χ^2 statistic based on observed (o) and expected, fitted or predicted (e) observations (Chapter 14):

$$\sum_{i=1}^{n} \frac{(o - e)^2}{e} = \sum_{i=1}^{n} \frac{(y_i - n\hat{\pi}_i)^2}{n\hat{\pi}_i(1 - \hat{\pi}_i)} \tag{13.20}$$

In Equation 13.20, y_i is the observed value of Y, $\hat{\pi}_i$ is the predicted or fitted value of Y for a given value of x_i and n is the number of observations. The use of the χ^2 statistic for logistic regression models is best visualized by treating the data as a two (binary response, Y) by n (different values of X) contingency table. The χ^2 statistic for goodness-of-fit is the usual χ^2 for contingency tables (Chapter 14).

The other is the G^2 statistic, which is:

$$\pm 2 \sum_{i=1}^{n} (o.\log(o/e)) = \pm 2 \left[\sum_{i=1}^{n} y_i \ln(y_i/n\hat{\pi}_i) + (n - y_i)\ln[(n - y_i)/n(1 - \hat{\pi}_i)] \right] \tag{13.21}$$

The terms in Equation 13.21 are as defined as in Equation 13.20. The G^2 statistic is also the deviance for a given model, defined in Section 13.2.1.

In both cases, low values indicate that the model is a better fit to the data, i.e. the observed and fitted values are similar. The Pearson χ^2 statis-

tic and the deviance G^2 statistic approximately follow a χ^2 distribution under certain assumptions. The most important assumption is that the minimum predicted frequency of either of the binary outcomes is not too small (see Chapter 14). When the predictors are continuous, however, there will usually be one or few observations of Y for each combination of values of the predictor variables ($n_i = 1$) so this assumption is not met and the Pearson χ^2 statistic and the deviance G^2 statistic will not have approximate χ^2 distributions. The statistics themselves are still valid measures of goodness-of-fit; it is just their P-values that are unreliable (Hosmer et al. 1997). Note also that when we have multiple observations for each combination of X-values, such as when the predictors are categorical, we will have a contingency table in which the expected frequencies are more likely to be reasonable (see Section 13.2.3 and Chapter 14) and the P-values associated with these statistics will be much more reliable. Note also that the calculation of deviance for categorical predictors depends on whether the saturated model is determined based on individual observations or groupings of observations (Siminoff 1998).

So, we cannot use the usual χ^2 or G^2 statistics to test null hypotheses about overall goodness-of-fit of a model when the predictors are continuous, although they are still useful as comparative measures of goodness-of-fit. Hosmer & Lemeshow (1989) developed a solution to the problem of testing goodness-of-fit for continuous predictors in logistic regression by grouping observations so that the minimum expected frequency of either of the binary outcomes is not too small. The Hosmer–Lemeshow statistic, also termed the deciles of risk (DC) statistic, is derived from aggregating the data into ten groups. The grouping is based on either each group having one tenth of the ordered predicted probabilities so the groups have equal numbers of observations, or the groups being separated by fixed cutpoints (e.g. first group having all probabilities ≤0.10, etc.). Both grouping methods produce a statistic ($\hat{C}$) which approximately follows a χ^2 distribution with df as the number of groups minus two.

Hosmer et al. (1997) reviewed many goodness-of-fit tests, including the Pearson χ^2 statistic and

$\hat{C}$, for assessing logistic regression models. They found that the χ^2 statistic performed well if based on the conditional mean and variance estimate and compared to a scaled χ^2 distribution; unfortunately, the computations required to modify the usual χ^2 statistic are not straightforward. They also recommended $\hat{C}$, as it is available in most statistical software and is powerful and we support their recommendation.

There has also been work on analogues of r^2 used as a measure of explained variance in OLS regression. Menard (2000) discussed a range of measures like r^2 for logistic regression and tentatively recommended:

$$r_L^2 = \frac{[\ln(L_0) - \ln(L_M)]}{\ln(L_0)} = 1 - \frac{\ln(L_M)}{\ln(L_0)} \qquad (13.22)$$

In Equation 13.22, L_0 is the likelihood for the model with only the intercept and L_M is the likelihood for the model with all predictors (one in the case of simple logistic regression).

13.2.6 Model diagnostics

As well as assessing the overall fit of the model, it is also important to evaluate the contribution of each observation, or group of observations, to the fit and deviations from the fit. In OLS linear models, we have emphasized the importance of residuals, the difference between each observed and fitted or predicted value. There are two types of residuals from logistic regression models. The first is the Pearson residual for an observation, which is the contribution of the difference between the observed and predicted value for an observation to the Pearson χ^2 statistic, and is usually expressed as a standardized residual (e_i):

$$e_i = \frac{y_i - n\hat{\pi}_i}{\sqrt{[n\hat{\pi}_i(1 - \hat{\pi}_i)]}} \qquad (13.23)$$

where y_i is the observed value of Y, $\hat{\pi}_i$ is the predicted or fitted value of Y for a given value of x_i and n is the number of observations. The second is the deviance residual for an observation, which is the contribution of the difference between the observed and predicted value for an observation to the total deviance.

The Pearson and deviance residuals approximately follow a normal distribution for larger sample sizes when the model is correct and residuals greater than about two indicate lack of fit (Agresti 1996, Hosmer & Lemeshow 1989, Menard 1995). When predictor variables are continuous and there is only a single value of Y for each combination of values of the predictor variables, then the large sample size condition will not hold and single residuals will be difficult to interpret. When the predictor variables are categorical and we have reasonable sample sizes for each combination of predictor variables, then residuals are easier to interpret and we will examine such residuals in the context of contingency tables in Chapter 14.

Diagnostics for influence of an observation, i.e. how much the estimates of the parameters change if the observation is deleted, are also available and are similar to those for OLS models (Chapter 5; see also Hosmer & Lemeshow 1989, Menard 1995). These include (i) leverage, which is measured in the same way as for OLS regression, and (ii) an analogue of Cook's statistic standardized by its standard error called Dfbeta (Agresti 1996) or $\Delta\beta$ (Hosmer & Lemeshow 1989), which measures the standardized change in the estimated logistic regression coefficient b_1 when an observation is deleted. The change in χ^2 or deviance when an observation is deleted can also be calculated. These diagnostics are standard output from many logistic regression routines in statistical software. Influential observations should always be checked and our recommendations from Chapters 4 and 5 apply here.

13.2.7 Model selection

As with OLS multiple linear regression, we often wish to know which of the two or more predictor variables in the logistic regression model contributes most to the pattern in the binary response variable. A related aim is to find the "best" model, one that provides the maximum fit for the fewest predictors. The criteria for assessing different models include the Pearson χ^2 or deviance (G^2) statistics, r_L^2 and information criteria like Akaike's (see Chapter 6). The Akaike Information Criterion (AIC) adjusts ("penalizes") the G^2 (deviance) for a given model for the number of predictor variables:

$$AIC = G^2 - n + 2p \qquad (13.24)$$

where n is the number of observations and p is the number of predictors. For categorical predictors:

$$\text{AIC} = G^2 - D + 2p \tag{13.25}$$

where D is the number of different combinations of the categorical predictors (Larntz 1993). Models with low AICs are the best fit and if many models have similarly low AICs, you should choose the one with the fewest model terms. For both continuous and categorical predictors, we prefer comparing full and reduced models to test individual terms rather than comparing the fit of all possible models to try and select the "best" one.

We will not discuss stepwise modeling for multiple logistic regression or more general logit models. Our reservations about stepwise procedures (see also James & McCulloch 1990) have been stated elsewhere (Chapter 6).

13.2.8 Software for logistic regression

Logistic regression models can be fitted using statistical software in two main ways. Most programs provide logistic regression modules, often as part of a general regression module. It is assumed that the response variable is binary and that a GLM is fitted with a binomial distribution for the error terms and a logit link function. Some software offers GLM routines and the error distribution and link function might need to be specified. The range of diagnostics is usually extensive but it is always worth running a known data set from a text like Christensen (1997) or Hosmer & Lemeshow (1989). Tabachnick & Fidell (1996) have provided an annotated comparison of output from four common programs.

13.3 | Poisson regression

Biologists often deal with data that are in the form of counts (e.g. number of organisms in a sampling unit, numbers of cells in a tissue section) and we commonly wish to model a response that is a count variable. Counts usually have a Poisson distribution, where the mean equals the variance and therefore linear models based on normal distributions may not be appropriate. One solution is to simply transform the response variable with a power transformation (e.g. $\sqrt{}$), which tends to remove any relationship between the mean and variance. An alternative is to use a GLM with a Poisson error term and a log link function that is called a log-linear model. Log-linear models are commonly used to analyze contingency tables (Chapter 14) but can also be used effectively when the predictors are continuous and the response variable is a count to produce a Poisson regression model:

$$\log(\mu) = \beta_0 + \beta_1 x_i \tag{13.26}$$

In model 13.26, μ is the mean of the Poisson distributed response variable, β_0 is the intercept (constant), β_1 is the regression coefficient and x_i is the value of a single predictor variable for observation i. The model predicts that a single unit increase in X results in Y increasing by a factor of e^{β_1} (Agresti 1996). A positive or negative value of β_1 represents Y increasing or decreasing respectively as X increases. Such models can be easily extended to include multiple predictors. For example, Speight et al. (1998) described the infestation of a scale insect Pulvinaria regalis in an urban area in England. They modeled egg code, the level of adult/egg infestation measured on a scale of one to ten, against seven predictor variables: tree species, tree diameter, distance to nearest infested tree, distance to nearest road, percentage impermeability of ground, tree vigor and distance from nearest building.

Nearly all the discussion in previous sections related to logistic regression, including estimation, model fitting and goodness-of-fit, and diagnostics, applies similarly to Poisson regression models. One additional problem that can occur when modeling count data is that we are assuming that the response has a Poisson distribution where the mean equals the variance. Often, however, the variance is greater than the mean, which is termed overdispersion (Agresti 1996). In GLMs, the dispersion parameter is now less than or greater than one (see Section 13.1). Standard errors of estimated regression coefficients will be smaller than they should and tests of hypotheses will have inflated probabilities of Type I error. Overdispersion is usually caused by other factors, which we have not measured, influencing our response variable in heterogeneous ways. For example, we might model number of plant species per plot against soil pH in a forest; if unmeasured nutrient levels also vary greatly between plots, then variance in the number of species may be greater than the mean. There are at least three possible ways of dealing with over-dispersion.

- We can correct the standard errors of the parameters by multiplying by $\sqrt{(\chi^2/df)}$, as suggested by Agresti (1996). Gardner et al. (1995) provide a complex adjustment based on an estimate of the dispersion parameter.
- We could use a more appropriate probability distribution, such as the negative binomial (Chapter 2, Gardner et al. 1995).
- We could use quasi-likelihood models where the dispersion parameter is estimated from the data rather than restricted to the value defined by a Poisson distribution.

Criteria for assessing the fit of GLMs, such as the likelihood ratio statistic and AIC, are also sensitive to overdispersion. Fitzmaurice (1997) suggested that such criteria could be simply scaled by a REML (restricted maximum likelihood) estimate of the degree of overdispersion.

13.4 | Generalized additive models

Generalized additive models (GAMs) are non-parametric modifications of GLMs where each predictor is included in the model as a non-parametric smoothing function (Hastie & Tibshirani 1990). In general terms, with a response variable and $j = 1$ to p predictor variables, a GLM can be written as:

$$g(\mu) = \beta_0 + \sum_{j=1}^{p} \beta_j X_j \qquad (13.27)$$

Note that we have summarized the systematic component representing the predictor variables as a sum of products between regression coefficients and predictors.

A GAM fits a more flexible model:

$$g(\mu) = \beta_0 + \sum_{j=1}^{p} f_j X_j \qquad (13.28)$$

$$g(\mu) = \beta_0 + f_1 x_{i1} + f_2 x_{i2} + \cdots + f_p x_{ip} \qquad (13.29)$$

In models 13.28 and 13.29, the f_j are non-parametric functions estimated using a smooth-

ing technique (Chapter 5). These smoothing functions, which are commonly Loess or cubic splines for GAMs, are usually estimated from exploratory scatterplots of the data (Yee & Mitchell 1991).

For example, recall the data from Loyn (1987) described in Chapter 6. These data were the abundances of birds from 56 forest patches in south-eastern Australia. Six predictor variables were recorded for each patch: area, distance to nearest patch, distance to nearest largest patch, grazing intensity, altitude and years since isolation. A GAM with all predictors (area and the two distances transformed to logs), using a normal probability distribution and identity link function and based on Loess smoothing functions for each predictor, would be:

$$g(\text{mean bird abundance})_i = \beta_0 +$$
$$f_1(\text{log patch area})_i + f_2(\text{years isolated})_i +$$
$$f_3(\text{log nearest patch distance})_i +$$
$$f_4(\text{log nearest large patch distance})_i +$$
$$f_5(\text{stock grazing})_i + f_6(\text{altitude})_i \qquad (13.30)$$

where f_j is a Loess smoothing function. Note that there is no requirement for the same criteria to be used for each smoothing function, e.g. Loess smoothers for X_1 and X_2 may use different smoothing parameters, or even for the same type of smoothing function to be used for each predictor, e.g. a Loess could be used for X_1 and a cubic spline for X_2. The smoothing function for each predictor is derived from the data separately from the smoothing function for any other predictor. We will illustrate the fit of a GAM to a subset of these data from Loyn (1987), incorporating only three predictors (log patch area, log nearest patch distance, years isolated), in Box 13.3.

The main difference between GLMs and GAMs is that the former fits models that are constrained to a parametric (linear) form whereas the latter can fit a broader range of non-parametric models determined from the observed data. A combination of the two types of models is termed semi-parametric. This is a linear model with non-parametric terms included for at least one but not all of the predictors. GAMs are termed additive because the response variable is modeled as the sum of the functions of each predictor with no interactions.

Like GLMs, GAMs need a link function defined

Box 13.3 | Worked example of generalized additive models: bird abundances in habitat fragments

We will use the data from Loyn (1987), first introduced in Chapter 6, to illustrate a simple application of GAMs. We will model the abundance of birds in 56 forest patches against three predictors: $\log_{10}$ patch area, $\log_{10}$ distance to nearest patch and years since patch isolation. The boxplot of bird abundance is symmetrical so we will use a normal (Gaussian) probability distribution and an identity link function. We will also use a Loess smoothing function for each of the predictors and keep the smoothing parameter the same for all three functions. We fitted the models using S-Plus 2000 for Windows software.

Full model:

$g(\text{mean bird abundance})_i = \beta_0 + f_1(\log_{10} \text{ patch area})_i + f_2(\text{years isolated})_i + f_3(\log_{10} \text{ nearest patch distance})_i$

Deviance for null model:	6337.929 with 55 degrees of freedom
Residual deviance from fitted model:	1454.314 with 40.529 degrees of freedom

Degrees of freedom and *F*-ratios for non-parametric effects for each predictor are tabulated below.

Term	Parametric df	Non-parametric df	Non-parametric F-ratio	P
Intercept	1			
$\log_{10}$ patch area	1	4.2	1.817	0.142
Years isolated	1	3.3	0.618	0.620
$\log_{10}$ nearest patch distance	1	4.1	2.576	0.051

None of the terms had significant non-parametric components, suggesting that the linear model we fitted in Chapter 6 was appropriate, at least for these three predictors. This is clear from the Loess fits to scatterplots of bird abundance against each predictor (Figure 13.3) with only $\log_{10}$ distance suggesting some nonlinearity.

Test of $\log_{10}$ patch area is as follows.

Model	$df_{Residual}$	$Deviance_{Residual}$
$\log_{10}$ patch area + years isolated + $\log_{10}$ nearest patch distance	40.529	1454.314
Years isolated + $\log_{10}$ nearest patch distance	45.683	3542.574

Difference in deviance $= -2088.26$, df $= -5.154$, approximate *F*-ratio $= 11.291$, $P < 0.001$.

Clearly, a model that includes $\log_{10}$ patch area was a significantly better fit than a reduced model that doesn't. Equivalent model comparisons could be done for the remaining two predictors.

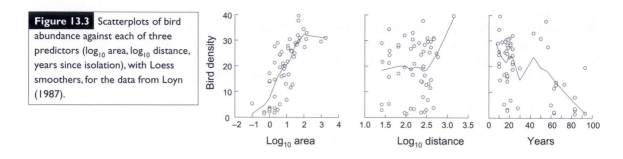

Figure 13.3 Scatterplots of bird abundance against each of three predictors ($\log_{10}$ area, $\log_{10}$ distance, years since isolation), with Loess smoothers, for the data from Loyn (1987).

and a probability distribution for the response variable that implies a probability distribution for the error terms from the model. The difficulty in specifying a probability distribution for the response variable and error terms is often overcome in GAMs by using quasi-likelihood models where only a relationship between mean and variance is specified and the dispersion parameter (i.e. the variance) is derived from the data (Section 13.1). The fit of a GAM is based on something called the local scoring algorithm, an extension of the Newton–Raphson algorithm used for fitting GLMs. Details of both can be found in Hastie & Tibshirani (1990) but basically local scoring uses a backfitting algorithm that iteratively fits a smoothing function, determines the partial residuals, and smooths these residuals. The details are complex and understanding them is not necessary to appreciate GAMs.

The important point is that we can measure the fit of a particular GAM, using measures like deviance and AIC, and also compare the fit of models with and without particular terms or combinations of terms. This allows us to assess the contribution of each predictor, modeled with its specific smoothing function, to the pattern in the response variable based on the usual analysis of deviance as used for GLMs. The difference in deviance between two hierarchical models (one with and one without the term being tested in the H_0) can be compared asymptotically to a χ^2 distribution. Hastie & Tibshirani (1990) also suggested that deviance statistics can be converted to approximate F-ratio statistics when the dispersion parameter is unknown and F tests are common output from software that fits GAMs. In summary, GAMs can be analyzed using the same framework as linear and generalized linear models.

There are some complexities when using

GAMs for inference that we do not find in linear and generalized linear models. The use of smoothing functions means that the degrees of freedom will usually not be an integer (Yee & Mitchell 1991). Additionally, the degrees of freedom for a smoothing term can be split into two components, that due to the parametric linear fit and that due to the non-parametric fit once the linear component has been removed. Some software also provides tests of the non-parametric component for individual terms in our model. This is very useful if GAMs are used as an exploratory tool because non-significant non-parametric fits suggest that linear models are appropriate for the data.

An example of the use of GAMs in biology comes from Berteaux & Boutin (2000) who modeled the breeding behavior of female red squirrels against 13 possible predictor variables, including minimum age of females, food abundance in same year as female behavior observed, food abundance in previous year, minimum number of middens owned by female, number of juveniles at weaning, and year of study. Their response variable was categorical, values being one, two or three: one was females keeping their territory and excluding juveniles after breeding, two was females sharing their territories with juveniles and three was females bequeathing their territories to juveniles. Berteaux & Boutin (2000) fitted GAMs with different combinations of predictors and with cubic splines as the smoothing functions. They used a quasi-likelihood model to estimate the variance in their response variable because a Poisson distribution was not quite appropriate. They also used the Akaike Information Criterion (AIC) to select the best model, which turned out to be the one with the predictors listed above but not including the remaining seven predictors. They also used logistic regression to model a binary response (females disperse or not disperse after breeding) against these previously described predictor variables; pretty much the same set of variables as for the GAM had the best fit in the logistic model.

Bjorndal *et al.* (2000) also used GAMs to model the growth rates (from mark–recapture data) of immature green turtles in the Bahamas against five predictor variables (sex, site, year, mean size and recapture interval). They used a similar modeling procedure to Bertaux & Boutin (2000), with quasi-likelihood models and cubic spline smoothing functions. However, they sensibly did not try to select a single best model, but rather estimated the fit and parameters for a model with all predictors, including specific contrasts between sexes (male vs female and male versus unknown) and between the three sites. They also tested for non-linear effects for some of the predictors (see also Yee & Mitchell 1991).

Although GAMs are very flexible models that can be fitted for a wide range of distributions of the response variable, especially exponential distributions, their application is not straightforward. First, we must choose a smoothing function for each predictor and also a smoothing parameter for each smoothing function. Second, we must make the same decisions as for GLMs: which probability distribution and link function combination is appropriate or use quasi-likelihood models. Third, we must have appropriate software and routines for fitting GAMs are not available in most commercial programs, although S-Plus is a noteable exception. With these limitations in mind, GAMs can be very useful, both as an exploratory tool that extends the idea of smoothing functions, and as a more formal model fitting procedure that lets the data determine many aspects of the final model structure.

13.5 | Models for correlated data

One of the most challenging data analysis tasks for biologists is dealing with correlated data. For example, repeated observations on the same sampling or experimental units, either under sequential treatment applications or simply through

time, cause difficulties for analysis. All the linear and additive models we have described so far assume independence of observations. If observations are correlated, then the variances and standard errors of estimated model parameters will be inappropriate. For example, positive correlations between observations will result in standard errors of parameter estimates being too low and increased Type I error probabilities for hypothesis tests and negative correlations will result in the converse effect (Dunlop 1994; see also Chapters 5 and 8 for discussion of effects of non-independence in linear regression and ANOVA models).

We have already described methods for dealing with correlated observations that are based on adjusting estimates and hypothesis tests depending on the degree of correlation. For example, the ANOVA models we used for repeated measures designs in Chapters 10 and 11 are basically standard partly nested models where we adjust the tests of significance in a conservative fashion to correct for inflated Type I errors resulting from the correlated observations. While allowing reliable significance tests for repeated measures designs, we would really like a method that fits predictive models that incorporate a mixture of continuous and categorical predictors in a general modeling framework. We will briefly describe two relatively recently developed modeling techniques that specifically address correlated data. Details of the methods are beyond the scope of this book, and our expertise. Their main application seems to have been in the medical literature, especially various types of clinical trials, and in education, although they clearly have potential application in biology given the prevalence of repeated measures designs in the literature. Our aim is simply to make biologists aware that there are methods based on linear and generalized linear models for dealing with correlated data, and to provide references to the literature that will help biologists wishing to investigate these methods further.

These two modeling approaches are just some of the many methods for dealing with correlated data, especially longitudinal data where we have repeated observations of sampling or experimental units. As well as the adjusted ANOVA models described in Chapters 10 and 11, there are growth models, structural equation models, Markov models, transition models and more formal non-linear time series analyses (see Chapter 5). These techniques, and the two described below, are reviewed by Bijleveld & van der Kamp (1998) and Diggle *et al.* (1994).

13.5.1 Multi-level (random effects) models

We often deal with observations from sampling or experimental units that are arranged hierarchically. In Chapter 9, we described nested ANOVA models for situations where we had categorical predictors (factors) that were nested within other factors. In those analyses, we used a single model that incorporated the top level factor plus a second level factor nested within the top level factor and so on. One assumption was that observations at the lowest level ("replicates") were independent of each other. Longitudinal, repeated measures, data can also be viewed as hierarchical with the repeated measurements being nested within an individual sampling or experimental unit and those units being nested within some other (between unit) factors. The difference from the classical nested design described in Chapter 9 is that the measurements nested within each unit are not independent of each other. Laird & Ware (1982) proposed using multi-level linear models with random effects for analyzing longitudinal data, including repeated measures designs. In fact, these models include both fixed and random effects and are therefore best described as multi-level mixed models (Bijleveld & van der Kamp 1998, Ware & Liang 1996).

Consider a fictitious study on growth rates of animals where we use a repeated measures design with a single between-subjects factor (sex) and time as the within-subjects factor. The subjects or units might be individual animals and the response variable might be body size. The basic idea is that we fit a model in two stages; we will mainly follow the terminology of Bijleveld & van der Kamp (1998). In the first stage, we model the response variable for the observations within each unit, against whichever predictor variables are represented by the different times. For example, the predictors may be simply time (in days, months or years) and/or some polynomial of time, or may represent successively applied treatments.

With usual linear or generalized linear modeling techniques, we estimate the fixed model parameters for the time effects within each unit and the random error terms:

$$y_i = \beta_i T + e_i \qquad (13.31)$$

In model 13.31, y_i is the vector of response variable values for each time for unit i, T is a matrix representing the different times, β_i is the vector of regression coefficients (intercept and slopes, usually only one slope if T contains only a single time variable) and e_i is the vector of random error terms. In the second stage, we treat the regression coefficients as random effects allowing the coefficients (slopes and/or intercepts) of the regressions against time to vary from unit to unit. We are assuming the observed regression coefficients for each unit are a sample from some probability distribution of coefficients. We now model these random coefficients against the predictor variables measured at the between-unit (or subject) level, which will be the between-subjects factor(s):

$$\beta_i = \gamma x_i + u_i \qquad (13.32)$$

In this stage two model, β_i is the vector of regression coefficients from stage one, x_i is the matrix of between-unit predictor variables, such as the between-subjects design structure, γ is the vector of coefficients relating the original regression coefficients to the between-subjects factor and u_i is the vector of random error terms.

These two stages can be combined into a single mixed model:

$$y_i = \gamma T x_i + T u_i + e_i \qquad (13.33)$$

There are two sets of random effects, the error term from the first level model (within units) and those from the second level model (between units). Different formulations of this model for situations where we allow the slopes or the intercepts or both to vary between units are provided by Burton *et al.* (1998), Cnaan *et al.* (1997) and Omar *et al.* (1999). These models can also be extended to three and more levels.

These multi-level models are usually fit using iterative least squares that result in REML estimates of parameters. The random effects are often estimated as variance components. Tests of particular terms in the model are based on comparing models with and without the term of interest with likelihood ratio (deviance) tests. For the fixed parameters, these deviances can be compared to a χ^2 distribution; for random parameters, using the χ^2 distribution will result in overly conservative tests (Burton *et al.* 1998).

Routines for fitting multi-level mixed models are becoming available, both as stand-alone programs (Burton *et al.* 1998) and in more general use statistical software (e.g. S-Plus). These multi-level mixed models are complex, the literature replete with slightly different formulations of what is basically the same set of model for a given number of levels. They are particularly useful if the relationship between the response variable and time for each sampling or experimental unit is of interest because this pattern can be modeled, allowing for different slopes and/or intercepts for each unit, against between-unit (between-subject) predictors (factors).

13.5.2 Generalized estimating equations

Generalized estimating equations (GEEs) were introduced by Liang & Zeger (1986) as an extension of GLMs to model correlated data. To understand the basics of GEEs, we need to examine how we fit GLMs in a little more detail. GLMs are fitted, and therefore parameters of the model are estimated, by solving complex likelihood equations using the iterative Newton–Raphson algorithm. If the response variable has a probability distribution from the exponential family, then the likelihood equations can be viewed as estimating equations (Agresti 1990), equations that are solved to produce ML estimates of model parameters. The normal equations that are solved to produce OLS estimates of linear regression models (Chapter 5) can also be considered as estimating equations. The estimating equations for GLMs are characterized by a covariance (or correlation) matrix that comprises zeros except along the diagonal, i.e. correlations between observations are zero (Dunlop 1994). Liang & Zeger (1986) generalized these estimating equations to allow for covariance matrices where correlations between observations on the same sampling or experimental unit ("subject") are not zero. Solving the GEEs results in estimates of model parameters with variances (and standard errors) that are robust to correlations between

observations (Burton *et al.* 1998). GEEs are not restricted to situations where the response variable has a probability distribution from the exponential family. In fact, quasi-likelihood methods are used where we only need to specify a relationship between the mean and variance for Y and we estimate the variance from the data (Section 13.1).

GEEs fit marginal models, where the relationship between the response variable and predictor variables is modeled separately from the correlation between observations within each experimental or sampling unit (Diggle *et al.* 1994). For example, imagine a data set where we have n sampling units (e.g. permanently marked plots in a forest) and we record a response variable (e.g. growth rate of plants) and a predictor variable (e.g. soil phosphorus concentration) at a number of times. Our main interest is probably the relationship between plant growth and soil P, but we want to estimate the parameters of a regression model between these variables accounting for the correlation between observations through time for the same plot. The GEE method will estimate the regression separately from the within-unit correlation. In a repeated measures design, we might have experimental units within a number of treatment groups but these units are observed repeatedly through time. A GEE approach to the analysis would estimate the correlation structure within units separately and use this when fitting a linear model of the response variable against the treatment variable. The correlation structure is treated as a nuisance parameter used to adjust the variance and standard errors of the parameter estimates (Omar *et al.* 1999).

Burton *et al.* (1998) summarized the steps in fitting a GEE. First, a GLM is fitted to all observations and the residuals calculated. These residuals are used to estimate the correlation between observations within each unit. The GLM is refitted but now incorporating the correlation matrix just estimated into the estimating equations. The residuals from this new fit are used to re-estimate the correlation structure and the steps repeated until the estimates stabilize. Hypothesis tests for individual parameters of the model are usually done with Wald tests (Section 13.2.1), where the estimate of the parameter is divided by its robust standard error estimated from the GEE model.

Besides finding software that will fit GEEs, the main difficulty is that the structure of correlations between observations (i.e. the covariance matrix) needs to be specified *a priori*. Burton *et al.* (1998) and Horton & Lipsitz (1999) suggested a range of working correlation structures.

- Independence, where there are no correlations between observations. Clearly, this is not a sensible choice when we have repeated observations.
- Exchangeable, where the correlations between different observations are identical, no matter how close they are in a time sequence. This is the equivalent of compound symmetry, described for analyses of repeated measures designs with ANOVA models in Chapters 10 and 11.
- Unstructured, where the correlations between pairs of observations can vary and are estimated from the data.
- Fixed, where we fix the correlations rather than estimating them from the data.
- Autoregressive, where correlations between observations closer together in a time sequence are more correlated than observations further apart. This is the situation we anticipate in repeated measures designs and why we usually need to adjust significance tests when fitting partly nested ANOVA models to repeated measures data (Chapters 10 and 11). This choice of correlation structure is used when the residuals from a linear model fit are used to estimate the correlations between observations.

All choices except an unstructured correlation matrix will constrain the pattern of estimated correlations between observations within the same unit. Horton & Lipsitz (1999) recommended an unstructured correlation matrix if the data set is balanced (no missing values) and the number of observations within a unit is small. It turns out that one of the strengths of GEEs is that, although correct specification of the correlation structure makes estimation more efficient, parameter estimates are usually consistent even if the wrong correlation structure is used, i.e. the estimates of model parameters are not very sensitive to the choice of correlation structure. Omar *et al.* (1999)

showed this for real data, where estimates and standard errors of between-subject treatment differences from a repeated measures design with repeated observations within subjects were similar for unstructured, exchangeable and autoregressive correlation structures.

While GEEs may not work as well for small sample sizes (Ware & Liang 1996), all model fitting methods have difficulties in this situation. GEEs can handle missing data effectively as long as the observations are missing completely at random (Chapters 4 and 15), and therefore provide a real alternative to classical ANOVA type models for repeated measures designs that do not handle missing observations very effectively (Chapters 10 and 11). GEEs can be used for any combination of categorical and continuous response variables and predictors and can make use of the GLM framework of specifying a link function, so that the GEEs can resemble logistic and log-linear models.

In a comparison of different methods for analyzing repeated measurement data, Omar *et al.* (1999) argued that GEEs are most applicable when the pattern of observations through time for sampling or experimental units is not the main research question. For example, in a repeated measures design, GEEs might be suitable when the main factor of interest was between subjects and the within-subjects component represents repeated observations through time. If the within-subjects component is a factor of specific interest, GEEs are less useful. GEEs are really best for estimating regression models where we have a mixture of repeated and independent observations or when the focus is on comparisons of groups where the units are independent between groups, even if there are also repeated observation within units.

13.6 | General issues and hints for analysis

13.6.1 General issues

- Generalized linear models (GLMs) provide a broad framework for testing linear models when the distribution of model error terms, and the response variable, is from the exponential family (e.g. normal, binomial, Poisson, etc.).

- Logistic regression is a GLM for modeling binary response variables against categorical or continuous predictors.
- GLMs such as logistic regression are parametric analyses. Choosing the correct probability distribution, and therefore mean and variance relationship, is important. Quasi-likelihood models are more flexible if you are not sure about the probability distribution or you have data that are underdispersed or overdispersed.
- Poisson regression is a GLM for modeling Poisson response variables (e.g. counts) against categorical or continuous predictors.
- Generalized additive models (GAMs) increase the flexibility of GLMs by permitting a range of non-parametric smoothing functions, rather than just linear relationships.
- For modeling correlated data, generalized estimating equations (GEEs) can provide estimates of parameters and robust standard errors that account for the correlations but are most suited to situations where the pattern through time is not of much interest.
- Multi-level mixed models fit linear models through time for each sampling and experimental unit (stage one) and then model the coefficients from those stage one models against between-unit predictor variables (stage two).

13.6.2 Hints for analysis

- Goodness-of-fit tests for logistic models with continuous predictors are difficult to interpret. The Hosmer–Lemeshow $\hat{C}$ statistic is recommended; do not rely on P values from standard χ^2 or G^2 statistics.
- Always compare GLMs with multiple predictors in a hierarchical fashion. If an interaction term is included, also include all lower-order terms. Check for collinearity if you have two or more predictor variables.
- Overdispersion in binomial or Poisson distributions (where the variance is greater than would be expected based on the chosen probability distribution) can affect parameter estimates and significance tests. Adjustments can be made or use quasi-likelihood models.
- When both the response variable and predictor variable(s) are categorical, log-linear models are easier to interpret if distinguishing a response variable is not essential.

Chapter 14

Analyzing frequencies

The previous chapter introduced logistic regression, a generalized linear model based on a binomial distribution and logit link function for modeling binary response variables. If the response has more than two categories, then it is likely to come from a multinomial distribution, of which the binomial is a special case. We can also model the count or frequency in each category as coming from a Poisson distribution when the total count (n) across all categories is not fixed. This chapter focuses on the analysis of one or more categorical variables, particularly when we have counts of observations in each combination of the variables. When there are two or more variables, each with two or more categories, the counts form a contingency table where the observations are cross-classified by the categorical variables. Contingency tables do not specifically distinguish response and predictor variables, although such a distinction can be important in model building and interpretation.

A fundamental statistic for the analysis of categorical data is the chi-square (χ^2) statistic, also called the Pearson χ^2 statistic, which is commonly used to compare observed and theoretical (i.e. expected) frequencies in categories:

$$\sum_{i=1}^{n} \frac{(o-e)^2}{e} \tag{14.1}$$

where o and e denote the observed and expected (or theoretical) frequencies respectively in each category or combination of categories and the summation is over all the categories. The degrees of freedom are a function of the number of categories minus one. Note that χ^2 basically measures the differences between the observed and expected values. It has a value of zero when the observed and expected values are the same. Null hypotheses in categorical analyses often imply that a sample of observations came from a population where the observed frequencies match some expected frequencies. The χ^2 statistic approximately follows a χ^2 distribution if the following assumptions hold.

1. Observations are classified into categories independently. This means that the category combination into which any observation is classified is independent of the category combination into which other observation is classified.

2. No more than 20% of the categories have expected frequencies less than about five (Agresti 1990, 1996). With smaller sample sizes, comparisons of the χ^2 statistic to a χ^2 distribution can produce misleading probabilities.

This chapter is an introduction to categorical data analyses; more detailed treatments can be found in Agresti (1990, 1996), Christensen (1997) and Tabachnick & Fidell (1996) among others. We will first illustrate some simple analyses based on the χ^2 statistic, although generalized linear models, especially log-linear models, are much more flexible for categorical data analysis. We will consider these later in the chapter.

Box 14.1	Worked example: goodness-of-fit tests for a single variable

For one of the few times in this book, we will use fictitious data. Ninety shrubs of a dioecious plant were sampled in a forest and each plant was classified as male or female. The observed counts and the predicted (expected) counts based on a theoretical 50:50 sex ratio were as follows.

	Female	Male	Total
Observed	40	50	90
Expected	45	45	

The H_0 is that this sample of plants came from a population with a sex ratio of 50:50. The expected values were derived from n and the H_0.

$$\chi^2 = 1.11, df = 1, P = 0.292.$$

There is no evidence that the observed sex ratio in the population is different from 50:50.

14.1 | Single variable goodness-of-fit tests

A simple goodness-of-fit test is where we test whether our observations come from a population with a particular distribution of frequencies in categories of a single variable. The general data layout for these tests is usually a single categorical variable with counts or frequencies for each category (Box 14.1). The expected values (if H_0 is true) are calculated from some theoretical or predicted frequency. The H_0 is that the observed data came from a population that has the theoretical or expected frequencies. We test this H_0 by calculating a χ^2 statistic with the equation described above. We then compare the calculated χ^2 to the χ^2 distribution with the degrees of freedom being the number of categories minus one. If the probability of obtaining the calculated χ^2, or one larger, when H_0 is true, is less than our chosen significance level, then H_0 should be rejected. This is the standard logic of testing a statistical null hypothesis (Chapter 3).

An alternative goodness-of-fit test for a single variable is the Kolmogorov–Smirnov (K–S) test, which compares observed and expected cumulative frequencies (Hays 1994). The test statistic (D) is just the largest difference between the observed and expected cumulative frequencies across all possible values of the categorical variable. This test is preferred to the χ^2 when there are a large number of categories and the categories can be ordered in some way. In particular, the K–S test is suited for comparing two frequency distributions, where one distribution acts as the observed and the other the expected. As with most biostatistical analyses, the K–S test is clearly described, with formulae, in Sokal & Rohlf (1995) and is available in most statistical software.

14.2 | Contingency tables

The most common form of categorical data analysis in the biological sciences is the analysis of contingency tables. These tables involve the cross-classification of sampling or experimental units by two or more variables (Table 14.1), with counts or frequencies of units in each combination of the variables, termed a cell, analogous to factorial ANOVA designs.

14.2.1 Two way tables
Tables where sampling or experimental units are cross-classified by two variables are termed two way tables. Generally, contingency tables are analyzed so that neither variable is considered as a

Table 14.1 General data layout for a two by two contingency table

Variable 2→ Variable 1↓	1	2	Marginal totals variable 1
1	n_{11} π_{11}	n_{12} π_{12}	n_{1j} π_{1j}
2	n_{21} π_{21}	n_{22} π_{22}	n_{2j} π_{2j}
Marginal totals variable 2	n_{i1} π_{i1}	n_{i2} π_{i2}	Grand total n

Note:
Variable 1 has two levels ($I = 2$), variable 2 has two levels ($J = 2$) with observed counts or frequencies (n_{ij}) for each combination (cell) of the two variables. The probability that an observation falls in any cell is π_{ij}; marginal probabilities are π_{i+} and π_{+j}.

predictor or a response variable. For example, French & Westoby (1996) cross-classified plant species following fire by two variables: whether they regenerated by seed only or vegetatively and whether they were ant or vertebrate dispersed. These two variables could not be distinguished as response or predictor since regeneration mechanisms could just as easily "affect" dispersal mode as vice versa. This was a two by two table (Table 14.2(a)) and its analysis is in Box 14.2.

In other situations, one variable can be envisaged as a response variable and the other as a predictor. For example, Roberts (1993) sampled quadrats on a floodplain and classified them by two variables: presence/absence of dead coolibah trees (*Eucalyptus coolibah*) and position along transect (top = dunes, bottom = lakeshore, middle = intermediate). In this example, position along the transect might be considered a predictor variable and with or without dead coolibah trees as a response variable. We might expect coolibah tree mortality to be affected by position but the converse is biologically unlikely. This was a two by three table (Table 14.2(b)) and its analysis is in Box 14.3. Another example is from Clinton & Le Boeuf (1994), who looked at the association between survivorship of male northern elephant seals

Table 14.2 Observed frequencies for two way contingency tables from (a) French & Westoby's (1996) study where plant species were cross-classified by dispersal mode and regeneration mechanism and (b) Roberts's (1993) cross-classification of quadrats on a floodplain by presence/absence of dead coolibah trees and position along transect

(a)

Regeneration	Dispersal mechanism		Total
	Ant	Vertebrate	
Seed only	25	6	31
Vegetative	36	21	57
Total	61	27	88

(b)

Position along transect	Dead coolibah trees		Total
	With	Without	
Bottom	15	13	28
Middle	4	8	12
Top	0	17	17
Total	19	38	57

(*Mirounga gustirostris*) and mating success (the number of females inseminated). This was a two by two contingency table with died/survived as the response variable, zero or greater than zero females inseminated as the predictor variable and the number of male seals were the frequencies in each category.

In practice, the analysis of contingency tables is not really changed by whether we can distinguish response and predictor variables. If the response variable is binary, then we can use logistic (i.e. logit) models with categorical predictors as described in Chapter 13. However, the distinction between response and predictor variables can be important for the interpretation of log-linear models for analyzing complex contingency tables (Section 14.2.2).

Table structure
The general data layout for a two way table (cross-classification of two variables) is illustrated in

Box 14.2	Worked example of analysis of independence in two way table: regeneration and seed dispersal mechanisms of plants

French & Westoby (1996) cross-classified plant species following fire by two variables: whether they regenerated by seed only or vegetatively and whether they were ant or vertebrate dispersed. The H_0 is that the dispersal mechanism is independent of mode of regeneration. The χ^2 statistic for testing this H_0 is 2.89 with one df and $P = 0.089$. We have no evidence to reject the H_0 of independence. The standardized residuals showed no strong patterns, although fewer species that regenerated only from seed were dispersed by vertebrates than expected by chance and the converse was true for seeds that regenerated vegetatively.

Standardized residuals are tabulated below.

	Dispersal mechanism	
Regeneration	Ant	Vertebrate
Seed only	0.757	−1.139
Vegetative	−0.559	0.840

The odds of being ant dispersed compared to being vertebrate dispersed for plants that regenerate by seed are 4.17. For plants that regenerate vegetatively, the odds are 1.71.

The sample odds ratio ($\hat{\theta}$) is:

$$\frac{n_{11}n_{22}}{n_{12}n_{21}} = \frac{25 \times 21}{36 \times 6} = 2.43$$

So the odds of being dispersed by ants is 2.43 times greater for plant species that regenerate by seed compared to those that regenerate vegetatively. We can convert $\hat{\theta}$ to logs, use Equation 14.10 to calculate the standard error of the log ($\hat{\theta}$), Equation 14.11 to calculate the 95% confidence interval for the log (θ) and back-transform this for a confidence interval for the θ.

Odds ratio	Log (odds ratio)	ASE log (odds ratio)	95% CI log (odds ratio)	95% CI (odds ratio)
2.43	0.89	0.53	± 1.04	0.86 to 6.89

The wide confidence interval includes one, indicating that odds of being dispersed by ants for plant species that regenerate by seed are not statistically different than for plant species that regenerate vegetatively.

Table 14.1. We will follow Agresti (1996) and use X ($i = 1$ to I categories) and Y ($j = 1$ to J categories) as labels for the two variables. For a two by two table, both I and J equal two. When one of the variables is clearly a response variable, it will be designated Y; otherwise, no particular significance should be ascribed to which variable is X and which is Y. The observed frequency in each cell is n_{ij} and the probability that an observation occurs in any cell is π_{ij}. We also have marginal totals (e.g. the total in row one is n_{1j}) and marginal probabilities (e.g. the probability that an observation occurs in row one is $\pi_{1j} = \pi_{11} + \pi_{12}$); these marginal probabilities are the probabilities that an observation occurs in a particular row or column.

Sokal & Rohlf (1995) described three different

Box 14.3 | Worked example of analysis of independence in two way table: coolibah trees on a floodplain

Roberts (1993) sampled quadrats on a floodplain and classified them by two variables: presence/absence of dead coolibah trees (*Eucalyptus coolibah*) and position along transect (top = dunes, bottom = lakeshore, middle = intermediate). The H_0 is that the presence/absence of dead coolibah trees is independent of position on the floodplain. The χ^2 statistic for the test of this H_0 is 13.66 with two df and $P = 0.001$. Therefore, we reject the H_0 of independence.

Standardized residuals are tabulated below.

	Dead coolibah trees	
Floodplain position	With	Without
Bottom	1.855	−1.312
Middle	0.000	0.000
Top	−2.380	1.683

It is clear from the residuals that there were more quadrats with dead trees at the bottom of the dunes than expected and fewer quadrats with dead trees at the top of the dunes than expected.

Odds of having dead trees versus not are as follows.

Position	Odds
Bottom of floodplain	1.15
Middle of floodplain	0.50
Top of floodplain	0.00

The odds of having dead coolibah trees were greater than not having them for quadrats at the bottom of the floodplain, but the odds of having dead coolibah trees were less than not having them for quadrats at the middle of the floodplain. Because there were no quadrats with dead coolibah trees at the top of the floodplain, odds cannot be calculated for this position.

Odds ratios were calculated using the modified formula that adds 0.5 to each cell to correct for zero observed frequencies.

	Odds ratio	Log (odds ratio)	ASE	95% CI (odds ratio)
Bottom versus middle	2.17	0.77	0.69	0.59 to 8.18
Bottom versus top	40.19	3.69	1.48	2.20 to 728.36
Middle versus top	18.53	2.92	1.55	0.89 to 386.84

The 95% CI for the odds ratios of having dead coolibah trees included one the comparison of the bottom of the floodplain versus the middle and the middle versus the top. The strongest pattern is that the odds of having dead coolibah trees were greater at the bottom of the floodplain compared with the top.

models for contingency tables, based on whether the investigator predetermines the marginal totals (i.e. row and column totals).

- Model I is when none of the marginal totals are fixed, the most common situation when a number of sampling or experimental units are sampled from a population of units and each unit is classified by one or more categorical variables. An underlying Poisson distribution for the counts in each cell is assumed. The three examples described above are Model I.
- Model II is when one set of marginal totals is fixed. For example, imagine an experiment where ten rats are allocated to three different drug treatments and the survivorship of each rat in recorded at the end of the experiment. Each rat is cross-classified by treatment (fixed marginal totals of ten) and lived/died (marginal totals not fixed). In Model II tables, the variable without fixed marginal totals is usually considered a response variable (Agresti 1996).
- Model III is when both sets of marginal totals are fixed, a very uncommon situation in biology. Fisher (1935) described such a model for an experiment to test whether someone could actually tell by tasting whether or not milk had been added first to a cup of tea (see also Agresti 1990, 1996).

Null hypothesis

The H_0 is one of independence, that the sampling or experimental units come from a population of units in which the two variables (rows and columns) are independent of each other in terms of the cell frequencies. This is often expressed as no association, or interaction, between the two variables. For example, French & Westoby (1996) tested whether the mechanism of seed regeneration (seed or vegetative) was independent of dispersal mechanism (ant or vertebrate) for a number of plant species (Box 14.2, Table 14.2). Usually, the H_0 is expressed in terms of a population from which the sampling or experimental units were obtained, a population that is difficult to envisage for the French & Westoby (1996) example. Roberts (1993) wished to test whether her quadrats came from a population of quadrats on the floodplain where presence/absence of dead coolibahs was independent of position along

transect (Box 14.3, Table 14.2). Clinton & Le Boeuf (1994) tested whether survivorship of male elephant seals (died or survived) was independent of whether the males had inseminated zero or more than zero females.

The H_0 can also be expressed as:

$$\pi_{ij} = \pi_{i+} \cap \pi_{+j} \tag{14.2}$$

i.e. the probability of an observation occurring in a cell equals the probability of it occurring in that row *and* that column.

We can test this H_0 using a χ^2 test by calculating the expected frequencies in each cell based on the H_0 being true and there being no association between the two variables. An expected cell frequency is simply the product of the probability of an observation occurring in that cell and the total sample size:

$$f_{ij} = n\pi_{ij} \tag{14.3}$$

We can elaborate on this as follows. If rows and columns are independent (i.e. H_0 is true), then the probability of an observation occurring in a specific cell (π_{ij}) is simply the probability of an observation occurring in the specific row (π_{i+}, estimated by row total divided by grand total) multiplied by the probability of it occurring in the specific column (π_{+j}, estimated by column total divided by grand total). Therefore, a general formula for calculating the expected frequency in each cell assuming independence of the two variables (i.e. under H_0) is:

[(row total)(column total) / grand total] (14.4)

We then calculate χ^2 based on Equation 14.1 where n_{ij} are observed frequencies and f_{ij} are expected frequencies under the H_0:

$$\chi^2 = \sum_{i=1}^{I} \sum_{j=1}^{J} \frac{(n_{ij} - f_{ij})^2}{f_{ij}} \tag{14.5}$$

We compare the χ^2 in 14.5 to a χ^2 distribution with $(I-1)(J-1)$ df. If the probability of obtaining the calculated χ^2 or one larger when H_0 is true is less than our chosen significance level, then H_0 should be rejected. For the French & Westoby (1996) example, we have no evidence to reject the H_0 that dispersal mode and regeneration mode are independent of each other (Box 14.2). For the Roberts (1993) example, we would reject the H_0

Box 14.4 | Worked example of log-linear models for two way table: coolibah trees on a floodplain

We will re-analyze the contingency table from Roberts (1993) using log-linear models to test the H_0 that quadrats came from a population of quadrats where presence/absence of dead coolibahs was independent of position along transect.

Reduced model:

Log f_{ij} = constant + $\lambda^{position}$ + $\lambda^{presence/absence}$

Log-likelihood for reduced model: -19.735, df = 2.

Full (and saturated) model:

Log f_{ij} = constant + $\lambda^{position}$ + $\lambda^{presence/absence}$ + $\lambda^{position \times presence/absence}$

Log-likelihood for full (and saturated) model: -10.429, df = 3.

$$G^2 = -2(\text{log-likelihood model} - \text{log-likelihood saturated model})$$
$$= -2 \times (-19.735 - (-10.429))$$
$$= 18.61, df = 1, P < 0.001.$$

Therefore we reject H_0.

---

that presence/absence of dead coolibah trees is independent of position on floodplain (Box 14.3).

Odds and odds ratios

Odds and odds ratios are important summary measures of association or lack of independence in contingency tables, just as they are for logistic regression models (Chapter 13). They can only be calculated for two by two tables but can also be used in larger tables by subdividing these tables into sets of two by two tables. We calculate the odds of one of the two possible categories (outcomes) of one variable for each level (j) of the other variable:

$$\frac{\pi_j}{1 - \pi_j} \tag{14.6}$$

where π_j is the probability of one of the two outcomes and one minus π_j is the probability of the other outcome.

For the French & Westoby (1996) example, the odds of being ant dispersed compared to being vertebrate dispersed for plants that regenerate by seed are 4.17 and for plants that regenerate vegetatively, the odds are 1.71 (Box 14.2). In the Roberts (1993) example, presence/absence of dead coolibah trees is the response variable and position on the floodplain is the predictor variable. The

estimated odds of having versus not having a dead coolibah for the bottom of the floodplain is 1.15; this indicates that having dead coolibah trees is more likely than not having them (Box 14.3 and Box 14.4). We can calculate odds of a quadrat having dead coolibah trees for the other two floodplain positions as well. For the middle of the floodplain, the odds are 0.50 and for the top of the floodplain, the odds are zero.

The odds ratio (θ) is simply the ratio of the odds of one outcome for one level of the second variable to the odds of the same outcome for another level of the second variable. The odds ratio is a population parameter (Agresti 1996):

$$\theta = \frac{\pi_1/(1 - \pi_1)}{\pi_2/(1 - \pi_2)} \tag{14.7}$$

The ML estimate of this odds ratio is the sample odds ratio:

$$\hat{\theta} = \frac{n_{11}n_{22}}{n_{12}n_{21}} \tag{14.8}$$

In Equation 14.8, each n_{ij} is the observed frequency in the cell based on the ith row and jth column, e.g. n_{12} is the observed frequency in the cell being the first row and first column.

Note that the odds ratio equals zero if any of the observed counts in the two by two subset table also equal zero. Agresti (1996) suggested a simple correction by adding 0.5 to each cell:

$$\hat{\theta} = \frac{(n_{11} + 0.5)(n_{22} + 0.5)}{(n_{12} + 0.5)(n_{21} + 0.5)} \quad (14.9)$$

You can see that odds ratios are much easier to interpret for two by two tables because there is only one odds ratio. For larger tables, there will be different odds ratios for different two by two subsets. These odds ratios are not independent (Agresti 1990) and, because of this redundancy, only $(I-1)(J-1)$ odds ratios are needed to summarize the lack of independence in an I by J table.

Odds ratios are important for interpreting lack of independence in contingency tables (Agresti 1996). If the probability of one outcome (e.g. having dead coolibah trees) is the same for two floodplain positions, i.e. the presence of dead coolibah trees is independent of position, then the odds ratio will be one. If the odds ratio is greater than one, as for the bottom vs middle floodplain positions, then the odds of having dead coolibah trees is greater for one level of the other variable (bottom) than the other (middle). The converse is true if the odds ratio is less than one.

The sampling distribution of odds ratios is usually very skewed, especially for small sample sizes (Agresti 1990, 1996). To calculate a standard error and confidence interval for an odds ratio, we need to transform it to logs, which results in its sampling distribution being approximately normal. Note that an odds ratio of one (H_0 true) is a log odds ratio of zero. The asymptotic standard error for the odds ratio is:

$$\text{ASE}(\log \hat{\theta}) = \sqrt{\frac{1}{n_{11}} + \frac{1}{n_{12}} + \frac{1}{n_{21}} + \frac{1}{n_{22}}} \quad (14.10)$$

Confidence intervals for the odds ratio are best calculated on the log odds ratio and then back-transformed. The 95% CI is:

$$\pm z_{0.95} \text{ ASE}(\log \text{ odds ratio}) \quad (14.11)$$

where z is the critical value from a standard normal distribution. The antilog of these confidence limits will provide the CI for the odds ratio.

In the French & Westoby (1997) example, there is only one odds ratio because it is a two by two table. The estimated ratio is 2.43, so the odds of being dispersed by ants are 2.43 times greater for

plant species that regenerate by seed than for those that regenerate vegetatively. However, the confidence interval for the odds ratio is wide (Box 14.2), which is not surprising since the test of independence was not significant. Note that the 95% CI includes one, indicating no evidence (at $\alpha = 0.05$) against the H_0 of independence.

For the Roberts (1993) two by three table, there can be three odds ratios for the presence of dead coolibah trees (bottom vs mid, bottom vs top, mid vs top). The odds of having dead coolibah trees were greater than one for all three comparisons (bottom versus middle, bottom versus top, middle versus top) but only for bottom versus top did the 95% CI for the odds ratio not include one (Box 14.3). So the major contribution to the lack of independence in Robert's (1993) data was the contrast between the bottom of the floodplain and the top of the floodplain.

Residuals

Another way of interpreting lack of independence in contingency tables is examining the pattern of the residuals, the difference between the observed and expected values ($n_{ij} - f_{ij}$). There will be a residual for each cell of the table and this is the same definition of a residual we used for linear models (e.g. Chapter 5). Absolute residuals are difficult to compare when the frequencies vary. For example, a ($n_{ij} - f_{ij}$) difference of five is more "important" when the frequencies are around ten than when the frequencies are around 100. Therefore, we usually standardize each residual by dividing by $\sqrt{f_{ij}}$:

$$\frac{(n_{ij} - f_{ij})}{\sqrt{f_{ij}}} \quad (14.12)$$

These are also called Pearson residuals (Agresti 1996) and are directly comparable irrespective of the absolute frequencies.

From the Roberts (1993) data, the standardized residuals showed that there were more quadrats with dead trees at the bottom of the dunes than expected and fewer quadrats with dead trees at the top of the dunes than expected (Box 14.3).

We can also calculate adjusted residuals as:

$$\frac{(n_{ij} - f_{ij})}{\sqrt{f_{ij}(1 - p_{i+})(1 - p_{+j})}} \quad (14.13)$$

where p_{i+} is the proportion of the total row observations in that cell and p_{+j} is the proportion of the total column observations in that cell. Large residuals indicate large deviations from independence and the sign (+ or −) indicates more or less observed than expected under the H_0.

Small sample sizes

The χ^2 statistic, and the log-linear G^2 statistic described in Section 14.3, are based on frequencies in categories and can only be compared validly to the continuous χ^2 distribution if the sample size is big enough. We mentioned at the start of this chapter that we assume that no more than 20% of the categories have expected frequencies less than about five. What if sample sizes are smaller, i.e. we have a sparse contingency table, one with many low or zero frequencies?

Yate's correction for continuity was developed to improve the accuracy of the χ^2 test for two by two tables with small frequencies but is of debatable value and is now not regarded as necessary (Agresti 1990, Manly 1992) because of the availability of "exact" tests.

Fisher's Exact test was designed for two by two tables with fixed marginal totals. It does not use the χ^2 distribution to test the H_0 of independence but instead answers the question "Given our fixed marginal totals, what is the probability of obtaining the observed cell frequencies and all cell frequencies that are further away from the expected?". The calculations are tedious for anything but the smallest sample sizes, but it is available in most statistical software. Although Fisher's Exact test strictly should be used in situations where we have fixed marginal totals, it is commonly used more generally as a solution for small sample sizes even when both marginal totals are not fixed (e.g. Clinton & Le Beouf 1994). There are other exact tests for contingency tables more complex than two by two. These tests use resampling procedures (randomization tests – see Chapter 3) to generate an exact distribution for the χ^2 statistic rather than assuming it follows a χ^2 distribution but they require special software.

Another solution to small observed frequencies is to collapse or combine some categories. For example, when the categories are evenly spaced size classes, there might be few individuals in some of the larger classes. They can be combined into a single category that will have adequate frequencies for analysis.

14.2.2 Three way tables

An obvious extension of two way contingency tables is the addition of a third variable in the cross-classification. Again following Agresti's (1996) terminology, the three variables are labeled X (i equals 1 to I categories), Y (j equals 1 to J categories), and Z (k equals 1 to K categories) and we will use Y in cases where there is clearly one response variable. Remember that analyses of contingency tables do not usually distinguish response and predictor variables, unless the analysis uses a logit (logistic) model. However, the interpretation of the generalized linear models (log-linear models) we commonly use for complex contingency tables can depend on whether we clearly distinguish a response variable.

Two examples from the recent literature will illustrate three way contingency tables in a biological context. Sinclair & Arcese (1995) cross-classified wildebeest carcasses from the Serengeti by three variables: sex (X with I equals two: male, female), cause of death (Y with J equals two: predation, non-predation) and bone marrow type (Z with K equals three: solid white fatty, opaque gelatinous, translucent gelatinous, with the first indicating a healthy animal that is not undernourished) – Table 14.3(a). In this example, it is not clear that any of the variables could be classified as a "response" variable. We have a random sample of carcasses cross-classified by three variables, all of which can be considered responses. The analysis of these data is presented in Box 14.5.

Taulman et al. (1998) examined the demography of southern flying squirrels in response to experimental logging in southern Arkansas. They had a response variable: age of squirrel (Y with J equals two: adult, young). The other two variables were treatment from which squirrels were caught (X with I equals two: control, logged) and year (Z with K equals three: 1994, 1995, 1996) – see Table 14.3(b). They had pre-treatment data from 1993 but we will only consider the post-treatment data. A logit model (Section 13.2) could have been fitted to these data, with age as the response variable and treatment and year as the two categorical

Table 14.3 | Observed frequencies for three way contingency tables from (a) Sinclair & Arcese's (1995) study on wildebeest carcasses cross-classified by cause of death, sex and marrow type and (b) Taulman *et al.*'s (1998) study on squirrels in logged and control stands over three years

(a)

Cause of death	Sex	Marrow type			Totals
		SWF	OG	TG	
Predation	Female	26	32	8	66
Predation	Male	14	43	10	67
Non-predation	Female	6	26	16	48
Non-predation	Male	7	12	26	45
Totals		53	113	60	226

(b)

Treatment	Year	Age		Totals
		Adult	Juvenile	
Control	1994	46	10	56
Harvest	1994	30	8	38
Control	1995	44	31	75
Harvest	1995	53	54	107
Control	1996	8	0	8
Harvest	1996	79	14	93
Totals		260	117	377

predictors. Note that there may be correlations between successive years in this study, although we will ignore these for the purposes of analysis. The analysis of these data is presented in Box 14.6.

In contrast to two way tables, there is more than one sort of (in)dependence between variables in three way tables. We can examine complete independence between all three variables (no interactions), various forms of conditional and marginal independence that we will describe in the next section, and also complete dependence where there is a three way interaction. While we can calculate expected cell frequencies and χ^2 statistics to test null hypotheses about these various forms of independence, it is more efficient to do so with log-linear models (Section 14.3.2).

Conditional independence and odds ratios

A three way table can be best interpreted by considering it as a set of partial tables, each of which is a two way table for each level of the third variable. For the wildebeest example, we can construct a partial table between sex and cause of death for each level of marrow type, i.e. partial table between X and Y for each level Z (Box 14.5). We could, of course, construct partial tables between Y and Z for each level of X and between X and Z for each level of Y. Conditional independence is where two variables are independent of each other given the level of (controlling for) the third variable, i.e. the two variables in each partial table are independent. For example, the proportions of wildebeest carcasses that suffered predation (or didn't) are independent of sex, for all marrow types. When two variables are not conditionally independent, we say they have a partial association, i.e. they are not independent for all levels of the third variable.

Odds ratios are important in the interpretation of conditional independence in three way

Box 14.5 Worked example of log-linear model for three way table: death in wildebeest (sex, predation and bone marrow type)

Sinclair & Arcese (1995) cross-classified 226 wildebeest carcasses from the Serengeti by three variables: sex (male, female), cause of death (predation, non-predation) and bone marrow type (solid white fatty, opaque gelatinous, translucent gelatinous, with the first indicating a healthy animal which is not undernourished).

We have fitted log-linear models with different combinations of terms. The fit of each model shown below is based on comparing observed and fitted cell frequencies and, equivalently, comparing the fit of each model to that of the saturated model with zero degrees of freedom. For hypothesis testing, we would fit these models hierarchically, starting with the most complex.

	Model	G^2	df	P	AIC
1	death + sex + marrow	42.76	7	<0.001	28.76
2	death $\times$ sex	42.68	6	<0.001	30.68
3	death $\times$ marrow	13.24	5	0.021	3.34
4	sex $\times$ marrow	37.98	5	<0.001	27.98
5	death $\times$ sex + death $\times$ marrow	13.16	4	0.011	5.16
6	death $\times$ sex + sex $\times$ marrow	37.89	4	<0.001	29.89
7	death $\times$ marrow + sex $\times$ marrow	8.46	3	0.037	2.46
8	death $\times$ sex + death $\times$ marrow + sex $\times$ marrow	7.19	2	0.027	3.19
9	Saturated (full) model	0	0		

The AIC chose model 7 as best fit, whereas G^2 chose model 8. The comparison of the fit of model 8 and the saturated model 9 is a test of the H_0 that there is no three way interaction. The G^2 deviance statistic results in rejection of this H_0. Standardized residuals under no three way interaction showed that more male wildebeest with SWF marrow and fewer with OG marrow were not killed by predators than expected.

		Marrow type		
Cause of death	Sex	SWF	OG	TG
Predation	Female	0.541	−0.730	0.719
Predation	Male	−0.641	0.709	−0.522
Non-predation	Female	−0.891	0.948	−0.425
Non-predation	Male	1.248	−1.088	0.364

We will also illustrate the tests for conditional independence and complete independence, although the presence of a three way interaction would usually preclude tests of two way interactions and the presence of both complete and conditional dependence would preclude testing complete independence. The relevant hierarchical comparisons of models are shown below.

Term	Models compared	G^2	df	P
Three way interaction				
death × sex × marrow	8 vs 9	7.19	2	0.027
Conditional independence				
death × sex	7 vs 8	1.28	1	0.259
death × marrow	6 vs 8	30.71	2	<0.001
sex × marrow	5 vs 8	5.97	2	0.051
Complete independence	1 vs 8	35.57	5	<0.001

This demonstrates that we would reject the H_0 of conditional independence of cause of death and marrow type.

The odds ratios for wildebeest killed by predation for each pair of marrow types separately for males and females are shown below.

	Odds ratio	95% CI
Male		
OG versus TG	0.107	0.041−0.283
SWF versus TG	0.192	0.060−0.616
SWF versus OG	0.558	0.184−1.693
Female		
OG versus TG	0.406	0.150−1.097
SWF versus TG	0.115	0.034−0.395
SWF versus OG	3.521	1.261−9.836

The conditional dependence is clearly shown by the complex pattern of odds ratios that is different for males and females. The odds of being killed by predation were less for male wildebeest with either OG or SWF marrow than TG marrow. The odds of males being killed by predators were the same for those with SWF marrow versus OG marrow. For females, the odds of being killed by predators were greater for those with SWF marrow than OG marrow but less for those with SWF marrow than TG. The odds of females being killed by predators were the same for those with OG marrow and TG marrow.

tables but are more difficult to calculate because we have three variables and odds ratios can only be calculated for two by two tables. Odds ratios can be derived for larger tables by breaking the table into two by two subsets so when the table dimensions are two by two by K, we can calculate conditional odds ratios for each set of partial tables (see Table 14.4).

One conditional odds ratio in the wildebeest study is the ratio of the odds that a male wildebeest carcass suffered predation to the odds that a female wildebeest carcass suffered predation, for one marrow type, i.e. if a carcass had marrow type SWG, are the odds of being eaten the same for males and females? Other odds ratios are the ratios of the odds that a male wildebeest carcass suffered predation to the odds that a female wildebeest carcass suffered predation for the other two marrow types. Conditional independence between Y and Z means that all the odds ratios between Y and Z equal one.

If conditional independence between two variables does not hold, then two possible patterns may occur. First, the odds ratios for two variables may all be different from one but still may be equal for all levels of the other variable, i.e. conditional dependence (association) exists between two variables but is the same for all levels of the third variable. For example, the ratio of the odds that a male wildebeest carcass suffered predation

Box 14.6 Worked example of log-linear model for three way table – demography of squirrels in response to disturbance: effects of logging and year on age

Taulman et al. (1998) examined the age of squirrels in relation to the treatment stand from which squirrels were caught (control, logged) and year (1994, 1995, 1996) – see Table 14.3(b). We considered age of squirrel as a response variable (treatment and year might affect the relative numbers of adult and young squirrels but not vice versa) so not all models were fitted. The interaction between treatment and year was never omitted because the investigator set these variables, so their conditional independence makes little sense.

	Model	G^2	df	P	AIC
1	treatment $\times$ year + age $\times$ year	4.13	3	0.248	0.00
2	treatment $\times$ age + treatment $\times$ year	46.27	4	<0.001	38.27
3	treatment $\times$ age + treatment $\times$ year + age $\times$ year	1.88	2	0.390	0.00
4	Saturated (full) model	0.00	0		

Either models 1 or 3 could have been chosen as best fit, with the G^2 suggesting model 3. Note that exclusion of both the three way interaction and the two way interaction between age and year results in a very poor fit. Since we have already shown that the three way interaction is not significant (model 3), this suggests that there is conditional dependence between age and year.

The relevant hierarchical comparisons of models for the tests for the three way interaction and the tests for conditional independence, with the interaction between treatment and caged years always in the models, are shown below.

Term	Models compared	G^2	df	P
Three way interaction				
treatment $\times$ age $\times$ year	3 vs 4	1.88	2	0.390
Conditional independence				
age $\times$ year	2 vs 3	44.39	2	<0.001
treatment $\times$ age	1 vs 3	2.24	1	0.134

There was no evidence to reject the hypothesis of conditional independence between age and treatment, i.e. squirrel age and treatment were independent for each year. In contrast, squirrel age and year were not independent, for control or logged treatments.

to the odds that a female wildebeest carcass suffered predation may be the same for each marrow type, even if the odds are greater for males than females consistently. This pattern is termed a homogeneous association between two variables. A homogeneous association implies no three variable interaction. Conditional independence is a special case of a homogeneous association.

Second, the pattern of dependence (association) between two variables may differ between levels of the third variable and, therefore, the odds ratios for two variables vary between the levels of the other variable. For example, the ratio of the odds that a male wildebeest carcass suffered predation to the odds that a female wildebeest carcass suffered predation are different for

Table 14.4 Partial table for $I = 2$ by $J = 2$ by K contingency table for $K = 1$ with observed frequencies

	I	$J = 1$	$J = 2$
$K = 1$	1	n_{11K}	n_{21K}
$K = 1$	2	n_{12K}	n_{22K}

the different marrow types. This pattern indicates an interaction between all three variables and that the two variable associations will not have a simple interpretation.

The odds ratio for an I equals two by J equals two by K table, for a given level k of K, can be estimated as:

$$\hat{\theta}_{XY(k)} = \frac{n_{11k} n_{22k}}{n_{12k} n_{21k}} \qquad (14.14)$$

The odds ratios for cause of death in relation to marrow type for male and female wildebeest are presented in Box 14.5. The only odds ratio that is clearly greater than one is for female wildebeest, where the odds of a SWF marrow type animal being killed by a predator are three and half times the odds of an OG marrow type animal being killed by a predator. This indicates conditional dependence between cause of death and marrow type, where the dependence is conditional on sex.

A test for conditional independence in two by two by K tables is the Cochran–Mantel–Haenszel (C–M–H) test (Sokal & Rohlf 1995), which basically tests the null hypothesis that the conditional odds ratios between X and Y equal one for all levels of Z. It is particularly appropriate when there is no three variable (XYZ) interaction (Agresti 1996). The C–M–H statistic is converted to a χ^2 and compared to a χ^2 distribution; it is available in most statistical software. It can also be generalized for I by J by K tables where I and J are greater than two but the formulae are complex (Agresti 1990). For the squirrel example, C–M–H statistic equals 1.18 with P equals 0.530, so the ratio of the odds of a squirrel being an adult on control stands and the odds of a squirrel being an adult on logged stands were not different from one for all three years. The C–M–H test also allows a form of meta-analysis to combine the results from a number of independent two by two tables.

Marginal independence and odds ratios

Marginal tables are two way tables completely ignoring the third variable, e.g. the frequencies for X by Y pooling levels of Z. Marginal independence is independence between the two variables in the marginal table, pooling the levels of the third variable. For the squirrel example, one marginal table would be age crossed with treatment, pooling year (Box 14.6). From this marginal table, we would assess marginal independence as the independence of age and treatment combining years. We can also calculate marginal odds ratios from the marginal table. The odds of a squirrel being an adult are almost identical ($\hat{\theta} = 0.996$) for control versus treatment stands, ignoring year.

Complete independence

The effects of the individual variables represent complete independence and no two or three way associations. For our two worked examples, the proportions of adult squirrels are independent of treatment and year and cause of death, sex and marrow type are completely independent of each other.

14.3 | Log-linear models

The best method for analyzing contingency tables is with log-linear models. Log-linear models treat the cell frequencies as counts distributed as a Poisson random variable. Log-linear models are examples of generalized linear models (GLMs; see Chapter 13); the expected cell frequencies are modeled against the variables using the log link and a Poisson error term (Agresti 1996). As with other GLMs, we fit log-linear models and estimate their parameters using maximum likelihood techniques. ML fits for most complex log-linear models do not have simple solutions so iterative methods like the Newton–Raphson algorithm (Chapter 13) are required. The fit of the models is measured by the log-likelihood.

Log-linear models do not distinguish response and predictor variables; all the variables are considered equally as response variables. However, there is a relationship between log-linear models and logit models (including logistic regression) discussed in Chapter 13. Logit models distinguish a response variable (with two categories in a logistic regression) and model it against predictors that can be continuous or categorical. A logit model with categorical predictors can also be analyzed as a log-linear model (Agresti 1996).

14.3.1 Two way tables

Two way tables were described in Section 14.2.1 and will be illustrated here with the example from Roberts (1993).

Full and reduced models

For a two way table (*I* by *J*), we can fit two log-linear models. The first is a saturated (full) model:

$$\log f_{ij} = \text{constant} + \lambda_i^X + \lambda_j^Y + \lambda_{ij}^{XY} \qquad (14.15)$$

For the data from Roberts (1993), the saturated (full) model is:

$$\log f_{ij} = \text{constant} + \lambda_i^{\text{coolibah}} + \lambda_j^{\text{position}} + \lambda_{ij}^{\text{coolibah*position}} \qquad (14.16)$$

In models 14.15 and 14.16:

f_{ij} is the expected frequency in cell *ij*, i.e. the expected number of quadrats in each combination of coolibah trees (alive, dead) and floodplain position (top, mid, low),

constant is the mean of the logs of all the expected frequencies,

λ_i^X is the effect of category *i* of variable *X*, i.e. the effect of coolibah trees being either alive or dead on the log expected frequency of quadrats in each cell,

λ_j^Y is the effect of category *j* of variable *Y*, i.e. the effect of floodplain position being top, mid or bottom on the log expected frequency of quadrats in each cell,

λ_{ij}^{XY} is the effect of any interaction between *X* and *Y*, i.e. an interactive effect of coolibah tree category and floodplain position on the log expected frequency of quadrats in each cell. The interaction measures deviations from independence of the two variables.

Models 14.15 and 14.16 fit the observed frequencies perfectly, hence the term saturated. Note that "effect" does not imply any causality, just the

influence of a variable or interaction between variables on the log of the expected number of observations in a cell.

The second log-linear model represents independence of the two variables (*X* and *Y*) and is a reduced model:

$$\log f_{ij} = \text{constant} + \lambda_i^X + \lambda_j^Y \qquad (14.17)$$

Again from Roberts (1993):

$$\log f_{ij} = \text{constant} + \lambda_i^{\text{coolibah}} + \lambda_j^{\text{position}} \qquad (14.18)$$

The interpretation of models 14.17 and 14.18 is that the log of the expected frequency in any cell is a function of the mean of the log of all the expected frequencies plus the effect of floodplain position and the effect of the presence/absence of dead coolibah trees. Note that log-linear models do not distinguish one of the variables as a response variable, they just model the log of the expected frequencies. This is an additive linear model with no interaction between the two variables.

The parameters of log-linear models are the effects of a particular category of each variable on the expected frequencies; a larger λ means that the expected frequencies will be larger for that variable, i.e. that row or that column (Agresti 1996). These parameters are also deviations from the mean of all the log expected frequencies, just like parameters in ANOVA linear models are deviations from the overall mean. When λ is greater than zero, then the mean log expected frequency for that variable (row or column) is greater than the mean of all the log expected frequencies (Agresti 1990).

Null hypothesis of independence

The H_0 of independence in a two way table (Section 14.2.1) is also a test of the H_0 that λ_{ij}^{XY} equals zero, i.e. there is no interaction between the two variables. We can test this H_0 by comparing the fit of the model without this term (14.17) to the saturated model that includes this term (14.15). We determine the fit of each model by calculating the expected frequencies under each model, comparing the observed and expected frequencies and calculating the log-likelihood of each model. We then compare the fit of the two models with the likelihood ratio statistic (Λ), that is the ratio of the two log-likelihoods. However, sampling distribution of Λ is not well known (Sokal & Rohlf 1995), so instead we calculate the G^2 statistic (Chapter 13):

$$G^2 = -2\log\Lambda \tag{14.19}$$

G^2 follows a χ^2 distribution for reasonable sample sizes and can be generalized to:

$$G^2 = -2(\text{log-likelihood reduced model} - \text{log-likelihood full model}) \tag{14.20}$$

This is also termed the deviance and measures the difference in fit of the two models. If the H_0 of independence is true, then the reduced (no interaction) model should fit as well as the full model and the deviance (G^2) will be close to zero. If the H_0 is false, then there should be a difference in the fit of the two models and the deviance (G^2) will be greater than zero. The calculated G^2 is compared to a χ^2 distribution with $(I-1)(J-1)$ df, just like the χ^2 test of independence described in Section 14.2.1. The df $[(I-1)(J-1)]$ is the difference between the df for the full model $[(IJ-1)]$ and the df for the reduced model $[(I-1)+(J-1)]$.

Note that, for two way tables, the saturated model acts as the full model for model comparisons. This is not the case for more complex tables where many different full and reduced models can be fitted. For two way contingency tables with large sample sizes, the χ^2 test and the G^2 test will give similar results. Note that G^2 is slightly more sensitive to small sample sizes than the χ^2 statistic. In most statistical software, fitting the reduced model for a two way table will automatically provide the difference in fit between the two models.

Interpretation of lack of independence in log-linear models can be done using odds ratios and residuals, just as described in Section 14.2.1. Various types of residuals are standard output from log-linear modeling routines in most statistical software.

14.3.2 Log-linear models for three way tables

We will provide an introduction to log-linear models for three way tables. Sokal & Rohlf (1995) is also a good introduction and they provide a detailed worked example for a three way table.

Agresti (1990) is a more statistically complete reference for log-linear modeling, although Agresti (1996) is a more readable version of that text for the mathematically disinclined.

Full and reduced models

For three way tables (X with I categories, Y with J categories, Z with K categories), there is a large number of full and reduced models for testing the different interactions and main effects. Like three factor ANOVA models, log-linear models for contingency tables with three variables include three main effects (X, Y, Z), three two variable interactions (XY, XZ, YZ) and one three variable interaction (XYZ). For a three way table (I by J by K), the saturated model is:

$$\log f_{ijk} = \text{constant} + \lambda_i^X + \lambda_j^Y + \lambda_k^Z + \lambda_{ij}^{XY} + \lambda_{ik}^{XZ} + \lambda_{jk}^{YZ} + \lambda_{ijk}^{XYZ} \tag{14.21}$$

For the wildebeest example (Sinclair & Arcese 1995), this saturated model is:

$$\log f_{ijk} = \text{constant} + \lambda^{\text{death}} + \lambda^{\text{sex}} + \lambda^{\text{marrow}} + \lambda^{\text{death} \times \text{sex}} + \lambda^{\text{death} \times \text{marrow}} + \lambda^{\text{sex} \times \text{marrow}} + \lambda^{\text{death} \times \text{sex} \times \text{marrow}} \tag{14.22}$$

In models 14.21 and 14.22:

f_{ijk} is the expected frequency in cell ijk, i.e. the expected number of carcasses in each combination of death (predation, non-predation), sex (male, female) and bone marrow type (solid white fatty, opaque gelatinous, translucent gelatinous),

constant is the mean of the logs of all the expected frequencies,

λ_i^X is the effect of category i of variable X, i.e. the effect of type of death on the log expected frequency of carcasses in each cell,

λ_j^Y is the effect of category j of variable Y, i.e. the effect of being male or female on the log expected frequency of carcasses in each cell,

λ_k^Z is the effect of category k of variable Z, i.e. the effect of bone marrow type on the log expected frequency of carcasses in each cell,

λ_{ij}^{XY} is the effect of any interaction between X and Y, i.e. an interactive effect of type of death and sex on the log expected frequency of carcasses in each cell,

λ_{ik}^{XZ} is the effect of any interaction between

Table 14.5 Some typical log-linear models fitted to a three way (X by Y by Z) table with their df: comparisons of models are tested with the difference between the relevant df

Log-linear model	df
$X + Y + Z$	$IJK - I - J - K + 2$
$X + Y + Z + XY$	$(K-1)(IJ-1)$
$X + Y + Z + XZ$	$(J-1)(IK-1)$
$X + Y + Z + YZ$	$(I-1)(JK-1)$
$X + Y + Z + XZ + YZ$	$K(I-1)(J-1)$
$X + Y + Z + XY + YZ$	$J(I-1)(K-1)$
$X + Y + Z + XY + XZ$	$I(J-1)(K-1)$
$X + Y + Z + XY + XZ + YZ$	$(I-1)(J-1)(K-1)$
Saturated model:	
$X + Y + Z + XY + XZ + YZ + XYZ$	0

X and Z, i.e. an interactive effect of type of death and bone marrow type on the log expected frequency of carcasses in each cell,

λ_{jk}^{YZ} is the effect of any interaction between Y and Z, i.e. an interactive effect of sex and bone marrow type on the log expected frequency of carcasses in each cell,

λ_{ijk}^{XYZ} is the effect of any interaction between X, Y, and Z, i.e. an interactive effect of type of death, sex and bone marrow type on the log expected frequency of carcasses in each cell.

Models 14.21 and 14.22 include all main effects, all two way interactions and the three way interaction and fit the observed frequencies perfectly.

Because the G^2 goodness-of-fit statistic for the saturated model 14.21 is zero, then the G^2 statistic for any model represents the difference in fit of that model to the fit of the saturated model 14.21, i.e. the deviance. We can also use criteria of fit that "penalize" the model for the number of parameters, such as the Akaike Information Criterion, which for a particular model equals (Christensen 1997):

$$\text{AIC} = G^2 - (\text{df}_{\text{Saturated model}} - 2\text{df}_{\text{Particular model}})$$
$$= G^2 - 2\text{df}_{\text{Test of model}} \qquad (14.23)$$

The choice of "best" model is that which minimizes either the G^2 or the AIC.

Log-linear models are usually fitted in a hier-archical fashion, i.e. the inclusion of a higher order term automatically includes all lower order terms with those variables. The model with the three variable interaction automatically includes all two way interactions and main effects. Similarly, a model which omits one or more two way interactions also must omit the three way interaction. The range of models that can be fitted for a three way table are listed in Table 14.5.

The saturated model allows for complete dependence of the three variables by including the three way interaction term. The remaining models each omit the three way interaction and one or more two way interactions. Three models omit both the three way interaction and one of the two way interactions. For example, consider the model:

$$\log f_{ijk} = \text{constant} + \lambda_i^X + \lambda_j^Y + \lambda_k^Z + \lambda_{ij}^{XY} + \lambda_{jk}^{YZ}$$
$$(14.24)$$

Model 14.24 implies that X and Z are conditionally independent, i.e. the odds ratios for the association between X and Z are equal to one for all levels of Y. The goodness-of-fit statistics for these models omitting a two variable interaction compare their fit to that of the saturated model and measure how much the absence of both the three way interaction and the particular two way interaction affects the fit of the model. If the three way interaction has been shown to be small, then the fit of these models really measures the effect of omitting the particular two way interaction, i.e. testing whether those two variables are conditionally independent.

In the wildebeest example from Sinclair & Arcese (1995), the model which includes death, sex, marrow, death × sex and sex × marrow is:

$$\log f_{ijk} = \text{constant} + \lambda^{\text{death}} + \lambda^{\text{sex}} + \lambda^{\text{marrow}} + \lambda^{\text{death} \times \text{sex}} + \lambda^{\text{sex} \times \text{marrow}} \qquad (14.25)$$

Model 14.25 implies that there is no partial association between cause of death and marrow type for any sex. For either males or females, whether a wildebeest is taken by a predator or not is independent of which marrow type they have.

In the study on the effects of logging on squirrel demography from Taulman *et al.* (1998), the variable squirrel age (adult, young) can be viewed as a response variable and therefore all models should include the interaction between the other two variables (treatment and year). These two variables are set by the investigators and it makes no sense for the interaction between them to be zero; their conditional independence (independence of treatment and year for adult or young squirrels) has no biological meaning (see also Agresti 1996, Sokal & Rohlf 1995). Therefore, the number of models to be fitted is less than for the wildebeest example (Box 14.6).

Therefore, we test the fit of models with the relevant two way interaction terms (treatment × age and year × age) omitted. These models imply that there is conditional independence between treatment and age for each year and conditional independence between age and year for each treatment.

Note that the comparison of models that omit one of the two way interactions to the saturated model are not the best for testing the absence of two way interactions (conditional independence). This is because the reduced model has omitted both a two way interaction and the three way interaction so any difference between this model and the saturated model could be due to either the two way or the three way interaction or both. In general, the comparison of models omitting interaction terms to the saturated model should be considered an initial exploratory or screening approach to analyzing a contingency table. The exception is the valid test of the three way interaction.

Three other models omit the three way interaction and two of the two way interactions. For example, the model:

$$\log f_{ijk} = \text{constant} + \lambda_i^X + \lambda_j^Y + \lambda_k^Z + \lambda_{ij}^{XY} \qquad (14.26)$$

implies that X and Z are conditionally independent for each level of Y and that Y and Z are conditionally independent for each level of X. Only X and Y can be conditionally dependent. So the model that includes death, sex, marrow and death × marrow:

$$\log f_{ijk} = \text{constant} + \lambda^{\text{death}} + \lambda^{\text{sex}} + \lambda^{\text{marrow}} + \lambda^{\text{death} \times \text{sex}} \qquad (14.27)$$

implies that cause of death and sex are conditionally independent for each level of marrow type and sex and marrow type are conditionally independent for each cause of death; only cause of death and marrow type are conditionally dependent.

The simplest possible model is one that assumes complete independence and excludes all interaction terms:

$$\log f_{ijk} = \text{constant} + \lambda_i^X + \lambda_j^Y + \lambda_k^Z \qquad (14.28)$$

Model 14.28 implies that each variable is completely independent of the other two, e.g. the cause of death is independent of sex and marrow type.

The fit of the different possible models is a useful exploratory step in analyzing complex contingency tables and we can determine the model that provides the best fit for the fewest parameters. For the wildebeest carcasses example (Box 14.5), the two criteria (G^2 and AIC) chose different models, although the difference in fit between models 3, 5, 7 and 8 was minor. Based on the AIC, we would choose the model 7:

$$\log f_{ijk} = \text{constant} + \lambda^{\text{death}} + \lambda^{\text{sex}} + \lambda^{\text{marrow}} + \lambda^{\text{death} \times \text{marrow}} + \lambda^{\text{sex} \times \text{marrow}} \qquad (14.29)$$

whereas based on the G^2, we would choose model 8:

$$\log f_{ijk} = \text{constant} + \lambda^{\text{death}} + \lambda^{\text{sex}} + \lambda^{\text{marrow}} + \lambda^{\text{death} \times \text{sex}} + \lambda^{\text{death} \times \text{marrow}} + \lambda^{\text{sex} \times \text{marrow}} \qquad (14.30)$$

The AIC chose a model with fewer parameters.

In practice, however, we are usually more interested in tests of individual terms in the models. Comparisons of reduced models to the saturated model only do this in the case of the three way interaction. For the remaining models, more than one term is being omitted. Testing individual terms relates to the different forms of independence (complete, conditional, marginal) discussed in Section 14.2.2 and these tests are done by comparing the fit of full (not saturated) and reduced models.

Tests for three way interaction: complete dependence

The test of the three way interaction is a test of complete dependence. If the H_0 of no three way interaction is true, we have either conditional independence between all pairs of variables or the pattern of conditional dependence between all pairs of variables is the same for all levels of the third variable. This is similar to the interpretation of a three way interaction in an ANOVA model (Chapter 9) where the interaction between two factors depends on the level of the third factor. We test the three way interaction by comparing the fit of the saturated model, which is also the full model for the test of this term:

$$\log f_{ijk} = \text{constant} + \lambda_i^X + \lambda_j^Y + \lambda_k^Z + \lambda_{ij}^{XY} + \lambda_{ik}^{XZ} + \lambda_{jk}^{YZ} + \lambda_{ijk}^{XYZ} \qquad (14.21)$$

to a reduced model that omits this term:

$$\log f_{ijk} = \text{constant} + \lambda_i^X + \lambda_j^Y + \lambda_k^Z + \lambda_{ij}^{XY} + \lambda_{ik}^{XZ} + \lambda_{jk}^{YZ} \qquad (14.31)$$

This tests the H_0 that the three way interaction term is zero. If this H_0 is true, then we have homogeneous association where each pair of variables can be conditionally dependent but this dependence is the same at each level of the third variable. If H_0 is true, we would expect models 14.21 and 14.31 to fit similarly; if the H_0 is false, we would expect the reduced model to fit significantly worse than the saturated model. We use the difference in G^2 for the reduced model and the saturated (full) model, i.e. the deviance, to test whether there is a significant three way interaction between the variables.

For the wildebeest example (Box 14.5),

omitting the three way interaction term (sex $\times$ death $\times$ marrow) results in significantly worse fit so we would reject the null hypothesis of no three way interaction. The conditional dependence of cause of death and sex depends on the type of marrow. Equivalently, the conditional dependence of cause of death and marrow type depends on sex and the conditional dependence of sex and marrow type depends on cause of death. As in factorial ANOVAs (Chapter 9), interactions in log-linear models are symmetric.

For the squirrel example (Box 14.6), it is clear that omitting the three way interaction term (treatment $\times$ age $\times$ year) makes little difference to the fit of the model, so we wouldn't reject the H_0 that the three way interaction term is zero. Any conditional dependence between age of captured squirrels and treatment does not depend on year and any conditional dependence between age of captured squirrels and year does not depend on treatment.

Testing and interpreting two way interactions

Whether we test other terms depends on whether we reject the H_0 of no three way interaction between the variables. In the wildebeest carcass example, the three way interaction was significant so we could proceed in two ways. First, by examining the residuals from the model without the three way interaction term to see which cells were causing the lack of independence among the three variables (Box 14.5). The largest residuals indicate that there are more male carcasses that were not killed by predation with SWF marrow and fewer with OG marrow. None of the residuals is near two so we would not consider any observations particularly unusual. We could also examine odds ratios by breaking the table into a series of two way tables, e.g. tables of marrow type by sex for each cause of death separately. Second, we could examine dependence of pairs of variables for each level of the third variable separately, analogous to simple interaction tests in three factor ANOVA models (Chapter 9).

Although the three way interaction was significant in the wildebeest example, we will test for conditional dependence of each pair of variables to illustrate the process. Conditional independence is tested by comparing the full model

$$\log f_{ijk} = \text{constant} + \lambda_i^X + \lambda_j^Y + \lambda_k^Z + \lambda_{ij}^{XY} +$$
$$\lambda_{ik}^{XZ} + \lambda_{jk}^{YZ} \qquad (14.31)$$

with each of the following reduced models

Test H_0: $\lambda_{ij}^{XY} = 0$ $\log f_{ijk} = \text{constant} + \lambda_i^X + \lambda_j^Y +$
$$\lambda_k^Z + \lambda_{ik}^{XZ} + \lambda_{jk}^{YZ} \qquad (14.32)$$

Test H_0: $\lambda_{ik}^{XZ} = 0$ $\log f_{ijk} = \text{constant} + \lambda_i^X + \lambda_j^Y +$
$$\lambda_k^Z + \lambda_{ij}^{XY} + \lambda_{jk}^{YZ} \qquad (14.33)$$

Test H_0: $\lambda_{jk}^{YZ} = 0$ $\log f_{ijk} = \text{constant} + \lambda_i^X + \lambda_j^Y +$
$$\lambda_k^Z + \lambda_{ij}^{XY} + \lambda_{ik}^{XZ} \qquad (14.34)$$

For the wildebeest example, we would only reject the H_0 of conditional independence for cause of death and marrow type for each sex separately (Box 14.5). This means that cause of death and marrow type are not independent for male wildebeest and female wildebeest carcasses and the odds ratios for the association between cause of death and marrow type are different for each sex. In contrast, the odds ratios for the cause of death and sex association equal one for all marrow types and the odds ratios for the sex and marrow type association equal one for all causes of death.

In the squirrel example, the absence of a three way interaction is not rejected so there is good justification for proceeding to examine simpler models (Box 14.6). Because the treatment and year variables are set by the investigators, the independence between these two variables is not tested. There was no evidence to reject the hypothesis of conditional independence between age and treatment, i.e. squirrel age and treatment were independent for each year. This indicates that logging does not alter the relative numbers of adult and young squirrels compared to control stands in any year. In contrast, squirrel age and year were not independent in both control and logged treatments and the odds ratios for the association between age and year are different for each treatment.

We can also test for marginal independence of two variables by creating a two way table ignoring the third variable. For example, the test for marginal independence of cause of death and marrow type, ignoring sex, is done with a test of independence of the two way cause of death and marrow type table pooling the two sexes:

$$G^2 = 29.52, \text{df} = 2, P < 0.001$$

In this example, cause of death and marrow type are not marginally independent, as they are not conditionally independent, although agreement between marginal and conditional independence does not always hold (see Agresti 1996).

Test for complete independence

If none of the two way interactions are significant, we could fit the model of complete independence (no interactions) among the three variables:

$$\log f_{ijk} = \text{constant} + \lambda_i^X + \lambda_j^Y + \lambda_k^Z \qquad (14.28)$$

Assuming there is no three way interaction, we can test the H_0 that all two way interactions equal zero (i.e. that the three variables are completely independent) by comparing model 14.28 to:

$$\log f_{ijk} = \text{constant} + \lambda_i^X + \lambda_j^Y + \lambda_k^Z + \lambda_{ij}^{XY} +$$
$$\lambda_{ik}^{XZ} + \lambda_{jk}^{YZ} \qquad (14.31)$$

This comparison tests that all three variables are completely independent of each other, both conditionally and marginally. In the wildebeest example, marrow type is completely independent of cause of death and sex, sex is completely independent of cause of death and marrow type, and cause of death is completely independent of sex and marrow type (Box 14.5). There are no conditional dependencies.

We would not do this test for the wildebeest example because there is a three way interaction, nor for the squirrel example because the interaction between treatment and year should always be included because these variables are set by the investigator and independence between them makes little sense.

Analysis of deviance tables

We can create a modified analysis of deviance table, which gives the difference in G^2 between hierarchical models, showing tests for the null hypotheses that specific terms equal zero (Chapter 13). It is always better to compare the fit of full and reduced models when testing specific terms in log-linear models. Simple goodness-of-fit statistics for a given model can overestimate the importance of specific terms and should be used as an exploratory tool (except for the three way interaction). Comparing full and reduced models in a hierarchical manner is the most common method of analyzing and presenting the results of log-linear modeling.

14.3.3 More complex tables

Log-linear models for four way and higher tables follow the logic described above, although interpretation of four way interactions is as difficult as the interpretation of four way interactions in complex ANOVA models (Chapter 9). Agresti (1990) has provided a worked example for a four way table using log-linear models.

14.4 | General issues and hints for analysis

14.4.1 General issues

- Contingency tables represent a cross-classification of sampling or experimental units by two or more variables so each cell in the table contains a number of units (frequency).
- Log-linear models are GLMs that relate the log of the expected frequencies to a linear combination of the variables and their interactions.
- For two way tables, the basic χ^2 test is for independence between the two variables.
- To test H_0 that a specific term equals zero, compare the fit of the full model with that term included to the reduced model with that term omitted, using the deviance.
- Conditional independence means that two variables are independent for all levels of the third variable. Odds ratios and standardized residuals are very important tools for interpreting lack of independence in contingency tables.
- Standard significance tests can be unreliable when expected frequencies are small (less than five). Use exact tests for two way contingency tables with small sample sizes.

14.4.2 Hints for analysis

- Remember that log-linear models do not distinguish a response variable. However, when one variable is clearly a response, then some log-linear models won't make much sense. If modeling a response variable is important, consider logit models.
- As an initial analysis, it is useful to test the goodness-of-fit of a range of possible models using the deviance and AIC.
- For a complex table, breaking it into two by two by K sub-tables will allow odds ratios for conditional dependence to be calculated.

Chapter 15

Introduction to multivariate analyses

15.1 | Multivariate data

A multivariate data set includes more than one variable recorded from a number of replicate sampling or experimental units, sometimes referred to as objects. If these objects are organisms, the variables might be morphological or physiological measurements; if the objects are ecological sampling units, the variables might be physicochemical measurements or species abundances. We have already considered multivariate data in linear models with two or more predictor variables, e.g. multiple regression (Chapter 6) and multifactor analysis of variance (Chapters 9–11). For these analyses, we have multiple predictor (independent) variables. The multivariate analyses we will discuss in the remaining chapters either deal with multiple response variables (e.g. MANOVA – Chapter 16) or multiple variables that could be response variables, predictor variables or a combination of both. This chapter will introduce some aspects of multivariate data and analysis that apply generally to many of the methods we will describe in the subsequent three chapters. We will illustrate these aspects with four data sets from the recent biological literature. For each data set, there are $i = 1$ to n objects with $j = 1$ to p variables measured for each object.

Chemistry of forested watersheds
In Chapter 2, we first described the study of Lovett et al. (2000) who examined the chemistry of forested watersheds in the Catskill Mountains in New York. They chose 39 first and second order streams (objects) and measured the concentrations of ten chemical variables (NO_3^-, total organic N, total N, NH_4^-, dissolved organic C, SO_2^{2-}, Cl^-, Ca^{2+}, Mg^{2+}, H^+), averaged over three years, and four watershed variables (maximum elevation, sample elevation, length of stream, watershed area).

Plant functional groups and leaf characters
In Chapter 9, we described the study of Reich et al. (1999) who examined the generality of leaf traits from different species across a range of ecosystems and geographic regions. We will use a subset of their data, Wisconsin forbs, with ten species as the objects. There were five variables measured for each species: specific leaf area, leaf nitrogen concentration, mass-based net photosynthetic capacity, area-based net photosynthetic capacity and leaf diffusive conductance at photosynthetic capacity.

Wildlife underpasses in Canada
Clevenger & Waltho (2000) reported on the effectiveness of road underpasses for wildlife in Banff National Park in Alberta, Canada. For part of their study, they quantified the human activity at the underpasses as numbers of people on bikes, on horses and on foot. The objects were the eleven underpasses and the variables were the three human activities and the data were counts.

Bats and African woodlands
Fenton et al. (1998) studied the effects of woodland disturbance on species richness and abundance of bats in northern Zimbabwe. They had four groups

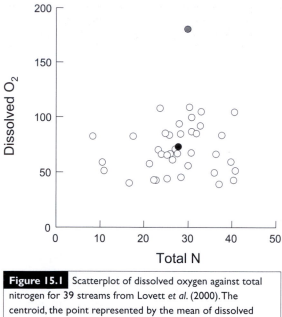

Figure 15.1 Scatterplot of dissolved oxygen against total nitrogen for 39 streams from Lovett et al. (2000). The centroid, the point represented by the mean of dissolved oxygen and total nitrogen, is filled. In this example, one object (grey fill) is an outlier for dissolved oxygen and also a multivariate outlier.

of sites: nine intact and nine impacted sites in Mana, six intact sites in Kanyati and six impacted sites in Matusadona. The sites within each area and disturbance category are not true replicates for assessing effects of disturbance so, like Fenton et al. (1998), we will combine the sites within each group. There were four objects (area and disturbance combinations) and 15 variables, species of bats. The data were numbers of each species of bat and there were numerous zero values, i.e. species absent.

15.2 | Distributions and associations

In a univariate context, we can describe the distribution of each variable and many of the parametric univariate analyses for estimating linear models and testing hypotheses about their parameters assume that the distribution of the response variable being analyzed is of a particular form (Chapters 5, 6, 8–14). For example, classical linear models assume normality (although the analyses are robust to this assumption under many circumstances), while generalized linear models allow

other distributions from the exponential family (e.g. binomial, Poisson, etc.). Although the multivariate analyses we will introduce in the next three chapters are mainly descriptive, interval estimation and hypothesis tests of parameters can also be relevant and usually require the assumption of multivariate normality, where all variables and linear combinations of variables are normally distributed (Tabachnick & Fidell 1996). The simplest multivariate normal distribution is the bivariate normal distribution described in Chapter 5. Other multivariate distributions are obviously possible, although less commonly used in multivariate analyses.

One measure of the center of a multivariate distribution is the centroid. In multivariate space where each dimension is a variable, the centroid is the point represented by the univariate means of the distributions of each of the variables (Figure 15.1). The centroid is not usually estimated by a single value but is used as a description of the center of a multivariate normal distribution and for detecting multivariate outliers (Section 15.9.1).

We can summarize variation in single variables by sums-of-squares (SS) and variances (Chapter 2). When we have more than one variable, we not only have variances for each variable but also covariances between variables. To represent variation in multivariate data sets, we must use some simple matrix algebra. A data matrix (**Y**) for n objects by p variables is represented in Table 15.1, and illustrated using the data from Reich et al. (1999) for Wisconsin shrubs.

With more than one variable, we calculate both sums-of-squares for each variable and sums-of-cross-products between variables to get a p by p sums-of-squares-and-cross-products (**SSCP** or **S**) matrix (Table 15.2). The rows and columns of this matrix represent the variables ($j = 1$ to p). The main diagonal of this matrix contains the sums-of-squares for each variable. The other entries are the sums-of-cross-products, the sum of the product of the deviations of the value for each variable from its sample mean. Note that this matrix is symmetrical, i.e. the sum-of-cross-products between Y_1 and Y_2 is the same as the sum-of-cross-products between Y_2 and Y_1.

We can convert this matrix to a p by p matrix of variances and covariances (**C**) by dividing the

Table 15.1 | Raw data matrix of p variables ($j = 1$ to p) for n objects ($i = 1$ to n), illustrated with data from Reich et al. (1999) for eleven species of Wisconsin forbs (objects) and five variables

$$\begin{bmatrix} y_{11} & y_{12} & \cdots & y_{1p} \\ y_{21} & y_{22} & \cdots & y_{2p} \\ \cdots & \cdots & y_{ij} & \cdots \\ y_{n1} & y_{n2} & \cdots & y_{np} \end{bmatrix}$$

	SLA (cm² g⁻¹)	Leaf N (mg g⁻¹)	A_{mass} (nmol g⁻¹ s⁻¹)	A_{area} (μmol m⁻² s⁻¹)	G_s (mmol m⁻² s⁻¹)
Caulophyllum thalictroides	425.0	58.2	254.0	5.9	134
Dentaria laciniate	297.0	53.0	432.0	14.2	227
Erythronium americanum	222.0	42.0	263.0	11.9	359
Silphium terebinthinaceum	133.0	14.4	175.0	13.4	615
Podophyllum peltatum	309.0	44.7	244.0	7.9	164
Baptisia leucophaea	106.3	35.9	159.0	15.0	481
Trillium grandiflora	357.0	51.6	209.0	5.8	499
Echinacea purpurea	128.5	15.0	122.9	9.8	480
Silphium integrifolium	116.3	16.6	116.0	10.0	478
Sanguinaria canadensis	321.0	53.6	255.0	7.9	208
Sarrachenia purpurea	78.1	11.4	22.8	2.9	144

Note:

SLA is specific leaf area, leaf N is leaf nitrogen concentration, A_{mass} is mass-based net photosynthetic capacity, A_{area} is area-based net photosynthetic capacity and G_s is leaf diffusive conductance at photosynthetic capacity.

sums-of-squares and sums-of-cross-products by their degrees of freedom ($n - 1$), where the main diagonal contains the variances for each variable and the other entries are the covariances between pairs of variables (Table 15.3). The covariance matrix can also be obtained directly from the raw data matrix **Y**, if each variable is centered (to a mean of zero), by $\mathbf{Y'Y}/(n-1)$, where $\mathbf{Y}^1$ is the transpose of the centered raw data matrix.

There are two ways we can summarize the variability of a multivariate data set based on the variance–covariance matrix (Jackson 1991).

- The determinant of a square matrix is a single number summary of the matrix. The determinant of the variance–covariance matrix ($|\mathbf{C}|$) represents the generalized variance of the matrix.
- The trace of the variance–covariance matrix (Tr(**C**)) is the sum of the diagonal values, i.e.

the sum of the variances of the centered individual variables.

Finally, we can also standardize these covariances by dividing by the standard deviations of the two variables involved to produce correlations and thus a correlation matrix (**R**), where r_{12} is the correlation coefficient between variables 1 and 2, etc. (Table 15.4). Note the main diagonal consists of ones because the correlation between each variable and itself is one. Covariances and correlations are measures of association between variables. Other measures of association include the χ^2 statistic, discussed in Chapter 14 as a measure of association for contingency tables.

If our objects occur in groups (e.g. experimental treatments), then we can calculate these matrices for between and within groups, analogous to analyses of variance in Chapters 8–11. Analyses based on multiple variance–covariance matrices

Table 15.2 Sums-of-squares-and-cross-products matrix between p variables ($j = 1$ to p) for n objects ($i = 1$ to n), illustrated with data from Reich *et al.* (1999)

$$\begin{bmatrix} \sum_{i=1}^{n}(y_{i1} - \bar{y}_1)^2 & \sum_{i=1}^{n}(y_{i2} - \bar{y}_2)(y_{i1} - \bar{y}_1) & \cdots & \sum_{i=1}^{n}(y_{ip} - \bar{y}_p)(y_{i1} - \bar{y}_1) \\ \sum_{i=1}^{n}(y_{i1} - \bar{y}_1)(y_{i2} - \bar{y}_2) & \sum_{i=1}^{n}(y_{i2} - \bar{y}_2)^2 & \cdots & \sum_{i=1}^{n}(y_{ip} - \bar{y}_p)(y_{i2} - \bar{y}_2) \\ \cdots & \cdots & \sum_{i=1}^{n}(y_{ij} - \bar{y}_j)^2 & \cdots \\ \sum_{i=1}^{n}(y_{i1} - \bar{y}_1)(y_{ip} - \bar{y}_p) & \sum_{i=1}^{n}(y_{i2} - \bar{y}_2)(y_{ip} - \bar{y}_p) & \cdots & \sum_{i=1}^{n}(y_{ip} - \bar{y}_p)^2 \end{bmatrix}$$

	SLA	Leaf N	A_{mass}	A_{area}	G_s
SLA	144 120.13				
Leaf N	19 873.03	3335.73			
A_{mass}	87 160.14	15 162.00	112 204.77		
A_{area}	−1290.94	−23.86	1635.93	148.98	
G_s	−97 696.97	−14 505.68	−50 261.55	3412.31	301 594.73

Note:
Main diagonal entries are sums-of-squares, off diagonal entries are sums-of-cross-products. Variables defined in Table 15.1.

Table 15.3 Variance–covariance matrix between p variables ($j = 1$ to p), illustrated with data from Reich *et al.* (1999)

$$\begin{bmatrix} s_1^2 & s_{12}^2 & \cdots & s_{p1}^2 \\ s_{12}^2 & s_2^2 & \cdots & s_{p2}^2 \\ \cdots & \cdots & s_j^2 & \cdots \\ s_{1p}^2 & s_{2p}^2 & \cdots & s_p^2 \end{bmatrix}$$

	SLA	Leaf N	A_{mass}	A_{area}	G_s
SLA	14 412.01				
Leaf N	1987.30	333.57			
A_{mass}	8716.01	1516.20	11 220.48		
A_{area}	−129.09	−2.39	163.59	14.89	
G_s	−9769.69	−1450.57	−5026.16	341.23	30 159.47

Note:
Main diagonal entries are variances, off diagonal entries are covariances. Variables defined in Table 15.1.

Table 15.4 Correlation matrix between p variables ($j = 1$ to p), illustrated with data from Reich *et al.* (1999)

$$
\begin{bmatrix}
1 & r_{21} & \cdots & r_{p1} \\
r_{12} & 1 & \cdots & r_{p2} \\
\cdots & \cdots & 1 & \cdots \\
r_{1p} & r_{2p} & \cdots & 1
\end{bmatrix}
$$

	SLA	Leaf N	A_{mass}	A_{area}	G_s
SLA	1.00				
Leaf N	0.91	1.00			
A_{mass}	0.69	0.78	1.00		
A_{area}	−0.28	−0.03	0.40	1.00	
G_s	−0.47	−0.46	−0.27	0.51	1.00

Note:
All entries are Pearson correlations. Variables defined in Table 15.1.

nearly always have the assumption that the within-groups matrices have equal variances and covariances.

15.3 | Linear combinations, eigenvectors and eigenvalues

15.3.1 Linear combinations of variables

One of the fundamental techniques in multivariate analyses is to derive linear combinations of the variables that summarize the variation in the original data set. Basically, we are "consolidating" (*sensu* Tabachnick & Fidell 1996) the variance from a data matrix into a new set of derived variables, each of which is a linear combination of the original variables. For $i = 1$ to n objects and $j = 1$ to p original variables:

$$z_{ik} = c_1 y_{i1} + c_2 y_{i2} + \cdots c_j y_{ij} + \cdots + c_p y_{ip} \quad (15.1)$$

In Equation 15.1, z_{ik} is the value of the new variable k for object i, y_{i1} to y_{ip} are the values of the original variables for object i and c_1 to c_p are weights or coefficients that indicate how much each original variable contributes to the linear combination. Depending on the analysis, these new variables are termed, variously, discriminant functions, canonical functions or variates, principal

components or factors. This linear combination is analogous to a regression equation. For some analyses, the linear combination may include a constant (an intercept in regression terminology):

$$z_{ik} = \text{constant} + c_1 y_{i1} + c_2 y_{i2} + \cdots c_j y_{ij} + \cdots + c_p y_{ip} \quad (15.2)$$

The form in Equation 15.2 is common when the variables are not standardized to zero mean and unit variance; if they are, then the constant becomes zero and Equation 15.1 is appropriate.

The derived variables are extracted so the first explains most of the variance in the original variables, the second explains most of the remaining variance after the first has been extracted but is uncorrelated with the first, the third explains most of the remaining variance after the first and second have been extracted but is uncorrelated with either the first or second, etc. The new derived variables are independent of, uncorrelated with, each other. The number of new derived variables is the same as the number of original variables (p), although the variance is usually consolidated in the first few derived variables.

15.3.2 Eigenvalues

Eigenvalues, also termed characteristic or latent roots ($\lambda_1, \lambda_2, \lambda_3, \ldots \lambda_k \ldots \lambda_p$), represent the amount of the original variance explained by each of the

$k = 1$ to p new derived variables. These eigenvalues are population parameters and we estimate them using maximum likelihood (ML) to produce $(l_1, l_2, l_3, \ldots l_k \ldots l_p)$ and can also determine their approximate standard errors. Note from Box 15.1 that if we use a covariance matrix and centered variables, then the sum of the eigenvalues is equal to the trace of the original covariance matrix, i.e. the sum of the variances of the original centered variables. If we use a correlation matrix and centered and standardized variables, the sum of the eigenvalues would equal the trace of the correlation matrix, i.e. the sum of the variances of the original standardized variables. We have simply rearranged the variance in the association matrix so

that the first few derived variables explain most of the variation that was present (between objects) in the original variables. The eigenvalues can also be expressed as proportions or percentages of the original variance explained by each new derived variable (component).

15.3.3 Eigenvectors

Eigenvectors (characteristic vectors) are lists of the coefficients or weights showing how much each original variable contributes to each new derived variable. In general terms, the eigenvectors contain the c_j in Equation 15.1 but these coefficients can be scaled in different ways so are often represented as u_j, v_j or w_j in matrix descriptions of

---

Box 15.1 | **Deriving components (modified from Jackson 1991)**

There are two different strategies for extracting eigenvectors (components) and their eigenvalues from multivariate data set of n objects by p variables. First, we can use a spectral decomposition of a p by p association matrix between variables. Second, we can use a singular value decomposition (SVD) of a n by p data matrix, with variables standardized as necessary. The SVD is more generally applicable (see Chapter 17) although most biologists are more familiar with obtaining eigenvectors and eigenvalues from a covariance or correlation matrix.

Consider the matrix (**Y**) of raw data from Clevenger & Waltho (2000) who recorded the numbers of people on bicycles, horses and on foot for eleven underpasses also used by wildlife in Alberta, Canada.

	Raw			Centered		
Underpass	Bicycle	Horse	Foot	Bicycle	Horse	Foot
1	0	6	7	−118.727	−37.273	−55.364
2	5	3	45	−113.727	−40.273	−17.364
3	6	6	14	−112.727	−37.273	−48.364
4	21	5	20	−97.727	−38.273	−42.364
5	189	42	34	70.273	−1.273	−28.364
6	8	138	77	−110.727	94.727	14.636
7	462	186	129	343.273	142.727	66.636
8	19	12	80	−99.727	−31.273	17.636
9	595	58	241	476.273	14.727	178.636
10	1	10	10	−117.727	−33.273	−52.364
11	0	10	29	−118.727	−33.273	−33.364

Spectral decomposition

We will illustrate spectral decomposition of a matrix of associations between variables (**Y′Y**). This might be a matrix of variances and covariances, **C**, among p variables based on n objects (Table 15.3).

	Bicycle	Horse	Foot
Bicycle	44 906.018		
Horse	7336.382	3862.018	
Foot	13 084.709	2205.191	4903.655

Note that we could also use a correlation matrix. Basically, we then derive two matrices, **L** and **U**, so that:

L = U′CU

U is a n by p matrix whose columns contain the eigenvectors (characteristic vectors), the coefficients of the linear combinations of the original variables. The elements of each eigenvector k are u_{jk}, the coefficient for the jth variable in the kth eigenvector. Note that we clearly need to have to some constraints imposed on the coefficients within each eigenvector, otherwise simply increasing the absolute sizes of the coefficients could increase the variance explained by each new variable. The simplest and most commonly used constraint is to restrict the sum of squared coefficients to zero, i.e. $\sum_{j=1}^{p} u_{jk}^2 = 1$. Eigenvectors that are independent and scaled to unity are termed orthonormal. Additional scaling options for the eigenvectors are available to make the variances of the eigenvectors similar (Jackson 1991), e.g. $v_{jk} = \sqrt{l_k} u_{jk}$ so the eigenvectors are in a **V** matrix and $w_{jk} = u_{jk}/\sqrt{l_k}$ so the eigenvectors are in a **W** matrix.

L is a p by p matrix whose diagonal contains the eigenvalues $l_1, l_2, \ldots l_k \ldots l_p$ (estimates of $\lambda_1, \lambda_2, \ldots \lambda_k \ldots \lambda_p$, the latent or characteristic roots) of **C**. The eigenvalues measure the variance explained by each of the eigenvectors. The number of eigenvalues is the same as the number of rows and columns in the covariance matrix and therefore the same as the number of original variables (p).

The matrix **L** for our example data set with the eigenvalues on the diagonal is:

$$\begin{matrix} 50\ 075.681 & 0 & 0 \\ 0 & 2592.350 & 0 \\ 0 & 0 & 1003.660 \end{matrix}$$

The trace of this matrix, the sum of its diagonal elements, is the sum of the variances of the original centered variables. The sum of the eigenvalues from an eigenanalysis of a sums-of-squares-and-cross-products matrix or a correlation matrix would equal the sum of the variances of the original variables or the centered and standardized variables respectively. The matrix **L** represents, therefore, a reorganization of the variances of the variables from the original data matrix. Each eigenvalue is associated with each eigenvector and it is clear that the eigenvectors are extracted in order of decreasing proportions of the total variance. We often convert these eigenvalues to percentages.

Eigenvector	1	2	3
Eigenvalue	50 075.681	2592.350	1003.660
Percentage of total variance	93.300	4.830	1.870

More formally, determination of the eigenvalues involves solving the characteristic equation:

$$|\mathbf{C} - l\mathbf{I}| = 0$$

where **I** is an identity matrix of equivalent dimensions to **C**. The resulting polynomial (pth degree) in l is used to obtain $l_1, l_2 \ldots l_p$.

Based on the three human activity variables (bicycle, horse, foot) for eleven underpasses in Alberta from Clevenger & Waltbo (2000), the matrix **U** is:

	1	2	3
Bicycle	0.945	0.160	0.284
Horse	0.164	−0.986	0.011
Foot	0.282	0.036	−0.959

Each column is an eigenvector (u_k where $k = 1$ to p), the values in the eigenvector representing the coefficients or weights for that linear combination of the original variables. For example, the linear combination comprising eigenvector 1 is:

$$(0.945)\text{Bicycle} + (0.164)\text{Horse} + (0.282)\text{Foot}$$

where the values of each variable are centered because we used the covariance matrix to extract the eigenvectors. These linear equations are often termed components or factors (Chapter 17) and represent new variables derived from the original variables. Note that each variable contributes differently to each component (different coefficients or weights) and that these coefficients will depend on the units of each variable and whether standardizations are used. These linear equations can be solved to produce a component score (z_{ik}) for each object or observation for each component. For example, the score for component 1 for underpass 1:

$$(0.945)(-118.727) + (0.164)(-37.273) + (0.282)(-55.364) = -133.946$$

Singular value decomposition (SVD)

The SVD of an n by p data matrix is based on the product of the characteristic vectors of a matrix of associations between variables, the characteristic vectors of a matrix of associations between objects and their characteristic roots (eigenvalues, which are the same for both association matrices). If **Y** is a matrix of centered data (as used for the covariance matrix above), then **Y′Y** is the covariance matrix between variables (matrix **C** above) and **YY′** is the covariance matrix between objects (note these would be SSCP matrices for raw data and correlation matrices for centered and standardized data). The characteristic roots (eigenvalues) of these two matrices are the same.

The SVD of **Y** is:

$$\mathbf{Y} = \mathbf{Z}\mathbf{L}^{1/2}\mathbf{U}'$$

where **L** contains the eigenvalues, **U** is a p by p containing the eigenvectors of **Y′Y** as defined above and **Z** is an n by p matrix of eigenvectors of **YY′** and are also the principal component scores for objects scaled by the square root of the eigenvalues. Note that we now have the square root of the eigenvalues because we are dealing with the original variables rather than covariances or correlations (Jackson 1991). If **Y** contains raw data, then **L** and **U** will be the equivalent to that from the spectral decomposition of the SSCP matrix. If **Y** contains centered data, then **L** and **U** will be the equivalent to that from the spectral decomposition of the covariance matrix. If **Y** contains centered and standardized data, then **L** and **U** will be the equivalent to that from the spectral decomposition of the correlation matrix. Note that we can determine the original variables (centered and standardized if appropriate) from the matrix of component scores and vice versa when all components are extracted.

The advantage of using SVD is that extraction of eigenvectors and their eigenvalues is a one step process and SVD can also be applied to association matrices that are not square, e.g. chi-square matrices from contingency tables as used in correspondence analysis (Chapter 17). The advantage of spectral decomposition is that the choice of matrix (e.g. covariance vs correlation) will automatically center or standardize the data. As most multivariate analyses require statistical software, we rarely have to make this choice in practice.

multivariate analyses – see Box 15.1. The eigenvectors are commonly scaled so the sum of squared coefficients equals one; other forms of scaling are possible. We estimate the coefficients with maximum likelihood and can determine approximate standard errors. These linear combinations can be solved to provide a score (z_{ik}) for each object for each new derived variable. Note that there is the same number of derived variables as there are original variables (p). The new derived variables, each with an eigenvector of coefficients and an eigenvalue, are extracted sequentially so that they are uncorrelated with each other.

15.3.4 Derivation of components

We can derive the new variables (components) with matrix algebra in two ways. We can use a spectral decomposition of a p by p square matrix of associations among variables (e.g. **SSCP**, **C** or **R** matrices) or we can use a singular value decomposition of the n by p original data matrix. The two approaches produce equivalent results if there is a match between the association matrix used and the standardization of variables in the data matrix. One of the biggest problems facing biologists trying to become familiar with multivariate statistical techniques is the bewildering range of terminology, with different textbooks using different terms for the same property and also different labels for the relevant matrices. We have tried to summarize these two approaches for extracting components from a multivariate data set in Box 15.1, following the terminology of Jackson (1991) where possible.

The usual derivation of components is from an association matrix of covariances or correlations between variables (Box 15.1). This is sometimes termed an *R*-mode analysis and we can calculate scores for the derived variables (components) for each object (Jackson 1991, Ludwig & Reynolds 1988). We could also derive components from matrices representing covariances or correlations between objects and the derived variables (components) are linear combinations of the objects. We can calculate component scores for each variable and this is termed a *Q*-mode analysis. These two sets of component scores are related via matrix algebra and we can obtain component scores for objects from the eigenvectors of the variables and vice versa (Jackson 1991). In practice, *Q*-mode analyses comparing objects are more commonly based on dissimilarity measures (Box 15.2; Figure 15.2; Section 15.4).

The calculation of eigenvectors and their eigenvalues for new derived variables (components) from a multivariate data set is fundamental to canonical correlation analysis, principal components analysis and correspondence analysis (Chapter 17). If our data set contains groups, we can extract the components in a way that maximizes the between-group differences and this is the basis of multivariate analysis of variance and discriminant function analysis (Chapter 16).

15.4 | Multivariate distance and dissimilarity measures

The methods described in the previous section deal with multivariate data sets by rearranging

Box 15.2 | Measures of dissimilarity between objects for continuous variables

Consider two objects ($i = 1$ and 2), e.g. two sampling units, and a number of variables ($j = 1$ to p) recorded from each object, e.g. abundances of p species from each sampling unit. The same variables are recorded from each object (even if some variables have zero values for an object). First, we need a few definitions:

- y_{1j} and y_{2j} are the values of variable j in object 1 and object 2,
- $\min(y_{1j}, y_{2j})$ is the lesser value of each variable when it is greater than zero in *both* objects,
- p is the number of variables, and
- q is the number of variables that are zero for objects 1 and 2.

For example, y_{1j} and y_{2j} might be the abundances of species j in sampling units 1 and 2, $\Sigma \min(y_{1j}, y_{2j})$ is the sum of the lesser abundance of species j when it is present in both sampling units, p is the number of species and q is the number of species that are missing (zero values) from both samples. The formulae presented below are from Faith *et al.* (1987), except we present a more common version of the Canberra measure (see Digby & Kempton 1987) and correct their typographical error for chi-square.

Dissimilarity	Equation
Minkowski	$\left(\sum_{j=1}^{p} \lvert y_{1j} - y_{2j} \rvert^{\lambda} \right)^{1/\lambda}$
Euclidean ($\lambda = 2$)	$\sqrt{\sum_{j=1}^{p} (y_{1j} - y_{2j})^2}$
City block (Manhattan: $\lambda = 1$)	$\sum_{j=1}^{p} \lvert (y_{1j} - y_{2j}) \rvert$
Canberra	$\dfrac{1}{p - q} \sum_{j=1}^{p} \dfrac{\lvert y_{1j} - y_{2j} \rvert}{(y_{1j} + y_{2j})}$
Bray–Curtis (Czekanowski)	$1 - \dfrac{2 \sum_{j=1}^{p} \min(y_{1j}, y_{2j})}{\sum_{j=1}^{p} (y_{1j} + y_{2j})} = \dfrac{\sum_{j=1}^{p} \lvert y_{1j} - y_{2j} \rvert}{\sum_{j=1}^{p} (y_{1j} + y_{2j})}$
Kulczynski	$1 - \dfrac{\left(\dfrac{\sum_{j=1}^{p} \min(y_{1j}, y_{2j})}{\sum_{j=1}^{p} (y_{1j})} + \dfrac{\sum_{j=1}^{p} \min(y_{1j}, y_{2j})}{\sum_{j=1}^{p} (y_{2j})} \right)}{2}$
Chi-square	$\sqrt{\sum_{j=1}^{p} \dfrac{\left(y_{1j} \left\lvert \sum_{j=1}^{p} y_{1j} - y_{2j} \right\rvert \sum_{j=1}^{p} y_{2j} \right)^2}{\sum_{i=1}^{n} y_i}}$

To illustrate these dissimilarity measures, we have calculated the dissimilarity between three species of Wisconsin forbs based on five leaf character variables from Reich *et al.* (1999). We have used the original variables and also variables centered and standardized to zero mean and unit variance.

Dissimilarity between	Euclidean	City block	Canberra	Bray–Curtis	Kulczynski
C. thalictroides vs *D. laciniata:*					
Raw data	238.355	82.500	0.231	0.217	0.212
Standardized data	2.992	1.143	NA	NA	NA
C. thalictroides vs *P. peltatum:*					
Raw data	121.005	34.300	0.111	0.104	0.100
Standardized data	1.337	0.498	NA	NA	NA
D. laciniata vs *P. peltatum:*					
Raw data	198.911	55.520	0.166	0.155	0.138
Standardized data	2.482	0.865	NA	NA	NA

Note that all measures show the same basic pattern, with the dissimilarity between *C. thalictroides* and *D. laciniata* the greatest and that between *C. thalictroides* and *P. peltatum* the least. Standardizing the variables to zero mean and unit variance doesn't change the relative dissimilarities although such a standardization cannot be applied to Canberra, Bray–Curtis and Kulczynski because they already include standardization as part of the calculation.

We also compared intact and impacted forest locations, based on the abundance of 15 species of bats, from Fenton *et al.* (1998). This data set allows us to include the chi-square measure, which requires integer values.

Dissimilarity between	Euclidean	City block	Canberra	Bray–Curtis	Kulczynski	Chi-square
Mana intact vs *Mana impacted:*						
Raw data	35.875	77.000	0.754	0.336	0.252	0.036
Standardized data	5.679	17.323	NA	NA	NA	NA
Range standardized data	2.720	8.255	0.835	0.770	0.435	0.428
Kanyati intact vs *Matusadona impacted:*						
Raw data	21.119	48.000	0.715	0.444	0.416	0.087
Standardized data	4.831	13.706	NA	NA	NA	NA
Range standardized data	2.390	6.663	0.792	0.719	0.703	0.491

Here the different dissimilarities produce different patterns. The intact vs impacted difference is greater for Mana than for Kanyati/Matusadona when measured with Euclidean, City block and Canberra but the reverse is true for Bray–Curtis, Kulczynski and chi-square. None of the standardizations changed the relative sizes for any of the measures except for Bray–Curtis.

Figure 15.2 Distinction in initial steps between *R*- and *Q*-mode analyses. A data matrix of *n* rows by *p* columns is converted to a *p* by *p* matrix of associations between variables (e.g. correlations) or a *n* by *n* matrix of dissimilarities between objects.

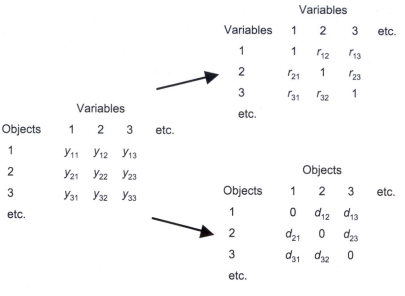

the variance based on the association (covariances or correlations) between the variables (*R*-mode analyses). Another approach to multivariate data analyses (*Q*-mode analyses) is based on a measure of similarity or dissimilarity, sometimes termed a resemblance measure (Ludwig & Reynolds 1988), between objects.

Similarity indices measure how alike objects are, e.g. how similar sampling units are in terms of species composition or how alike specimens are in morphology. Dissimilarity indices measure how different objects are and should represent multivariate distance – if each variable is represented by an axis (or dimension) then multivariate distance is how far apart the objects are in multidimensional space. These dissimilarity indices are also called distances and are calculated for every possible pair of objects. There are numerous dissimilarity indices and the preferred ones are those that most closely represent biologically meaningful differences between objects. Particular difficulties arise when variables are measured on very different scales or when some of the variables include zero values, e.g. the variables are abundances of species of organisms and many objects have zero abundance for one or more species.

We usually represent the dissimilarities between objects as a dissimilarity matrix, converting an *n* rows by *p* columns data matrix to an *n* rows by *n* columns dissimilarity matrix. Like the covariance and correlation matrices described in Section 15.2, dissimilarity matrices are identical above and below the diagonal, which will be zeros indicating zero dissimilarity between an object and itself.

15.4.1 Dissimilarity measures for continuous variables

There is a broad range of measures of dissimilarity between objects based on continuous variables (see Digby & Kempton 1987, Faith *et al.* 1987, Legendre & Legendre 1998, Ludwig & Reynolds 1988). Their proliferation is partly due to the requirement by ecologists for measures of dissimilarity between sampling units in species composition that best represent underlying environmental gradients. We illustrate some of the commonly used measures in Box 15.2 and describe them briefly below. Legendre & Legendre (1998) provide a very thorough coverage.

Euclidean
This is based on simple geometry as a measure of the distance between two objects in multidimensional space. It is the square root of the sum, over all the variables, of the square of the difference between the values of each variable for the two objects. It is only bounded by zero for two objects with exactly the same values for all variables and has no upper limit, even when two objects have no variables in common with positive values.

City block or Manhattan
This is the sum (across variables) of the absolute differences in the value of each variable between two objects. It has properties similar to Euclidean

distance and will be dominated by variables with large values.

Minkowski

Euclidean and City block are both versions of the more general Minkowski metric. Some software will, by default, "normalize" both measures by dividing by the sample size, i.e. the number of variables that contribute to the distance measure. This is only relevant if you wish to compare dissimilarities between data sets with different numbers of variables.

Canberra

This is the City block measure above, except that the difference between objects for each variable is divided by the sum of the variable values in the two objects before summing across variables. To ensure it has an upper limit of one, we standardize it by the number of variables that are greater than zero in both objects, e.g. the number of species present in at least one of the objects. This standardization is not always provided in texts (e.g. see Digby & Kempton 1988). The Canberra measure is less influenced by variables with very large values (Krebs 1989) than the City block measure.

Bray–Curtis

Developed by botanists in Wisconsin, this is also a modification of the Manhattan measure where the sum of differences between objects across variables is standardized by the sum of the variable values across objects, also summed across variables. Equivalently, it can be calculated as one minus twice the sum of the lesser value of each variable when it is greater than zero in both objects, standardized by the sum of the values of all variables in both objects. It ranges between zero (same variables and values in both objects – completely similar) and one (no variables in common with positive values – completely dissimilar) and is sometimes called percent dissimilarity (when expressed as a percentage; Ludwig & Reynolds 1988) or Czekanowski's coefficient. It is well suited to species abundance data because it ignores variables that have zeros for both objects (joint absences). Its value is determined mainly by variables with high values (e.g. species with high

abundances; see Krebs 1989) because these variables are likely to be more different between the objects.

Kulczynski

This complicated measure, also termed the quantitative symmetric measure, was introduced to biologists by Faith *et al.* (1987). Like Bray–Curtis, it ranges between zero and one and has similar properties.

Chi-square

This dissimilarity measure, implicit in some multivariate analyses (e.g. correspondence analysis – Chapter 17), is only applicable when the variables are counts, such as species abundances. It is based on differences between objects in the proportional representation of each species, also adjusted for species totals.

15.4.2 Dissimilarity measures for dichotomous (binary) variables

Another group of dissimilarity coefficients has been developed for variables measured on a binary scale (e.g. presence and absence). Let a be the number of variables with non-zero values in both objects, b is the number of variables with non-zero values in object 1 and c is the number of variables with non-zero values in object 2. A simple measure of dissimilarity between two objects is Jaccard's coefficient:

$$1 - \frac{a}{(a+b+c)} \tag{15.3}$$

A slight modification is Sorensen's coefficient, which replaces a by $2a$. Sorensen's coefficient is identical to the Bray–Curtis measure for dichotomous variables.

15.4.3 General dissimilarity measures for mixed variables

Gower (1971) introduced a general dissimilarity measure that is useful for situations that include a mixture of continuous and categorical variables:

$$\frac{\sum_{j=1}^{p} W_{12j} S_{12j}}{\sum_{j=1}^{p} W_{12j}} \tag{15.4}$$

In Equation 15.4, s_{12j} is the similarity between objects 1 and 2 based on variable j and w_{12j} equals one if the two objects can be compared for variable j and zero if they can't. So Gower's coefficient is "an average over all possible similarities" (Cox & Cox 1994) for objects 1 and 2. Gower's coefficient handles a mixture of variable types by calculating similarity for each variable separately (using appropriate coefficients for binary and continuous variables), then averaging those similarities. With all continuous variables, Gower's coefficient becomes (Cox & Cox 1994, Faith *et al.* 1987):

$$\sum_{j=1}^{p} \frac{|y_{1j} - y_{2j}|}{(\max_j - \min_j)} \tag{15.5}$$

15.4.4 Comparison of dissimilarity measures

One characteristic of dissimilarities is whether they meet the criterion of being metric. A dissimilarity coefficient is metric if the dissimilarity between objects 1 and 2 is less than the sum of the dissimilarities between objects 1 and 3 and 2 and 3. This means that it is possible to construct a triangle whose sides match the three dissimilarities between three objects. Dissimilarity measures that meet the condition of being metric are commonly termed dissimilarity metrics. Not all dissimilarity measures are metric, e.g. Minkowski and chi-square are, but Bray–Curtis is not. If the dissimilarity is to be used in linear models (see Chapter 18), then being metric is important but otherwise the choice of dissimilarity measure for the analyses we describe in Chapter 18 is not usually based on whether it is metric or not.

Which of the many dissimilarity measures to use depends on the purpose of the analysis, the nature of the data and is closely linked to standardizations discussed in Section 15.6. When variables are measured on similar scales and have no zero values, Euclidean, City block or Canberra are good measures of dissimilarity between objects. If the scales of measurement are not consistent for different variables (e.g. the leaf characteristics from Reich *et al.* 1999), then the data need to be standardized before calculating these dissimilarities. Where the variables are species abundances (i.e. counts), an ideal dissimilarity coefficient should reach a constant maximum value when

two sampling units have no species in common (i.e. it doesn't classify sampling units as similar because they have no species in common). Bray–Curtis, Kulczynski and Canberra meet this criterion, whereas Euclidean and chi-square do not. For this and other reasons, Faith *et al.* (1987) recommended the Bray–Curtis or Kulczynski coefficients for comparing objects when the variables are abundances of different species, as simulations showed these measures best matched ecological gradients. The suitability of some multivariate analyses for certain types of data is closely linked to the chosen or implicit dissimilarity measure that is used; we will discuss this further in the next two chapters.

For binary data, Kent & Coker (1992) argued that Sorenson's coefficient is preferred because it weights species (variables) in common higher than species absences (see also Krebs 1989). Remember that Sorenson's coefficient is the same as the Bray–Curtis measure with binary variables.

The general Gower dissimilarity measure is particularly useful when the data are a mixture of binary and continuous variables or when there are missing observations (but see Section 15.9.2), although Faith *et al.* (1997) showed that the version for continuous variables did not represent underlying ecological distances very well.

15.5 | Comparing distance and/or dissimilarity matrices

Biologists often wish to test whether two or more matrices, or at least their corresponding elements, are correlated with each other. Such questions are particularly relevant when we are dealing with distance and/or dissimilarity matrices. For example, Sokal & Rohlf (1995) compared the matrix of genetic distances between ten villages of the Yanomama Amerindians in South America to the matrix of geographic distances between the villages. Fortin & Gurevitch (1993) emphasized the importance of examining spatial structure in field experiments, where one matrix might be differences in response of experimental units and the other might be the actual physical distances between the units.

Mantel's test is used for testing null hypotheses about correlations between matrices. It uses a randomization procedure (Chapter 3) to test whether the relationship between two matrices is more different than we would expect by chance (Manly 1997, Sokal & Rohlf 1996). We simply calculate the correlation coefficient between the corresponding elements of the two matrices, using only the lower (or upper) half of each matrix because they are symmetrical. However, the dissimilarities or distances within each matrix are not independent of each other (the dissimilarity between object 1 and 2 uses some of the same information as the dissimilarity between object 1 and 3, etc.). This is why we use a randomization test (Chapter 3) for the H_0 that the correlation between the two matrices is no different than we would expect by chance. Other statistics equivalent to the correlation coefficient for testing the H_0 in Mantel's test include Z (the sum of the products of the corresponding elements in the two matrices) and the regression coefficient (slope) for elements in one matrix regressed against elements in the other matrix. If the distances in the two matrices are standardized to zero mean and unit variance (Chapter 4), the values of the correlation coefficient, the regression slope and Z/m, where m is the number of elements in each matrix, will be the same (Manly 1997).

McCue *et al.* (1996) described genetic structure of a rare annual plant (*Clarkia springvillensis*) in California. They identified eight subpopulations and calculated Cavalli–Svorza genetic distances between subpopulations from isozyme analysis of tissue samples. They had two distance matrices – one for genetic distances between subpopulations and one for geographic distance (in meters) between subpopulations. The correlation coefficient between the two matrices was 0.632 with a randomization P-value of 0.032 and we would conclude that there is a statistically significant positive relationship between genetic and geographic distance for populations of *C. springvillensis*. Note that, in this example, the subpopulations were either really close (<500 m) or around 8000 m apart so our interpretation of the relationship between genetic and geographic distance is constrained by the absence of data for separations between 500 and 8000 m.

The correlations can be extended to more than two matrices, using an analogue of the coefficient of multiple correlation (r^2) and partial correlations, called partial Mantel's test (Manly 1997). For example, Sklenar & Jorgensen (1999) measured floristic similarity between six mountains in Ecuador using Sorenson's index for presence–absence data. They used Mantel's test to show that there was a significant correlation between floristic similarity and differences in sampling intensity and they used a partial Mantel's test to test for a correlation between floristics and distance, holding sampling intensity constant.

15.6 | Data standardization

Transformations, which change the scale of measurement of the data, were discussed in Chapter 4 in relation to meeting the normality assumption of parametric analyses and the homogeneity of variance assumption of most of these analyses. Transformations are particularly important for multivariate procedures based on eigenanalysis (e.g. principal components analysis – see Chapter 17) because covariances and correlations measure linear relationships between variables. Transformations that improve linearity will increase the efficiency with which the eigenanalysis extracts the eigenvectors.

Transformations such as log or square root will normalize positively skewed data and also reduce the influence of variables with high values (e.g. very abundant species) in multivariate procedures based on dissimilarity indices (Digby & Kempton 1987). Clarke & Warwick (1994) argued that fourth-root transformations should always be used for species abundance data before calculating dissimilarities to reduce the influence of very abundant species. One difficulty with this approach is that the effect of the transformation will depend on the underlying distributions of the variables (e.g. species) and therefore the degree of reduction of influence of very abundant species will be inconsistent. Cao *et al.* (1999) also had concerns about log transformation of water quality variables, pointing out that this transformation "indiscriminately increases the importance of a low range across all variables".

Standardizations work slightly differently

from transformations by adjusting the data so that means and/or variances or totals for each variable are the same. The following are examples (see also Table 15.5).

- Centering the data subtracts the variable mean from each observation for each variable, resulting in all variables having a mean of zero. Spectral decomposition of a covariance matrix extracts components from centered data.
- Standardizing the data divides the centered observations by the standard deviation for each variable, resulting in all variables having a mean of zero and a standard deviation (and variance) of one. Spectral decomposition of a correlation matrix extracts components from standardized data.
- Data can also be standardized so that each observation is expressed relative to the maximum value of that variable across all objects. This standardization results in observations being expressed as a proportion of the largest value for a variable, and is basically standardization based on the range within a variable.
- Cao *et al.* (1999) proposed a novel standardization for water quality data, whereby each variable is standardized in relation to the water

quality standard of that variable and its range. Although acknowledging problems with their new standardization, they argued that it does allow natural variability in each variable to contribute to the results of a multivariate analysis.

These standardizations of variables are important if variables are measured in very different units or scales, because otherwise those variables with larger values or larger variances will often be more influential on the results of an analysis than variables with smaller values or smaller variances. Standardization of variables is essential if the variables are measured in very different units. For species abundances, such standardizations make all species have similar "importance" and thus "avoids a strong weighting by a few highly abundant species" (Ludwig & Reynolds 1988, p. 215). Without this standardization, rare species are often making little contribution to dissimilarities – of course, this may be the most biologically sensible interpretation.

In the same way that variables could be standardized, objects (e.g. sampling units) can also be standardized so the value for any variable for each object is expressed relative to the maximum value for that object in the whole data matrix. For

Table 15.5 Comparison of unstandardized, centered (zero mean) and standardized (zero mean and unit variance) observations for leaf N concentration for the eleven species of Wisconsin forbs from the study by Reich *et al.* (1999)

	Unstandardized	Centered	Standardized
Caulophyllum thalictroides	58.20	22.16	1.21
Dentaria laciniate	53.00	16.96	0.93
Erythronium americanum	42.00	5.96	0.33
Silphium terebinthinaceum	14.40	−21.64	−1.18
Podophyllum peltatum	44.70	8.66	0.47
Baptisia leucophaea	35.90	−0.14	−0.01
Trillium grandiflora	51.60	15.56	0.85
Echinacea purpurea	15.00	−21.04	−1.15
Silphium integrifolium	16.60	−19.44	−1.06
Sanguinaria canadensis	53.60	17.56	0.96
Sarrachenia purpurea	11.40	−24.64	−1.35
Mean	36.04	0.00	0.00
Standard deviation	18.26	18.26	1.00

species abundance data, this standardization is very important if the size of the sampling unit, and hence the total number of individuals, varies because it removes any effect of different total abundances in different sampling units, i.e. all sampling units are considered to have the same total abundance across all species.

Finally, converting abundance data to presence and absence might be considered an extreme combination of transformation and standardization. There are specific dissimilarity measures for such binary data (see Section 15.4.2).

It is often useful to analyze the same data with different standardizations, particularly in ecological research. For example, comparing the results of an analysis using raw data with one using sample-standardized data will indicate what influence different total abundances in samples have. Raw data versus species-standardized data will illustrate what influence the most abundant species have (simply leaving out different combinations of rarer species will provide similar information). Finally, to remove all effects of abundance, we can analyze just presence–absence data.

15.7 Standardization, association and dissimilarity

Measures of association between variables described in Section 15.2 have implicit standardizations (see also Chapter 5). Covariances measure the linear relationships between centered variables whereas correlations measure the linear relationships between standardized (zero mean and unit variance) variables. The choice of association matrix on which to base subsequent multivariate analyses (Chapter 17) depends on whether differences in variances between variables represent important biological information that you don't wish to lose. Standardizations are also important for dissimilarity measures. Some dissimilarity measures are implicitly standardized and are unaffected by data standardizations (Faith et al. 1987). Some become identical after data standardization, e.g. Bray–Curtis, Kulczynski and City block are identical for count data if objects are standardized to the same total abundance.

Others, e.g. Bray–Curtis and Kulczynski, produce nonsensical values when standardization is to zero mean (centering) or zero mean and unit variance (because of negative values). Standardizing by the range is a better option for these measures if you wish to reduce the influence of very abundant variables (e.g. species).

15.8 Multivariate graphics

Many of the exploratory data analysis techniques described in Chapter 4 are very applicable to multivariate data sets. In particular, describing distributions and checking for outliers for each variable separately with boxplots and examining bivariate relationships between variables with scatterplot matrices (SPLOMS) are always useful.

We may also wish to represent each observation or object in symbolic form, so that each symbol describes the relative value of all of the variables. A number of approaches have been developed to represent the different variables in a single "icon". The best known method is using Chernoff faces, where different features of the face represent different variables (Chernoff 1973; see also Everitt & Dunn 1991, Flury & Riedwyl 1988). These plots have been criticized, primarily because of the difficulty of rationally assigning variables to face features (Cox 1978), but they also have their supporters (Everitt & Dunn 1991, Flury & Riedwyl 1988). We illustrate these face plots with the Wisconsin forb data from Reich et al. (1999) in Figure 15.3, for both raw and standardized data. The differences between species are more noticeable for standardized variables, especially nose features representing mass-based and area-based photosynthetic capacity. Nonetheless, practice on known data sets is required to become familiar with recognizing similar and dissimilar faces.

An alternative, less "cartoonish", icon plot is to represent each object with a star, where each variable is represented by a point on the star, and the value of the variable is indicated by how far the point is from the center. There are no limits to the number of points, and therefore variables, for each star although the stars become difficult to interpret when there are too many variables. The

(a)   (b)

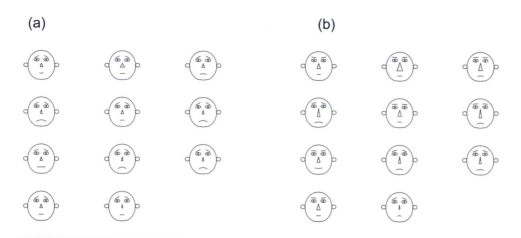

Figure 15.3 Chernoff face representation of the eleven species of Wisconsin forbs for five leaf characteristics based on raw data (a) and standardized data (b) from Reich *et al.* (1999). The features of the Chernoff faces are curvature of mouth for specific leaf area, angle of brow for leaf nitrogen concentration, width of nose for mass-based net photosynthetic capacity, length of nose for area-based net photosynthetic capacity, and length of mouth for leaf diffusive conductance at photosynthetic capacity. The species are, from left to right and row by row: *Caulophyllum thalictroides*, *Dentaria laciniate*, *Erythronium americanum*, *Silphium terebinthinaceum*, *Podophyllum peltatum*, *Baptisia leucophaea*, *Trillium grandiflora*, *Echinacea purpurea*, *Silphium integrifolium*, *Sanguinaria canadensis*, and *Sarrachenia purpurea*.

the relationships between sampling or experimental units based on species composition, where they are termed "ordination" plots, the term ordination being derived from attempts to order units along some environmental gradient (Digby & Kempton 1987). Ordination is not a term familiar to most statisticians, or even non-ecological biologists, so we will call such plots of objects "scaling plots".

15.9 | Screening multivariate data sets

In Chapter 4, we emphasized the importance of exploratory data analyses before proceeding with univariate statistical procedures, especially those with distributional assumptions. We also pointed out that unusual values (outliers) can have very influential effects on the conclusions from a statistical analysis, both in terms of estimation and hypothesis testing, and checking for outliers is an important precursor to any formal analysis. The need for exploratory screening of data is even more important for multivariate data sets because their complexity means that visual inspection of the raw data is likely to miss unusual patterns or observations. Additionally, the issue of missing observations is much more critical for the analyses we will describe in the next three chapters.

All of the univariate procedures we described in Chapter 4, especially graphical explorations (see previous section), can and should be used for

difference between raw and standardized variables is often very obvious on star plots. In Figure 15.4, we again illustrate the Wisconsin forb data from Reich *et al.* (1999). It is clear that *S. purpurea* is very different from the remaining species and *S. terebinthinaceum*, *P. peltatum*, *B. leucophaea* and *T. grandiflora* have larger values for leaf diffusive conductance at photosynthetic capacity, indicated by the extension of their stars to the left.

Finally, a very common method of graphing relationships between objects is to use a scatterplot where the axes represent the new derived variables from an eigenanalysis. These plots are common in the analyses described in Chapters 16 and 17, especially discriminant function analysis, principal components analysis and correspondence analysis. Alternatively, we can graphically represent a dissimilarity matrix between objects in a scatterplot, the basis of multidimensional scaling described in Chapter 18. Both types of plots are used especially by ecologists to represent

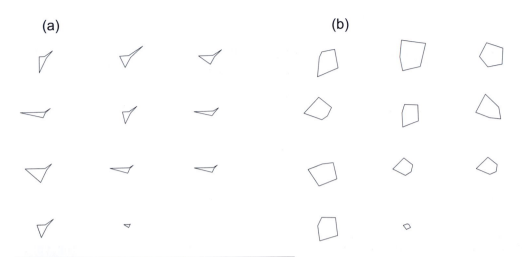

Figure 15.4 Star plot representation of the eleven species of Wisconsin forbs for five leaf characteristics based on raw data (a) and standardized data (b) from Reich *et al.* (1999). The features of the stars are, clockwise from the top, specific leaf area, leaf nitrogen concentration, mass-based net photosynthetic capacity, area-based net photosynthetic capacity, leaf diffusive conductance at photosynthetic capacity. The species are, from left to right and row by row: *Caulophyllum thalictroides, Dentaria laciniate, Erythronium americanum, Silphium terebinthinaceum, Podophyllum peltatum, Baptisia leucophaea, Trillium grandiflora, Echinacea purpurea, Silphium integrifolium, Sanguinaria canadensis,* and *Sarrachenia purpurea.*

multivariate data sets. In this section, we will focus on two particular issues: detecting multivariate outliers and dealing with missing observations.

15.9.1 Multivariate outliers

We discussed in Chapter 4 how unusually extreme values can influence the outcome of a statistical analysis. Multivariate outliers are more difficult to detect because they may not be univariate outliers for any of the individual variables (Jobson 1992). Additionally, outliers are often defined as large departures from a fitted statistical, usually linear, model to our data. For example, an observation may be an outlier from a fitted regression model (Chapters 5 and 6) and may have undue influence on the estimates of model parameters and tests of hypotheses about these parameters. In contrast, many of the multivariate techniques we will introduce in the next three chapters are more

descriptive in nature, although new summary variables are often derived and can be used as response or predictor variables in subsequent linear models.

A multivariate outlier is an object with an unusual pattern of values for the variables (Tabachnick & Fidell 1996) and can be detected by measuring its distance, in multivariate space, from the centroid (Figure 15.1). The square of this distance (d_i^2 for object i) is called Mahalanobis distance (see Flury & Riedwyl 1988, Jackson 1991, Jobson 1992 for computational details) and is provided by most software in one or more of the multivariate analysis routines. If multivariate normality holds, the d_i^2 follow a χ^2 distribution with p (the number of variables) df (Manly 1994) so we can test for outliers, possibly using a strict significance level like 0.001 (Tabachnick & Fidell 1996).

Dealing with univariate outliers has been described in Chapter 4. The options for multivariate outliers are similar. If we decide that an object has such an unusual pattern of values for one or more variables that it is unlikely to be part of the population of objects we wish to describe or make inferences about, then we might delete that object from the analysis. Transformations of the variable(s) can also reduce the influence of outliers if they are extreme values in a positively skewed distribution.

15.9.2 Missing observations

Occasionally, we will have missing observations in our data set, i.e. no value was recorded for one or more variables for one or more objects. The approaches for dealing with missing observations depend on the missing data mechanism, as introduced in Chapter 4 (see also Heitjan 1997, Little & Rubin 1987, Roth 1994). If the probability that an observation is missing is independent of the observed and missing values, the missing observations are termed missing completely at random (MCAR). This implies that the missing observations are a random subset of the data. The probability that an observation is missing might not depend on the unobserved missing value but be dependent on the values of the other variables for that object. For example, the pattern of missing data may depend on the group in which the object occurs, where another variable classifies objects into groups. This is termed missing at random (MAR). Finally, the missing values might be non-ignorable because whether an observation is missing depends on its value.

Consider the data set from Lovett et al. (2000) and imagine that one stream was missing a value for concentration of H^+. If the value is missing because of a random malfunction of a meter or a mistake by a researcher who forgot to write the value down then this observation might be MCAR. Our experience is MCAR is a common missing data mechanism in ecological sampling programs. If the value is missing because the stream was at a high altitude and weather conditions precluded access, then the observation might be MAR because the value of another variable (elevation), but not the unobserved H^+ value, determines the probability of it being missing. Finally, if the value is missing because the original H^+ reading was so high (e.g. Winnisook Creek) that the researcher assumed that the reading was a mistake and ignored it, the missing value is clearly non-ignorable. This situation is more common in situations when the observations depend on responses from subjects, such as in marketing surveys or clinical trials, although studies on animal behavior may suffer from this type of non-response. MCAR and MAR are much easier to deal with.

Basically, there are three approaches to dealing with missing observations (Little & Rubin 1987, Roth 1994). Our objective in this section is simply to make biologists aware that there are alternatives to simply "omitting whole rows of data", although some of the methods are sophisticated and usually require advice from statisticians experienced with their use. It is important to remember that avoiding missing data is the best solution because all of the alternatives are imperfect. We illustrate the results from some of the methods for dealing with missing observations in using a subset of the data from Reich et al. (1999). Our emphasis is not on the calculations, as these require appropriate software, but on the interpretation of the different methods.

Deletion

The simplest approach is to delete the entire object that has the missing value. This may be an appropriate strategy when the proportion of objects with missing values is low and the pattern is MCAR. It does result in loss of information because the non-missing values of variables for the object with the missing value are also excluded from the analysis. This is sometimes termed listwise deletion and is often the default for multivariate analyses in statistical software. If the analysis is based on pairwise associations between variables (e.g. correlations), an alternative is to use pairwise deletion. Here an object is only excluded for the calculation of the association between the two variables for which one value is missing but not excluded for the calculation of associations between other variables. This is the preferred deletion strategy when pairwise associations are the basis for the analysis.

Imputation

Imputation involves replacing (substituting) the missing values with some estimate of what the values might have been. There have been three common methods for imputing missing observations. The first is to replace the observation with the mean value of the variable calculated from the non-missing observations. Unfortunately, this tends to result in an underestimate of the true variance for that variable because these means do not contribute to the sum of squared deviations (Roth 1994). The second is to use a regression model to predict the imputed observation from other variables in the data. For example, we could determine which variable has the highest correlation with the variable with missing values from the complete objects and develop a regression model where the variable with missing values is the response variable and the other variable is the predictor. For the object with the missing value, the observed value of the predictor could then be used to predict the missing value from this regression model. Alternatively, we could use two or more predictors in a multiple regression model. Generalized linear models could be used if the assumption of normal error terms for the regressions was untenable or even generalized additive models if the shape of the relationship between the variables is not linear, although we have not seen either of these used in practice. Finally, hot-deck imputation simply replaces the missing value with the actual value from an object with similar characteristics (Roth 1994).

There are two main difficulties with these imputation methods. The first is that the imputed values are not independent of the observed data for a given variable and the precision (variances and standard errors) of the estimates of parameters based on these imputed values is generally underestimated. The second problem is that imputing a single value provides no indication of the effect that different imputed values have on the estimation of the relevant parameter (e.g. correlation), i.e. no measure of imputation uncertainty (Little 1999). Rubin (1987) developed a method termed multiple imputation as a solution to the second problem (see also Schafer 1999). Multiple imputation basically imputes a range of values for each missing observation, these values being simulated from a specific distribution for the missing values. The complete data sets (observed and imputed values) are then analyzed in the usual manner. The estimate of any parameter is simply the mean of estimates from the analyses of the imputed data sets. The standard error of this average estimate includes both the variance between imputations and the variance within each data set. Multiple imputation is clearly a sensible approach and a considerable improvement over single imputation, giving us some indication of how different imputed values affect the outcome of our analysis. The really tricky bit is developing the distribution of

values from which the multiple imputations are derived. Rubin (1987) recommended a Bayesian strategy whereby the posterior distribution of missing values is conditional on the prior distribution of observed values, although the computations are complex (Schafer 1999). Multiple imputation routines are not readily available in commonly used statistical software but specialist products do exist and macros for some programs are available (see Rubin 1996 and references therein).

Maximum likelihood and EM

A different approach is to use maximum likelihood (ML) techniques to estimate the parameters of interest (e.g. means, correlation coefficients) from the observed, incomplete data (Little & Rubin 1987). Basically we use the distribution of the observed data and the conditional distribution of the pattern of missing data given the observed data. The likelihood function for any parameter can be complex with missing data so Little & Rubin (1987) also proposed methods based on factoring the likelihoods. The likelihood for a given parameter is decomposed into the sum of the likelihoods of distinct parameters given complete subsets of the data. These ML methods can estimate the missing observations once the parameters are estimated but do not use imputed values to estimate the parameters.

A combination of imputation and ML estimation is the Expectation–Maximization (EM) algorithm. This is an iterative procedure whereby the missing values are imputed, the parameters are estimated by ML, the missing values are re-estimated and imputed, the parameters re-estimated by ML, etc., until convergence of the likelihood of the parameter given the observed data is achieved. Technically, the missing values are not directly imputed using the EM method, but some function of the missing data like a predictive distribution is incorporated into the likelihood function (Little & Rubin 1987, Schafer 1999). The EM algorithm is now available in some commonly used statistical software. Multiple imputation may be more robust than EM methods for small data sets (Schafer 1999). Both straight ML and the EM method require the missing data to be at least MAR. See also Box 15.3.

Box 15.3 | Dealing with missing data

The data set on physiological variables for a range of plant species from different locations and functional groups from Reich et al. (1999) will be used to illustrate some of the methods for handling missing observations. We will use a subset of their data, trees from Venezuela, where there were 22 species (objects). There were five variables: specific leaf area (SLA), leaf nitrogen concentration (Leaf N), mass-based net photosynthetic capacity (A_{mass}), area-based net photosynthetic capacity (A_{area}) and leaf diffusive conductance at photosynthetic capacity (G_s). Five of the possible 110 observations were missing: SLA and A_{area} for *Eperua purpurea* and A_{mass}, A_{area} and G_s for *Micropholis maguirei*. We will assume these values are at least MAR and use listwise and pairwise deletion, regression imputation (using all other variables with complete data as predictor variables) and the EM algorithm to estimate means, standard deviations and pairwise correlations between variables. The EM algorithm converged in four iterations with −2(log-likelihood) of 650.85.

Means (standard deviations)

	SLA (cm² g⁻¹)	Leaf N (mg g⁻¹)	A_{mass} (nmol g⁻¹ s⁻¹)	A_{area} (μmol m⁻² s⁻¹)	G_s (mmol m⁻² s⁻¹)
Listwise	89.85 (24.04)	14.29 (4.71)	78.96 (55.23)	8.28 (3.68)	622.60 (535.76)
All values	88.20 (24.62)	14.04 (4.68)	77.82 (54.09)	8.28 (3.68)	602.90 (529.94)
EM	88.15 (24.18)	14.04 (4.68)	74.49 (55.39)	8.01 (3.67)	580.68 (535.92)
Regression	89.85 (24.04)	14.29 (4.71)	78.96 (55.23)	8.28 (3.68)	622.60 (535.76)

Correlations based on deletions

	SLA List	SLA Pair	Leaf N List	Leaf N Pair	A_{mass} List	A_{mass} Pair	A_{area} List	A_{area} Pair	G_s List	G_s Pair
SLA	1.000	1.000								
Leaf N	0.569	0.607	1.000	1.000						
A_{mass}	0.789	0.789	0.708	0.699	1.000	1.000				
A_{area}	0.550	0.550	0.684	0.684	0.931	0.931	1.000	1.000		
G_s	0.498	0.498	0.546	0.530	0.851	0.851	0.894	0.894	1.000	1.000

Note that only the correlation between SLA and Leaf N differs much between the two methods of deletion.

Correlations based on regression imputation and EM

	SLA Regress	SLA EM	Leaf N Regress	Leaf N EM	A_{mass} Regress	A_{mass} EM	A_{area} Regress	A_{area} EM	G_s Regress	G_s EM
SLA	1.000	1.000								
Leaf N	0.601	0.602	1.000	1.000						
A_{mass}	0.789	0.795	0.714	0.719	1.000	1.000				
A_{area}	0.555	0.563	0.681	0.685	0.931	0.932	1.000	1.000		
G_s	0.503	0.511	0.541	0.546	0.853	0.854	0.893	0.895	1.000	1.000

There are differences between the estimated correlations based on the two methods but, for these data, the differences are small.

Observed data with regression and EM imputed values (in bold)

SLA	Leaf N	A_{mass}	A_{area}	G_s
144.60	24.70	252.20	17.70	2272.00
114.30	17.90	159.30	13.80	889.00
126.40	16.50	115.50	9.10	597.00
105.40	16.40	140.40	12.80	975.00
78.10	16.90	111.50	14.00	1707.00
129.90	15.10	99.00	7.80	300.00
103.10	18.40	65.00	6.40	479.00
90.30	15.90	91.80	10.30	1009.00
82.80	6.80	46.50	5.60	490.00
75.20	7.80	47.20	6.20	693.00
86.60	8.60	34.70	4.00	321.00
82.60	10.70	52.20	6.50	411.00
82.00	17.70	67.20	8.20	381.00
67.80	9.30	38.80	5.70	241.00
76.80	15.00	44.90	5.90	329.00
67.30	13.00	53.80	8.00	378.00
86.20 (Regress) **87.10 (EM)**	15.20	55.10	**6.40 (Regress)** **6.32 (EM)**	209.00
95.10	12.50	35.10	3.70	173.00
72.10	21.40	47.70	6.70	235.00
58.40	10.80	43.30	7.40	298.00
55.30	8.00	**4.76 (Regress)** **20.94 (EM)**	**4.26 (Regress)** **5.01 (EM)**	**114.03 (Regress)** **247.29 (EM)**
58.10	10.30	33.00	5.70	274.00

Note that the regression and EM imputed values are similar for *Eperua purpurea* (row 17) but very different for A_{mass} and G_s for *Micropholis maguirei* (row 21). The latter differences probably reflect the fact that only two predictor variables are available for this species for predicting the missing observations using a regression and the observed values for both of those variables are at the low end of the range for those variables. The EM imputed values are probably more reliable for this species.

15.10 | General issues and hints for analysis

15.10.1 General issues

- Variation within, and linear relationships between, two or more variables can be summarized with a sums-of-squares-and-cross-products matrix (raw data), covariance matrix (centered data) or a correlation matrix (standardized data).

- Spectral decomposition of one of these matrices produces new derived variables (components), extracted so the first explains most of the original variation, the second most of what is left, etc., and so that the new variables are uncorrelated with each other. Equivalent results are obtained from a singular value decomposition of the original data matrix, appropriately standardized.
- These new variables are linear combinations of the original variables and the coefficients

(summarized as an eigenvector) indicate the contribution of each original variable to the new variable.

- Differences between pairs of objects are measured with dissimilarities that are based on the sum of the differences for each variable between objects, often standardized so they range between zero and one.

- For measurement variables, either Euclidean or one of its modifications (City block or Canberra) are reliable dissimilarity measures, usually based on standardized data. For species abundances (counts with possible zero values), Bray–Curtis or Kulczynski are recommended.

- Graphical representations of multivariate data are available. SPLOMs display pairwise bivariate relationships and icon plots (Chernoff faces or stars) visually represent objects in terms of the relative values for the variables.

- The default for handling missing data with most software is to omit whole objects. Other approaches are generally preferred unless the sample size is large and the observations are missing completely at random.

15.10.2 Hints for analysis

- Before extracting components or determination of dissimilarities between objects when variables are measured in different scales or units, some type of standardization (based on standard deviation or range) is recommended.

- For species abundance, i.e. count, variables, different standardizations can provide useful comparative information. Standardizing objects to equal totals corrects for different sized sampling units, standardizing species to equal totals means that the most abundant species do not dominate the dissimilarity measure.

- Some standardizations can result in Bray–Curtis and Kulczynski dissimilarities not being bounded by one; standardize by range rather than by standard deviations when using these measures.

- We prefer standardizations to transformations for reducing the influence of variables with large values, although transforming variables may be relevant to improve linearity or if univariate analyses on the same variables also require transformation.

Chapter 16

Multivariate analysis of variance and discriminant analysis

In this chapter, we will examine the relationship between two or more response variables and one or more categorical predictor variables. We are primarily interested in two research questions. First, are there differences between groups based on all the response variables taken together and, second, can we successfully classify observations, particularly new observations, into the correct group.

16.1 | Multivariate analysis of variance (MANOVA)

There are many situations where we record more than one response variable from each sampling or experimental unit and where these units are allocated to or occur in treatment groups. Ecologists often record the abundances of many species from each sampling or experimental unit and physiologists commonly measure more than one variable (e.g. blood pressure, heart rate, etc.) on experimental animals. For example, Peckarsky *et al.* (1993) examined the sub-lethal responses of mayfly larvae in streams to three different predator treatments (no predator and normal food, no predator and reduced food, one predatory mayfly (*Megarcys*) and normal food). There were five response variables recorded for each mayfly: body mass, egg mass, percentage of eggs, total mass, and maturation time. Botanists and zoologists also often measure many morphological variables when describing organisms from different locations or to compare organisms that may or may not be taxonomically different.

If each response variable is of inherent biological interest, our research questions might be whether there are group or treatment effects on each variable separately. Then the appropriate strategy is to analyze each variable using a separate univariate ANOVA to test for differences between groups. Some statisticians have argued that there is an inherent disadvantage to this approach. Because the response variables are measured from the same experimental or sampling units and may be highly correlated, the multiple ANOVA tests are not independent of each other and this can make interpretation difficult. Also, the number of univariate tests can get large if we have many variables so the family-wise Type I error rate may be very high for the collection of tests (Harris 1993; see also Chapter 3). A common recommendation is to adjust the significance level of each ANOVA test by using a Bonferroni-type correction so the family-wise Type I error rate stays at or below 0.05 (or whatever *a priori* significance level you choose). Unfortunately, with many response variables, this can result in unacceptably low power for each univariate test.

With multiple response variables, we might be more interested in whether there are group differences on all the response variables considered simultaneously. This is the aim of multivariate analysis of variance (MANOVA), the analogue of univariate ANOVA when we have multiple response variables for each experimental or sampling unit. Basically our hypothesis is now about group effects on a combination of the response variables and instead of comparing group means on a single variable, we now compare group centroids for two or more variables. In the Peckarsky et al. (1993) example, we would test whether there is an effect of predator treatment on a combination of body mass, egg mass, percentage of eggs, total mass, and maturation time of individual mayflies.

We will illustrate MANOVA with two examples from the biological literature.

Trace metals in marine sediments

Haynes et al. (1995) carried out a pilot study to test for differences between sites in trace metal concentrations in marine sediments off the Victorian coast in southern Australia. They had three sites: Delray Beach, site of a proposed wastewater outfall, and two possible control sites, Seaspray and Woodside. At each site, they had four randomly chosen stations and at each station, two randomly chosen cores of sediment. They recorded the concentrations of copper, chromium, cadmium, lead, iron, nickel, manganese and mercury. We will test for the effects of site on a subset of these response variables taken together. Although this is strictly a nested design, site would be tested against the random station effect so we will average the replicate cores for each station and use a single factor MANOVA for comparing sites. The analysis of these data is presented in Box 16.1.

Plant functional groups and leaf characters

In Chapters 9 and 15, we described the study of Reich et al. (1999) who examined the generality of leaf traits from different species across a range of ecosystems and geographic regions. We will analyze a subset of their data (to avoid missing cells), with two locations (Colorado and Wisconsin) and two functional groups (forbs and shrubs) in a crossed design. There were between three and eleven species in each cell and five response variables were measured: specific leaf area ($\log_{10}$ transformed), leaf nitrogen concentration, mass-based net photosynthetic capacity, area-based net photosynthetic capacity and leaf diffusive conductance at photosynthetic capacity. We will test for the effects of location and functional group, and their interaction, on these five response variables taken together. The analysis of these data is presented in Box 16.2.

16.1.1 Single factor MANOVA

Linear combination

The simplest design where a MANOVA is appropriate is when we have n replicate experimental or sampling units ("objects" from Chapter 15) allocated to two or more levels of a factor (groups) and we record p (where p is greater than two) response variables from each unit. The MANOVA is based on a linear combination (z) of the p response variables as defined in Chapter 15 (see Equations 15.1 and 15.2). In the example from Haynes et al. (1995), there were n equals four replicate stations in each of three groups (sites) with p equals four response variables (trace metals). The MANOVA uses the linear combination (z) of response variables, out of the infinite number of possible linear combinations, which maximizes the ratio of between-group and within-group variances of z. This linear combination is also called the discriminant function for the difference between groups and is used in discriminant function analysis (see Section 16.2):

$$z_{ik} = \text{constant} + c_1 y_{i1} + c_2 y_{i2} + \ldots c_j y_{ij} + \ldots + c_p y_{ip} \quad (16.1)$$

For example, from Haynes et al. (1995):

$$z_{ik} = \text{constant} + c_1 (\log_{10} \text{Cu})_i + c_2 (\log_{10} \text{Pb})_i + c_3 (\log_{10} \text{Ni})_i + c_4 (\log_{10} \text{Mn})_i \quad (16.2)$$

From Reich et al. (1999):

$$z_{ik} = \text{constant} + c_1 (\log_{10} \text{specific leaf area})_i + c_2 (\text{leaf N})_i + c_3 (\text{mass-based photosynthetic capacity})_i + c_4 (\text{area-based photosynthetic capacity})_i + c_5 (\text{leaf diffusive capacity})_i \quad (16.3)$$

In Equations 16.1, 16.2 and 16.3, z_{ik} are the values for object i for linear combination k, the combination that maximizes the ratio of between-group and within-group variances of z_{ik}. From Haynes et al. (1995), this is the value for station i from solving Equation 16.2 for linear combination k. The coefficients (c_j) are the weights measuring the relative contribution of each variable to the linear combination. As described in Box 15.1, these coefficients will be scaled in some form and will be represented in matrix descriptions of MANOVA as elements of a matrix of eigenvectors (Box 15.1). Note that if the variables are

Box 16.1 | Worked example of MANOVA: heavy metals in marine sediments

Haynes *et al.* (1995) carried out a pilot study to test for differences between sites in trace metal concentrations in marine sediments off the Victorian coast in southern Australia. They had three sites: Delray Beach, site of a proposed wastewater outfall, and two possible control sites, Seaspray and Woodside. At each site, they recorded the concentrations of copper, chromium, cadmium, lead, iron, nickel, manganese and mercury (means of two sediment cores) at four randomly chosen stations. We used only the 1991 data in our analyses. There were strong correlations among some of the metals (e.g. Cu and Cr, Fe and Ni) so only four variables (Cu, Ni, Pb, Mn) were included in the analysis. There was strong indication of skewness for the four variables, so all were $\log_{10}$-transformed. There were a few cases with significant ($P < 0.001$) Mahalanobis distances ($D_{ij}^2 > 16.3$) but these were not extreme and remained in the analysis. All variables except Cu (Levene's test, $P = 0.023$) had similar variances between groups.

The multivariate test statistics all result in rejection of the H_0 that there is no difference in site group centroids.

	Statistic	df	F	P
Wilk's λ	0.058	8, 12	4.728	0.008
Pillai trace	1.272	8, 14	3.058	0.033
Hotelling–Lawley trace	10.549	8, 10	6.593	0.004

Pairwise contrasts among the sites, with a sequential Bonferroni (Holm's method) adjustment of P values, indicated that only the difference between Delray Beach and Woodside was significant.

Contrast	Pillai trace	df	F	P	Adj P
Delray vs Seaspray	0.713	4, 6	3.719	0.074	0.078
Delray vs Woodside	0.909	4, 6	14.924	0.003	0.009
Seaspray vs Woodside	0.772	4, 6	5.092	0.039	0.078

The univariate F tests indicate significant differences between sites for all four metals.

Source	df	MS	F	P
Log Cu				
Site	2	0.098	5.208	0.031
Residual	9	0.019		
Log Pb				
Site	2	0.136	4.834	0.038
Residual	9	0.028		
Log Ni				
Site	2	0.083	8.655	0.008
Residual	9	0.009		
Log Mn				
Site	2	0.244	23.608	<0.001
Residual	9	0.010		

The raw and standardized coefficients for the discriminant function obviously differ but because the variables were $\log_{10}$-transformed, the difference in scales between the variables is not great and the basic pattern is the same. The standardized coefficients suggest that lead contributes least to the difference between sites and manganese the most. The loadings simply reflect the univariate F-ratio statistics from above, and the pattern is the same as for the coefficients. Mn and Ni are most important, and Pb least important, at separating the sites.

Variable	Raw coefficient	Standardized coefficient	Loading
Constant	−29.013		
Log Cu	1.253	0.172	0.334
Log Pb	−0.494	−0.083	0.258
Log Ni	6.690	0.653	0.428
Log Mn	9.308	0.945	0.724

We had no theoretical basis for ordering our variables so we entered them in a step-down analysis in order of their univariate F-ratios. Log Mn entered first, then we tested log Ni with log Mn as a covariate, then log Cu with log Mn and log Ni as covariates and finally log Pb with log Mn, log Ni and log Cu as covariates. We were not interested in testing hypotheses about the covariates and adjusted the significance levels for the site effects with a Holm correction (Chapter 3).

Source	df	MS	F	P(Adj P)
Log Mn				
Site	2	0.244	23.608	<0.001 (0.004)
Residual	9	0.010		
Log Ni				
Site	2	0.034	3.407	0.085 (0.255)
Log Mn	1	0.007		
Residual	8	0.010		
Log Cu				
Site	2	0.011	0.512	0.620 (0.910)
Log Mn	1	<0.001		
Log Ni	1	0.023		
Residual	7	0.021		
Log Pb				
Site	2	0.033	0.901	0.455 (0.910)
Log Mn	1	0.021		
Log Ni	1	0.022		
Log Cu	1	0.002		
Residual	6	0.037		

The step-down analysis suggests that none of the variables contributes significantly to the difference between groups when entered after log Mn, i.e. none of the site effects for any variable is significant once log Mn is included as a covariate.

Box 16.2 | **Worked example of MANOVA: plant functional groups and leaf characters**

Reich et al. (1999) examined the generality of leaf traits from different species across a range of ecosystems and geographic regions. We will use two of their locations (Colorado and Wisconsin) and two of their functional groups (forbs and shrubs) in a crossed design. There were between three and eleven species in each cell and five response variables were measured: specific leaf area ($\log_{10}$-transformed), leaf nitrogen concentration, mass-based net photosynthetic capacity, area-based net photosynthetic capacity and leaf diffusive conductance at photosynthetic capacity.

There is some concern about the assumption of homogeneity of variances and covariances, especially as Levene's test for homogeneity of variances was statistically significant for three (log specific leaf area, leaf N and G_s) out of the five variables.

There were no significant multivariate test statistics for either main effect or the interaction. Note that since there were only two levels of each factor, the df, the approximate F-ratios and the P values were identical for each term for all three multivariate statistics.

	Wilk's λ	Pillai trace	Hotelling–Lawley trace	df	F	P
Location	0.573	0.427	0.745	5, 16	2.384	0.085
Functional group	0.549	0.450	0.819	5, 16	2.622	0.065
Interaction	0.836	0.164	0.196	5, 16	0.626	0.682

The univariate F tests indicate that the only significant effect was that of functional group for nitrogen concentration in leaves, although the effect of functional group for mass-based net photosynethetic capacity and of location for leaf diffusive conductance were marginal.

Source	df	F	P
Location	1, 19		
Log specific leaf area		0.880	0.359
Leaf N		0.005	0.947
A_{mass}		1.025	0.323
A_{area}		0.042	0.841
G_s		3.756	0.069
Functional group	1, 20		
Log specific leaf area		2.299	0.145
Leaf N		5.305	0.032
A_{mass}		3.254	0.086
A_{area}		1.148	0.297
G_s		2.645	0.119
Interaction	1, 20		
Log specific leaf area		1.979	0.175
Leaf N		0.774	0.389
A_{mass}		1.624	0.217
A_{area}		0.065	0.802
G_s		1.112	0.304

The standardized discriminant function coefficients for each main effect and interaction would not normally be of much interest given that there were no significant effects from the MANOVA. We present them simply to illustrate that there is a separate discriminant function for each effect in the model and we can interpret these coefficients just as we would for single factor MANOVAs.

Variable	Location	Functional group	Interaction
Log specific leaf area	−2.002	−1.721	1.309
Leaf N	1.798	1.499	−1.294
A_{mass}	0.612	1.409	0.479
A_{area}	−1.489	−1.615	0.338
G_s	1.436	1.472	−0.709

standardized to zero mean and unit variance, the constant equals zero.

The determination of the linear combination that maximizes the ratio of between-group and within-group variances is best done using simple matrix algebra, some of which we have already described in Chapter 15. The steps for a single factor MANOVA are as follows.

1. The between-groups, within-groups and total SS used in an ANOVA are replaced by sums-of-squares-and-cross-products matrices (SSCP or **S**; see Chapter 15), one matrix for between groups (the hypothesis or effect matrix, **H**), one for within groups (the error or residual matrix, **E**) and one for total (the total matrix, **T**). The values in the main diagonal of these matrices are the univariate sums-of-squares for each variable, either between group means (**H**) or pooled across replicates within groups (**E**). The other elements are the sums-of-cross-products between any two of the variables. For example, the cross product for the between-groups matrix for two variables is the sum of (i) the product of the differences between each group mean and the overall mean for one variable and (ii) the differences between each value and the mean for the other variable – see Table 16.1.

2. We multiply **H** by the inverse of **E** (i.e. **HE**$^{-1}$). Matrix inversion is the multivariate analogue of division so what we are really doing here is "dividing" **H** by **E**, the between-groups SSCP matrix "divided by" the within-groups SSCP matrix.

3. We then decompose the resulting matrix product (Box 15.1) to calculate characteristic roots or eigenvalues of each linear combination (eigenvector). The eigenvalues measure how much of the total between-group variance in the variables (the sum of the between-group variances of each of the variables) is explained by each linear combination or eigenvector. The eigenvectors contain the coefficients for each linear combination.

4. The linear combination producing the largest eigenvalue is the linear combination that maximizes the ratio of between-group and within-group variance (i.e. maximizes the explained variance between groups) and the eigenvector is a vector of coefficients or weights for that linear combination.

Null hypothesis

The H_0 for a single factor MANOVA is that the population effect of the groups or treatments is zero with respect to all linear combinations of the response variables. This is equivalent to no difference between population centroids (multivariate means). This H_0 can be tested by using statistics based on one of the measures of variance of a matrix, such as the determinant or the trace (Chapter 15; see also Harris 1985, Johnson & Field 1993, Stevens 1992, Tabachnick & Fidell 1996).

• Wilk's lambda (λ), which is the ratio of the determinants of the within-groups SSCP and the total SSCP: $|\mathbf{E}|/|\mathbf{T}|$. Remember that the determinant of a matrix is a measure of generalized variance for that matrix (Chapter

Table 16.1 Groups (a) and residual (b) and total (c) sums-of-squares-and-cross-products matrices for data from Haynes *et al.* (1995)

(a)

	Log_{10} Cu	Log_{10} Pb	Log_{10} Ni	Log_{10} Mn
Log_{10} Cu	0.196			
Log_{10} Pb	0.152	0.273		
Log_{10} Ni	0.164	0.192	0.165	
Log_{10} Mn	0.306	0.275	0.273	0.487

(b)

	Log_{10} Cu	Log_{10} Pb	Log_{10} Ni	Log_{10} Mn
Log_{10} Cu	0.169			
Log_{10} Pb	0.001	0.254		
Log_{10} Ni	0.045	0.031	0.086	
Log_{10} Mn	−0.011	0.033	−0.026	0.093

(c)

	Log_{10} Cu	Log_{10} Pb	Log_{10} Ni	Log_{10} Mn
Log_{10} Cu	0.369			
Log_{10} Pb	0.153	0.523		
Log_{10} Ni	0.209	0.223	0.251	
Log_{10} Mn	0.295	0.308	0.247	0.579

Note:

The main diagonals are sums-of-squares between groups, within groups and total and the other elements are cross-products.

15), so Wilk's λ is a measure of how much of the total variance is due to the residual, with smaller values indicating larger group differences.

- Hotelling–Lawley trace, which is the ratio of the determinants of the between-groups SSCP and the within-groups SSCP: $|H|/|E|$. This is also the sum of the eigenvalues (trace) of the matrix product HE^{-1}. Larger values indicate greater differences between group centroids.
- Pillai trace, which is the sum of the eigenvalues (trace) of HT^{-1}, i.e. the variance between groups.
- Roy's largest root, which is the largest eigenvalue of HE^{-1}, i.e. the eigenvalue of the linear combination that explains most of the variance and covariance between groups. This statistic is less commonly provided by statistical software.

The sampling distributions of these statistics are not well understood and they are usually converted to approximate F-ratio statistics (Tabachnick & Fidell 1996). Wilk's, Hotelling's and Pillai's statistics produce identical F tests when there are only two groups and become Hotelling's T^2 statistic – see example based on plant functional group data in Box 16.2. This is the multivariate extension of the t test for comparing two groups (Harris 1985, Tabachnick & Fidell 1996). They will generally produce similar results with more than two groups, although Pillai's trace seems to be the most robust of the tests (Johnson & Field 1993), especially when the assumption of similar variance–covariance matrices might be violated (Section 16.1.4). In our two worked examples (Box 16.1 and Box 16.2), the conclusions from Wilk's, Hotelling's and Pillai's statistics were the same. Most statistical software will provide H, E, maximum λ and all the multivariate test statistics with their approximate F tests.

16.1.2 Specific comparisons

Most statistical software allow contrasts among the factor levels in MANOVA, analogous to planned contrasts in the univariate ANOVA (Chapter 8). Unplanned multiple comparisons are a more difficult problem, although use of Bonferroni-adjusted (see Chapter 3) pairwise MANOVAs is one conservative solution. Harris (1993) and Johnson & Field (1993) have reviewed other approaches for comparing specific groups after a MANOVA.

16.1.3 Relative importance of each response variable

If the null hypothesis of no difference between group centroids is rejected, we usually are interested in which of the response variables contributes most to the group differences. There are several methods of assessing the relative contribution of each response variable to the difference between groups in a MANOVA.

Univariate ANOVAs

We can examine the univariate ANOVAs on each response variable separately. Indeed, univariate hypotheses about group differences for each response variable will often be relevant. These univariate results do not necessarily indicate the relative contribution of each variable to the MANOVA result because they ignore correlations between variables. Correlations between variables can have marked effects on the power of MANOVA tests (Cole *et al.* 1994). Some authors (e.g. Harris 1985, 1993) also emphasize the problem of increasing family-wise Type I error rates when doing multiple univariate ANOVAs, a problem inherent in any multiple testing situation (see Chapter 3).

Step-down analysis

Step-down analysis is an analogue of forward selection stepwise multiple regression (Chapter 6) but taking into account the group structure (Tabachnick & Fidell 1996). This procedure relies on ordering the response variables based on theoretical expectations of their importance or using univariate analyses to choose the variable that shows the greatest difference between groups. First, the response variable with the highest priority is decided; for example, this might be the variable with the largest F-ratio from univariate ANOVAs on all the response variables. Each response variable is then tested sequentially, in the order determined *a priori*, in an ANCOVA model (Chapter 12), with groups as the categorical predictor and the higher priority response variables as covariates. We are interested in how much each additional variable adds to the variance explained by the variables already included.

Automated step-down analysis is available in some statistical software; otherwise, it must done with a series of ANCOVAs. Step-down analysis suffers from the problems we described in Chapter 6 for stepwise multiple regression, although we are not trying to find the "best" model in this situation, just assess the relative importance of each of the response variables. Step-down analysis also results in numerous unplanned significance tests so you need to be aware of the high family-wise Type I error rate. Huberty (1994) describes similar approaches, such as deleting variables one at a time and running a MANOVA on each set of the $p-1$ remaining variables. The variables can be ordered based on the size of the change in MANOVA test statistic for each set.

Coefficients of linear combination

A more subjective approach is based on examining the discriminant function, i.e. the linear combination of the response variables that maximizes the ratio of between-group to within-group variance. There is a coefficient for each variable in the discriminant function, plus one for the grand mean (i.e. intercept or constant). If the different variables are measured on comparable scales (or we have values of a single variable recorded repeatedly through time in a repeated measures design), then the relative size of these coefficients (also termed "weights") provides a comparable measure of the contribution of each variable to the variance explained by the discriminant function and thus the difference between groups. If the variables are measured on very different scales, then we need to standardize them so that the coefficients can be compared. The simplest method is to standardize the discriminant function by the within-group variances, although whether this produces coefficients that are directly comparable is debatable (see Harris 1985 and Huberty 1994 for differing opinions). Standard errors can be estimated for each discriminant function coefficient (Flury & Riedwyl 1988), although they are rarely provided by statistical software.

Loadings

Loadings are the correlations between each variable and the discriminant function (see Chapters 15 and 17). These simply represent the correlations between the value of a variable and the score for the discriminant function with the units as replicates. The loadings of each variable on each discriminant function can be found by multiplying the within-group correlation matrix between variables (pooled across groups) by the matrix of standardized discriminant function coefficients (Tabachnick & Fidell 1996). Correlations automatically standardize the variables and examining loadings is popular because correlation coefficients are familiar and easily interpretable. However, these loadings are directly proportional to the univariate F-ratio statistics for each variable tested between groups so they ignore any relationships between the variables (Harris 1985). Note that one of the effects of highly correlated response variables can be a contradictory pattern when coefficients are compared with loadings.

Comments

Most statistical software will provide all of these coefficients and the loadings, either in MANOVA output or as part of a discriminant function analysis. The terminology used in the output does, however, vary considerably between programs and Tabachnick & Fidell (1996) provide a detailed comparison of the major software. Our experience is that unless there are many variables with some high correlations, the different approaches will produce a similar pattern. In our worked example of trace metals in sediments (Haynes *et al.* 1995; Box 16.1), the variables were log-transformed but not standardized. The univariate F-ratios, loadings and function coefficients showed the same pattern, with the order of importance being log Mn, followed by log Ni, log Cu and log Pb. The step-down analysis showed that none

of the variables contributed significantly to site differences besides log Mn.

16.1.4 Assumptions of MANOVA

It is important to check normality, homogeneity of variance, and outliers for each response variable using univariate exploratory data analysis procedures (boxplots, residual plots, pplots, etc.; see Chapter 4). Given that the multivariate tests (especially Pillai's trace) are relatively robust to deviations from multivariate normality, particularly if each response variable has approximate univariate normality and sample sizes are equal, two multivariate assumptions are of major concern (Johnson & Field 1993, Tabachnick & Fidell 1996).

First, MANOVA tests are sensitive to multivariate outliers, which are cases with an unusual pattern of values for all the response variables considered simultaneously. Mahalanobis distance, the distance of each observation from the centroid or multivariate mean, can be used to detect multivariate outliers and is provided by most statistical software (Chapter 15).

Second, homogeneity of variances and covariances (i.e. equality of the variance–covariance matrices for each group) is an important assumption – this is the multivariate extension of univariate homogeneity of within-group variances. If this assumption is not met, then the pooled within-group matrix (E) will be misleading. Box's M test can test the H_0 of equal variance–covariance matrices but it is very sensitive to deviations from multivariate normality and is not recommended. There is no easy check for this assumption (but see discussion in Johnson & Field 1993), although it is more likely to be met when univariate homogeneity holds for each response variable. Like univariate ANOVA tests, MANOVA tests are more reliable when sample sizes are equal. Reducing the dimensionality (reducing the number of variables) of the analysis improves the robustness of all the MANOVA tests statistics (Johnson & Field 1993).

Johnson & Field (1993) provided strong evidence from simulation studies that Pillai's trace statistic is the most robust to deviations from the assumption of homogeneity of the variance–covariance matrices across groups. Suitable transformations of individual variables should

Table 16.2 MANOVA results from Juenger & Bergelson (2000) who tested the effects of clipping, emasculation and their interaction on four response variables (flower, fruit, and seed production, total seed mass) of the perennial wildflower, the scarlet gilia

Source	df	Wilk's λ	F	P
Clipping (C)	4, 56	0.467	23.950	<0.001
Emasculation (E)	4, 45	0.936	3.251	0.439
C × E	4, 56	0.826	2.768	0.029

also be used where appropriate and including quadratic terms in the discriminant function can also help (Section 16.2.3).

Collinearity between variables is also a problem in the same way as for multiple regression (Chapter 6). The discriminant function coefficients, just like multiple regression coefficients, will be sensitive to which variables are included or excluded when variables are highly correlated. Most statistical software provides collinearity diagnostics, such as tolerance or variance inflation factors, and examinations of pairwise correlations between variables will be informative. Not including highly correlated (redundant) variables will help lessen the impact of collinearity and, since it reduces the dimensionality of the data matrix, will also make the MANOVA more robust to heterogeneous variance–covariance matrices (see above).

16.1.5 Robust MANOVA
Approaches to MANOVA that are robust to the underlying assumptions of multivariate normality and homogeneity of the variance–covariance matrices have been based on randomization procedures (Johnson & Field 1993). Edgington (1995) and Manly (1997) describe numerous possible test statistics for randomization MANOVA tests. These include a test based on Wilk's lambda, one using the sum of the logs of the univariate t or F statistics for each variable and one that compares the sum of squared Euclidean distances between objects and their sample centroids between groups and within groups. Manly (1997) pointed out that with large data sets (many variables and/or observations), only a subsample of all possible randomizations of observations on all variables to groups will be possible.

Another type of test is to determine distances or dissimilarities between all pairs of objects and compare the between-groups and within-groups dissimilarities. These tests will be described in Chapter 18 when we consider in detail multivariate analyses based on dissimilarities.

16.1.6 More complex designs
MANOVAs can also be used to test null hypotheses about combinations of variables in more complex designs. The matrix calculations described in Section 16.1.1 are done for each effect and error term that would have been used if univariate ANOVA models were fitted (Harris 1985). Separate linear combinations of variables are thus constructed for each main effect and interaction (Box 16.2) and the contribution of each variable needs to be assessed separately for each effect and its appropriate discriminant function. An ecological example is from Juenger & Bergelson (2000), who studied interactions between herbivory and pollination on various aspects of reproduction in the perennial wildflower *Ipomopsis aggregata* ssp. candida (the scarlet gilia) in Colorado, USA. Their experimental design had two factors: artificial grazing or clipping (two levels: control vs experimentally clipped) and male function (two levels: control vs emasculation, i.e. anther removal). There were 20 replicate plants in each combination (cell) of the two factor crossed design and a number of response variables were measured for each plant: total number of flowers, fruits and undamaged seeds and total seed mass. They used Wilk's lambda to test the two main effects and the interaction effect on the combination of the four response variables (Table 16.2).

Table 16.3 | MANOVA results from Pennings & Calloway (1996) who set up an experiment in a saltmarsh with three factors: *Cuscuta* infection by the parasitic plant *Cuscuta salina*, zone within saltmarsh and size of patch. They recorded the biomass of three non-parasitic plant species and analyzed these three response variables with a three factor (infection, marsh zone, patch size) crossed MANOVA

Source	df	Pillai's trace	F	P
Infected or not	3, 54	0.58	24.43	<0.001
Marsh zone	3, 54	0.38	11.00	<0.001
Patch size	3, 54	0.51	18.56	<0.001
Infection × zone	3, 54	0.19	4.12	0.010
Infection × size	3, 54	0.41	12.60	<0.001
Zone × size	3, 54	0.13	2.60	0.062
Infection × zone × size	3, 54	0.09	1.84	0.150

A more complex factorial MANOVA was used by Pennings & Callaway (1996), who studied the effects of a parasitic plant (*Cuscuta salina*) on a saltmarsh community. They set up an experiment with three factors: *Cuscuta* infection, zone within saltmarsh and size of patch. They recorded the biomass of three non-parasitic plant species and analyzed these three response variables with a three factor (infection, marsh zone, patch size) crossed MANOVA and tested the hypotheses for each main effect and interaction using Pillai's trace statistic (Table 16.3).

Note that one of the commonest applications of MANOVA in biology is in the analysis of repeated measures designs (Chapters 10 and 11), where the differences between pairs of repeated measurements are analyzed as multiple response variables using MANOVA statistics.

16.2 | Discriminant function analysis

Discriminant function analysis (DFA) is a "classification" technique, introduced by Fisher (1936) and recently reviewed by Huberty (1994). DFA is used when we have observations from pre-determined groups with two or more response variables recorded for each observation. DFA generates a linear combination of variables that maximizes the probability of correctly assigning observations to their pre-determined groups and can also be used to classify new observations into one of the groups. We might also wish to have some measure of the likelihood of success of our classification. Examples of DFA are common in the biological literature. For example, Skelly (1995) used DFA to test how well three variables (survivorship, size and larval period) could be used to classify individuals of two species of frogs (chorus frogs and spring peepers). Petit & Petit (1996) used DFA to separate four habitats based on ten variables (canopy cover, canopy height, density of various stem sizes) measured around nest boxes occupied by warblers along the Tennessee River.

We will illustrate DFA with the same two data sets we used for MANOVA.

Trace metals in marine sediments

We will analyze the data from Haynes *et al.* (1995), previously used in Box 16.1 for a MANOVA, with a discriminant function analysis. Our aim is to classify stations to each of the three sites (Delray Beach, Seaspray, Woodside) based on trace metal concentrations in marine sediments off the Victorian coast in southern Australia. The DFA of these data is in Box 16.3.

Plant functional groups and leaf characters

We will also analyze the data from Reich *et al.* (1999), used in Box 16.2 for a MANOVA, with a discriminant function analysis to classify species into one of four location and plant functional group combinations (Colorado–forb, Colorado–shrub,

Box 16.3 | Worked example of discriminant function analysis: trace metals in marine sediments

We will illustrate a discriminant function analysis using the data from Haynes *et al.* (1995) – see Box 16.1. The aim here is to try and predict site membership of stations based on the four variables recorded for each station. The variance explained by each discriminant function was as follows.

	Eigenvalue	Percentage of variance
Function 1	9.979	94.6
Function 2	0.570	5.4

The first discriminant function explains most of the between-group (between-site) variance. The MANOVA test showed a significant difference between sites in the first discriminant function (Pillai trace = 1.272, df = 8, 14, *F*-ratio = 3.058, *P* = 0.033; see Box 16.1).

The relative contributions of each of the four trace metals to each discriminant function were as follows.

	Raw coefficient		Standardized coefficient		Loading	
	1	2	1	2	1	2
Constant	−29.013	−0.822	0	0		
Log Cu	1.253	3.030	0.172	0.415	0.334	−0.271
Log Pb	−0.494	−5.042	−0.083	−0.847	0.258	0.845
Log Ni	6.690	−3.126	0.653	−0.305	0.428	0.409
Log Mn	9.308	2.864	0.945	0.291	0.724	−0.159

The general pattern is the same for raw and standardized coefficients and loadings. Manganese and nickel contribute the most to the first function (Box 16.1), whereas lead contributes most to the second function. Note that within a discriminant function, the direction of the sign for each variable is arbitrary, i.e. the positives and negatives could be reversed with no change in interpretation.

The classification functions for each site are tabulated below.

	Delray	Seaspray	Woodside
Constant	−339.675	−421.174	−534.398
Log Cu	14.723	14.191	22.851
Log Pb	−24.237	−18.519	−27.090
Log Ni	171.225	195.893	216.269
Log Mn	258.338	282.345	320.356

These classification functions were solved for each station and each station classified to the site with the highest value.

	Delray	Seaspray	Woodside	Percentage correct
Delray	4	0	0	100
Seaspray	0	4	0	100
Woodside	0	0	4	100
Total	4	4	4	100

Note that percentage successful prediction is perfect. The classification matrix produced using a jackknife technique was as follows.

	Delray	Seaspray	Woodside	Percentage correct
Delray	3	1	0	74
Seaspray	1	3	0	75
Woodside	1	1	2	50
Total	5	5	2	67

Note that the jackknifed model results in lower percentage successful prediction but these percentages may be a more reliable indicator of classification success because we have excluded each observation when calculating the classification coefficients.

A discriminant function plot using group mean scores showed that the three sites discriminate clearly along function 1 but there is little separation along function 2, not surprisingly since function 1 explained nearly all of the variation between sites (Figure 16.1).

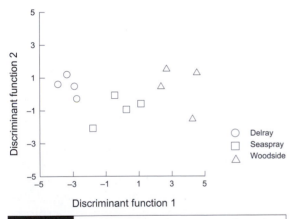

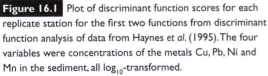

Figure 16.1 Plot of discriminant function scores for each replicate station for the first two functions from discriminant function analysis of data from Haynes et al. (1995). The four variables were concentrations of the metals Cu, Pb, Ni and Mn in the sediment, all $\log_{10}$-transformed.

although the former emphasizes classification and prediction rather than tests of hypotheses about group differences. However, the first step in any DFA is to derive discriminant functions (also called canonical discriminant functions) that are linear combinations of the original variables. The first discriminant function is the linear combination of variables that maximizes the ratio of between-groups to within-groups variance (i.e. maximizes the differences between groups) and is the linear combination used for the MANOVA test of no differences between group centroids derived in Section 16.1.1. The second discriminant function is independent of (uncorrelated with) the first and best separates groups using the variation remaining (the residual variation) after the first discriminant function has been determined, and so on for the third, fourth, etc., discriminant functions.

The number of discriminant functions that can be extracted depends on the number of groups and the number of variables – it is the lesser of the degrees of freedom for groups (number of groups minus one) and the number of variables (Tabachnick & Fidell 1996). In the example from Haynes et al. (1995), with three groups (sites) and four variables, there can be only two discriminant functions. Even in situations when there are more functions, the first one or two usually have the most discriminating power. Most statistical software also provides eigenvalues

Wisconsin–forb, Wisconsin–shrub) based on five response variables: specific leaf area ($\log_{10}$-transformed), leaf nitrogen concentration, mass-based net photosynthetic capacity, area-based net photosynthetic capacity and leaf diffusive conductance at photosynthetic capacity. The DFA of these data is in Box 16.4.

16.2.1 Description and hypothesis testing

Discriminant function analysis (DFA) is mathematically identical to a single factor MANOVA,

Box 16.4 | Worked example of discriminant function analysis: plant functional groups and leaf characters

We examined our ability to discriminate between the four location and functional group combinations for species of plants on which Reich *et al.* (1999) measured five variables – see Box 16.2. Like the two factor MANOVA earlier, the multivariate tests indicated no significant differences between the four groups (e.g. Pillai Trace = 0.902, df = 15, 54, *F*-ratio = 1.548, *P* = 0.121) for the first discriminant function.

The following classification functions were solved for each species (object).

	Colorado forb	Colorado shrub	Wisconsin forb	Wisconsin shrub
Constant	−535.136	−570.858	−576.439	−593.038
Log specific leaf area	557.743	580.616	582.442	592.914
Leaf N	−2.688	−2.981	−3.010	−3.129
A_{mass}	−1.126	−1.154	−1.134	−1.173
A_{area}	24.450	25.467	25.356	26.184
G_s	−0.227	−0.249	−0.248	−0.262

Each species was classified to the location and functional group combination with the highest value for the classification function. The classification matrices showed that we could more correctly classify species to some combinations than others.

	Colorado forb	Colorado shrub	Wisconsin forb	Wisconsin shrub	Percentage correct
Colorado forb	3	0	0	0	100
Colorado shrub	0	3	0	1	75
Wisconsin forb	1	3	6	1	55
Wisconsin shrub	0	1	0	5	83
Total	4	7	6	7	71

The jackknifed classification matrix was as follows.

	Colorado forb	Colorado shrub	Wisconsin forb	Wisconsin shrub	Percentage correct
Colorado forb	3	0	0	0	100
Colorado shrub	2	0	0	2	0
Wisconsin forb	2	2	5	2	45
Wisconsin shrub	0	2	0	4	67
Total	7	4	5	8	50

We were most successful at classifying species from the Colorado–forb combination and least from the Colorado–shrub combination.

The plot of the scores for the first two discriminant functions shows that there is considerable overlap between the different groups for both functions (Figure 16.2). Colorado forbs were the tightest group and we were most successful at classifying these species.

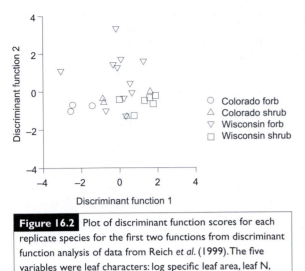

Discriminant function 2 (y-axis, from −4 to 4)

Discriminant function 1 (x-axis, from −4 to 4)

○ Colorado forb
△ Colorado shrub
▽ Wisconsin forb
□ Wisconsin shrub

Figure 16.2 Plot of discriminant function scores for each replicate species for the first two functions from discriminant function analysis of data from Reich et al. (1999). The five variables were leaf characters: log specific leaf area, leaf N, A_{mass}, A_{area}, and G_s.

(how much of the between-group variance is explained by each function) and the proportion of total variance explained.

Determining which variables contribute most to discriminant functions, and therefore to group separation, is done in the same way as for MANOVA (Section 16.1.3). The relative sizes of the standardized coefficients for each discriminant function indicate which variables are more important to each discriminant function. Also useful are loadings, which measure the correlation between each variable and each discriminant function, although they ignore any correlation between variables. With a large number of variables, stepwise discriminant function analysis can be used, similar to stepwise multiple regression. The stepwise approach enters and removes variables in a model-building process to try and produce a discriminant function with only the "important" variables. Our criticisms of stepwise procedures (see Chapter 6) are just as applicable here and we do not recommend stepwise discriminant analysis.

The test of the H_0 of no difference between group centroids (MANOVA) is usually the first step in a discriminant function analysis because if it is not significant, the discriminant functions will not be very useful for separating groups and therefore classifying observations. Successive discriminant functions can be tested for significance

(the second one is tested after the first has been extracted) using the MANOVA tests described in Section 16.1.1.

We can calculate discriminant function scores (z_{ik}) for each observation on each function (k) by simply solving each discriminant function as in Equation 16.1. These scores can be used in a linear discriminant function (LDF) plot (Huberty 1994), with the first discriminant function scores on one axis and the second discriminant function scores on the other axis. Either individual observations or centroids can be plotted. These plots indicate subjectively how similar or different groups are in terms of the discriminant functions. For example, there was a clear separation between sites from Haynes et al. (1995) when the first two discriminant functions were plotted (Figure 16.1), although most of the difference was for function one.

LDFs can also be presented as biplots where the loadings (correlations) of each variable on each function are plotted as vectors, scaled so that the vectors are commensurate with the scale of functions scores. The direction of the vectors indicates an increase in the values of the variable towards those objects in that direction on the plot, and the length of the vector indicates the rate of increase. Biplots will be explored in more detail in Chapter 17.

16.2.2 Classification and prediction

The second purpose of a DFA is to classify each observation into one of the groups and assess the success of the classification. A classification equation is derived for each group and is a linear combination of variables like a discriminant function, including a constant (Equation 16.1).

For example, for Delray using the variables from Haynes et al. (1995):

$$C_{\text{Delray}} = \text{constant} + c_1(\log_{10} \text{Cu}) + c_2(\log_{10} \text{Pb}) + c_3(\log_{10} \text{Ni}) + c_4(\log_{10} \text{Mn}) \quad (16.4)$$

There are four steps in determining and using the classification function for any group.

• The coefficients (c) of the classification equation are termed classification coefficients (Tabachnick & Fidell 1996) and are found by multiplying the within-group covariance matrix (pooled across all groups) by the matrix of means for each variable for that group.

- The constant for a group is determined by multiplying the matrix of classification coefficients for that group (i.e. the coefficients for each variable) again by the matrix of means for each variable for that group.
- A classification score for each observation for each group is then calculated by using the actual values for each variable to solve the classification equation for that group.
- Each observation is formally classified into the group for which it has the highest score. This may or may not be the actual group from which the observation came.

Tabachnick & Fidell (1996) have provided a fully worked example of the calculations and Huberty (1994) has a more detailed theoretical background.

Discriminant analysis routines in most statistical software provide classification matrices that indicate to which group each observation was classified and whether that classification was correct. The success of classifications of observations will be greater if the groups were clearly distinguishable on the first discriminant function. For example, the stations from Haynes *et al.* (1995) were clearly separable into groups (highly significant MANOVA) and the classification success was also high (Box 16.3). In contrast, there was no significant separation of groups in the Reich *et al.* (1999) data and the classification success was lower (e.g. only six out eleven species correctly classified as being from forbs from Wisconsin – Box 16.4).

One difficulty with the classification methodology we just described is that the classification functions are calculated using all observations and these functions are then used to classify the same observations, i.e. we classify each observation with an equation that already used that observation. One way of avoiding the resulting inherent bias is to use a jackknife procedure (Chapter 2). The classification of each observation is based on group classification functions that are determined when the observation is omitted and only the remaining observations are used to calculate coefficients and constants. In our examples,

Table 16.4 Discriminant function analysis from Skelly (1995). The grouping variable was frog species (*Pseudoacris triseriata* and *P. crucifer*) and standardized coefficients and loadings for the three variables on the first discriminant function are provided. Larval period contributed most to the separation between species

Variable	Standardized coefficient	Loading (correlation)
Survivorship	0.208	0.015
Size	0.634	0.593
Larval period	1.015	0.757

the jackknife classifications were less successful, but probably more robust, than the usual classifications using all observations (Box 16.3 and Box 16.4). The biggest difference between the usual and jackknifed classifications will often be for groups with the smallest sample size, again illustrated for the classification of the Reich *et al.* (1999) data where our classification success for Colorado shrubs went from 75% to 0% when the jackknife approach was used (Box 16.4).

Most uses of DFA we have found in the biological literature have focused on description and hypothesis testing, rather than classification. For example, Petit & Petit (1996) derived three discriminant functions to separate four habitats based on ten variables (canopy cover, canopy height, density of various stem sizes) measured around nest boxes occupied by warblers along the Tennessee River. They found that the first function explained 96.7% of the variance and canopy cover was the variable most highly correlated (loading = 0.84) with this first discriminant function. Skelly (1995) used a number of discriminant function analyses in his study of tadpole behaviour and performance. In one, he tested how well three variables (survivorship, size, and larval period) classified individuals into one of two species of frogs (chorus frogs and spring peepers). He presented a single discriminant function, which significantly separated the two species (MANOVA). Larval period had the highest coefficient (1.015) and loading (0.76) for this function, i.e. larval period separated the species more than size and survivorship (Table 16.4).

16.2.3 Assumptions of discriminant function analysis

DFA has the same assumptions as MANOVA (Section 16.1.4). The most important of these assumptions is homogeneity of the within-group variance–covariance matrices, especially for the classification part of discriminant analysis because this is quite sensitive to heterogeneous variance–covariance matrices between groups. This assumption is very difficult to test formally and Tabachnick & Fidell (1996) suggested plotting the scores for each observation for the first two discriminant functions (e.g. Figure 16.1) and checking if the spread of points is similar among the groups. Transformations of variables will often help.

If there is clear heterogeneity across the within-group variance–covariance matrices, you can try fitting quadratic functions instead of the usual linear ones. Quadratic functions include coefficients for squares of the variables and do not assume equal within-group covariances; statistical software usually offers quadratic functions as an option. Quadratic terms are usually highly correlated with the linear term for the same variable. This can result in collinearity problems (Section 16.1.4) and centered variables may need to be used (Chapter 6).

16.2.4 More complex designs

Because DFA is identical to a MANOVA, DFA can be extended to more complex designs, such as factorial designs, as described in Section 16.1.6. However, when focusing on classification, we usually treat each combination of factor levels (cell) as a separate group and use methods developed for single factor designs.

16.3 | MANOVA vs discriminant function analysis

MANOVA and DFA are mathematically identical (Tabachnik & Fidell 1996), although the terminology used in the two procedures often differs. In MANOVA, we test whether population centroids, based on a number of response variables, are different between groups. In DFA, we use the response variables to try and predict group membership and also to classify new observations to one or other of the groups with some measure of success of that classification. The linear combination of variables that maximizes the ratio of between-group to within-group variation in MANOVA is the first discriminant function. Discriminant function analysis goes further than MANOVA, however, by calculating additional discriminant functions and using the functions to classify observations to groups.

16.4 | General issues and hints for analysis

16.4.1 General issues

- MANOVA can be used to analyze any design where there is more than one response variable and one or more categorical predictor variables and the question of interest concerns the response variables considered simultaneously.
- MANOVA is also used when analyzing partly nested models for "repeated measures" designs where the differences between levels of the within-subjects factor are treated as multiple response variables.
- Although checking the assumptions is more difficult for multivariate analyses compared with univariate analyses, the former are also more sensitive to departures from the assumptions.
- MANOVA and DFA are functionally equivalent, the former emphasizing between-group differences on a single discriminant function, the latter using more than one discriminant function and focusing on classification.

16.4.2 Hints for analysis

- Homogeneity of between-group variances and covariances is important. Keep sample sizes similar and at least ensure homogeneity of variances for each variable separately. Check for outliers with Mahalanobis distance, tested against a χ^2 distribution with p df and a strict significance level (0.001).

- Pillai's trace is the most robust of the test statistics for MANOVA and is recommended.
- The contribution of each variable to a discriminant function is best measured by the standardized coefficients.
- Loadings for each variable on each discriminant function ignore correlations between variables and will have the same pattern between groups as the univariate F tests for each variable
- Jackknifed classifications of each observation to each group are probably more reliable than standard classifications because the former do not include the observation being classified when calculating the classification score.

Chapter 17

Principal components and correspondence analysis

This chapter and the next deal with analyses of multiple variables recorded from multiple objects where there are two primary aims. The first is to reduce many variables to a smaller number of new derived variables that adequately summarize the original information and can be used for further analysis, i.e. variable reduction. Multivariate analysis of variance and discriminant function analysis described in the previous chapter also have this aim. The discriminant functions represented the new derived variables that are extracted while explicitly accounting for group structure in the data set. Comparison of groups in the methods covered in this chapter and the next require subsequent analyses because the extraction of the summary variables does not consider group structure.

The second aim is to reveal patterns in the data, especially among objects, that could not be found by analyzing each variable separately. One way of detecting these patterns is to plot the objects in multidimensional space, the dimensions being the new derived variables. This is termed scaling, or multidimensional scaling, and the objects are ordered along each axis and the distance between objects in multidimensional space represents their biological dissimilarity (Chapter 15). Ecologists often use the term "ordination" instead of scaling, particularly for analyses that arrange sampling or experimental units in terms of species composition or environmental characteristics. Ordination is sometimes considered as a subset of gradient analysis (Kent & Coker 1992). Direct gradient analysis displays sampling units directly in relation to one or more underlying environmental characteristics. Indirect gradient analysis displays sampling units in relation to a reduced set of variables, usually based on species composition, and then relates the pattern in sampling units to the underlying environmental characteristics.

There are many different approaches to achieving the aims of variable reduction and scaling (ordination). In this chapter, we will describe methods based on extracting eigenvectors and eigenvalues from matrices of associations between variables or objects (Chapter 15). Methods based on measures of dissimilarity between objects will be the subject of Chapter 18.

17.1 | Principal components analysis

Principal components analysis (PCA) is one of the most commonly used multivariate statistical techniques and it is also the basis for some others. For $i = 1$ to n objects, PCA transforms $j = 1$ to p variables ($Y_1, Y_2, Y_3,...,Y_p$) into $k = 1$ to p new uncorrelated variables ($Z_1, Z_2, Z_3,..., Z_p$) called principal components or factors (Chapter 15). The scores for each object on each component are called z-scores (Jackson 1991). For example, Naiman et al. (1994) examined the influence of beavers on aquatic biogeochemistry. Four habitats were sampled for soil and pore water constituents. Variables were N, nitrate-N, ammonium-N, P, K, Ca, Mg, Fe, sulfate, pH, Eh, percentage of organic matter, bulk density, N fixation, moisture, redox. Three components explained 75% of the variation, with component 1 representing N and P, component 2 representing moisture and organic matter, and component 3 representing ammonium-N and redox.

We will use two data sets from previous chapters, plus a new one, to illustrate principal components analysis.

Chemistry of forested watersheds

In Chapters 2 and 15, we described the work of Lovett *et al.* (2000) who studied the chemistry of forested watersheds in the Catskill Mountains in New York. They chose 39 first and second order streams (objects) and measured the concentrations of ten chemical variables (NO_3^-, total organic N, total N, NH_4^-, dissolved organic C, SO_2^{2-}, Cl^-, Ca^{2+}, Mg^{2+}, and H^+), averaged over three years, and four watershed variables (maximum elevation, sample elevation, length of stream, and watershed area). We will use PCA to reduce these variables to a smaller number of components and use these components to examine the relationships between the 39 streams (Box 17.1).

Box 17.1 | **Worked example of principal components analysis (PCA): chemistry of forested watersheds**

The variables in the study of 39 stream sites in New York state by Lovett *et al.* (2000) fell into two groups measured at different spatial scales – watershed variables (elevation, stream length and area) and chemical variables for a site averaged across sampling dates. We only used the chemical variables for the PCA, as a PCA using all variables together was very difficult to interpret. Preliminary checks of the data showed that one stream, Winnisook Brook, was severely acidified with a concentration of H far in excess of the other streams so this site was omitted from further analysis. Additionally, three variables (dissolved organic C, Cl and H) were very strongly skewed and were transformed to log_{10}. Summary statistics for each variable were as follows.

Variable	Mean	Standard deviation
NO_3	22.85	8.61
Total organic N	4.97	1.28
Total N	27.89	8.10
NH_4	1.65	0.73
Log_{10} dissolved organic C	1.83	0.15
SO_4	62.08	5.22
Log_{10} Cl	1.33	0.16
Ca	65.13	13.96
Mg	22.86	5.12
Log_{10} H	−0.67	0.29

First, the PCA was done on all ten chemical variables and 38 streams. We used a correlation matrix because the variables had very different variances, with the variance in Ca concentration much greater than for all other variables, and we did not wish these variances to influence the analysis. Three components had eigenvalues greater than one and explained over 70% of the total variance.

Component	Eigenvalue	Percentage variance
1	3.424	34.239
2	2.473	24.729
3	1.171	11.711

Analysis of the residuals from retaining three components indicated that there were no Q values very different from the rest and all P values were >0.100.

The coefficients of the first three eigenvectors, with their standard errors, are shown below. Note that many of the standard errors are relatively large, some exceeding the value of the coefficient. Considering these standard errors, it appears that SO_4, $\log_{10}$ Cl, Mg (all +ve) and $\log_{10}$ H (−ve) contribute consistently to eigenvector 1. NO_3, total N, and Ca contribute consistently (−ve) to eigenvector 2. Finally, eigenvector 3 contrasts $\log_{10}$ dissolved organic C (+ve) with NH_4 (−ve), although the latter has low precision (large standard error).

Variable	Eigenvector 1	Eigenvector 2	Eigenvector 3
NO_3	-0.261 ± 0.260	-0.519 ± 0.138	0.049 ± 0.212
Total organic N	0.147 ± 0.181	0.299 ± 0.164	0.515 ± 0.404
Total N	-0.228 ± 0.258	-0.510 ± 0.133	0.154 ± 0.274
NH_4	0.228 ± 0.116	0.075 ± 0.192	-0.487 ± 0.478
$\log_{10}$ dissolved organic C	-0.288 ± 0.123	0.147 ± 0.201	0.562 ± 0.198
SO_4	0.368 ± 0.133	-0.225 ± 0.207	0.242 ± 0.221
$\log_{10}$ Cl	0.358 ± 0.110	0.158 ± 0.204	-0.018 ± 0.269
Ca	0.281 ± 0.227	-0.446 ± 0.156	0.081 ± 0.225
Mg	0.472 ± 0.058	-0.015 ± 0.247	0.301 ± 0.145
$\log_{10}$ H	-0.397 ± 0.150	0.281 ± 0.210	0.006 ± 0.218

The loadings (correlations) of each variable on each component reveal a similar pattern to the coefficients of the eigenvectors, although measures of sampling error are not available. Mg (+ve), $\log_{10}$ H (−ve), SO_4 (+ve) and $\log_{10}$ Cl (+ve) correlate highest with component 1, NO_3 (−ve), total N (−ve), and Ca (−ve) correlate with component 2 and $\log_{10}$ dissolved organic C (+ve) correlates with component 3, as do total organic N (+ve) and NH_4 (−ve) slightly less. Note that there are many variables that have moderate correlations (0.4 to 0.6) with the three components.

Variable	Component 1	Component 2	Component 3
NO_3	-0.483	-0.816	0.053
Total organic N	0.272	0.471	0.557
Total N	-0.423	-0.802	0.166
NH_4	0.422	0.118	-0.527
$\log_{10}$ dissolved organic C	-0.533	0.231	0.608
SO_4	0.682	-0.354	0.262
$\log_{10}$ Cl	0.662	0.248	-0.019
Ca	0.520	-0.701	0.087
Mg	0.873	-0.024	0.326
$\log_{10}$ H	-0.735	0.443	0.006

To see if we could get better simple structure for the components, we also applied a varimax (orthogonal) rotation to these eigenvectors. The total variance explained by the first three eigenvectors is the same as before.

Component	Eigenvalue	Percentage variance
1	2.908	29.081
2	2.719	27.185
3	1.441	14.413

The loadings (correlations) of each variable on each rotated component reveal an improved simple structure. SO_4 (+ve), Mg (+ve), log_{10} H (−ve) and Ca (+ve) correlate strongly with rotated component 1, NO_3 (−ve) and total N (−ve) stand out for component 2, and log_{10} dissolved organic C (+ve) and NH_4 (−ve) for component 3. The number of variables that have moderate correlations (0.4–0.6) with components has decreased from nine in the unrotated solution to four in the rotated solution.

Variable	Component 1	Component 2	Component 3
NO_3	0.046	−0.943	0.104
Total organic N	0.175	0.578	0.491
Total N	0.126	−0.893	0.192
NH_4	0.090	0.284	−0.617
Log_{10} dissolved organic C	−0.324	−0.038	0.775
SO_4	0.808	0.064	−0.028
Log_{10} Cl	0.393	0.551	−0.206
Ca	0.794	−0.327	−0.182
Mg	0.817	0.448	0.011
Log_{10} H	−0.801	0.002	0.307

We also calculated component scores for each stream for each component based on the rotated solution and correlated the first three components with the watershed variables, adjusting the P-values with Holm's sequential Bonferroni method (Chapter 3). Elevation was negatively correlated with component 2. NO_3 and total N load negatively on component 2, indicating that streams with lower elevations also have lower concentrations of nitrogen.

	Max. elevation		Sample elevation		Stream length		Watershed area	
	r	P	r	P	r	P	r	P
Component 1	−0.330	0.387	−0.414	0.100	−0.165	1.000	−0.170	1.000
Component 2	−0.528	0.012	−0.496	0.022	−0.066	1.000	−0.048	1.000
Component 3	−0.084	1.000	−0.064	1.000	−0.229	1.000	−0.284	0.664

We also extracted the components based on a covariance matrix, to illustrate the influence that differences in variances have when using a covariance matrix compared with a correlation matrix for a PCA. A much higher proportion of the total variance is explained by the first three components. The eigenvalues are considerably larger than for the correlation matrix because the variables are not standardized to unit variance.

Component	Eigenvalue	Percentage variance
1	223.510	57.262
2	128.595	32.945
3	29.681	7.604

The loadings are now covariances rather than correlations and their pattern among variables is quite different from that based on a correlation matrix. Note that Ca dominates component 1 and this is the variable with the largest variance, with contributions from NO_3 and total N, both with next largest variances. These two variables also structure component 2, as with the correlation-based PCA, and SO_4 and Mg make up component 3, whereas $\log_{10}$ dissolved organic C did so for the correlation-based PCA.

Note that our preference with these data would be to use a correlation matrix because we did not want the large differences in variances to contribute to our interpretation of components.

Variable	Component 1	Component 2	Component 3
NO_3	4.386	−7.373	0.499
Total organic N	−0.286	0.371	0.342
Total N	4.275	−6.729	1.215
NH_4	0.001	0.164	0.045
$\log_{10}$ dissolved organic C	−0.033	−0.040	−0.026
SO_4	2.514	2.022	3.741
$\log_{10}$ Cl	0.006	0.084	0.025
Ca	13.212	3.853	−1.638
Mg	1.532	3.135	3.340
$\log_{10}$ H	−0.207	−0.143	0.009

Habitat fragmentation and rodents

In Chapter 13, we introduced the study of Bolger *et al.* (1997) who surveyed the abundance of seven native and two exotic species of rodents in 25 urban habitat fragments and three mainland control sites in coastal southern California. Besides the variables representing the species, other variables recorded for each fragment and mainland site included area (ha), percentage shrub cover, age (years), distance to nearest large source canyon and distance to nearest fragment of equal or greater size. We will use PCA to reduce the species variables to a smaller number of components and use these components to examine the relationships between the habitat fragments and mainland sites (Box 17.2).

Geographic variation and forest bird assemblages

Mac Nally (1989) described the patterns of bird diversity and abundance across 37 sites in southeastern Australia. We will analyze the maximum abundance for each species for each site from the four seasons surveyed. There were 102 species of birds and we will use a PCA to try and reduce those 102 variables to a smaller number of components and use these components to examine the relationship between the 37 sites (Box 17.3).

17.1.1 Deriving components

Axis rotation

The simplest way to understand PCA is in terms of axis rotation (see Kent & Coker 1992, Legendre & Legendre 1998). Consider the study of Green (1997), who studied the ecology of red land crabs on Christmas Island (see Chapter 5). Part of that study measured two variables (total biomass of crabs and number of burrows) in ten quadrats in a forested site on the island. A scatterplot of these data is in Figure 17.1, with biomass on the vertical axis and burrow number on the horizontal axis. PCA can be viewed as a rotation of these principal axes, after centering to the mean of biomass and the mean of burrow number, so that the first "new" axis explains most of the variation and the second axis is orthogonal (right angles) to the first (see Figure 17.1). The first new axis is called principal component 1 and the second is called principal component 2. The first component is actually a "line-of-best-fit" that is halfway between the least squares estimate of the linear regression model of biomass on burrow number and the regression model of burrow number on biomass. This is the estimate of the Model II regression (Chapter 5) and is the line represented by the correlation between

Box 17.2 | Worked example of principal components analysis (PCA): habitat fragmentation and rodents

Bolger *et al.* (1997) surveyed the abundance of seven native and two exotic species of rodents in 25 urban habitat fragments and three mainland control sites in coastal southern California. Our aim is to reduce the nine species variables to fewer principal components and examine the relationships between the sites in terms of these components. All species variables were strongly skewed and the variances were very different between variables with many zeros. A fourth root transformation improved normality but did not consistently improve the strength of the linear correlations between variables, so we analyzed raw data. We did separate analyses using covariance and correlation matrices, the latter to remove the effects of the very different variances. With the correlation matrix, the first three components explained over 79% of the variation. With a covariance matrix, more of the variance was contained within component 1 and the first three components explained more than 90% of the variation.

	Correlation		Covariance	
Component	Eigenvalue	Percentage variance	Eigenvalue	Percentage variance
1	4.387	48.746	697.522	78.101
2	1.565	17.393	136.580	15.293
3	1.173	13.029	31.149	3.488

Varimax rotation resulted in different structures, especially for components 1 and 2, but these were not necessarily easier to interpret so we will discuss the unrotated solutions. The loadings (correlations) from a PCA based on a correlation matrix showed that component 1 represented a contrast between the two exotic species and the seven native species and component 3 was a contrast between the two exotics. Component 2 was a little harder to interpret, mainly involving *P. eremicus* and *N. lepida* (+ve) and *N. fuscipes* and *P. fallax* (−ve). Not surprisingly, the loadings (covariances) from a PCA based on a covariance matrix emphasized the species with large variances in their abundances. Component 1 was mainly the two *Peromyscus* species and component 2 was dominated by *P. eremicus*. None of the covariances for component 3 were very strong.

	Correlation			Covariance		
Variable	1	2	3	1	2	3
R. rattus	−0.350	0.293	0.664	−0.252	0.017	−0.249
M. musculus	−0.307	−0.146	−0.800	−1.355	0.013	0.009
P. californicus	0.836	−0.101	0.144	23.697	−3.753	−1.534
P. eremicus	0.750	0.575	−0.139	9.096	10.704	0.499
R. megalotis	0.852	0.051	0.025	3.471	0.283	0.245
N. fuscipes	0.825	−0.509	0.091	5.924	−1.752	4.520
N. lepida	0.685	0.626	−0.163	1.377	1.811	−0.047
P. fallax	0.573	−0.678	0.096	1.427	−1.174	2.799
M. californicus	0.840	0.057	−0.082	0.532	0.333	0.396

The scaling (ordination) scatterplots of component scores for each site from a PCA based on the correlation matrix show that three sites, Sandmark, Alta La Jolla, and Balboa Terrace, stood out from the rest, particularly along components 1 and 2 (Figure 17.3). A biplot of components 1 and 2 including loading vectors for six of the species (Figure 17.3(a)) showed that Sandmark and Alta La Jolla were in the opposite direction of the vector for *M. musculus* and Balboa Terrace was in the opposite direction of the vector for *R. rattus*. So these were sites with high abundance native species and few of the two exotics. Sandmark and Alta La Jolla were at the opposite extreme from Balboa Terrace for component 2, indicating very different numbers of *P. eremicus*, *N. lepida*, *N. fuscipes* and *P. fallax*. Sites with similar patterns for the two exotic species group together on component 3. For all three components, the control mainland sites were not obviously different from the spread of the urban fragments.

Box 17.3 | Worked example of principal components analysis (PCA): geographic variation and forest bird assemblages

The data set from Mac Nally (1989) contains the maximum seasonal abundance of 102 species of birds across 37 sites in southeastern Australia. Our main interest is whether we can summarize the relationships between sites based on a small number of components representing the 102 species. This example illustrates problems often faced by ecologists trying to explore multivariate data sets – a large number of variables relative to objects and most of the variables having numerous zero values. We don't present detailed output from the analysis but the PCA based on a matrix of correlations between species showed that 25 components had eigenvalues greater than one and the first five components only explained about 48% of the variation in the original 102 variables. The components themselves were difficult to interpret because of the number of variables, many of them loading moderately on many components (although rotation did help).

A plot of the standardized component scores for the first two components also illustrates the problem of a horseshoe or arch in the pattern of sites along component 1, whereby sites at the extremes are compressed in their relationship to other sites (Figure 17.4). The extremes of this axis represented sites in central Victoria at one end and sites in the Dandenong Ranges close to Melbourne at the other. We will discuss this arch effect further in Chapter 18. Clearly, PCA is not a particularly efficient or interpretable method for examining patterns among sites for these data.

---

burrow number and biomass (either raw or centered) and is also called the major axis. If the variables are standardized (to zero mean and unit standard deviation), then the first principal component represents the reduced major axis (Chapter 5). The second component is completely independent of, or uncorrelated with, the first component.

Decomposing an association matrix

When there are more than two variables, it is difficult (or impossible) to represent the rotation procedure graphically. In practice, the components are extracted either by a spectral decomposition of a sums-of-squares-and-cross-products matrix, a covariance matrix or a correlation matrix among variables or by a singular value

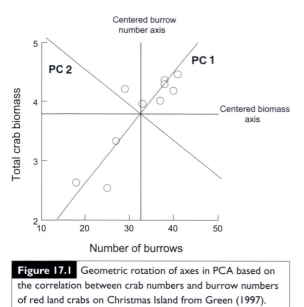

Figure 17.1 Geometric rotation of axes in PCA based on the correlation between crab numbers and burrow numbers of red land crabs on Christmas Island from Green (1997).

decomposition of the raw data matrix with variables standardized as necessary (see Chapter 15 and Box 15.1). Which matrix to use will be discussed in Section 17.1.2. There will be $k = 1$ to p principal components, each of which is a linear combination of the original variables:

$$z_{ik} = c_1 y_{i1} + c_2 y_{i2} + \ldots c_j y_{ij} + \ldots + c_p y_{ip} \tag{17.1}$$

From Lovett *et al.* (2000):

$$z_{ik} = c_1(NO_3)_i + c_2(\text{total organic N})_i + c_3(\text{total N})_i + c_4(NH_4)_i + c_5(\log_{10} \text{ dissolved organic C})_i + c_6(SO_4)_i + c_7(\log_{10} \text{ Cl})_i + c_8(Ca)_i + c_9(Mg)_i + c_{10}(\log_{10} H)_i \tag{17.2}$$

In Equations 17.1 and 17.2, z_{ik} is the value or score for component k for object i, y_{i1} to y_{ip} are the values of the original variables for object i and c_1 to c_p are weights or coefficients that indicate how much each original variable contributes to the linear combination forming this component. Although the number of components that can be derived is equal to the number of original variables, p, we hope that the first few components summarize most of the variation in the original variables.

The matrix approach to deriving components produces two important pieces of information – see Box 15.1. The eigenvectors contain the estimates of the coefficients for each principal component (the c_js in equation 17.1). Eigenvector 1

contains the coefficients for principal component 1, eigenvector 2 for principal component 2, etc. As described in Box 15.1, the eigenvectors are usually scaled so that the sum of squared coefficients for each eigenvector equals one, although additional scaling is also sometimes used.

Estimates of the eigenvalues (or latent roots, λ_k) provide relative measures of how much of the variation between the objects, summed over the variables in the data set, is explained by each principal component. The components are extracted so that the first explains the maximum amount of variation, the second explains the maximum amount of that unexplained by the first, etc. If there are some associations between the variables, the first two or three components will usually explain most of the variation present in the original variables, so we can summarize the patterns in the original data based on a smaller number of components (variable reduction). In the analysis of the data from Lovett *et al.* (2000), the first three components comprised over 70% of the original variation (Box 17.1). If the original variables are uncorrelated, then PCA will not extract components that explain more of the variation than the same number of original variables – see analysis of data from Mac Nally (1989) in Box 17.3. Note that the sum of all the eigenvalues equals the total variation in the original data set, the sum of the variances of the original variables. PCA rearranges the variance in the original variables so it is concentrated in the first few new components.

17.1.2 Which association matrix to use?

The choice of association matrix between variables is an important one. The choice basically comes down to choosing between the covariance and the correlation matrix, because using the sums-of-squares-and-cross-products matrix makes the resulting PCA sensitive to differences in mean values of the variables, even when they are measured in the same units and on the same scale. The covariance matrix is based on mean-centered variables and is appropriate when the variables are measured in comparable units and differences in variance between variables make an important contribution to interpretation. The correlation matrix is based on variables standardized to zero mean and unit variance and is necessary when the variables are measured in very different units and we wish to ignore differences between variances.

Most statistical software uses a correlation matrix by default in their PCA routines, although all should offer the covariance matrix as an alternative. Our experience is that most biologists use the correlation matrix but rarely consider the implications of analyzing variables standardized to zero mean and unit variance. For example, a PCA using the chemical data from Lovett et al. (2000) might be best based on a correlation matrix. Although the units of the variables are the same (μmol l^{-1}), the absolute values and variances are very different and we cannot attach an obvious biological interpretation to these very different variances (Box 17.1). In contrast, we might compare the results from using a covariance matrix with those from using a correlation matrix on the species abundance data from Bolger et al. (1998) to see if the different patterns of variance in abundance of species across fragments is important (Box 17.2). We argued in Chapter 15 that analyzing data with different forms of standardization can assist in interpretation. The message for using PCA is that using covariances will not produce the same components as using correlations (Jackson 1991, James & McCulloch 1990), and the choice depends on how much we want different variances among variables to influence our results.

17.1.3 Interpreting the components

The value of the components, and any subsequent use of them in further analyses, depends on their interpretation in terms of the original variables. The eigenvectors provide the coefficients (c_js) for each variable in the linear combination for each component. The further each coefficient is from zero, the greater the contribution that variable makes to that component. Approximate standard errors can be calculated for the coefficients (Flury & Riedwyl 1988, Jackson 1991), although the calculations are tedious for more than a few variables. Fortunately, these standard errors are default output from good statistical software and should be used when comparing the relative sizes of these coefficients. These standard errors are asymptotic only (i.e. approximate) and assume multivariate normality (Flury & Riedwyl 1988). The size of the standard errors can be relatively large compared to the size of the coefficients (Box 17.1).

Component loadings are simple correlations (using Pearson's r) between the components (i.e. component scores for each object) and the original variables. If we use centered and standardized data (i.e. a correlation matrix), the loadings are provided directly by scaled eigenvectors in the V matrix (see Box 15.1). If we use just centered data (i.e. a covariance matrix), the V matrix will contain covariances rather than correlations, although true correlations can be determined (Jackson 1991). High loadings indicate that a variable is strongly correlated with (strongly loads on) a particular component. The loadings and the coefficients will show a similar pattern (although their absolute values will obviously differ) and either can be used to examine which of the original variables contribute strongly to each component. Tabachnick & Fidell (1996) warn against placing much emphasis on components that are determined by only one or two variables.

Ideally what we would like is a situation where each variable loads strongly on only one component and the loadings (correlations) are close to plus/minus one (strong correlation) or zero (no correlation). It is also easier to interpret the components if all the strongly correlated variables have the same sign (+ve or −ve) on each component (which ones are +ve compared to −ve is actually arbitrary). What we usually get is much messier than this, with some variables loading strongly on a couple of components and many variables with loadings of about 0.5.

17.1.4 Rotation of components

The common situation where numerous variables load moderately on each component can sometimes be alleviated by a second rotation of the components after the initial PCA. The aim of this additional rotation is to obtain simple structure, where the coefficients within a component are as close to one or zero as possible (Jackson 1991). Rotation can be of two types. Orthogonal rotation keeps the rotated components orthogonal to, or uncorrelated with, each other after rotation. This includes varimax, quartimax, equimax methods, the first being the most commonly used. Oblique rotation produces new components that are no longer orthogonal to each other. Orthogonal rotation is simplest and maintains the independence of the components, although some (e.g. Richman 1986) have recommended oblique methods based on the results of simulation studies. Tabachnick & Fidell (1996) also argue that oblique rotation methods may be more realistic since the underlying processes represented by the components are unlikely to be independent.

The PCA on the chemical data for streams from Lovett *et al.* (2000) illustrates the advantages of secondary rotation, with more variables strongly correlated with just one of the retained components than with the unrotated solution (Box 17.1). This will not always be the case, but in our experience with biological variables, rotation often improves the interpretability of the components extracted by a PCA.

If the aim of the PCA is to produce components that will be used as predictor or response variables in subsequent analyses, and those analyses require that the variables are independent of each other (e.g. predictor variables in multiple linear regression models; Chapter 6), then oblique rotation methods should be avoided. Harris (1985), Jackson (1991) and Richman (1986) provide the equations and statistical detail underlying rotations.

17.1.5 How many components to retain?

Although there are a number of approaches to determining how many components to keep (Jackson 1991, Jackson 1993), there is no single best method. It is important to examine the interpretability of the components and make sure that those providing a biologically interpretable result are retained. For example, there is little point retaining components with which no variables are strongly correlated, because these components will be difficult to interpret.

Eigenvalue equals one rule
We can use the eigenvalue equals one rule, which simply says to keep any component that has an eigenvalue greater than one when the PCA is based on a correlation matrix (Norman & Streiner 1994). The logic here is that the total amount of

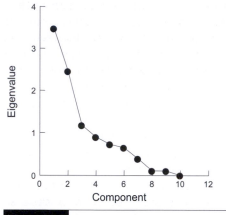

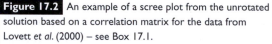

Figure 17.2 An example of a scree plot from the unrotated solution based on a correlation matrix for the data from Lovett *et al.* (2000) – see Box 17.1.

variance to be explained equals the number of variables (because using a correlation matrix standardizes the variables to a mean of zero and standard deviation of one), so by chance each component would have an eigenvalue of one. In the analysis of the water chemistry data from Lovett *et al.* (2000), three out of the ten possible components had eigenvalues greater than one (Box 17.1). In contrast, the analysis of the bird abundance data from Mac Nally (1989) resulted in 25 out of the 102 possible components with eigenvalues greater than one (Box 17.3).

Scree diagram
We can also examine the scree diagram, which simply plots the eigenvalues for each component against the component number. We are looking for an obvious break (or elbow) where the first couple of components explain most of the variation and the remaining group of components don't explain much more of the variation (Figure 17.2). The rule of thumb is to keep all components up to and including the first in that remaining group. Our experience is that scree diagrams don't offer more in interpretability than just simply examining the successive numerical eigenvalues for each component.

Tests of eigenvalue equality
There are tests for equality of a set of successive eigenvalues derived from a covariance matrix,

such as Bartlett's and Lawley's tests (Jackson 1991, Jobson 1992), and we might use one of these to test the null hypothesis that the eigenvalues of the components not retained are equal. Bartlett's test is most common (and available in most statistical software as part of correlation or PCA routines) and the test statistic is compared to a χ^2 distribution. We usually test in a sequential manner, first testing that the eigenvalues of all components are equal (Bartlett's test is then a test of sphericity of a covariance matrix – see Chapters 10 and 11). If this is rejected, we then test equality of eigenvalues of all components except the first, and so on. Once we do not reject the null hypothesis, we retain all components above those being tested. This is a multiple testing situation so some adjustment of significance levels may be warranted (Chapter 3). Bartlett's and Lawley's tests are not applicable when using a correlation matrix because the test statistics do not follow a χ^2 distribution; approximate methods when using correlations are suggested by Jackson (1991).

Analysis of residuals

Residual analysis is also useful for PCA, just like for linear models. Remember that we can extract p components from the original (appropriately standardized) data and we can also reconstruct the original data from the p components. If we extract less than p components, then we can only estimate the original data and there will be some of the information in the original data not explained by the components – this is the residual. When we retain fewer than all p components, we are fitting a model analogous to a linear model (Jackson 1991) with the original data (with variables usually standardized to unit variance) represented as a multivariate mean (centroid) plus a contribution due to the retained components plus a residual. This residual measures the difference between the observed value of a variable for an object and the value of a variable for that object predicted by our model with less than p components. Alternatively, we can measure the difference between the observed correlations or covariances and the predicted (reconstructed) correlations or covariances based on the less than p components – this is termed the residual correlation or covariance

matrix (Tabachnick & Fidell 1996; see also Chapter 16).

We have a residual term for each variable for each object and the sum (across variables) of squares of the residuals, often termed Q (Jackson 1991), can be derived for each object. If the variances differ between the variables and some objects have much larger values for some variables, then the residuals, and Q-values, for those objects will probably be larger for a PCA based on a covariance matrix than one based on a correlation matrix.

Whichever matrix is used, unusually large values of Q for any observation are an indication that the less than p components we have retained do not adequately represent the original data set for that object. Q-values can be compared to an approximate sampling distribution for Q to determine P-values (the probability that a particular Q-value or one more extreme came from the sampling distribution of Q). When we retained three components from a PCA on the correlation matrix of the water chemistry data from Lovett et al. (2000), none of the residual values were statistically significant (Box 17.1).

However, formal statistical testing seems not very useful when exploring a multivariate data set for unusual values – just check unusual values relative to the rest. This is the same process for checking for outliers using residuals from linear models. Objects with large Q-values may be particularly influential in the interpretation of the PCA and a number of such objects would suggest that too few components have been retained to adequately describe the original data. These objects can be further examined to see which variable(s) contribute most to the large Q-value, i.e. which variables have the large difference between observed and predicted values.

17.1.6 Assumptions

Because it uses covariances or correlations as a measure of variable association, PCA is more effective as a variable reduction procedure when there are linear relationships between variables. Nonlinear relationships are common between biological variables and under these circumstances, PCA will be less efficient at extracting components. Transformations can often improve the linearity of relationships between variables (see Chapter 4, Tabachnick & Fidell 1989).

There are no distributional assumptions associated with the ML estimation of eigenvalues and eigenvectors and the determination of component scores (the descriptive use of PCA). However, calculation of confidence intervals and tests of hypotheses about these parameters, such as a test that some of the eigenvalues are equal (see Section 17.1.5; also Jackson 1991, Jobson 1992), do assume multivariate normality. Outliers can also influence the descriptive results from a PCA, especially when based on a covariance matrix where the variances of variables contribute to the component structure. Multivariate outliers can be identified using Mahalanobis distances (Chapter 15).

When normality is questionable, because we have skewed univariate distributions of variables for example, then bootstrap standard errors and confidence intervals might be used. Alternatively, transformations of variables to achieve univariate normality might also improve multivariate normality, reduce the influence of outliers and also improve the linearity of the associations between variables.

Like all multivariate analyses, missing data are a real problem. The default setting for PCA routines in most statistical software is to omit whole objects that contain one or more missing observations. Unless the sample size (number of objects) is large and the objects with missing values are a random sample from the complete data set, then pairwise deletion, multiple imputation or estimation based on the EM algorithm are more appropriate for dealing with missing observations (see Chapter 15).

17.1.7 Robust PCA

Robust PCA techniques allow us to derive components that are less sensitive to outliers. Two approaches have been suggested in the literature. The first is to use robust estimates of covariances or correlations (Jackson 1991). For example, we could use correlations based on ranked variable values, such as Spearman's rank correlation, for the PCA (Jobson 1992). Alternatively, we could calculate each correlation (or covariance) independently of the others, using trimmed observations

or M-estimators, such as Huber's, that downweight extreme observations (Chapter 2). Calculating each pairwise covariance or correlation independently of the others, using all the available data for each pair of variables, is also an effective means of handling missing data (Chapter 15). The second approach is to use robust methods to derive components directly from the original data (Jackson 1991), although these are more complex to compute and there are no obvious criteria for choosing between the methods.

17.1.8 Graphical representations

Scaling (ordination)

The eigenvectors can be used to calculate a new score (z-score) on each component for each object. This is achieved by solving the linear combination for each object for each component (Equation 17.1), using mean centered or standardized variables if the eigenvectors came from covariance or correlation matrices respectively (see Box 15.1). These scores can also be further standardized by dividing by the square root of the eigenvalue for the relevant component so that the variance of the scores for each component is one:

$$z_{ik}^* = \frac{z_{ik}}{\sqrt{l_k}} \tag{17.3}$$

Some software may produce these standardized scores, rather than the original z-scores.

The objects can then be positioned on a scatterplot based on their scores with the first two or three principal components as axes (Figure 17.3). It doesn't matter whether z- or z*-scores are used for the basic plot of objects, although some authors recommend that standardized scores should be used if the PCA is based on a correlation matrix (Jobson 1992). The interpretation of these plots is straightforward but subjective. Objects close together on the plot are more similar in terms of their variable values based on the components being a summary of the original variables; conversely for objects further apart. For a PCA on the data from Bolger et al. (1997), the sites Sandmark and Alta La Jolla are similar to each other but different from other sites in terms of native rodent species composition (Figure 17.3).

This type of graphical representation of objects

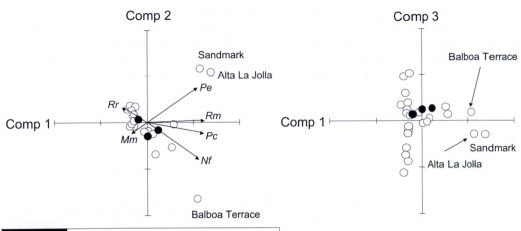

Figure 17.3 PCA scaling (ordination) plots of the 28 sites from Bolger *et al.* (1997) based on a correlation matrix of association between rodent species abundances. Solid circles are mainland control sites, open circles are urban fragments, all axes range from −4 to +4. The left-hand plot is a biplot and vectors of loadings for six of the species have been included, scaled by three. *Rr* is *Rattus rattus*, *Mm* is *Mus musculus*, *Pc* is *Peromyscus californicus*, *Pe* is *Peromyscus eremicus*, *Rm* is *Reithrodontomys megalotis* and *Nf* is *Neotoma fuscipes*.

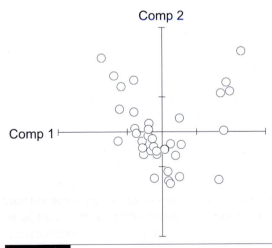

Figure 17.4 PCA scaling (ordination) plot of the 37 sites from Mac Nally (1988) based on a correlation matrix of association between bird species abundances. Axes range from −3 to +3. Note the arch ("horseshoe") pattern in the plot.

from a multivariate analysis is termed scaling. When the objects are sampling units and the variables are species abundances, then ecologists describe analyses that produce such plots as ordinations and the plot an ordination plot.

Clearly, we could plot each object using the original variables as axes, but such a plot is impractical beyond three variables. The plot of the component scores allows us to show the relationship between the objects based on the new derived components, given that the first two or three components can usually be interpreted in terms of the original variables and explain most of the original variance.

It is well known by ecologists that when we are dealing with data for species abundances for different sampling units (e.g. plots, sites, etc.), then the scaling plot of the sampling units (objects) for the first two components of a PCA often shows an arching pattern (the "arch" and "horseshoe" effects). This arching is most apparent when the sampling units cover a long ecological gradient and those at each end of the gradient have few species in common (Minchin 1987, Wartenberg *et al.* 1987). For example, the scaling of the bird abundance data from Mac Nally (1989) shows a strong arch when sites are plotted for the first two principal component axes (Box 17.3; Figure 17.4). Although this arching may indicate the true ecological dissimilarities between the extreme sampling units, there is evidence that it distorts the true underlying pattern. One explanation for the arching is that the implicit measure of dissimilarity between objects that PCA uses, Euclidean distance, does not reach a constant maximum value when two sampling units have no species in common and thus can imply that two objects are similar due to joint absences. Sampling units with few or no species in common are most likely to occur at the extremes of an environmental or geographical gradient so the underlying relationship between dissimilarity and the environmental gradient is nonlinear. The inability to represent nonlinear relationships between dissimilarity and some gradient without distortion is not unique to PCA; correspondence analysis (Section 17.3) also has this problem. We will compare different approaches to scaling/ordination in Chapter 18.

We have described an R-mode analysis, where associations between variables are used to extract components. The PCA could be done as a Q-mode analysis where a matrix of associations between the objects is calculated (Legendre & Legendre 1998). Components can be extracted from either matrix and object scores derived from variable eigenvectors and eigenvalues and vice versa. Any differences relate to how variables or objects are standardized, since an R-mode PCA based on a correlation matrix standardizes variables to zero mean and unit variance. More commonly, Q-mode analyses are based on measured dissimilarities between objects (Chapter 18). It turns out that using the techniques in Chapter 18 to examine the relationship between objects based on a matrix of dissimilarities will produce almost identical scaling (ordination) plots to those produced by an R-mode PCA if we use Euclidean distance as the dissimilarity measure.

Biplots

One particular form of a scaling/ordination plot is called a biplot (Gower & Hand 1996), where both objects and variables (hence the "bi") are included on a single scaling plot. Biplots can use more than two axes although they are commonly plotted in two dimensions. The usual form of a biplot is a point–vector plot where the objects are points and the variables are represented by vectors (lines) drawn from the origin of the scaling plot. Biplots are possible because the singular value decomposition of a data matrix allows us to relate eigenvectors from a matrix of associations between variables to the eigenvectors from a matrix of associations between objects through the eigenvalues for the components (Box 15.1). The most common form of the biplot will use the component scores for objects as points and the variables are represented by the eigenvectors relating each variable

to each component. If the PCA is based on a correlation matrix (i.e. centered and standardized variables), then the biplot will often use z^*-scores for the objects and component loadings to represent the variables on the biplot. In any case, some scaling of the eigenvectors or loadings for variables will usually be required so that the vectors are commensurate with the range of object scores.

Biplots are commonly used by ecologists in situations where the objects represent sampling units or sites and the variables are species abundances (e.g. Digby & Kempton 1987, Legendre & Legendre 1998). We have illustrated a PCA biplot for the 28 sites from the study of the effects of habitat fragmentation on rodents by Bolger et al. 1997 (left-hand plot in Figure 17.3; see also Box 17.2). We have included loading vectors for six of the species (vectors for all species resulted in a plot that was very crowded and difficult to read). The ends of the vectors represent the correlations of each species with each component, although the correlations have been scaled by three so they are roughly commensurate with site scores. For these point–vector biplots, it is not how close the head of the variable vector is to the object points on a biplot that is relevant because we usually have to scale the vectors in some way. It is the direction and relative length of these vectors that are important. The direction indicates that the values of the variable increase in that direction and the length indicates the rate of increase – long vectors are more gradual increases, short vectors are faster increases. So, the vector for R. rattus in Figure 17.3 indicates that this species increases rapidly in abundance in the opposite direction from Balboa Terrace. The vector for P. eremicus indicates that this species increases more gradually in abundance in the direction of Sandmark and Alta La Jolla.

17.1.9 Other uses of components

One problem we face with many statistical analyses, particularly linear models, is dealing with numerous correlated response or predictor variables. We usually analyze each response variable separately with univariate regression or ANOVA techniques, which causes Type I error rate problems due to multiple testing, and we have difficulties using correlated predictor variables in these models because of the effects of collinearity on our parameter estimates and hypothesis tests. PCA may help in both situations because we can often reduce a large number of correlated variables down to a smaller number of components without losing much information and our linear model analyses can use these components as response or predictor variables.

Relationship to MANOVA

When we have multiple response variables in a design that we would usually analyze with an ANOVA model to estimate and test for differences between groups, there are two approaches we can use. The first is multivariate analysis of variance (MANOVA) that we described in Chapter 16. Basically, we analyze a component (discriminant function) that is extracted so it maximizes the explained variance between groups and the hypothesis being tested is about group differences on a linear combination of variables or differences between group centroids. The second approach is initially to ignore group differences and do a PCA on the whole data set, i.e. all objects, and then use as many of the derived components as deemed interpretable as response variables in univariate ANOVA models to test for group differences. The components are obviously independent of each other, although the F tests from univariate ANOVAs on these components technically are not (Jackson 1991).

The two approaches (MANOVA and ANOVA on components) will produce different results, although the broad patterns of group differences are likely to be similar. Analyzing components using ANOVA has some advantages. MANOVA is commonly described in terms of the first discriminant function and deriving output from software for other functions, especially for complex designs, is difficult. In contrast, ANOVA on components can analyze the second, third, etc., components if they offer useful interpretations of the original variables. Also, *post hoc* comparisons of groups are more straightforward under a univariate ANOVA framework.

Principal components regression

In Chapter 6, we discussed the problems caused by collinearity among predictor variables when fitting multiple regression models, especially the inflated standard errors of regression coefficients and the sensitivity of estimates of regression coefficients to which predictors are included in the model. One strategy sometimes suggested as a solution to this problem is principal components regression (Chaterjee & Price 1991, Lafi & Kaneene 1992, Rawlings *et al*. 1998). If there are serious correlations among the predictor variables, we can do a PCA on the predictors, usually centered (and maybe standardized), to extract the p components. We could then fit a regression model that uses all the components as the predictors, but such a model will predict the response variable with the same precision as a model based on the original variables. Usually, we fit a simpler model based on fewer than p components, although the choice of which components to retain is problematical (see below). If the components are easily interpretable, then principal components regression might be better than the original multiple regression because the components are orthogonal so there is no collinearity and no instability in the estimates of the regression coefficients.

We can also recalculate regression coefficients in terms of the original variables based on the relationship (Jackson 1991, Lafi & Kaneene 1992):

$$\mathbf{b} = \mathbf{U}\mathbf{b}_z \tag{17.4}$$

In Equation 17.4, $\mathbf{b}$ is a matrix of regression coefficients on the original standardized variables, $\mathbf{b}_z$ is a matrix of regression coefficients on the principal components (derived using a correlation matrix) and $\mathbf{U}$ is the matrix of eigenvectors from the PCA on the predictor variables (see Box 15.1). When the PCA is based on a matrix of correlations between the predictors, then regression coefficients in $\mathbf{b}$ are standardized coefficients and relate to standardized predictor variables. Covariances could be used with just centered predictor variables.

Equation 17.4 simply states that we can obtain regression coefficients in terms of the original variables from the product of the regression coefficients for the principal components and the eigenvectors from the PCA. Using eigenvectors from the $\mathbf{U}$ matrix scales the coefficients so that the sum of squared coefficients equals one (Box 15.1).

The standard error of the regression coefficient for the kth principal component is (Chaterjee & Price 1991, Jackson 1991):

$$s_{b_k} = \sqrt{\frac{MS_{Residual}}{l_k}} \tag{17.5}$$

In Equation 17.5, $MS_{Residual}$ is from the linear regression on the p principal components. So the standard errors are inversely proportional to the eigenvalues and the first principal components will have smaller standard errors than later components.

If all p components are used, then the regression coefficients in **b** will be the same as those from the regression on the original (standardized) variables. If less than p components are used, then the regression coefficients in **b** will be different from the regression coefficients on the original (standardized) variables. These new coefficients will be biased, the bias increasing the fewer components we retain. In both cases (p or less than p components retained), the standard errors of the recalculated regression coefficients will also be smaller than those from the original multiple regression (Jackson 1991).

Chaterjee & Price (1991) provide a clear example of the calculations involved in principal components regression. Despite its attractiveness as a way of overcoming collinearity in multiple linear regression models, there are limitations to principal components regression. Hadi & Ling (1998) pointed out that the components that explain most of the variance in the predictor variables, i.e. the first few components derived using PCA, might not be the most important in explaining the variance in the response variable in a multiple regression model. The choice of which components to use in principal components regression should be based on their contributions to the $SS_{Regression}$, not just their eigenvalues from the original PCA.

17.2 | Factor analysis

In Section 17.1.5, we pointed out that we can reconstruct the original data from the principal components but if we retain less than p components, we can only approximate the original data.

The residual represents information in the original data not included within the less than p retained components. Factor analysis (FA) formalizes this into a structured model and we now use the term factors instead of components. FA is based on a correlation matrix, or less commonly a covariance matrix. The correlation matrix for the original variables is separated into two parts (Jackson 1991, Jobson 1992). The first is that generated by the common factors, those factors that explain all the correlations among the original variables. The second is that due to the unique factors, those factors representing information in the correlation matrix that is not explained by the common factors. So we have a model that basically includes explained and unexplained (residual) variability, although FA is "explaining" the correlation structure in the data rather than just the variance. The term communality is used for the variance of a variable explained by common factors.

The mechanics of FA are pretty much the same as for PCA, although the procedure is more complex because we need to estimate both common factors and the residual variability associated with the unique factors. Jackson (1991) describes different approaches to estimation, the most commonly used called principal factor analysis where the matrix of correlations between the variables is modified so that the diagonal contains estimates of the communalities. A spectral decomposition is then applied to this new matrix to extract eigenvectors and eigenvalues.

The common factors are estimates of latent variables, the true variables causing the correlation structure in the data. Structural equation modeling (also termed latent variable analysis or causal modeling) combines FA with multiple regression so that the response and predictor variables may be measured variables or common factors (Tabachnick & Fidell 1996). When only measured variables are used, we have multiple regression modeling and the possible causal relationships between response and predictor variables can be displayed as a path diagram (Chapter 6). When we have factors on either side of our regression model, we have structural equation modeling and the path diagrams are more sophisticated. We strongly recommend Tabachnick &

Fidell (1996) for a readable introduction to structural equation modeling.

Jackson (1991) summarized the differences between PCA and FA. The most fundamental is that PCA is trying to extract components that explain the variability in the original variables whereas FA is trying to explain correlations among the original variables. FA is not commonly used in biological research, probably because biologists are trying to extract a small number of new variables that explain most of the variability in the original variables and use these new variables in scaling or ordination plots. PCA is clearly more appropriate than FA for these purposes. Jackson (1991) and Manly (1994) include good introductions to FA and Tabachnick & Fidell (1996) compare some of the common statistical software routines for FA and PCA.

17.3 | Correspondence analysis

Correspondence analysis (CA) was developed as a method for decomposing contingency tables of counts (see Chapter 14) into a small number of summary variables and representing the lack of independence between rows and columns of the contingency table as a low dimensional plot. CA is based on a raw data matrix of counts, classified by n rows (objects) and p columns (variables). In Chapter 14, we described tests for independence of rows and columns in a two way contingency table of counts. A simple test was based on the χ^2 statistic calculated as:

$$\chi^2_{(n-1)(p-1)} = \sum_{i=1}^{n} \sum_{j=1}^{p} \frac{(o_{ij} - e_{ij})^2}{e_{ij}} \qquad (17.6)$$

where o_{ij} are the observed cell counts and e_{ij} are the expected cell counts under independence. Large values of this statistic indicate lack of independence between rows and columns, i.e. the proportion of counts in different columns depends on the row and vice versa. The main purpose of CA is to summarize the lack of independence between rows (objects) and columns (variables) of a contingency table as a small number of derived variables, sometimes called principal axes. The maximum number of derived variables is the minimum of $(n-1)$ and $(p-1)$, although usually

only two axes are derived. The scores for each object and each variable on these axes are used in the scaling (ordination) plot, often with objects and variables plotted jointly.

We will illustrate the use of CA to scale jointly the 28 sites and nine species of rodents from the habitat fragmentation study of Bolger et al. (1997). This CA is presented in Box 17.4.

17.3.1 Mechanics

CA proceeds by a double transformation of the observed minus expected counts, dividing by the product of the square roots of the row totals (r_i) and column totals (c_j). This is equivalent to using standardized residuals from the model of independence for a two way contingency table, adjusted by the total frequency:

$$\frac{1}{\sqrt{N}} \frac{(o_{ij} - e_{ij})}{\sqrt{e_{ij}}} = \frac{(o_{ij} - e_{ij})}{\sqrt{r_i} \sqrt{c_j}} \qquad (17.7)$$

We could just use the observed counts in the numerator of Equation 17.7 (Jackson 1991, Ludwig & Reynolds 1988) and the basic results of the CA are the same except that the first principal axis becomes trivial and is ignored in interpretation. The matrix approach to CA can be of two forms, like PCA. First, we can use a SVD on the matrix of transformed counts (H):

$$H = U^* L^{1/2} U' \qquad (17.8)$$

In Equation 17.8, U^* represents the eigenvectors for each component with coefficients for variables, U represents the eigenvectors for each component with coefficients for objects and L represents a diagonal matrix containing the eigenvalues for each component (Box 15.1). Therefore, we have two sets of eigenvectors, one for objects and one for variables. Second, we can convert H into two association matrices, one between variables ($H'H$) and the other between objects (HH') and use spectral decomposition of both these association matrices to extract the same eigenvectors and eigenvalues.

Because the eigenvectors for objects and variables are extracted jointly, after a double transformation of counts to contributions to the χ^2 statistic for lack of independence, the eigenvalues associated with the principal axes for rows and columns are the same. The sum of these

Box 17.4 | **Worked example of correspondence analysis (CA): habitat fragmentation and rodents**

In this example, we will treat the abundances of each species in each fragment/site from Bolger et al. (1997) as a two way contingency table. Although the fragment and mainland sites were very different size, there was little difference in the pattern in the final joint plot of sites and species using raw abundances compared with that based on standardized ("relativized") abundances so that the total abundance at each site was one. Remember that CA partitions the total χ^2 after standardizing by row and column totals so its not surprising that data standardizations do not have much effect. We will just present the analyses of the unstandardized data.

The χ^2 statistic for independence of species and sites is 1722.777 (216 df, $P < 0.001$) and total inertia is 1722.777 / 1002 = 1.719. We used the program PC-ORD to run a CA on these data. The total inertia was 1.702, slightly different from above and reflecting the different precision used by different software and possibly the difference between reciprocal averaging and the matrix approach to CA. Don't be surprised by minor variations in output for CA from different programs.

The CA extracted a total of eight eigenvectors (number of species minus one) and the first two explained over 70% of the total inertia.

Axis (component)	Eigenvalue	Percentage intertia
I	0.746	43.41
2	0.459	26.70
3	0.288	16.73
4 to 8	0.227	13.17
Total inertia	1.719	100.00

The joint CA plot of sites and species is in Figure 17.5. We have not included scales on the axes because different software will scale the scores differently – the basic patterns should be similar, however. In contrast to the PCA scaling, where the native species were most influential, the CA scaling emphasizes the two introduced species because there tended to be more of these than expected at a number of sites. It is clear that El Mac and Acuna sites were most different from the remaining sites, with 54th Street also separating out. These sites are associated with the abundance of R. rattus, this species having higher than expected abundance at these sites. A number of sites (including 32nd Street Sth, 60th Street, Canon, Florida, Juan, Laurel, Titus and Washington) had similar scores and also had higher than expected abundance of M. musculus. Few sites showed marked differences between observed and expected numbers for native species. The mainland sites could not be distinguished from numerous fragments that were associated with the seven native species. It appears that the ecological gradient across these 28 sites is not long and there is no evidence of an arching effect in the scaling plot.

eigenvalues is equal to the overall χ^2 statistic divided by the total frequency and is called total inertia, a measure of lack of independence. The eigenvalues are interpreted similarly to those from a PCA, with the percentage of the total inertia explained by the successive axes usually presented. The first axis should explain a high proportion of the lack of independence between objects and variables. The axes are extracted in CA so that the correlation between variable and object scores is as high as possible. The axes are also orthogonal (independent) of each other.

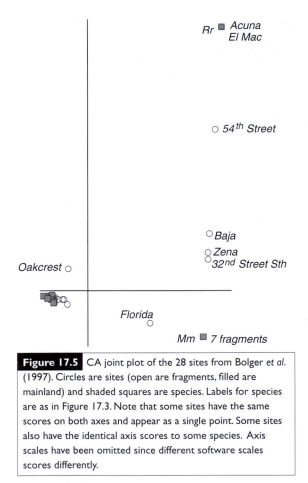

Figure 17.5 CA joint plot of the 28 sites from Bolger *et al.* (1997). Circles are sites (open are fragments, filled are mainland) and shaded squares are species. Labels for species are as in Figure 17.3. Note that some sites have the same scores on both axes and appear as a single point. Some sites also have the identical axis scores to some species. Axis scales have been omitted since different software scales scores differently.

17.3.2 Scaling and joint plots

The eigenvectors are used to determine a score for each principal axis for each object and for each variable. These scores are used for the scaling (ordination) plots. Commonly, objects and variables are plotted together as a joint plot (a "point–point" plot). The biggest difficulty in interpreting these joint plots from a CA is the numerous options for scaling (or standardizing) the object and variable eigenvectors and subsequent scores. As with PCA, the scores are scaled by a measure based on $\sqrt{l}$, where l is the estimated eigenvalue for that axis. An alternative scaling (Hill's method) uses $\sqrt{(l(1-l))}$. The different scaling options result in "minor, but irritating, variants in presenting CA results" (Gower 1996, p. 162), a problem exacerbated by the different terminology used by statisticians and biologists, especially ecologists. These different forms of

scaling don't change the order of objects or species along the axes but do change their relative positions because the underlying dissimilarity measure differs. Not all the types of scaling allow sensible joint plots (see below).

Jackson (1991) described scaling options for objects and variables that result in the implicit dissimilarity between points being Euclidean distance (Chapter 15; see also Legendre & Legendre 1998). More commonly, especially for biological applications, we scale objects and/or variables so that the implicit dissimilarity between points is the chi-square metric (Chapter 15), and this is the usual output from CA routines in software. The distances between objects and/or variables in the scaling plot are proportional to their chi-square distances. Three common scalings available in specialist software used for ecological applications (sampling units by species abundances) produce scores that can be used in biplots (see Legendre & Legendre 1998).

- Scores for sampling units are scaled so that they are positioned at the centroids of the species scores. The distances between sampling units are proportional to their chi-square distances and this scaling is appropriate when the main focus is on relative positions of sampling units (objects).
- Scores for species are scaled so they are positioned at the centroids of the sampling unit scores. The distances between species are proportional to their chi-square distances and this scaling is appropriate when the main focus is on relative positions of species (variables).
- Compromise scaling tries to scale sampling unit and species scores comparatively with a method "half-way" between the first two.

It often doesn't matter which scaling is chosen because the pattern of objects and variables in the joint plots will be similar – just the absolute scores are different and the values of the axis scores are not of much practical use. Note that some software plots either objects or variables as points and the other as vectors, as in a biplot, although CA actually produces a point–point plot of objects and variables jointly, not a true biplot. You also occasionally see the point–point joint plots called biplots. Finally, some programs do not scale scores in a manner that allows sensible joint plots, especially CA routines in general statistical software (Legendre & Legendre 1998).

The interpretation of the joint plot of object and variable scores is different from a biplot. In CA, objects and variables that occur together on the plot indicate that the variables have values greater than predicted under independence for those objects, or conversely, objects have greater values than predicted for those variables. Examining the joint plot in conjunction with a matrix of residuals from the independence model for the contingency table will be helpful since we can see which cells have large deviations from expected values. We would expect combinations of objects and variables with large positive deviations to be near each other on the plot, whereas combinations with large negative deviations to be in opposite quadrants of the plot. With the scaling options described above, those variables (e.g. species) contributing most to the position of the objects (e.g. sampling units) will be the ones closest to the particular object on the plot.

The scores produced by a CA can be used, like principal components scores, as response variables in subsequent analyses. For example, we could correlate the sampling unit scores from a CA with other environmental variables recorded for each unit or use the sampling unit scores to examine difference between groups of units.

17.3.3 Reciprocal averaging

Scaling the eigenvectors so that dissimilarities between points are chi-square distances also relates to an alternative approach to CA, termed reciprocal averaging (Hill 1973, 1974; see descriptions in Digby & Kempton 1987, Ludwig & Reynolds 1988). This is an iterative procedure that calculates object scores for the first axis as a weighted average of variable scores and vice versa. At each step, the object and variable scores are rescaled so they are comparable. Final scores are obtained when there is little change in scores between iterations and convergence is usually quick. The process is then repeated for the second axis. The reciprocal averaging procedure is tedious and produces the similar scores (given rounding error) as the much more efficient matrix approach

to CA when the two methods are used with the equivalent scaling. However, the default settings will often be different between programs that use the reciprocal averaging algorithm and programs that use the matrix approach – don't be surprised by variations in output from competing software. The reciprocal averaging algorithm is particularly useful when we wish to constrain the axis scores by additional variables, as in canonical correspondence analysis (Section 17.6).

17.3.4 Use of CA with ecological data

The most common users of CA in biology are community ecologists, who often deal with data sets consisting of n objects (sampling units, sites, etc.) and p variables (species abundances) – see Section 17.1. By treating these data sets as two-way contingency tables, CA can be used to scale objects and variables simultaneously by plotting the scores for sampling units and species. These data sets are often based on sampling units along ecological gradients so that units at each end of the gradient (i.e. units furthest apart spatially or temporally or most different along some underlying environmental gradient) have few or no species in common. Ecologists describe this as high beta diversity, i.e. large changes in species diversity along environmental gradients (Ludwig & Reynolds 1988). We have already pointed out that under these conditions, PCA can produce a distorted scaling/ordination plot of sampling units (objects) so that units at the ends of the gradient are closer together than they should be ("arch" effect) and may even curve back in ("horseshoe" effect) – see Legendre & Legendre (1998) for an excellent summary. This effect is partly because the PCA scaling plot is trying to display a potentially complex and nonlinear relationship between dissimilarity and true ecological distance in a simple form (two or three dimensions), using a dissimilarity measure (Euclidean) that does not represent these distances very well.

CA also suffers from this problem (Legendre & Legendre 1998), because the implied dissimilarity measure is chi-square distance and, like Euclidean, this does not reach a constant maximum value when two sampling units have no species in common (Chapter 15). Also, because chi-square distance is measuring differences in proportional representation of species between sampling units, it tends to weight rarer species higher in the calculation of dissimilarity than their overall abundance warrants (Minchin 1987). Therefore, sampling units with few or no species in common may appear more similar relative to other sampling units in the CA plot than we would expect from their species composition and abundance (Wartenberg *et al.* 1987). If we are using the CA scaling plot to look for underlying ecological gradients, then this distortion can make interpretation difficult, especially for the second axis, because patterns of sampling units related to a second gradient (assuming the first is displayed along the first axis) may be obscured. The second axis is a quadratic distortion of the first axis, rather than reflecting a second ecological gradient (Kent & Coker 1992). Van Groenewald (1992) simulated ecological data with clear gradients and showed that CA does not recover underlying gradients beyond the primary one very well if they are nearly as strong as the primary gradient. Therefore, we cannot recommend CA as an appropriate method for scaling sampling units across long ecological gradients.

17.3.5 Detrending

Hill & Gauch (1980) proposed detrended correspondence analysis (DCA) as a solution to the arching problem. Detrending breaks the first axis up into a number of segments, the number determined by the user, and rescales the second axis so its average is the same for all segments. Detrending is applied to the reciprocal averaging algorithm, with rescaling occurring at each iteration. While this method is effective at removing the arch effect, different numbers of segments used in the detrending process can affect the results (Jackson & Somers 1991). Also, the method assumes that the arch effect is an artifact of the CA, and not a real pattern in the data (Minchin 1987). Simulations by Minchin (1987) showed that DCA performed poorly relative to other methods (e.g. non-metric multidimensional scaling; see Chapter 18) in trying to recover known ecological gradients, although this was due to both the instability of the results to detrending and the implicit chi-square dissimilarity measure. Therefore, we cannot recommend DCA as a scaling/ordination technique because of the arbitrary nature of detrending, its sensitivity to the number of segments chosen and even problems with order of data entry for some versions of the algorithm (Okansen & Minchin 1997).

17.4 | Canonical correlation analysis

Biologists may have a data set where they wish to examine the correlation between one set of variables and another set of variables for the same objects. For example, consider the data from Lovett *et al.* (2000) described in Section 17.1. The variables recorded from each of the 39 stream sites were of two types: ten chemical variables (NO_3^-, total organic N, total N, NH_4^-, dissolved organic C, SO_4^{2-}, Cl^-, Ca^{2+}, Mg^{2+}, H^+), averaged over three years, and four watershed variables (maximum elevation, sample elevation, length of stream, watershed area) – see Box 17.5. We might wish to examine the correlation between the set of chemical variables and the set of watershed variables. We could do this by examining all the pairwise correlations between the variables (30

| **Box 17.5** | Worked example of canonical correlation analysis: chemistry of forested watersheds |

We were interested in testing for correlations between the set of ten chemical variables (Box 17.1) and the set of four watershed variables (maximum elevation, site elevation, stream length and watershed area) for the 39 stream sites in New York state studied by Lovett *et al.* (2000). We omitted the acidified Winnisook site with its extreme concentration of H. We also tried to minimize collinearities by not including highly correlated variables within either set. For the chemical variables, we omitted total N as it was highly correlated with NO_3 and for the watershed variable, we omitted stream length as it was highly correlated with catchment area. Three of the chemical variables (dissolved organic C, Cl^-, H) and catchment area were transformed to $\log_{10}$ to correct skewness.

Only summaries of the extensive output from statistical software will be presented. Three canonical variate pairs were extracted (only three watershed variables). The correlations for the pairs of canonical variates were as follows.

Canonical variate pair	1	2	3
Canonical correlation	0.874	0.733	0.524

Bartlett's tests of these correlations were as follows.

All three canonical correlations: χ^2 statistic $= 77.387$, df $= 27$, $P < 0.001$.
The two sets of variables are not independent so at least the first canonical variate pair is significantly correlated.
Canonical correlations 2 and 3: χ^2 statistic $= 33.258$, df $= 16$, $P = 0.007$.
Once the most correlated canonical variate pair (number one) is removed, at least the second canonical variate pair is also correlated, but more weakly.
Canonical correlation 3: χ^2 statistic $= 9.775$, df $= 7$, $P = 0.202$.
After removing the first two pairs, the third canonical variate pair is not correlated. In summary, only the first two canonical variate pairs are significantly correlated.

The canonical loadings for the chemical variables (correlations between the canonical variates and the ten chemical variables) were as follows.

Variable	Variate 1	Variate 2
NO_3	−0.740	−0.007
Total organic N	0.098	−0.563
NH_4	−0.058	−0.287
$\log_{10}$ dissolved organic C	−0.262	−0.311
SO_4	0.540	−0.339
$\log_{10}$ Cl	0.616	−0.358
Ca	0.192	0.110
Mg	0.641	−0.551
$\log_{10}$ H	0.331	0.016

The canonical loadings for the watershed variables (correlations between the canonical variates and the four watershed variables) were as follows.

Variable	Variate 1	Variate 2
Max. elevation	−0.862	0.073
Site elevation	−0.699	0.477
$\log_{10}$ area	0.139	0.393

The strong canonical correlation for the first canonical variate pair represents a correlation between a variate contrasting NO_3 with SO_4, $\log_{10}$ Cl and Mg and a variate combining maximum and sample elevation. Sites with higher elevations have greater concentrations of NO_3 and lower concentrations of SO_4, Cl and Mg.

pairwise correlations). Alternatively, we could use canonical correlation analysis where we extract linear combinations of variables (components) from the two sets of variables so that first component for one set has the maximum correlation with the first component from the second set. The components are termed canonical variates and the first component from each set forms one pair of canonical variates, the second component from each set forms a second pair, etc. The number of canonical variates, and therefore pairs, is the number of variables in the smallest set.

The basic equation for canonical correlation analysis is:

$$\mathbf{R} = \mathbf{R}_{11}^{-1}\mathbf{R}_{12}\mathbf{R}_{22}^{-1}\mathbf{R}_{21} \tag{17.9}$$

In Equation 17.9, $\mathbf{R}$ is the matrix of canonical correlations, $\mathbf{R}_{12}$ and $\mathbf{R}_{21}$ are the correlation matrices between sets 1 and 2 and between sets 2 and 1 respectively, and $\mathbf{R}_{11}$ and $\mathbf{R}_{22}$ are the correlation matrices within sets 1 and 2 respectively. Basically, this is an eigenvalue–eigenvector problem similar to that outlined for PCA (Box 15.1), with the constraint that the canonical variates are paired so they have the maximum correlation among all possible pairs of canonical variates. The matrix calculations are tedious but described in detail by Jackson (1991), Jobson (1992), Manly (1994) and Tabachnick & Fidell (1996). In some software, canonical correlation analysis can be set up as a regression problem with one set of variables being the response set and the other set being the predictor set.

The output from running a canonical correlation analysis in most software will be familiar once you are used to eigenvalues, eigenvectors and component scores from PCA (Box 17.5). The descriptive output usually includes matrices of correlations within and between the two sets and regression statistics for each response variable regressed against each predictor variable (these are based on standardized variables because we are using correlations).

Output related specifically to the canonical correlation analysis includes eigenvectors and loadings for the canonical variates from each set, interpreted in the same way as eigenvectors and loadings from PCA. Remember that we are using correlation matrices here so the comparable PCA

interpretation is for centered and standardized variables. The relative signs associated with eigenvector coefficients and loadings are arbitrary within a variate but the interpretation of the canonical correlations between variates depends on the signs associated with the variables within each variate. For example, the analysis of the correlation between the set of chemical variables and the set watershed variables from Lovett *et al.* (2000) showed negative loadings for NO_3 and negative loadings for maximum and site elevation for canonical variate 1. The interpretation here is that large values of NO_3 are associated with large values of maximum and site elevation. Positive loadings for variables in one set and negative loadings for variables in the other for a canonical variate indicate that large values of the variables in one set are associated with small values of the variables in the other. Always check your interpretation by examining the univariate correlations to make sure your interpretation of the direction of the multivariate relationship makes sense.

We also get a test of the H_0 that there is no correlation between any of the pairs of the canonical variates, usually provided as Bartlett's χ^2 statistic. If this H_0 is rejected, then we know that at least the first pair of canonical variates is significantly correlated. Most software then provides tests for the subsequent pairs, usually sequentially by testing the remaining pairs after the first has been removed, then those still remaining after the first two have been removed, etc.

Like PCA (Section 17.1.3), the interpretation of canonical correlation analysis really depends on how easily the canonical variates can be interpreted in terms of the original variables. Also like PCA (Section 17.1.4), rotation of the canonical variates is possible and may improve the simple structure for each pair of variates.

The nature of the matrix calculations in canonical correlation analysis means that it is very sensitive to collinearity among the variables in either set, especially when one or both sets have many variables (see Tabachnick & Fidell 1996). In these circumstances, omitting one or two variables can cause marked differences (instability) in the magnitude and signs of the variable loadings on the canonical variates. This is a similar problem that affects multiple regression (Chapter

6) and multivariate analysis of variance (Chapter 16) and other procedures that require matrix inversion. Removing redundant variables (those highly correlated with others) is about the only option. A method for assessing correlations between two sets of variables that is sensitive to correlations between pairs of variables within or between the sets must have limited applicability to real world data.

We have not found many examples of canonical correlation analyses in the biological literature, nor have we had much cause to consider using it ourselves. This may be because biologists are most interested in hypotheses about correlations between specific pairs of variables, rather than sets of variables or exploratory descriptions of relationships between objects based on some form of scaling (ordination).

17.5 | Redundancy analysis

An obvious extension of canonical correlation analysis would be to distinguish response and predictor variables and develop a predictive model whereby we predict a linear combination of response variables from a linear combination of predictor variables. The proportion of the total variance in the response variables that can be explained by (predicted from or extracted by) a linear combination of the predictor variables is termed redundancy (Tabachnick & Fidell 1996). The statistical procedure for estimating this variance and developing the predictive model is termed redundancy analysis (RDA: van den Wollenberg 1977). Legendre & Legendre (1998) and Legendre & Anderson (1999a) provide excellent descriptions of RDA. A multiple linear regression model relating each response variable to the set of predictor variables is estimated and a matrix of predicted Y-values for the response variables determined. This matrix is just like the raw data matrix comprising n objects by p variables, except that the values for each variable are those predicted by the regression model. This matrix of predicted Y-values is then subjected to a PCA via spectral decomposition of the covariance matrix of the predicted values (see Box 15.1) to extract eigenvectors and their "canonical" eigenvalues.

The redundancy, the variance in the response variables explained by the predictor variables, is the sum of these eigenvalues. The eigenvectors can be used to calculate scores for each object and can be used as axes for scaling/ordination of the objects.

The contrast with PCA is important (Legendre & Legendre 1998). In a PCA, a covariance (or correlation) matrix of the response variables would be decomposed into eigenvectors and their eigenvalues, principal component scores determined for each object based on these eigenvectors and a scaling/ordination plot derived from these scores. In RDA, the response variables are first constrained to be a linear combination of some set of predictor variables, using multiple regression, and then the eigenvectors and their eigenvalues are extracted, object scores calculated and a scaling/ordination plot derived. The RDA eigenvectors are constrained to be a linear combination of the predictor variables, whereas the PCA eigenvectors are not related to predictor variables in any way (Jongman *et al.* 1995, Legendre & Anderson 1999a).

RDA can therefore be viewed as an extension of canonical correlation analysis that explicitly models multiple response variables against multiple predictor variables. However, ecologists commonly use RDA as a modification of PCA to produce eigenvectors and component scores for sampling units that are constrained to a linear combination of environmental variables recorded for each sampling unit (Legendre & Legendre 1998). For example, Verschuren *et al.* (2000) examined the composition of the fossil invertebrate community in different levels of a core taken from a lake bed in Kenya and used RDA to incorporate three environmental variables: salinity, lake level and papyrus-swamp development. The significance of the overall model relating the species abundance data set and the predictor variables, and also of individual predictor variables, can be tested using randomization procedures (Legendre & Anderson 1999a; Manly 1997). The predictor variables do not have to be continuous and an important application of RDA is when the predictors are dummy variables representing categories of categorical factors and their interactions (Legendre & Anderson 1999a; Chapter 18).

In the context of scaling/ordination, the logic

of RDA can be illustrated with the data from Bolger *et al.* (1997). The response variables would be the abundance of the different rodent species for 28 fragments (objects) and the predictor variables would be the other fragment characteristics, such as area, percentage of shrubs, age, etc. The scaling of the fragments in terms of species abundances would be constrained so that the components were linear combinations of the predictor variables. An alternative way of constraining axes of a scaling/ordination plot is within the context of correspondence analysis and will be described in the next section.

17.6 | Canonical correspondence analysis

As indicated in the previous section, ecologists who work with data sets of species abundances for a number of sampling units sometimes also have additional variables (covariates) recorded for each sampling unit. For example, in the study of rodents in habitat fragments, Bolger *et al.* (1997) also recorded the area of the fragment, the percentage of the area covered with shrubs, the age of the fragment, the distance to the nearest large "source" canyon and the distance to the nearest canyon fragment of equal or greater size. We might be interested not only in scaling the sampling unit and species, such as with CA, but also in examining how the relative positions of sampling unit and species are related to the values of the additional covariates for each sampling unit. Canonical correspondence analysis (CCA) is a modification of CA where the principal axes are extracted not only so they explain most of the total inertia (lack of independence between objects and variables) but also so that their correlation with additional variables is maximized (Jongman *et al.* 1995, Kent & Coker 1992, Legendre & Legendre 1998, ter Braak & Verdonschot 1995).

CCA uses the reciprocal averaging algorithm for CA. At each step when sampling unit scores are determined, they are constrained to be a linear combination of environmental variables (usually standardized) using OLS multiple regression techniques (Chapter 6). The predicted values of the sampling unit scores from this multiple regression are then used to calculate species scores and the iterative process continues (Jongman *et al.* 1995). Incorporating the environmental variables in this way also ensures that the extracted axes maximize the dispersion of the species scores based on the linear combination of environmental variables. The axes in CA also maximize the dispersion of species scores but independently of any environmental variables.

The main decisions for users of software for CCA are about standardizations or transformations of species and/or environmental variables and standardization and scaling of sampling unit and species scores. Linear relationships between environmental variables and scores may be improved by transforming environmental variables so they have closer to a symmetrical distribution. The options for scaling the scores for CCA are similar to those for CA (Section 17.3.2) and the choice of scaling needs to be made carefully if the objects and variables are to be included in a joint plot.

The CCA algorithm produces axes that represent maximum correlations with linear combinations of the environmental variables, with the second axis being uncorrelated with the first. CCA produces two sets of sampling unit scores. The first are those produced without being constrained by the environmental variables, although for some reason these are different when produced by CCA than when the same data are analyzed by CA. The second are those produced by the multiple regression of the above scores on the linear combination of environmental variables. Palmer (1993) termed these WA and LC scores respectively, and described them as the observed sampling unit scores, as weighted averages of species scores, and those sampling unit scores predicted from the multiple regression on the environmental variables. He recommended plotting the LC scores, arguing that the meaning of the WA scores is unclear and they differ from the scores from a straight CA anyway. The relative positions of sampling unit based on the three types of scores (CCA WA scores, CCA LC scores, CA scores) is usually different, although broad patterns are comparable.

Output from CCA algorithms includes axis scores for sampling unit and species and vectors representing the correlations between the

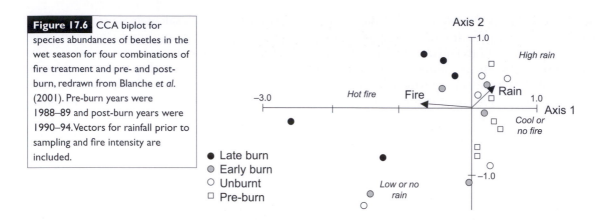

Figure 17.6 CCA biplot for species abundances of beetles in the wet season for four combinations of fire treatment and pre- and post-burn, redrawn from Blanche *et al.* (2001). Pre-burn years were 1988–89 and post-burn years were 1990–94. Vectors for rainfall prior to sampling and fire intensity are included.

● Late burn
◒ Early burn
○ Unburnt
□ Pre-burn

environmental variables and principal axes can also be included on these plots, creating a biplot. Canonical weights for the final multiple regression model are provided as well as correlations between the environmental variables and species and sampling unit scores. CCA can be run with the detrending option although, as discussed in Section 17.3.5, detrending is difficult to justify. The big advantage of CCA is the simultaneous scaling of sampling unit and species (like CA) while at the same time maximizing the correlations between the principal axes and linear combinations of environmental variables. Its disadvantages are those of CA described in Section 17.3.4, especially the chi-squared distance measure, and the limited availability of software; CCA is not available in any of the common commercial programs and specialist ecological software like CANOCO is required.

Blanche *et al.* (2001) illustrate the use of CCA in their experimental study of the effects of fire on the community of ground-active beetles in tropical savannahs of Kakadu National Park in northern Australia. There were three fire treatments (unburnt, early-season burn each dry season, late-season burn each dry season) and six years of sampling (pre-burn in 1988–89 and post-burn from 1990 to 1994). Abundances of ground-dwelling beetles, sorted to family and species, in each of three replicate 15–20 km² experimental compartments (small catchments) for each treatment in each year were measured with pitfall traps. The replicate compartments were combined for the analysis and two environmental covariates were also recorded for each year–treatment combination: fire intensity and rainfall just prior to sam-

pling. The CCA showed that the effects of treatment were contingent on both sampling rainfall and fire intensity (Figure 17.6). Treatment– year combinations favored by high rainfall tended to be pre-burn years and unburnt treatments and late-burn treatments were correlated with less rainfall and more intense fires.

We illustrate a worked example of CCA based on the rodent data from Bolger *et al.* (1997) in Box 17.6. The 25 habitat fragments were scaled based on the abundances of nine rodent species, with three variables used to constrain the ordination: area of the fragment (ha), the age of the fragment (years), and the distance to the nearest large "source" canyon (m). All three variables were important in determining the associations of fragments with species (Figure 17.7) and the biplot was quite different to that produced by a CA on the same data, ignoring the environmental variables (compare Figure 17.7 with Figure 17.8).

The logic of CCA is to include the environmental variables as part of the sampling unit and species scaling (ordination). An alternative approach is to scale the sampling unit separately and then examine which species contribute most to the pattern and also relationships with environmental variables. We will discuss these approaches in Chapter 18.

17.7 | Constrained and partial "ordination"

Both RDA and CCA are known as constrained scaling procedures because the relative positioning

Box 17.6 | Worked example of canonical correspondence analysis (CCA): habitat fragmentation and rodents

We repeated the CA on the rodent data from Bolger *et al.* (1997), but now constrained the axes to be correlated with environmental variables that were also recorded for each site. There were high correlations between the percentage of the area covered with shrubs and the age of the fragment and between the distance to the nearest large source canyon and the distance to the nearest canyon fragment of equal or greater size. To avoid problems with collinearity, only three variables were included: the area of the fragment (ha), the distance to the nearest large source canyon (m) and the age of the fragment (years). Only the 25 habitat fragments were used because the three mainland sites did not have values for the distance measure or age.

The fragments were very different in size so as for the CA presented in Box 17.4, we compared the scaling pattern based on raw abundances and also based on abundances standardized so that all sites had a total abundance of one. The broad pattern in the biplot was the same for both forms of the data so we just present the results for the raw data.

We used the program PC-ORD to do a CCA with the site and species scores standardized to zero mean and unit variance and scaled using the compromise approach between species scores positioned at centroid of site scores and vice versa. The total inertia in the data was 1.702 (as with the CA) and three principal axes were derived.

	Axis 1	Axis 2	Axis 3
Eigenvalue	0.595	0.083	0.039
Percentage inertia (variance)	35.0	4.9	2.3

The CCA biplot (Figure 17.7) shows that the introduced mouse *M. musculus* is associated with older fragments that are further away from source canyons. The other introduced species, *R. rattus*, is more common on small fragments, occurring in the opposite quadrant from the vector for area. Three native taxa (*P. eremicus, M. californianus, N. lepida*) were also more associated with larger fragments. The remaining native taxa occurred more commonly on younger fragments that were closer to source canyons.

The correlations between each CCA axis and the environmental variables showed that the first axis mainly represented fragment age and to a lesser extent distance to nearest source – the vector for age is longer than that for distance in Figure 17.7. This axis is negatively correlated with area – fragments with high scores on this axis are smaller. Axis 2 is positively correlated with all three variables, but more so with area.

Variable	Axis 1	Axis 2
Area	−0.458	0.887
Distance	0.480	0.439
Age	0.806	0.532

A CA on the same 25 fragments revealed a similar pattern as the CA on all 28 sites in Box 17.4.

	Axis 1	Axis 2	Axis 3
Eigenvalue	0.743	0.459	0.279
Percentage inertia (variance)	43.6	26.9	16.4

The first axis of the CA explained 44% of the total inertia, more than for the CCA on the same data with the environmental variables included (35%). The second and third axes also contributed more than in the CCA. This is usually the case when comparing CCA and CA results for the same data set (Jongman *et al.* 1996). The joint plot (Figure 17.8) was almost identical to that in Figure 17.5, indicating that the removal of the mainland sites had little effect on the results of the CA. In contrast to the CCA, Acuna, El Mac and 54th Street stand out as different from the other fragments. Their association with *R. rattus* is also stronger than in the constrained ordination.

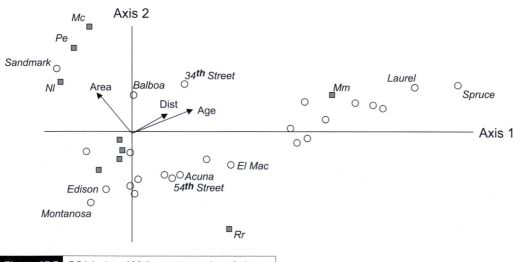

Figure 17.7 CCA biplot of 25 fragment sites from Bolger *et al.* (1997) using LC scores for sites and final scores for species. Circles are sites and shaded squares are species. Labels for species as in Figure 17.3. Axis scales have been omitted since different software scales scores differently.

of the objects in the scaling (ordination) plot is constrained by a set of covariates. In an ecological setting, we usually have sampling units being scaled based on the abundances of multiple species, with the covariates being environmental variables recorded for each sampling unit or even spatial coordinates of each sampling unit. These constrained methods are very informative because they allow the relationship between the environ-

mental variables and scaling of sampling units or species to be explored simultaneously. RDA, like PCA, is most appropriate when the relationship between species abundances and underlying environmental gradients is linear. This is unlikely in practice, especially for long environmental gradients, so CCA, like CA, is more suited when the relationship between species abundances and underlying environmental gradients is unimodal (Jongman *et al.* 1995). Forms of scaling/ordination that have fewer assumptions about the relationship between species abundances and underlying gradients, such as non-metric multidimensional scaling, will be described in Chapter 18.

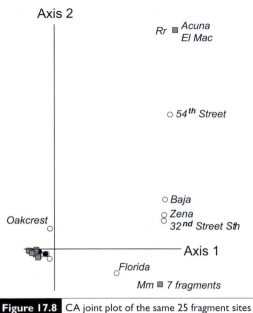

Axis 2

Rr ■ *Acuna*
El Mac

○ *54th Street*

○ *Baja*
○ *Zena*
○ *32nd Street Sth*

Oakcrest
○

Axis 1

○ *Florida*

Mm ■ *7 fragments*

Figure 17.8 CA joint plot of the same 25 fragment sites from Bolger *et al.* (1997) as in Figure 17.7. Note that some sites have the same scores on both axes and appear as a single point. Some sites also have the identical axis scores to some species. The seven fragments associated with *M. musculus* (bottom right quadrant) are Laurel, Canon, Washington, 60th, Juan, Titus and 32nd Street Nth. Axis scales have been omitted since different software scales scores differently.

An interesting development that can be applied to any of the constrained scaling/ordination methods is partial ordination (Legendre & Legendre 1998). Imagine a situation where we have two sets of environmental variables, and we wish to use one set to constrain a scaling of sampling units based on species abundance after eliminating the effects of the second set. An example given by Jongman *et al.* (1995) is where there is one or more "impact" variables representing effects of some human activity and one or more covariates representing other sources of variation we are less interested in, such as seasonal factors (ter Braak & Versonschot 1995). A partial scaling of sampling units would use the impact variables after removing the effects of the other covariates. This would be achieved by fitting multiple regression models with each of the covariates of prime interest (e.g. impact variables) as the response variable and the secondary covariates we are partialing out as the predictor variables. The residuals from each of these

models represent the variation in each of the primary covariates that is not explained by the linear relationship with the secondary covariates. These residuals are then used instead of the original primary covariates in a CCA or RDA.

These partial ordination techniques allow us to examine the relationships between a scaling based on species abundances and some environmental variables after partialing out the effects of other covariates. For example, Verschuren *et al.* (2000) examined the fossil invertebrate communities in a core of sediment from a lake in Kenya. They used RDA to examine the relationships between the scaling of sampling units (sections of the core) and three environmental variables (salinity, lake level, papyrus-swamp development) and used partial RDA to look at the effects of each of these covariates after removing one or both of the remaining ones. We might also be interested in how much of the variation between sampling units in abundances of multiple species can be attributed to a set of environmental variables, a set of spatial coordinates, the variation shared by the environmental and spatial components and the undetermined (residual) variation. Borcard *et al.* (1992) described a method based on either partial RDA or CCA to determine the variation in the original sampling units by species data matrix into these four components. The residuals from multiple regression models of either environmental variables on spatial coordinates or vice versa are used to examine the contribution of the environmental variables and spatial coordinates independently of each other. Note that for partial RDA, it is variance being partitioned; for partial CCA, it is inertia. In both cases, percentage contributions can be determined.

17.8 | General issues and hints for analysis

17.8.1 General issues

• The implicit dissimilarity measures used in scaling/ordination techniques, such as Euclidean for PCA and RDA and chi-square for CA and CCA, may not be best suited to all types of data, especially species abundance data.

- The choice between covariance and correlation for the association matrix in a PCA is important. Use covariance if you wish differences in variance for each variable to contribute to the analysis. Use correlation if the variables are measured on different scales and you do not wish differences in variance for each variable to have any influence on the analysis.
- Eigenvector coefficients and component loadings indicate the contribution of each variable to each component. They should be interpreted in conjunction with their standard errors.
- CA jointly scales objects and variables, based on counts, and emphasizes proportional representation of variables (e.g. species) in objects (e.g. sampling units).
- RDA and CCA constrain the scaling of objects and variables to a linear combination of covariates; for ecological data, this directly incorporates environmental variables in the scaling/ordination of species abundance data.

17.8.2 Hints for analysis

- Secondary rotation of components after an initial PCA will often improve simple structure and interpretability of components.
- Transformation of variables may improve linear relationships between variables and improve the effectiveness of component extraction in PCA.
- Examination of residuals from a PCA can help assess whether the number of retained components is adequate.
- Biplots can be used to represent scaling of objects in PCA, RDA, CA and CCA with correlations of original variables to each component indicated by vectors. It is not the closeness of the end of the vector to objects in the configuration that is important, but the length and angle of the vectors relative to the axes.

Chapter 18

Multidimensional scaling and cluster analysis

In the previous chapter, we were mainly interested in R-mode analyses that were based on associations between variables and scaled objects indirectly, although correspondence analysis scaled both objects and variables simultaneously. In this chapter, the primary focus is Q-mode analyses that directly scale objects based on similarities or dissimilarities between them. The techniques based on dissimilarities attempt to display the dissimilarities between objects graphically, with the distance between objects on the plot (inter-object distances) representing their relative dissimilarity. The scores for objects on the axes of these scaling plots can be used as variables in subsequent analyses so the techniques in this chapter are also methods for variable reduction. Remember that objects represent sampling or experimental units, such as plots, organisms, aquaria, sites, etc.

Some of the dissimilarity measures for dichotomous and continuous variables were outlined in Chapter 15 (and see Legendre & Legendre 1998 for a much more complete treatment) and all of those dissimilarities can be used with the analyses in this chapter. However, the choice of dissimilarities is a crucial one and different dissimilarities can result in very different patterns in, and interpretations of, the analyses we will describe. Additionally, the form of transformation and/or standardization of variables and/or objects, combined with the dissimilarity measure, can also be very influential.

18.1 | Multidimensional scaling

Multidimensional scaling (MDS) refers to a broad class of procedures that scale objects based on a reduced set of new variables derived from the original variables (Cox & Cox 1994). As the name suggests, MDS is specifically designed to graphically represent relationships between objects in multidimensional space. The objects are represented on a plot with the new variables as axes and the relationship between the objects on the plot should represent their underlying dissimilarity. The methods we described in Chapter 17 achieve this scaling indirectly, although MDS is more commonly based on similarities or dissimilarities between objects and was termed "similarities MDS" by Jackson (1991).

The basic data structure we will use in this chapter is similar to that from Chapter 17, a data matrix of i equals 1 to n objects by j equals 1 to p variables. Any two objects will be identified as h and i (*sensu* Legendre & Legendre 1998). The dissimilarities between objects calculated from our data are termed d, so that the dissimilarity between any two objects is d_{hi}. We will call the distance between any two objects (inter-object distances) in the scaling (configuration) plot $d_{hi}^{\sim}$ and it is usually measured as simple Euclidean distance. Unfortunately, there is some inconsistency in the symbols used for dissimilarity and inter-object distance in the literature, with δ commonly used for dissimilarity. This seems inappropriate as Greek letters are usually reserved for unknown parameters.

MDS can be based on any of the measures of dissimilarity described in Chapter 15 but is not restricted to these. For example, Guiller *et al.* (1998) calculated genetic dissimilarities (Nei's and Rogers' indices) between 30 North African populations of the snail *Helix aspersa*, based on 17 enzyme loci. They used MDS to examine the relationships between the populations.

We will illustrate MDS using some recent data sets from the biological literature.

Genetic structure of a rare plant

In Chapter 15, we described the work of McCue *et al.* (1996), who measured the genetic structure of a rare annual plant (*Clarkia springvillensis*) in California. They identified eight subpopulations and calculated Cavalli–Sforza genetic distances between subpopulations from isozyme analysis of tissue samples. We will use their genetic distances as dissimilarities and examine the relationships between the subpopulations using MDS.

Habitat fragmentation and rodents

In Chapter 13, we introduced the study of Bolger *et al.* (1997) who surveyed the abundance of seven native and two exotic species of rodents in 25 urban habitat fragments and three mainland control sites in coastal southern California. Besides the variables representing the species, other variables recorded for each fragment and mainland site included area (ha), percentage shrub cover, age (years), distance to nearest large source canyon and distance to nearest fragment of equal or greater size (m). We will first calculate dissimilarities in species composition between the 25 fragments and three mainland sites and use MDS to represent the relationship between these objects. We will then examine relationships with other fragment characteristics such as area for the 25 fragments.

Geographic variation and forest bird assemblages

Mac Nally's (1989) study on forest birds was first used in Chapter 17. The data set consisted of the maximum abundance (from four seasons) for 102 species of birds for 37 sites in southeastern Australia. These sites were actually replicates of five different forest types, four each of Gippsland manna gum, montane forest, foothills woodland, box-ironbark and river redgum with the remaining 17 sites not able to be classified into one of the habitats. An obvious question is whether the five habitat types are different in the composition of their bird assemblages.

18.1.1 Classical scaling – principal coordinates analysis (PCoA)

Principal coordinates analysis (PCoA) is closely related to PCA (Chapter 17) and is sometimes called classical scaling. We will only provide a brief introduction to PCoA here (see Legendre & Legendre 1998 for complete details), mainly because it is not used that much as a scaling (ordination) technique in biology. The steps in PCoA are as follows.

- Create an n by n matrix of dissimilarities between objects (d_{hi}), based on any of the dissimilarity measures described in Chapter 15.
- Transform these dissimilarities to $-0.5d_{hi}^2$. This transformation maintains the original dissimilarities during subsequent calculations (Legendre & Legendre 1998).
- These transformed dissimilarities are double centered by subtracting the means for the relevant row and column and adding the overall mean from the dissimilarity matrix. This centering removes the first, and trivial, eigenvector in the next step. The relative positions of the objects in the final configuration won't be affected by the double centering.
- This symmetric n by n matrix of transformed dissimilarities is then subjected to a spectral decomposition to obtain the eigenvectors and their eigenvalues, in exactly the same way as we treated a matrix of associations (covariances or correlations) between variables in a R-mode PCA. Most of the information (as measured by the eigenvalues) in the dissimilarity matrix will be in the first few eigenvectors (Box 18.1).
- As with PCA (Chapter 17), the eigenvectors are scaled, usually by the square roots of the eigenvalues (Legendre & Legendre 1998).
- The coefficients of these eigenvectors are then used to position the objects relative to each other on the scaling plot (Figure 18.1).

Box 18.1	**Worked example of PCoA: habitat fragmentation and rodents**

We will use the data on rodent numbers from 25 canyon fragment and three mainland sites in California from Bolger *et al.* (1997) to illustrate PCoA. Because the sites were very different in size, we standardized the total abundance for each site to range between zero and one and calculated a matrix of Bray–Curtis dissimilarities between the sites. This matrix was then used for the PCoA. Of the 28 possible eigenvectors, ten had zero eigenvalues and seven had negative eigenvalues but nearly 90% of the variance was explained by the first two components so only these were used for the scaling plot of sites.

	Axis 1	Axis 2
Eigenvalues	5.255	1.724
Percentage variation	66.081	21.681
Cumulative percentage variation	66.081	87.762

The PCoA scaling plot of the 28 sites based on the original Bray–Curtis dissimilarities of data range standardized by site is shown in Figure 18.1. When corrected for total abundance at a site, the three mainland sites were almost identical and were not distinguishable from most of the canyon fragments. Acuna, El Mac and 54th Street separated from the other sites, especially along axis 2. These three sites also stood out from the others in the scaling plot from a CA of these 28 sites (Chapter 17, Figure 17.5). The agreement with CA is because the latter emphasizes proportional abundance of species at each site, as does the PCoA when the dissimilarity is calculated on abundances standardized to the same maximum value at a site. Note, however, that the CA did separate the three mainland sites from each other, a pattern not observed in the PCoA, probably reflecting differences in the sensitivity of the two dissimilarity measures (chi-square and Bray–Curtis) to changes in proportional abundance.

If the original data were centered by variable means and Euclidean distance was used to create the matrix of dissimilarities between objects, the relative positions of objects in the PCoA scaling will be similar to those for the scaling plot from a PCA based on a matrix of covariances between variables. If the original data were double transformed by row and column totals so that chi-square distance was used to create the dissimilarity matrix, the relative positions of objects in the PCoA scaling will be similar to those for the scaling plot from a CA. So PCoA can be viewed as a generalization of PCA that allows a much wider range of dissimilarity measures to be used.

Another way of viewing PCoA is a translation of dissimilarities between objects into Euclidean distances, the actual distances between objects in multidimensional space (Legendre & Anderson 1999a). If the original dissimilarities were metric (such as Euclidean or chi-square), and all eigenvectors are retained, then the distances in principal coordinate space are the same as the original dissimilarities because all the variance in the original dissimilarity matrix is retained in the principal coordinates. In contrast, biologists often use non-metric dissimilarities, like Bray–Curtis for species abundance data, and the principal coordinates represent only part of the variation in the original dissimilarities. Unfortunately, the remainder may be represented by negative eigenvalues, which are very difficult to interpret. This may not be a problem if we are using PCoA as a variable reduction technique because the first few eigenvalues will be positive. However, if we wish to use all the principal coordinates derived from a non-metric dissimilarity matrix, such as in

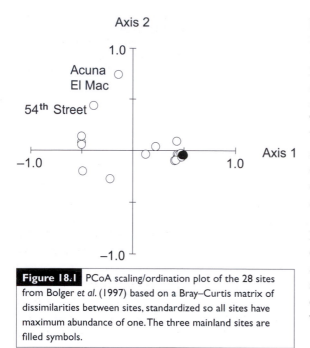

Figure 18.1 PCoA scaling/ordination plot of the 28 sites from Bolger *et al.* (1997) based on a Bray–Curtis matrix of dissimilarities between sites, standardized so all sites have maximum abundance of one. The three mainland sites are filled symbols.

distance-based redundancy analysis (db-RDA; see Section 18.1.3), then we usually have to correct for the negative eigenvalues. These corrections are somewhat technical (Legendre & Legendre 1998, Legendre & Anderson 1999a) and may result in conservative tests of complex hypotheses (McArdle & Anderson (2001).

When dealing with species abundance data, Minchin (1987) showed that the scaling plots of sampling units produced by PCoA could distort underlying ecological gradients. In particular, PCoA would force long gradients (i.e. with considerable species turnover from one end to the other) into curved patterns in the configuration in second and higher dimensions. This distortion occurred even when more robust dissimilarity measures like Bray–Curtis were used and Minchin (1987) argued that this was because PCoA, like PCA, is based on a linear relationship between dissimilarity and ecological distance, whereas the relationship was nonlinear, particularly for large dissimilarities. Also, PCoA does not provide a simple way of interpreting the new coordinates in terms of the original variables (Legendre & Legendre 1998). Although these problems do not rule out PCoA as a scaling technique for other types of data, biologists don't use PCoA very much

by itself because modern desktop computers make enhanced scaling techniques (Section 18.1.2) so accessible. However, PCoA was used by Rundle & Jackson (1996) who measured the abundance of 15 species of littoral zone fish from five sites in each of three lakes in Ontario, Canada. They calculated Bray–Curtis dissimilarities between the 15 sites and then subjected the dissimilarity matrix to a PCoA. The first two axes explained over 69% of the variation in the original dissimilarity matrix and one lake clearly separated from the other two along the first axis.

We illustrate the use of PCoA on the data from Bolger *et al.* (1997), who recorded the abundance of nine species of rodents in 25 habitat fragments and three mainland sites in southern California – see Box 18.1. We calculated a matrix of Bray–Curtis dissimilarities between sites. Close to 90% of the variation was explained by the first two axes.

18.1.2 Enhanced multidimensional scaling

Enhanced algorithm
Methods for MDS more familiar to biologists involve additional steps, beyond the initial scaling used by PCoA, to improve the fit between the observed dissimilarities between objects (d_{hi}) and the inter-object distances in the configuration ($d_{hi}^{\sim}$). Jackson (1991) termed these methods "enhanced multidimensional scaling". Basically, these methods iteratively reposition the objects in the configuration using an algorithm that improves the fit between the dissimilarities and the inter-object distances, the latter measured by a form of Minkowski metric such as Euclidean distance. The most commonly used algorithm for enhanced MDS is KYST, developed from methods first proposed by Kruskal (1964a,b), although some software offers the alternative ALSCAL program. The approach is surprisingly simple, although the computations would be very tedious without computer software. The steps for an enhanced MDS are as follows (Figure 18.2).

1. Set up a data matrix and make decisions about transformations or standardizations of the data.

2. Calculate a matrix of dissimilarities between objects (d_{hi}) using any of the dissimilari-

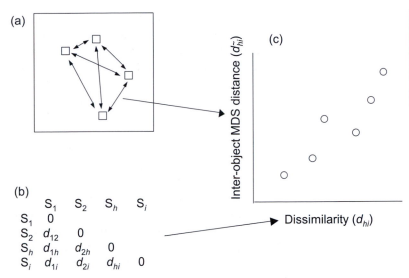

(a)

(b)

	S_1	S_2	S_h	S_i
S_1	0			
S_2	d_{12}	0		
S_h	d_{1h}	d_{2h}	0	
S_i	d_{1i}	d_{2i}	d_{hi}	0

(c)

Inter-object MDS distance ($d_{hi}^{\sim}$)

Dissimilarity (d_{hi})

Figure 18.2 Illustration of the links between (a) configuration (scaling/ordination) plot, (b) dissimilarity matrix and (c) Shepard plot in enhanced MDS. S_1, S_2, etc., are objects, e.g. sampling units.

ties described in Chapter 15. Similarities could also be used; it makes no difference in the subsequent steps.

3. Decide on the number (k) of dimensions (i.e. axes) for the scaling, which will be a compromise between the need to get the fit between dissimilarities and inter-object distances as good as possible and minimizing the number of scaling dimensions for simple interpretation.

4. Arrange the objects in a starting configuration in the k-dimensional space (i.e. on the plot), either at random or more commonly using coordinates from a PCoA or even a PCA.

5. Move the location of objects in the k-dimensional space iteratively so that at each step, the match between the inter-object distances in the configuration ($d_{hi}^{\sim}$) and the actual dissimilarities (d_{hi}) improves. The iterative procedure uses the method of steepest descent (see Kruskal 1964a,b for details).

6. The final position of the objects and therefore the final configuration plot is achieved when further iterative moving of the objects can no longer improve the match between the inter-object distances in the configuration and the actual dissimilarities.

We can show the relationship between inter-object distance and dissimilarity for all pairs of objects in a Shepard diagram, which is simply a scatterplot with dissimilarity (d_{hi}) on the horizon-tal axis and inter-object distance ($d_{hi}^{\sim}$) on the vertical axis (Figure 18.2(c)). Now consider a linear or nonlinear regression model relating inter-object Euclidean distance ($d_{hi}^{\sim}$) as the response variable to dissimilarity (d_{hi}) as the predictor variable. The differences between the observed inter-object distances and those predicted by the regression model ($\hat{d}_{hi}^{\sim}$, sometimes termed "disparities" in the MDS literature) are the residuals from the regression model. These residuals can be used to measure the match between the calculated dissimilarities and the inter-object distances in the configuration.

One measure of fit is Kruskal's stress:

$$\sqrt{\frac{\sum (d_{hi}^{\sim} - \hat{d}_{hi}^{\sim})^2}{\sum d_{hi}^{\sim 2}}} \quad (18.1)$$

In Equation 18.1, the summation is over all possible $n(n-1)/2$ pairwise distances and dissimilarities. If there is a perfect metric match between inter-object distance and dissimilarity (i.e. they are directly proportional to each other), then the residuals and stress will be zero. The lower the stress value, the better the match. There are other versions of stress used to measure fit (e.g. see Jackson 1991) and it is important to know which your software uses because they are scaled, and therefore interpreted, differently. The version in Equation 18.1 is the one usually incorporated in the KYST algorithm and most commonly used by biologists. When stress is based on a parametric linear or nonlinear regression model relating inter-object distances to dissimilarities, we have metric MDS.

It is common for the Shepard plot to show a nonlinear relationship between inter-object distance and dissimilarity (Figure 18.3(b)). While this

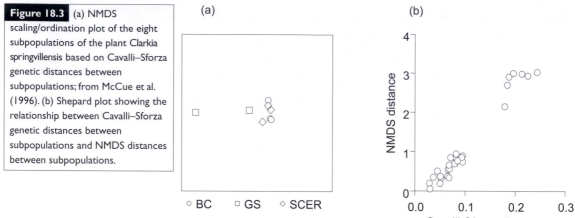

Figure 18.3 (a) NMDS scaling/ordination plot of the eight subpopulations of the plant Clarkia springvillensis based on Cavalli–Sforza genetic distances between subpopulations; from McCue et al. (1996). (b) Shepard plot showing the relationship between Cavalli–Sforza genetic distances between subpopulations and NMDS distances between subpopulations.

might suggest that a nonlinear model relating inter-object distance and dissimilarity is most appropriate, a more robust approach is to fit a monotonic regression. This is a form of nonparametric regression that relates the rank orders of the two variables (Chapter 5). So stress now measures the concordance in the rank order of the observed inter-object distances and those predicted from the dissimilarities. When stress is based on rank orders, we have non-metric MDS (NMDS).

A third type of MDS has been developed by Faith et al. (1987) and is termed hybrid MDS (HMDS). They noted that for species abundance data, sampling units at the ends of long ecological gradients often have few or no species in common and this can result in the nonlinear relationship between dissimilarity and inter-object ("ecological") distance mentioned in the previous paragraph. Importantly, it seemed that a linear relationship between dissimilarity and inter-object distance was appropriate for small dissimilarities but inappropriate for larger dissimilarities. Their hybrid approach generates two dissimilarity matrices. The first deletes dissimilarities above a threshold value and then uses a metric (linear) MDS to measure stress. The second matrix uses all the dissimilarities and uses a non-metric MDS to measure stress. The final configuration is the one that minimizes the combination of the two stress values. The choice of dissimilarity threshold is a difficult one, with Faith et al. (1987) originally proposing 0.8 (for Bray–Curtis or Kulczynski dissimilarities) but also

suggesting that some continuous function could also be used. Our experience is that HMDS does not offer much advantage over NMDS, even for ecological data sets, and is only available in specialized software anyway.

Interpretation of final configuration

We illustrate the use of NMDS with the data set on genetic differences between subpopulations of a species of plant from McCue et al. (1996) in Box 18.2, the habitat fragmentation study of Bolger et al. (1997) in Box 18.3 and the forest bird community study from Mac Nally (1995) in Box 18.4. The final configuration is the scatterplot of objects in a scaling or ordination diagram (Figure 18.3, Figure 18.4, Figure 18.5). The interpretation of this plot depends on how good a representation it is of the actual dissimilarities, i.e. how low the stress value is. Clarke (1993) provided some guidelines for stress values based on ecological (species abundance) data. Stress values greater than 0.3 indicate the configuration is no better than arbitrary and we should not try and interpret configurations unless stress values are less than 0.2, and ideally less than 0.1. These thresholds are for Kruskal's stress formula in Equation 18.1, while some software may use different versions that require different guidelines. We can always reduce the stress value, i.e. improve the fit between dissimilarities and inter-object distances, by increasing the number of dimensions in the scaling. However, the more dimensions we use, the more difficult the display and interpretation of the final configuration, so we are trying to achieve a compromise

Box 18.2 | Worked example of enhanced MDS: genetic structure of a rare plant

McCue et al. (1996) sampled eight subpopulations of the rare annual plant (*Clarkia springvillensis*) from three sites along the Tule River in California. Two sites, Bear Creek (BC) with three subpopulations and the Springville Clarkia Ecological Reserve (SCER) with three subpopulations, were separated by about 300 m and the third site, Gauging Station (GS) with two subpopulations, is approximately 8 km apart. The non-metric MDS algorithm produced identical configurations from all random starts and the stress of the final configuration was 0.045, indicating that the scaling/ordination of the subpopulations closely matched the Cavalli–Sforza genetic distances between the subpopulations. The final scaling plot of the subpopulations (Figure 18.3) indicates that the two Gauging Station subpopulations are genetically different from the remaining subpopulations, with subpopulation GS1 being the most distinct.

Box 18.3 | Worked example of enhanced MDS: habitat fragmentation and rodents

We will use the data on rodent numbers from 25 canyon fragment and three mainland sites in California from Bolger et al. (1997) to illustrate NMDS. Because the sites were very different in size, the data were standardized so that each site had a maximum total abundance of rodents of one. We were interested in comparing sites based on species composition and abundance but without patterns being confounded by very different areas.

A matrix of Bray–Curtis dissimilarities between all 28 sites was calculated and subjected to non-metric MDS. From 20 random starts in two dimensions, the minimum stress value of 0.054 was achieved from four starts, although all 20 starts produced very similar final configurations, one of which is displayed in Figure 18.4, with a small range of stress values (0.054–0.059). The mainland sites were not clearly separate from the fragments and the pattern of sites was similar to that in the PCoA plot. The same fragment sites were close to the mainland sites and Acuna, El Mac and 54th Street were most different to the mainland sites (Figure 18.4). It is interesting to compare the pattern from the NMDS to that from the CA on the same data described in Chapter 17 (Figure 17.5). Although the distances between the sites are different in the two plots, the broad pattern of Acuna, El Mac and 54th Street being separate was consistent in both analyses.

Correlations were calculated between the two dimensional configuration (scores) of sites and each of the six habitat variables (total area, shrub area, percentage area of shrubs, distance to nearest large source canyon and distance to nearest fragment of equal or greater size, age). Randomization testing showed that only percentage of shrub was significantly related to the configuration of sites, although the result for age suggested a pattern worth investigating further.

Variable	n	r	P
Area	28	0.28	0.380
Shrub	28	0.33	0.250
Percentage shrub	28	0.69	0.010
Distance nearest source	25	0.18	0.740
Distance nearest fragment	25	0.20	0.640
Age	25	0.47	0.050

Box 18.4 | Worked example of enhanced MDS: geographic variation and forest bird assemblages

The data set from Mac Nally (1989) consisted of the maximum abundance (from four seasons) for 102 species of birds for 37 sites in southeastern Australia. A matrix of Bray–Curtis dissimilarities between sites was constructed. No standardization was used because the data were densities of birds, rather than absolute counts. This means that species with high densities will dominate the dissimilarities between sites. A non-metric MDS in two dimensions, using 20 random starts, resulted in a stress value of 0.14. Using three dimensions, a stress value of 0.08 was achieved from 12 of the 20 random starts, so the three dimensional solution was used. The scaling/ordination plot of the 37 sites in the first two of the three dimensions (Figure 18.5(a)) showed clear separation of sites dominated by Gippsland Manna Gum and River Red Gum, and to a lesser extent Box-Ironbark. The remaining habitat types (Foothills woodland and Montane forest) could not be easily distinguished from the unclassified sites. If we had no evidence for prior groupings in these data, we might use a minimum spanning tree to further examine relative closeness of sites (Figure 18.5(b)). The three longest spans would roughly separate the River Red Gum and Gippsland Manna Gum habitats from the rest, with two of the unclassified sites intermediate.

Mac Nally (1996) was able to classify the sites *a priori* into five habitat types so we were able to test the H_0 of no difference between the five habitat types using a single factor ANOSIM procedure. We used the program PRIMER. The global R statistic was 0.914 and the probability of obtaining a value this great or greater, based on a randomization test, was less than 0.001. We concluded there were statistically significant differences in bird assemblages between habitats. Pairwise ANOSIM tests were difficult to interpret because there were only four observations in each group which only allowed 35 possible permutations for each pairwise randomization test and thus P values were ± approximately 0.029. However, only two of the pairwise comparisons had R values less than one, Montane forest versus Foothills woodland and Box-Ironbark versus Foothills woodland.

We also used the non-parametric MANOVA procedure of Anderson (2001) to test the H_0 of no difference between the five habitat types. We used the program NP-MANOVA, kindly supplied by M.J. Anderson from the University of Auckland. The single factor MANOVA test was based on Bray–Curtis dissimilarities between sites and we used 10 000 permutations.

Source	SS	df	MS	F	P	Possible number of permutations
Habitat	28 964.903	4	7241.226	9.619	<0.001	2.55×10^9
Residual	11 292.165	15	752.811			
Total	40 257.068	19				

Clearly, we would reject the H_0 and conclude that there is a significant difference across the five habitats in the Bray–Curtis dissimilarities between sites. We then ran pairwise comparisons, based on t statistics ($\sqrt{F}$ from non-parametric MANOVA comparing two groups). All comparisons were significant, except Foothills woodland v Montane forest. indicating that this procedure is more powerful than the ANOSIM tests, although Holm's adjustment to the P values to control the family-wise Type I error rate resulted in no significant differences (all $P = 0.280$).

Comparison	t	P
Box-Ironbark v Foothills woodland	1.702	0.031
Box-Ironbark v Gippsland Manna Gum	3.227	0.028
Box-Ironbark v Montane forest	2.676	0.028
Box-Ironbark v River Red Gum	3.639	0.028
Foothills woodland v Gippsland Manna Gum	2.954	0.031
Foothills woodland v Montane forest	1.520	0.054
Foothills woodland v River Red Gum	3.550	0.028
Gippsland Manna Gum v Montane forest	3.262	0.029
Gippsland Manna Gum v River Red Gum	3.361	0.028
Montane forest v River Red Gum	4.287	0.030

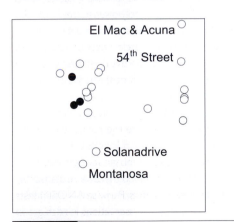

Figure 18.4 NMDS scaling/ordination plot of the 28 sites from Bolger et al. (1997) based on a Bray–Curtis matrix of dissimilarities between sites, standardized so all sites have maximum abundance of one. The three mainland sites are filled symbols.

between objects that are relevant to interpretation in MDS. It is preferable to rotate the final configuration so that the first axis lies along the direction of maximum variation. This can be achieved by a PCA on the MDS axis scores (Clarke & Warwick 1994) and will often be done automatically by MDS software. Note that actual values of the object scores are also arbitrary and these can be scaled in a number of ways; only the relative distances between the objects is important. Plots of the final configuration do not need scales on the axes as long as the axes are scaled identically.

Basically, the interpretation of final scaling (ordination) plot is subjective. Objects closer together are more similar (e.g. in species composition) than those further apart. A useful addition to the plot is a minimum spanning tree, where the objects are joined by lines so that the sum of line lengths is the smallest possible and there are no closed loops (Figure 18.5(b)). Minimum spanning trees can be applied to any scatterplot of points. For MDS configurations, objects joined by the shortest spans are closest on the plot and those separated by longest spans are furthest

between minimizing stress and minimizing the number of dimensions. Our experience with ecological data is that two or three dimensions will usually produce adequate configurations.

The final orientation of the configuration is arbitrary and it is only the relative distances

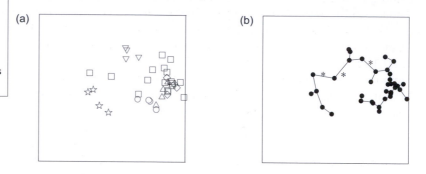

Figure 18.5 NMDS scaling/ordination plots of the 37 sites from Mac Nally (1989) based on a Bray–Curtis matrix of dissimilarities between sites. In (a), the different habitats are identified by different symbols. In (b), a minimum spanning tree joins all sites with longest spans indicated by *.

○ Box-Ironbark △ Foothills woodland ▽ Gippsland Manna Gum ◇ Montane Forest ☆ River Red Gum □ Unclassified

apart; the latter may separate different groups of objects (see Digby & Kempton 1987). Minimum spanning trees can be plotted in three dimensions, although they become ugly to interpret.

We may also have formal hypotheses we wish to test. For example, are dissimilarities between objects related to other differences, such as geographic distances? If the data consist of replicate objects within pre-defined natural (e.g. polluted area vs non-polluted area) or experimental (e.g. different nutrient treatments) groups, then we would probably test whether objects within a group are closer together than objects from different groups. Testing these hypotheses will be considered in Sections 18.1.3 and 18.1.5.

Convergence problems

The algorithms for enhanced MDS converge to the final configuration iteratively and the number of iterations depends on the complexity of the data. More rapid convergence can be achieved if the coordinates from an initial PCA or PCoA scaling are used rather than a random starting configuration and some software for MDS defaults to a preliminary PCoA before iterating. The iterative nature of the various algorithms for enhanced MDS means that the iterations can converge to a "local" solution that is not the configuration that best matches inter-object distances with dissimilarities. The only solution to this problem is to repeat the MDS a number of times, using a new random starting configuration each time, and then compare the different configurations for stress and axis coordinates. We can only be confident of the final configuration if it occurs from a majority of random starts. Comparison of different configurations can be achieved through Procrustes analysis (Digby & Kempton 1987), where one configuration is rotated and rescaled to most closely match a second configuration of the same objects. The fit is measured by the sum of squared distances between the corresponding objects in the two configurations.

18.1.3 Dissimilarities and testing hypotheses about groups of objects

It is common for biologists to have recorded multiple variables from objects in a sampling or experimental design where the objects fall into pre-defined groups. The design might have a single factor or be multifactorial with factors either crossed or nested. We would often be interested in testing null hypotheses about differences between groups in these designs, as we would using linear ANOVA models if we had just a single response variable. In the multivariate context, the methods for testing such hypotheses proposed in the literature are based on the original variables, the scores for each object in scaling (ordination) space or the dissimilarities between objects.

Tests based on dissimilarities are not straightforward for two reasons. First, the dissimilarities between objects are not always independent of each other (the dissimilarities between objects 1 and 2 and 2 and 3 are not independent of the dissimilarity between objects 1 and 3), so randomization (permutation) testing procedures are required (Chapter 3). Second, if we wish to use the dissimilarities in linear models, we require sums-of-squares based on the difference between each observation and the mean of the observations, or the centroid in the multivariate context. When dealing with metric dissimilarities (e.g. Euclidean distance), the centroid of a group of observations and the sum of squared deviations from this centroid are straightforward to calculate and interpret. This is not the case when dealing with non-metric dissimilarities like Bray–Curtis and a limitation of some approaches is their inability to deal with non-metric dissimilarities (see Anderson 2001).

MANOVA based on original variables

We could use a multivariate analysis of variance (MANOVA; see Chapter 16), a multivariate analogue of the univariate ANOVA, to test the null hypothesis of no difference between groups in some linear combination of variables. While MANOVA may be useful in some situations, it has quite restrictive assumptions about variances and covariances that are difficult to test (Chapter 16) and are unlikely to be met when the variables are species abundances with lots of zeros. A robust non-parametric form of MANOVA (NPMANOVA) that uses dissimilarities has recently been described by Anderson (2001) and will be discussed below. MANOVA comparing groups of objects is also restricted to data sets where the number of variables does not greatly exceed the number of objects, whereas ecological data sets often comprise many variables (species) and fewer objects (sampling untis).

(M)ANOVA based on axis scores

Another approach is to use any of the scaling procedures from Chapter 17 or this chapter that provide scores for each object on derived variables (components or axes). These scores could be used as response variables in linear models, as described for PCA in Chapter 17, to test hypotheses about group differences. There are some problems with this method. With MDS, we have to decide which axes to use; maybe scores from multiple axes (i.e. the first two or three dimensions if stress is adequate) could be used with a MANOVA? The axes themselves are also not a linear combination of variables like the components from a PCA or axes from a CA so are more difficult to relate to the original variables. Finally, the MDS axes

simply define the relative positions of the objects in multidimensional space so as to represent the observed dissimilarities. Tests of hypotheses about group differences might be better based on these actual dissimilarities rather than some approximation of them.

Mantel test

The Mantel test described in Chapter 15 can be used to correlate a dissimilarity matrix between objects with another dissimilarity matrix that simply separates objects into groups (Manly 1997, Schnell et al. 1985). This second matrix is termed the model or design matrix (Legendre & Legendre 1998, Sokal & Rohlf 1995). The main limitation of using the Mantel test in this way is that it is difficult to test more complex models such as those including interaction terms.

Rundle & Jackson (1996) used a Mantel test to test for differences in the fish communities of the littoral zones of three lakes in Canada based on five sites in each lake. They constructed a Bray–Curtis dissimilarity matrix between the 15 sites. To test whether the variation in fish communities was primarily between lakes rather than within lakes, they used Mantel test to assess whether the Bray–Curtis matrix based on fish was associated with a matrix containing zeros for within-lake distances between sites and ones for between-lake distances between sites.

Multi-response permutation procedures

Mielke et al. (1976, see also Mielke 1985) proposed multi-response permutation procedures (MRPP) that test hypotheses about group differences in Euclidean distances, and Zimmerman et al. (1985) illustrated their application to biological data sets, such as n sampling units by p species. Basically, the MRPP determines the mean of the Euclidean distances between objects within each group and calculates an MRPP statistic (delta) that is a linear combination of these mean within-group Euclidean distances. The statistic produces a weighted average (based on sample size) of the within-group mean Euclidean distances. Small values of the statistic indicate that objects tend to be found in groups. The probability distribution of the MRPP statistic is determined by randomizing the allocation of all objects to the groups, keeping the original sample sizes, with the null hypothesis being that all random allocations are equally likely. We compare our observed value of the MRPP statistic to the probability distribution generated under randomization to get the probability of obtaining the observed value of the statistic or one smaller under the null hypothesis. The MRPP can be used for a range of hypotheses including those associated with paired comparisons and randomized block designs.

MRPPs have been traditionally based on Euclidean distance and their use with more robust non-metric dissimilarities would be tricky because of the difficulty of defining the centroid and calculating the mean within-group dissimilarity. Nonetheless, McCune & Mefford (1999) have suggested that MRPPs might work well with other dissimilarity measures, such as Bray–Curtis. Since Euclidan distance is not a particularly appropriate measure of dissimilarity for some types of biological data, e.g. species abundances (Chapter 15), we could use the inter-object distances from classical (PCoA) or enhanced scaling (NMDS) in a MRPP. This is not an ideal solution because we know that these distances are an imperfect representation of the actual dissimilarities, and correction for negative eigenvalues would be required for PCoA. This approach is used, although not for MRPP, in distance-based redundancy analysis (Legendre & Anderson 1999a) and discussed below.

Analysis of similarities

ANOSIM (Analysis of Similarities; Clarke 1993, Clarke & Warwick 1994) is a hypothesis testing procedure that uses Bray–Curtis dissimilarities, although it could use any dissimilarity measure. This procedure uses a test statistic (R) based on the difference between the average of all the rank dissimilarities between objects between groups ($\bar{r}_B$) and the average of all the rank dissimilarities between objects within groups ($\bar{r}_W$):

$$R = \frac{\bar{r}_B - \bar{r}_W}{n(n-1)/4} \tag{18.2}$$

This is analogous to an ANOVA comparing between-group and within-group variation. The use of rank dissimilarities rather than actual dissimilarities is in keeping with the spirit of non-metric MDS.

The H_0 being tested by ANOSIM is that the average of the rank dissimilarities between all possible pairs of objects in different groups is the same as the average of the rank dissimilarities between pairs of objects in the same groups. R is scaled to be within the range +1 to −1. Differences between groups would be suggested by R values greater than zero where objects are more dissimilar between groups than within groups. R values of zero indicate that the null hypothesis is true. Negative R values indicate that dissimilarities within groups are greater than dissimilarities between groups, an outcome Clarke & Warwick (1994) considered unlikely. However, Chapman & Underwood (1999) showed that negative R values can occur, especially when groups had high levels of within-group variability that were similar between groups and when outliers were present. They argued that negative R values could be a useful diagnostic, indicating an inappropriate completely random sampling design when stratified sampling would be more appropriate.

Like the MRPP, ANOSIM uses a randomization procedure to randomly allocate objects to groups to generate the distribution of R under the null hypothesis that all random allocations are equally likely. Clarke & Warwick (1994) described the use of ANOSIM procedures for nested designs where averaging over the subsampling levels produces a series of single factor tests for each factor. They also proposed ANOSIM for testing main effects in factorial designs by simply treating each main effect as a single factor test, averaging over the other factor. Legendre & Legendre (1998) pointed out that ANOSIM is very similar to a Mantel test using a model matrix to define the groups specified in the hypothesis and the two methods should produce similar P values for the same hypothesis.

Both MRPP and ANOSIM use some measure of average dissimilarity within and between groups. Van Sickle (1997) described a useful graphical display for representing the relative strength of the differences in dissimilarity between groups, called a mean similarity dendogram. In its simplest form, a mean similarity dendogram for two or more groups would have branches for each group originating at the between-group mean dissimilarity and the length of each branch representing the within-group mean dissimilarities. Alternatively, the origin of each group branch could be staggered, with the mean between-group dissimilarity for each pair of groups plotted separately. Displays for multifactor designs are also possible (Van Sickle 1997). Mean similarity dendograms use the actual mean dissimilarities, rather than their rank orders, for plotting and therefore do not provide a direct graphical representation of the ANOSIM results.

One of the limitations of both MRPP and the ANOSIM procedure is that complex tests, such as interaction terms in linear models, are not available. This is in part because tests of interactions are difficult in the randomization context, since the interaction hypothesis cannot be simply expressed in terms of a random reallocation of observations to groups (see slightly differing opinions in Edgington 1995 and Manly 1997). Interactions are most sensibly tested in a linear model framework that also considers main effects. Unfortunately, if non-metric dissimilarities like Bray–Curtis are used, it is not straightforward to partition the variance (sum-of-squares) from fitting a multivariate linear model because of the difficulty of defining deviations from the centroid of the observations (Anderson 2001, Legendre & Anderson 1999a).

Distance-based redundancy analysis

Because of the difficulties in using MRPP or ANOSIM tests for designs with interactions, Legendre & Anderson (1999a; see 1999b for minor correction) proposed an alternative approach for testing group differences in dissimilarities, called distance-based redundancy analysis (db-RDA). Their method uses PCoA to convert the original dissimilarities into their equivalent Euclidean distances, correcting for negative eigenvalues (Section 18.1.1). The matrix of n objects by p principal coordinates is then related to grouping factors using redundancy analysis (RDA; Chapter 17), where the grouping factors are represented by a matrix of dummy variables (Chapter 5) and the relationship is tested by a linear model using randomization tests (Chapters 3 and 8). This makes it easy for testing interactions because the analysis just becomes a multiple linear regression model

and any combination of crossed and nested, fixed and random factors can be included.

It turns out that we can get the same results by simply doing a MANOVA test on the corrected principal coordinates, although Legendre & Anderson (1999a) argued that db-RDA has the advantages of more robust randomization tests and does not require more objects than variables in the original data matrix. The latter advantage is important because ecological data sets nearly always have more species (variables) than sampling units (objects). The main limitation of db-RDA is its complexity and the need to have software for the RDA component.

Non-parametric MANOVA

Distance-based RDA was developed to translate various non-metric measures of dissimilarity into their equivalent distance in Euclidean space using PCoA. We can then relate these distances to a design matrix using linear models (e.g. RDA) and calculate sum-of-squared deviations between observations and their centroid. McArdle & Anderson (2001) and Anderson (2001) have recently shown that the partitioning of sums-of-squares (SS) and variances used for testing linear models can also be applied directly to dissimilarities, even non-metric ones like Bray–Curtis. This method means that using PCoA on the original dissimilarities is not necessary and the negative eigenvalues produced by db-RDA correspond to negative SS. The correction for negative eigenvalues in db-RDA described by Legendre & Anderson (1999a) actually produces overly conservative tests when random factors are included in the design (McArdle & Anderson 2001).

The non-parametric MANOVA described by McArdle & Anderson (2001) and Anderson (2001) is elegantly simple and can be applied to any design structure. The main difficulty is developing a randomization test for complex terms like interactions (Chapter 9; see Manly 1997). Our view is that the non-parametric MANOVA is so widely applicable in the biological sciences that we will describe it in some detail.

Consider a single factor design with p groups and n objects in each group so the total number of objects is $N = pn$. For the equations below, any two objects are termed h ($h = 1$ to N) and i ($i = 1$ to N).

From an N by N matrix of dissimilarities (d_{hi} e.g. Bray–Curtis) between all pairs of objects, we calculate three SS.

The first is the sum of squared dissimilarities between all pairs of objects divided by N:

$$SS_{Total} = \frac{1}{N} \sum_{h=1}^{N-1} \sum_{i=h+1}^{N} d_{hi}^2 \qquad (18.3)$$

Note that only the lower (or upper) diagonal of the dissimilarity matrix is used. The dissimilarity between objects h and i is the same as between i and h and is only counted once in the calculation of SS_{Total}.

The second is the within-groups SS. The $SS_{Residual}$ is the sum of squared dissimilarities between objects within each group, summed over the groups:

$$SS_{Residual} = \frac{1}{N} \sum_{h=1}^{N-1} \sum_{i=h+1}^{N} d_{hi}^2 e_{hi} \qquad (18.4)$$

In Equation 18.4, e_{hi} equals one if object h and i are in the same group and zero if they are in different groups (just like the design matrix in the Mantel test above).

The between-groups SS is determined from the usual additive partitioning of the total SS described for ANOVA models in Chapter 8:

$$SS_{Groups} = SS_{Total} - SS_{Residual} \qquad (18.5)$$

The approximate F-ratio statistic for testing the H_0 that all allocations of objects, and therefore dissimilarities between objects, between groups are equally likely is:

$$F = \frac{SS_{Groups}/(p-1)}{SS_{Residual}/(N-p)} \qquad (18.6)$$

This is analogous to the F-ratio statistic for a single factor ANOVA model. The randomization test is then done in the same manner as described for single factor ANOVA tests in Chapter 8, using a subset of all possible permutations for anything except very small p and n.

Pairwise contrasts of specific groups, either planned or unplanned, can be done using the same test statistic. If there are many contrasts, the significance levels may need to be adjusted to control family-wise Type I error rate, using one of the Bonferroni corrections described in Chapter 3.

However, the main advantage of this non-parametric MANOVA is that it can handle more complex designs, especially those that include interactions. Anderson (2001) provides appropriate formulae for factorial designs but the logic is straightforward. The SS_{Total} are calculated using Equation 18.3. The main change from a single factor design is that we need to calculate within-groups SS for each factor separately, ignoring the other factor. The SS for each main effect are simply the difference between the SS_{Total} and within-groups SS for that factor. The $SS_{Residual}$ are calculated using Equation 18.4 except that each combination of the two factors (each cell) is considered a single group. So the e_{hi} equals one if the objects are in the same cell (combination of factors) and zero if they are in different cells. The $SS_{Interaction}$ are what is left after the main effects and residual SS are subtracted from the total. The F-ratios are determined following Equation 18.6, although the denominator may need to be changed if either factor is random (see Chapter 9).

As we discussed in Chapter 9, there are different approaches to randomization tests in factorial designs and some debate about whether randomization tests for interaction terms are possible. Manly (1997) summarized these different approaches, including whether to randomize observations or residuals and whether to impose restrictions on which objects are randomized for tests of different terms. He argued that the different methods produced comparable results.

We illustrate the use of a single factor non-parametric MANOVA with the bird community data from Mac Nally (1989) – see Box 18.4. There were four replicate sites for each of five forest habitats types; unclassified sites were not included in the comparison. There was a significant difference between habitats, although like the ANOSIM procedure, the small number of possible permutations with only four replicates per group meant that pairwise comparisons were difficult to interpret after adjusting significance levels. Based on raw P values, the non-parametric MANOVA procedure seemed more powerful than the ANOSIM comparisons.

The two main advantages of the non-parametric MANOVA introduced by McArdle & Anderson

(2001) and Anderson (2001) are that any dissimilarity measure can be used and the tests are based on the partitioning of sums-of-squares as used in classical linear models. This means that the method can be used for any design structure that can be formulated as a linear model (see Chapters 5, 6, 8–12) and can accommodate fixed and random factors by using different denominators in the approximate F-ratios. The only limitation is the difficulty of determining the appropriate randomization test procedure for complex designs.

18.1.4 Relating MDS to original variables

Another question of interest in scaling (ordination) procedures is to determine which variables contribute most to the observed pattern among objects, e.g. which species contribute most to the separation among sampling units or which morphological variables contribute most to the separation of organisms. As described in Section 18.1.3, we will often be using a sampling or experimental design that includes groups of objects and our interest will be which variables contribute most to the any separation among groups. When we scale using one of the R-mode methods described in the previous chapter, then we obtain loadings for each variable on each derived component (axis of the scaling plot) as in PCA or can plot object and variable scores jointly to examine correlations as in CA.

Scaling techniques that are based directly on dissimilarities, such as MDS, do not provide correlations between derived axis scores and variables as part of the algorithm but there are alternative ways of investigating how the variables contribute to the final configuration of objects. We could simply correlate the axis scores from an MDS with each variable or linear combination of variables. This is not an ideal solution because, besides the problem of increasing Type I error rates from multiple testing if we do numerous correlations, we have to decide how many and which dimensions from the MDS we use. Additionally, we know that the scores, or at least the distances between objects, are imperfect representations of the actual dissimilarities so a method that uses these dissimilarities directly would be preferable.

Clarke & Warwick (1994) described a procedure for ecological data termed SIMPER (similarity percentages) for determining which species (variables) are contributing most to the dissimilarity between groups of object (sampling units). For example, the Bray–Curtis dissimilarity for a pair of sampling units is basically the differences between the units for each species, summed over all the species. SIMPER computes the percentage contribution of each species to the dissimilarities between all pairs of sampling units in different groups and the percentage contribution of each species to the similarities between all pairs of sampling units within each group. It then calculates the average of these percentage contributions, with its standard deviation. Species with a large ratio of average/standard deviation percentage contribution to dissimilarity between sampling units in different groups are those species that best discriminate between the groups. Note that there are no formal tests of hypotheses with SIMPER, just a list of species in order of their percentage contributions to dissimilarities between groups or similarities within groups.

18.1.5 Relating MDS to covariates

In ecological data sets, we often have two types of variable recorded for each sampling unit, species abundances (or presence/absence) and environmental characteristics (covariates). In these circumstances, we might wish to relate the dissimilarities between sampling units, or groups of sampling units, based on the species variables to differences in the environmental characteristics. Are sampling units that are very different from others in terms of species composition also very different in terms of one or more environmental variables? There are numerous ways of relating dissimilarities between sampling units to environmental variables, two of which we have already described. We could examine correlations between, or fit regression models to, the scores for each axis from the MDS and the environmental variable(s) (Ludwig & Reynolds 1988), just as we described for component scores from a PCA in Chapter 17. These correlations can be represented as vectors on the MDS plot, producing a biplot, and tests of the correlations are best done in a randomization context. The problems with relating environmental variables (covariates) to axis scores are the same as outlined in Sections 18.1.3 and

18.1.4, i.e. the problem of multiple testing, axis scores being an imperfect representation of the actual dissimilarities, deciding how many and which dimensions to use.

Clarke & Ainsworth (1993) proposed a procedure for ecological data that basically measures the correlation between dissimilarities between sampling units based on species composition and the dissimilarities between sampling units based on environmental variables. They provided an algorithm called BIO-ENV that first calculates a dissimilarity matrix (e.g. Bray–Curtis) between sampling units based on species abundances and a separate dissimilarity matrix (e.g. Euclidean distance) between sampling units based on environmental variables. It then measures any correlation between the rank-orders of these two matrices using the Spearman rank correlation coefficient. Each pair of observations for the correlation will be the rank of the Bray–Curtis dissimilarity (from species abundances) between objects h and i and the rank of the Euclidean distance (from environmental variables) between objects h and i.

Legendre & Legendre (1998) pointed out that the BIO-ENV procedure basically calculates the same correlation as a Mantel test (Chapter 15 and Section 18.1.3), except the former is based on rank transformed data. The Mantel test could be used for the global test of no correlation between the two matrices, or even between the dissimilarities based on species composition and differences between sampling units for each environmental variable separately. It can also be extended to compare more than two matrices (Diniz-Filho & Bini 1996).

Clarke & Ainsworth (1993) and Clarke & Warwick (1994) incorporated a stepwise routine into their BIO-ENV procedure, to find the combinations of environmental variables that produce dissimilarities between sampling units with the highest correlations with dissimilarities between sampling units based on species composition. They argued that their implementation of the Mantel test is not suitable for hypothesis testing, both because the dissmilarities for both sets of variables are not independent and also because their stepwise procedure would produce numerous significance tests that are difficult to interpret (see Chapter 6).

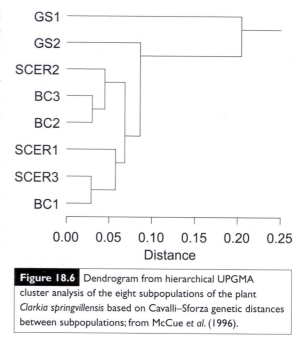

Figure 18.6 Dendrogram from hierarchical UPGMA cluster analysis of the eight subpopulations of the plant *Clarkia springvillensis* based on Cavalli–Sforza genetic distances between subpopulations; from McCue et al. (1996).

Procrustes analysis (Section 18.1.2; Digby & Kempton 1987, Legendre & Legendre 1998) can also provide a descriptive measure of the fit of a configuration between objects based on one set of variables (e.g. species abundances) and a configuration between the same objects based on a separate set of variables (e.g. environmental characteristics).

18.2 | Classification

The aim of classification is to group together a number of objects based on their attributes or variables to produce groups of objects where each object within a group is more similar to other objects in that group than to objects in other groups. One form of classification analysis is discriminant function analysis (DFA; Chapter 16) where the number of groups was known *a priori*. In this section, we are interested in classification methods where the number of groups is not known and must be determined from the data.

18.2.1 Cluster analysis
Cluster analysis is a method for combining similar objects into groups or clusters, which can usually be displayed in a tree-like diagram, called a dendrogram (Figure 18.6). Legendre & Legendre

(a)

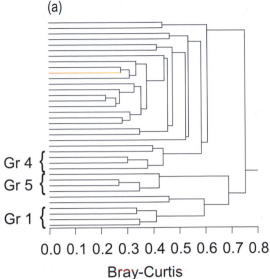

Gr 4

Gr 5

Gr 1

0.0 0.1 0.2 0.3 0.4 0.5 0.6 0.7 0.8

Bray-Curtis

(b)

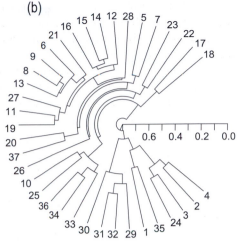

Figure 18.7 Dendrograms from hierarchical UPGMA cluster analysis of the 37 sites from Mac Nally (1995) based on a Bray–Curtis matrix of dissimilarities between sites. In (a), the usual dendrogram is displayed with clusters identified for Gippsland Manna Gum (Gr 1), Box-Ironbark (Gr 4) and River Red Gum (Gr 5). In (b), the polar representation of the dendrogram is displayed, with site numbers. Gippsland Manna Gum includes sites 2, 3, 4 and 24; Montane forest sites 9, 11, 12, 15; Foothills woodland sites 10, 20, 21, 37; Box-Ironbark sites 25, 33, 34, 36; River Red Gum sites 29, 30, 31, 32; remaining sites unclassified.

(1998) provide a recent, very thorough, discussion. Cluster analyses are used commonly by biologists. For example, Crews *et al.* (1995) examined plant species in montane rainforest in Hawaii. They compared six sites (varying in age) using the cover–abundance measures for numerous plant species. The objects were sites, the variables were species abundances and cluster analysis was used to place the sites into like groups. Koenig *et al.* (1994) studied acorn production in oak trees in California. They clustered five species of oaks (objects) based on twelve mean annual values of acorn production (variables). Probably the most important use of cluster analysis in biology is taxonomic and phylogenetic research, where the dissimilarity measures are often morphological or genetic/molecular differences between organisms, species, etc., and the dendrogram represents a possible evolutionary sequence.

Agglomerative hierarchical clustering

Agglomerative methods start with individual objects and join objects and then objects and groups together until all the objects are in one big group. This is the form of cluster analysis familiar to most biologists. Usually objects are clustered but sometimes you may wish to cluster variables (e.g. species). Most algorithms for agglomerative cluster analysis start with a matrix of pairwise similarities or dissimilarities between the objects and the steps are as follows.

1. Calculate a matrix of dissimilarities (d_{hi}) between all pairs of objects.

2. The first cluster is formed between the two objects with the smallest dissimilarity.

3. The dissimilarities between this cluster and the remaining objects are then recalculated.

4. A second cluster is formed between cluster 1 and the object most similar to cluster 1.

5. The procedure continues until all objects are linked in clusters.

The graphical representation of the cluster analysis is a dendrogram (Figure 18.6, Figure 18.7(a)), showing the links between groups of objects with the lengths of the lines representing dissimilarity. If there are many objects, the standard dendrogram can be very long and difficult to represent on a single page. An alternative representation is the polar dendrogram (Figure 18.7(b)),

Box 18.5 | Worked example of cluster analysis: genetic structure of a rare plant

Like MDS, hierarchical cluster analysis can be based on any type of dissimilarity matrix. We clustered the data on the eight subpopulations of the rare annual plant (*Clarkia springvillensis*) in California based on Cavalli–Sforza genetic distances between the subpopulations (McCue *et al*. 1996). We used UPGMA and the dendrogram is shown in Figure 18.6. The two Gauging Station subpopulations (GS) split off first; these were most different in the NMDS scaling plot based on the same matrix – see Box 18.2. Then the second of the Springville Clarkia Ecological Reserve (SCER) subpopulations grouped with the second and third Bear Creek (BC) subpopulations and the first BC subpopulation grouped with the first and third SCER subpopulations.

where the objects are arranged in a circle and their distance from the center of the circle represents dissimilarities between objects and groups of objects. Like scaling (ordination) plots, the interpretation of the groupings in the dendrogram is subjective and the decision about which groups to report is usually based on some arbitrary cut-off value for dissimilarity.

The major difference between the variety of available hierarchical agglomerative clustering methods is how the dissimilarities between clusters and between clusters and objects (step 3) are recalculated. These are termed linkage methods, and three common ones are as follows.

- Single linkage (nearest neighbour), where the dissimilarity between two clusters is measured by the minimum dissimilarity between all combinations of two objects, one from each cluster.
- Complete linkage (furthest neighbour), where the dissimilarity between two clusters is measured by the maximum dissimilarity between all combinations of two objects, one from each cluster.
- Average linkage (group average or mean), where the dissimilarity between two clusters is measured by the average of all the dissimilarities between all combinations of two objects, one from each cluster. The group mean (or average) linkage strategy, commonly called unweighted pair-groups method using arithmetic averages (UPGMA), is often recom-

mended. There is a weighted version of UPGMA (WPGMA), which weights the original dissimilarities differently, and unweighted clustering based on centroids (UPGMC), which is equivalent to UPGMA except that centroids instead of means are used.

Kent & Coker (1992), Legendre & Legendre (1998) and Ludwig & Reynolds (1988) discuss the pros and cons of these different linkage methods. If there are "strong" (i.e. very dissimilar) groups in your data, then the different methods will produce similar dendrograms; in contrast, the different linkage strategies can produce very different patterns for data with weak structure (Ludwig & Reynolds 1988). Belbin *et al*. (1993) proposed a flexible modification of UPGMA that allowed the clusters to be better, if artificially, defined and this method effectively recovered true groups in the data based on simulation studies (Belbin & McDonald 1993).

Box 18.5 illustrates a cluster analysis of the subpopulations of *Clarkia springvillensis* based on genetic differences recorded by McCue *et al*. (1996). A cluster analysis of the 37 sites in southeastern Australia, using Bray–Curtis dissimilarities based on the densities of 102 species of forest birds (Mac Nally 1989), is presented in Box 18.6.

Agglomerative cluster analysis does have some disadvantages, primarily related to the interpretation of the dendrogram. The hierarchical approach means that once a group or cluster is formed from two or more objects, that group cannot be broken later in the process. As a result,

Box 18.6 | Worked example of cluster analysis: geographic variation and forest bird assemblages

A matrix of Bray–Curtis dissimilarities, based on densities of 102 species of birds, between sites was used to hierarchically structure the 37 sites in southeastern Australia (Mac Nally 1989). No standardization was used because the data were densities of birds, rather than absolute counts. The UPGMA clustering procedure produced the dendrogram shown in Figure 18.7(a), although representing this in polar form (Figure 18.7(b)) makes presentation a little easier. The Gippsland Manna Gum sites, the River Red Gum sites and the Box-Ironbark sites grouped into clear clusters, whereas the remaining habitat types (Foothills woodland and Montane forest) were not in separate clusters. This interpretation is similar to that from the NMDS on the same matrix of dissimilarities (Box 18.5).

the dendrogram is not a representation of all pairwise dissimilarities between objects like in multidimensional scaling (MDS). A misleading cluster formed early in the process will influence the remaining clusters. Also, the analysis forces objects into clusters and it would be easy for naïve biologists to place too much emphasis on these clusters without examining the actual dissimilarities. We much prefer MDS as a method for graphically representing relationships between objects based on dissimilarities.

Divisive hierarchical clustering

Divisive methods have a long history for clustering ecological data. They basically start with the objects in a single group and split them up into smaller and smaller groups until each group is a single object. One method popular with ecologists is two-way indicator species analysis (TWINSPAN), a complex procedure that uses the reciprocal averaging algorithm of correspondence analysis (Chapter 17) to successively divide the first axis for both sampling units and species into smaller groups. The output includes a two-way table that orders the sampling units and species and shows the groupings and the relative abundances of species for each sampling unit. The actual computations are tedious, although a detailed description can be found in Kent & Coker (1992). Van Groenewood (1992) and Belbin & McDonald (1993) provided simulation results that showed that TWINSPAN is not particularly good at detecting true clusters in ecological data and the problems

that affect correspondence analysis, particularly the distortion of sampling units along the first axis, also affect TWINSPAN.

Non-hierarchical clustering

Non-hierarchical methods do not represent the relationship between objects in hierarchical form. Basically, they start with a single object and cluster other objects that are similar to the first one. In contrast to hierarchical clustering, objects can be reassigned to clusters during the clustering process. One method common in statistical software is K-means clustering – see Legendre & Legendre (1998) for a detailed description. K-means works by splitting the objects into a predefined number (K) of clusters, and then cluster membership of objects is iteratively re-evaluated by some criterion, such as to maximize the ratio of between-cluster to within-cluster variance. Another method is additive tree clustering, which develops a tree-like network (dendrogram) where the dissimilarity between objects within a cluster is represented by the sum of the lengths of the branches joining them (Gower 1996) and may be more suited to non-metric dissimilarity measures.

18.3 | Scaling (ordination) and clustering for biological data

When the main purpose of the multivariate analysis is to scale objects, what ecologists term ordination, numerous techniques are available. There have been many evaluations and comparisons of these techniques, particularly for ecological data in the form of species abundances across sampling units. Differing opinions on the relative merits of different techniques can be found in Faith *et al.* (1987), Jackson & Somers (1991), Minchin (1987), Palmer (1993), Peet *et al.* (1988), ter Braak & Verdonschot (1995), van Groenewood (1992), and Wartenberg *et al.* (1987), among others. In our view, the choice of method depends on the nature of the data, the implicit measure of dissimilarity used by each method, and, not surprisingly, the biological question being addressed. Our preferred approach is to use a method that is applicable to a range of data types, is amenable to various user-defined standardizations and transformations of the data, is flexible in terms of which dissimilarity measure is used, and can be used for describing patterns and testing *a priori* hypotheses. Multidimensional scaling (MDS), especially the robust non-metric version (NMDS), meets all these criteria. Any measure of dissimilarity can be used, thereby allowing dissimilarities between objects based on continuous, binary and mixed variables under nearly every combination of transformation and standardization. The scaling or ordination has been shown to be robust for a range of data types, accurately representing underlying true dissimilarities and recovering ecological gradients, and hypothesis tests can be based on the dissimilarities. For ecological data, NMDS also appears to be the most robust for nonlinear relationships of species abundances across sampling units along long ecological gradients, which can result in misleading arching of second and higher dimensions in some methods.

The most obvious competing technique is correspondence analysis (CA) or the more sophisticated canonical version (CCA). The strengths of these methods are also their weaknesses. By implicitly using the chi-square metric as the dissimilarity measure, they allow joint scaling plots of objects and variables and when axes are scaled similarly, relative positions of objects and variables can be compared. Unfortunately, the restriction to the chi-square metric also reduces flexibility and this dissimilarity measure may not be ideal for some forms of data (Faith *et al.* 1987).

There are also decisions to be made about how to scale the axis scores, although the different scalings don't often alter the general pattern from the joint plot.

Constrained ordinations like CCA and redundancy analysis (RDA) also allow for biplots, where covariates can be included on the scaling plot showing which axes are correlated with which covariates. This is probably the main reason for the popularity of these methods, especially CCA. Relationships between dissimilarities and covariates under the MDS framework can also be evaluated although not in the same direct manner as in CCA and RDA. Finally, we shouldn't forget the oldest of these techniques, principal components analysis (PCA). While not always suitable as a scaling/ordination procedure, PCA is still a very important method for variable reduction, especially when linear relationships between variables are expected.

You may have inferred from Section 18.2.1 that we are not big users of cluster analysis, especially for representing dissimilarities between objects. Clustering procedures do not really use all pairwise dissimilarities for grouping objects so the dendrogram is not necessarily a good representation of a dissimilarity matrix. The main use of clustering procedures in biology is to display possible evolutionary and phylogenetic relationships, where the objects are organisms or taxonomic groups and the dissimilarities are morphological or genetic differences. Cluster analysis has less applicability for analyzing species abundance data to show relationships among sampling units. Ecologists sometimes use an initial cluster analysis to identify groups in a data set and then indicate those groups on a subsequent scaling plot. This approach has never made much sense to us, the cluster analysis almost certainly being a less efficient way of representing dissimilarities between objects than a method like enhanced MDS (but see Legendre & Legendre 1998 for an alternative view). Certainly, it is inappropriate to test hypotheses about differences between these groups; hypothesis tests cannot be validly used to compare groups that were defined by the same data.

18.4 | General issues and hints for analysis

18.4.1 General issues

- Principal coordinates analysis (PCoA) is a useful metric scaling procedure but has generally been superseded by enhanced, iterative scaling procedures.
- Our preferred technique for scaling or ordination of ecological data, when there are numerous zeros and extracting underlying ecological gradients is important, is a combination of a suitable dissimilarity measure, like Bray–Curtis, and robust non-metric multidimensional scaling.
- Non-metric MDS is probably more robust than metric MDS, especially when the relationship between dissimilarities and inter-object distances is nonlinear. Hybrid MDS may offer a slight advantage.
- Hierarchical cluster analysis is not as useful as MDS for representing a dissimilarity matrix and has the disadvantage of forcing all objects into clusters that cannot be reassessed during the clustering procedure.

18.4.2 Hints for analysis

- Final enhanced MDS configurations should not be interpreted without examining stress values. Make sure you know which version of stress your software uses. Values for version one of Kruskal's stress should be less than 0.15, ideally less than 0.10, for configurations of objects to be considered reliable.
- Multiple runs from random starting configurations should be compared with enhanced MDS, to ensure that any configuration does not represent a local, unrepeatable, pattern. With large data sets, i.e. many objects, using an initial PCoA to determine a starting configuration may help convergence.
- Analysis of similarities (ANOSIM) or multi-response permutation procedures (MRPP) are useful ways of testing hypotheses about group differences in a multivariate context, the former retaining the underlying philosophy of NMDS. For pairwise comparisons of groups, n greater than four per group is needed for the randomization tests. For more complex hypotheses, especially tests of interactions, the non-parametric MANOVA of Anderson (2001) offers great promise.
- The unweighted pair-groups method using arithmetic averages (UPGMA) is usually recommended as a linkage strategy for agglomerative clustering. Non-hierarchical methods may offer more flexibility because clusters are not fixed once formed.

Chapter 19

Presentation of results

A central part of reporting any scientific work is the presentation of the results, in either tabular or, more commonly, graphical form, and a considerable literature has accumulated about the appropriate ways for displaying quantitative data (e.g. Cleveland 1993, Tufte 1983, 1990, and some recent issues of *The American Statistician*). Much of this literature focuses on clarity of graphs and it is an issue that has become increasingly important as biologists do multifactorial experiments, often with complex underlying statistical models. We then face the problem of explaining those complex results to an audience that is pressed for time, and deluged by the number of papers published in any given month. In this environment, the presentation of your results becomes almost as important as the work itself, as you must convince a reader that he or she should persist with reading your paper, in the face of the many other demands on their time.

In many cases, the decision whether to read a paper completely is based initially on the title and abstract, which are provided by many of the electronic databases and the web. Having decided to look more closely at the paper, the next decision made is whether to persist with reading it. That decision will be made based in part on how clearly you express your ideas, and there is a long tradition of convincing scientists to write clearly, with several excellent and essential guides (e.g. Pechenik 2001, Strunk & White 1979, Williams 1997).

As a result of these issues, many of us think carefully about our writing style. In contrast, there is not such a long history of thinking about how to present the data, although there are some examples of creative ways to present the raw data from a study in a very complex appendix. Because the data and accompanying analyses determine whether the audience believes the story you are telling, it is critical that you present those results as clearly as possible, drawing attention to the most important features of the results, rather than submerging them in a sea of extraneous material. In this chapter, we present some simple ways to present analytical results and display results graphically, as well as making suggestions of ways not to present results. Our aim is not to be prescriptive about presentation, but to encourage you to think more about how to report your work.

19.1 | Presentation of analyses

We will deal with some of the most common analyses, although many of these concerns and suggestions apply to a range of other statistical analyses.

19.1.1 Linear models

Regression analyses
Analyses of linear regression models are a clear example of where most statistics packages generate extensive output, but much of the information can be omitted. In the case of a simple linear regression with a single predictor variable, you will get an output similar to the one in Table 19.1 from most statistics packages.

The regression model examines the relationship between the number of limpets in a quadrat

| Table 19.1 | Standard regression output from a major statistics package. The example is from SYSTAT version 6 |

```
Dep Var: LOGLIMP N: 40 Multiple R: 0.30.345 Squared multiple R: 0.119
Adjusted squared multiple R: 0.096
Standard error of estimate: 0.373


Effect    Coeff    SE      StdC   Tol   t        P
CONSTANT   1.072   0.083    0.0   .      12.994  0.000
ALGAE     -0.006   0.003   -0.3   1.0   -2.265   0.029


                         Analysis of Variance
Source         SS     DF   MS      F      P
Regression   0.713    1    0.713   5.129  0.029
Residual     5.282   38    0.139
```

(log-transformed, LOGLIMP) and the cover of algae (ALGAE), and the output gives us the estimated regression line, some measures of how precisely the parameters of the line – slope and intercept – have been estimated, and tests of hypotheses about the slope and intercept (by default, that each equals zero). Some or all of this material could be added into a table, but we can present most of the information in the text in standardized form.

First, in a simple regression, there is considerable redundancy. Most statistics packages are written to deal with complex regression models, and a simple regression is treated as just a special case of the general linear model. The bottom half of the output is an ANOVA table, testing whether the regression model (i.e. the set of predictor variables) explains significant amounts of the variation in the dependent variable. The top section of the table also shows tests of hypotheses – t tests for the slope and intercept. With only one predictor variable, the ANOVA F test and the t test for the effect of algae are identical, and you can see on the output that the F-ratio of 5.129 is the square of t (= 2.265), and the two P-values are identical (Chapter 5). There is, in this case, no point in reporting both values. Other parts of this output only become relevant when we have more predictor variables, e.g. tolerance, adjusted multiple r^2 (see Chapter 6). In most cases, we are interested

only in whether the regression is significant, the estimates of the model parameters (which gives an idea whether the relationship is likely to be important), and some measure of how well the model fits the data. The t or F tests for the effects of the predictor variable provide the first information. The intercept and slope are listed under "Coeff" in the output table above ("CONSTANT" is often used to indicate the intercept of the regression model), and the simplest measure of the scatter of points around the line is the r^2, provided at the top of the output. We could therefore reduce that table of output to a single sentence in the text, using just the information highlighted on the output table:

The number of limpets fell as algal cover increased, although algal cover only explained 12% of the variation in limpet abundance (equation: log(limpets) = 1.076 − 0.006 × algal cover, $F_{1,38} = 5.129$, $P = 0.029$, $r^2 = 0.119$).

This format is a standard one; and you could expect a reader to be familiar with the estimates of the parameters of the regression model, etc. – assuming that you've mentioned somewhere that it's a linear regression! If not, that information could be added inside the parentheses. Again, if we wished to be true minimalists or maximize the data density, we could omit the r^2 or even the F-ratio. As we discuss below if you know the df and

P, you can back-calculate the F-ratio, so the P and F are technically redundant. In the same fashion, for a simple regression, the r^2 can also be calculated from the ANOVA table – it's the $SS_{Regression}/(SS_{Regression} + SS_{Residual})$, so the P-value is enough for a desperate reader to calculate the r^2. We recommend this as overkill – most readers are comfortable with the information given in the previous paragraph. The only additional information might be interval estimates for the model parameters, such as confidence intervals.

The information from more complex regressions can also generally be compressed, although not to the same degree, and most complex regressions are presented in tables.

ANOVA

The simplest way of presenting the results of a linear model with categorical predictor variables (i.e. a classical ANOVA model) is to display the complete ANOVA table. However, in many publication outlets, space is at a premium and there is usually pressure on authors of scientific papers in biology to reduce the amount of journal space devoted to results of statistical analyses. With this in mind, we should consider ways of presenting ANOVA results more efficiently without sacrificing information. We suggest the following.

- The degrees of freedom should always be presented, as they indicate the sample size. Therefore, we do not need both SS and MS, as one can be calculated from the other using the df.
- As long as the $MS_{Residual}$ and F-ratios are provided, we don't need the MS for groups or specific contrasts as these can be calculated from the F-ratio, the degrees of freedom, and the $MS_{Residual}$. This step does require that you have described the statistical model adequately in the Methods section.
- As discussed in Chapter 3, we prefer P-values to be presented (at least for $P \geq 0.001$), as they allow readers to use their own significance level for testing H_0.

Single factor models

For a single factor ANOVA model, there is generally no need to report your findings in a table; there is only one way to calculate the F-ratio. You can report your analysis in the text of your results, giving results in a standardized form:

"Attending a stats course by the authors of this book did not markedly improve the quality of students' analyses ($F_{1,4} = 1.23$, $P = 0.546$)"

The information in parentheses tells a reader that the conclusion is based on an F test with numerator $df = 1$, denominator with $df = 4$, that the F-ratio is 1.23 (and hence the ratio of MS_{Groups} to $MS_{Residual}$ is 1.23), and gives the probability of this value of F, or one larger, under the null hypothesis. There is no need for further information (except, perhaps, why this particular null hypothesis is retained). Of course, a real minimalist might argue that the value of the F-ratio is unnecessary; it follows automatically from the P-value and the two degrees of freedom.

If your analysis includes planned comparisons within an overall analysis, you can specify them in the same way, or you could include the analyses in a table. If you have listed the $df_{Residual}$ and $MS_{Residual}$ in the table, all you need to describe for most planned comparisons is the P-value. The vast majority of planned comparisons have numerator $df = 1$, and you have provided the other information (df, MS). In most cases, planned contrasts and trend analyses are best incorporated into the body of the ANOVA tables since they represent partitioning of the SS (see Chapter 8).

Multiple comparison results are commonly presented in two ways (i) labeling means in graphs and tables with the same letter or symbol if they are not significantly different, and (ii) listing the means (or group labels) in order and joining those not significantly different with an underline (see Chapter 8). The results can also be presented in the text, e.g. "a Tukey's test (with $\alpha = 0.05$) showed that the two highest densities had slower growth rates than the two lowest densities".

Complex ANOVA models

Two other issues are relevant for multifactor ANOVAs.

- When random factors are included, it is often useful to indicate the different error terms used in the ANOVA table unless it is a standard design. When the number of factors gets very large, there can be many possible (and actual) denominators, and a reader may not wish to derive the expected mean squares (e.g. Keough & Quinn 1998, for a very complex example).

- Measures of explained variance (e.g. variance components) are often incorporated into ANOVA tables when random factors are included.

19.1.2 Other analyses

Many other statistical methods also produce voluminous output with lots of redundancy, and you can generally reduce the volume of analytical results, without sacrificing information. There are also often conventions of how to report particular analyses – which pieces of information are critical to assure a reader that you know what you're talking about, and that you have results that he or she should believe. We will not go into details on these other analyses here, but, in the earlier chapters, you will find that the examples we cite can also be used as guides for how to report those kinds of analyses. Unfortunately, in some of the analyses that are only now making their way into the biological literature, such as randomization tests, including bootstraps and jackknifes, logistic regression, etc., there are no conventions for presenting analyses, and inspection of the literature shows great variation in how results are reported.

19.2 | Layout of tables

Once you have decided which information to incorporate into a table, there is the matter of how the table can be laid out. Many current software packages allow you a wide range of formatting options, and, just like the discussion on graphic design in Section 19.3, some of those options improve the appearance of your text, while others produce hideous results. The table should be laid out to make the reader's job as easy as possible. Look at the examples in Box 19.1, and see which table provides the clearest layout of simple information. The tables present the results of testing for the effects of existing ascidians on settlement of marine invertebrates larvae. The analyses are single factor ANOVAs, and the table shows the P value from each analysis, together with an estimate of the residual variance and power values (to detect a 50% change in settle-

ment rate). We had already decided to omit SS, MS, and F-ratios. The table is laid out simply, with no unusual formatting. The degrees of freedom were constant across species, and were detailed in the legend of the table.

We could improve the readability of the table by a few changes – there are three statistically significant results, and they can be highlighted by a bold typeface. The table shows results from two polychaetes, a species of barnacle, and a few bryozoans. If we want a reader to see them in their natural groups, and, perhaps, to contrast the results for different groups, we could either put faint lines between the groups or put some space between some of the lines. A reader then sees that all of the significant results fall in the same taxonomic group. In contrast, the lower panel shows one of the worst formatting styles, and we have buried the important information behind a large number of completely unnecessary grid lines. There is nothing to draw a reader's attention to the most important bits of information, in this case the tests of hypotheses, although we could equally have decided to highlight the power values.

In some cases, complex sets of results can best be displayed using non-standard table designs. For example, if there are many analyses of the same kind, such as analyses on a large number of species, the point of interest may be the patterns of significance, power, etc. For example, Table 19.2 shows an even simpler table, taken from Keough & Raimondi (1996), summarizing results from a whole suite of experiments. The experiments cover the effects of microbial films, and at issue is whether particular films stimulate, inhibit, or have no effect on settlement of larvae. In this table, the authors chose to use ticks and crosses to indicate positive and negative results and circles to indicate cases of no effect. A few weak or equivocal results are indicated by the "~". Blanks indicate that the species in question didn't settle during the particular experiment. Dotted lines separate groups belonging to different phyla. The table summarizes a large number of analyses from three papers.

These examples aren't an exhaustive list, nor are they necessarily the best ways to present information, but they do emphasize that there are alternatives to tedious standard ANOVA tables from complex models!

Box 19.1 | Different arrangements of a table

Taxon	P	$\sqrt{MS}_{Residual}$	Power (ES = 50%)
Serpulids	0.348	20.32	100
Spirorbids	0.455	2.60	47
Elminius	0.531	24.89	71
Cryptosula	0.025	1.90	48
Scruparia	0.789	0.62	61
Tricellaria	0.017	4.72	98
Watersipora	0.525	3.45	94
Bugula neritina	0.118	10.36	69
Bugula stolonifera	0.042	18.60	100

Taxon	P	$\sqrt{MS}_{Residual}$	Power (ES = 50%)
Serpulids	0.348	20.32	100
Spirorbids	0.455	2.60	47
Elminius	0.531	24.89	71
Cryptosula	**0.025**	1.90	48
Scruparia	0.789	0.62	61
Tricellaria	**0.017**	4.72	98
Watersipora	0.525	3.45	94
Bugula neritina	0.118	10.36	69
Bugula stolonifera	**0.042**	18.60	100

Taxon	P	$\sqrt{MS}_{Residual}$	Power (ES = 50%)
Serpulids	0.348	20.32	100
Spirorbids	0.455	2.60	47
Elminius	0.531	24.89	71
Cryptosula	0.025	1.90	48
Scruparia	0.789	0.62	61
Tricellaria	0.017	4.72	98
Watersipora	0.525	3.45	94
Bugula neritina	0.118	10.36	69
Bugula stolonifera	0.042	18.60	100

19.3 | Displaying summaries of the data[1]

We will describe a number of different types of graphical display that biologists commonly use for summarizing numerical information and presenting results. In general, too little information is paid to the layout of these graphs, despite their being the sections of the paper that readers' attention is often drawn to first. There is a substantial literature on production of graphical display of information, including the excellent books by Tufte (1983, 1990), especially his wonderful 1983 book, and Cleveland (1994). The manual for the graphics component of the statistics package SYSTAT (SPSS 1999) includes an introductory chapter by Leland Wilkinson that is a clear discussion of graphic design.

---

1 In presenting the following, often hideous, graphs, you should be aware that we generally used the default settings of one or more common graphics packages, rather than trying hard to create awful graphs!

Table 19.2 | Layout of summary table highlighting results from several experiments

SETTLERS	Variation in microbial cues			
	presence absence	Short time (0–6 d)	Long time (0–4 wk)	Large spatial (10s of km)
Serpulid polych.	✓	✓	✓	✓
Spirorbid polych.	✓	✓	○	~
Elminius modestus	✗	✗	○	○
Balanus variegatus	~	✗	✓	○
Bugula neritina	~	~	✓	✓
Bugula dentata	✓	✓	✓	○
Bugula stolonifera	~	✓	✓	○
Tricellaria	~		✓	✓
Encrusting bryozoans	✓	✓	✓	✓
Trididemnum	○			○
Botryllus schlosseri	~	○		○
Didemnum	○	○	○	○
Diplosoma	○	○	○	○
Pyura stolonifera	○	○		
Ascidia	○			○
Ciona intestinalis	○	○		~
Sponges	✓	✓		○
Electroma	○	○		
Total recruitment	✓	✓	✓	✓

Note:
Ticks and crosses indicate positive and negative effects, circles for no effect and tildes for weak or equivocal results.

The guiding principle in constructing graphs is to produce clear, unambiguous, representations of your results. These representations should draw a reader's attention to what you consider the most important aspects of your results, and should be free of distracting elements. In most cases, this will mean simple, clean graphics, rather than the wonderfully ornate productions possible in many graphics packages. For complex experiments or sampling programs, this will entail decisions about which factors to include, which to highlight, etc.

Tufte coined phrases for some of what he saw as important problems.

• Data:ink ratios reflect the amount of ink need to present a given amount of data – high values are desirable.

• Data density is similar to the data:ink ratio, but reflects the space taken, rather than the ink used.

• Chartjunk is extraneous ornamentation that puts fancy things all around, but doesn't help explain your results. This a particular problem in many graphics packages used to prepare talks.

The way in which the information is presented will also vary with your target audience – a figure in a paper can be more complex than one that you might show at a conference, because the reader can sit and digest the information. Similarly, careful or thoughtful use of color can help an oral presentation, but most journals either don't permit colored graphs or impose an extra charge for colored figures. Newer electronic journals or

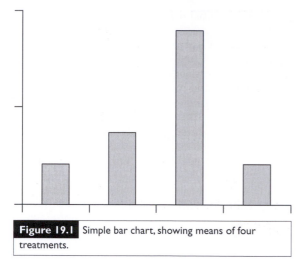

Figure 19.1 Simple bar chart, showing means of four treatments.

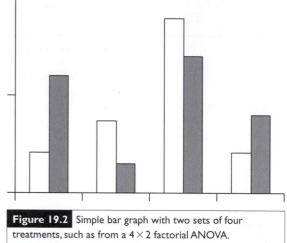

Figure 19.2 Simple bar graph with two sets of four treatments, such as from a 4 × 2 factorial ANOVA.

similar outlets may permit color and reports, such as those from consultancies that involve a smaller number of copies, can use color to great advantage.

The technical limitations of the medium will also influence how you construct graphs. For example, in presenting a computer-based talk, you need to bear in mind that most computer projection facilities are still relatively low resolution (typically 640 × 480 or 800 × 600 pixels), and you can put less detail than on a high-resolution 35 mm slide. Similarly, many laser printers don't reproduce solid colors very well, and rather than solid black as a filling pattern, you may be better using hatched or stippled fill patterns. The same cross-hatched patterns may look awful as part of a computer presentation, when solid colors work much better. Tufte refers to some of the unfortunate choices of fill patterns as "unintentional optical art"!

In talking about graphics, we focus on the most common ways of displaying information.

19.3.1 Bar graph

A bar graph is used to plot some quantitative variable on the *Y*-axis against a grouping (categorical) variable on the *X*-axis, where the value of the variable for each category is represented by the height of a rectangular bar (Figure 19.1). The width of the bars can be altered to improve aesthetic appearance. The top of the bar may represent a single value or it may represent a summary

statistic, such as a mean. In the latter case, some measure of variation or precision should be provided using error bars (Figure 19.14; also see discussion on error bars below).

If there is a second grouping variable, then it can be represented by adjacent bars, with different fill patterns or colors, at each level of the first grouping variable (Figure 19.2). A variation on bar graphs sometimes used in business presentations is called a pictogram (Snee & Pfeifer 1983), where the bar is replaced by objects which illustrate the variable being plotted, e.g. some product. We eschew pictograms because the actual value represented by the object is sometimes difficult to determine (see, for example, Chapter 2 of Tufte 1983), and there is no sensible way to include error bars.

Some attention should be paid to the fill patterns, too – as lamented by Tufte, most modern software packages give you access to a wide range of fill patterns, many of them appearing to have been designed while blindfolded. Fill patterns should not distract the reader – remember that particular kinds of hatching can cause adjacent bars to blur, or make it difficult to see where objects really end. For example, Figure 19.3 shows some samples of awful fill patterns or a poor choice of fill patterns to be alongside each other. Again, we've done nothing special here – these patterns are standard options of a common software package. On the left-hand panel, adjacent bars with poor cross-hatching make the information

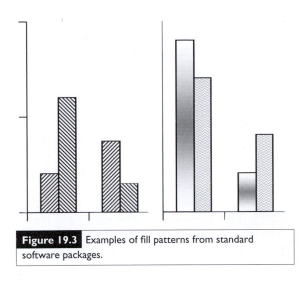

Figure 19.3 Examples of fill patterns from standard software packages.

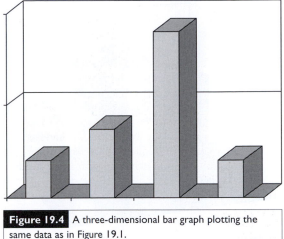

Figure 19.4 A three-dimensional bar graph plotting the same data as in Figure 19.1.

hard to read, while on the right-hand panel, some poorly chosen gradient fills make the tops of the bars hard to identify. In the first case, different fill patterns would make the comparison of bars clearer, whereas the gradient fills could be fixed by removing them completely, leaving the bars empty.

The choice of fill patterns, etc., will also be influenced by the printers available – be aware that many laser printers don't do a particularly good job of printing solid black, especially if the toner is running low, or if there is wear on some of the internal parts. The same is true of photocopiers, which use the same technology. Unless you are confident that you'll get uniform colours, try using a densely stippled pattern or densely packed cross-hatching. These patterns will print out evenly, even on worn printers. This advice doesn't apply to computer presentations for talks, when solid fills appear much clearer than cross-hatching, etc.

A fault that has been made more common by the availability of graphics software designed for business presentations is the three-dimensional representation of two-dimensional data. This is particularly noticeable for bar graphs and pie charts, although we will emphasize bar graphs here because even two-dimensional pie charts are not much use. A "three-dimensional bar" graph is shown in Figure 19.4. There are many problems with this graph, the most serious being that it is very difficult to tell what value along the Y-axis is displayed by the top of the bars.

Note that this is not a three-dimensional graph – only the bars are three-dimensional. The graph in Figure 19.4 shows only two variables, and just adds a third dimension to the graph, without adding any new information. Note also that we haven't even tried to include error bars on this type of graph – the error bars would start somewhere on the tops of each of the bars below, and it would be very hard to see exactly how much overlap there is between means and errors of our groups. As a rule of thumb, or, more usefully, an absolute rule(!):

do **NOT** use three-dimensional graphs for two-dimensional data!!!

There may, however, be occasions when we want to display data with three variables, and may need three axes. Even then, though, it may still be just as good to plot that information in two dimensions. Consider the example on Figure 19.2; it shows the results of measurements on two different factors, but the results can be displayed as a three-dimensional bar graph (Figure 19.5). There is little doubt that the pattern has become less clear. We've now reached almost the peak of obscuring our information, although there is worse to come, and we should also bear in mind Tufte's nomination for the worst graph ever published (Tufte 1983, p. 118).

If we were concerned about the waste of space or ink, we could reduce the simple bar graph even further – a minimalist might argue that we could

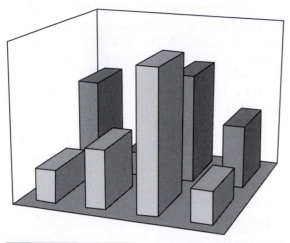

Figure 19.5 Three-dimensional plot of same data as in Figure 19.2. See how one of the groups is almost completely obscured.

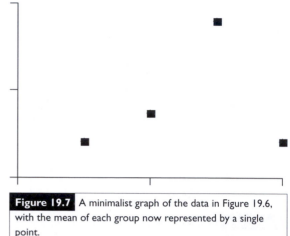

Figure 19.7 A minimalist graph of the data in Figure 19.6, with the mean of each group now represented by a single point.

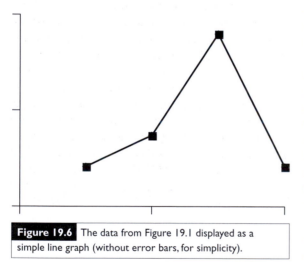

Figure 19.6 The data from Figure 19.1 displayed as a simple line graph (without error bars, for simplicity).

replace the bar by a single point, without losing any information). In Tufte's terminology, we'd be improving the data:ink ratio – the amount of information conveyed, relative to the amount of ink needed to print it.

19.3.2 Line graph (category plot)
Line graphs are like bar graphs except the top of the bar is replaced by a symbol and the adjacent symbols are joined by straight lines (Figure 19.6). They are used when the categorical variable on the X-axis can be ordered, or is quantitative, particularly to plot time series. The symbol can represent a single value or the sample mean (or

median, etc.) – the comments in Section 19.4 about error bars also apply here. These plots are most often used for interaction plots (Chapter 9), and they work very well for this purpose.

It is very important to appreciate that the lines in this case may simply indicate a trend in the (mean) values, without any interpolation. This is particularly the case for interaction plots for fixed effects in analyses of variance – there are by definition no other categories other than those used in the analysis. The line connecting the symbols does not represent any sort of formal relationship between Y and X, and could be omitted (Figure 19.7).

If we wish to include a second grouping variable, then it can be represented by an additional series of points, with different symbols (or different colors – see Fig. 1 in Cleveland 1994) and/or line styles (Figure 19.8).

19.3.3 Scatterplots
We have already discussed scatterplots as an exploratory tool in Chapters 4 and 5. They can also be very effective ways of presenting a bivariate relationship. For example, the scatterplot can include a line that represents a regression or smoothing function fitted to the observations (Figure 19.9). Note that the line in Figure 19.9 extends only to the edge of the range of X-values. Many computer graphics packages default to drawing the fitted curve across the entire X-axis (see Figure 19.10). This is inappropriate, as we have

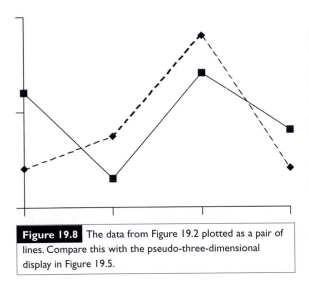

Figure 19.8 The data from Figure 19.2 plotted as a pair of lines. Compare this with the pseudo-three-dimensional display in Figure 19.5.

We could also plot confidence intervals about the regression lines or confidence ellipses (Figure 19.11; Sokal & Rohlf 1995) and non-parametric confidence kernels (Silverman 1986) can be included to indicate our level of confidence in the centroid (the mean of the two variables in multi-dimensional space). Details on these methods were provided in Chapter 5.

Multiple groups can be indicated on the scatterplot by simply using different symbols (or fill patterns or colors) for each group.

19.3.4 Pie charts

A pie chart is a circle (or a "pie") where each category's value is represented by a size of its section or slice of the circle (Figure 19.12). The different sections can be further emphasized by different fill patterns or colors.

Pie charts are very commonly used in business graphics (hence their presence in most presentation graphics software) but have a much reduced role in scientific graphics and none in statistical graphics. Tufte (1983) argued that they should never be used because their "data-density" is low and they fail to order numbers along a visual dimension. A reader can't be sure whether to look at the angle or the area to get an idea of how big each group is. Contrast that with a bar or line chart, where there is only one interpretation of the height of the bar or point. It becomes even worse if you allow the software to produce a

no information about the relationship beyond the largest and smallest X-values in our sample – even a simple linear relationship might change shape outside our range. A good example of that phenomenon is when we estimate regresssion models for relationships that logically must pass through the origin (e.g. amount of food vs number of limpets m^{-2}, mass vs length, etc.), but where the estimated line has a non-zero intercept. The model may be estimated reliably for the range of our data, and because we know that the curve passes through the origin, we therefore know that the line must change slope or shape outside that data range (Figure 19.10; see also Chapter 5).

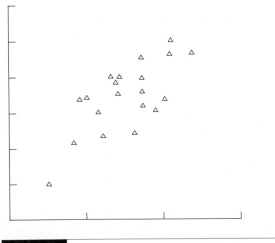

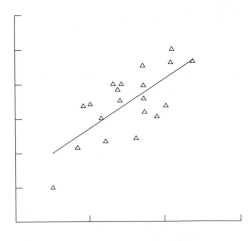

Figure 19.9 A basic scatterplot, with a least-squares straight line fitted through the observations.

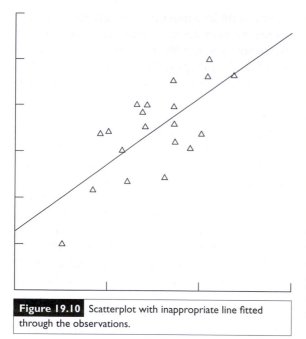

Figure 19.10 Scatterplot with inappropriate line fitted through the observations.

three-dimensional aspect to this information (Figure 19.13)

19.4 | Error bars

Any graphical or tabular representation of means should include some measure of the error associated with the estimate of the mean. Common measures of error include the standard deviation (a measure of variability between observations in the sample), the standard error (a measure of precision for the sample mean) and 95% or 99% confidence intervals (Chapter 2). Error bars on graphs are usually represented by a straight line that is symmetrical on either side of the mean. If we are using a bar graph with filled bars, one-sided error bars can be used. The length of the line in each direction indicates one standard deviation or one standard error so the total error bar is two standard errors or, alternatively, the 95% confidence interval.

One problem with error bars on complex graphs with many plotting symbols is that the error bars overlap with each other and other plotting symbols, making the graph messy and difficult to read. In such cases, one alternative is to present the largest and smallest error bars only in one section of the plot to indicate the range of variability or precision in the data.

Where a plot of means relates to a specific analysis, such as a simple ANOVA model, illustrating individual standard deviations or standard errors may not be crucial. In doing the ANOVA, you have assumed that the variances of the different groups are similar and have compared the groups using a pooled estimate of the variation within groups (i.e. the $MS_{Residual}$ term). In showing a single error bar, you may be representing more accurately the variation used in the analysis, whereas the individual errors for the particular treatments may differ from this pooled value, and give the

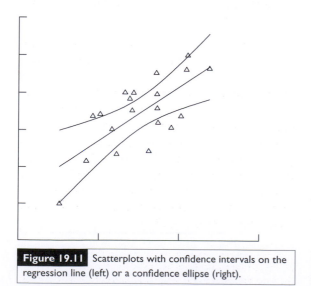
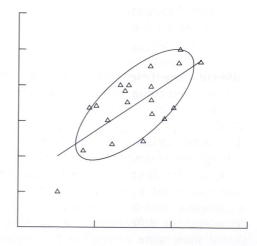

Figure 19.11 Scatterplots with confidence intervals on the regression line (left) or a confidence ellipse (right).

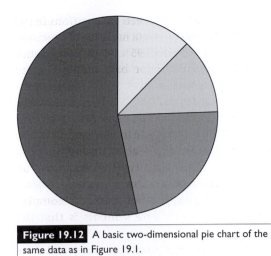

Figure 19.12 A basic two-dimensional pie chart of the same data as in Figure 19.1.

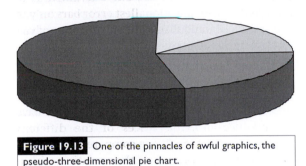

Figure 19.13 One of the pinnacles of awful graphics, the pseudo-three-dimensional pie chart.

reader an indication of whether the assumption of homogeneous variance is appropriate.

In some more complex linear models, particularly for designs involving nested factors (including repeated measures designs) or combinations of fixed and random factors, a simple standard error or the $MS_{Residual}$ may provide misleading information. As discussed in Chapters 9–12, many different hypotheses are tested in complex models, often using different error terms. As a simple example, consider a two-level nested ANOVA design, with groups as the main factor, plots nested within groups as the nested factor, and replicate observations within plots (Chapter 9). We test the effects of groups against variation among plots within groups, rather than using the within-plots variation. Therefore, if we are describing the differences between groups, we should show some measure of the appropriate variation within groups.

If we use the raw data file (or even the $MS_{Residual}$

from the ANOVA), and plot means and standard errors using common statistical packages, the means may be reliable, but the error bars that are produced by this procedure may bear little relation to the variances used to test particular hypotheses.

The problem is best illustrated with an example. Figure 19.14 shows the graphical summary from three simulated data sets for a nested ANOVA design. All three data sets have four groups, four subgroups within each group, and four replicates per subgroup. The group means were the same across the data sets, as was the variation within subgroups (i.e., the $MS_{Residual}$ was constant). The level of variation between subgroups varied between the data sets, and the graphs show two measures of error.

- The left hand error bar represents the output from a standard statistics package (SYSTAT)[2], from the raw data file. In this figure, the standard error is calculated from all observations within each main group, regardless of the subgroups, i.e., it pools replicate and subgroup variances, and uses the total number of observations in each group as the sample size.
- The right-hand error bar of each pair is based on the variation among subgroups, and was obtained by taking the means for each subgroup, providing a single value for each subgroup, and then plotting means and errors from those data.

The most important thing to note is that the two error bars are similar in some cases, but very different in others, depending on the patterns of variance in a particular data set. When the variation among plots is highest, the "standard" error bars are completely misleading. In the three data sets, the means based on pooling across subgroups will be the same as those calculated from the subgroup means, as long as the number of replicates per subgroup is constant. If the design is unbalanced, the means obtained by the two methods will also be different.

2 The error bars calculated by SYSTAT ignore the structure of the data, and pool all the subgroups into one set of replicates.

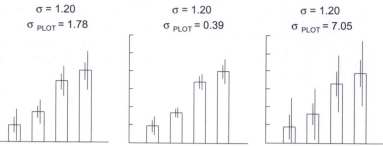

Figure 19.14 Depiction of error bars for three simulated data sets, from a nested ANOVA design.

This situation becomes more complex if we consider, for example, groups by trials or repeated measures designs (Chapter 11). The test of the an interaction involving the between-subjects and within-subjects factors is made using the variation among subjects across the repeated factor. For example, if the repeated factor is time, the groups by time effect, i.e. the variation in temporal profiles between groups, is tested using the variation through time of the subjects within groups. An overall residual error term will be worthless in this case, and the default output from most software packages would be for error bars to depict the variation among subjects at each level of the within-subjects factor. These error bars might be appropriate for a completely randomized design, but will not have any clear relationship to the denominators used to test the terms of most interest.

19.4.1 Alternative approaches

Our strongest recommendation is that you think about the message you want the reader to get, and then think about the measure of variance that is appropriate for this message. The best indication comes from the error term used to test the hypothesis in question, in the case of ANOVA models.

The correct alternative will not always be obvious. To return to the example of the nested ANOVA design, we can identify at least five different error terms that we could calculate.

1. The $\sqrt{MS_{Residual}}$ from the ANOVA.
2. Standard deviations from individual groups, from the raw data file.
3. Standard deviations from a file of means for each subgroup or plot.
4. The $\sqrt{MS_{Subgroup}}$ term from the ANOVA, which averages the variation among subgroups across the groups.

5. The square root of the variance component associated with groups, extracted from the $MS_{Subgroups}$.[3]

As argued earlier, option 1 is incorrect, as is option 2, since they use error terms unrelated to the hypothesis in question. Option 3 provides one correct answer, and results in different error bars for each group. Option 4 is a reasonable approximation, but it leads to an error term that, like option 2, includes two kinds of variation (see Footnote 3). Depending on the relative sizes of the two variances involved, this option may or may not produce an error close to the correct one. Option 5, like option 3, generates an appropriate error, and will produce similar results – given equal sample sizes, it is a pooled estimate of the variation among subgroups, and will be close to the average of the set of subgroup variances.

To see how these options produce different answers, we have used the artificial data sets seen already on Figure 19.14 to produce the data in Table 19.3. You should note that in going from standard deviations to standard errors, options 1 and 2 use the total sample size, i.e. number of subgroups $\times$ number of replicates per subgroup. In the above example, with four and four, respectively, the standard errors become quite different. If we take options 3 and 5 as being appropriate, you can see that the other options provide erratic, and misleading error calculations.

Given that most readers tend to look at graphs, and interpret your results for themselves, based on the differences among groups and the error

---

3 Recall that the Expected Mean Squares for subgroups in a nested ANOVA model is given by $\sigma_\varepsilon^2 + n\sigma^2_{subgroups}$, and then $\sigma^2_{subgroups}$ can be calculated by $(MS_{Subgroup} - MS_{Residual})/n$.

Table 19.3 | Error bars produced by five different methods, for a two factor nested design, with three different data sets

Option	Data set 1	Data set 2	Data set 3
1	1.10	1.10	1.10
2	1.60	1.22	2.60
3	1.42	0.79	2.70
4	2.88	1.66	5.42
5	1.33	0.63	1.33

Note:
The numbers are standard deviations.

bars, you risk distracting the readers, or having a reader sceptical of your results, just because you provided other than the most relevant data.

19.5 | Oral presentations

Although publishing our work in peer-reviewed outlets such as scientific journals is the primary way of making contributions to the field (and of assessing our productivity), talking about our work is a crucial part of publicizing that work, telling colleagues about work in progress, and "advertising" yourself when in the market for scientific jobs. Presenting information clearly and without distractions is just as important for oral papers, with a few additional considerations. There is a range of books and papers offering thoughts on how to construct an effective talk, and, here, we focus on how you display your data and analyses.

Most scientists now prepare talks using a range of graphics packages, most of us lack any training in graphical design, and a substantial number of us have poor taste. These three factors can combine to produce a wide range of distracting graphical displays. While we don't pretend to be style gurus (or may pretend, but unconvincingly!), we can offer some thoughts about preparing audiovisual aids.

19.5.1 Slides, computers, or overheads?

One of the first decisions to make is the kinds of tools you'll use to display the information. You will have three main options, assuming that most of us won't use the blackboard for a conference talk or seminar. Computer-based presentations are becoming easier, as more and more venues offer computer projections. Slides remain a very reliable, compact way of presenting information, and offer very high resolution, while overhead projection sheets are completely reliable, and also high resolution.

When deciding which of these you should use, you should consider the following.

- The venue.
  * How big is the room? Many overhead projectors don't produce large images, because they can't be moved far enough from the stage, so you might want to avoid them in big venues.
  * Is the room likely to have good lighting controls? If it can't be darkened, as can be the case at some convention facilities, you may find that your slides can't be seen, and that overheads are much brighter.
  * What is your target audience familiar with? In the past, most people giving talks at scientific conferences used slides. Meetings involving government or industry people, and less formal academic meetings, typically involved overhead projections, with slides being rare. This difference would not affect your preparation of the talk, it was a guide to the kinds of facilities you could expect when you arrived to speak. Now, it is very common to have computer projection facilities available, regardless of the venue.
  * Do you have confidence in the computer facilities? When you turn up for your talk, you may find a beautifully equipped room, with a computer with the latest version of your graphics package, and you'll just need to insert your disk (or even drag your presentation over the internet). Alternatively, you may find that
    - "computer projection facilities" means a plug in the wall, and you are expected to bring a computer with you, or
    - there's an antique Macintosh, when you prepared your talk using the newest

version of a Windows graphics package,or

- you love an obscure graphics package, used it to prepare your talk, but the computers in the venue lack that program, or
- you scanned some beautiful images into your presentation, then needed a special high-capacity disk to store your talk. The computer in the room won't read those disks, or
- . . . you can add a range of other, real-world disasters to this list.

• What kind of talk is it? Will you give it once, or is it to be a travelling show that you expect to give a few times, such as a talk about your PhD research? You are likely to give a PhD talk for at least a year or two, and it's probably worth making slides, but, later in your career, you may be asked to give more general or synthetic talks, on a range of topics, and you might write a new talk each time, with little intention of repeating it. One advantage of computer-based presentations is that they can be changed at no cost, while changing a slide costs money and time. It may also be that working in this way encourages you to create a fresh talk, rather than planning your talk based on the slides that you happen to have available.

• How organized are you? If you do everything at the last moment, computer-based presentations offer the most flexibility. It's even possible to change your overheads in response to some profound (or inflammatory) thought offered by the speaker preceding you in the program. You can also fix the spelling error you discovered when running through your talk.

• Where are you going to speak? Slides are the most secure option – they are compact, can be carried with you on planes, aren't affected by magnetic fields, etc. Computer disks are the least stable option, but you can improve things by making sure that you can get another copy of your presentation over the internet if the worst happens, and you can take multiple copies, spread through your baggage, in the heel of your shoe, etc.

19.5.2 Graphics packages

Whatever medium you choose, you will almost certainly use one of the common graphics packages to construct your audiovisuals. These packages are written for business users, and the software developers apparently think that business users love to use extraneous, garishly colored graphics as backgrounds. These packages also often lack many of the things we need for scientific purposes – for example, most lack the capacity to plot error bars easily.

We offer a few pieces of opinion (based on extensive, highly selective sampling of our colleagues' biases) about ways to put together a presentation.

• Keep the backgrounds simple. Use a uniform or lightly graded background. Complex, multicolored backgrounds will obscure parts of the text.
• Keep the number of fonts to a minimum.
• Strange transitions between slides – blinds, curtains to the left, checkerboards – and text flying in from all directions can be done easily from most software packages. It tends to polarize your audience. Mixing different transitions and patterns of appearance of objects should be avoided. Doing this demonstrates to the audience that you know how to use the bells and whistles of the software, but it also tells the audience something else about you . . . almost certainly an impression you'd like to avoid.

19.5.3 Working with color

As a general rule, graphics packages offer sets of colors that are recommended for producing a particular overall look for your presentation.

• We suggest that you choose a particular set, and use exactly those colors, rather than designing your own combination. The color combinations that you select are, with all due respect, likely to be awful, and consist of colors that shouldn't be combined, no matter what your drunken friends think. In addition, many packages offer an option to switch from a color scheme for 35 mm slides or computer graphics (often a dark background and light text), to one designed for overhead projection (a light background, dark text). This switch can be made with a single mouse click, but if you have redefined the color palette, you may lose this ability.

- There is a substantial literature on color perception, and a good understanding of working color combinations. You may want to read some of that literature, and, again, consult Tufte (1983) as an entry point.
- Remember color blindness and its incidence among the general population. There are some color combinations that are offered by many of the graphics packages, particularly red and green, which will be indistinguishable to as many of 20% of your audience (especially if you are in a particularly male-dominated forum).
- As a general rule, use solid fill patterns, and distinguish groups by different colors for audiovisuals (cf. contrasting fill patterns for printed material).

19.5.4 Scanned images

To avoid switching between slides and computer, you may decide to scan some images into your presentation. Scanned images are very large, especially if they are stored with fine color detail (e.g. 16.7 million colors on the palette). Individual images can be quite a few megabytes, but you may not need high resolution everywhere.

- If you are converting your presentation into slides, you should scan any images at the highest resolution possible, because 35 mm film is capable of fine details.
- If you are preparing overheads, the resolution will depend on the capabilities of your printer. Use high resolution.
- If you are using computer projection, most systems operate at only 800×600 pixel resolution. Therefore, if your scanned image exceeds this size, the finer details can't be displayed. You should reduce the resolution to something only slightly finer (i.e. slightly more pixels) than will be displayed. Most images are also scanned with many colors. Reducing the number of colors can dramatically decrease the file size; try reducing the number of colors, and see if the image is degraded. The net result will be a presentation file that is more compact, and fits onto fewer computer disks (at least using twentieth-century technology).

Finally, remember that graphics file types vary in whether they compress the information. Some store the raw graphics information, with no compression. Others compress the file size by searching the image for blocks of identical color, and replacing information about individual pixels with a description of the boundaries of the block and the color. Other file formats, such as JPEG, sacrifice some information for compaction.

19.5.5 Information content

Bear in mind that, in a printed paper, we can place large amounts of information on a figure, with the reader having time to digest that information. When presenting the material orally, there's usually less time for the audience to assimilate the information. More importantly, you are speaking more or less continuously, and if you produce an audiovisual with large amounts of information, you'll notice a large part of the audience immediately shift their focus away from you, to concentrate on reading. At that time, you've lost control of the audience, and they won't be listening to you. They may also not be getting the information that you want them to.

In general, you should remove all extraneous information from the figures. As part of your talk, you should guide the audience through the particular figure – show them the key patterns, explain what the different symbols represent, and so on. That way, you control the emphasis that is placed on the information, and the audience feels that they are getting a scientist's view of some information, rather than reading another paper.

You probably do not need to show results of statistical tests on the figure. For example, a regression equation, together with F-ratios and P-values, adds unneccesary clutter to a scatterplot, and there is often a collective groan in the audience when the next slide is an analysis of variance table. Our strong view is that, ethically, if you talk about a pattern in your data – a difference in groups, a correlation, etc. – you are describing the results of a significant analysis. The audience takes this on trust, and adding the analytical results to your figure or table doesn't help. During the talk, there is no chance to scrutinize your experimental design and analysis, to check that you did everything appropriately, so they must take the analysis on trust, anyway.

19.6   General issues and hints

- Presenting results clearly is a neglected part of publicizing scientific work.
- Most statistical packages produce considerable redundancy in their output, and omitting elements of redundancy produces cleaner, more concise, descriptions of results.
- Most graphics packages produce styles of graphs and allow choices of fill pattern and ornamentation that obscure, rather than clarify, results.
- Graphical illustration of results should be tailored to the audience, and optimal use of colors, fill patterns, and explanatory text will be very different for published scientific papers and oral presentations.
- In preparing illustrations, decide what pattern in the data you wish to illustrate, then identify the kind of variation that was the background against which the particular patterns were assessed. This variation is an appropriate candidate for error bars.

References

Abrahams, M.V. & Townsend, L.D. (1993) Bioluminescence in dinoflagellates: a test of the burglar alarm hypothesis. *Ecology* **74**: 258–260.

Abrams, M.D., Kubiske, M.E. & Mostoller, S.A. (1994) Relating wet and dry year ecophysiology to leaf structure in contrasting temperate tree species. *Ecology* **75**: 123–133.

Agresti, A. (1990) *Categorical Data Analysis*. Wiley, New York.

Agresti, A. (1996) *An Introduction to Categorical Data Analysis*. Wiley, New York.

Aguiar, M.R. & Sala, O.E. (1997) Seed distribution constrains the dynamics of the Patagonian steppe. *Ecology* **78**: 93–100.

Aiken, L.S. & West, S.G. (1991) *Multiple Regression: Testing and Interpreting Interactions*. Sage, Newbury Park.

Akaike, H. (1978) A Bayesian analysis of the minimum AIC procedure. *Annals of the Institute of Statistical Mathematics* **30**: 9–14.

Akritas, M.G. (1991) Limitations of the rank transform procedure: a study of repeated measures designs, part 1. *Journal of the American Statistical Association* **86**: 457–460.

Akritas, M.G., Ruscitti, T.F. & Patil, G.P. (1994) Statistical analysis of censored environmental data. In: *Handbook of Statistics Vol. 12 Environmental Statistics* (Patil, G.P. & Rao, C.R. eds.), pp. 221–242. North Holland, Amsterdam.

Allchin, D. (1999) Negative results as positive knowledge, and zeroing in on significant problems. *Marine Ecology Progress Series* **191**: 303–305.

Andersen, P.K. & Keiding, N. (1996) Survival analysis. In: *Advances in Biometry* (Armitage, P. & David, H.A. eds.), pp. 177–199. Wiley, New York.

Anderson, J.L. (1998) Embracing uncertainty: the interface of Bayesian statistics and cognitive psychology. *Conservation Ecology* **2**(2): http: //www.consecol.org/vol2/iss1/art2

Anderson, M.J. (2001) A new method for non-parametric multivariate analysis of variance. *Australian Ecology* **26**: 32–46.

Anderson-Sprecher, R. (1994) Model comparisons and R^2. *The American Statistician* **48**: 113–117.

Andrew, N.L. & Mapstone, B.D. (1987) Sampling and the description of spatial pattern in marine ecology. *Oceanography and Marine Biology Annual Review* **25**: 39–90.

Andrew, N.L. & Underwood, A.J. (1993) Density-dependent foraging in the sea urchin *Centrostephanus rodgersii* on shallow subtidal reefs in New South Wales, Australia. *Marine Ecology Progress Series* **99**: 89–98.

Anscombe, F.J. (1973) Graphs in statistical analysis. *The American Statistician* **27**: 17–21.

Antelman, G. (1997) *Elementary Bayesian Statistics* (Madansky, A. & McCulloch, R. eds.). Edward Elgar, Cheltenham, UK.

Ayres, M.P. & Scriber, J.M. (1994) Local adaptation to regional climates in *Papilo canadensis* (Lepidoptera: Papilionidae). *Ecological Monographs* **64**: 465–482.

Ayres, M.P. & Thomas, D.L. (1990) Alternative formulations of the mixed-model ANOVA applied to quantitative genetics. *Evolution* **44**: 221–226.

Barnett, V. (1999) *Comparative Statistical Inference*, 3rd edition. Wiley, New York.

Beck, M.W. (1995) Size-specific shelter limitation in stone crabs: a test of the demographic bottleneck hypothesis. *Ecology* **76**: 968–980.

Beck, M.W. (1997) Inference and generality in ecology: current problems and an experimental solution. *Oikos* **78**: 265–273.

Becker, B.J. (1994) Combining significance levels. In: *The Handbook of Research Synthesis* (Cooper, H. & Hedges, L.V. eds.), pp. 215–230. Russell Sage Foundation, New York.

Begon, M., Harper, J.L. & Townsend, C.R. (1996) *Ecology: Individuals, Populations and Communities*, 3rd edition. Blackwell Scientific Publications, London.

Belbin, L. & McDonald, C. (1993) Comparing three classification strategies for use in ecology. *Journal of Vegetation Science* **4**: 341–348.

Belbin, L., Faith, D.P. & Milligan, G.W. (1993) A comparison of two approaches to beta-flexible clustering. *Multivariate Behavioral Research* **27**: 417–433.

Bellgrove, A., Clayton, M.N. & Quinn, G.P. (1997) Effects of secondarily treated sewage effluent on intertidal macroalgal recruitment processes. *Marine and Freshwater Research* **48**: 137–146.

Belsley, D.A., Kuh, E. & Welsch, R.E. (1980) *Regression Diagnostics: Identifying Influential Data and Sources of Collinearity*. Wiley, New York.

Bence, J.R. (1995) Analysis of short time series: correcting for autocorrelation. *Ecology* **76**: 628–639.

Benjamini, Y. & Hochberg, Y. (1995) Controlling the false discovery rate: a practical and powerful approach to multiple testing. *Journal of the Royal Statistical Society* **B** **57**: 289–300.

Berger, J.O. & Berry, D.A. (1988) Statistical analysis and the illusion of objectivity. *American Scientist* **76**: 159–165.

Berger, J.O. & Sellke, T. (1987) Testing a point null hypothesis: the irreconcilability of P values and evidence. *Journal of the American Statistical Association* **82**: 112–122.

Bergerud, W.A. (1996) Displaying factor relationships in experiments. *The American Statistician* **50**: 228–233.

Bergmann, R., Ludbrook, J. & Spooren, W.P.J.M. (2000) Different outcomes of the Wilcoxon–Mann–Whitney test from different statistics packages. *The American Statistician* **54**: 72–77.

Berk, K. (1987) Computing for incomplete repeated measures. *Biometrics* **43**: 385–398.

Berk, R.A. (1990) A primer on robust regression. In: *Modern Methods of Data Analysis* (Fox, J. & Long, J.S. eds.), pp. 292–334. Sage, Newbury Park.

Berry, D.A. (1987) Logarithmic transformations in ANOVA. *Biometrics* **43**: 439–456.

Berry, D.A. (1996) *Statistics: A Bayesian Perspective.* Duxbury Press, Belmont.

Berry, D.A. & Stangl, D.K. (1996) Bayesian methods in health-related research. In: *Bayesian Biostatistics* (Berry, D.A. & Stangl, D.K. eds.), pp. 3–66. Marcel Dekker, New York.

Berteaux, D. & Boutin, S. (2000) Breeding dispersal in female North American red squirrels. *Ecology* **81**: 1311–1326.

Bijleveld, C.C.J.H. & van der Kamp, L.J.Th. (1998) *Longitudinal Data Analysis: Designs, Models and Methods.* Sage, London.

Birkes, D. & Dodge, Y. (1993) *Alternative Methods of Regression.* Wiley, New York.

Bjorndal, K.A., & Bolten, A.B. & Chaloupka, M.Y. (2000) Green turtle somatic growth model: evidence for density dependence. *Ecological Applications* **10**: 269–282.

Blackwell, T., Brown, C. & Mosteller, F. (1991) Which denominator? In: *Fundamentals of Exploratory Analysis of Variance* (Hoaglin, D.C., Mosteller, F. & Tukey, J.W. eds.), pp. 252–294. Wiley, New York.

Blake, J.G., Hanowski, J.M., Niemi, G.J. & Collins, P.T. (1994) Annual variation in bird populations of mixed conifer-northern hardwood forests. *The Condor* **96**: 381–399.

Blanche, K.R., Andersen, A.N. & Ludwig, J.A. (2001) Rainfall-contingent detection of fire impacts: responses of beetles to experimental fire regimes. *Ecological Applications* **11**: 86–96.

Boik, R.J. (1979) A priori tests in repeated measures designs: effects of nonsphericity. *Psychometrika* **46**: 241–255.

Boik, R.J. (1987) The Fisher–Pitman permutation test: a non-robust alternative to the normal theory *F* tests when variances are heterogeneous. *British Journal of Mathematical and Statistical Psychology* **40**: 26–42.

Bolger, D.T., Alberts, A.C., Sauvajot, R.M., Potenza, P., McCalvin, C., Tran, D., Mazzoni, S. & Soule, M. (1997) Response of rodents to habitat fragmentation on coastal southern California. *Ecological Applications* **7**: 552–563.

Bollen, K.A. & Jackman, R.W. (1990) Regression diagnostics: an expository treatment of outliers and influential cases. In: *Modern Methods of Data Analysis* (Fox, J. & Long, J.S. eds.), pp. 257–291. Sage, Newbury Park.

Borcard, D., Legendre, P. & Drapeau, P. (1992) Partialling out the spatial component of ecological variation. *Ecology* **73**: 1045–1055.

Bowerman, B.L. & O'Connell, R.T. (1990) *Linear Statistical Models: An Applied Approach.* Duxbury Press, California.

Box, G.E.P. (1954) Some theorems on quadratic forms applied in the study of analysis of variance problems, II. Effects of inequality of variance and correlation between errors in the two-way classification. *Annals of Mathematical Statistics* **25**: 484–498.

Box, G.E.P. & Tiao, G.C. (1973) *Bayesian Inference in Statistical Analysis.* Wiley, New York.

Box, G.E.P., Hunter, W.G. & Hunter, J.S. (1978) *Statistics for Experimenters. An Introduction to Design, Data Analysis, and Model Building.* Wiley, New York.

Brieman, L., Friedman, J.H., Olshen, R.A. & Stone, C.J. (1984) *Classification and Regression Trees.* Wadsworth, Belmont.

Bring, J. (1994) How to standardise regression coefficients. *The American Statistician* **48**: 209–213.

Brown, C. & Mosteller, F. (1991) Components of variance. In: *Fundamentals of Exploratory Analysis of Variance* (Hoaglin, D.C., Mosteller, F. & Tukey, J.W. eds.). Wiley, New York.

Brownie, C., Bowman, D.T. & Burton, J.W. (1993) Estimating spatial variation in analysis of data from yield trials: a comparison of methods. *Agronomy Journal* **85**: 1244–1253.

Brunet, J. (1996) Male reproductive success and variation in fruit and seed set in *Aquilegia caerula* (Rarunculaceae). *Ecology* **77**: 2458–2471.

Brunkow, P.E. & Collins, J.P. (1996) Effects of individual variation in size on growth and development of larval salamanders. *Ecology* **77**: 1483–1492.

Burdick, R.K. (1994) Using confidence intervals to test variance components. *Journal of Quality Technology* **26**: 30–38.

Burdick, R.K. & Graybill, F.A. (1992) *Confidence Intervals on Variance Components.* Marcel Dekker, New York.

Burton, P., Gurrin, L. & Sly, P. (1998) Extending the simple linear regression model to account for correlated responses: an introduction to generalized estimating equations and multi-level mixed modelling. *Statistics in Medicine* **17**: 1261–1291.

Cade, B.S & Terrell, J.W. (1997) Comment: cautions on forcing regression equations through the origin. *North American Journal of Fisheries Management* 17: 225–227.

Caley, M.J. & Schluter, D. (1997) The relationship between local and regional diversity. *Ecology* **78**: 70–80.

Cao, Y., Williams, D.D. & Williams, N.E. (1999) Data

transformation and standardization in the multivariate analysis of river water quality. *Ecological Applications* 9: 669–677.

Carpenter, S.R., Bolgrien, D., Lathrop, R.C., Stow, C.A., Reed, T. & Wilson, M.A. (1998) Ecological and economic analysis of lake eutrophication by nonpoint pollution. *Australian Journal of Ecology* 23: 68–79.

Carpenter, S.R. (1990) Large-scale perturbations: opportunities for innovation. *Ecology* 71: 2038–2043.

Carpenter, S.R. (1996) Microcosm experiments have limited relevance for community and ecosystem ecology. *Ecology* 77: 677–680.

Carpenter, S.R., Chisholm, S.W., Krebs, C.J., Schindler, D.W. & Wright, R.F. (1995) Ecosystem experiments. *Science* 269: 324–327.

Carver, R.P. (1978) The case against statistical significance testing. *Harvard Educational Review* 48: 378–399.

Carver, R.P. (1993) The case against statistical significance testing, revisited. *Journal of Experimental Education* 61: 287–292.

Casella, G. & Berger, R.L. (1987) Reconciling Bayesian and frequentist evidence in the one-sided testing problem. *Journal of the American Statistical Association* 82: 106–111.

Caselle, J.E. & Warner, R.R. (1996) Variability in recruitment of coral reef fishes: the importance of habitat at two spatial scales. *Ecology* 77: 2488–2504.

Chalmers, A.F. (1999) *What Is This Thing Called Science?*, 3rd edition. Hackett Publishing Co., Indianapolis.

Chapman, M.G. (1986) Assessment of some controls in experimental transplants of intertidal gastropods. *Journal of Experimental Marine Biology and Ecology* 103: 181–201.

Chapman, M.G. & Underwood, A.J. (1999) Ecological patterns in multivariate assemblages: information and interpretation of negative value in ANOSIM tests. *Marine Ecology – Progress Series* 180: 257–265.

Chatterjee, S. & Price, B. (1991) *Regression Analysis by Example*, 2nd edition. Wiley, New York.

Chatfield, C. (1989) *The Analysis of Time Series: An Introduction*, 4th edition. Chapman & Hall, London.

Chernoff, H. (1973) The use of faces to represent points in k-dimensional space graphically. *Journal of the American Statistical Association* 68: 361–368.

Chevan, A. & Sutherland, M. (1991) Hierarchical partitioning. *The American Statistician* 45: 90–96.

Chow, S.L. (1988) Significance test or effect size? *Psychological Bulletin* 103: 105–110.

Chow, S.L. (1991) Some reservations about power analysis. *American Psychologist* 46: 1088.

Christensen, D.L., Herwig, B.R., Schindler, D.E. & Carpenter, S.R. (1996) Impacts of lakeshore residential development on coarse woody debris in north temperate lakes. *Ecological Applications* 64: 1143–1149.

Christensen, R. (1997) *Log-Linear Models and Logistic Regression*, 2nd edition. Springer, New York.

Clarke, K.R. (1993). Non-parametric multivariate analyses of changes in community structure. *Australian Journal of Ecology* 18: 117–143.

Clarke, K.R. and Ainsworth, M. (1993) A method of linking multivariate community structure to environmental variables. *Marine Ecology Progress Series* 92: 205–219.

Clarke, K.R. & Warwick, R.M. (1994) *Change in Marine Communities: an Approach to Statistical Analysis and Interpretation*. Natural Environment Research Council, UK.

Clarke, M.R.B. (1980) The reduced major axis of a bivariate sample. *Biometrika* 67: 441–446.

Cleveland, W.S. (1979) Robust locally weighted regression and smoothing scatterplots. *Journal of the American Statistical Association* 74: 829–836.

Cleveland, W.S. (1993) *Visualizing Data*. Hobart Press, Summit, NJ.

Cleveland, W.S. (1994) *The Elements of Graphing Data*. Hobart Press, Summit, NJ.

Clevenger, A.P. & Waltho, N. (2000) Factors influencing the effectiveness of wildlife underpasses in Banff National Park, Alberta, Canada. *Conservation Biology* 14: 47–56.

Clinton, W.L. & Le Beouf, B.J. (1994) Sexual selection's effects on male life history and the pattern of male mortality. *Ecology* 74: 1884–1892.

Cnaan, A., Laird, N.M. & Slasor, P. (1997) Using the general linear model to analyse unbalanced repeated measures and longitudinal data. *Statistics in Medicine* 16: 2349–2380.

Cochran, W.G. & Cox, G.M. (1957) *Experimental Designs*, 2nd edition. Wiley, New York.

Cohen, J. (1988) *Statistical Power Analysis for the Behavioral Sciences*, 2nd edition. Lawrence Erlbaum, Hillsdale, NJ.

Cohen, J. (1990) Things I have learned (so far). *American Psychologist* 45: 1304–1312.

Cohen, J. (1992) A power primer. *Psychological Bulletin* 112: 155–159.

Cohen, J. (1994) The earth is round ($p < .05$). *American Psychologist* 49: 997–1003.

Cohen, J. & Cohen, P. (1983) *Applied Multiple Regression/Correlation Analysis for the Behavioral Sciences*, 2nd edition. Lawrence Erlbaum Associates, Hillsdale, NJ.

Cole, D.A., Maxwell, S.E., Arvey, R. & Salas, E. (1994) How the power of MANOVA can both increase and decrease as a function of the intercorrelations among the dependent variables. *Psychological Bulletin* 115: 465–474.

Collier, R.O., Baker, F.B., Mandeville, G.K. & Hayes, T.F. (1967) Estimates of test size for several test procedures based on conventional variance ratios in the repeated measures design. *Psychometrika* 32: 339–353.

Conover, W.J. & Iman, R.L. (1981) Rank transform as a bridge between parametric and nonparametric statistics. *The American Statistician* **35**: 124–133.

Conover, W.J., Johnson, M.E. & Johnson, M.M. (1981) A comparative study of tests for homogeneity of variances, with applications to the outer continental shelf bidding data. *Technometrics* **23**: 351–361.

Constable, A.J. (1993) The role of sutures in shrinking of the test in *Heliocidaris erythrogramma* (Echinoidea: Echinometridae). *Marine Biology* **117**: 423–430.

Cook, R.D. & Weisberg, S. (1982) *Residuals and Influence in Regression*. Chapman & Hall, New York.

Coombs, W.T., Algina, J. & Oltman, D.O. (1996) Univariate and multivariate omnibus hypothesis tests selected to control Type I error rates when population variances are not necessarily equal. *Review of Educational Research* **66**: 137–179.

Cooper, H. & Hedges, L.V. (eds.) (1994) *The Handbook of Research Synthesis*. Russell Sage Foundation, New York.

Corti, D., Kohler, S.L. & Sparks, R.E. (1997) Effects of hydroperiod and predation on a Mississippi River floodplain invertebrate community. *Oecologia* **109**: 154–165.

Cox, D.R. (1978) Some remarks on the role in statistics of graphical methods. *Applied Statistics* **27**: 4–9.

Cox, T.F. & Cox, M.A.A. (1994) *Multidimensional Scaling*. Chapman & Hall, London.

Crews, T.E., Kitayama, K., Fownes, J.H., Riley, R.H., Herbert, D.A., Mueller-Dombois, D. & Vitousek, P.M. (1995) Changes in soil phosphorus fractions and ecosystem dynamics across a long chronosequence in Hawaii. *Ecology* **75**: 1407–1424.

Crome, F.H.J., Thomas, M.R. & Moore, L.A. (1996) A novel Bayesian approach to assessing impacts of rain forest logging. *Ecological Applications* **6**: 1104–1123.

Crowder, M.J. & Hand, D.J. (1990) *Analysis of Repeated Measures*. Chapman & Hall, London.

Crowley, P.H. (1992) Resampling methods for computation-intensive data analysis in ecology and evolution. *Annual Review of Ecology and Systematics* **23**: 405–447.

Darlington, R.B. (1990) *Regression and Linear Models*. McGraw-Hill, New York.

Day, R.W. & Quinn, G.P. (1989) Comparison of treatments after an analysis of variance in ecology. *Ecological Monographs* **59**: 433–463.

De'ath, G. & Fabricius, K.E. (2000) Classification and regression trees: a powerful yet simple technique for ecological data analysis. *Ecology* **81**: 3178–3192.

Dennis, B. (1996) Discussion: should ecologists become Bayesians? *Ecological Applications* **6**: 1095–1103.

Digby, P.G.N. & Kempton, R.A. (1987) *Multivariate Analysis of Ecological Communities*. Chapman & Hall, London.

Diggle, P.J. (1990) *Time Series: A Biostatistical Introduction*. Oxford University Press, Oxford.

Diggle, P.J. (1996) Spatial analysis in biometry. In: *Advances in Biometry* (Armitage, P. & David, H.A. eds.), pp. 363–384. Wiley, New York.

Diggle, P.J., Liang, K.-Y. & Zeger, S.L. (1994) *Analysis of Longitudinal Data*. Oxford University Press, Oxford.

Diniz-Filho, J.A.F. & Bini, L.M. (1996) Assessing the relationship between multivariate community structure and environmental variables. *Marine Ecology Progress Series* **143**: 303–306.

Dixon, P.M. (1993) The bootstrap and the jackknife: describing the precision of ecological indices. In: *Design and Analysis of Ecological Experiments* (Scheiner, S. & Gurevitch, J. eds.), pp. 290–318. Chapman & Hall, New York.

Dobson, A.J. (1990) *An Introduction to Generalized Linear Models*. Chapman & Hall, London.

Downes, B.J., Lake, P.S. & Schreiber, E.S.G. (1993) Spatial variation in the distribution of stream invertebrates – implications of patchiness for models of community organization. *Freshwater Biology* **30**: 119–132.

Downes, B.J., Barmuta, L.A.,. Fairweather, P.G., Faith, D.P., Keough, M.J., Lake, P.S., Mapstone, B.D. & Quinn, G.P. (2002) *Assessing Ecological Impacts. Applications in Flowing Waters*. Cambridge University Press, Cambridge.

Driscoll, D.A. & Roberts, J.D. (1997) Impact of fuel-reduction burning on the frog *Geocrinia lutea* in southwest Western Australia. *Australian Journal of Ecology* **22**: 334–339.

Dufour, P. & Berland, B. (1999) Nutrient control of phytoplanktonic biomass in atoll lagoons and Pacific ocean waters: studies with factorial enrichment bioassays. *Journal of Experimental Marine Biology and Ecology* **234**: 147–166.

Dunham, A.E. & Beaupre, S.J. (1998) Ecological experiments: scale, phenomonology, mechanism and the illusion of generality. In: *Experimental Ecology: Issues and Perspectives* (Resetarits, W.J. & Bernado, J. eds.), pp. 27–49. Oxford University Press, New York.

Dunlop, D.D. (1994) Regression for longitudinal data: a bridge from least squares regression. *The American Statistican* **48**: 299–303.

Edgington, E.S. (1995) *Randomization Tests*, 3rd edition. Marcel Dekker, New York.

Edwards, D. (1996) Comment: the first data analysis should be journalistic. *Ecological Applications* **6**: 1090–1094.

Edwards, L.K. (1993) Analysis of time-dependent observations. In: *Applied Analysis of Variance in Behavioral Science* (Edwards, L.K. ed.), pp. 437–457. Marcel Dekker, New York.

Efron, B. (1982) The jackknife, the bootstrap and other resampling methods. *Society for Industrial and Applied Mathematics, CBMS-NSF Monograph 38*, Philadelphia.

Efron, B. & Gong, G. (1983) A leisurely look at the boot-strap, the jackknife, and cross-validation. *The American Statistician* **37**: 36–48.

Efron, B. & Tibshirani, R. (1991) Statistical data analysis in the computer age. *Science* **253**: 390–395.

Elgar, M.A., Allan, R.A. & Evans, T.A. (1996) Foraging strategies in orb-spinning spiders: ambient light and silk decorations in *Argiope aetherea Walckenaer* (Araneae: Araneoidea). *Australian Journal of Ecology* **21**: 464–467.

Eliason, S.R. (1993) *Maximum Likelihood Estimation Logic and Practice*. Sage Publications, Newbury Park.

Ellison, A.M. (1993) Exploratory data analysis and graphic display. In: *Design and Analysis of Ecological Experiments* (Scheiner, S.M. & Gurevitch, J. eds.). Chapman & Hall, New York.

Ellison, A.M. (1996) An introduction to Bayesian inference for ecological research and environmental decision-making. *Ecological Applications* **64**: 1036–1046.

Emerson, J.D. (1991) Introduction to transformation. In: *Fundamentals of Exploratory Analysis of Variance* (Hoaglin, D.C., Mosteller, F. & Tukey, J.W. eds.), pp. 365–400. Wiley, New York.

Emerson, J.D. & Hoaglin, D.C. (1983) Analysis of two-way tables by medians. In: *Understanding Robust and Exploratory Data Analysis* (Hoaglin, D.C., Mosteller, F. & Tukey, J.W. eds.), pp. 166–210. Wiley, New York.

Emerson, J.D. & Wong, G.Y. (1985) Resistant nonadditive fits for two-way tables. In: *Exploring Data Tables, Trends, and Shapes* (Hoaglin, D.C., Mosteller, F. & Tukey, J.W. eds.), pp. 67–124. Wiley, New York.

Evans, E.W. & England, S. (1996) Indirect interactions in biological control of insects: pests and natural enemies in alfalfa. *Ecological Applications* **6**: 920–930.

Evans, M., Hastings, N. & Peacock, B. (2000) *Statistical Distributions*, 3rd edition. Wiley, New York.

Everitt, B.S. & Dunn, G. (1991) *Applied Multivariate Data Analysis*. Edward Arnold, London.

Faeth, S.H. (1992) Interspecific and intraspecific interactions via plant responses to folivory: an experimental field test. *Ecology* **73**: 1802–1813.

Fairweather, P.G. (1991) Statistical power and design requirements for environmental monitoring. *Australian Journal of Marine and Freshwater Research* **42**: 555–567.

Faith, D.P., Minchin, P.R. & Belbin, L. (1987). Compositional dissimilarity as a robust measure of ecological distance. *Vegetatio* **69**: 57–68.

Federer, W.T. & Meredith, M.P. (1992) Covariance analysis for split-plot and split-block designs. *The American Statistician* **46**: 155–162.

Feinsinger, P., Tiebout III, H.M. & Young, B.M. (1991) Do tropical bird-pollinated plants exhibit density-dependent interactions? Field experiments. *Ecology* **72**: 1953–1963.

Fenton, M.B., Cumming, D.H.M., Rautenbach, I.L.,

Cumming, G.S., Cumming, M.S., Ford, G., Taylor, R.D., Dunlop, J., Hovorka, M.D., Johnston, D.S., Portfors, C.V., Kalcounis, M.C. & Mahlanga, Z. (1998) Bast and the loss of tree canopy in African woodlands. *Conservation Biology* **12**: 399–407.

Fisher, R.A. (1935; numerous subsequent editions) *The Design of Experiments*. Oliver & Boyd, Edinburgh.

Fisher, R.A. (1936) The use of multiple measurement in taxonomic problems. *Annals of Eugenics* **7**: 179–188.

Fisher, R.A. (1954) *Statistical Methods for Research Workers*. Oliver & Boyd, Edinburgh.

Fisher, R.A. (1956) *Statistical Methods and Scientific Inference*. Oliver & Boyd, Edinburgh.

Fitzmaurice, G.M. (1997) Model selection with overdispersed data. *The Statistician* **1**: 81–91.

Flack, V.F. & Chang, P.C. (1987) Frequency of selecting noise variables in subset regression analysis: a simulation study. *The American Statistician* **41**: 84–86.

Fligner, M.A. & Killeen, T.J. (1976) Distribution-free two-sample tests for scale. *Journal of the American Statistical Association* **71**: 210–213.

Flury, B. & Riedwyl, H. (1988) *Multivariate Statistics: a Practical Approach*. Chapman & Hall, London, 296 pp.

Ford, E.D. (2000) *Scientific Method for Ecological Research*. Cambridge University Press, Cambridge.

Fortin, M.-J. & Gurevitch, J. (1993) Mantel tests: spatial structure in field experiments. In: *Design and Analysis of Ecological Experiments* (Scheiner, S.M. & Gurevitch, J. eds.), pp. 342–359. Chapman & Hall, New York.

Fox, G.A. (1993) Failure-time analysis: emergence, flowering, survivorship, and other waiting times. In: *Design and Analysis of Ecological Experiments* (Scheiner, S.M. & Gurevitch, J. eds.), pp. 253–289. Chapman & Hall, New York.

French, K. & Westoby, M. (1996) Vertebrate-dispersed species in a fire-prone environment. *Australian Journal of Ecology* **21**: 379–385.

Frick, R.W. (1995) Accepting the null hypothesis. *Memory & Cognition* **23**: 132–138.

Fry, J.D. (1992) The mixed-model analysis of variance applied to quantitative genetics: biological meaning of the parameters. *Evolution* **46**: 540–550.

Furness, R.W. & Bryant, D.M. (1996) Effect of wind on field metabolic rates of breeding Northern Fulmars. *Ecology* **77**: 1181–1188.

Gange, A.C. (1995) Aphid performance in an alder (*Alnus*) hybrid zone. *Ecology* **76**: 2074–2083.

Gardner, W., Mulvey, E.P. & Shaw, E.C. (1995) Regression analyses of counts and rates: Poisson, overdispersed Poisson, and negative binomial models. *Psychological Bulletin* **118**: 392–404.

Gates, C.E. (1995) What really is experimental error in block designs? *The American Statistician* **49**: 362–363.

Gauch, H.G. (1982) *Multivariate Analysis in Community Ecology*. Cambridge University Press, New York.

Gelman, A., Carlin, J.B., Stern, H.S. & Rubin, D.B. (1995) *Bayesian Data Analysis*. Chapman & Hall, London.

Gigerenzer, G. (1993) The superego, the ego and the id in statistical reasoning. In: *A Handbook for Data Analysis in the Behavioral Sciences – Methodological Issues* (Keren, G. & Lewis, C. eds.), pp. 311–339. Lawrence Erlbaum Associates, New Jersey.

Glass, G.V. & Hakstian, A.R. (1969) Measures of association in comparative experiment: their development and interpretation. *American Educational Research Journal* **6**: 404–414.

Glass, G.V., Peckham, P.D. & Sanders, J.R. (1972) Consequences of failure to meet assumptions underlying the fixed effects analysis of variance and covariance. *Review of Educational Research* **42**: 237–288.

Glitzenstein, J.S., Platt, W.J. & Streng, D.R. (1995) Effects of fire regime and habitat on tree dynamics in north Florida longleaf pine savannas. *Ecological Monographs* **65**: 441–476.

Golden, D.M. & Crist, T.O. (1999) Experimental effects of habitat fragmentation on old-field canopy insects: community, guild and species responses. *Oecologia* **118**: 371–380.

Gonzalez, L. & Manly, B.F.J. (1998) Analysis of variance by randomization with small data sets. *Environmetrics* **9**: 53–65.

Goodall, C. (1990) A survey of smoothing techniques. In: *Modern Methods of Data Analysis* (Fox, J. & Long, J.S. eds.), pp. 126–176. Sage, Newbury Park.

Gough, L. & Grace, J.B. (1998) Herbivore effects on plant species density at varying productivity levels. *Ecology* **79**: 1586–1594.

Gower, B. (1997) *Scientific Method. A Historical and Philosophical Introduction*. Routledge, London.

Gower, J.C. (1971) A general coefficient of similarity and some of its properties. *Biometrics* **27**: 857–871.

Gower, J.C. (1996) Multivariate and multidimensional analysis. In: *Advances in Biometry* (Armitage, P. & David, H.A., eds.), pp. 149–175. Wiley, New York.

Gower, J.C. & Hand, D.J. (1996) *Biplots*. Chapman & Hall, London.

Green, P.T. (1997) Red crabs in rain forest on Christmas Island, Indian Ocean: activity patterns, density and biomass. *Journal of Tropical Ecology* **13**: 17–38.

Green, R.H. (1979) *Sampling Design and Statistical Methods for Environmental Biologists*. Wiley-Interscience Thesis, New York.

Green, S.B. (1991) How many subjects does it take to do regression analysis? *Multivariate Behavioral Research* **26**: 499–510.

Guiller, A., Bellido, A. & Madec, L. (1998) Genetic distance and ordination – the land snail *Helix aspersa* in North Africa as a test case. *Systematic Biology* **47**: 208–227.

Gumpertz, M.L. & Brownie, C. (1993) Repeated measures in randomized block and split-plot experiments. *Canadian Journal of Forest Research* **23**: 625–639.

Gurevitch, J. & Hedges, L.V. (1993) Meta-analysis: combining the results of independent experiments. In: *Design and Analysis of Ecological Experiments* (Scheiner, S.M. & Gurevitch, J. eds.), pp. 378–398. Chapman & Hall, New York.

Gurevitch, J., Morrow, L.L., Wallace, A. & Walsh, J.S. (1992) A meta-analysis of field experiments on competition. *American Naturalist* **140**: 539–572.

Hadi, A.S. & Ling, R.F. (1998) Some cautionary notes on the use of principal components regression. *The American Statistician* **52**: 15–19.

Hairston, N.G. (1980) The experimental test of an analysis of field distributions: competition in terrestrial salamanders. *Ecology* **61**: 817–826.

Hairston, N.G. (1989) *Ecological Experiments. Purpose, Design and Execution*. Cambridge University Press, Cambridge.

Hall, S.J., Gray, S.A. & Hammett, Z.L. (2000) Biodiversity–productivity relations: an experimental evaluation of mechanisms. *Oecologia* **122**: 545–555.

Hancock, G.R. & Klockars, A.J. (1996) The quest for α: developments in multiple comparison procedures in the quarter century since Games (1971). *Review of Educational Research* **66**: 269–306.

Hanley, J.A. & Shapiro, S.H. (1994) Sexual activity and the lifespan of male fruitflies: a dataset that gets attention. *Journal of Statistics Education* **2**(1). http://www.amsat.org/publications/jse/

Hansson, B., Bensch, S. & Hasselquist, D. (2000) Patterns of nest predation to polygyny in the Great Reed Warbler. *Ecology* **81**: 319–328.

Harlow, L.L., Mulaik, S.A. & Steiger, J.H. (1997) *What If There Were No Significance Tests?* Lawrence Erlbaum, New Jersey.

Harris, R.J. (1985) *Primer of Multivariate Statistics*, 2nd edition. Academic Press, New York.

Harris, R.J. (1993) Multivariate analysis of variance. In: *Applied Analysis of Variance in Behavioral Science* (Edwards, L.K. ed.), pp. 691–716. Marcel Dekker, New York.

Harrison, S.R. & Tamaschke, H.U. (1984) *Applied Statistical Analysis*. Prentice-Hall, Sydney.

Hasselblad, V. (1994) Meta-analysis in environmental studies. In: *Environmental Statistics* Vol. 12 (Patil, G.P. & Rao, C.R. eds.). North Holland, Amsterdam.

Hastie, T.J. & Tibshirani, R.J. (1990) *Generalized Additive Models*. Chapman & Hall, London.

Haynes, D., Toohey, D., Clarke, D. & Marney, D. (1995) Temporal and spatial variation in concentrations of trace metals in coastal sediments from the ninety mile beach, Victoria, Australia. *Marine Pollution Bulletin* **30**: 414–418.

Hays, W.L. (1994) *Statistics*, 5th edition. Harcourt Brace, Fort Worth.

Hedges, L.V. & Olkin, I. (1985) *Statistical Methods for Meta-Analysis*. Academic Press, New York.

Heitjan, D.F. (1997) Annotation: What can be done about missing data? Approaches to imputation. *American Journal of Public Health* **87**: 548–549.

Herrera, C.M. (1992) Interspecific variation in fruit shape: allometry, physlogeny, and adaptation to dispersal agents. *Ecology* **73**: 1832–1841.

Heschel, M.S. & Paige, K.N. (1995) Inbreeding depression, environmental stress, and population size variation in scarlet gilia (*Ipomopsis aggregata*). *Conservation Biology* **9**: 126–133.

Hicks, C.R. & Turner, K.V. (1999) *Fundamental Concepts in the Design of Experiments*, 5th edition. Oxford University Press, Oxford.

Hilbe, J.M. (1993) Generalized additive models software. *The American Statistician* **47**: 59–64.

Hilborn, R. & Mangel, M. (1997) *The Ecological Detective: Confronting Models with Data*. Princeton University Press, Princeton, New Jersey.

Hill, M.O. (1973) Reciprocal averaging: an eigenvector method of ordination. *Journal of Ecology* **61**: 237–249.

Hill, M.O. (1974) Correspondence analysis: a neglected multivariate method. *Applied Statistics* **23**: 340–354.

Hill, M.O. & Gauch, H.G. (1980) Detrended correspondence analysis, an improved ordination technique. *Vegetatio* **42**: 47–58.

Hines, W.G.S. (1996) Pragmatics of pooling in ANOVA tables. *The American Statistician* **50**: 127–139.

Hoaglin, D.C & Welsch, R.E. (1978) The hat matrix in regression and ANOVA. *The American Statistician* **32**: 17–22.

Hoaglin, J.D., Mosteller, F. & Tukey, J.W. (1983) *Understanding Robust and Exploratory Data Analysis*. Wiley, New York.

Hochberg, Y. (1988) A sharper Bonferroni procedure for multiple tests of significance. *Biometrika* **75**: 800–802.

Hochberg, Y. & Tamhane, A.C. (1987) *Multiple Comparison Procedures*. Wiley, New York.

Hocking, R.R. (1985) *The Analysis of Linear Models*. Brooks-Cole, California.

Hocking, R.R. (1993) Variance component estimation in mixed linear models. In: *Applied Analysis of Variance in Behavioral Science* (Edwards, L.K. ed.), pp. 541–571. Marcel Dekker, New York.

Hocking, R.R. (1996) *Methods and Applications of Linear Models: Regression and the Analysis of Variance*. Wiley, New York.

Hoenig, J.M. & Heisey, D.M. (2001) The abuse of power: the pervasive fallacy of power calculations for data analysis. *The American Statistician* **55**: 19–24.

Hollander, M. & Wolfe, D.A. (1999) *Nonparametric Statistical Methods*, 2nd edition. Wiley, New York.

Holm, S. (1979) A simple sequentially rejective multiple test procedure. *Scandinavian Journal of Statistics* **6**: 65–70.

Horton, N.J. & Lipsitz, S.R. (1999) Review of software to fit generalized estimating equation regression models. *The American Statistician* **53**: 160–169.

Hosmer, D.W. & Lemeshow, S. (1989) *Applied Logistic Regression*. Wiley, New York.

Hosmer, D.W., Hosmer, T., Le Cessie, S. & Lemeshow, S. (1997) A comparison of goodness-of-fit tests for the logistic regression model. *Statistics in Medicine* **16**: 965–980.

Huber, P.J. (1981) *Robust Statistics*. Wiley, New York.

Huberty, C.J. (1993) Historical origins of statistical testing practices: the treatment of Fisher versus Neyman–Pearson views in textbooks. *Journal of Experimental Education* **61**: 317–333.

Huberty, C.J. (1994) *Applied Discriminant Analysis*. Wiley, New York.

Huitema, B.E. (1980) *The Analysis of Covariance and Its Alternatives*. Wiley, New York.

Hull, D.L. (1999) The role of negative evidence in science. *Marine Ecology Progress Series* **191**: 305–307.

Hurlbert, S.J. (1984) Pseudoreplication and design of ecological field experiments. *Ecological Monographs* **54**: 187–211.

Hyndman, R.J. (1996) Computing and graphing highest density regions. *The American Statistician* **50**: 120–126.

Inman, H.F. (1994) Karl Perason and R.A. Fisher on statistical tests: a 1935 exchange from *Nature*. *The American Statistician* **48**: 2–11.

Jaccard, J., Turrisi, R. & Wan, C.K. (1990) *Interaction Effects in Multiple Regression*. Sage Publications, Newbury Park.

Jackson, D.A. (1993). Principal components analysis: how many components are nontrivial and interpretable? *Ecology* **74**: 2204–2214.

Jackson, D.A. & Somers, K.M. (1991). Putting things in order – the ups and downs of detrended correspondence analysis. *American Naturalist* **137**: 704–712.

Jackson, J.E. (1991). *A User's Guide to Principal Components*. Wiley, New York.

Jackson, P.R. (1986) Robust methods in statistics. In: *New Developments in Statistics for Psychology and the Social Sciences* (Lovie, A.D. ed.), pp. 22–43. BPS and Methuen, London.

James, F.C. & McCulloch, C.E. (1985) Data analysis and the design of experiments in ornithology. In: *Current Ornithology* Vol. 2 (Johnston, R.F. ed.), pp. 1–63. Plenum Press, New York.

James, F.C. & McCulloch, C.E. (1990) Multivariate analysis in ecology and systematics: Panacea or Pandora's box? *Annual Review of Ecology and Systematics* **21**: 129–166.

Janky, D.G. (2000) Sometimes pooling for analysis of variance hypothesis tests: a review and study of a split-plot model. *The American Statistician* **54**: 269–279.

Jobson, J.D. (1992) *Applied Multivariate Data Analysis*, Vol. 2. Springer-Verlag, New York.

Johnson, C.R. & Field, C.A. (1993) Using fixed-effects model multivariate analysis of variance in marine biology and ecology. *Oceanography and Marine Biology Annual Review* **31**: 177–221.

Johnson, D.H. (1999) The insignificance of statistical significance testing. *Journal of Wildlife Management* **63**: 763–772.

Johnson, P.O. & Neyman, J. (1936) Tests of certain linear hypotheses and their application to some educational problems. *Statistical Research Memoirs* **1**: 57–93.

Jones, D. & Matloff, N. (1986) Statistical hypothesis testing in biology: a contradiction in terms. *Journal of Economic Entomology* **79**: 1156–1160.

Jongman, R.H.G., ter Braak, C.J.F. & van Tongeren, O.F.R. (1995) *Data Analysis in Community and Landscape Ecology*. Cambridge University Press, Cambridge.

Judd, C.M., McClelland, G.H. & Culhane, S.E. (1995) Data analysis: continuing issues in the everyday analysis of psychological data. *Annual Review of Psychology* **46**: 433–465.

Juenger, T. & Bergelson, J. (2000) Does early season browsing influence the effect of self-pollination in scarlet gilia. *Ecology* **81**: 41–48.

Kass, R.E. & Raftery, A.E. (1995) Bayes factors. *Journal of the American Statistical Association* **90**: 773–795.

Kause, A., Haukioja, E. & Hanhimäki, S. (1999) Phenotypic plasticity in foraging behavior of sawfly larvae. *Ecology* **80**: 1230–1241.

Keene, O.N. (1995) The log transformation is special. *Statistics in Medicine* **14**: 811–819.

Kenny, D.A. & Judd, C.M. (1986) Consequences of violating the independence assumption in analysis of variance. *Psychological Bulletin* **99**: 422–431.

Kent, M. & Coker, P. (1992). *Vegetation Description and Analysis: a Practical Approach*. CRC Press, Boca Raton, Florida.

Keough, M.J. & King, A. (1991) Recommendations for monitoring of marine plant and animal populations in Wilsons Promontory Marine National Park and the Bunurong Marine Park. Department of Conservation and Environment, Melbourne, Victoria. (Unpublished report).

Keough, M.J. & Mapstone, B.D. (1995) Protocols for designing marine ecological monitoring programs associated with BEK mills. Technical Report No. 11, National Pulp Mills Program. CSIRO, Canberra, 177 pp.

Keough, M.J. & Mapstone, B.D. (1997) Designing environmental monitoring for pulp mills in Australia. *Water Science and Technology* **35**: 397–404.

Keough, M.J. & Quinn, G.P. (1998) Effects of periodic disturbances from trampling on rocky intertidal algal beds. *Ecological Applications* **8**: 141–161.

Keough, M.J. & Raimondi, P.T. (1995) Responses of settling invertebrate larvae to bioorganic films: effects of different types of films. *Journal of Experimental Marine Biology and Ecology* **185**: 235–253.

Keough, M.J. & Raimondi, P.T. (1996) Responses of settling invertebrate larvae to biofilms: a comparison of the effects of local and "foreign" films at three sites. *Journal of Experimental Marine Biology and Ecology* **207**: 59–78.

Keough, M.J., Quinn, G.P. & King, A. (1993) Correlations between human collecting and intertidal mollusc populations on rocky shores. *Conservation Biology* **7**: 378–391.

Keppel, G. (1991) *Design and Analysis: A Researcher's Handbook*. Prentice-Hall, Englewood Cliffs, NJ.

Keselman, H.J. & Keselman, J.C. (1993) Analysis of repeated measurements. In: *Applied Analysis of Variance in Behavioral Science* (Edwards, L.K. ed.), pp. 105–145. Marcel Dekker, New York.

Keselman, H.J., Keselman, J.C. & Lix, L.M. (1995) The analysis of repeated measurements: univariate tests, multivariate tests, or both? *British Journal of Mathematical and Statistical Psychology* **48**: 319–338.

Kingsolver, J.G. & Schemske, D.W. (1991) Path analyses of selection. *Trends in Ecology and Evolution* **6**: 276–280.

Kirk, R.E. (1995) *Experimental Design*. Brooks/Cole, Pacific Grove.

Kleinbaum, D.G., Kupper, L.L. & Muller, K.E. (1988) *Applied Regression Analysis and Other Multivariable Methods*. PWS-Kent, Boston, Mass.

Kleinbaum, D.G., Kupper, L.L. & Muller, K.E. (1997) *Applied Regression Analysis and Other Multivariable Methods*, 3rd edition Duxbury Press.

Koenig, W.D. (1999) Spatial autocorrelation of ecological phenomena. *Trends in Ecology and Evolution* **14**: 22–26.

Koenig, W.D., Mumme, R.L., Carmen, W.J. & Stanback, M.T. (1994) Acorn production by oaks in central coastal California: variation within and among years. *Ecology* **75**: 99–109.

Krebs, C.J. (1989) *Ecological Methodology*. Harper-Collins, New York.

Krupnick, G.A. & Weis, A.E. (1999) The effect of floral herbivory on male and female reproductive success in *Isomeris arborea*. *Ecology* **80**: 135–149.

Kruskal, J.B. (1964a) Multidimensional scaling by optimizing goodness of fit to a nonmetric hypotheses. *Psychometrika* **29**: 1–27.

Kruskal, J.B. (1964b) Nonmetric multidimensional scaling: a numerical method. *Psychometrika* **29**: 115–129.

Kuhn, T.S. (1970) *The Structure of Scientific Revolutions*, 2nd edition. University of Chicago Press, Chicago.

Kvalseth, T. (1985) Cautionary note about R^2. *The American Statistician* **39**: 279–285.

LaBarbera, M. (1989) Analyzing body size as a factor in ecology and evolution. *Annual Review of Ecology and Systematics* **20**: 97–117.

Lafi, S.Q. & Kaneene, J.B. (1992) An explanation of the use of principal-components analysis to detect and correct for multicollinearity. *Preventive Veterinary Medicine* **13**: 261–275.

Laird, N.M. & Ware, J.H. (1982) Random effects models for longitudinal data. *Biometrics* **38**: 963–974.

Lakatos, I. (1978) *The Methodology of Scientific Research Programmes*. Cambridge University Press, New York.

Larntz, K. (1993) Analysis of categorical response variables. In: *Applied Analysis of Variance in Behavioral Science* (Edwards, L.K. ed.). Marcel Dekker, New York.

Legendre, P. (1993) Spatial autocorrelation: trouble or new paradigm. *Ecology* **74**: 1659–1673.

Legendre, P. & Anderson, M.J. (1999a) Distance-based redundancy analysis: testing multispecies responses in multifactorial ecological experiments. *Ecological Monographs* **69**: 1–24.

Legendre, P. & Anderson, M.J. (1999b) Distance-based redundancy analysis: testing multispecies responses in multifactorial ecological experiments. *Ecological Monographs* **69**: 1–24.

Legendre, P. & Legendre, L. (1998) *Numerical Ecology*, 2nd English edition. Elsevier Science, Amsterdam.

Lehmann, E.L. (1993) The Fisher, Neyman–Pearson theories of testing hypotheses: one theory or two. *Journal of the American Statistical Association* **88**: 1242–1249.

Lentner, M., Arnold, J.C. & Hinkelmann, K. (1989) The efficiency of blocking: how to use MS(Blocks)/MS(Error) correctly. *The American Statistician* **43**: 106–108.

Leonard, G.H., Bertness, M.D. & Yund, P.O. (1999) Crab predation, waterborne cues, and inducible defences in the blue mussel, *Mytilus edulis*. *Ecology* **80**: 1–14.

Letourneau, D.K. & Dyer, L.A. (1998) Experimental test in lowland tropical forest shows top-down effects through four trophic levels. *Ecology* **79**: 1678–1687.

Levin, J.R. (1998) To test or not to test H_0? *Educational and Psychological Measurement* **58**: 313–333.

Levy, P.S. & Lemeshow, S. (1991) *Sampling of Populations*. Wiley, New York.

Liang, K.-Y. & Zeger, S.L. (1986) Longitudinal data analysis using generalized linear models. *Biometrika* **73**: 13–22.

Lindsey, J.C. & Ryan, L.M. (1998) Tutorial in biostatistics – methods for interval-censored data. *Statistics in Medicine* **17**: 219–238.

Little, R.J.A. (1999) Methods for handling missing values in clinical trials. *The Journal of Rheumatology* **26**: 1654–1656.

Little, R.J.A. & Rubin, D.B. (1987) *Statistical Analysis with Missing Data*. Wiley, New York.

Loehle, C.J. (1987) Hypothesis testing in ecology: psychological aspects and the importance of theory maturation. *Quarterly Review of Biology* **62**: 397–409.

Loehle, C.J. (1990) Proper statistical treatment of species-area data. *Oikos* **57**: 143–145.

Looney, S.W. & Stanley, W.B. (1989) Exploratory repeated measures analysis for two or more groups. *The American Statistician* **43**: 220–225.

Losos, E. (1995) Habitat specificity of two palm species: experimental transplantation in Amazonian successional forests. *Ecology* **76**: 2595–2606.

Lovett, G.M., Weathers, K.C. & Sobczak, W.V. (2000) Nitrogen saturation and retention in forested watersheds of the Catskill Mountains, New York. *Ecological Applications* **10**: 73–84.

Loyn, R.H. (1987) Effects of patch area and habitat on bird abundances, species numbers and tree health in fragmented Victorian forests. In: *Nature Conservation: the Role of Remnants of Native Vegetation* (Saunders, D.A., Arnold, G.W., Burbidge, A.A. & Hopkins, A.J.M. eds.), pp. 65–77. Surrey Beatty & Sons, Chipping Norton, NSW.

Ludbrook, J. & Dudley, H. (1998) Why permutation tests are superior to *t* and *F* tests in biomedical research. *The American Statistician* **52**: 127–132.

Ludwig, J.A. & Reynolds, J.F. (1988) *Statistical Ecology: a Primer on Methods and Computing*. Wiley, New York.

Mac Nally, R.C. (1989) The relationship between habitat breadth, habitat position, and abundance in forest and woodland birds along a continental gradient. *Oikos* **54**: 44–54.

Mac Nally, R. (1996) Hierarchical partitioning as an interpretive tool in multivariate inference. *Australian Journal of Ecology* **21**: 224–228

Mac Nally, R. (2000) Regression and model-building in conservation biology, biogeography and ecology: The distinction between, and reconciliation of, predictive and explanatory models. *Biodiversity and Conservation* **9**: 655–671.

Manly, B.F.J. (1992) *The Design and Analysis of Research Studies*. Cambridge University Press, Cambridge.

Manly, B.F.J. (1994) *Multivariate Statistical Methods: A Primer*. 2nd edition. Chapman & Hall, London.

Manly, B.F.J. (1997) *Randomization and Monte Carlo Methods in Biology*, 2nd edition. Chapman & Hall, London.

Manly, B.F.J. (2001) *Statistics for Environmental Science and Management*. Chapman & Hall / CRC, Boca Raton, Florida.

Mapstone, B.D. (1995) Scalable decision rules for environmental impact studies: effect size, Type I, and Type II errors. *Ecological Applications* **5**: 401–410.

Maret, T.J. & Collins, J.P. (1996) Effect of prey vulnerability on population size structure of a gape-limited predator. *Ecology* **77**: 320–324.

Markowski, C.A. & Markowski, E.P. (1990) Conditions for the effectiveness of a preliminary test of variance. *The American Statistician* **44**: 322–326.

Marshall, P. & Keough, M.J. (1994) Asymmetry in intraspecific competition in the limpet *Cellana tramoserica* (Sowerby). *Journal of Experimental Marine Biology and Ecology* **177**: 121–138.

Matlack, G.R. (1994) Plant species migration in a mixed-history forest landscape in eastern North America. *Ecology* 75: 1491–1502.

Matloff, N.S. (1991) Statistical hypothesis testing: problems and alternatives. *Environmental Entomology* 20: 1246–1250.

Maxwell, S.E. & Delaney, H.D. (1990) *Designing Experiments and Analyzing Data: a Model Comparison Perspective.* Wadsworth Publishing, Belmont, California.

Maxwell, S.E., O'Callaghan, M.F. & Delaney, H.D. (1993) Analysis of covariance. In *Applied Analysis of Variance in Behavioral Science* (Edwards, L.K. ed.), pp. 63–104. Marcel Dekker, New York.

Mayo, D.G. (1996) *Error and the Growth of Experimental Knowledge.* University of Chicago Press, Chicago.

McArdle, B.H. (1988) The structural relationship: regression in biology. *Canadian Journal of Zoology* 66: 2329–2339.

McArdle, B.H. (1996) Levels of evidence in studies of competition, predation and disease. *New Zealand Journal of Ecology* 20: 7–15.

McArdle, B.H. & Anderson, M.J. (2001) Fitting multivariate models to community data: a comment on distance-based redundancy analysis. *Ecology* 82: 290–297.

McCue, K.A., Buckler, E.S. & Holtsford, T.P. (1996) A hierarchical view of genetic structure in the rare annual plant *Clarkia springvillensis. Conservation Biology* 10: 1424–1434.

McCullough, P. & Nelder, J.A. (1989) *Generalized Linear Models*, 2nd edition. Chapman & Hall, New York.

McCune, B. & Mefford, M.J. (1999) *Multivariate Analysis of Ecological Data*, Version 4.10, MjM Software, Gleneden Beach, Oregon, USA.

McGoldrick, J.M. & Mac Nally, R.C. (1998) Impact of flowering on bird community dynamics in some central Victorian eucalypt forests. *Ecological Research* 13: 125–139.

McKean, J.W. & Vidmar, T.J. (1994) A comparison of two rank-based methods for the analysis of linear models. *The American Statistician* 48: 220–229.

McLean, R.A., Sanders, W.L. & Stroup, W.W. (1991) A unified approach to mixed linear models. *The American Statistician* 45: 54–64.

McShane, P. & Smith, M.G. (1990) Direct measurement of fishing mortality in abalone (*Haliotis rubraech*) off southeastern Australia. *Fisheries Research* 8: 93–102.

McShane, P., Smith, M.G. & Beinssen, K.H.H. (1988) Growth and morphometry in abalone (*Haliotis rubra* Leach) from Victoria. *Australian Journal of Marine and Freshwater Research* 39: 161–166.

Mead, R. (1988) *The Design of Experiments.* Cambridge University Press, Cambridge.

Medley, C.N. & Clements, W.H. (1998) Responses of diatom communities to heavy metals in streams: the influence of longitudinal variation. *Ecological Applications* 8: 631–644.

Menard, S. (1995) *Applied Logistic Regression Analysis.* Sage Publications, Thousand Oaks, California.

Menard, S. (2000) Coefficients of determination for multiple logistic regression. *The American Statistician* 54: 17–24.

Mentis, M.T. (1988) Hypothetico-deductive and inductive approaches in ecology. *Functional Ecology* 12: 5–14.

Meredith, M.P. & Stehman, S.V. (1991) Repeated measures experiments in forestry: focus on analysis of response curves. *Canadian Journal of Forest Research* 21: 957–965.

Meserve, P.L., Gutierrez, J.R., Yunger, J.A., Conteras, L.C. & Jaksic, F.M. (1996) Role of biotic interactions in a small mammal assemblage in semiarid Chile. *Ecology* 77: 133–148.

Mielke, P.W. (1985) Multiresponse permutation procedures. In: *Encyclopedia of Statistical Sciences*, vol. 5 (Kotz, S. & Johnson, N.L. eds.), pp. 724–727. Wiley, New York.

Mielke, P.W., Berry, K.J. & Johnson, E.J. (1976) Multiresponse permutation procedures for *a priori* classifications. *Communications in Statistics – Theory and Methods* A5: 1409–1424.

Millard, S.P. & Deverel, S.J. (1988) Nonparametric statistical methods for comparing two sites based on data with multiple nondetect limits. *Water Resources Research* 24: 2087–2098.

Miller, J.N. (1993) Outliers in experimental data and their treatment. *Analyst* 118: 455–461.

Miller, R.G. (1981) *Simultaneous Statistical Inference*, 2nd edition. Springer, New York.

Milliken, G.A. & Johnson, D.E. (1984) *Analysis of Messy Data. Vol. 1: Designed Experiments.* Van Nostrand Reinhold, New York.

Mills, K.E. & Bever, J.D. (1998) Maintenance of diversity within plant communities: soil pathogens as agents of negative feedback. *Ecology* 79: 1595–1601.

Minchin, P.R. (1987). An evaluation of the relative robustness of techniques for ecological ordination. *Vegetatio* 69: 89–107.

Minchinton, T.E. & Ross, P.M. (1999) Oysters as habitat for limpets in a temperate mangrove forest. *Australian Journal of Ecology* 24: 157–170.

Mitchell, R.J. (1992) Testing evolutionary and ecological hypotheses using path analysis and structural equation modelling. *Functional Ecology* 6: 123–129.

Mitchell, R.J. (1993) Path analysis: pollination. In: *Design and Analysis of Ecological Experiments* (Scheiner, S.M. & Gurevitch, J. eds.), pp. 211–231. Chapman & Hall, New York.

Morris, C.N. (1987) Comment. *Journal of the American Statistical Association* 82: 131–133.

Morris, D.W. (1996) Coexistence of specialist and generalist rodents via habitat selection. *Ecology* 77: 2351–2364.

Morrison, D. (1991) Personal Type I error rates in the ecological sciences. *Bulletin of the Ecological Society of Australia* 21: 49–53.

Morse, S.R. & Bazzaz, F.A. (1994) Elevated CO_2 and temperature alter recruitment and size hierarchies in C_3 and C_4 annuals. *Ecology* 75: 966–975.

Mothershead, K. & Marquis, R.J. (2000) Fitness impacts of herbivory through indirect effects of plant–pollinator interactions in *Oenothera macrocarpa*. *Ecology* 81: 30–40.

Mulaik, S.A., Raju, N.S. & Harshman, R.A. (1997) There is a time and a place for significance testing. In: *What if there were no significance tests?* (Harlow, L.L., Mulaik, S.A. & Steiger, J.H. eds.), pp. 65–115. Lawrence Erlbaum, New Jersey.

Mullens, A. (1993) The effects of inspired oxygen on the pattern of ventilation in the Cane Toad (*Bufo marinus*) and the Salt Water Crocodile (*Crocodylus porosus*). Honours Thesis. University of Melbourne, Australia.

Murdoch, D.J. & Chow, E.D. (1996) A graphical display of large correlation matrices. *The American Statistician* 50: 178–180.

Myers, R.H. (1990) *Classical and Modern Regression Analysis with Applications*. Duxbury, Belmont.

Myers, R.H. & Montgomery, D.C. (1997) A tutorial on generalized linear models. *Journal of Quality Technology* 29: 274–291.

Naiman, R.J., Pinay, G., Johnston, C.A. & Pastor, J. (1994) Beaver influences on the long-term biogeochemical characteristics of boreal forest drainage networks. *Ecology* 75: 905–921.

National Research Council (1990) *Managing Troubled Waters. The Role of Marine Environmental Monitoring*. National Academy of Sciences, Washington, DC.

Nelder, J. & Wedderburn, R.W.M. (1972) Generalized linear models. *Journal of the Royal Statistical Society* A135: 370–384.

Nelder, J.A. & Lane, P.W. (1995) The computer analysis of factorial experiments: in memoriam – Frank Yates. *The American Statistician* 49: 382–385.

Nester, M.R. (1996) An applied statistician's creed. *Applied Statistics* 45: 401–410.

Neter, J., Kutner, M.H., Nachtsheim, C.J. & Wasserman, W. (1996) *Applied Linear Statistical Models*, 4th edition. Irwin, Illinois.

Newman, J.A., Bergelson, J. & Grafen, A. (1997) Blocking factors and hypothesis tests in ecology: is your statistics text wrong? *Ecology* 78: 1312–1320.

Newman, M.C., Dixon, P.M., Looney, B.B. & Pinder, J.E. (1989) Estimating mean and variance for environmental samples with below detection limit observations. *Water Resources Bulletin* 25: 905–916.

Newman, R.A. (1994) Effects of changing density and food level on metamorphosis of a desert amphibian, *Scaphiopus couchii*. *Ecology* 75: 1085–1096.

Neyman, J. & Pearson, E. (1928) On the use and interpretation of certain test criteria for purposes of statistical inference: Part I. *Biometrika* 20A: 175–240.

Neyman, J. & Pearson, E.S. (1933) On the problem of the most efficient tests of statistical hypotheses. *Philosophical Transactions of the Royal Society of London*, Series A 231: 289–337.

Noreen, E.W. (1989) *Computer-Intensive Methods for Testing Hypotheses : An Introduction*. Wiley, New York.

Norman, G.R. & Streiner, D.L. (1994) *Biostatistics: The Bare Essentials*. Mosby, St Louis.

O'Hear, A. (1989) *An Introduction to the Philosophy of Science*. Oxford University Press, Oxford.

Oakes, M. (1986) *Statistical Inference: a Commentary for the Social and Behavioural Sciences*. Wiley, Chichester.

Okansen, J. & Minchin, P.R. (1997) Instability of ordination results under changes in input order: explanations and remedies. *Journal of Vegetation Science* 8: 447–454.

Olejnik, S.F. & Algina, S.L. (1987) An analysis of statistical power for parametric ANCOVA and rank transform ANCOVA. *Communications in Statistics – Theory and Methods* A16: 1923–1949.

Omar, R.Z., Wright, E.M., Turner, R.M. & Thompson, S.G. (1999) Analysing repeated measurements data: a practical comparison of methods. *Statistics in Medicine* 18: 1587–1603.

Osenberg, C.W., Schmitt, R.J., Holbrook, S.J., Abu-Saba, K.E. & Flegal, A.R. (1996). Detection of ecological impacts: natural variability, effect size, and power analysis. In *The Design of Ecological Impact Studies: Conceptual Issues and Application in Coastal Marine Habitats*, (Schmitt R.J. & Osenberg, C.W. eds.) pp. 83–108. Academic Press, San Diego.

Ouborg, N.J. & van Groenendael, J.M. (1996) Demography, genetics, or statistics: comments on a paper by Heschel and Paige. *Conservation Biology* 10: 1290–1291.

Ozaydin, F., van Leeuwen, D.M., Miller, C.S. & Schroeder, J. (1999) Factor effects on the variance in a replicated two-way treatment structure in an agricultural system. *Journal of Agricultural, Biological, and Environmental Statistics* 4: 166–184.

Paige, K.N. & Heschel, M.S. (1996) Inbreeding depression in scarlet gilia: a reply to Ouborg and van Groenendael. *Conservation Biology* 10: 1292–1294.

Palmer, M.W. (1993). Putting things in even better order: the advantages of canonical correspondence analysis. *Ecology* 74: 2215–2230.

Papineau, D. (1994) The virtues of randomization. *British Journal for the Philosophy of Science* 45: 437–450.

Partridge, L. & Farquhar, M. (1981) Sexual activity and the lifespan of male fruitflies. *Nature* 294: 580–581.

Paruelo, J.M. & Lauenroth, W.K. (1996) Relative abundance of plant functional types in grasslands and shrublands of North America. *Ecological Applications* **6**: 1212–1224.

Peake, A.J. & Quinn, G.P. (1993) Temporal variation in species–area curves for invertebrates in clumps of an intertidal mussel. *Ecography* **16**: 269–277.

Pechenik, J. (2001) *A Short Guide to Writing About Biology*, 4th edition. Longman, New York.

Peckarsky, B.L., Cowan, C.A., Penton, M.A. & Anderson, C. (1993) Sublethal consequences of stream-dwelling predatory stoneflies on mayfly growth and fecundity. *Ecology* **74**: 1836–1846.

Peet, R.K., Knox, R.G.; Case, S.J. & Allen, R.B. (1988) Putting things in order: the advantages of detrended correspondence analysis. *American Naturalist* **131**: 924–934.

Pennings, S.C. & Callaway, R.M. (1996) Impact of a parasitic plant on the structure and dynamics of salt marsh vegetation. *Ecology* **77**: 1410–1419.

Peterman, R. (1990a) The importance of reporting statistical power: the forest decline and acidic deposition example. *Ecology* **71**: 2024–2027.

Peterman, R. (1990b) Statistical power analysis can improve fisheries research and management. *Canadian Journal of Fisheries and Aquatic Sciences* **47**: 2–15.

Peterman, R.M. (1989) Application of statistical power analysis on the Oregon coho salmon problem. *Canadian Journal of Fisheries and Aquatic Sciences* **46**: 1183–1187.

Peters, R.H. (1991) *A Critique for Ecology*. Cambridge University Press, Cambridge.

Petit, L.J. & Petit, D.R. (1996) Factors governing habitat selection by prothonotary warblers: field test of the Fretwell–Lucas models. *Ecological Monographs* **66**: 367–387.

Petraitis, P.S. (1998) How can we compare the importance of ecological processes if we never ask, "compared to what?". In: *Experimental Ecology: Issues and Perspectives* (Resetarits, W.J. & Bernado, J. eds.), pp. 183–201. Oxford University Press, New York.

Petraitis, P.S., Dunham, A.E. & Niewiarowski, P.H. (1996) Inferring multiple causality: the limitations of path analysis. *Functional Ecology* **10**: 421–431.

Philippi, T.E. (1993) Multiple regression: herbivory. In: *Design and Analysis of Ecological Experiments* (Scheiner, S. & Gurevitch, J. eds.), pp. 183–210. Chapman & Hall, New York.

Platt, J.R. (1964) Strong inference. *Science* **146**: 347–353.

Polis, G.A., Hurd, S.D., Jackson, C.D. & Sanchez-Piñero, F. (1998) Multifactor population limitation: variable spatial and temporal control of spiders on Gulf of California islands. *Ecology* **79**: 490–502.

Popper, K.R. (1968) *The Logic of Scientific Discovery*. Hutchinson, London.

Popper, K.R. (1969) *Conjectures and Refutations*. Routledge and Kegan Paul, London.

Posten, H.O. (1984) Robustness of the two-sample *t*-test. In: *Robustness of Statistical Methods and Nonparametric Statistics* (Rasch, D. & Tiku, M.L. eds.). D. Reidel, Dordrecht, German Democratic Republic.

Potvin, C. (1993) ANOVA: Experiments in controlled environments. In: *Design and Analysis of Ecological Experiments* (Scheiner, S. & Gurevitch, J. eds.), pp. 46–68. Chapman & Hall, New York.

Potvin, C. & Roff, D.A. (1993) Distribution-free and robust statistical methods: viable alternatives to parametric statistics? *Ecology* **74**: 1617–1628.

Potvin, C., Lechowicz, M.J. & Tradif, S. (1990) The statistical analysis of ecophysiological response curves obtained from experiments involving repeated measures. *Ecology* **71**: 1389–1400.

Poulson, T.L. & Platt, W.J. (1996) Replacement patterns of beech and sugar maple in Warren Woods, Michigan. *Ecology* **77**: 1234–1253.

Prairie, Y.T., Peter, R.H. & Bird, D.F. (1995) Natural variability and the estimation of empirical relationships: a reassessment of regression methods. *Canadian Journal of Fisheries and Aquatic Sciences* **52**: 788–798.

Pugusek, B.H. & Grace, J.B. (1998) On the utility of path modelling for ecological and evolutionary studies. *Functional Ecology* **12**: 843–856.

Puri, M.L. & Sen, P.K. (1969) Analysis of covariance based on general rank scores. *Annals of Mathematical Statistics* **40**: 610–618.

Quinn, G.P. (1988) Ecology of the intertidal pulmonate limpet *Siphonaria diemenensis* Quoy et Gaimard. II Reproductive patterns and energetics. *Journal of Experimental Marine Biology and Ecology* **117**: 137–156.

Quinn, G.P. & Keough, M.J. (1993) Potential effect of enclosure size on field experiments with herbivorous intertidal gastropods. *Marine Ecology Progress Series* **98**: 199–201.

Radwan, M.A., Shumway, J.S., DeBell, D.S. & Kraft, J.M. (1992) Variance in response of pole-size trees and seedlings of Douglas-fir wetern hemlock to nitrogen and phosphorous fertilizers. *Canadian Journal of Forest Research* **21**: 1431–1438.

Ramsey, P.H. (1993) Multiple comparisons of independent means. In: *Applied Analysis of Variance in Behavioral Science* (Edwards, L.K. ed.). Marcel Dekker, New York.

Rasmussen, J.L. (1989) Parameteric and non-parametric analysis of groups by trials under variance–covariance inhomogeneity. *British Journal of Mathematical and Statistical Psychology* **42**: 91–102.

Ratkowsky, D.A. (1990) *Handbook of Nonlinear Regression Models*. Marcel Dekker, New York.

Ratkowsky, D.A., Evans, M.A. & Alldredge, J.R. (1993) *Cross-Over Experiments : Design, Analysis, and Application*. Marcel Dekker, New York.

Rawlings, J.O., Pantula, S.G. & Dickey, D.A. (1998) *Applied Regression Analysis; A Research Tool*, 2nd edition. Springer-Verlag, New York.

Reckhow, K.H. (1990) Bayesian inference in non-replicated ecological studies. *Ecology* 71: 2053–2059.

Reich, P.B., Ellsworth, D.S., Walters, M.B., Vose, J.M., Gresham, C., Volin, J.C. & Bowman, W.D. (1999) Generality of leaf trait relationships: a test across six biomes. *Ecology* 80: 1955–1969.

Rejwan, C., Collins, N.C., Brunner, L.J., Shuter, B.J. & Ridgeway, M.S. (1999) Tree regression analysis on the nesting habitat of smallmouth bass. *Ecology* 80: 341–348.

Rencher, A.C. & Pun, F.C. (1980) Inflation of R^2 in best subset regression. *Technometrics* 22: 49–53.

Resetarits, W.J. & Fauth, J.E. (1998) From cattle tanks to Carolina bays: the utility of model systems for understanding natural communities. In: *Experimental Ecology: Issues and Perspectives* (Resetarits, W.J. & Bernado, J. eds.), pp. 133–151. Oxford University Press, New York.

Reynolds, H.L., Hungate, B.A., Chapin III, F.S. & D'Antonio, C.M. (1997) Soil heterogeneity and plant competition in an annual grassland. *Ecology* 78: 2076–2090.

Rice, W.R. (1989) Analyzing tables of statistical tests. *Evolution* 43: 223–225.

Richman, M.B. (1986) Rotation of principal components. *Journal of Climatology* 6: 293–335.

Rivest, L.-P. (1986) Bartlett's, Cochran's, and Hartley's tests on variances are liberal when the underlying distribution is long-tailed. *Journal of the American Statistical Association* 81: 124–128.

Roberts, J. (1993) Regeneration and growth of coolibah, *Eucalyptus coolabah* subsp. *arida*, a riparian tree, in the Cooper Creek region of South Australia. *Australian Journal of Ecology* 18: 345–350.

Robertson, C. (1991) Computationally intensive statistics. In: *New Developments in Statistics for Psychology and the Social Sciences* Vol. 2 (Lovie, P. & Lovie, A.D. eds.), pp. 49–80. BPS and Routledge, London.

Robles, C.J., Sherwood-Stephens, R. & Alvarado, M. (1995) Responses of a key intertidal predator to varying recruitment of its prey. *Ecology* 76: 565–579.

Rodgers, J.L. & Nicewander, W.A. (1988) Thirteen ways to look at the correlation coefficient. *The American Statistician* 42: 59–66.

Rogosa, D.R. (1980) Comparing non-parallel regression lines. *Psychological Bulletin* 88: 307–321.

Rohlf, F.J. & Sokal, R.R. (1969) *Statistical Tables*. W.H. Freeman, San Francisco.

Rosenthal, R. (1994) Parametric measures of effect size. In: *The Handbook of Research Synthesis* (Cooper, H. & Hedges, L.V. eds.), pp. 231–244. Russell Sage Foundation, New York.

Rossi, R.E., Mulla, D.J., Journel, A.G. & Franz, E.H. (1992) Geostatistical tools for modeling and interpreting ecological spatial dependence. *Ecological Monographs* 62: 277–314.

Roth, P.L. (1994) Missing data: a conceptual review for applied psychologists. *Personnel Psychology* 47: 537–560.

Rousseeuw, P.J., Ruts, I. & Tukey, J.W. (1999) The bagplot: a bivariate boxplot. *The American Statistician* 53: 382–387.

Rovine, M.J. & Delaney, M. (1990) Missing data estimation in developmental research. In: *Statistical Methods in Longitudinal Research* (von Eye, A. ed.), pp. 35–79. Academic Press, San Diego.

Royall, R.M. (1997) *Statistical Evidence. A Likelihood Paradigm*. Chapman & Hall, London.

Rubin, D.B. (1987) *Multiple Imputation for Nonresponse in Surveys*. Wiley, New York.

Rubin, D.B. (1996) Multiple imputation after 18+ years. *Journal of the American Statistical Association* 91: 473–489.

Rundle, H.D. & Jackson, D.A. (1996) Spatial and temporal variation in littoral-zone fish communities: a new statistical approach. *Canadian Journal of Fisheries and Aquatic Sciences* 53: 2167–2176.

Ruse, M. (1999) When is a negative result anomalous? *Marine Ecology Progress Series* 191: 302–303.

Salsburg, D.S. (1985) The religion of statistics as practiced in medical journals. *The American Statistician* 39: 220–257.

Salter, K.C. & Fawcett, R.F. (1993) A robust and powerful rank test of interaction in factorial models. *Communications in Statistics – Simulation and Computation* B22: 137–153.

Samuels, M.L., Casella, G. & McCabe, G.P. (1991) Interpreting blocks and random factors. *Journal of the American Statistical Association* 86: 798–808.

Sasieni, P.D. & Royston, P. (1996) Dotplots. *Applied Statistics* 45: 219–234.

Schafer, J.L. (1999) Multiple imputation: a primer. *Statistical Methods in Medical Research* 8: 3–15.

Scheffé, H. (1959) *The Analysis of Variance*. Wiley, New York.

Scheiner, S.M. (1993) Introduction: theories, hypotheses, and statistics. In *Design and Analysis of Ecological Experiments* (Scheiner, S.M. & Gurevitch, J. eds.), pp. 1–13. Chapman & Hall, New York.

Schervish, M.J. (1996) *P* values: what they are and what they are not. *The American Statistician* 50: 203–206.

Schmid, C.H. (1991) Value splitting: taking the data apart. In: *Fundamentals of Exploratory Analysis of Variance* (Hoaglin, D.C., Mosteller, F. & Tukey, J.W. eds.). Wiley, New York.

Schnell, G.D., Watt, D.J. & Douglas, M.E. (1985) Statistical comparison of proximity matrices: applications in animal behavior. *Animal Behavior* 33: 239–253.

Schwartz, M.W., Hermann, S.M. & Vogel, C.S. (1995) The

catastrophic loss of *Torreya taxifolia*: assessing environmental induction of disease hypotheses. *Ecological Applications* **5**: 501–516.

Schwarz, C.J. (1993) The mixed model ANOVA: the truth, the computer packages, the books. Part I: balanced data. *The American Statistician* **47**: 48–59.

Schwarz, G. (1978) Estimating the dimension of a model. *Annals of Statistics* **6**: 461–464.

Scott, A. & Wild, C. (1991) Transformations and R^2. *The American Statistician* **45**: 127–129.

Seaman, J.W., Walls, S.C., Wise, S.E. & Jaeger, R.G. (1994) Caveat emptor: rank transform methods and interaction. *Trends in Ecology and Evolution* **9**: 261–263.

Searle, S.R. (1988) Parallel lines in residual plots. *The American Statistician* **42**: 211.

Searle, S.R. (1993) Unbalanced data and cell means models. In: *Applied Analysis of Variance in Behavioral Science* (Edwards, L.K. ed.), pp. 375–420. Marcel Dekker, New York.

Searle, S.R., Casella, G. & McCulloch, C.E. (1992) *Variance Components*. Wiley, New York.

Shaffer, J.P. (1995) Multiple hypothesis testing. *Annual Review of Psychology* **46**: 561–584.

Sharpe, A. & Keough, M.J. (1998) An investigation of the indirect effects of intertidal shellfish collection. *Journal of Experimental Marine Biology and Ecology* **223**: 19–38.

Shaver, J.P. (1993) What statistical significance testing is, and what it is not. *Journal of Experimental Education* **61**: 293–316.

Shaw, R.G. & Mitchell-Olds, T. (1993) ANOVA for unbalanced data: an overview. *Ecology* **74**: 1638–1645.

Siegel, S. & Castellan, J.J. (1988) *Nonparametric Statistics for the Behavioral Sciences*, 2nd edition. McGraw-Hill, New York.

Silverman, B.W. (1986) *Density Estimation for Statistics and Data Analysis*. Chapman & Hall, London.

Siminoff, J.S. (1998) Logistic regression, categorical predictors, and goodness-of-fit: it depends on who you ask. *The American Statistician* **52**: 10–14.

Sinclair, A.R.E. & Arcese, P. (1995) Population consequences of predation-sensitive foraging: the Serengeti wildebeest. *Ecology* **76**: 882–891.

Skelly, D.S. (1995) A behavioural trade-off and its consequences for the distribution of *Pseudacris* treefrog larvae. *Ecology* **76**: 150–164.

Sklenar, P. & Jorgensen, P.M. (1999) Distribution patterns of paramo plants in Ecuador. *Journal of Biogeography* **26**: 681–691.

Smith, F.A., Brown, J.H. & Valone, T.J. (1997) Path analysis: a critical evaluation using long-term experimental data. *The American Naturalist* **149**: 29–42.

Smith, P.L. (1982) Measures of variance accounted for: theory and practice. In: *Statistical and Methodological Issues in Psychology and Social Sciences Research* (Keren, G.

ed), pp. 101–129. Lawrence Erlbaum Associates, Hillsdale, New Jersey.

Snedecor, G.W. & Cochran, W.G. (1989) *Statistical Methods*, 8th edition. Iowa State College Press, Ames, Iowa.

Snee, R.D. & Pfeifer, C.G. (1983) Graphical representation of data. In: *Encyclopedia of Statistical Sciences* Vol. 3 (Kotz, S. & Johnson, N.L. eds.), pp. 488–511. Wiley, New York.

Sokal, R.R. & Rohlf, F.J. (1995) *Biometry*. 3rd edition. W.H. Freeman, New York.

Speight, M.R. Hails, R.S., Gilbert, M. & Foggo, A. (1998) Horse chestnut scale (*Pulvinaria regalis*) (Homoptera: Coccidae) and urban tree host environment. *Ecology* **79**(5): 1503–1513.

Sprent, P. (1993). *Applied Nonparametric Statistical Methods*, 2nd edition. Chapman & Hall, London.

SPSS. (1999) *SYSTAT 9 Graphics*. SPSS, Chicago.

Stehman, S.V. & Meredith, M.P. (1995) Practical analysis of factorial experiments in forestry. *Canadian Journal of Forest Research* **25**: 446–461.

Stevens, J. (1992) *Applied Multivariate Statistics for the Social Sciences*, 2nd edition. Lawrence Erlbaum, Hillsdale, NJ.

Stewart-Oaten, A. (1995) Rules and judgements in statistics: three examples. *Ecology* **76**: 2001–2009.

Stewart-Oaten, A. (1996). Goals in environmental monitoring. In: *The Design of Ecological Impact Studies: Conceptual Issues and Application in Coastal Marine Habitats*, (Schmitt, R.J. & Osenberg, C.W., eds.), pp. 17–28. Academic Press, San Diego.

Stewart-Oaten, A., Bence, J.R. & Osenberg, C.W. (1992) Assessing effects of unreplicated perturbations: no simple solutions. *Ecology* **73**: 1396–1404.

Stewart-Oaten, A., Murdoch, W.W. & Parker, K.R. (1986). Environmental impact assessment: "pseudoreplication" in time? *Ecology* **67**: 929–940

Stow, C.A., Carpenter, S.R. & Cottingham, K.L. (1995) Resource vs. ratio-dependent consumer-resource models: a Bayesian perspective. *Ecology* **76**: 1986–1990.

Strunk, W. & White, E.B. (1979) *The Elements of Style*, 3rd edition. Macmillan, New York.

Tabachnick, B. & Fidell, L. (1996) *Using Multivariate Statistics*, 3rd edition. Harper & Row, New York.

Taulman, J.F., Smith, K.G. & Thill, R.E. (1998) Demographic and behavioral responses of southern flying squirrels to experimental logging in Arkansas. *Ecological Applications* **8**: 1144–1155.

ter Braak, C.J.F. & Verdonschot, P.F.M. (1995) Canonical correspondence analysis and related multivariate methods in aquatic ecology. *Aquatic Sciences* **57**: 255–289.

Thomas, L. (1997) Retrospective power analysis. *Conservation Biology* **11**: 276–280.

Thompson, B. (1993) The use of statistical significance tests in research: bootstrap and other alternatives. *Journal of Experimental Education* **61**: 361–377.

Thompson, G.L. (1991a) A note on the rank transformation for interactions. *Biometrika* **78**: 697–701.

Thompson, G.L. (1991b) A unified approach to rank tests for multivariate and repeated measures designs. *Journal of the American Statistical Association* **86**: 410–419.

Thompson, S.K. (1992) *Sampling*. Wiley, New York.

Thompson, S.K. & Seber, G.A.F. (1995) *Adaptive Sampling*. Wiley, New York.

Todd, C.D. & Keough, M.J. (1994) Larval settlement in hard substratum epifaunal assemblages: a manipulative field study of the effects of substratum filming and the presence of incumbents. *Journal of Experimental Marine Biology and Ecology* **181**: 159–187.

Tollrian, R. (1995) Predator-induced morphological defenses: costs, life history shifts, and maternal effects in *Daphnia pulex*. *Ecology* **76**: 1691–1705.

Toothaker, L.E. (1993) *Multiple Comparison Procedures*. Sage Publications, Newbury Park, California.

Trexler, J.C. & Travis, J. (1993) Nontraditonal regression analyses. *Ecology* **74**: 1629–1637.

Trussell, G.C. (1997) Phenotypic plasticity in the foot size of an intertidal snail. *Ecology* **78**: 1033–1048.

Tufte, E.R. (1983) *The Visual Display of Quantitative Information*. Graphics Press, Cheshire, Cleveland.

Tufte, E.R. (1990) *Envisioning Information*. Graphics Press, Cheshire, Connecticut.

Tukey, J.W. (1949) One degree of freedom for nonadditivity. *Biometrics* **5**: 232–242.

Tukey, J.W. (1977) *Exploratory Data Analysis*. Addison-Wesley, Reading.

Twombly, S. (1996) Timing of metamorphosis in a freshwater crustacean: comparison with anuran models. *Ecology* **77**: 1855–1866.

Underwood, A.J. (1981) Techniques of analysis of variance in experimental marine biology and ecology. *Oceanography and Marine Biology Annual Review* **19**: 513–605.

Underwood, A.J. (1990) Experiments in ecology and management: their logics, functions and interpretations. *Australian Journal of Ecology* **14**: 365–389.

Underwood, A.J. (1991) The logic of ecological experiments: a case history from studies of the distribution of macro-algae on rocky intertidal shores. *Journal of the Marine Biological Association of the United Kingdom* **71**: 841–866.

Underwood, A.J. (1997) *Experiments in Ecology. Their Logical Design and Interpretation Using Analysis of Variance*. Cambridge University Press, Cambridge.

Underwood, A.J. (1999) Publication of so-called "negative" results in marine ecology. *Marine Ecology Progress Series* **191**: 307–309.

Underwood, A.J. & Petraitis, P.S. (1993) Structure of intertidal assemblages in different locations: how can local processes be compared? In: *Species Diversity in Ecological Communities: Historical and Geographical Perspectives*. (Ricklefs, R.E. & Schluter, D. eds.), pp. 38–51. University of Chicago Press, Chicago.

Urbach, P. (1984) Randomization and the design of experiments. *Philosophy of Science* **52**: 256–272.

van den Wollenberg, A.L. (1977) Redundancy analysis. An alternative for canonical correlation analysis. *Psychometrika* **42**: 207–219.

van Groenewood, H. (1992). The robustness of correspondence, detrended correspondence and twinspan analysis. *Journal of Vegetation Science* 3: 239–246.

Van Sickle, J. (1997) Using mean similarity dendograms to evaluate classifications. *Journal of Agricultural, Biological and Environmental Statistics* 2: 370–388.

Vasquez, R.A. (1996) Patch utilization by three species of Chilean rodents differing in body size and mode of locomotion. *Ecology* **77**: 2343–2351.

Ver Hoef, J.M. & Cressie, N. (1993) Spatial statistics: analysis of field experiments. In: *Design and Analysis of Ecological Field Experiments* (Scheiner, S.M. & Gurevitch, J. eds.), pp. 319–341. Chapman & Hall, New York.

Verschuren, D., Tibby, J., Sabbe, K. & Roberts, N. (2000) Effects of depth, salinity, and substrate on the invertebrate community of a fluctuating tropical lake. *Ecology* **81**: 164–182.

von Ende, C.N. (1993) Repeated-measures analysis: growth and other time-dependent measures. In: *Design and Analysis of Ecological Experiments* (Scheiner, S. & Gurevitch, J. eds.), pp. 113–137. Chapman & Hall, New York.

Voss, D.T. (1999) Resolving the mixed models controversy. *The American Statistician* **53**: 352–356.

Wagner, J.D. & Wise, D.H. (1996) Cannabilism regulates densities of young wolf spiders: evidence from field and laboratory experiments. *Ecology* **77**: 639–652.

Walter, D.E. & O'Dowd, D.J. (1992) Leaves with domatia have more mites. *Ecology* **73**: 1514–1518.

Ward, S. & Quinn, G.P. (1988) Preliminary investigations of the ecology of the predatory gastropod *Lepsiella vinosa* (Lamarck) (Gastropoda Muricidae). *Journal of Molluscan Studies* **54**: 109–117.

Ware, J.H. & Liang, K.-Y. (1996) The design and analysis of longitudinal studies: a historical perspective. In: *Advances in Biometry* (Armitage, P. & David, H.A. eds.), pp. 339–362. Wiley, New York.

Wartenberg, D., Ferson, S. and Rohlf, F.J. (1987). Putting things in order: a critique of detrended correspondence analysis. *The American Naturalist* **129**: 434–448.

Werner, E.E. (1998) Ecological experiments and a research program in community ecology. In: *Experimental Ecology: Issues and Perspectives* (Resetarits, W.J. & Bernado, J. eds.), pp. 3–26. Oxford University Press, New York.

Westfall, P.H. & Young, S.S. (1993a) *Resampling-Based Multiple Testing: Examples and Methods for P-Value Adjustment*. Wiley, New York.

Westfall, P.H. & Young, S.S. (1993b) On adjusting *P*-values for multiplicity. *Biometrics* **49**: 941–945.

Westly, L.C. (1993) The effect of inflorescence bud removal on tuber production in *Helianthus tuberosus* L. (Asteraceae). *Ecology* **74**: 2136–2144.

White, G.C. & Bennetts, R.E. (1996) Analysis of count data using the negative binomial distribution. *Ecology* **77**: 2549–2557.

Wilcox, R.R. (1987a) New designs in analysis of variance. *Annual Review of Psychology* **38**: 29–60.

Wilcox, R.R. (1987b) Pairwise comparisons of J independent regression lines over a finite interval, simultaneous pairwise comparisons of their parameter, and the Johnson–Neyman procedure. *British Journal of Mathematical and Statistical Psychology* **40**: 80–93.

Wilcox, R.R. (1993) Robustness in ANOVA. In: *Applied Analysis of Variance in Behavioral Science* (Edwards, L.K. ed.), pp. 345–374. Marcel Dekker, New York.

Wilcox, R.R. (1997) *Introduction to Robust Estimation and Hypothesis Testing*. Academic Press, San Diego.

Wilcox, R.R., Charlin, V. & Thompson, K. (1986) New Monte Carlo results on the robustness of the ANOVA F, W and F* statistics. *Communications in Statistics – Simulation and Computation* **B15**: 933–944.

Wilkinson, L. (1999) Dot plots. *The American Statistician* **53**: 276–281.

Williams, J.M. (1997) *Style. Ten lessons in Clarity and Grace*. Longman, New York.

Winer, B.J., Brown, D.R. & Michels, K.M. (1991) *Statistical Principles in Experimental Design*, 3rd edition. McGraw-Hill, New York.

Winkler, R.L. (1993) Bayesian statistics: an overview. In: *A Handbook for Data Analysis in the Behavioral Sciences – Statistical Issues* (Keren, G. & Lewis, C. eds.), pp. 201–232. Lawrence Erlbaum Associates, New Jersey.

Wiser, S.K., Allen, R.B., Clinton, P.W. & Platt, K.H. (1998) Community structure and forest invasion by an exotic herb over 23 years. *Ecology* **79**: 2071–2081.

Wissinger, S.A., Sparks, G.B., Rouse, G.L., Brown, W.S. & Steltzer, H. (1996) Intraguild predation and cannabilism among larvae of detritivorous caddisflies in subalpine wetlands. *Ecology* **77**: 2421–2430.

Wright, S. (1920) The relative importance of heredity and environment in determining the piebald pattern of guinea pigs. *Proceedings of the National Academy of Science, USA* **6**: 320–332.

Wright, S. (1934) The method of path coefficients. *Annals of Mathematics and Statistics* **5**: 161–215.

Yandell, B.S. (1997) *Practical Data Analysis for Designed Experiment*. Chapman & Hall, London.

Yee, T.W. & Mitchell, N.D. (1991) Generalized additive models in plant ecology. *Journal of Vegetation Science* **2**: 587–602.

Zar, J.H. (1996) *Biostatistical Analysis*, 3rd edition. Prentice Hall, Upper Saddle River, NJ.

Zimmerman, D.W. (1994) A note on the influence of outliers on parametric and nonparametric tests. *The Journal of General Psychology* **121**: 391–401.

Zimmerman, D.W. & Zumbo, B.D. (1993) The relative power of parametric and nonparametric statistical methods. In: *A Handbook for Data Analysis in the Behavioral Sciences – Statistical Issues* (Keren, G. & Lewis, C. eds.), pp. 481–517. Lawrence Erlbaum Associates, New Jersey.

Zimmerman, G.M., Goetz, H. & Mielke, P.W. (1985) Use of an improved statistical method for group comparisons to study effects of prairie fire. *Ecology* **66**: 606–611.

Index